THIRD EDITION

The Norton
Field Guide
to Writing

with readings

Richard Bullock

WRIGHT STATE UNIVERSITY

Maureen Daly Goggin

ARIZONA STATE UNIVERSITY

W. W. NORTON & COMPANY

New York • London

W. W. Norton & Company has been independent since its founding in 1923, when William Warder Norton and Mary D. Herter Norton first published lectures delivered at the People's Institute, the adult education division of New York City's Cooper Union. The firm soon expanded its program beyond the Institute, publishing books by celebrated academics from America and abroad. By mid-century, the two major pillars of Norton's publishing program—trade books and college texts—were firmly established. In the 1950s, the Norton family transferred control of the company to its employees, and today—with a staff of four hundred and a comparable number of trade, college, and professional titles published each year—W. W. Norton & Company stands as the largest and oldest publishing house owned wholly by its employees.

Editor: Marilyn Moller
Developmental editor: John Elliott
Project editor: Rebecca Homiski
Editorial assistants: Tenyia Lee, Erica Wnek
Production manager: Andrew Ensor
Emedia editor: Cliff Landesman
Marketing Manager: Lib Triplett
Text Design: Anna Palchik
Composition: Cenveo Publisher Services
Manufacturing: R. R. Donnelley—Crawfordsville

ISBN: 978-0-393-91957-8

The Library of Congress has cataloged another edition as follows:

Bullock, Richard H. (Richard Harvey)
    The Norton field guide to writing / Richard Bullock, Wright State University. — Third Edition.
        pages   cm.
    Includes bibliographical references and index.
    ISBN: 978-0-393-91956-1 (pbk.)
    1. English language—Rhetoric—Handbooks, manuals, etc.   2. English language—
Grammar—Handbooks, manuals, etc.   3. Report writing—Handbooks, manuals, etc.   I. Title.
    PE1408.B883824 2013
    808'.042—dc23   2012047959

W. W. Norton & Company, Inc., 500 Fifth Avenue, New York, NY 10110-0017
wwnorton.com

W. W. Norton & Company Ltd., Castle House, 75/76 Wells Street, London W1T 3QT

3 4 5 6 7 8 9 0

Preface

The Norton Field Guide to Writing began as an attempt to offer the kind of writing guides found in the best rhetorics in a format as user-friendly as the best handbooks, and on top of that, to be as brief as could be. We wanted to create a handy guide to help college students with all their written work. Just as there are field guides for bird watchers, for gardeners, and for accountants, this would be one for writers. In its first two editions, the book obviously touched a chord with many writing instructors, and it became the best-selling college rhetoric — a success that leaves us humbled and grateful. Those teachers, though, have often asked for a little more coverage here and there, especially on choosing genres and the distinctive challenges of writing online, creating multimodal texts, and writing in academic contexts. So we're happy now to offer a third edition that answers those requests.

The Norton Field Guide still aims to offer both the guidance new teachers and first-year writers need and the flexibility many experienced teachers want. From our own experiences as teachers and WPAs, we've seen how well explicit guides to writing work for students and novice teachers. But too often, writing textbooks provide far more information than students need or instructors can assign and as a result are bigger and more expensive than they should be. So we've tried to provide enough structure without too much detail—to give the information college writers need to know while resisting the temptation to tell them everything there is to know.

Most of all, we've tried to make the book easy to use. To that end, it includes menus, directories, a glossary/index, and color-coded links to make it simple for students to find what they're looking for and navigate the parts. The links are also the key to keeping the book brief: chapters are short, but the links send students to pages elsewhere in the book if they need more detail.

What's in the Book

The Norton Field Guide covers 14 genres often assigned in college. Much of the book is in the form of guidelines, designed to help students consider the choices they have as writers. The book is organized into seven parts:

1. RHETORICAL SITUATIONS. Chapters 1–6 focus on purpose, audience, genre, stance, media and design, and writing in academic contexts. In addition, almost every chapter includes a short list of tips to help students focus on their particular rhetorical situation.

2. GENRES. Chapters 7–21 cover 14 genres, 4 of them — literacy narrative, textual analysis, report, and argument — treated in greater detail. Chapter 21 helps students choose genres when they need to.

3. PROCESSES. Chapters 22–29 offer advice for generating ideas and text, drafting, revising and rewriting, editing, proofreading, compiling a portfolio, collaborating with others, and writing as inquiry.

4. STRATEGIES. Chapters 30–42 cover familiar ways of developing and organizing text — writing effective beginnings and endings, coming up with good titles and developing effective thesis statements, comparing, describing, and using dialogue. Chapters 41 and 42 offer strategies for reading and taking essay exams.

5. RESEARCH/DOCUMENTATION. Chapters 43–51 offer advice on how to do academic research; work with sources; quote, paraphrase, and summarize source materials; and document sources using MLA and APA styles.

6. MEDIA/DESIGN. Chapters 52–56 give guidance on choosing the appropriate print, electronic, or spoken medium; designing text; using images and sound; giving spoken presentations; and writing online.

7. READINGS. Chapters 57–66 provide readings in nine of the genres, plus one chapter of readings that mix genres. Discussion questions help students engage with the text and are color-coded to refer students to relevant details elsewhere in the book.

What's Online

The Norton Field Guide to Go. A brief, quick-reference version will be available in a digital format for smartphones and other handheld devices. Portable, searchable, and interactive, it will be free with the purchase of the book — and $10 net otherwise.

Ebooks. All versions of *The Norton Field Guide* are available as ebooks and include all the readings and images found in the print books. Offered at less than half the price of the print books, the ebooks are completely searchable and allow readers to highlight and attach sticky notes.

A companion website includes model papers, exercises and quizzes, and more. Access the site at wwnorton.com/write/fieldguide.

norton/write. A free and open site with author bios, plagiarism tutorials, exercises — and more. Access the site at wwnorton.com/write.

What's Available for Instructors

A Guide to Teaching with **The Norton Field Guides.** Written by Richard Bullock and several other teachers, this is a comprehensive guide to teaching first-year writing, from developing a syllabus to facilitating group work, teaching multimodal writing to assessing student writing. Free of charge.

Coursepacks are available absolutely free and in a variety of formats, including *Blackboard, Desire2Learn, Moodle, Canvas,* and *Angel.* The *Field Guide* Coursepack includes model papers, quizzes and exercises, video tutorials, documentation guidelines, and more — all of it fully customizable. You can choose the content you want to use, rearrange it, add to it, edit it as you wish to suit your course — and your students. Access the Coursepack at wwnorton.com/instructors.

FRED. An online commenting system that allows you to respond to drafts in writing — and with audio or video. Created by CritiqueIt and customized for college writing classes.

Highlights

It's easy to use. Menus, directories, and a glossary/index make it easy for students to find what they're looking for. Color-coded templates and documentation maps even make MLA and APA documentation easy.

It has just enough detail, with short chapters that include color-coded links sending students to more detail *if* they need more.

It's uniquely flexible for teachers. Short chapters can be assigned in any order — and color-coded links help draw from other chapters as need be.

What's New

A new chapter on writing in academic contexts, helping students understand what's expected of their writing in college. (Chapter 6)

A new chapter on choosing genres. (Chapter 21)

42 new readings, including 14 multimodal readings.

New reading strategies helping students assess their knowledge of a topic, deal with difficult texts, and use a coding system for responding to a text. (Chapter 41)

A new chapter on choosing media, helping students decide which media (print, electronic, or spoken) and which modes (words, images, video, audio, hyperlinks) best suit their needs. (Chapter 52)

A new chapter on designing text. (Chapter 53)

A new chapter on incorporating images and sound — photographs, graphs, charts, videos, sound effects, and more. (Chapter 54)

A new chapter on writing online, with advice on managing files; LMS's; and using email, blogs, and social media in academic contexts. (Chapter 55)

Ways of Teaching with *The Norton Field Guide to Writing*

The Norton Field Guide is designed to give you both support and flexibility. It has clear assignment sequences if you want them, or you can create your own. If, for example, you assign a position paper, there's a full chapter. If you want students to use sources, add the appropriate research chapters. If you want them to submit a topic proposal, add that chapter.

If you're a new teacher, the genre chapters offer explicit assignment sequences — and the color-coded links will remind you of other detail that you may want to bring in. The instructor's manual is designed for new teachers, with advice on creating a syllabus, responding to writing, and more.

If you focus on genres, there are complete chapters on all the genres college students are often assigned. Color-coded links will help you bring in details about research or other writing strategies as you wish.

If you organize your course thematically, a Thematic Guide will lead you to readings on 25 themes. Chapter 24 on generating ideas can help get students thinking about a theme. You can also assign them to do research on the theme, starting with Chapter 44 on finding sources, or perhaps with Chapter 22 on writing as inquiry. If they then write in a particular genre, there will be a chapter to guide them.

If you want students to do research, there are 9 chapters on the research process, including guidelines and sample papers demonstrating MLA and APA documentation.

If you focus on modes, you'll find chapters on narration, description, and so on. The chapters assume these to be strategies that a writer might use for many writing purposes, and also include links that lead students through the process of writing an essay organized around a particular mode.

If you teach online, the book is available as an ebook — and in a quick-reference version for use on mobile devices. In addition, a companion Coursepack includes exercises, quizzes, video tutorials, and more.

Acknowledgments

As we've traveled around the country and met many of the students, teachers, and WPAs who are using *The Norton Field Guide*, we've been gratified to hear that so many find it helpful, to the point that some students tell us that they aren't going to sell it back to the bookstore when the term ends — the highest form of praise. As much as we like the positive response, though, we are especially grateful when we receive suggestions for ways the book might be improved. In this third edition, as we did in the second edition, we have tried to respond to the many good suggestions we've gotten from students, colleagues, reviewers, and editors. Thank you all, both for your kind words and for your good suggestions.

Some people need to be singled out for thanks, especially Marilyn Moller, the guiding editorial spirit of the *Field Guide* through all three editions. When we presented Marilyn with the idea for this book, she encouraged us and helped us conceptualize it — and then taught us how to write a textbook. The quality of the *Field Guide* is due in large part to her knowledge of the field of composition, her formidable editing and writing skills, her sometimes uncanny ability to see the future of the teaching of writing — and her equally formidable, if not uncanny, stamina.

Development editor John Elliott has shepherded the third edition through its revisions and additions with a careful hand and a clear eye for appropriate content and language. His painstaking editing of every chapter shows throughout the book, and we're grateful for his ability to make us appear to be better writers than we are.

Many others have contributed, too. Thanks to project editor Rebecca Homiski for her energy, patience, and great skill in coordinating the tightly scheduled production process for the book and her wonderful talent for researching and handling the new images. Erica Wnek helped find readings, managed the reviewing process, and contributed to the planning of the new edition; Lisa Moore provided valuable editorial help with the new coverage of digital writing; Tenyia Lee helped find photos, check pageproofs, and more. Anna Palchik designed the award-winning, user-friendly, and attractive interior, and Kimberly Glyder created the beautiful new cover design. Francine Weinberg wrote the ingenious documentation chapters and the glossary, and did heavy lifting on much of the first edition. Jane Searle and Andy Ensor transformed a scribbled-over manuscript into a finished product with admirable speed and precision, while Jude Grant copyedited and Mark Gallaher proofread. Megan Jackson and Bethany Salminen cleared text permissions, coping efficiently with ongoing changes, and Michael Fodera cleared permission for the images. Juliana Fidler, our excellent intern, located author images and updated manuscript files. Cliff Landesman planned, designed, and produced the sensational website with help from Stefani Wallace. Steve Dunn and especially Lib Triplett helped us all keep our eyes on the market. Thanks to all, and to Roby Harrington, Drake McFeely, and Julia Reidhead for supporting this project in the first place.

Rich has many, many people at Wright State University to thank for their support and assistance. Jane Blakelock has taught Rich most of what he knows about electronic text and writing on and for the web and has assembled an impressive list of useful links for the book's website. Adrienne Cassel, now at Sinclair Community College, and Catherine Crowley read and commented on many drafts. Peggy Lindsey shared her students' work and the idea of using charts to show how various genres might be organized. Brady Allen, Debbie Bertsch (now at Columbus State Community College), Vicki Burke, Melissa Carrion, Jimmy Chesire, Carol Cornett, Byron Crews, Deborah Crusan, Sally DeThomas, Stephanie Dickey, Scott Geisel, Karen Hayes, Chuck Holmes, Beth Klaisner, Nancy Mack, Marty Maner, Cynthia Marshall, Sarah McGinley, Kristie McKiernan, Michelle Metzner, Kristie Rowe, Bobby Rubin, Cathy Sayer, David Seitz, Caroline Simmons, Tracy Smith, Rick Strader, Mary Van Loveren, and A. J. Williams responded to drafts, submitted good models of student writing, contributed to the instructor's manual, tested the *Field Guide* in their classes, provided support, and shared some of their best teaching ideas. Henry Limouze and then Carol Loranger, chairs of the English Department, gave him room to work on this project with patience and good humor. Sandy Trimboli, Becky Traxler, and Lynn Morgan, the secretaries to the writing programs, kept him anchored. And he thanks especially the more than 300 graduate teaching assistants and 10,000 first-year students who class-tested various editions of the *Field Guide* and whose experiences helped — and continue to help — to shape it.

At Arizona State, Maureen wants to acknowledge the unwavering support of Neal A. Lester, Vice President of Humanities and Arts and former chair of the English Department, and the assistance of Jason Diller, her former graduate research assistant, and Judy Holiday, her former graduate mentee, for their reading suggestions. She thanks her colleagues, all exemplary teachers and mentors, for creating a supportive intellectual environment, especially Patricia Boyd, Peter Goggin, Mark Hannah, Kathleen Lamp, Elenore Long, Paul Matsuda, Keith Miller, Ersula Ore, Alice Robison, Shirley Rose, and Doris Warriner. Thanks also go to ASU instructors and first-year students who have used the *Field Guide* and have offered good suggestions. Finally, Maureen wants to pay tribute to her students, who are themselves among her best teachers.

Thanks to the teachers across the country who reviewed the second edition of the *Field Guide* and helped shape this third edition: Brock Adams, University of South Carolina Upstate; Jill Adams, University of South Carolina Upstate; Steven Adkison, Wallace Community College; Stevens Russell Amidon, Indiana University–Purdue University Fort Wayne; Irene Anders, Indiana University–Purdue University Fort Wayne; Susan Barkley, Dallas County Community College District; Scott Bayer, Purdue University North Central; James Beitler, Roger Williams University; Kay Berg, Sinclair Community College; Scott Berzon, St. Louis School; Jacqueline Blackwell, Thomas Nelson Community College; Sheena D. Boran, University of Mississippi; Ehel Bowden, Central Maine Community College; Kimberly Britt, Horry Georgetown Technical College; Adrienne Cassel, Sinclair Community College; Jill Channing, Mitchell Community College; Benjamin Child, University of Mississippi; Angie Cook, Cisco College; Robert E. Cummings, University of Mississippi; Judy Deisler, Pasco-Hernando Community College; Alexandra DeSiato, Alamance Community College; Gordon H. Dunkin III, University of Mississippi; Gloria Dyc, University of New Mexico; Jeremiah Dyehouse, University of Rhode Island; Sean Ennis, University of Mississippi; Jason Faulkner, East Carolina University; Shanna Flaschka, University of Mississippi; Shawnda Floyd, Brookdale Community College; Catherine Fox, St. Cloud State University; Robert B. Galin, University of New Mexico–Gallup; Anne Gray, Ivy Tech Community College, Bloomington; Jennifer Gray, College of Coastal Georgia; Wendy Howard Gray, J. Sargeant Reynolds Community College; Shauna Gobble, Northampton Community College; Esther Godfrey, University of Southern California Upstate; Deborah Goodwyn, Virginia State University; Timothy Hackett, East Carolina University; Audley Hall, Northwest Arkansas Community College; Anne Helms, Alamance Community College; Furaha Henry-Jones, Sinclair Community College; Mildred Ann Henson, Moraine Valley Community College; Mark Horstmeyer, Moraine Valley Community College; Susan E. Howard, Ivy Tech Community College; Yi-Wen Huang, University of New Mexico–Gallup; Jo Johnson, Ivy Tech Community College; Amy Jorgensen, North Carolina State

University; Sara Kaplan, Del Mar College; Bridget R. Kozlow, North Carolina State University; Celena Kusch, University of South Carolina Upstate; Sharon Gavin Levy, Northampton Community College; Chantelle MacPhee, Elizabeth City State University; Sarah K. McKinney Maddalena, North Carolina State University; Terri Mann, El Paso Community College; Stephen March, Elizabeth City State University; Stephen L. Mathewson, Central New Mexico Community College; Jeanne McDonald, Waubonsee Community College; Tom McLaren, University of New Mexico at Gallup; Tara L. McLellan, University of Mississippi; Mary Pat McQueeney, Johnson County Community College; Robert Mellin, Purdue University North Central; Dodie M. Miller, Ivy Tech Community College; Don Miller, Alamance Community College; Moraine Valley Community College Foundation; Roxanne Munch, Joliet Junior College; Denise Nemec, Northwest Arkansas Community College; James O'Brien, University of Mississippi; Kristina Onder, Sinclair Community College; Michael Pennell, University of Rhode Island; Brietta Perez, Alvin Community College; Staci Perryman-Clark, Western Michigan University; Daniel Portincaso, Waubonsee Community College; Nancy Riecken, Ivy Tech Community College; Mauricio Rodriguez, El Paso Community College; DaRelle M. Rollins, Hampton University; Theodore (Ted) Rollins, Johnson County Community College; Brian Royse, Ivy Tech Community College; Matthew W. Schmeer, Johnson County Community College; Danielle Sellers, University of Mississippi; Marilyn M. Senter, Johnson County Community College; Brandi Smith Wallace, Wallace Community College; Jennifer Stewart, Indiana University–Purdue University Fort Wayne; Danielle Sullivan, San Juan College; Martha Tolleson, Collin County College; Sara Webb-Sunderhaus, Indiana University–Purdue University Fort Wayne; George H. Williams, University of South Carolina Upstate; Leah Williams, University of New Hampshire; Glenda O. Yount, Alamance Community College.

Thanks also to the many teachers across the country who have reviewed various previous versions and offered valuable input and encouragement: Alan Ainsworth, Houston Community College; Jonathan Alexander, University of California at Irvine; Althea Allard, Community College of Rhode Island; James Allen, College of DuPage; Cathryn Amdahl, Harrisburg Area Community College; Jeff Andelora, Mesa Community College; Anne Beaufort, University of Washington, Tacoma; Sue Beebe, Texas State University; Patrick Bizzaro, East Carolina University; Kevin Brooks, North Dakota State University; Ron Brooks, Oklahoma State University; Cheryl Brown,

Towson University; Gina Caison, University of Alabama, Birmingham; Jill Channing, Mitchell Community College; Ron Christiansen, Salt Lake Community College; Susan Cochran-Miller, North Carolina State University at Raleigh Durham; Billye Currie, Samford University; Paul C. Davis, Northland Community and Technical College; Pat Densby, San Jacinto College Central; Marvin Diogenes, Stanford University; Sarah Duerdan, Arizona State University; Russel Durst, University of Cincinnati; Sylvia Edwards, Longview Community College; Karen Fitts, West Chester University; Paul Formisano, University of New Mexico; Lloren A. Foster, Hampton University; Ivonne M. Garcia, Ohio State University; Anne Gervasi, DeVry University; Gregory Glau, Arizona State University; Emily Golson, University of Northern Colorado; Richard Hansen, California State Fresno; Susanmarie Harrington, University of Vermont; Lory Hawkes, DeVry Institute of Technology; Gary Hawkins, Warren Wilson College; Paul Heilker, Virginia Polytechnic Institute and State University; Hal Hellwig, Idaho State University; Michael Hennessy, Texas State University; Cheryl Huff, Germanna Community College; Maurice Hunt, Baylor University; Teresa James, South Florida Community College; Kim Jameson, Oklahoma City Community College; Peggy Jolly, University of Alabama, Birmingham; Mitzi Walker Jones, University of Arkansas, Fort Smith; Jeanne Kelly, Holmes Community College; Rhonda Kyncl, University of Oklahoma; Sally Lahmon, Sinclair Community College; Erin Lebacqz, University of New Mexico; Paul Lynch, Purdue University; T. Michael Mackey, Community College of Denver; Magdalena Maczynska, Marymount Manhattan College; Leigh A. Martin, Community College of Rhode Island; Deborah McCollister, Dallas Baptist University; Miles McCrimmon, J. Sargeant Reynolds Community College; Jeanne McDonald, Waubonsee Community College; Jacqueline McGrath, College of DuPage; Pat McQueeny, Johnson County Community College; Shellie Michael, Volunteer State Community College; Thomas Miller, University of Arizona; Bryan Moore, Arkansas State University; Mary Ellen Muesing, University of North Carolina, Charlotte; Roxanne Munch, Joliet Junior College; Terry Novak, Johnson & Wales University; Peggy Oliver, San Jacinto College; Amy Patrick, Western Illinois University; Ann Pearson, San Jacinto College; Irv Peckham, Louisiana State University; K. J. Peters, Loyola Marymount University; Deirdre Pettipiece, University of the Sciences; Donna Qualley, Western Washington University; Daniela Ragusa, Southern Connecticut State University; Dana Resente, Montgomery County Community College; Nedra Reynolds, University of

Rhode Island; Althea Rhodes, University of Arkansas, Fort Smith; Mauricio Rodriguez, El Paso Community College; Gardner Rogers, University of Illinois at Urbana-Champaign; Tony Russell, Purdue University; Matthew Samra, Kellogg Community College; Lisa L. Sandoval, Joliet Junior College; Lisa M. Schwerdt, California University of Pennsylvania; Michelle Sidler, Auburn University; William H. Smith, Weatherford College; Leah Sneider, University of New Mexico; Jeffrey Larsen Snodgrass, Prince George's Community College; Jean Sorensen, Grayson County College; Brady J. Spangenberg, Purdue University; Candace Stewart, Ohio University; Jennifer Stewart, Indiana University–Purdue University, Fort Wayne; Amy Ferdinandt Stolley, Purdue University; Mary Stripling, Dallas Baptist University; Martha Swearingen, University of District Columbia; Elyssa Tardiff, Purdue University; Linda Tetzlaff, Normandale Community College; John M. Thomson, Johnson County Community College; Monica Parrish Trent, Montgomery College, Rockville Campus; Griselda Valerio, University of Texas at Brownsville; Jarica Watts, University of Utah; Scott Weeden, Indiana University–Purdue University Fort Wayne; Candice Welhausen, University of New Mexico; Carol Westcamp, University of Arkansas, Fort Smith; Barbara Whitehead, Hampton University; Melissa E. Whiting, University of Arkansas, Fort Smith; and Anne-Marie Yerks, University of Michigan. Thanks especially to Avon Crismore's students at Indiana University–Purdue University Fort Wayne for their thoughtful (and well-written) evaluations.

The Norton Field Guide has also benefited from the good advice and conversations we've had with writing teachers across the country, including (among many others) Maureen Mathison, Susan Miller, Tom Huckin, Gae Lyn Henderson, and Sundy Watanabe at the University of Utah; Christa Albrecht-Crane, Doug Downs, and Brian Whaley at Utah Valley State College; Anne Dvorak and Anya Morrissey at Longview Community University; Jeff Andelora at Mesa Community College; Robin Calitri at Merced College; Lori Gallinger, Rose Hawkins, Jennifer Nelson, Georgia Standish, and John Ziebell at the Community College of Southern Nevada; Stuart Blythe at Indiana University–Purdue University Fort Wayne; Janice Kelly at Arizona State University; Jeanne McDonald at Waubonsee Community College; Web Newbold, Mary Clark-Upchurch, Megan Auffart, Matt Balk, Edward James Chambers, Sarah Chavez, Desiree Dighton, Ashley Ellison, Theresa Evans, Keith Heller, Ellie Isenhart, Angela Jackson-Brown, Naoko Kato, Yuanyuan Liao, Claire Lutkewitte, Yeno Matuki, Casey McArdle,

Tibor Munkacsi, Dani Nier-Weber, Karen Neubauer, Craig O'Hara, Martha Payne, Sarah Sandman, and Kellie Weiss at Ball State University; Patrick Tompkins at Tyler Community College; George Kanieski and Pamela Hardman at Cuyahoga Community College; Daniela Regusa, Jeff Partridge, and Lydia Vine at Capital Community College; Elizabeth Woodworth, Auburn University–Montgomery; Stephanie Eason at Enterprise Community College; and Kate Geiselman at Sinclair Community College.

We wouldn't have met most of these people without the help of the Norton travelers, the representatives who spend their days visiting faculty, showing and discussing the *Field Guide* and Norton's many other fine textbooks. Thanks especially to Kathy Church, Scott Cook, John Darger, Peter Wentz, Mary Helen Willett, Lauren Winkler, and all the other Norton travelers. And we'd especially like to thank Mike Wright, Lib Triplett, Ashley Cain, and Doug Day for promoting this book so enthusiastically and professionally.

It's customary to conclude by expressing gratitude to one's spouse and family, and for good reason. Writing and revising *The Norton Field Guide* over the past several years, we have enjoyed the loving and unconditional support of our spouses, Barb and Peter, who provide the foundation for all we do. Thank you. We couldn't have done it without you.

How to Use This Book

There's no one way to do anything, and writing is no exception. Some people need to do a lot of planning on paper; others write entire drafts in their heads. Some writers compose quickly and loosely, going back later to revise; others work on one sentence until they're satisfied with it, then move on to the next. And writers' needs vary from task to task, too: sometimes you know what you're going to write about and why, but need to figure out how to do it; other times your first job is to come up with a topic. *The Norton Field Guide* is designed to allow you to chart your own course as a writer, offering guidelines that suit your writing needs. It is organized in seven parts:

1. **RHETORICAL SITUATIONS**: No matter what you're writing, it will always have some purpose, audience, genre, stance, and medium and design. This part will help you consider each of these elements, as well as the particular kinds of rhetorical situations created by academic assignments.

2. **GENRES**: Use these chapters for help with specific kinds of writing, from abstracts to lab reports to memoirs and more. You'll find more detailed guidance for four especially common assignments: literacy narratives, textual analyses, reports, and arguments. There's also help with choosing which genre to use when an assignment doesn't specify one.

3. **PROCESSES**: These chapters offer general advice for all writing situations — from generating ideas and text to drafting, revising and rewriting, compiling a portfolio — and more.

4. **STRATEGIES**: Use the advice in this part to develop and organize your writing — to write effective beginnings and endings, to guide readers through your text, and to use comparison, description, dialogue, and other strategies as appropriate.

5. RESEARCH / DOCUMENTATION: Use this section for advice on how to do research, work with sources, and compose and document research-based texts using MLA and APA styles.

6. MEDIA / DESIGN: This section offers guidance in designing your work and using visuals and sound, and in deciding whether and how to deliver what you write on paper, on screen, or in person.

7. READINGS: This section includes readings in 9 genres, and one chapter of texts that mix genres — 50 readings in all that provide good examples of the kinds of writing you yourself may be assigned to do.

Ways into the Book

The Norton Field Guide gives you the writing advice you need, along with the flexibility to write in the way that works best for you. Here are some of the ways you can find what you need in the book.

Brief menus.   Inside the front cover you'll find a list of all the chapters; start here if you are looking for a chapter on a certain kind of writing or a general writing issue. Inside the back cover is a menu of all the readings in the book.

Complete contents.   Pages xviii–xxxvi contain a detailed table of contents. Look here if you need to find a reading or a specific section in a chapter.

Guides to writing.   If you know the kind of writing you need to do, you'll find guides to writing 14 common genres in Part 2. These guides are designed to help you through all the decisions you have to make — from coming up with a topic to editing and proofreading your final draft.

Color-coding.   The parts of this book are color-coded for easy reference: red for RHETORICAL SITUATIONS, green for GENRES, lavender for PROCESSES, orange for STRATEGIES, blue for RESEARCH / DOCUMENTATION, gold for MEDIA / DESIGN, and apple green for the READINGS. You'll find a key to the colors on the front cover flap and also at the foot of each left-hand page. When you see a word highlighted in a color, that tells you where you can find additional detail on the topic.

Glossary / index. At the back of the book is a combined glossary and index, where you'll find full definitions of key terms and topics, along with a list of the pages where everything is covered in detail.

Directories to MLA and APA documentation. A brief directory at the back of the book will lead you to guidelines on citing sources and composing a list of references or works cited. The documentation models are color-coded so you can easily see the key details.

The website. You can also start at wwnorton.com/write/fieldguide. There you'll find model essays; worksheets; MLA and APA guidelines; more than 1,000 exercises focused on sentences, language, and punctuation; an online handbook; and more.

Ways of Getting Started

If you know your genre, simply turn to the appropriate genre chapter. There you'll find model readings, a description of the genre's Key Features, and a Guide to Writing that will help you come up with a topic, generate text, organize and write a draft, get response, revise, edit, and proofread. The genre chapters also point out places where you might need to do research, use certain writing strategies, design your text a certain way — and direct you to the exact pages in the book where you can find help doing so.

If you know your topic, you might start with some of the activities in Chapter 24, Generating Ideas and Text. From there, you might turn to Chapter 44, for help Finding Sources on the topic. When it comes time to narrow your topic and come up with a thesis statement, Chapter 31 can help. If you get stuck at any point, you might turn to Chapter 22, Writing as Inquiry; it provides tips that can get you beyond what you already know about your topic. If your assignment or your thesis defines your genre, turn to that chapter; if not, consult Chapter 21 for help determining the appropriate genre, and then turn to that genre chapter. The genre chapters point out places where you might need to do more research, use certain writing strategies, design your text a certain way — and direct you to the exact pages in the book where you can find help doing so.

Contents

Part 1   Rhetorical Situations   *1*

Part 2   Genres   25

Contents   **xxiii**

Part 3   Processes *249*

Part 4   Strategies   *297*

Part 5   Doing Research   *419*

Part 7   Readings   *621*

Thematic Guide to the Readings

Entertainment and the Arts

Humor and Satire

Identity

Language and Literacy

Nature and the Environment

Race and Ethnicity

part 1

Rhetorical Situations

Whenever we write, whether it's a text to a friend or a toast for a wedding, an English essay or a résumé, we face some kind of rhetorical situation. We have a PURPOSE, a certain AUDIENCE, a particular STANCE, a GENRE, and a MEDIUM to consider — and often as not a DESIGN. All are important elements that we need to think about carefully. The following chapters offer brief discussions of those elements of the rhetorical situation, along with questions that can help you make the choices you need to as you write. A chapter on WRITING IN ACADEMIC CONTEXTS offers help with the demands of college writing. See also the fourteen GENRES chapters for guidelines for considering your rhetorical situation in each of these specific kinds of writing.

Rhetorical Situations

Purpose 1

All writing has a purpose. We write to explore our thoughts and emotions, to express ourselves, to entertain; we write to record words and events, to communicate with others, to try to persuade others to believe as we do or to behave in certain ways. In fact, we often have several purposes at the same time. We may write an essay in which we try to explain something to an audience, but at the same time we may be trying to persuade that audience of something. Look, for example, at this passage from a 2012 *New York Times* op-ed essay by economist and editorial columnist Paul Krugman about social and economic trends among "the traditional working-class family" — declining rates of marriage and of male participation in the labor force and increasing numbers of out-of-wedlock births. Krugman asserts that the primary reason for those statistics is a "drastic reduction in the work opportunities available to less-educated men":

> Most of the numbers you see about income trends in America focus on households rather than individuals, which makes sense for some purposes. But when you see a modest rise in incomes for the lower tiers of the income distribution, you have to realize that all — yes, all — of this rise comes from the women, both because more women are in the paid labor force and because women's wages aren't as much below male wages as they used to be.
>
> For lower-education working men, however, it has been all negative. Adjusted for inflation, entry-level wages of male high school graduates have fallen 23 percent since 1973. Meanwhile, employment benefits have collapsed. In 1980, 65 percent of recent high-school graduates working in the private sector had health benefits, but, by 2009, that was down to 29 percent.
>
> So we have become a society in which less-educated men have great difficulty finding jobs with decent wages and good benefits.
>
> —Paul Krugman, "Money and Morals"

Krugman is reporting information here, outlining how the earnings and benefits of less-educated men have dropped over the last forty years. He is also making an argument, that these economic setbacks are the cause of the social ills among working-class Americans and not, as some would have it, the result of them. (Krugman, writing for a newspaper, is also using a style — including dashes, contractions, and other informal elements — that strives to be engaging while it informs and argues.)

Even though our purposes may be many, knowing our primary reason for writing can help us shape that writing and understand how to proceed with it. Our purpose can determine the genre we choose, our audience, even the way we design what we write.

Identify your purpose. While a piece of writing often has many purposes, a writer usually focuses on one. When you get an assignment or see a need to write, ask yourself what the primary purpose of the writing task is: to entertain? to inform? to persuade? to demonstrate your knowledge or your writing ability? What are your own goals? What are your audience's expectations, and do they affect the way you define your purpose?

Thinking about Purpose

- *What do you want your audience to do, think, or feel?* How will they use what you tell them?

- *What does this writing task call on you to do?* Do you need to show that you have mastered certain content or skills? Do you have an assignment that specifies a particular **STRATEGY** or **GENRE** — to compare two things, perhaps, or to argue a position?

- *What are the best ways to achieve your purpose?* What kind of **STANCE** should you take? Should you write in a particular genre? Do you have a choice of **MEDIUM,** and does your text require any special format or **DESIGN** elements?

297 ◆
25 ▲
12–15 ■
575 ☐

Audience 2

Who will read (or hear) what you are writing? A seemingly obvious but crucially important question. Your audience affects your writing in various ways. Consider a piece of writing as simple as a text from a mother to her son:

> *Pls. take chicken out to thaw and feed Annye. Remember Dr. Wong at 4.*

On the surface, this brief note is a straightforward reminder to do three things. But in fact it is a complex message filled with compressed information for a specific audience. The writer (the mother) counts on the reader (her son) to know a lot that can be left unsaid. She expects that he knows that the chicken is in the freezer and needs to thaw in time to be cooked for dinner; she knows that he knows who Annye is (a pet?), what he or she is fed, and how much; she assumes that he knows who (and where) Dr. Wong is. She doesn't need to spell any of that out because she knows what her son knows and what he needs to know—and in her text she can be brief. She understands her audience. Think how different such a reminder would be were it written to another audience—a babysitter, perhaps, or a friend helping out while Mom is out of town.

What you write, how much you write, how you phrase it, even your choice of **GENRE** (memo, essay, email, note, speech)—all are influenced by the audience you envision. And your audience will interpret your writing according to their own expectations and experiences, not yours.

9–11

When you are a student, your audience is most often your teachers, so you need to be aware of their expectations and know the conventions (rules, often unstated) for writing in specific academic fields. You may make statements that seem obvious to you, not realizing that your instructors may consider them assertions that must be proved with evidence of one sort or another. Or you may write more or less formally than teachers expect. Understanding your audience's expectations — by asking outright, by reading materials in your field of study, by trial and error — is important to your success as a college writer.

This point is worth dwelling on. You are probably reading this textbook for a writing course. As a student, you will be expected to produce essays with few or no errors. If as part of your job or among friends and family you correspond using email and texts you may question such standards; after all, many of the messages you get in these contexts are not grammatically perfect. But in a writing class, the instructor needs to see your best work. Whatever the rhetorical situation, your writing must meet the expectations of your audience.

Identify your audience.   Audiences may be defined as *known, multiple,* or *unknown. Known audiences* can include people with whom you're familiar as well as people you don't know personally but whose needs and expectations you do know. You yourself are a known, familiar audience, and you write to and for yourself often. Class notes, to-do lists, reminders, and journals are all written primarily for an audience of one: you. For that reason, they are often in shorthand, full of references and code that you alone understand.

Other known, familiar audiences include anyone you actually know — friends, relatives, teachers, classmates — and whose needs and expectations you understand. You can also know what certain readers want and need, even if you've never met them personally, if you write for them within a specific shared context. Such a known audience might include PC gamers who read cheat codes that you have posted on the Internet for beating a game; you don't know those people, but you know roughly what they know about the game and what they need to know, and you know how to write about it in ways they will understand.

You often have to write for *multiple audiences*. Business memos or reports may be written initially for a supervisor, but he or she may pass them along to others. Grant proposals may be reviewed by four to six levels of readers — each, of course, with its own expectations and perspectives.

rhetorical situations   genres   processes   strategies   research MLA / APA   media / design   readings

Even writing for a class might involve multiple audiences: your instructor and your classmates.

Unknown audiences can be the most difficult to address since you can't be sure what they know, what they need to know, how they'll react. Such an audience could be your downstairs neighbor, with whom you're chatted occasionally in the laundry room. How will she respond to your letter asking her to sponsor you in an upcoming charity walk? Another unknown audience — perhaps surprisingly — might be many of your instructors, who want — and expect! — you to write in ways that are new to you. While you can benefit from analyzing any audience, you need to think most carefully about those you don't know.

Thinking about Audience

- *Whom do you want to reach?* To whom are you writing (or speaking)?
- *What is your audience's background — their education and life experiences?* It may be important for you to know, for example, whether your readers attended college, fought in a war, or have young children.
- *What are their interests?* What do they like? What motivates them? What do they care about?
- *Is there any demographic information that you should keep in mind?* Consider whether race, gender, sexual orientation, disabilities, occupations, religious beliefs, economic status, and so on should affect what or how you write. For example, writers for *Men's Health*, *InStyle*, and *Out* must consider the particular interests of each magazine's readers.
- *What political circumstances may affect their reading?* What attitudes — opinions, special interests, biases — may affect the way your audience reads your piece? Are your readers conservative, liberal, or middle of the road? Politics may take many other forms as well — retirees on a fixed income may object to increased school taxes, so a letter arguing for such an increase would need to appeal to them differently than would a similar letter sent to parents of young children.

- *What does your audience already know — or believe — about your topic? What do you need to tell them? What is the best way to do so?* Those retirees who oppose school taxes already know that taxes are a burden for them; they may need to know why schools are justified in asking for more money every few years. A good way to explain this may be with a bar graph showing how property values benefit from good schools with adequate funding. Consider which **STRATEGIES** will be effective — narrative, comparison, something else?

297 ◆

- *What's your relationship with your audience, and how should it affect your language and tone?* Do you know them, or not? Are they friends? Colleagues? Mentors? Adversaries? Strangers? Will they likely share your **STANCE?** In general, you need to write more formally when you're addressing readers you don't know, and you may address friends and colleagues more informally than you would a boss.

12–15 ■

- *What does your audience need and expect from you?* Your history professor, for example, may need to know how well you can discuss the economy of the late Middle Ages in order to assess your learning; he may expect you to write a carefully reasoned argument, drawing conclusions from various sources, with a readily identifiable thesis in the first paragraph. Your boss, on the other hand, may need an informal email that briefly lists your sales contacts for the day; she may expect that you list the contacts in the order in which you saw them, that you clearly identify each one, and that you briefly say how well each contact went. What **GENRE** is most appropriate?

25 ▲

- *What kind of response do you want?* Do you want readers to believe or do something? To accept as valid your information on a topic? To understand why an experience you once had matters to you?

575 ☐

- *How can you best appeal to your audience?* Is there a particular **MEDIUM** that will best reach them? Are there any **DESIGN** requirements? (Elderly readers may need larger type, for instance.)

Genre 3

Genres are kinds of writing. Letters, profiles, reports, position papers, poems, blog posts, instructions, parodies—even jokes—are genres. For example, here is the beginning of a **PROFILE** of a mechanic who repairs a specific kind of automobile:

▲ 191–204

> Her business card reads Shirley Barnes, M.D., and she's a doctor, all right—a Metropolitan Doctor. Her passion is the Nash Metropolitan, the little car produced by Austin of England for American Motors between 1954 and 1962. Barnes is a legend among southern California Met lovers—an icon, a beacon, and a font of useful knowledge and freely offered opinions.

A profile offers a written portrait of someone or something that informs and sometimes entertains, often examining its subject from a particular angle—in this case, as a female mechanic who fixes Nash Metropolitans. While the language in this example is informal and lively ("she's a doctor, all right"), the focus is on the subject, Shirley Barnes, "M.D." If this same excerpt were presented as a poem, however, the new genre would change our reading:

> Her business card reads
> Shirley Barnes, M.D.,
> and she's a doctor, all right
> —a Metropolitan Doctor.
> Her passion is the Nash Metropolitan,
> the little car produced by Austin of England
> for American Motors between 1954 and 1962.
> Barnes is a legend
> among southern California Met lovers
> — an icon,

> a beacon,
> and a font of useful knowledge and
> freely offered opinions.

The content hasn't changed, but the different presentation invites us to read not only to learn about Shirley Barnes but also to explore the significance of the words and phrases on each line, to read for deeper meaning and greater appreciation of language. The genre thus determines how we read and how we interpret what we read.

Genres help us write by establishing features for conveying certain kinds of content. They give readers clues about what sort of information they're likely to find and so help them figure out how to read ("This article begins with an abstract, so it's probably a scholarly source" or "Thank goodness! I found the instructions for editing videos on my phone"). At the same time, writers sometimes challenge genre conventions, reshaping them as communicative needs and technologies change. For example, computers have enabled us to add audio and video content to texts that once could appear only on paper.

25

Identify your genre. Does your writing situation call for a certain **GENRE?** A memo? A report? A proposal? A letter? Academic assignments generally specify the genre ("take a position," "analyze the text"), but if not, see

243–48

Chapter 21 for help **CHOOSING GENRES** — or ask your instructor.

Thinking about Genre

- *What is your genre, and how does it affect what content you can or should include?* Objective information? Researched source material? Your own opinions? Personal experience?

297
173–82

- *Does your genre call for any specific* **STRATEGIES?** Profiles, for example, usually include some narration; **LAB REPORTS** often explain a process.

205–13

- *Does your genre require a certain organization?* Most **PROPOSALS,** for instance, first identify a problem and then offer a solution. Some genres leave room for choice. Business letters delivering good news might be organized differently than those making sales pitches.

rhetorical situations   genres   processes   strategies   research MLA / APA   media / design   readings

- *Does your genre affect your tone?* An abstract of a scholarly paper calls for a different TONE than a memoir. Should your words sound serious and scholarly? Brisk and to the point? Objective? Opinionated? Sometimes your genre affects the way you communicate your STANCE.

■ 13

■ 12–15

- *Does the genre require formal (or informal) language?* A letter to the mother of a friend asking for a summer job in her bookstore calls for more formal language than does an email to the friend thanking him for the lead.

- *Do you have a choice of medium?* Some genres call for print; others for an electronic medium. Sometimes you have a choice: a résumé, for instance, can be printed to bring to an interview, or it may be emailed. Some teachers want reports turned in on paper; others prefer that they be emailed or posted in the class course management system. If you're not sure what MEDIUM you can use, ask.

☐ 575

- *Does your genre have any design requirements?* Some genres call for paragraphs; others require lists. Some require certain kinds of fonts — you wouldn't use **Impact** for a personal narrative, nor would you likely use Chiller for an invitation to Grandma's sixty-fifth birthday party. Different genres call for different DESIGN elements.

☐ 575

4 Stance

Whenever you write, you have a certain stance, an attitude toward your topic. The way you express that stance affects the way you come across to your audience as a writer and a person. This email from a college student to his father, for example, shows a thoughtful, reasonable stance for a carefully researched argument:

> Hi Dad,
> I'll get right to the point: I'd like to buy a car. I saved over $3500 from working this summer, and I've found three different cars that I can get for under $3000. That'll leave me $400 to cover the insurance. I can park in Lot J, over behind Monte Hall, for $75 for both semesters. And I can earn gas and repair money by upping my hours at the cafeteria. It won't cost you any more, and if I have a car, you won't have to come and pick me up when I want to come home. May I buy it?
> Love,
> Michael

While such a stance can't guarantee that Dad will give permission, it's more likely to produce results than this version:

> Hi Dad,
> I'm buying a car. A guy in my Western Civ course has a cool Chevy he wants to get rid of. I've got $3500 saved from working this summer, it's mine, and I'm going to use it to get some wheels. Mom said you'd blow your top if I did, but I want this car. OK?
> Michael

The writer of the first email respects his reader and offers reasoned arguments and evidence of research to convince him that buying a car is an action that will benefit them both. The writer of the second, by contrast, seems impulsive, ready to buy the first car that comes along, and defiant—he's picking a fight. Each email reflects a certain stance that shows the writer as a certain kind of person dealing with a topic in a certain way and establishing a certain relationship with his audience.

Identify your stance.   What is your attitude toward your topic? Objective? Critical? Curious? Opinionated? Passionate? Indifferent? Your stance may be affected by your relationship to your AUDIENCE. How do you want them to see you? As a colleague sharing information? As a good student showing what you can do? As an advocate for a position? Often your stance is affected by your GENRE: for example, lab reports require an objective, unemotional stance that emphasizes the content and minimizes the writer's own attitudes. Memoir, by comparison, allows you to reveal your feelings about your topic. Your stance is also affected by your PURPOSE, as the two emails about cars show. Your stance in a piece written to entertain will likely differ from the stance you'd adopt to persuade.

5–8

25

3–4

You communicate (or downplay) your stance through your tone — through the words you use and other ways your text expresses an attitude toward your subject and audience. For example, in an academic essay you would state your position directly — "the *Real Housewives* series reflects the values of American society today"—a confident, assertive tone. In contrast, using qualifiers like "might" or "I think" can give your writing a wishy-washy, uncertain tone: "I think the *Real Housewives* series might reflect some of the values of American society today." The following paragraph, from an essay analyzing a text, has a sarcastic tone that might be appropriate for a comment on a blog post, but that isn't right for an academic essay:

> In "Just Be Nice," Stephen M. Carter complains about a boy who wore his pants too low, showing his underwear. Is that really something people should worry about? We have wars raging and terrorism happening every day, and he wants to talk about how inconsiderate it is for someone to wear his pants too low? If by that boy pulling his pants up, the world would be a better place and peace would break out in the Middle East, I'm sure everyone would buy a belt.

This writer clearly thinks Carter's complaint is trivial in comparison with the larger issues of the day, but her sarcastic tone belittles Carter's argument instead of answering it with a serious counterargument. Like every other element of writing, your tone must be appropriate for your rhetorical situation.

Just as you likely alter what you say depending on whether you're speaking to a boss, an instructor, a parent, or a good friend, so you need to make similar adjustments as a writer. It's a question of appropriateness: we behave in certain ways in various social situations, and writing is a social situation. You might sign an email to a friend with an x and an o, but in an email to your supervisor you'll likely sign off with a "Many thanks" or "Sincerely." To write well, you need to write with integrity, to say as much as possible what you wish to say; yet you also must understand that in writing, as in speaking, your stance and tone need to suit your purpose, your relationship to your audience, the way in which you wish your audience to perceive you, and your medium. In writing as in other aspects of life, the Golden Rule applies: "Do unto audiences as you would have them do unto you." Address readers respectfully if you want them to respond to your words with respect.

Thinking about Stance

- *What is your stance, and how does it relate to your purpose for writing?* If you feel strongly about your topic and are writing an argument that tries to persuade your audience to feel the same way, your stance and your **PURPOSE** fit naturally together. But suppose you are writing about the same topic with a different purpose — to demonstrate the depth of your knowledge about the topic, for example, or your ability to consider it in a detached, objective way. You will need to adjust your stance to meet the demands of this different purpose.

- *How should your stance be reflected in your tone?* Can your tone grow directly out of your stance, or do you need to "tone down" your attitude toward the topic or take a different tone altogether? Do you want to be seen as reasonable? Angry? Thoughtful? Gentle? Funny? Ironic? If you're writing about something you want to be seen as taking very

3–4 ■

seriously, be sure that your language and even your font reflect that seriousness. Check your writing for words that reflect the tone you want to convey — and for ones that do not (and revise as necessary).

- *How is your stance likely to be received by your audience?* Your tone and especially the attitude it projects toward your **AUDIENCE** will affect how they react to the content of what you say.

  5–8

- *Should you openly reveal your stance?* Do you want or need to announce your own perspective on your topic? Will doing so help you reach your audience, or would it be better not to say directly where you're coming from?

5 Media/Design

In its broadest sense, a medium is a go-between: a way for information to be conveyed from one person to another. We communicate through many media, verbal and nonverbal: our bodies (we catch someone's eye, wave, nod); our voices (we whisper, talk, shout, groan); and various technologies, including handwriting, print, telephone, radio, CD, film, and computer.

Each medium has unique characteristics that influence both what and how we communicate. As an example, consider this message: "I haven't told you this before, but I love you." Most of the time, we communicate such a message in person, using the medium of voice (with, presumably, help from eye contact and touch). A phone call will do, though most of us would think it a poor second choice, and a handwritten letter or note would be acceptable, if necessary. Few of us would break such news on a website, with a tweet, or during a radio call-in program.

By contrast, imagine whispering the following sentence in a darkened room: "By the last decades of the nineteenth century, the territorial expansion of the United States had left almost all Indians confined to reservations." That sentence starts a chapter in a history textbook, and it would be strange indeed to whisper it into someone's ear. It is appropriate, however, in the textbook, in print or in an e-book, or on a *PowerPoint* slide accompanying an oral presentation.

As you can see, we can often choose among various media depending on our purpose and audience. In addition, we can often combine media to create **MULTIMEDIA** texts. And different media allow us to use different ways or modes of expressing meaning, from words to images to sound to hyperlinks, that can be combined into **MULTIMODAL** formats.

No matter the medium or media, a text's design affects the way it is received and understood. A typed letter on official letterhead sends a different message than the same words handwritten on pastel stationery.

579

rhetorical situations

genres

processes

strategies

research MLA / APA

media / design

readings

Classic type sends a different message than *flowery italics*. Some genres and media (and audiences) demand **PHOTOS, DIAGRAMS,** or color. Some information is easier to explain—and read—in the form of a **PIE CHART** or a **BAR GRAPH** than in the form of a paragraph. Some reports and documents are so long and complex that they need to be divided into sections, which are then best labeled with **HEADINGS.** These are some of the elements to consider when you are thinking about how to design what you write.

☐ 593–95

☐ 588–89

Identify your media and design needs.   Does your writing situation call for a certain medium and design? A printed essay? An oral report with visual aids? A blog? A podcast? Academic assignments often assume a particular medium and design, but if you're unsure about your options or the degree of flexibility you have, check with your instructor.

Thinking about Media

- *What medium are you using*— print? spoken? electronic? a combination? —and how does it affect the way you will create your text? A printed résumé is usually no more than one page long; a scannable résumé sent via email has no length limits. An oral presentation should contain detailed information; accompanying slides should provide only an outline.

- *How does your medium affect your organization and* **STRATEGIES?** Long paragraphs are fine on paper but don't work well on the web. On presentation slides, phrases or key words work better than sentences. In print, you need to define unfamiliar terms; on the Web, you can sometimes just add a link to a definition found elsewhere.

◆ 297

- *How does your medium affect your language?* Some print documents require a more formal voice than spoken media; email and texting often invite greater informality.

- *How does your medium affect what elements besides words you include?* Should your text include photos, graphics, audio or video files, or links? Do you need slides, handouts, or other visuals to accompany an oral presentation?

Thinking about Design

1

- *What's the appropriate look for your* RHETORICAL SITUATION? Should your text look serious? Whimsical? Personal? Something else? What design elements will suit your audience, purpose, genre, and medium?

- *What elements need to be designed?* Is there any information you would like to highlight by putting it in a box? Are there any key terms that should be boldfaced? Do you need navigation buttons? How should you indicate links?

- *What font(s) are appropriate* to your audience, purpose, genre, and medium?

591–99
5–8

- *Are you including any* VISUALS? Should you? Will your AUDIENCE expect or need any? Is there any information in your text that would be easier to understand as a chart or graph? If you need to include video or audio clips, how should the links be presented?

9–11
17

- *Should you include headings?* Would they help you organize your materials and help readers follow the text? Does your GENRE or MEDIUM require them?

Writing in Academic Contexts   **6**

In an introductory psychology course, you're assigned to write an essay taking a position on whether genes or environment do more to determine people's intelligence. Your environmental science instructor asks you to research and write a report on the environmental effects of electricity-generating windmills. Your marketing professor requires you to write a proposal, including a multimedia presentation, for a sales campaign. Academic writing serves many purposes: you may write to explore a topic, to explain what's known about it, to outline what others have said about it, to say what you think about it and why — or for various other purposes. Whatever your topic or purpose, academic writing is a way of adding your voice to some larger conversation. This chapter will help you think about some of the key features expected in academic contexts.

Key Features of Academic Writing

Evidence that you've carefully considered the subject. Whether you're writing a personal narrative, a report, or an argument, you need to demonstrate that you've thought seriously about the topic and done any necessary research. You can use a variety of ways to show that you've considered the subject thoughtfully, from citing authoritative sources to incorporating information you learned in class to pointing out connections among ideas.

A clear, appropriately qualified THESIS. When you write in an academic   313–15
context, you're expected to state your main point explicitly, often in a thesis statement. MIT student Joanna MacKay states her thesis clearly in her

19

314–15 ◆

essay "Organ Sales Will Save Lives": "Governments should not ban the sale of human organs; they should regulate it." Often, you'll need to **QUALIFY** your thesis statement to acknowledge that the subject is complicated and there may be more than one way of seeing it, or exceptions to the generalization you're making about it. Here, for example, is a qualified thesis, from an essay about whether texting affects writing by Michaela Cullington, a student at Marywood University: "Although some believe that texting has either a positive or negative effect on writing, it in fact seems likely that texting has no significant effect on student writing." The beginning of the sentence acknowledges other views, and the use of words like *seems likely* and *significant* indicates that Cullington is not making an absolute, unqualified claim that texting has no effect at all.

A response to what others have said. Whatever your topic, it is unlikely that you'll be the first one to write about it. And if, as this chapter assumes, all academic writing is part of a larger conversation, you are in a way adding your own voice to that conversation. One good way of doing that is to present your ideas as a response to what others have said about your topic — to begin by quoting, paraphrasing, or summarizing what others have said and then to agree, disagree, or both.

For example, in an essay arguing that the American Dream is alive and well, Brandon King presents the views of two economists who say that because wealth is concentrated in the hands "of a rich minority . . . the American Dream is no longer possible for most Americans." He then responds by disagreeing, arguing that "the American Dream . . . is based on perception, on the way someone *imagines* how to be successful."

326–35 ◆

Good reasons supported by evidence. You need to provide good **REASONS** for your thesis and **EVIDENCE** to support those reasons. For example, MacKay offers several reasons why sales of human kidneys should be legalized: there is a surplus of kidneys, the risk to the donor is not great, and legalization would allow the trade in kidneys to be regulated. Evidence to support your reasons sometimes comes from your own experience, but more often from published research and scholarship, research you do yourself, or first-hand accounts by others.

Compared with other kinds of writing, academic writing is generally expected to be more detached and objective and less personal and emotional. You may find *Romeo and Juliet* deeply moving or cry when you watch *Titanic* — but when you write about the play or the film for a class, you must do so using evidence from the text to support your thesis. Similarly, you may find someone's ideas deeply offensive, but you should respond to them primarily with reason, rather than with emotional appeals or personal attacks.

Acknowledgment of multiple perspectives. Debates and arguments in popular media are often framed in "pro/con" terms, a view in which there are only two sides to an issue. Once you begin seriously studying a topic, though, you're likely to find that there are several sides, and that each of them deserves serious consideration. In your academic writing, you need to represent fairly the range of perspectives on your topic — to explore three, four, or more positions on it as you research and write. King, for instance, looks at the American Dream from several angles: the ways it is defined, the effects of taxes and other government policies on the ability of people to achieve the Dream, the role of education, and more.

Carefully documented sources. Clearly acknowledging sources and DOCUMENTING them carefully and correctly is a basic requirement of academic writing. When you use the words or ideas of others — including visuals, video, or audio — those sources must be documented both in the text and in a works cited or references list at the end. (If you're writing something that will appear online, you may also refer readers to your sources by using hyperlinks in the text; check with your instructor first, and ask if you need to include a list of references or works cited.)

480–83

A confident, authoritative STANCE. Since one of the goals of academic writing is to contribute to a larger conversation, your tone should convey confidence and establish your authority to write about your subject. Ways to achieve such a tone include using active verbs ("X claims" rather than "it seems"), avoiding such phrases as "in my opinion" and "I think," and

12–15

writing in a straightforward, direct style. For example, here is the final paragraph of Cullington's essay on texting and writing:

> On the basis of my own research, expert research, and personal observations, I can confidently state that texting is not interfering with students' use of standard written English and has no effect on their writing abilities in general. It is interesting to look at the dynamics of the arguments over these issues. Teachers and parents who claim that they are seeing a decline in the writing abilities of their students and children mainly support the negative-impact argument. Other teachers and researchers suggest that texting provides a way for teens to practice writing in a casual setting and thus helps prepare them to write formally. Experts and students themselves, however, report that they see no effect, positive or negative. Anecdotal experiences should not overshadow the actual evidence.

Cullington's use of simple, declarative sentences ("Other teachers and researchers suggest . . . ," "Anecdotal experiences should not overshadow . . .") and her straightforward summary of the arguments surrounding texting, along with her strong, unequivocal ending ("texting is not interfering with students' use of standard written English") lend her writing a confident tone. Her stance sends the message that she's done the research and knows what she's talking about.

An indication of why your topic matters. You need to help your readers understand why your topic is worth exploring and why your writing is worth reading. Even if you are writing in response to an assigned topic, you can better make your point and achieve your purpose by showing your readers why your topic is important and why they should care about it. For example, in "Throwing Like a Girl," James Fallows explains why his topic, the differences between the ways men and women throw a baseball, is worth writing about:

> The phrase "throwing like a girl" has become an embattled and offensive one. Feminists smart at its implication that to do something "like a girl" is to do it the wrong way. Recently, on the heels of the O. J. Simpson case, a book appeared in which the phrase was used to help explain why male athletes, especially football players, were involved in

so many assaults against women. Having been trained (like most American boys) to dread the accusation of doing anything "like a girl," athletes were said to grow into the assumption that women were valueless, and natural prey.

By explaining that the topic matters because it reflects attitudes about gender that have potentially serious consequences, he gives readers reason to read on about the mechanics of "throwing like a girl."

Careful attention to correctness. Whether you're writing something formal or informal, in an essay or an email, you should almost always write in complete sentences, use appropriate capitalization and punctuation, and check that your spelling is correct. In general, academic writing is no place for or texting abbreviations. If you're quoting someone, you can reproduce that person's language exactly, but in your own writing you should try hard to be correct — and always proofread carefully.

Thinking about an Academic Rhetorical Situation

- *What* GENRE *does the assignment require?* An essay? If so, is it a narrative, a report, a reflection, an analysis, an argument, or something else? Does the assignment specify the genre, or if not, can you figure out what's required from the verb or other key terms in the assignment wording? If not, do you get to CHOOSE YOUR GENRE? 9–11

  243–48

- *What do you see as your instructor's purpose for this assignment?* To have you demonstrate learning of some kind? Show your understanding of course material? Discuss ideas, concepts, or facts? Explore ideas and look for connections among them? Have you been given a description of what your writing should include?

- *What is your* PURPOSE *as the writer, apart from fulfilling your instructor's expectations?* To persuade your audience to do or believe something? To inform them about something and help them understand it? To play with ideas and see where they lead? 3–4

5–8
- *Who is your* AUDIENCE? Your instructor? your classmates? others? How much does the audience know about the topic? Are they in an academic field with particular conventions you need to follow?

12–15
- *How can you convey a confident, authoritative* STANCE? By showing that you understand the larger context of your topic? By showing confidence in what you say? By stating your claims forthrightly and clearly? By adopting a tone appropriate for your genre?

16–18
- *What* MEDIA *are available, permitted, and appropriate? Are any required?* Will you present your work as a paper document? As a digital text? As an oral presentation? Can you — and should you — use photos, drawings, charts, graphs, or slides or embed audio or video files?

16–18
- *What* DESIGN *issues need to be considered?* Should you assume that your written text should follow MLA or APA formatting guidelines? Do you need to include any visual or audio elements? How much freedom do you have to design your work?

rhetorical situations

genres

processes

strategies

research MLA / APA

media / design

readings

part 2

Genres

When we make a shopping list, we automatically write each item we need in a single column. When we email a friend, we begin with a salutation: "Hi, Brian." Whether we are writing a letter, a résumé, a lab report, or a proposal, we know generally what it should contain and what it should look like because we are familiar with each of those genres. Genres are kinds of writing, and texts in any given genre share goals and features — a proposal, for instance, generally starts out by identifying a problem and then suggests a certain solution. The chapters in this part provide guidelines for writing in thirteen common academic genres. First come detailed chapters on four genres often assigned in writing classes: LITERACY NARRATIVES, essays ANALYZING TEXTS, REPORTS, and ARGUMENTS, followed by brief chapters on NINE OTHER GENRES and two on MIXING and CHOOSING GENRES.

Genres

Writing a Literacy Narrative   **7**

Narratives are stories, and we read and tell them for many different purposes. Parents read their children bedtime stories as an evening ritual. Preachers base their Sunday sermons on Bible stories to teach lessons about moral behavior. Grandparents tell how things used to be (sometimes the same stories year after year). Schoolchildren tell teachers that their dog ate their homework. College applicants write about significant moments in their lives. Writing students are often called upon to compose literacy narratives to explore their experiences with reading and writing. This chapter provides detailed guidelines for writing a literacy narrative. We'll begin with four good examples, the first annotated to point out the key features found in most literacy narratives.

EMILY VALLOWE

Write or Wrong Identity

Emily Vallowe wrote this literacy narrative for a writing class at the University of Mary Washington in Virginia. In it, she explores her lifelong identity as a writer — and her doubts about that identity.

I'm sitting in the woods with a bunch of Catholic people I just met yesterday. Suddenly, they ask me to name one of the talents God has given me. I panic for a split second and then breathe an internal sigh of relief. I tell them I'm a writer. As the group leaders move on to question someone else, I sit trying to mentally catch my breath. It will take a moment before the terror leaves my forearms, chest, and stomach,

Attention-getting opening.

rhetorical situations • genres • processes • strategies • research MLA / APA • media / design • readings but I tell myself that I have nothing to fear. I am a writer. Yes, I most definitely am a writer. *Now breathe,* I tell myself . . . *and suppress that horrifying suspicion that you are actually not a writer at all.*

The retreat that prepared me for my eighth-grade confirmation was not the first time I found myself pulling out the old "I'm a writer" card and wondering whether I was worthy enough to carry this sacred card in the wallet of my identity. Such things happen to people with identity crises.

In kindergarten I wrote about thirty books. They were each about five pages long, with one sentence and a picture on each page. They were held together with three staples on the left side or top and had construction paper covers with the book's title and the phrase "By Emily Vallowe" written out in neat kindergarten-teacher handwriting. My mom still has all of these books in a box at the bottom of her closet.

Clearly described details.

One day at the very end of the school year, my kindergarten teacher took me to meet my future first-grade teacher, Mrs. Meadows. I got to make a special trip to meet her because I had been absent on the day the rest of the kindergarteners had gone to meet their future teachers. Mrs. Meadows's classroom was big and blue and different from the kindergarten class, complete with bigger, different kids (I think Mrs. Meadows had been teaching third or fourth graders that year, so her students were much older than I was). During this visit, Mrs. Meadows showed me a special writing desk, complete with a small, old-fashioned desk lamp (with a lamp shade and everything). I'm not sure if I understood why she was showing me this writing area. She may have said that she'd heard good things about me.

Vallowe traces her identity as a writer through her life.

This handful of images is all I can remember about the most sig- 5 nificant event in my writing life. I'm not sure why I connect the memory of my kindergarten books with the image of me sitting in Mrs. Meadows's old classroom (for by the time I had her she was in a room on the opposite side of the school). I guess I don't even know exactly when this major event happened. Was it kindergarten? First grade? Somewhere in between? All I know is that some event occurred in early elementary school that made me want to be a writer. I don't even clearly remember what this event was, but it is something that has actively affected me for the fourteen years since then.

I have wanted to be a writer my entire life — or at least that's what I tell people. Looking back, I don't know if I ever *wanted* to be a writer. The idea might never have even occurred to me. Yet somehow I was marked as a writer. My teachers must have seen something in my writing that impressed them and clued me in on it. Teachers like to recognize kids for their strengths, and at the age of five, I probably started to notice that different kids were good at different things: Bobby was good at t-ball; Sally was good at drawing; Jenny could run really fast. I was probably starting to panic at the thought that I might not be good at anything — and then a teacher came along and told me I was good at writing. Someone gave me a compliment, and I ran with it. I declared myself to be a writer and have clung to this writer identity ever since.

There are certain drawbacks to clinging to one unchanging identity since the age of five. Constant panic is one of these drawbacks. It is a strange feeling to grow up defining yourself as something when you don't know if that something is actually true. By the time I got to middle school, I could no longer remember having become a writer; I had just always been one — and had been one without any proof that I deserved to be called one. By the age of ten, I was facing a seasoned writer's terror of "am I any good?!" and this terror has followed me throughout my entire life since then. Every writing assignment I ever had was a test — a test to see if I was a real writer, to prove myself to teachers, to classmates, to myself. I approached every writing assignment thinking, "I am supposed to be good at this," not "I am going to try to make this good," and such an attitude is not a healthy way to approach anything.

It doesn't help that, if I am a writer, I am a very slow one. I can't sit down and instantly write something beautiful like some people I know can. I have been fortunate to go to school with some very smart classmates, some of whom can whip out a great piece of writing in minutes. I still find these people threatening. If they are faster than I am, does that make them better writers than I am? *I thought I was supposed to be "the writer"!*

My obsession with being "the" writer stems from my understanding of what it means to be "the" anything. My childhood was marked by a belief in many abstract absolutes that I am only now allowing to crumble. I was born in Chicago (and was thus the fourth

> *Ongoing discussion of the central issue: is she a writer or not?*

generation of my family to live there), but I grew up in northern Virginia. I came to look down on my Virginia surroundings because I had been taught to view Chicago as this great Mecca — the world's most amazing city to which I must someday return, and to which all other places on earth pale in comparison. Throughout my childhood, I gathered that Chicago is a real city in which average people live and which has an economy historically based in shipping and manufacturing; Washington, D.C., on the other hand, where my dad works, has a population that includes a bizarre mix of impoverished people and the most influential leaders and diplomats in the world — and so manufactures nothing but political power. People in Chicago know how to deal with snow; Virginians panic at the *possibility* of snow. Chicago rests on soil that is so fertile it's *black*; Virginia does not even have soil — it has reddish clay suitable for growing nothing except tobacco. Even Chicago's tap water tastes amazing; D.C.'s tap water is poisoned with lead. I grew up thinking that every aspect of Chicago was perfect — so perfect that Chicago became glorious to the point of abstraction. No other city could compare, and after a while I forgot *why* no other city could compare. I just knew that Chicago was "the" city . . . and that if "the" city exists, there must also be an abstract "the" everything.

I grew up with this and many other abstract ideals that I would 10 defend against my friends' attacks . . . until I learned that they were just abstractions — and so was I. My writing identity was just another ideal, an absolute that I clung to without any basis in fact. I used to use writing as an easy way to define myself on those over-simplistic surveys teachers always asked us to fill out in elementary and middle school — the surveys that assumed that someone could know all about me simply by finding out my favorite color, my favorite TV show, or my hobbies. I used to casually throw out the "I'm a writer" card just to get these silly surveys over with. "I'm a writer" was just an easy answer to the complicated question, "Who are you?" I always thought the surveys avoided asking this question, but maybe I was the one avoiding it. For years, I had been defining myself as "the writer" without really pondering what this writer identity meant. Is a writer simply someone who writes all the time? Well, I often went through long stretches in which I did not write anything, so this definition did not seem to suit me. Is a writer someone who is good at writing? Well, I've already mentioned that I've been having "am I any good?!" thoughts

Vallowe examines the roots of her identity as a writer — and why she questions that identity.

since elementary school, so this definition didn't seem to fit me, either. I was identifying myself as "the writer" as an abstraction, without any just cause to do so.

The funny thing is that I recognized my writing identity as an abstract ideal before I recognized any of the other ideals I was clinging to, but that didn't make the situation any better. It is one thing to learn that dead people have been voting in Chicago elections for decades, and so perhaps Chicago isn't the perfect city, but what happens when the absolute ideal is you? More important, what would happen if *this* absolute were to crumble? It was terrifying to think that I might discover that I was not a writer because to not be a writer was to suddenly be nothing. If a writer was the only thing that I had ever been, what would happen if writing was a lie? I would vanish. Looking back, the logical part of my brain tells me that, if I am not a writer, I am still plenty of other things: I am a Catholic; I am a Vallowe; people tell me that I have other good qualities. But when facing these horrifying spells of writer's doubt, my brain doesn't see these other things. I am driven only by the fear of nothingness and the thought that I have to be a writer because I'm not good at anything else.

Am I really not good at anything else? I used to blame this entire writer's complex on whoever it was that told me I was a writer. If that person hadn't channeled this burdensome identity into me, I might never have expected great literary things from myself, and life would have been easier. I had these thoughts until one day in high school I mentioned something to my mom about the fact that I'd been writing since I was five years old. My mom corrected me by saying that I'd been writing since I was three years old. At the age of three I couldn't even physically form letters, but apparently I would dictate stories to my mom on a regular basis. My mom explained to me how I would run to her and say, "Mommy, Mommy, write my story for me!"

This new information was both comforting and unsettling. On one hand, it was a great relief to know that I had been a writer all along— that I would have been a writer even if no one had told me that I was one. On the other hand, the knowledge that I had been a writer all along drove me into an entirely new realm of panic.

I've been a writer my entire life?

WHAT?!

She continues to explore her identity as a writer.

15

I've been a writer since I was three? Three? *Three* years old: How is that even possible? I didn't know it was possible to be anything at age three, let alone the thing that might define me for my entire life.

I have been taught that each person has a vocation — a calling that he or she must use to spread God's love to others. Yet I've also assumed that one must go on some sort of journey to figure out what this vocation is. If I found my vocation at the age of three, have I skipped this journey? And if I've skipped the journey, does that mean that the vocation isn't real? Or am I just really lucky for having found my vocation so early? Was I really born a writer? Was I born to do one thing and will I do that one thing for my entire life? Can anything be that consistent? That simple? And if I am living out some divine vocation, is that any comfort at all? If I am channeling some divine being in my writing, and everything I write comes from some outside source, where does that leave me? Am I nothing even if I am a writer?

This questioning has not led me to any comforting conclusions. I still wonder if my writer identity has been thrust upon me, and what it means to have someone else determine who I am. If I am a writer, then I am someone who passionately seeks originality — someone who gets pleasure from inventing entire fictional worlds. Yet if someone — either a teacher or a divine being — is channeling an identity into me, then I am no more original than the characters that I create in my fiction. If my identity is not original, then this identity is not real, and if I am not real . . . I can't even finish this sentence.

I don't know if I really wrote thirty books in kindergarten. It might have been twenty — or fifteen — or ten — or five. I might have made up that part about the special writing desk in Mrs. Meadows's old classroom. I don't know if God predestined me to write masterpieces or if a teacher just casually mentioned that I wrote well and I completely overreacted to the compliment. Questioning my identity as "the writer" has led me to new levels of fear and uncertainty, but this questioning is not going to stop. Even if I one day sit, withered and gray, with a Nobel Prize for Literature proudly displayed on my desk as I try to crank out one last novel at the age of ninety-two, my thoughts will probably drift back to Mrs. Meadows and those books I wrote in kindergarten. In my old age, I still might not understand my writer identity,

Ending refers back to the opening anecdote.

Conclusion is tentative (since the end of the story is decades in the future).

but maybe by that point, I will have written a novel about a character with an identity crisis — and maybe the character will have come through all right.

In this literacy narrative, Vallowe reflects on the origins of her identity as a writer: her early teachers, her parents, God, herself. The significance of her story lies in her inability to settle on any one of these possibilities.

MARJORIE AGOSÍN

Always Living in Spanish: Recovering the Familiar, through Language

Marjorie Agosín, a Spanish professor at Wellesley College, wrote this literacy narrative for Poets & Writers *magazine in 1999. Originally written in Spanish, it tells of Agosín's Chilean childhood and her continuing connection to the Spanish language.*

In the evenings in the northern hemisphere, I repeat the ancient ritual that I observed as a child in the southern hemisphere: going out while the night is still warm and trying to recognize the stars as it begins to grow dark silently. In the sky of my country, Chile, that long and wide stretch of land that the poets blessed and dictators abused, I could easily name the stars: the three Marias, the Southern Cross, and the three Lilies, names of beloved and courageous women.

But here in the United States, where I have lived since I was a young girl, the solitude of exile makes me feel that so little is mine, that not even the sky has the same constellations, the trees and the fauna the same names or sounds, or the rubbish the same smell. How does one recover the familiar? How does one name the unfamiliar? How can one be another or live in a foreign language? These are the dilemmas of one who writes in Spanish and lives in translation.

Since my earliest childhood in Chile I lived with the tempos and the melodies of a multiplicity of tongues: German, Yiddish, Russian, Turkish, and many Latin songs. Because everyone was from somewhere else, my relatives laughed, sang, and fought in a Babylon of languages. Spanish was reserved for matters of extreme seriousness, for commercial transactions, or for illnesses, but everyone's mother tongue was always associated with the memory of spaces inhabited in the past: the shtetl, the flowering and vast Vienna avenues, the minarets of Turkey, and the Ladino whispers of Toledo. When my paternal grandmother sang old songs in Turkish, her voice and body assumed the passion of one who was there in the city of Istanbul, gazing by turns toward the west and the east.

Destiny and the always ambiguous nature of history continued my family's enforced migration, and because of it I, too, became one who had to live and speak in translation. The disappearances, torture, and clandestine deaths in my country in the early seventies drove us to the United States, that other America that looked with suspicion at those who did not speak English and especially those who came from the supposedly uncivilized regions of Latin America. I had left a dangerous place that was my home, only to arrive in a dangerous place that was not: a high school in the small town of Athens, Georgia, where my poor English and my accent were the cause of ridicule and insult. The only way I could recover my usurped country and my Chilean childhood was by continuing to write in Spanish, the same way my grandparents had sung in their own tongues in diasporic sites.

The new and learned English language did not fit with the visceral emotions and themes that my poetry contained, but by writing in Spanish I could recover fragrances, spoken rhythms, and the passion of my own identity. Daily I felt the need to translate myself for the strangers living all around me, to tell them why we were in Georgia, why we are different, why we had fled, why my accent was so thick, and why I did not look Hispanic. Only at night, writing poems in Spanish, could I return to my senses, and soothe my own sorrow over what I had left behind. 5

This is how I became a Chilean poet who wrote in Spanish and lived in the southern United States. And then, one day, a poem of mine was translated and published in the English language. Finally, for the first time since I had left Chile, I felt I didn't have to explain myself. My poem, expressed in another language, spoke for itself . . . and for me.

Sometimes the austere sounds of English help me bear the solitude of knowing that I am foreign and so far away from those about whom

rhetorical situations | genres | processes | strategies | research MLA / APA | media / design | readings

I write. I must admit I would like more opportunities to read in Spanish to people whose language and culture is also mine, to join in our common heritage and in the feast of our sounds. I would also like readers of English to understand the beauty of the spoken word in Spanish, that constant flow of oxytonic and paraoxytonic syllables (*Vérde qué té quiéro vérde*),* the joy of writing — of dancing — in another language. I believe that many exiles share the unresolvable torment of not being able to live in the language of their childhood.

I miss that undulating and sensuous language of mine, those baroque descriptions, the sense of being and feeling that Spanish gives me. It is perhaps for this reason that I have chosen and will always choose to write in Spanish. Nothing else from my childhood world remains. My country seems to be frozen in gestures of silence and oblivion. My relatives have died, and I have grown up not knowing a young generation of cousins and nieces and nephews. Many of my friends were disappeared, others were tortured, and the most fortunate, like me, became guardians of memory. For us, to write in Spanish is to always be in active pursuit of memory. I seek to recapture a world lost to me on that sorrowful afternoon when the blue electric sky and the Andean cordillera bade me farewell. On that, my last Chilean day, I carried under my arm my innocence recorded in a little blue notebook I kept even then. Gradually that diary filled with memoranda, poems written in free verse, descriptions of dreams and of the thresholds of my house surrounded by cherry trees and gardenias. To write in Spanish is for me a gesture of survival. And because of translation, my memory has now become a part of the memory of many others.

Translators are not traitors, as the proverb says, but rather splendid friends in this great human community of language.

Agosín's narrative uses vivid detail to bring her childhood in Chile to life for her readers. Her love for her homeland and its people is clear, as is the significance of her narrative — with her childhood home gone, to write in Spanish is a "gesture of survival."

---

*"Vérde qué té quiéro vérde" ("Green, how I want you, green") is the opening line of a famous Spanish poem that demonstrates the interplay of words with the main stress on the final syllable (oxytonic) and those with the main stress on the next-to-last syllable (paroxytonic) in Spanish. [Editor's note]

SHANNON NICHOLS

"Proficiency"

In the following literacy narrative, Shannon Nichols, a student at Wright State University, describes her experience taking the standardized writing proficiency test that high school students in Ohio must pass to graduate. She wrote this essay for a college writing course, where her audience included her classmates and instructor.

The first time I took the ninth-grade proficiency test was in March of eighth grade. The test ultimately determines whether students may receive a high school diploma. After months of preparation and anxiety, the pressure was on. Throughout my elementary and middle school years, I was a strong student, always on the honor roll. I never had a GPA below 3.0. I was smart, and I knew it. That is, until I got the results of the proficiency test.

Although the test was challenging, covering reading, writing, math, and citizenship, I was sure I had passed every part. To my surprise, I did pass every part—except writing. "Writing! Yeah right! How did I manage to fail writing, and by half a point, no less?" I thought to myself in disbelief. Seeing my test results brought tears to my eyes. I honestly could not believe it. To make matters worse, most of my classmates, including some who were barely passing eighth-grade English, passed that part.

Until that time, I loved writing just as much as I loved math. It was one of my strengths. I was good at it, and I enjoyed it. If anything, I thought I might fail citizenship. How could I have screwed up writing? I surely spelled every word correctly, used good grammar, and even used big words in the proper context. How could I have failed?

Finally I got over it and decided it was no big deal. Surely I would pass the next time. In my honors English class I worked diligently, passing with an A. By October I'd be ready to conquer that writing test. Well, guess what? I failed the test again, again with only 4.5 of the 5 points needed to pass. That time I did cry, and even went to my English teacher, Mrs. Brown, and asked, "How can I get A's in all my English classes but fail the writing part of the proficiency test twice?" She couldn't answer my question. Even my friends and classmates were confused. I felt like

a failure. I had disappointed my family and seriously let myself down. Worst of all, I still couldn't figure out what I was doing wrong.

I decided to quit trying so hard. Apparently—I told myself—the people grading the tests didn't have the slightest clue about what constituted good writing. I continued to excel in class and passed the test on the third try. But I never again felt the same love of reading and writing.

This experience showed me just how differently my writing could be judged by various readers. Obviously all my English teachers and many others enjoyed or at least appreciated my writing. A poem I wrote was put on television once. I must have been a pretty good writer. Unfortunately the graders of the ninth-grade proficiency test didn't feel the same, and when students fail the test, the state of Ohio doesn't offer any explanation.

After I failed the test the first time, I began to hate writing, and I started to doubt myself. I doubted my ability and the ideas I wrote about. Failing the second time made things worse, so perhaps to protect myself from my doubts, I stopped taking English seriously. Perhaps because of that lack of seriousness, I earned a 2 on the Advanced Placement English Exam, barely passed the twelfth-grade proficiency test, and was placed in developmental writing in college. I wish I knew why I failed that test because then I might have written what was expected on the second try, maintained my enthusiasm for writing, and continued to do well.

Nichols's narrative focuses on her emotional reaction to failing a test that she should have passed easily. The contrast between her demonstrated writing ability and her repeated failures creates a tension that captures readers' attention. We want to know what will happen to her.

SOFIA GOMEZ

Mother Goose in Monterrey

In this literacy narrative from Ohio State's Digital Archive of Literacy Narratives, Sofia Gomez describes how she learned English, both at home and at school, in her native Mexico. In the online version, available via wwnorton.com/write/ fieldguidelinks, she also includes the video of herself and her brother and sister that she describes in the text.

I wish that I could memorize my class curriculum as easily as I memorized Timon and Pumba's arguments, or Iago's witty complaints, or Pocahontas's explanation of her strange dream. I know these things (by heart) now because as a little girl, I used to watch Disney movies over and over. At the time it seemed like a great pastime, but looking back, I'm grateful to see that these movies did way more than just entertain me: they helped me learn English.

When you're a child, everything around you is a learning experience. So when you're exposed to foreign things, like a new language, they are assimilated as much as any other lesson like learning manners or learning to count. I think that introducing a second language for children is an advantage, since their minds are much more receptive to new things than when they're adults.

My English education started mainly at home. I grew up in a small town called Montemorelos, an hour away from Monterrey, Mexico's second-largest industrial city. Being so close to the American border, my family made very frequent shopping trips to Texas. Every so often, we would go to McAllen, Texas, to buy some clothes, household items, and if we were lucky, a new movie. At home we didn't have cable, so if we watched anything on TV it would be a movie, probably a Disney classic or a *Sesame Street* video. If I look them up now, we're probably missing only a couple of movies from the entire classics collection.

We children loved watching movies in English so much that we would hate it when we got a translated version of an American movie. As we grew older (before DVD was invented), we would avoid buying movies in Mexico because the dialogue wasn't the same for us if it wasn't in the original language: English. In fact, we only had two movies in Spanish — *Pocahontas* and *The Aristocats* — and eventually we were insistent enough that we got a second copy of them in English.

We also read a lot in English. One of my aunts was the head of the English department of a school in Monterrey, so every time she ordered English textbooks, my mom would ask her to order a few extra ones for me and my siblings. Every night we read an English book and a Spanish book, to the point of memorizing them. So I knew all the traditional Mexican nursery rhymes, like Cri Cri and others, but I also learned about Mother Goose and other classic English children's

5

rhetorical situations

genres

processes

strategies

research MLA / APA

media / design

readings

stories like "Five Little Monkeys," "The Wheels on the Bus," "Three Little Kittens," and "The Little Red Hen." We also had Disney books about the movies we watched and about other stories as well. (I dare anyone to challenge me on Disney trivia, because I'll probably kick their butts.)

We read like crazy. At some point, my mom would take her jumbo clear Scotch tape and reinforce the bindings on each page because some books were falling apart from so much use. We even had several copies of the same book, either by chance or because my mom thought that four children in the same household might need a bigger library. There's a very funny home video in which my younger brother and sister are arguing about holding a book, and I randomly cross the frame, storm away frustrated from hearing them bicker, come back with the second copy of the book, give it to them so they would stop arguing, and then without a word walk away to return to whatever I was doing.

A scene from the video Gomez included with her written narrative.

I attended a very small and conservative Catholic school, in Montemorelos, where I received very basic English lessons for only a couple of hours a week. My parents wanted us to learn more English, so we took private afternoon lessons with a good teacher from Canada. We also traveled twice to Canada to attend YMCA summer camps, and where my brothers and I got the opportunity of being immersed into an English-speaking environment. The first time, I remember being struck by the fact that everyone around me was speaking English and that I had no choice but to make an effort and do so myself. The second time, however, I found myself much more comfortable being around children who didn't speak my first language, and even though I wasn't as fluent as I am now, I managed to make lots of friends in spite of my limited English.

All this experience came in handy when my family decided to move to the big city and pursue a better grade school education for us. Private schools in Monterrey are very expensive, competitive, and selective. My parents worked hard to find the right one for us, and more important, to get us accepted into it. After an arduous search, they narrowed the choice down to two schools. One of them, very highly regarded, rejected us out of hand. The people in charge of admissions said we did not have the necessary bilingual education to catch up with the rest of the students, although they didn't bother to test us on our English or on other subjects, for that matter. All they saw was the name of our small Catholic school, and they turned us down. The other school, however, the American Institute of Monterrey (AIM), opened its doors to us, assisting us in the transition from a monolingual to a bilingual school. I was very nervous about being a new student, not only because I had to meet new people and try to fit in but also because the AIM was bigger, bolder, and quite frankly, so foreign compared to our little small-town Catholic school.

The summer we moved to Monterrey, we were assigned teachers by the AIM to prepare us to enter a bilingual school. I was assigned to Miss Ale, who taught in her house, in a ranch a few minutes outside the city. She instructed me in some math and spelling but mostly in English grammar. What I remember the most about her lessons were her two black Doberman dogs, which were always around and scared the English out of me. At times, she would let me work by myself on

rhetorical situations

genres

processes

strategies

research MLA / APA

media / design

readings

short assignments and would leave the room. The dogs would watch me work, sometimes circle the table a few times, and every once in a while growl to each other. I felt like they were judging me, and their presence would force me to concentrate on my work. I remember trying to finish faster and accurately so as to get Miss Ale to come back and spare me the guard dogs. It wasn't until five weeks later, when Miss Ale talked to my mother about my progress and how well I worked by myself, that I realized I had greatly improved my English skills. The day of our last lesson, my older brother came along. While Miss Ale and I wrapped up our remedial course, he played outside with the dogs. When my lesson was over, I found myself going out and joining them. The dogs weren't so scary anymore, and neither was entering a new bilingual school.

Literacy transitions are always complicated. As Mike Rose points out in *Lives on the Boundary*, struggling with writing or reading does not mark a person as "illiterate." In his book, he discusses some students in remedial classes he observed who participated very effectively in the classroom, contributing valuable points to the lesson. "These are [supposedly] the truly illiterate among us," Rose remarks. His story resonates with mine and helped me understand that aptitude is not always measured by grades but by life experiences and the education one receives at home when growing up. Just because I needed help adapting to a new environment, especially one involving a second language, doesn't mean I was poorly educated.

10

I started my AIM life in August 1998, as I entered the fifth grade. Four years later, the Monterrey Institute of Technology and Superior Studies (ITESM), the largest combined high school and university in all of Mexico, granted me an Excellence Scholarship for high school, an honor given to the graduating secondary (middle-school) student of each private school in Monterrey with the highest grade in his or her class. After secondary school, most students in Monterrey who go on to high school attend the same one: ITESM. I was surprised to find out that Lili Tello, the student in the ITESM class with the Excellence Scholarship from that school that had rejected us four years ago, had a lower grade than I. My mother likes to brag about this, but I like to think of it as a way of showing how things are not always what they seem, and that education, especially early education, comes from many places (mostly home) and not just from school.

Today, Lili and I are great friends. We developed a strong partnership in high school, working together on projects and such since we have similar temperaments regarding school. It's a shame I didn't get to meet her sooner (in her school) when we first moved to Monterrey, but I wouldn't trade my AIM experience, or any other English preparation I had, for the world.

For five more literacy narratives, see CHAPTER 57.

Gomez's narrative tells of her parents' efforts to give their children a good education and strong grounding in English. Vivid details, from the tape holding the family's books together to a teacher's Dobermans, bring her narrative to life — as does the video of her brother and sister fighting over a book.

Key Features / Literacy Narratives

A well-told story.   As with most narratives, those about literacy often set up some sort of situation that needs to be resolved. That need for resolution makes readers want to keep reading. We want to know whether Nichols ultimately will pass the proficiency test. Some literacy narratives simply explore the role that reading or writing played at some time in someone's life—assuming, perhaps, that learning to read or write is a challenge to be met.

Vivid detail.   Details can bring a narrative to life for readers by giving them vivid mental sensations of the sights, sounds, smells, tastes, and textures of the world in which your story takes place. The details you use when describing something can help readers picture places, people, and events; dialogue can help them hear what is being said. We get a picture of Agosín's Chilean childhood when she writes of the "blue electric sky" and her "little blue notebook" in which she described her "house surrounded by cherry trees and gardenias." We can see the tutor's dogs circling the table where Gomez was trying to work and hear them "growl to each other." Similarly, we can picture and hear Vallowe as a little girl running to her mother and saying, "Mommy, Mommy, write my story for me!"

rhetorical situations

genres

processes

strategies

research MLA / APA

media / design

readings

Sometimes you can provide detail through visuals or audio, as Gomez does with her home video.

Some indication of the narrative's significance. By definition, a literacy narrative tells something the writer remembers about learning to read or write. In addition, the writer needs to make clear why the incident matters to him or her. You may reveal its significance in various ways. Nichols does it when she says she no longer loves to read or write. Agosín points out that she writes in Spanish because "nothing else from my childhood world remains. . . . To write in Spanish is for me a gesture of survival." The trick is to avoid tacking a brief statement about your narrative's significance onto the end as if it were a kind of moral of the story. Vallowe's narrative would be less effective if, instead of questioning her identity as a writer from several perspectives, she had simply said, "I became a writer at the age of three."

A GUIDE TO WRITING LITERACY NARRATIVES

Choosing a Topic

In general, it's a good idea to focus on a single event that took place during a relatively brief period of time. For example:

- any early memory about writing or reading that you recall vividly
- someone who taught you to read or write
- a book or other text that has been significant for you in some way
- an event at school that was related to reading or writing and that you found interesting, humorous, or embarrassing
- a writing or reading task that you found (or still find) especially difficult or challenging
- a memento that represents an important moment in your literacy development (perhaps the start of a LITERACY PORTFOLIO) ○ 295–96
- the origins of your current attitudes about writing or reading

- learning to text, learning to write email appropriately, creating and maintaining a *Facebook* page or blog

Make a list of possible topics, and then choose one that you think will be interesting to you and to others — and that you're willing to share with others. If several seem promising, try them out on a friend or classmate. Or just choose one and see where it leads; you can switch to another if need be. If you have trouble coming up with a topic, try FREEWRITING, LISTING, CLUSTERING, or LOOPING.

259–62

Considering the Rhetorical Situation

3–4

PURPOSE

Why do you want to tell this story? To share a memory with others? To fulfill an assignment? To teach a lesson? To explore your past learning? Think about the reasons for your choice and how they will shape what you write.

5–8

AUDIENCE

Are your readers likely to have had similar experiences? Would they tell similar stories? How much explaining will you have to do to help them understand your narrative? Can you assume that they will share your attitudes toward your story, or will you have to work at making them see your perspective? How much about your life are you willing to share with this audience?

12–15

STANCE

What attitude do you want to project? Affectionate? Neutral? Critical? Do you wish to be sincere? serious? humorously detached? self-critical? self-effacing? something else? How do you want your readers to see you?

16–18

MEDIA / DESIGN

Will your narrative be in print? presented orally? online? Should you use photos, tables, graphs, or video or audio clips? Is there a font that conveys the right tone? Do you need headings?

Generating Ideas and Text

Good literacy narratives share certain elements that make them interesting and compelling for readers. Remember that your goals are to tell the story as clearly and vividly as you can and to convey the meaning the incident has for you today. Start by writing out what you remember about the setting and those involved, perhaps trying out some of the methods in the chapter on GENERATING IDEAS AND TEXT. You may also want to INTERVIEW a teacher or parent who figures in your narrative.

259–65
448–49

Describe the setting.   Where does your narrative take place? List the places where your story unfolds. For each place, write informally for a few minutes, DESCRIBING what you remember:

367–75

- *What do you see?* If you're inside, what color are the walls? What's hanging on them? What can you see out any windows? What else do you see? Books? Lined paper? Red ink? Are there people? places to sit? a desk or a table?

- *What do you hear?* A radiator hissing? Leaves rustling? The wind howling? Rain? Someone reading aloud? Shouts? Cheers? Children playing? Music? The zing of an instant message arriving?

- *What do you smell?* Sweat? Perfume? Incense? Food cooking?

- *How and what do you feel?* Nervous? Happy? Cold? Hot? A scratchy wool sweater? Tight shoes? Rough wood on a bench?

- *What do you taste?* Gum? Mints? Graham crackers? Juice? Coffee?

Think about the key people.   Narratives include people whose actions play an important role in the story. In your literacy narrative, you are probably one of those people. A good way to develop your understanding of the people in your narrative is to write about them:

- *Describe each person in a paragraph or so.* What do the people look like? How do they dress? How do they speak? Quickly? Slowly? With an accent? Do they speak clearly, or do they mumble? Do they use any distinctive words or phrases? You might begin by describing their movements, their posture, their bearing, their facial expressions. Do they have a distinctive scent?

376–81

- *Recall (or imagine) some characteristic dialogue.* A good way to bring people to life and move a story along is with **DIALOGUE**, to let readers hear them rather than just hearing about them. Try writing six to ten lines of dialogue between two people in your narrative. If you can't remember an actual conversation, make up one that could have happened. (After all, you are telling the story, and you get to decide how it is to be told.) Try to remember (and write down) some of the characteristic words or phrases that the people in your narrative used.

387–95

Write about "what happened."   At the heart of every good **NARRATIVE** is the answer to the question "What happened?" The action in a literacy narrative may be as dramatic as winning a spelling bee or as subtle as a conversation between two friends; both contain action, movement, or change that the narrative tries to capture for readers. A good story dramatizes the

407–8

action. Try **SUMMARIZING** the action in your narrative in a paragraph — try to capture what happened. Use active and specific verbs (*pondered*, *shouted*, *laughed*) to describe the action as vividly as possible.

Consider the significance of the narrative.   You need to make clear the ways in which any event you are writing about is significant for you now. Write a page or so about the meaning it has for you. How did it change or otherwise affect you? What aspects of your life now can you trace to that event? How might your life have been different if this event had not happened or had turned out differently? Why does this story matter to you?

Ways of Organizing a Literacy Narrative

263–64

Start by **OUTLINING** the main events in your narrative. Then think about how you want to tell the story. Don't assume that the only way to tell your story is just as it happened. That's one way — starting at the beginning of the action and continuing to the end. But you could also start in the middle — or even at the end. Shannon Nichols, for example, could have begun her narrative by telling how she finally passed the proficiency test and then gone back to tell about the times she tried to pass it, even as she was an A student in an honors English class. Several ways of organizing a narrative follow.

[Chronologically, from beginning to end]

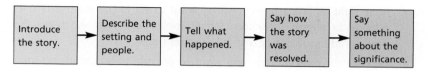

Introduce the story. → Describe the setting and people. → Tell what happened. → Say how the story was resolved. → Say something about the significance.

[Beginning in the middle]

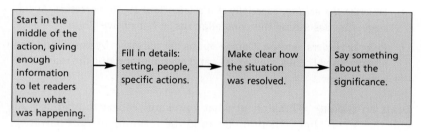

Start in the middle of the action, giving enough information to let readers know what was happening. → Fill in details: setting, people, specific actions. → Make clear how the situation was resolved. → Say something about the significance.

[Beginning at the end]

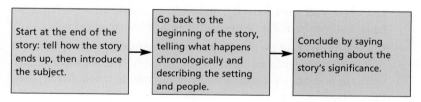

Start at the end of the story: tell how the story ends up, then introduce the subject. → Go back to the beginning of the story, telling what happens chronologically and describing the setting and people. → Conclude by saying something about the story's significance.

Writing Out a Draft

Once you have generated ideas and thought about how you want to organize your narrative, it's time to begin **DRAFTING.** Do this quickly—try to write a complete draft in one sitting, concentrating on getting the story on paper or screen and on putting in as much detail as you can. Some writers find

266–68

it helpful to work on the beginning or ending first. Others write out the main event first and then draft the beginning and ending.

299–306
Draft a BEGINNING. A good narrative grabs readers' attention right from the start. Here are some ways of beginning:

- *Jump right in.* Sometimes you may want to get to the main action as quickly as possible. Nichols, for example, begins as she takes the ninth-grade proficiency test for the first time.

- *Describe the context.* You may want to provide background information at the start of your narrative, as Vallowe does with an anecdote exposing her fears that she may not be who she thinks she is.

- *Describe the setting, especially if it's important to the narrative.* Agosín begins by describing the constellations in her native Chile.

- *Provoke readers' interest.* Gomez opens her narrative by describing how she watched Disney movies over and over, memorizing the main characters' lines.

306–10
Draft an ENDING. Think about what you want readers to read last. An effective ending helps them understand the meaning of your narrative. Here are some possibilities:

- *End where your story ends.* It's up to you to decide where a narrative ends. Vallowe ends far in the future, in her imagined old age.

- *Say something about the significance of your narrative.* Nichols observes that she no longer loves to write, for example. The trick is to touch upon the narrative's significance without stating it too directly, like the moral of a fable.

- *Refer back to the beginning.* Vallowe refers back to her kindergarten writing; Nichols ends by contemplating the negative effects of failing the proficiency test.

- *End on a surprising note.* Agosín catches our attention when she tells us of the deaths and disappearances of her friends and relatives.

Come up with a title. A good TITLE indicates something about the subject of your narrative — and makes readers want to take a look. Nichols's title, " 'Proficiency,' " is also her subject; her use of quote marks around this word calls its meaning into question in a way that might make readers wonder — and read on. Vallowe focuses on the significance of her narrative: "Write or Wrong Identity." Agosín makes her title an expression of her sense of identity: "Always Living in Spanish."

312–13

Considering Matters of Design

You'll probably write your narrative in paragraph form, but think about the information you're presenting and how you can design it to enhance your story and appeal to your audience.

- What would be an appropriate FONT? Something serious, like Times Roman? Something whimsical, like Comic Sans? Something else?

585–86

- Would it help your readers if you added HEADINGS in order to divide your narrative into shorter sections?

588–89

- Would photographs or other VISUALS show details better than you can describe them with words alone? If you're writing about learning to read, for example, you might scan in an image of one of the first books you read. Or if your topic is learning to write, you could include something you wrote. You could even include a family video, as Gomez does. Would your narrative best be conveyed as a multimodal composition that combines written text, images, and video or audio?

591–99

Getting Response and Revising

The following questions can help you study your draft with a critical eye. GETTING RESPONSE from others is always good, and these questions can guide their reading, too. Make sure they know your purpose and audience.

275–76

- Do the title and first few sentences make readers want to read on? If not, how else might you begin?

- Is the sequence of events in the narrative clear? Does it flow, and are there effective transitions? Does the narrative get sidetracked at any point?
- Is anything confusing?
- Is there enough detail, and is it interesting? Will readers be able to imagine the setting? Can they picture the characters and sense what they're like? Would it help to add some dialogue, so that readers can "hear" them?
- Are visuals used effectively and integrated smoothly with the written text? If there are no visuals, would using some strengthen the narrative?
- Have you made the narrative meaningful enough for readers so that they wonder and care about what will happen?
- Do you narrate any actions clearly? vividly? Does the action keep readers engaged?
- Is the significance of the narrative clear?
- Is the ending satisfying? What are readers left thinking?

276–79 ○ The preceding questions should identify aspects of your narrative you need to work on. When it's time to **REVISE**, make sure your text appeals to your audience and achieves your purpose as successfully as possible.

Editing and Proofreading

282–85 ○ Readers equate correctness with competence. Once you've revised your draft, follow these guidelines for **EDITING** a narrative:

387–95 ◆
317
- Make sure events are **NARRATED** in a clear order and include appropriate time markers, **TRANSITIONS**, and summary phrases to link the parts and show the passing of time.
- Be careful that verb tenses are consistent throughout. If you start your narrative in the past tense ("he *taught* me how to use a computer"), be careful not to switch to the present ("So I *look* at him and *say* . . . ") along the way.

- Check to see that verb tenses correctly indicate when an action took place. If one action took place before another action in the past, for example, you should use the past perfect tense: "I forgot to dot my i's, a mistake I *had made* many times before."

- Punctuate DIALOGUE correctly. Whenever someone speaks, surround the speech with quotation marks ("No way," I said). Periods and commas go inside quotation marks; exclamation points and question marks go inside if they're part of the quotation, outside if they're part of the whole sentence:

376–81

INSIDE	Opening the door, Ms. Cordell announced, "Pop quiz!"
OUTSIDE	It wasn't my intention to announce "I hate to read"!

- PROOFREAD your finished narrative carefully before turning it in.

285–86

Taking Stock of Your Work

- How well do you think you told the story?
- What did you do especially well?
- What could still be improved?
- How did you go about coming up with ideas and generating text?
- How did you go about drafting your narrative?
- Did you use photographs or any other visual or audio elements? What did they add? Can you think of such elements you might have used?
- How did others' responses influence your writing?
- What would you do differently next time?

IF YOU NEED MORE HELP

See also MEMOIRS (Chapter 15), a kind of narrative that focuses more generally on a significant event from your past, and REFLECTIONS (Chapter 18), a kind of essay for thinking about a topic in writing. See Chapter 29 if you are required to submit your literacy narrative as part of a writing PORTFOLIO.

183–90
214–21

287–98

8 Analyzing Texts

Both the *Huffington Post* and *National Review Online* cover the same events, but each one interprets them differently. All toothpaste ads claim to make teeth "the whitest." The Environmental Protection Agency is a guardian of America's air, water, and soil — or an unconstitutional impediment to economic growth, depending on which politician is speaking. Those are but three examples that demonstrate why we need to be careful, analytical readers of magazines, newspapers, blogs, websites, ads, political documents, even textbooks. Not only does text convey information, but it also influences how and what we think. We need to read, then, to understand not only what texts say but also how they say it and how they try to persuade or influence us.

Because understanding how texts say what they say and achieve their effects is so crucial, assignments in many disciplines ask you to analyze texts. You may be asked to analyze candidates' speeches in a political science course or to analyze imagery in James Joyce's story "Araby" for a literature class. In a statistics course, you might analyze a set of data—a numerical text—to find the standard deviation from the mean. This chapter offers detailed guidelines for writing an essay that closely examines a text both for what it says and for how it does so, with the goal of demonstrating for readers how—and how well—the text achieves its effects. We'll begin with four good examples, the first annotated to point out the key features found in most textual analyses.

HANNAH BERRY

The Fashion Industry: Free to Be an Individual

Hannah Berry wrote this analysis of two shoe ads for a first-year writing course at Wright State University.

As young women, we have always been told through the medium of advertisement that we must use certain products to make ourselves beautiful. For decades, ads for things like soap, makeup, and mouthwash have established a sort of misplaced control over our lives, telling us what will make us attractive and what will not. Recently, however, a new generation of advertisement has emerged in the fashion industry, one that cleverly equates the products shown in the ads with the quest for confident individuality. Ads such as the two for Clarks and Sorel discussed below encourage us to break free from the standard beauty mold and be ourselves; using mostly imagery, they remind us that being unique is the true origin of beauty.

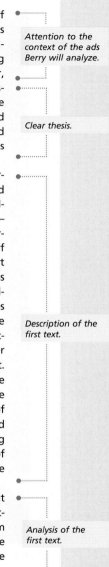

Attention to the context of the ads Berry will analyze.

Clear thesis.

The first ad promotes Clarks fashion as band geek chic, quite literally raising a unique personality onto a pedestal, with the subject poised on a decorative stone platform as shown in fig. 1. Photographed in standing profile, this quirky-looking young woman is doing what she loves — playing some kind of trumpet — and looks great doing it. She is wearing her hair in a French twist with a strand tucked behind her ear, as if she recently moved it out of her face to play the music she loves without distraction. The downturn of her nose points to the short gray-black dress that stops several inches above her knees but covers her chest and shoulders modestly, with a collar situated at the base of her neck and sleeves that reach for her elbows. The dress is plain, but it is a perfect fit for the personality implied in the photo. Set against the background of a light-tan wall, the model leans back slightly as if supporting the weight of her instrument. Her right knee is bent while her left knee remains straight. The positioning of her legs not only accentuates her unbalanced posture but also points out the pair of simple brown pumps that complete the look. She wears the shoes with a pair of socks in a much darker shade of brown pulled up around her shins. Around her ankles are sandy-colored rings of shaggy fabric that are most likely attached to the socks, giving the whole outfit a sense of nerdy flair. Her expression is a simple mix of calm and concentration. It's as if the photographer happened to take the picture while she was practicing for a school recital.

Description of the first text.

Clarks has taken what looks like your average high school student and dressed her in an outfit that speaks to her own distinctive character and talents. The image sparks the idea that her beauty comes from an internal base of secure self-confidence and moves outward to infuse her physical appearance and sense of style. This ad urges us to celebrate individuality with the right look. Using an image alone, Clarks advertises

Analysis of the first text.

Fig. 1. Clarks ad shows a band geek doing what she loves (Clarks).

rhetorical situations　genres　processes　strategies　research MLA / APA　media / design　readings

its products with the simple promise that they will support you in doing what you love and keep you original.

Taking a narrower perspective on originality, the ad for Sorel boots shown in fig. 2 dramatizes the idea that spontaneity is key to a distinctive personal identity. This abstract idea is depicted in a vividly concrete way, using the featured fur-topped boots as a base for encouraging a bold sense of self. The ad dares us to break free from the mold of society and do something "fearless" (Sorel). It shows us a dark-haired, red-lipped woman sitting in a formal French upholstered chair in a dark-blue, elaborately paneled parlor. An expression of triumph and mischief adorns her sultry visage. She's wearing a revealing short white dress that overlaps slightly around her chest and falls strategically over her hips so that large portions of her upper thighs are visible. Feathers in autumn colors cover her shoulders, and a gold belt accentuates her waist. Next to her is a polished wood table supporting a lighted candle, a small glass vase of pink and white flowers, and a black-and-white-patterned orb. There is a dormant, ornate fireplace to her left. But what makes this scene extraordinary is what seems to have taken place moments before the picture was taken. One of the young woman's feet, clad in the devil-red black-laced boots being advertised, rests defiantly on top of the shattered remains of a crystal chandelier. In her right hand, the woman holds an old-looking shotgun with her forefinger still resting on the trigger.

Description of the second text.

In Sorel's explosive ad, it is apparent that the woman not only shot 5 down the ceiling fixture but also has no regrets about doing so. Her white dress represents a sort of purity and innocence that is completely contradicted by the way she wears it — and by the boots. They gave her the power to shoot down the chandelier, the push she needed to give in to a long-held desire that perhaps she couldn't have indulged in without the extra help. They symbolize her liberty to decide to be herself and do what she wants. Along with the white dress, the formal decor represents the bounds that society tells her she must fit into — but that she decides to take a potshot at instead. Focusing on the beauty of inner power, not just the power of outer beauty, this Sorel ad punctuates its bold visual statement with a single verbal phrase: "Après anything" (Sorel). In the French language, the word *après* means "after." So, the ad suggests, no matter what outrageous or outlandish deed you do, the Sorel boots will be there for you, suitable for slipping into afterward like a negligee.

Analysis of the second text.

See the full story at sorel.com/fearless

Après anything. SOREL

Fig. 2. Sorel ad flaunts devil-red boots worn by a fearless woman with a shotgun (Sorel).

rhetorical
situations

genres

processes

strategies

research
MLA / APA

media /
design

readings

With these pioneering fashion ads that celebrate blowing your own horn or shooting up fancy French lighting fixtures for fun, young women are told to accessorize their inner beauty with articles of clothing geared toward their distinctive individual desires. "You don't have to just try to be beautiful in the ways other women do," they say; "you can strike out on your own, and our products will help you do it." The extent to which women will respond to these messages remains to be seen, but certainly the ads themselves achieve a strikingly different look. Whether celebrating individual talents or random acts of defiance in our everyday lives, they dare us to accessorize our personalities.

Conclusion ties together the strands of her analysis.

Works Cited
Clarks. Advertisement. *Lucky*. Sept. 2011: 55. Print.
Sorel. Advertisement. *Lucky*. Sept. 2011: 65. Print.

Berry summarizes each ad clearly and focuses her analysis on a theme running through both ads: that clothing is an expression of one's individuality. She describes patterns of images in both ads as evidence.

EMILY NUSSBAUM

In Defense of Liz Lemon

Emily Nussbaum explores the evolution of Liz Lemon, 30 Rock's main character, in this analysis from the New Yorker.

Judging from my Twitter feed, there's been a backlash to *30 Rock* this season, particularly the character of Liz Lemon, played by Tina Fey. . . . The argument in all these pieces (many by writers I respect) is pretty much the same: *30 Rock* used to be funny, but now it's sour and negative. Liz Lemon was once our heroine — a sassy, confident, if somewhat neurotic single career lady. Now she's become infantilized and dumb. She behaves as if Jack Donaghy (Alec Baldwin) is her daddy. She doesn't trust her own judgment, she's bad at her job, and there's something awfully misogynist about all this! Liz Lemon is pathetic.

Tina Fey as Liz Lemon.

rhetorical situations

genres

processes

strategies

research MLA / APA

media / design

readings

Well, I can't get on board the hate train, especially after last week's tour-de-force episode, in which Liz morphed from a crazy old subway lady (every New Yorker's dream: she gets her way at every turn) into Heath Ledger's Joker. Someone needs to speak up for the Lemon, and for the Fey. Because from the beginning Liz Lemon was pathetic. That was what was enthralling, and even revolutionary, about the character. Unlike some other adorable or slutty-fabulous characters I could name, Liz only superficially resembled the protagonist of a romantic comedy, ready to remove her glasses and be loved. Beneath that, she was something way more interesting: a strange, specific, workaholic, NPR-worshipping, white-guilt-infected, sardonic, curmudgeonly, hyper-nerdy New Yorker. In the first episode, Jack nails her on sight as "a New York third-wave feminist, college-educated, single-and-pretending-to-be-happy-about-it, over-scheduled, undersexed, you buy any magazine that says 'healthy body image' on the cover and every two years you take up knitting for . . . a week." Even Liz had to admit he scored a point.

That was why the show worked: it rarely made Liz an empowering role model, although many women certainly identified with her. The show let her be the George Costanza, not the Mary Richards. And, refreshingly, this appeal had little to do with sex or relationships: a lot of it was about her job. Liz was professionally successful, but she was a sellout. The lady-centric pitch for her show — it was supposed to be *The Girlie Show,* a showcase for her best friend, Jenna — had been commercialized into TGS, a mediocre SNL ripoff, with low ratings and fart gags. Liz needed Jack because her life was a mess, but their rapport wasn't primarily based around gender: it was about the cocky powerful suits versus the smug weakling creatives, although this satire was done (for once) with a woman at the center. In its apocalyptic view of the TV industry, *30 Rock* famously faced off against another show that premiered in the fall of 2006, Aaron Sorkin's accidentally hilarious *Studio 60 on the Sunset Strip.* Sorkin's show was a drama (or really, a temper tantrum) about two male comedy writers portrayed as heroic geniuses. In contrast, *30 Rock* was a brilliant comedy about a stupid comedy, a feminist sitcom about a woman whose feminism was endlessly lampooned.

Sure, Liz had tiny moments of triumph — as when she showed Jack how hard it was to be an actor — but she lost most battles from the start, because that's the nature of network TV: compromise, compromise, compromise. (She didn't win that "Followship" award for nothing.) Also, Liz's nerdliness was not cute, and, over time, it was often quite disgusting: she wore Duane Reade bags for underwear, she binged on cheese, she was pathologically prudish. In the first season, she lived with a beeper salesman, Dennis, whose nickname for her was "Dummy." After finally getting the guts to end it with Dennis, Liz had several promising relationships, including one great one, when she dated an ex-alcoholic named Floyd. But he moved away to Cleveland and got engaged to someone else, which I thought was fantastic: sometimes, that's what happens. In her late thirties, Liz dated a white British guy named Wesley Snipes, who was endlessly thrown at her in classic rom-com soulmate style. She refused to settle. And she got her dream: airline pilot Carol Burnett, who was too similar to Liz in the end, since he shared her cranky, unforgiving bent. The relationship climaxed with one of the best scenes on the show, a crazy screaming match down the aisle of Carol's airplane in which Liz nearly killed an elderly hostage in order to win an argument.

That has always been one of the most radical things about *30 Rock*, the way it has continually punctured Liz's image of herself as a spunky brunette underdog. Early on, she went to her high-school reunion and discovered that she had not in fact been the overlooked nerd — she had been the sarcastic bully, throwing zingers at women she envied (an insight Tina Fey has regularly expressed about herself). When her old boyfriend Floyd came back to town, he got drunk and blurted out the truth about why he prefers his young aerobics-instructor fiancée: "She's alive! Like a deer who runs and sniffs and jumps and stares. Not like the badger, with her glasses and her rules about weekday sex."

All that stuff was true about Liz, and I thought it was great when, last season, in the "Reaganing" episode, Liz finally confronted her own anxieties about sex, a hallmark of the character from the beginning. (The episode featured a montage of every prudish remark Liz has made.) In the midst of a massive run in which he fixes the problems of everyone around him, Jack helps Liz flash back to a childhood masturbation trauma, which, with typical wackiness, involved roller skates and posters of Grizzly Adams and Tug McGraw. The anti-Lemon squad might not like that Jack was the one who guided Liz to that insight, but after all, his life has changed too: yes, he's married and a father, but from the perspective of Jack's future self, he's a pathetic failure, currently running a worthless network bought by the lame Philadelphia conglomerate Kabletown.

And the thing is, Liz's confrontations with her worst qualities have actually strengthened her. That's what so odd about the backlash. This season, Liz is happier than ever — and for once, she's *rejecting* Jack's influence, finding her own bliss, embracing her oddball nature, going

5

on the Oprah-style vacations she feels like taking. Unbeknownst to Jack, she began dating a cute younger guy who made no money, had a stupid career path, but treated her well. Of course, when Jack found out, he judged her for this, got inside her head, and made fun of her boyfriend's name (which is, to be fair, Criss Chros). But then Liz realized that she actually likes Criss and was an idiot to dump him for shallow reasons; i.e., Jack's reasons. She goes back to him, against Jack's advice.

On Valentine's Day, she and Criss have a fight at IKEA and she assumes they've broken up. Instead, when she goes home, he's made dinner. "You wanted a table, I wasn't super-helpful, who cares?" he says. "I tend to care," she admits. "I let little things ruin stuff. I stopped shopping at Kmart because I found out Kathy Ireland didn't design any of her signature socks." Liz tells him that, at forty-one, she can finally change, but Criss thinks that's ridiculous. "Eh, why bother. You can get mad at dumb stuff, that's your thing. I'll get over it, that's my thing. It's kind of perfect." And he gives her a table he made from a Herman Cain poster and fallen branches from Riverside Park.

As for her career, while Liz was once a people-pleasing, prickly, masochistic workaholic, she's gotten awfully laissez-faire. This is not a bad thing. She's in her forties now and she's stopped obsessing about whether she'll have a baby or whether her job is ideal. She took a fun hobby that Jack would never approve of, shaking her butt as a middle-aged cheerleader for the Liberty. She used Jack's negotiating tricks against him, getting him so exasperated that he negotiated against himself on her behalf. She's now paid well (while Liz used to be bad with money, she's now outright rich) and she's more chill and she's getting laid with a handsome, nice guy. I'm not seeing what's so pathetic. In fact, the show seems to recognize how good her life has become, because they brought in the excellent Kristen Schaal as a female intern who is so impressed by Liz she wishes she could wear her lips as a mask. In *30 Rock* terms, that's a huge compliment.

Still, maybe the best thing about Liz Lemon is that all her idiosyncrasies—her sourness, her prudishness, her love of *The Real Housewives*—don't have to mean as much, anyway. When the show started, every bespectacled, slovenly, overworked media chick was delighted to finally have a character who reflected her. (I should know.) But we're living in a golden age for female comedy, post-*Bridesmaids* and post–*Young Adult* (a movie I loved, but we can argue about that later). On TV in particular, this season has been a fat sweep of sitcoms starring or made by women, some of which I deeply enjoy, some of which I hate: *New Girl,* 10

Suburgatory, Whitney, Up All Night, Two Broke Girls, that Chelsea Handler disaster, and the upcoming *Don't Trust the B— in Apt 23.* There are amazing female characters on *Raising Hope, Cougar Town, Community, Happy Endings, The Middle, The Office,* and *It's Always Sunny in Philadelphia.* Actually, Jenna Maroney of *30 Rock* has also had a solid recent plot arc, one of the kinkiest and most sex-positive I've ever seen on TV. Plus, Lena Dunham's terrific new series *Girls* launches on HBO in April.

And then there is Leslie Knope, of *Parks and Recreation,* a very different character from Liz Lemon — sunny and positive and eyes-on-the-prize and currently juggling more than one man. I love them both. We all know this has always been the goal: enough female funny out there that each one doesn't have to hold the banner quite so high. As for me, I'm still on Team Lemon. Or, to quote the woman herself, "Man, do my feet hurt in heels sometimes . . . and other things women talk about."

Nussbaum analyzes the success of 30 Rock *in terms of its refusal to portray Liz Lemon as a stereotypical career woman — "A spunky brunette underdog" — instead showing her as a deeply flawed person, just like her viewers.*

WILLIAM SAFIRE

A Spirit Reborn

Just before the first anniversary of September 11, 2001, New York Times columnist William Safire analyzed the Gettysburg Address for what it meant to Americans after 9/11.

Abraham Lincoln's words at the dedication of the Gettysburg cemetery will be the speech repeated at the commemoration of September 11 by the governor of New York and by countless other speakers across the nation.

The lips of many listeners will silently form many of the famous phrases. "Four score and seven years ago" — a sonorous way of recalling the founding of the nation eighty-seven years before he spoke — is a phrase many now recite by rote, as is "the last full measure of devotion."

But the selection of this poetic political sermon as the oratorical centerpiece of our observance need not be only an exercise in historical evocation, nonpolitical correctness, and patriotic solemnity. What makes this particular speech so relevant for repetition on this first anniversary of the worst bloodbath on our territory since Antietam Creek's waters ran red is this: now, as then, a national spirit rose from the ashes of destruction.

Here is how to listen to Lincoln's all-too-familiar speech with new ears.

In those 236 words, you will hear the word *dedicate* five times. The first two times refer to the nation's dedication to two ideals mentioned in the Declaration of Independence, the original ideal of "liberty" and the ideal that became central to the Civil War: "that all men are created equal."

The third, or middle, *dedication* is directed to the specific conse-cration of the site of the battle of Gettysburg: "to dedicate a portion of that field as a final resting place." The fourth and fifth times Lincoln repeated *dedicate* reaffirmed those dual ideals for which the dead being honored fought: "to the unfinished work" and then "to the great task remaining before us" of securing freedom and equality.

Those five pillars of dedication rested on a fundament of religious metaphor. From a president not known for his piety — indeed, often criticized for his supposed lack of faith — came a speech rooted in the theme of national resurrection. The speech is grounded in conception, birth, death, and rebirth.

Consider the barrage of images of birth in the opening sentence. The nation was "conceived in liberty" and "brought forth" — that is, delivered into life — by "our fathers" with all "created" equal. (In the nineteenth century, both "men" and "fathers" were taken to embrace women and mothers.) The nation was born.

Then, in the middle dedication, to those who sacrificed themselves, come images of death: "final resting place" and "brave men, living and dead."

Finally, the nation's spirit rises from this scene of death: "that this nation, under God, shall have a new birth of freedom." Conception, birth, death, rebirth. The nation, purified in this fiery trial of war, is resurrected. Through the sacrifice of its sons, the sundered nation would be reborn as one.

An irreverent aside: All speechwriters stand on the shoulders of ora-tors past. Lincoln's memorable conclusion was taken from a fine oration by the Reverend Theodore Parker at an 1850 Boston antislavery convention. That social reformer defined the transcendental "idea of freedom" to be "a government of all the people, by all the people, for all the people."

Lincoln, thirteen years later, dropped the "alls" and made the phrase his own. (A little judicious borrowing by presidents from previous orators shall not perish from the earth.) In delivering that final note, the Union's defender is said to have thrice stressed the noun "people" rather than the prepositions "of," "by," and "for." What is to be emphasized is not rhetorical rhythm but the reminder that our government's legitimacy springs from America's citizens; the people, not the rulers, are sovereign. Not all nations have yet grasped that.

Do not listen on September 11 only to Lincoln's famous words and comforting cadences. Think about how Lincoln's message encompasses but goes beyond paying "fitting and proper" respect to the dead and the bereaved. His sermon at Gettysburg reminds "us the living" of our "unfinished work" and "the great task remaining before us" — to resolve that this generation's response to the deaths of thousands of our people leads to "a new birth of freedom."

Safire's analysis focuses on patterns of specific words and images—he identifies dedicate *as a key term and analyzes how its meaning changes and develops each time it is used. He shows how Lincoln shaped his text around images of birth, death, and resurrection to assert that although a nation's soldiers die, their deaths permit the rebirth of the nation. In doing so, Safire builds an argument linking Lincoln's words to current circumstances.*

SAM ANDERSON

Just One More Game . . . : Angry Birds, Farmville, and Other Hyperaddictive Stupid Games

Journalist and critic Sam Anderson analyzes the lure of video games in this essay, which appeared in print in the New York Times Sunday Magazine *and simultaneously online at NYTimes.com. In addition to the text reproduced here, the online version, available via* wwnorton.com/write/fieldguidelinks, *includes illustrations, a simulation of the online game Kick Ass, and personal narratives of Anderson's video gaming experiences.*

In 1989, as communism was beginning to crumble across Eastern Europe, just a few months before protesters started pecking away at the Berlin Wall, the Japanese game-making giant Nintendo reached across the world to unleash upon America its own version of freedom. The new product was the Game Boy — a

hand-held, battery-powered plastic slab that promised to set gamers loose, after all those decades of sweaty bondage, from the tyranny of rec rooms and pizza parlors and arcades.

The unit came bundled with a single cartridge: Tetris, a simple but addictive puzzle game whose goal was to rotate falling blocks — over and over and over and over and over and over and over — in order to build the most efficient possible walls. (Well, it was complicated. You were both building walls and not building walls; if you built them right, the walls disappeared, thereby ceasing to be walls.) This turned out to be a perfect symbiosis of game and platform. Tetris's graphics were simple enough to work on the Game Boy's small gray-scale screen; its motion was slow enough not to blur; its action was a repetitive, storyless puzzle that could be picked up, with no loss of potency, at any moment, in any situation. The pairing went on to sell more than 70 million copies, spreading the freedom of compulsive wall-building into every breakfast nook and bank line in the country.

And so a tradition was born: a tradition I am going to call (half descriptively, half out of revenge for all the hours I've lost to them) "stupid games." In the nearly 30 years since Tetris's invention — and especially over the last five, with the rise of smartphones — Tetris and its offspring (Angry Birds, Bejeweled, Fruit Ninja, etc.) have colonized our pockets and our brains and shifted the entire economic model of the video-game industry. Today we are living, for better and worse, in a world of stupid games.

Game-studies scholars (there are such things) like to point out that games tend to reflect the societies in which they are created and played. Monopoly, for instance, makes perfect sense as a product of the 1930s — it allowed anyone, in the middle of the Depression, to play at being a tycoon. Risk, released in the 1950s, is a stunningly literal expression of cold-war realpolitik. Twister is the translation, onto a game board, of the mid-1960s sexual revolution. One critic called it "sex in a box."

Tetris was invented exactly when and where you would expect — in a Soviet 5 computer lab in 1984 — and its game play reflects this origin. The enemy in Tetris is not some identifiable villain (Donkey Kong, Mike Tyson, Carmen Sandiego) but a faceless, ceaseless, reasonless force that threatens constantly to overwhelm you, a churning production of blocks against which your only defense is a repetitive, meaningless sorting. It is bureaucracy in pure form, busywork with no aim or end, impossible to avoid or escape. And the game's final insult is that it annihilates free will. Despite its obvious futility, somehow we can't make ourselves stop rotating blocks. Tetris, like all the stupid games it spawned, forces us to choose to punish ourselves.

In 2009, 25 years after the invention of Tetris, a nearly bankrupt Finnish company called Rovio hit upon a similarly perfect fusion of game and device: Angry Birds. The game involves launching peevish birds at green pigs hiding inside flimsy structures. Its basic mechanism — using your index finger to pull back a slingshot, over and over and over and over and over and over and over — was the perfect use of the new technology of the touch screen: simple enough to lure a suddenly immense new market of casual gamers, satisfying enough to hook them.

Within months, Angry Birds became the most popular game on the iPhone, then spread across every other available platform. Today it has been downloaded, in its various forms, more than 700 million times. It has also inspired a disturbingly robust merchandising empire: films, T-shirts, novelty slippers, even plans for Angry Birds "activity parks" featuring play equipment for kids. For months, a sign outside my local auto-repair shop promised, "Free Angry Birds pen with service." The game's latest iteration, Angry Birds Space, appeared a couple weeks ago with a promotional push from Wal-Mart, T-Mobile, National Geographic Books, MTV and NASA. (There was an announcement on the International Space Station.) Angry Birds, it seems, is our Tetris: the string of digital prayer beads that our entire culture can twiddle in moments of rapture or anxiety — economic, political or existential. . . .

Humans have always played stupid games. Dice are older than recorded history. Ancient Egyptians played a board game called Senet, which archaeologists believe was something like sacred backgammon. We have rock-paper-scissors, tick-tack-toe, checkers, dominoes and solitaire — small, abstract games in which sets of simple rules play out in increasingly complex scenarios. (Chess, you might say, is the king of stupid games: the tide line where stupid games meet genius.)

But pre-Tetris games were different in a primal way. They required human opponents or at least equipment — the manipulation of three-dimensional objects in space. When you sat down to play them, chances were you meant to sit down and play them.

Stupid games, on the other hand, are rarely occasions in themselves. They are designed to push their way through the cracks of other occasions. We play them incidentally, ambivalently, compulsively, almost accidentally. They're less an activity in our day than a blank space in our day; less a pursuit than a distraction from other pursuits. You glance down to check your calendar and suddenly it's 40 minutes later and there's only one level left before you jump to the next stage, so you might as well just launch another bird. . . .

Then, in 2007, the iPhone appeared. Games were much easier to develop and easier to distribute through Apple's app store. Instead of just passing their work

10

around to one another on blogs, independent game designers suddenly had a way to reach everyone — not just hard-core gamers, but their mothers, their mail-men and their college professors. Consumers who never would have put a quarter into an arcade or even set eyes on an Xbox 360 were now carrying a sophisticated game console with them, all the time, in their pockets or their purses.

This had a profound impact on game design. In the era of consoles, most games were designed to come to life on a stationary piece of furniture — a television or a desktop computer. The games were built accordingly, around long narratives (quests, wars, the rise and fall of civilizations) that could be explored comfortably while sitting cross-legged on a living-room carpet.

Smartphone games are built on a very different model. The iPhone's screen is roughly the size of a playing card; it responds not to the fast-twitch button combos of a controller but to more intuitive and intimate motions: poking, pinching, tapping, tickling. This has encouraged a very different kind of game: Tetris-like little puzzles, broken into discrete bits, designed to be played anywhere, in any context, without a manual, by any level of player. (Charles Pratt, a researcher in New York University's Game Center, refers to such games as "knitting games.") You could argue that these are *pure* games: perfectly designed minisystems engineered to take us directly to the core of gaming pleasure without the distraction of narrative. The Angry Birds creators like to compare their game with Super Mario Brothers. But the first and simplest level of Super Mario Brothers takes about a minute and a half to finish. The first level of Angry Birds takes around 10 seconds. . . .

There are people who see the proliferation of stupid games as a good thing. In fact, they believe that games may be the answer to all of humanity's problems. In her book "Reality Is Broken," Jane McGonigal argues that play is possibly the best, healthiest, most productive activity a human can undertake — a gateway to our ideal psychological state. Games aren't an escape from reality, McGonigal contends, they are an optimal form of engaging it. In fact, if we could just find a way to impose game mechanics on top of everyday life, humans would be infinitely better off. We might even use these approaches to help solve real-world problems like obesity, education and government abuse. Some proponents point to successful examples of games applied to everyday life: Weight Watchers and frequent-flier miles, for example.

Corporations, of course, have been using similar strategies for decades, hooking consumers on products by giving them constant small victories for spending money (think of the old Monopoly game promotion at McDonald's). The buzzword for this is "gamification" and the ubiquity of computers and smartphones has only supercharged these tendencies. Gartner, a technology research firm, 15 predicted last year that, in the near future, "a gamified service for consumer-goods marketing and customer retention will become as important as Facebook, eBay or Amazon." Companies have already used online games to sneakily advertise sugary cereals directly to children.

Although there is a certain utopian appeal to McGonigal's "games for change" model, I worry about the dystopic potential of gamification. Instead of just bombarding us with jingles, corporations will be able to inject their messages directly into our minds with ads disguised as games. Gamification seeks to turn the world into one giant chore chart covered with achievement stickers — the kind of thing parents design for their children — though it raises the potentially terrifying question of who the parents are. This, I fear, is the dystopian future of stupid games: amoral corporations hiring teams of behavioral psychologists to laser-target our addiction cycles for profit. . . .

[Game designer Frank] Lantz seemed undisturbed by the dark side of stupid games, like addiction or cynical corporate hijacking. He said that real games are far too fragile and complex to be engineered by corporations and that their appeal goes much deeper than reward schedules. "It's as hard to make a really good game as it is to make a really good movie or opera or hat," he told me. "Sure, there's mathematics to it, but it's also a piece of culture. The type of game you play is also a part of how you think about yourself as a person. There's no formula that's going to solve that equation. It's impossible, because it's infinitely deep and wonderful."

As for my nightmare vision of a world splintered by addiction to stupid games, Lantz had a different perspective. He said that he liked to think Drop7 [a game Lantz designed that combines elements of Tetris and Sudoku] was not only addictive but also, on some level, about addiction. Games, he told me, are like "home-brew neuroscience" — "a little digital drug you can use to run experiments on your own brain." Part of the point of letting them seduce you, as Lantz sees it, is to come out the other side a more interesting and self-aware person; more conscious of your habits, weaknesses, desires and strengths. "It's like heroin that is abstracted or compressed or stylized," he said. "It gives you a window into your brain that doesn't crush your brain."

I tried to think about what — if anything — I had learned from this window into my brain. Like their spiritual forefather, Tetris, most stupid games are about walls: building them, scaling them, knocking them down. Walls made of numbers, walls made of digital bricks, walls with green pigs hiding behind them. They're like miniature boot camps of containment. Ultimately, I realized, these games are also about a more subtle and mysterious form of wall-building: the internal walls we build to compartmentalize our time, our attention, our lives. The legendary game designer Sid Meier once defined a game as, simply, "a series of interesting choices." Maybe that's the secret genius of stupid games: they force us to make a series of interesting choices about what matters, moment to moment, in our lives. . . .

Anderson describes Tetris *and other games clearly and outlines their relationship to older "stupid games." He interprets the "gamification" of American culture positively and provides evidence from experts as well as the games themselves, including the playable online* Kick Ass *game, to support his interpretation.*

> For five more textual analyses, see CHAPTER 58.

Key Features / Textual Analysis

A summary of the text. Your readers may not know the text you are analyzing, so you need to include it or tell them about it before you can analyze it. Because Safire's text is so well known, he describes it only briefly as "Abraham Lincoln's words at the dedication of the Gettysburg cemetery." Texts that are not so well known require a more detailed summary. Berry includes the ads she analyzes and also describes them in detail.

Attention to the context. Texts don't exist in isolation: they are influenced by and contribute to ongoing conversations, controversies, or debates, so to understand a particular text, you need to understand its larger context. Nussbaum opens by describing fans' critical response to the evolution of *30 Rock's* main character. Safire notes the source of the phrase "of the people, by the people, for the people" and is clearly writing in the context of the United States after 9/11.

A clear interpretation or judgment. Your goal in analyzing a text is to lead readers through careful examination of the text to some kind of interpretation or reasoned judgment, sometimes announced clearly in a thesis statement. When you interpret something, you explain what you think it means, as Berry does when she argues that the two ads suggest that our clothing choices enhance our individuality. She might instead have chosen to judge the effectiveness of the ads, perhaps noting that they promise the impossible: uniqueness through mass-produced clothing. Anderson judges "stupid games" to be positive, as "they force us to make a series of interesting choices about what matters, moment to moment, in our lives."

Reasonable support for your conclusions. Written analysis of a text is generally supported by evidence from the text itself and sometimes from other sources. The writer might support his or her interpretation by quoting words or passages from a written text or referring to images in a visual text. Safire, for example, looks at Lincoln's repetition of the word "dedicate" in the Gettysburg Address as a way of arguing that the speech was still relevant in 2002, on the anniversary of the 9/11 attacks. Berry examines patterns of both language and images in her analysis of the two ads. Nussbaum describes several scenes and plotlines from *30 Rock*. Note that the support you offer for your interpretation need only be "reasonable" — there is never any one way to interpret something.

A GUIDE TO WRITING TEXTUAL ANALYSES

Choosing a Text to Analyze

Most of the time, you will be assigned a text or a type of text to analyze: a poem in a literature class, the work of a political philosopher in a political science class, a speech in a history or communications course, a painting or sculpture in an art class, a piece of music in a music theory course. If you must choose a text to analyze, look for one that suits the demands of the assignment — one that is neither too large or complex to analyze thoroughly (a Dickens novel or a Beethoven symphony is probably too big) nor too brief or limited to generate sufficient material (a ten-second TV news brief or a paragraph from *Moneyball* would probably be too small). You might also choose to analyze three or four texts by examining elements common to all. Be sure you understand what the assignment asks you to do, and ask your instructor for clarification if you're not sure.

Considering the Rhetorical Situation

3–4 ■ | **PURPOSE** | Why are you analyzing this text? To demonstrate that you understand it? To show how its argument works — or doesn't? Or are you using the text as a way to make some other point?

AUDIENCE   Are your readers likely to know your text? How much detail will you need to supply?

5–8

STANCE   What interests you (or not) about your text? Why? What do you know or believe about it, and how will your own beliefs affect your analysis?

12–15

MEDIA / DESIGN   Will your analysis appear in print? on the web? How will your medium affect your analysis? If you are analyzing a visual text, you will probably need to include an image of it.

16–18

Generating Ideas and Text

In analyzing a text, your goal is to understand what it says, how it works, and what it means. To do so, you may find it helpful to follow a certain sequence: read, respond, summarize, analyze, and draw conclusions from your analysis.

Read to see what the text says.   Start by reading carefully, to get a sense of what it says. This means first skimming to PREVIEW THE TEXT, rereading for the main ideas, then questioning and ANNOTATING.

399
400–401
400

Consider your INITIAL RESPONSE. Once you have a sense of what the text says, what do you think? What's your reaction to the argument, the tone, the language, the images? Do you find the text difficult? puzzling? Do you agree with what the writer says? disagree? agree *and* disagree? Your reaction to a text can color your analysis, so start by thinking about how you react—and why. Consider both your intellectual and any emotional reactions. Identify places in the text that trigger or account for those reactions. If you think that you have no particular reaction or response, try to articulate why. Whatever your response, think about what accounts for it.

Next, consolidate your understanding of the text by SUMMARIZING (or, if it's a visual text, DESCRIBING) what it says in your own words. You may find it helpful to OUTLINE its main ideas. See, for instance, how Hannah Berry carefully described what the shoe ads she was analyzing show and say. Some of this analysis ended up in her essay.

470–71
367–75
263–64

Photographed in standing profile, this quirky-looking young woman is doing what she loves — playing some kind of trumpet — and looks great doing it. She is wearing her hair in a French twist with a strand tucked behind her ear, as if she recently moved it out of her face to play the music she loves without distraction. The downturn of her nose points to the short gray-black dress that stops several inches above her knees but covers her chest and shoulders modestly, with a collar situated at the base of her neck and sleeves that reach for her elbows. The dress is plain, but it is a perfect fit for the personality implied in the photo. Set against the background of a light-tan wall, the model leans back slightly as if supporting the weight of her instrument. Her right knee is bent while her left knee remains straight. The positioning of her legs not only accentuates her unbalanced posture but also points out the pair of simple brown pumps that complete the look. She wears the shoes with a pair of socks in a much darker shade of brown pulled up around her shins. Around her ankles are sandy-colored rings of shaggy fabric that are most likely attached to the socks, giving the whole outfit a sense of nerdy flair. Her expression is a simple mix of calm and concentration. It's as if the photographer happened to take the picture while she was practicing for a school recital.

Decide what you want to analyze.   Having read the text carefully, think about what you find most interesting or intriguing and why. Does the argument interest you? its logic? its attempt to create an emotional response? its reliance on the writer's credibility or reputation? its use of design to achieve its aims? its context? Does the text's language, imagery, or structure intrigue you? something else? You might begin your analysis by exploring what attracted your notice.

Think about the larger context.   All texts are part of larger conversations with other texts that have dealt with the same topic. An essay arguing for handgun trigger locks is part of an ongoing conversation about gun control, which is itself part of a conversation on individual rights and responsibilities. Academic texts include documentation in part to weave in voices from the conversation. And, in fact, any time you're reading to learn, you're probably reading for some larger context. Whatever your reading goals, being aware of that larger context can help you better understand

rhetorical situations

genres

processes

strategies

research MLA / APA

media / design

readings

what you're reading. Here are some specific aspects of the text to pay attention to:

- *Who else cares about this topic?* Especially when you're reading in order to learn about a topic, the texts you read will often reveal which people or groups are part of the conversation — and might be sources of further reading. For example, an essay describing the formation of Mammoth Cave could be of interest to geologists, spelunkers, travel writers, or tourists. If you're reading such an essay while doing research on the cave, you should consider how the audience addressed determines the nature of the information provided — and its suitability as a source for your research.

- *Ideas.* Does the text refer to any concepts or ideas that give you some sense that it's part of a larger conversation? An argument on airport security measures, for example, is part of larger conversations about government response to terrorism, the limits of freedom in a democracy, and the possibilities of using technology to detect weapons and explosives, among others.

- *Terms.* Is there any terminology or specialized language that reflects the writer's allegiance to a particular group or academic discipline? If you run across words like *false consciousness, ideology,* and *hegemony,* for example, you might guess the text was written by a Marxist scholar.

- *Citations.* Whom does the writer cite? Do the other writers have a particular academic specialty, belong to an identifiable intellectual school, share similar political leanings? If an article on politics cites Michael Moore and Barbara Ehrenreich in support of its argument, you might assume the writer holds liberal opinions; if it cites Rush Limbaugh and Sean Hannity, the writer is likely a conservative.

Write a brief paragraph describing the larger context surrounding the text and how that context affects your understanding of the text.

Consider what you know about the writer or artist. What you know about the person who created a text can influence your understanding of it. His or her CREDENTIALS, other work, reputation, stance, and beliefs are all useful windows into understanding a text.

● 454

Then write a sentence or two summarizing what you know about the writer and how that information affects your understanding of the text.

Study how the text works.   Written texts are made up of various components, including words, sentences, paragraphs, headings, lists, punctuation — and sometimes images as well. Visual texts might be made up of images, lines, angles, color, light and shadow, and sometimes words. To analyze these elements, look for patterns in the way they're used and try to decide what those patterns reveal about the text. How do they affect its message? See the sections on **THINKING ABOUT HOW THE TEXT WORKS** and **IDENTIFYING PATTERNS** for specific guidelines on examining patterns this way. Then write a sentence or two describing the patterns you've discovered and how they contribute to what the text says.

405–7
408–11

Analyze the argument.   Every text makes an argument. Both verbal and visual texts make certain assertions and provide some kind of support for those claims. An important part of understanding any text is to recognize its argument — what the writer or artist wants the audience to believe, feel, or do. Here are some questions you'll want to consider when you analyze an argument:

- *What is the claim?*   What is the main point the writer is trying to make? Is there a clearly stated **THESIS**, or is the thesis merely implied? Is it appropriately qualified?

313–15

- *What support does the writer offer for the claim?*   What **REASONS** are given to support the claim? What **EVIDENCE** backs up those reasons? Facts? Statistics? Examples? Testimonials by authorities? Appropriate anecdotes or stories? Are the reasons and evidence appropriate, plausible, and sufficient? Are you convinced by them? If not, why not?

326–35

- *How does the writer appeal to readers?*   Does he or she appeal to your **EMOTIONS?** rely on **LOGIC?** try to establish **COMMON GROUND?** demonstrate **CREDIBILITY?**

338
324–34
334–35
334–37

- *How evenhandedly does the writer present the argument?*   Is there any mention of **COUNTERARGUMENTS?** If so, how does the writer deal with them? By refuting them? By acknowledging them and responding to them reasonably? Does the writer treat other arguments respectfully? dismissively? 336–37

- *Does the writer use any logical* **FALLACIES?**   Are the arguments or beliefs of others distorted or exaggerated? Is the logic faulty? 338–40

- *What authorities or other sources of outside information does the writer use?* How are they used? How credible are they? Are they in any way biased or otherwise unreliable? Are they current?

- *How does the writer address you as the reader?*   Does the writer assume that readers know something about what is being discussed? Does his or her language include you or exclude you? (Hint: If you see the word *we,* do you feel included?) Do you sense that you and the writer share any beliefs or attitudes? If the writer is not writing to you, what audience is the target? How do you know?

Then write a brief paragraph summarizing the argument the text makes and the main way the writer argues it, along with your reactions to or questions about that argument.

Come up with a thesis.   When you analyze a text, you are basically **ARGUING** that the text should be read in a certain way. Once you've studied the text thoroughly, you need to identify your analytical goal: do you want to show that the text has a certain meaning? uses certain techniques to achieve its purposes? tries to influence its audience in particular ways? relates to some larger context in some significant manner? should be taken seriously—or not? something else? Come up with a tentative **THESIS** to guide your thinking and analyzing—but be aware that your thesis may change as you continue to work. 323–41

313–15

Ways of Organizing a Textual Analysis

263–64 ○

Examine the information you have to see how it supports or complicates your thesis. Look for clusters of related information that you can use to structure an **OUTLINE**. Your analysis might be structured in at least two ways. You might, as Safire does, discuss patterns or themes that run through the text. Alternatively, you might analyze each text or section of text separately, as Berry does. Following are graphic representations of some ways of organizing a textual analysis.

[Thematically]

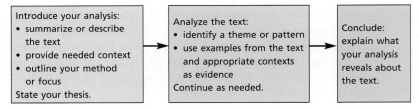

Introduce your analysis:
• summarize or describe the text
• provide needed context
• outline your method or focus
State your thesis.

Analyze the text:
• identify a theme or pattern
• use examples from the text and appropriate contexts as evidence
Continue as needed.

Conclude: explain what your analysis reveals about the text.

[Part by part, or text by text]

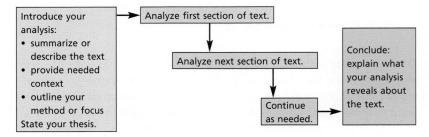

Introduce your analysis:
• summarize or describe the text
• provide needed context
• outline your method or focus
State your thesis.

Analyze first section of text.

Analyze next section of text.

Continue as needed.

Conclude: explain what your analysis reveals about the text.

Writing Out a Draft

In drafting your analysis, your goal should be to integrate the various parts into a smoothly flowing, logically organized essay. However, it's

easy to get bogged down in the details. Consider writing one section of the analysis first, then another and another until you've drafted the entire middle; then draft your beginning and ending. Alternatively, start by summarizing the text and moving from there to your analysis and then to your ending. However you do it, you need to support your analysis with evidence: from the text itself (as Berry's analysis of advertisements and Nussbaum's analysis of *30 Rock* do), or from **RESEARCH** on the larger context of the text (as Safire does), or by incorporating various experts' views of your subject (as Anderson does).

419

Draft a BEGINNING. The beginning of an essay that analyzes a text generally has several tasks: to introduce or summarize the text for your readers, to offer any necessary information on the larger context, and to present your thesis.

299–306

- *Summarize the text.* If the text is one your readers don't know, you need to give a brief **SUMMARY** early on that introduces it to them and shows that you understand it fully. For example, Berry begins each analysis of a shoe advertisement with a brief summary of its content.

470–71

- *Show the text.* If you're analyzing a visual text or any text that is available online, consider starting off with an image, a video, or a link to it or something similar, as Anderson does by illustrating his essay with a playable video game.

- *Provide a context for your analysis.* If there is a larger context that is significant for your analysis, you might mention it in your introduction. Safire does this when he frames his analysis of the Gettysburg Address as a "centerpiece" of 9/11 commemorations.

- *State your thesis.* Berry ends her first paragraph by stating the **THESIS** of her analysis: These ads for Clarks and Sorel encourage us to break free from the standard beauty mold and be ourselves; "using mostly imagery, they remind us that being unique is the true origin of beauty."

313–15

306–10
Draft an ENDING. Think about what you want your readers to take away from your analysis, and end by getting them to focus on those thoughts.

- *Restate your thesis — and say why it matters.* Berry, for example, ends by asserting that the ads she examines invite women to "be ourselves" by "accessoriz[ing] our personalities."

- *Explain what your analysis reveals.* Your analysis should tell your readers something about the way the text works or about the meaning of the text. Safire, for example, states that "[Lincoln's] sermon at Gettysburg reminds 'us the living' of our 'unfinished work' and 'the great task remaining before us' — to resolve that this generation's response to the deaths of thousands of our people leads to 'a new birth of freedom.'"

312–13
Come up with a TITLE. A good title indicates something about the subject of your analysis — and makes readers want to see what you have to say about it. Nussbaum's title forthrightly declares her topic. And Berry's title provides a preview of her thesis that the ads she is analyzing are selling a vision of clothing as a vehicle for being unique.

Considering Matters of Design

480–83
588–89
- If you cite written text as evidence, be sure to set long quotations and **DOCUMENTATION** according to the style you're using.

- If your essay is lengthy, consider whether **HEADINGS** would make your analysis easier for readers to follow.

- If you're analyzing a visual text, include a copy of the image and a caption identifying it.

- If you're submitting your essay electronically, provide links to the text, image, webpage, or other material you are analyzing.

- If you're analyzing an image or a screen shot, consider annotating elements of it, as is done in the following editorial cartoon about the September 11, 2012, attack on the U.S. Consulate in Benghazi, Lybia.

rhetorical situations
genres
processes
strategies
research MLA / APA
media / design
readings

In 2011, a wave of protest demonstrations led to the overthrow of several governments in the Arab world. This movement was called the "Arab Spring" and a common cartoonist's symbol for it was a flower growing in the desert.

Frost kills flowers, and the cartoonist is suggesting that not only are the U.S. officials to be mourned, but that the attack signals the end of the Arab Spring itself.

Ambassador Christopher Stevens, Sean Smith, Glen Doherty, and Tyrone Woods (the unnamed "Diplomat") were killed during the attack on the U.S. Consulate in Benghazi, Libya.

The attack was carried out by armed terrorists, which the cartoonist labels "Extremists."

— Jeff Darcy *The Plain Dealer*

Getting Response and Revising

The following questions can help you and others study your draft with a critical eye. Make sure that anyone you ask to read and **RESPOND** to your text knows your purpose and audience.

275–76

- Is the beginning effective? Does it make a reader want to continue?
- Does the introduction provide an overview of your analysis and conclusions? Is your thesis clear?
- Is the text described or summarized clearly and sufficiently?
- Is the analysis well organized and easy to follow? Do the parts fit together coherently? Does it read like an essay rather than a collection of separate bits of analysis?
- Does each part of the analysis relate to the thesis?
- Is anything confusing or in need of more explanation?
- Are all quotations accurate and correctly documented?
- Is it clear how the analysis leads to the interpretation? Is there adequate evidence to support the interpretation?
- Does the ending make clear what your findings mean?

276–00 Then it's time to **REVISE.** Make sure your text appeals to your audience and achieves your purpose as successfully as possible.

Editing and Proofreading

Readers equate correctness with competence. Once you've revised your draft, edit carefully:

313–15
- Is your **THESIS** clearly stated?
462–74
480–83
- Check all **QUOTATIONS**, **PARAPHRASES**, and **SUMMARIES** for accuracy and form. Be sure that each has the required **DOCUMENTATION.**

rhetorical situations · genres · processes · strategies · research MLA / APA · media / design · readings

- Make sure that your analysis flows clearly from one point to the next and that you use TRANSITIONS to help readers move through your text.

◆ 317

- PROOFREAD your finished analysis carefully before turning it in.

◯ 285–86

Taking Stock of Your Work

Take stock of what you've written and learned by writing out answers to these questions:

- How did you go about analyzing the text? What methods did you use—and which ones were most helpful?
- How did you go about drafting your essay?
- How well did you organize your written analysis? What, if anything, could you do to make it easier to read?
- Did you provide sufficient evidence to support your analysis?
- What did you do especially well?
- What could still be improved?
- Did you use any visuals, and if so, what did they add? Could you have shown the same thing with words?
- How did other readers' responses influence your writing?
- What would you do differently next time?
- Are you pleased with your analysis? What did it teach you about the text you analyzed? Did it make you want to study more works by the same writer or artist?

LITERARY ANALYSES

Literary analyses are essays in which we examine literary texts closely to understand their messages, interpret their meanings, and appreciate their writers' techniques. You might read *Macbeth* and notice that Shakespeare's play contains a pattern of images of blood. You could explore the distinctive point of view in Ambrose Bierce's story "An Occurrence at Owl Creek Bridge." Or you could point out the differences between Stephen King's *The Shining* and Stanley Kubrick's screenplay based on that novel. In all these cases, you use specific analytical tools to go below the surface of the work to deepen your understanding of how it works and what it means. Here is a sonnet by the nineteenth-century English Romantic poet Percy Bysshe Shelley, followed by one student's analysis of it written for a literature course at Wright State University.

PERCY BYSSHE SHELLEY

Sonnet: "Lift not the painted veil which those who live"

Lift not the painted veil which those who live
Call Life: though unreal shapes be pictured there,
And it but mimic all we would believe
With colours idly spread, — behind, lurk Fear
And Hope, twin Destinies; who ever weave   5
Their shadows, o'er the chasm, sightless and drear.
I knew one who had lifted it — he sought,
For his lost heart was tender, things to love,
But found them not, alas! nor was there aught
The world contains, the which he could approve. 10
Through the unheeding many he did move,
A splendour among shadows, a bright blot
Upon this gloomy scene, a Spirit that strove
For truth, and like the Preacher found it not.

STEPHANIE HUFF

Metaphor and Society in Shelley's "Sonnet"

In his sonnet "Lift not the painted veil which those who live," Percy Bysshe Shelley introduces us to a bleak world that exists behind veils

and shadows. We see that although fear and hope both exist, truth is dishearteningly absent. This absence of truth is exactly what Shelley chooses to address as he uses metaphors of grim distortion and radiant incandescence to expose the counterfeit nature of our world.

The speaker of Shelley's poem presents bold assertions about the nature of our society. In the opening lines of the poem, he warns the reader, "Lift not the painted veil which those who live / Call Life" (lines 1–2). Here, the "painted veil" serves as a grim metaphor for life. More specifically, the speaker equates the veil with what people like to *call* life. In this sense, the speaker asserts that what we believe to be pure reality is actually nothing more than a covering that masks what really lies beneath. Truth is covered by a veil of falsehood and is made opaque with the paint of people's lies.

This painted veil does not completely obstruct our view but rather distorts what we can see. All that can be viewed through it are "unreal shapes" (2) that metaphorically represent the people that make up this counterfeit society. These shapes are not to be taken for truth. They are unreal, twisted, deformed figures of humanity, people full of falsities and misrepresentations.

Most people, however, do not realize that the shapes and images seen through the veil are distorted because all they know of life is the veil—this life we see as reality only "mimic[s] all we would believe" (3), using "colours idly spread" (4) to create pictures that bear little resemblance to that which they claim to portray. All pure truths are covered up and painted over until they are mere mockeries. The lies that cloak the truth are not even carefully constructed, but are created idly, with little attention to detail. The paint is not applied carefully but merely spread across the top. This idea of spreading brings to mind images of paint slopped on so heavily that the truth beneath becomes nearly impossible to find. Even the metaphor of color suggests only superficial beauty—"idly spread" (4)—rather than any sort of pure beauty that could penetrate the surface of appearances.

What really lies behind this facade are fear and hope, both of which 5 "weave / Their shadows, o'er the chasm, sightless and drear" (5–6). These two realities are never truly seen or experienced, though. They exist only as shadows. Just as shadows appear only at certain times of day, cast only sham images of what they reflect, and are paid little attention, so too do these emotions of hope and fear appear only as brief, ignored imitations of themselves when they enter the artificiality of this chasmlike world. Peering into a chasm, one cannot hope to make out what lies at the bottom. At best one could perhaps make out shadows and even that cannot be done with any certainty as to true appearance. The world is so large, so caught up in itself and its counterfeit ways, that it can no longer see even the simple truths of hope and fear. Individuals and civilizations have become sightless, dreary, and as enormously empty as a chasm.

This chasm does not include *all* people, however, as we are introduced to one individual, in line 7, who is trying to bring to light whatever truth may yet remain. This one person, who defies the rest of the world, is portrayed with metaphors of light, clearly standing out among the dark representations of the rest of mankind. He is first presented to us as possessing a "lost heart" (8) and seeking things to love. It is important that the first metaphor applied to him be a heart because this is the organ with which we associate love, passion, and purity. We associate it with brightness of the soul, making it the most radiant spot of the body. He is then described as a "splendour among shadows" (12), his purity and truth brilliantly shining through the darkness of the majority's falsehood. Finally, he is equated with "a bright blot / Upon this gloomy scene" (12–13), his own bright blaze of authenticity burning in stark contrast to the murky phoniness of the rest of the world.

These metaphors of light are few, however, in comparison to those of grim distortion. So, too, are this one individual's radiance and zeal too little to alter the warped darkness they temporarily pierce. This one person, though bright, is not bright enough to light up the rest of civilization and create real change. The light simply confirms the dark falsity that comprises the rest of the world. Shelley gives us one flame of hope, only to reveal to us what little chance it has under the suffocating veil. Both the metaphors of grim distortion and those of radiant incandescence work together in this poem to highlight the world's counterfeit nature.

Huff focuses her analysis on patterns in Shelley's imagery. In addition, she pays careful attention to individual words and to how, as the poem unfolds, they create a certain meaning. That meaning is her interpretation.

rhetorical situations   genres   processes   strategies   research MLA / APA   media / design   readings

Key Features / Literary Analyses

An arguable thesis.   A literary analysis is a form of argument; you are arguing that your analysis of a literary work is valid. Your thesis, then, should be arguable, as Huff's is: "[Shelley] uses metaphors of grim distortion and radiant incandescence to expose the counterfeit nature of our world." A mere summary—"Shelley writes about a person who sees reality and seeks love but never finds it"—would not be arguable and therefore is not a good thesis.

Careful attention to the language of the text.   The key to analyzing a text is looking carefully at the language, which is the foundation of its meaning. Specific words, images, metaphors—these are where analysis begins. You may also bring in contextual information, such as cultural, historical, or biographical facts, or you may refer to similar texts. But the words, phrases, and sentences that make up the text you are analyzing are your primary source when dealing with texts. That's what literature teachers mean by "close reading": reading with the assumption that every word of a text is meaningful.

Attention to patterns or themes.   Literary analyses are usually built on evidence of meaningful patterns or themes within a text or among several texts. These patterns and themes reveal meaning. In Shelley's poem, images of light and shadow and artifice and reality create patterns of meaning, while the poem's many half rhymes (*live/believe, love/approve*) create patterns of sound that may contribute to the overall meaning.

A clear interpretation.   A literary analysis demonstrates the plausibility of its thesis by using evidence from the text and, sometimes, relevant contextual evidence to explain how the language and patterns found there support a particular interpretation. When you write a literary analysis, you show readers one way the text may be read and understood; that is your interpretation.

MLA style. Literary analyses usually follow MLA style. Even though Huff's essay has no works-cited list, it refers to line numbers using MLA style.

Considering the Rhetorical Situation

3–4 **PURPOSE**

What do you need to do? Show that you have examined the text carefully? Offer your own interpretation? Demonstrate a particular analytical technique? Or some combination? If you're responding to an assignment, does it specify what you need to do?

5–8 **AUDIENCE**

What do you need to do to convince your readers that your interpretation is plausible and based on sound analysis? Can you assume that readers are already familiar with the text you are analyzing, or do you need to tell them about it?

12–15 **STANCE**

How can you see your subject through interested, curious eyes — and then step back in order to see what your observations might *mean*?

16–18 **MEDIA / DESIGN**

Will your analysis focus on an essentially verbal text or one that has significant visual content, such as a graphic novel? Will you need to show visual elements in your analysis? Will it be delivered in a print, spoken, or electronic medium? Are you required to follow MLA or some other style?

IF YOU NEED MORE HELP

266–68
269–74
275–81
282–86
287–98

See Chapter 25 for guidelines on **DRAFTING,** Chapter 26 on **ASSESSING YOUR OWN WRITING,** Chapter 27 on **GETTING RESPONSE AND REVISING,** and Chapter 28 on **EDITING AND PROOFREADING.** See Chapter 29 if you are required to submit your analysis in a writing **PORTFOLIO.**

Reporting Information

Many kinds of writing report information. Newspapers report on local and world events; textbooks give information about biology, history, writing; websites provide information about products (*jcrew.com*), people (*justinbiebermusic.com*), institutions (*smithsonian.org*). We write out a lot of information ourselves, from a note we post on our door saying we've gone to choir practice to an essay we're assigned to write for a history class, reporting what we've learned about the state of U.S. diplomacy in the days before the bombing of Pearl Harbor. This chapter focuses on reports that are written to inform readers about a particular topic. Very often this kind of writing calls for some kind of research: you need to know your subject in order to report on it! When you write to report information, you are the expert. This chapter offers guidelines for writing essays that inform. We'll begin with four good examples, the first annotated to show the key features found in most reports.

MICHAELA CULLINGTON

Does Texting Affect Writing?

This essay by a student at Marywood University was published in Young Scholars in Writing, *a journal of undergraduate writing published by the University of Missouri–Kansas City.*

> It's taking over our lives. We can do it almost anywhere — walking to class, waiting in line at the grocery store, or hanging out at home. It's

quick, easy, and convenient. It has become a concern of doctors, parents, and teachers alike. What is it? It's texting!

Text messaging — or texting, as it's more commonly called — is the process of sending and receiving typed messages via a cellular phone. It is a common means of communication among teenagers and is even becoming popular in the business world because it allows quick messages to be sent without people having to commit to a telephone conversation. A person is able to say what is needed, and the other person will receive the information and respond when it's convenient to do so.

In order to more quickly type what they are trying to say, many people use abbreviations instead of words. The language created by these abbreviations is called textspeak. Some people believe that using these abbreviations is hindering the writing abilities of students, and others argue that texting is actually having a positive effect on writing. In fact, it seems likely that texting has no significant effect on student writing.

Definitions of key terms.

Here's the thesis.

Concerns about Textspeak

A September 2008 article in *USA Today* entitled "Texting, Testing Destroys Kids' Writing Style" summarizes many of the most common complaints about the effect of texting. It states that according to the National Center for Education Statistics, only 25% of high school seniors are "proficient" writers. The article quotes Jacquie Ream, a former teacher and author of *K.I.S.S.— Keep It Short and Simple*, a guide for writing more effectively. Ream states, "[W]e have a whole generation being raised without communication skills." She blames the use of acronyms and shorthand in text messages for students' inability to spell and ultimately to write well. Ream also points out that students struggle to convey emotion in their writing because, as she states, in text messages "emotions are always sideways smiley faces."

Analysis of causes and effects.

This debate became prominent after some teachers began to 5 believe they were seeing a decline in the writing abilities of their students. Many attributed this perceived decline to the increasing popularity of text messaging and its use of abbreviations. Naomi Baron, a linguistics professor at American University, blames texting for what she sees as the fact that "so much of American society has become sloppy and laissez faire about the mechanics of writing" ("Should We Worry or LOL?"). Teachers report finding "2" for "to," "gr8" for

"great," "dat" for "that," and "wut" for "what," among other examples of textspeak, in their students' writing. A Minnesota teacher of the seventh and ninth grades says that she has to spend extra time in class editing papers and must "explicitly" remind her students that it is not acceptable to use text slang and abbreviations in writing (Walsh). Another English teacher believes that text language has become "second nature" to her students (Carey); they are so used to it that they do not even catch themselves doing it.

Many also complain that because texting does not stress the importance of punctuation, students are neglecting it in their formal writing. Teachers say that their students are forgetting commas, apostrophes, and even capital letters to begin sentences. Another complaint is that text messages lack emotion. Many argue that texts lack feeling because of their tendency to be short, brief, and to the point. Because students are not able to communicate emotion effectively through texts, some teachers worry, they may lose the ability to do so in writing.

To get a more personal perspective on the question of how teachers perceive texting to be influencing student writing, I interviewed two of my former high school teachers — my junior-year English teacher and my senior-year theology teacher. Both teachers stress the importance of writing in their courses. They maintain that they notice text abbreviations in their students' writing often. To correct this problem, they point it out when it occurs and take points off for its use. They also remind their students to use proper sentence structure and complete sentences. The English teacher says that she believes texting inhibits good writing — it reinforces simplistic writing that may be acceptable for conversation but is "not so good for critical thinking or analysis." She suggests that texting tends to generate topic sentences without emphasizing the following explanation. According to these teachers, then, texting is inhibiting good writing. However, their evidence is limited, based on just a few personal experiences rather than on a significant amount of research.

Responses to Concerns about Textspeak

In response to these complaints that texting is having a negative impact on student writing, others insist that texting should be viewed as beneficial because it provides students with motivation to write, practice in specific writing skills, and an opportunity to gain confidence in their writing. For example, Sternberg, Kaplan, and Borck argue that texting is a good way to motivate students: teens enjoy texting, and if they frequently write through texts, they will be more motivated to write formally. Texting also helps to spark students' creativity, these authors argue, because they are always coming up with new ways to express their ideas (417).

In addition, because they are engaging in written communication rather than oral speech, texting teens learn how to convey their message to a reader in as few words as possible. In his book *Txtng: The Gr8 Db8*, David Crystal discusses a study that concludes that texting actually helps foster "the ability to summarize and express oneself concisely" in writing (168). Furthermore, Crystal explains that texting actually helps people to "sharpen their diplomatic skills . . . [because] it allows more time to formulate their thoughts and express them carefully" (168). One language arts teacher from Minnesota believes that texting helps students develop their own "individual voice" (qtd. in Walsh). Perfecting such a voice allows the writer to offer personal insights and express feelings that will interest and engage readers.

Synthesis of various sources of information.

Supporters of texting also argue that it not only teaches elements of writing but provides extra practice to those who struggle with the conventions of writing. As Crystal points out, children who struggle with literacy will not choose to use a technology that requires them to do something that is difficult for them. However, if they do choose to text, the experience will help them "overcome their awkwardness and develop their social and communication skills" (*Txtng* 171). Shirley Holm, a junior high school teacher, describes texting as a "comfortable form of communication" (qtd. in Walsh). Teenagers are used to texting, enjoy doing so, and as a result are always writing. Through this experience of writing in ways they enjoy, they can learn to take pleasure in writing formally. If students are continually writing in some form, they will eventually develop better skills.

Furthermore, those who favor texting explain that with practice comes the confidence and courage to try new things, which some observers believe they are seeing happen with writing as a result of texting. Teenagers have, for example, created an entirely new language — one that uses abbreviations and symbols instead of words, does not require punctuation, and uses short, incomplete phrases throughout the

10

entire conversation. It's a way of speaking that is a language in and of itself. Crystal, among others, sees this "language evolution" as a positive effect of texting; he seems, in fact, fascinated that teenagers are capable of creating such a phenomenon, which he describes as the "latest manifestation of the human ability" (*Txtng* 175). David Warlick, a teacher and author of books about technology in the classroom, would agree with Crystal. He believes students should be given credit for "inventing a new language ideal for communicating in a high-tech world" (qtd. in Carey).

Methods

I decided to conduct my own research into this controversy. I wanted to get different, more personal, perspectives on the issue. First, I surveyed seven students on their opinions about the impact of texting on writing. Second, I questioned two high school teachers, as noted above. Finally, in an effort to compare what students are actually doing to people's perceptions of what they are doing, I analyzed student writing samples for instances of textspeak.[1]

To let students speak for themselves, I created a list of questions for seven high school and college students, some of my closest and most reliable friends. Although the number of respondents was small, I could trust my knowledge of them to help me interpret their responses. In addition, these students are very different from one another, and I believed their differences would allow for a wide array of thoughts and opinions on the issue. I was thus confident in the reliability and diversity of their answers but was cautious not to make too many assumptions because of the small sample size.

Firsthand research: interviews and survey.

I asked the students how long they had been texting; how often they texted; what types of abbreviations they used most and how often they used them; and whether they noticed themselves using any type of textspeak in their formal writing. In analyzing their responses, I looked for commonalities to help me draw conclusions about the students' texting habits and if/how they believed their writing was affected.

I created a list of questions for teachers similar to the one for the students and asked two of my high school teachers to provide their input. I asked if they had noticed their students using textspeak in their writing assignments and, if so, how they dealt with it. I also asked if they believed texting had a positive or negative effect on writing. Next, I asked if they were texters themselves. And, finally, I solicited their

15

opinions on what they believed should be done to prevent teens from using text abbreviations and other textspeak in their writing.

I was surprised at how different the students' replies and opinions were from the teachers'. I decided to find out for myself whose impressions were more accurate by comparing some students' actual writing with students' and teachers' perceptions of that writing. To do this I looked at twenty samples of student writing — end-of-semester research arguments written in two first-year college writing courses with different instructors. The topics varied from increased airport security after September 11 to the weapons of the Vietnam War to autism, and lengths ranged from eight to ten pages. To analyze the papers for the presence of textspeak, I looked closely for use of abbreviations and other common slang terms, especially those usages which the students had stated in their surveys were most common. These included "hbu" ("How about you?"); "gtg" ("Got to go"); and "cuz" ("because"). I also looked for the numbers 2 and 4 used instead of the words "to" and "for."

Comparison and contrast.

Discussion of Findings

My research suggests that texting actually has a minimal effect on student writing. It showed that students do not believe textspeak is appropriate in formal writing assignments. They recognize the difference between texting friends and writing formally and know what is appropriate in each situation. This was proven true in the student samples, in which no examples of textspeak were used. Many experts would agree that there is no harm in textspeak, as long as students continue to be taught and reminded that occasions where formal language is expected are not the place for it. As Crystal explains, the purpose of the abbreviations used in text messages is not to replace language but rather to make quick communications shorter and easier, since in a standard text message, the texter is allowed only 160 characters for a communication ("Texting" 81).

Summary and quotations of sources.

Dennis Baron, an English and linguistics professor at the University of Illinois, has done much research on the effect of technology on writing, and his findings are aligned with those of my own study. In his book *A Better Pencil: Readers, Writers, and the Digital Revolution,* he concludes that students do not use textspeak in their writing. In fact, he suggests students do not even use abbreviations in their text messages very often. Baron says that college students have "put away such

childish things, and many of them had already abandoned such signs of middle-school immaturity in high school" (qtd. in Golden A Better Pencil).

In surveying the high school and college students, I found that most have been texting for a few years, usually starting around ninth grade. The students said they generally text between thirty and a hundred messages every day but use abbreviations only occasionally, with the most common being "lol" ("Laugh out loud"), "gtg" ("Got to go"), "hbu" ("How about you?"), "cuz" ("because"), and "jk" ("Just kidding"). None of them believed texting abbreviations were acceptable in formal writing. In fact, research has found that most students report that they do not use textspeak in formal writing. As one Minnesota high school student says, "[T]here is a time and a place for everything," and formal writing is not the place for communicating the way she would if she were texting her friends (qtd. in Walsh). Another student admits that in writing for school she sometimes finds herself using these abbreviations. However, she notices and corrects them before handing in her final paper (Carey). One teacher reports that, despite texting, her students' "formal writing remains solid." She occasionally sees an abbreviation; however, it is in informal, "warm-up" writing. She believes that what students choose to use in everyday types of writing is up to them as long as they use standard English in formal writing (qtd. in Walsh).

Summary of survey results with quotations.

Also supporting my own research findings are those from a study which took place at a midwestern research university. This study involved eighty-six students who were taking an Introduction to Education course at the university. The participants were asked to complete a questionnaire that included questions about their texting habits, the spelling instruction they had received, and their proficiency at spelling. They also took a standardized spelling test. Before starting the study, the researchers had hypothesized that texting and the use of abbreviations would have a negative impact on the spelling abilities of the students. However, they found that the results did not support their hypothesis. The researchers did note that text messaging is continuing to increase in popularity; therefore, this issue should continue to be examined (Shaw, Carlson, and Waxman).

20

Summary of research that supports her own.

I myself am a frequent texter. I chat with my friends from home every day through texting. I also use texting to communicate with my school friends, perhaps to discuss what time we are going to meet for dinner or to ask quick questions about homework. According to my cell phone bill, I send and receive around 6,400 texts a month. In the messages I send, I rarely notice myself using abbreviations. The only time I use them is if I do not have time to write out the complete phrase. However, sometimes I find it more time-consuming to try to figure out how to abbreviate something so that my message will still be comprehensible.

Pertinent personal experience.

Since I rarely use abbreviations in my texting, I never use them in my formal writing. I know that they are unacceptable and that it would make me look unintelligent if I included acronyms and symbols instead of proper and formal language. I also have not noticed an effect on my spelling as a result of texting. I am confident in my spelling abilities, and even when I use an abbreviation, I know how to spell the word(s) it stands for.

On the basis of my own research, expert research, and personal observations, I can confidently state that texting is not interfering with students' use of standard written English and has no effect on their writing abilities in general. It is interesting to look at the dynamics of the arguments over these issues. Teachers and parents who claim that they are seeing a decline in the writing abilities of their students and children mainly support the negative-impact argument. Other teachers and researchers suggest that texting provides a way for teens to practice writing in a casual setting and thus helps prepare them to write formally. Experts and students themselves, however, report that they see no effect, positive or negative. Anecdotal experiences should not overshadow the actual evidence.

Conclusion: summary of research and restatement of claim.

Note

1. All participants in the study have given permission for their responses to be published.

Works Cited

Baron, Dennis. *A Better Pencil: Readers, Writers, and the Digital Revolution.* Oxford: Oxford UP, 2009. Print.

Carey, Bridget. "The Rise of Text, Instant Messaging Vernacular Slips into Schoolwork." *Miami Herald* 6 Mar. 2007: n. pag. *Academic Search Elite.* Web. 27 Oct. 2009.

Crystal, David. "Texting." *ELT Journal* 62.1 (2008): 77–83. *WilsonWeb.* Web. 8 Nov. 2009.

———. *Txtng: The Gr8 Db8*. Oxford: Oxford UP, 2008. Print.

Golden, Serena. Rev. of *A Better Pencil*. *Inside Higher Ed*, 18 Sept. 2009: n. pag. Web. 9 Nov. 2009.

Shaw, Donita M., Carolyn Carlson, and Mickey Waxman. "An Exploratory Investigation into the Relationship between Text Messaging and Spelling." *New England Reading Association Journal* 43 (2007): 57–62. *WilsonWeb*. Web. 8 Nov. 2009.

"Should We Worry or LOL?" *NEA Today* Mar. 2004: 12. *Academic Search Elite*. Web. 27 Oct. 2009.

Sternberg, Betty, Karen A. Kaplan, and Jennifer E. Borck. "Enhancing Adolescent Literacy Achievement through Integration of Technology in the Classroom." *Reading Research Quarterly* 42 (2007): 416–20. *WilsonWeb*. Web. 8 Nov. 2009.

"Texting, Testing Destroys Kids' Writing Style." *USA Today* 137.2760 (2008): 8. *Academic Search Elite*. Web. 9 Nov. 2009.

Walsh, James. "Txt Msgs Creep in2 class; Some Say That's gr8." *Star Tribune* 23 Oct. 2007: n. pag. *Academic Search Elite*. *Web*. 27 Oct. 2009.

Cullington's essay examines whether or not texting affects students' writing. Her information is based on both published scholarship and a small survey of students and teachers.

NICHOLAS CARR

Rural > City > Cyberspace: The Biggest Migration in Human History

In this essay, from The Shallows: What the Internet Is Doing to Our Brains, *cultural critic Nicholas Carr explains how our wired environment is shaping our thinking.*

It was a warm summer morning in Concord, Massachusetts. The year was 1844. An aspiring novelist named Nathaniel Hawthorne was sitting in a small clearing in the woods, a particularly peaceful spot known around town as Sleepy Hollow. Deep in concentration, he was attending to every passing impression, turning himself into what Emerson, the leader of Concord's Transcendentalist movement, had eight years earlier termed a "transparent eyeball." Hawthorne saw, as he would record in his notebook later that day, how "sunshine glimmers through shadow, and shadow effaces sunshine, imaging that pleasant mood of mind where gayety and pensiveness intermingle." He felt a slight breeze, "the gentlest sigh imaginable, yet with a spiritual potency, insomuch that it seems to penetrate, with its mild, ethereal coolness, through the outward clay, and breathe upon the spirit itself, which shivers with gentle delight." He smelled on the breeze a hint of "the fragrance of the white pines." He heard "the striking of the village clock" and "at a distance mowers whetting their scythes," though "these sounds of labor, when at a proper remoteness, do but increase the quiet of one who lies at his ease, all in a mist of his own musings."

Abruptly, his reverie was broken:

> But, hark! there is the whistle of the locomotive, — the long shriek, harsh above all other harshness, for the space of a mile cannot mollify it into harmony. It tells a story of busy men, citizens from the hot street, who have come to spend a day in a country village, — men of business, — in short, of all unquietness; and no wonder that it gives such a startling shriek, since it brings the noisy world into the midst of our slumbrous peace. (qtd. in Hawthorne 503)

. . .

What exactly was going on in Hawthorne's head as he sat in the green seclusion of Sleepy Hollow and lost himself in contemplation? And how was it different from what was going through the minds of the city dwellers on that crowded, noisy train? A series of psychological studies over the past twenty years has revealed that after spending time in a quiet rural setting, close to nature, people exhibit greater attentiveness, stronger memory, and generally improved cognition. Their brains become both calmer and sharper. The reason, according to attention restoration theory, or ART, is that when people aren't being bombarded by external stimuli, their brains can, in effect, relax. They no longer have to tax their working memories by processing a stream of bottom-up distractions. The resulting state of contemplativeness strengthens their ability to control their mind.

The results of the most recent such study were published in *Psychological Science* at the end of 2008. A team of University of Michigan researchers, led by psychologist Marc Berman, recruited some three dozen people and subjected them to a rigorous, and mentally fatiguing, series of tests designed to measure the capacity of their working memory and their ability to exert top-down control over their attention. The subjects were then divided into two groups. Half of them spent about an hour walking through a secluded woodland park, and the other half spent an equal amount of time walking along busy downtown streets. Both groups then took the tests a second time. Spending time in the park, the researchers found, "significantly improved" people's performance on the cognitive tests, indicating a substantial increase in attentiveness. Walking in the city, by contrast, led to no improvement in test results.

The researchers then conducted a similar experiment with another   5
set of people. Rather than taking walks between the rounds of testing, these subjects simply looked at photographs of either calm rural scenes or busy urban ones. The results were the same. The people who looked at pictures of nature scenes were able to exert substantially stronger control over their attention, while those who looked at city scenes showed no improvement in their attentiveness. "In sum," concluded the researchers, "simple and brief interactions with nature can produce marked increases in cognitive control." Spending time in the natural world seems to be of "vital importance" to "effective cognitive functioning" (1212).

There is no Sleepy Hollow on the Internet, no peaceful spot where contemplativeness can work its restorative magic. There is only the endless, mesmerizing buzz of the urban street. The stimulations of the Net, like those of the city, can be invigorating and inspiring. We wouldn't want to give them up. But they are, as well, exhausting and distracting. They can easily, as Hawthorne understood, overwhelm all quieter modes of thought. One of the greatest dangers we face as we automate the work of our minds, as we cede control over the flow of our thoughts and memories to a powerful electronic system, is the one that informs the fears of both the scientist Joseph Weizenbaum and the artist Richard Foreman: a slow erosion of our humanness and our humanity.

It's not only deep thinking that requires a calm, attentive mind. It's also empathy and compassion. Psychologists have long studied how people experience fear and react to physical threats, but it's only recently that they've begun researching the sources of our nobler instincts. What they're finding is that, as Antonio Damasio, the director of USC's Brain and Creativity Institute, explains, the higher emotions emerge from neural processes that "are inherently slow" (qtd. in Marzali). In one recent experiment, Damasio and his colleagues had subjects listen to stories describing people experiencing physical or psychological pain. The subjects were then put into a magnetic resonance imaging machine and their brains were scanned as they were asked to remember the stories. The experiment revealed that while the human brain reacts very quickly to demonstrations of physical pain — when you see someone injured, the primitive pain centers in your own brain activate almost instantaneously — the more sophisticated mental process of empathizing with psychological suffering unfolds much more slowly. It takes time, the researchers discovered, for the brain "to transcend immediate involvement of the body" and begin to understand and to feel "the psychological and moral dimensions of a situation" (Immordino-Yang, McColl, Damasio, and Damasio 8025).

The experiment, say the scholars, indicates that the more distracted we become, the less able we are to experience the subtlest, most distinctively human forms of empathy, compassion, and other emotions. "For some kinds of thoughts, especially moral decision-making about other people's social and psychological situations, we need to allow for adequate time and reflection," cautions Mary Helen Immordino-Yang, a member of the research team. "If things are happening too fast, you may not ever fully experience emotions about other people's psychological states" (qtd. in Marzali). It would be rash to jump to the conclusion that the Internet is undermining our moral sense. It would not be rash to suggest that as the Net reroutes our vital paths and diminishes our capacity for contemplation, it is altering the depth of our emotions as well as our thoughts.

There are those who are heartened by the ease with which our minds are adapting to the Web's intellectual ethic. "Technological progress does not reverse," writes a *Wall Street Journal* columnist, "so the trend toward multitasking and consuming many different types of information will only continue." We need not worry, though, because our "human software" will in time "catch up to the machine technology that made the information abundance possible." We'll "evolve"

rhetorical situations

genres

processes

strategies

research MLA / APA

media / design

readings

to become more agile consumers of data (Crovitz A11). The writer of a cover story in *New York* magazine says that as we become used to "the 21st-century task" of "flitting" among bits of online information, "the wiring of the brain will inevitably change to deal more efficiently with more information." We may lose our capacity "to concentrate on a complex task from beginning to end," but in recompense we'll gain new skills, such as the ability to "conduct 34 conversations simultaneously across six different media" (Anderson). A prominent economist writes, cheerily, that "the web allows us to borrow cognitive strengths from autism and to be better infovores" (Cowen 10). An *Atlantic* author suggests that our "technology-induced ADD" may be "a short-term problem," stemming from our reliance on "cognitive habits evolved and perfected in an era of limited information flow." Developing new cognitive habits is "the only viable approach to navigating the age of constant connectivity" (Cascio).

These writers are certainly correct in arguing that we're being molded by our new information environment. Our mental adaptability, built into the deepest workings of our brains, is a keynote of intellectual history. But if there's comfort in their reassurances, it's of a very cold sort. Adaptation leaves us better suited to our circumstances, but qualitatively it's a neutral process. What matters in the end is not our becoming but what we become. In the 1950s, Martin Heidegger observed that the looming "tide of technological revolution" could "so captivate, bewitch, dazzle, and beguile man that calculative thinking may someday come to be accepted and practiced *as the only* way of thinking." Our ability to engage in "meditative thinking," which he saw as the very essence of our humanity, might become a victim of headlong progress (*Discourse* 56). The tumultuous advance of technology could, like the arrival of the locomotive at the Concord station, drown out the refined perceptions, thoughts, and emotions that arise only through contemplation and reflection. The "frenziedness of technology," Heidegger wrote, threatens to "entrench itself everywhere" (*The Question* 35).

It may be that we are now entering the final stage of that entrenchment. We are welcoming the frenziedness into our souls.

Works Cited

Anderson, Sam. "In Defense of Distraction." *New York*. New York Magazine, 25 May 2009. Web. 11 Feb. 2012.

Berman, Marc G., John Jonides, and Stephen Kaplan. "The Cognitive Benefits of Interacting with Nature." *Psychological Science* 19.12 (2008): 1207–12. Print.

Cascio, Jamais. "Get Smarter." *TheAtlantic.com*. Atlantic Monthly Group, July/Aug. 2009. Web. 11 Feb. 2012.

Cowen, Tyler. *Create Your Own Economy*. New York: Dutton, 2009. Print.

Crovitz, L. Gordon. "Information Overload? Relax." *Wall Street Journal*, 6 July 2009: A11. Print.

Hawthorne, Julian. *Nathaniel Hawthorne and His Wife: A Biography*. Vol. 1. Boston: Osgood, 1885. Print.

Heidegger, Martin. *Discourse on Thinking*. New York: Harper, 1966. Print.

———. *The Question concerning Technology and Other Essays*. New York: Harper, 1977. Print.

Immordino-Yang, Mary Helen, Andrea McColl, Hanna Damasio, and Antonio Damasio. "Neural Correlates of Admiration and Compassion." *Proceedings of the National Academy of Sciences* 106.19 (2009): 8021–26. Print.

Marziali, Carl. "Nobler Instincts Take Time." *USC Dornsife*. U of Southern California, 14 Apr. 2009. Web. 11 Feb. 2012.

This report explores the effects of distraction and the way we interact with the internet on our abilities to think and even feel. Carr relies primarily on the results of two research studies to establish the basis for his assertions and then offers several perspectives, positive and negative, on our increasing loss of the ability to contemplate.

JAMES FALLOWS

Throwing Like a Girl

In the following report for the Atlantic, *national correspondent James Fallows explores the art of throwing a baseball and the misconceptions that lead to the phrase "throwing like a girl."*

rhetorical situations

genres

processes

strategies

research MLA / APA

media / design

readings

Most people remember the 1994 baseball season for the way it ended—with a strike rather than a World Series. I keep thinking about the way it began. On opening day, April 4, Bill Clinton went to Cleveland and, like many Presidents before him, threw out a ceremonial first pitch. That same day Hillary Rodham Clinton went to Chicago and, like no First Lady before her, also threw out a first ball, at a Cubs game in Wrigley Field.

The next day photos of the Clintons in action appeared in newspapers around the country. Many papers, including the *New York Times* and the *Washington Post*, chose the same two photos to run. The one of Bill Clinton showed him wearing an Indians cap and warm-up jacket. The President, throwing lefty, had turned his shoulders sideways to the plate in preparation for delivery. He was bringing the ball forward from behind his head in a clean-looking throwing action as the photo was snapped. Hillary Clinton was pictured wearing a dark jacket, a scarf, and an oversized Cubs hat. In preparation for her throw she was standing directly facing the plate. A right-hander, she had the elbow of her throwing arm pointed out in front of her. Her forearm was tilted back, toward her shoulder. The ball rested on her upturned palm. As the picture was taken, she was in the middle of an action that can only be described as throwing like a girl.

Hillary and Bill Clinton throw the first ball of the season at two games in 1994.

The phrase "throwing like a girl" has become an embattled and offensive one. Feminists smart at its implication that to do something "like a girl" is to do it the wrong way. Recently, on the heels of the O. J. Simpson case, a book appeared in which the phrase was used to help explain why male athletes, especially football players, were involved in so many assaults against women. Having been trained (like most American boys) to dread the accusation of doing anything "like a girl," athletes were said to grow into the assumption that women were valueless, and natural prey.

I grant the justice of such complaints. I am attuned to the hurt caused by similar broad-brush stereotypes when they apply to groups I belong to — "dancing like a white man," for instance, or "speaking foreign languages like an American," or "thinking like a Washingtonian."

Still, whatever we want to call it, the difference between the two 5 Clintons in what they were doing that day is real, and it is instantly recognizable. And since seeing those photos I have been wondering, Why, exactly, do so many women throw "like a girl"? If the motion were easy to change, presumably a woman as motivated and self-possessed as Hillary Clinton would have changed it. (According to her press secretary, Lisa Caputo, Mrs. Clinton spent the weekend before opening day tossing a ball in the Rose Garden with her husband, for practice.) Presumably, too, the answer to the question cannot be anything quite as simple as, Because they *are* girls.

A surprising number of people think that there is a structural difference between male and female arms or shoulders — in the famous "rotator cuff," perhaps — that dictates different throwing motions. "It's in the shoulder joint," a well-educated woman told me recently. "They're hinged differently." Someone researchers may find evidence to support a biological theory of throwing actions. For now, what you'll hear if you ask an orthopedist, an anatomist, or (especially) the coach of a women's softball team is that there is no structural reason why men and women should throw in different ways. This point will be obvious to any male who grew up around girls who liked to play baseball and became good at it. It should be obvious on a larger scale this summer, in broadcasts of the Olympic Games. This year [1996], for the first time, women's fast-pitch softball teams will compete in the Olympics. Although the pitchers in these games will deliver the ball underhand, viewers will see female shortstops, center fielders, catchers, and so on

pegging the ball to one another at speeds few male viewers could match.

Even women's tennis is a constant if indirect reminder that men's and women's shoulders are "hinged" the same way. The serving motion in tennis is like a throw—but more difficult, because it must be coordinated with the toss of the tennis ball. The men in professional tennis serve harder than the women, because they are bigger and stronger. But women pros serve harder than most male amateurs have ever done, and the service motion for good players is the same for men and women alike. There is no expectation in college or pro tennis that because of their anatomy female players must "serve like a girl." "I know many women who can throw a lot harder and better than the normal male," says Linda Wells, the coach of the highly successful women's softball team at Arizona State University. "It's not gender that makes the difference in how they throw."

At a superficial level it's easy to tick off the traits of an awkward-looking throw. The fundamental mistake is the one Mrs. Clinton appeared to be making in the photo: trying to throw a ball with your body facing the target, rather than rotating your shoulders and hips ninety degrees away from the target and then swinging them around in order to accelerate the ball. A throw looks bad if your elbow is lower than your shoulder as your arm comes forward (unless you're throwing sidearm). A throw looks really bad if, as the ball leaves your hand, your wrist is "inside your elbow"—that is, your elbow joint is bent in such a way that your forearm angles back toward your body and your wrist is closer to your head than your elbow is. Slow-motion film of big-league pitchers shows that when they release the ball, the throwing arm is fully extended and straight from shoulder to wrist. The combination of these three elements—head-on stance, dropped elbow, and wrist inside the elbow—mechanically dictates a pushing rather than a hurling motion, creating the familiar pattern of "throwing like a girl."

It is surprisingly hard to find in the literature of baseball a deeper explanation of the mechanics of good and bad throws. Tom Seaver's pitching for the Mets and the White Sox got him into the Hall of Fame, but his book *The Art of Pitching* is full of bromides that hardly clarify the process of throwing, even if they might mean something to accomplished pitchers. His chapter "The Absolutes of Pitching Mechanics," for instance, lays out these four unhelpful principles: "Keep the Front Leg Flexible!" "Rub Up the Baseball!" "Hide the Baseball!" "Get It Out, Get It Up!" (The fourth refers to the need to get the ball out of the glove and into the throwing hand in a quick motion.)

A variety of other instructional documents, from *Little League's Official How-to-Play Baseball Book* to *Softball for Girls & Women*, mainly reveal the difficulty of finding words to describe a simple motor activity that everyone can recognize. The challenge, I suppose, is like that of writing a manual on how to ride a bike, or how to kiss. Indeed, the most useful description I've found of the mechanics of throwing comes from a man whose specialty is another sport: Vic Braden made his name as a tennis coach, but he has attempted to analyze the physics of a wide variety of sports so that they all will be easier to teach.

Braden says that an effective throw involves connecting a series of links in a "kinetic chain." The kinetic chain, which is Braden's tool for analyzing most sporting activity, operates on a principle like that of crack-the-whip. Momentum builds up in one part of the body. When that part is suddenly stopped, as the end of the "whip" is stopped in crack-the-whip, the momentum is transferred to and concentrated in the next link in the chain. A good throw uses six links of chain, Braden says. The first two links involve the lower body, from feet to waist. The first motion of a throw (after the body has been rotated away from the target) is to rotate the legs and hips back in the direction of the throw, building up momentum as large muscles move body mass. Then those links stop—a pitcher stops turning his hips once they face the plate—and the momentum is transferred to the next link. This is the torso, from waist to shoulders, and since its mass is less than that of the legs, momentum makes it rotate faster than the hips and legs did. The torso stops when it is facing the plate, and the momentum is transferred to the next link—the upper arm. As the upper arm comes past the head, it stops moving forward, and the momentum goes into the final links—the forearm and wrist, which snap forward at tremendous speed.

This may sound arcane and jerkily mechanical, but it makes perfect sense when one sees Braden's slow-mo movies of pitchers in action. And it explains why people do, or don't, learn how to throw. The implication of Braden's analysis is that throwing is a perfectly natural action (millions and millions of people can do it), but not at all innate. A

rhetorical situations   genres   processes   strategies   research MLA / APA   media / design   readings

successful throw involves an intricate series of actions coordinated among muscle groups, as each link of the chain is timed to interact with the next. Like bike riding or skating, it can be learned by any-one — male or female. No one starts out knowing how to ride a bike or throw a ball. Everyone has to learn.

Fallows describes in detail what distinguishes a successful baseball throw from an awkward-looking one, concluding with the point that throwing a baseball effectively is a learned activity. He draws on various sources — including a women's softball coach, a tennis coach, and his own observations — to support his claim. Notice how he establishes the context for his essay by focusing on the differences between the stances of the Clintons when photographed throwing a baseball.

MATTHEW O'BRIEN

The Strange Economics of Engagement Rings

Writing in his blog on TheAtlantic.com, Matthew O'Brien looks at the economic reasons behind the tradition of giving diamond engagement rings. The words and phrases underlined here represent links to other websites from the online version of the essay, which is available via wwnorton.com/write/ fieldguidelinks.

Why do men buy diamond rings for our fiancées? There's the emotional story. We enjoy making grand gestures of commitment to the people we love. Behind that, there's the marketing story. DeBeers' his-toric ad campaign, crafted by the real-life mad men at N. W. Ayers, convinced generations of lovers that diamond bands were synonymous with eternal devotion. But behind that, there is economic story that is just as important and fascinating.

Once upon a time, diamond rings weren't just gifts. They were, frankly, virginity insurance.

A recent DeBeers ad bearing their classic "a diamond is forever" tagline.

 rhetorical situations

 genres

 processes

 strategies

 research
MLA / APA

 media /
design

readings

A now-obsolete law called the "Breach of Promise to Marry" once allowed women to sue men for breaking off an engagement. Back then, there was a high premium on women being virgins when they married — or at least when they got engaged. Surveys from the 1940s show that roughly half of engaged couples reported being intimate before the big day. If the groom-to-be walked out after he and the bride-to-be had sex, that left her in a precarious position. From a social angle, she had been permanently "damaged." From an economic angle, she had lost her market value. So Breach of Promise to Marry was born.

But in the 1930s, states began striking down the "Breach of Promise to Marry" law. By 1945, 16 states representing nearly half of the nation's population had made Breach of Promise a historical relic. At the same time, the diamond engagement ring began its transformation from decorative to de rigueur. Legal scholar Margaret Brinig doesn't think that's a coincidence, and she has the math to prove it. Regressing the percent of people living in states without Breach of Promise against a handful of other variables — including advertising, per capita income and the price of diamonds — Brinig found that this legal change was actually the *most* significant factor in the rise of the diamond engagement ring. It's historically plausible. The initial mini-surge in

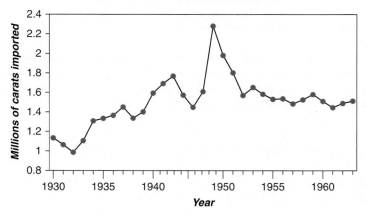

Diamond Imports by Year, 1930–63

diamond imports came in 1935, four years before DeBeers launched its celebrated advertising campaign. What's going on here?

Let's think like an economist. An engaged couple aren't all that   5
different from a borrower and a lender. The woman is lending her hand in marriage to the man, who promises to tie the knot at a later date. In the days of Breach of Promise, the woman would do this on an unsecured basis — that is, the man didn't have to pledge any collateral — because the law provided her something akin to bankruptcy protection. Put simply, if the man didn't fulfill his obligation to marry, the woman had legal recourse. This calculus changed once the law changed. Suddenly, women wanted an upfront financial assurance from their men. Basically, collateral. That way, if the couple never made it down the aisle, she'd at least be left with *something*. And that something was almost always small and shiny. The diamond ring was insurance.

So, should a jilted bride give back the engagement ring? Today, the answer is often yes. But back when rings first came into vogue, part of the point was that she wouldn't. It was a security against a default on the engagement. The good news is that this seems so alien to us today. Women have their own careers. They earn more degrees. And, for the younger generation, they <u>out-earn</u> men. More importantly, the stigma against premarital sex has disappeared. A broken engagement isn't a lasting financial disaster for a woman like it was before. The diamond engagement ring has itself undergone a transformation. It's no longer a security. It's just about <u>signaling</u> nowadays. It's anachronistic. But don't try telling your girlfriend that.

▌▌ For five more reports, see CHAPTER 59.

O'Brien explains the evolution of the symbolism of engagement rings by presenting a narrative of their history over the last century, coupled with an image of a ring, a chart showing diamond imports by year, and several links to websites that define important terms or offer additional information.

Key Features / Reports

A tightly focused topic.   The goal of this kind of writing is to inform readers about something without digressing—and without, in general,

bringing in the writer's own opinions. All four examples focus on a particular topic—texting, the mental effects of the internet, throwing a baseball, and diamond engagement rings — and present information about the topics evenhandedly.

Accurate, well-researched information. Reports usually require some research. The kind of research depends on the topic. Library research to locate scholarly sources may be necessary for some topics—Cullington, for example, uses various sources available through her library's database. Other topics may require field research—interviews, observations, and so on. Fallows interviewed two coaches in addition to reading several books on pitching baseballs.

Various writing strategies. Presenting information usually requires various organizing patterns—defining, comparing, classifying, explaining processes, analyzing causes and effects, and so on. Fallows explains the process governing throwing a baseball and classifies different ways of throwing. Carr describes several psychological experiments, and Cullington analyzes the effects (or lack of effects) of texting on students' writing ability.

Clear definitions. Reports need to provide clear definitions of any key terms that their audience may not know. Cullington defines both *texting* and *textspeak*. Fallows defines several pitching terms, such as *inside your elbow*. And O'Brien defines *collateral* as it applies to wedding rings.

Appropriate design. Reports often combine paragraphs with information presented in lists, tables, diagrams, and other illustrations. When you're presenting information, you need to think carefully about how to design it—numerical data, for instance, can be easier to understand and remember in a table than in a paragraph. Often a photograph can bring a subject to life, as do the photos on page 101, which accompany "Throwing Like a Girl." The caption provides important information that is explained more fully in the essay itself. Online reports offer the possibility of video and audio clips as well as links to source materials and more detailed information.

A GUIDE TO WRITING REPORTS

Choosing a Topic

Whether you get to choose your topic or are working with an assigned one, see if you can approach the topic from an angle that interests you.

If you get to choose. What interests you? What do you wish you knew more about? The possible topics for informational reports are limitless, but the topics that you're most likely to write well on are those that engage you. They may be academic in nature or reflect your personal interests or both. If you're not sure where to begin, here are some places to start:

- an intriguing technology: hybrid cars, smartphones, roller coasters
- sports: soccer, snowboarding, ultimate Frisbee, basketball
- an important world event: the Arab Spring, the fall of Rome, the Black Death
- a historical period: the African diaspora, the Middle Ages, the Ming dynasty, the Great Depression
- a common object: hoodies, gel pens, mascara, Post-it notes
- a significant environmental issue: Arctic oil drilling, deer overpopulation, mercury and the fish supply
- the arts: hip-hop, outsider art, the Crystal Bridges Museum of American Art, Savion Glover, Mary Cassatt

260–61 **LIST** a few possibilities, and then choose one that you'd like to know more about—and that your audience might find interesting, too. You might start out by phrasing your topic as a question that your research will attempt to answer. For example:

> How is Google different from Yahoo!?
> How was the Great Pyramid constructed?
> What kind of training do football referees receive?

rhetorical situations

genres

processes

strategies

research MLA / APA

media / design

readings

If your topic is assigned.   If your assignment is broad — "Explain some aspect of the U.S. government" — try focusing on a more limited topic within the larger topic: federalism, majority rule, political parties, states' rights. Even if an assignment seems to offer little flexibility — "Explain the physics of roller coasters" — your task is to decide how to research the topic — and sometimes even narrow topics can be shaped to fit your own interests and those of your audience.

Considering the Rhetorical Situation

PURPOSE	Why are you presenting this information? To teach readers about the subject? To demonstrate your research and writing skills? For some other reason?	◼ 3–4
AUDIENCE	Who will read this report? What do they already know about the topic? What background information do they need in order to understand it? Will you need to define any terms? What do they want or need to know about the topic? Why should they care about it? How can you attract their interest?	◼ 5–8
STANCE	What is your own attitude toward your subject? What interests you most about it? What about it seems important?	◼ 12–15
MEDIA / DESIGN	What medium are you using? What is the best way to present the information? Will it all be in paragraph form, or is there information that is best presented as a chart or a table? Do you need headings? Would diagrams, photographs, or other illustrations help you explain the information?	◼ 16–18

Generating Ideas and Text

Good reports share certain features that make them useful and interesting to readers. Remember that your goal is to present information clearly and accurately. Start by exploring your topic.

Explore what you already know about your topic. Write out whatever you know or want to know about your topic, perhaps by **FREEWRITING, LISTING,** or **CLUSTERING.** Why are you interested in this topic? What questions do you have about it? Such questions can help you decide what you'd like to focus on and how you need to direct your research efforts.

259–62 ◐

Narrow your topic. To write a good report, you need to narrow your focus — and to narrow your focus, you need to know a fair amount about your subject. If you are assigned to write on a subject like biodiversity, for example, you need to know what it is, what the key issues are, and so on. If you do, you can simply list or brainstorm possibilities, choose one, and start your research. If you don't know much about the subject, though, you need to do some research to discover focused, workable topics. This research may shape your thinking and change your focus. Start with **SOURCES** that can give you a general sense of the subject, such as an encyclopedia entry, a magazine article, a website, perhaps an interview with an expert. Your goal at this point is simply to find out what issues your topic might include and then to focus your efforts on an aspect of the topic you will be able to cover.

432–52 ●

Come up with a tentative thesis. Once you narrow your topic, write out a statement that explains what you plan to report or explain. A good **THESIS** is potentially interesting (to you and your readers) and limits your topic enough to make it manageable. Fallows phrases his thesis as a question: "Why, exactly, do so many women throw 'like a girl'?" Cullington frames her thesis in relation to the context surrounding her topic: "Some people believe that using these abbreviations is hindering the writing abilities of students, and others argue that texting is actually having a positive effect on writing. In fact, it seems likely that texting has no significant effect on student writing." At this point, however, you need only a tentative thesis that will help focus any research you do.

313–15 ◆

Do any necessary research, and revise your thesis. To focus your research efforts, **OUTLINE** the aspects of your topic that you expect to discuss. Identify any aspects that require additional research and **DEVELOP A RESEARCH PLAN.** Expect to revise your outline as you do your research,

263–64 ◐
421–31 ●

since more information will be available for some aspects of your topic than others, some may prove irrelevant to your topic, and some may turn out to be more than you need. You'll need to revisit your tentative thesis once you've done any research, to finalize your statement.

Ways of Organizing a Report

Reports can be organized in various ways. Here are three common ones:

[Reports on topics that are unfamiliar to readers]

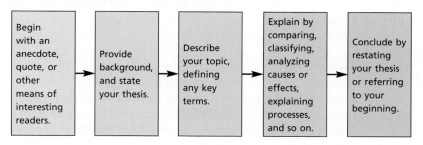

Begin with an anecdote, quote, or other means of interesting readers. → Provide background, and state your thesis. → Describe your topic, defining any key terms. → Explain by comparing, classifying, analyzing causes or effects, explaining processes, and so on. → Conclude by restating your thesis or referring to your beginning.

[Reports on an event]

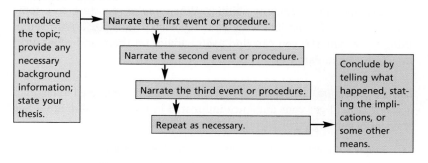

Introduce the topic; provide any necessary background information; state your thesis. → Narrate the first event or procedure. ↓ Narrate the second event or procedure. ↓ Narrate the third event or procedure. ↓ Repeat as necessary. → Conclude by telling what happened, stating the implications, or some other means.

[Reports that compare and contrast]

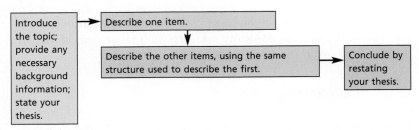

Many reports use a combination of organizational structures; don't be afraid to use whatever method of organization best suits your material and your purpose.

Writing Out a Draft

266–68 ○

Once you have generated ideas and thought about how you want to organize your report, it's time to start **DRAFTING**. Do this quickly—try to write a complete draft in one sitting, concentrating on getting the report on paper or screen and on putting in as much detail as you can.

382–86 ◆
318–22
348–55

Writing that reports information often calls for certain writing strategies. The report on throwing a baseball, for example, **EXPLAINS THE PROCESS** of throwing, whereas the report on cyberspace **ANALYZES THE EFFECTS** of multitasking on our thinking abilities. When you're reporting on a topic your readers aren't familiar with, you may wish to **COMPARE** it with something more familiar; you can find useful advice on these and other writing strategies in Part 4 of this book.

299–306 ◆

Draft a **BEGINNING**.   Essays that report information often need to begin in a way that will get your audience interested in the topic. Here are a few ways of beginning:

- *Simply state your thesis.* Cullington states her thesis about texting after only a brief introduction. Opening with a thesis works well when you

can assume your readers have enough familiarity with your topic that you don't need to give much detailed background information.

- *Start with something that will provoke readers' interest.* O'Brien's report begins by provocatively describing diamond rings as more than "just gifts. They were, frankly, virginity insurance." Such a surprising characterization of a common symbol of being engaged to be married is likely to make readers curious to read further.

- *Begin with an illustrative example.* Fallows uses the contrasting photographs of the Clintons throwing baseballs as a way of defining "throwing like a girl."

Draft an ENDING. Think about what you want your readers to read last. An effective ending leaves them thinking about your topic.

306–10

- *Summarize your main points.* This is a good way to end when you've presented several key points you want readers to remember. Cullington ends this way, summarizing the debate about texting's effects and the results of her research.

- *Point out the implications of your report.* Carr ends with the gloomy suggestion that the "technological revolution" of computers and the internet has already made contemplation and deep thinking obsolete.

- *Frame your report by referring to its introduction.* Cullington begins and ends her report by referring to the positive or negative effects of texting on student writing.

- *Tell what happened.* If you are reporting on an event, you could conclude by telling how it turns out.

Come up with a title. You'll want a title that tells readers something about your subject—and makes them want to know more. Cullington's title, "Does Texting Affect Writing?," is a straightforward description of what's to come. O'Brien's title, "The Strange Economics of Engagement Rings," gets our interest by its intriguing wording (What's strange about it?) and by its relevance to anyone who is or might become engaged. See the

312–17
chapter on **GUIDING YOUR READER** for tips on coming up with titles that are informative and enticing enough to make readers wish to read on.

Considering Matters of Design

You'll probably write the main text of your report in paragraph form, but think about what kind of information you're presenting and how you can design and format it to make it as easy as possible for your readers to understand. You might ask yourself these questions:

585–86
- What is an appropriate **FONT?** Something serious like Times Roman, something traditional like `Courier`, something else?

588–89
- Would it help your readers if you divided your report into shorter sections and added **HEADINGS?**

587
- Is there any information that would be easier to follow in a **LIST?**

593–95
- Could any of your information be summarized in a **TABLE** or **FIGURE?**

593–95
- Do you have any data that readers would more easily understand in the form of a bar **GRAPH,** line graph, or pie chart?

591–99
- Would **ILLUSTRATIONS** (diagrams, photos, drawings, and so on), video or audio clips, or links help you explain anything in your report?

Getting Response and Revising

The following questions can help you study your draft with a critical eye. **GETTING RESPONSE** from others is always good, and these questions can guide their reading, too. Make sure they know your purpose and audience.
275–76

- Do the title and opening sentences get readers' interest? If not, how might they do so?

- What information does this text provide, and for what purpose?

- Does the introduction explain why this information is being presented? Does it place the topic in a larger context?

- Are all key terms defined that need to be?

rhetorical situations   genres   processes   strategies   research MLA / APA   media / design   readings

- Do you have any questions? Where might more explanation or an example help you understand something better?

- Is any information presented visually, with a chart, graph, table, drawing, or photograph? If so, is it clear how the illustration relates to the written text? Is there any text that would be more easily understood if it were presented visually?

- Is any information presented through digital media, such as hyperlinks, video clips, or audio files? If so, is the relation of these elements to the written text made clear? Would any aspect of the report be clearer if presented using such elements?

- Does the organization help make sense of the information? Does the text include description, comparison, or any other writing strategies? Does the topic or rhetorical situation call for any particular strategies that should be added?

- If the report cites any sources, are they quoted, paraphrased, or summarized effectively (and with appropriate documentation)?

- Does the report end in a satisfying way? What are readers left thinking?

These questions should identify aspects of your report you need to work on. When it's time to **REVISE,** make sure your report appeals to your audience and achieves your purpose as successfully as possible.

○ 276–79

Editing and Proofreading

Readers equate correctness with the writer's competence. Once you've revised your draft, follow these guidelines for **EDITING** a report:

○ 282–85

- Check your use of key terms. Repeating key words is acceptable in reports; using synonyms for unfamiliar words may confuse readers, while the repetition of key words or the use of clearly identified pronouns for them can be genuinely helpful.

- Check to be sure you have **TRANSITIONS** where you need them.

◆ 317

- If you have included **HEADINGS,** make sure they're parallel in structure and consistent in design.

□ 588–89

591–99 □
- Make sure that any photos or other **ILLUSTRATIONS** have captions, that charts and graphs have headings — and that all are referred to in the main text. Use white space as necessary to separate sections of your report and to highlight graphic elements.

480–83 ●
- Check any **DOCUMENTATION** to see that it follows the appropriate style without mistakes.

285–86 ○
- **PROOFREAD** and spell-check your report carefully.

Taking Stock of Your Work

- How well did you convey the information? Is it complete enough for your audience's needs?
- What strategies did you rely on, and how did they help you achieve your purpose?
- How well did you organize the report?
- How did you go about researching the information for this piece?
- How did you go about drafting this piece?
- Did you use any tables, graphs, diagrams, photographs, illustrations, or other graphics effectively?
- How did others' responses influence your writing?
- What did you do especially well?
- What could still be improved?
- What would you do differently next time?

IF YOU NEED MORE HELP

287–96 ○
150–54 ▲
173–82
191–204
See Chapter 29 if you are required to submit your report in a writing **PORTFOLIO.** See also Chapter 11 on **ABSTRACTS** if your report requires one; Chapter 14 on **LAB REPORTS,** a kind of report written in the sciences; and Chapter 16 on **PROFILES,** a report based on firsthand research.

Arguing a Position 10

Everything we say or do presents some kind of argument, takes some kind of position. Often we take overt positions: "Everyone in the United States is entitled to affordable health care." "The university needs to offer more language courses." "Photoshopped images should carry disclosure notices." But arguments can be less direct and specific as well, from yellow ribbons that honor U.S. troops to a yellow smiley face, which might be said to argue for a good day. In college course work, you are constantly called on to argue positions: in an English class, you may argue for a certain interpretation of a poem; in a business course, you may argue for the merits of a flat tax; in a linguistics class, you may argue that English is now a global language. All of those positions are arguable—people of goodwill can agree or disagree with them and present reasons and evidence to support their positions. This chapter provides guidelines for writing an essay that argues a position. We'll begin with four good examples, the first one annotated to point out key features of this kind of writing.

JOANNA MACKAY

Organ Sales Will Save Lives

In this essay, written for a class on ethics and politics in science, MIT student Joanna MacKay argues that the sale of human organs should be legal.

There are thousands of people dying to buy a kidney and thousands of people dying to sell a kidney. It seems a match made in heaven. So why are we standing in the way? Governments should not ban the sale of human organs; they should regulate it. Lives should not be wasted; they should be saved.

Clear and arguable position.

About 350,000 Americans suffer from end-stage renal disease, a state of kidney disorder so advanced that the organ stops functioning altogether. There are no miracle drugs that can revive a failed kidney, leaving dialysis and kidney transplantation as the only possible treatments (McDonnell and Mallon, Pars. 2 and 3).

Dialysis is harsh, expensive, and, worst of all, only temporary. Acting as an artificial kidney, dialysis mechanically filters the blood of a patient. It works, but not well. With treatment sessions lasting three hours, several times a week, those dependent on dialysis are, in a sense, shackled to a machine for the rest of their lives. Adding excessive stress to the body, dialysis causes patients to feel increasingly faint and tired, usually keeping them from work and other normal activities.

Kidney transplantation, on the other hand, is the closest thing to a cure that anyone could hope for. Today the procedure is both safe and reliable, causing few complications. With better technology for confirming tissue matches and new anti-rejection drugs, the surgery is relatively simple.

Necessary background information.

But those hoping for a new kidney have high hopes indeed. In the year 2000 alone, 2,583 Americans died while waiting for a kidney transplant; worldwide the number of deaths is around 50,000 (Finkel 27). With the sale of organs outlawed in almost every country, the number of living donors willing to part with a kidney for free is small. When no family member is a suitable candidate for donation, the patient is placed on a deceased donors list, relying on the organs from people dying of old age or accidents. The list is long. With over 60,000 people in line in the United States alone, the average wait for a cadaverous kidney is ten long years.

Daunted by the low odds, some have turned to an alternative solution: purchasing kidneys on the black market. For about $150,000, they can buy a fresh kidney from a healthy, living donor. There are no lines, no waits. Arranged through a broker, the entire procedure is carefully planned out. The buyer, seller, surgeons, and nurses are flown to a predetermined hospital in a foreign country. The operations are performed, and then all are flown back to their respective homes. There is no follow-up, no paperwork to sign (Finkel 27).

The illegal kidney trade is attractive not only because of the promptness but also because of the chance at a living donor. An organ from a cadaver will most likely be old or damaged, estimated to function for about ten years at most. A kidney from a living donor can last

5

over twice as long. Once a person's transplanted cadaverous kidney stops functioning, he or she must get back on the donors list, this time probably at the end of the line. A transplanted living kidney, however, could last a person a lifetime.

While there may seem to be a shortage of kidneys, in reality there is a surplus. In third world countries, there are people willing to do anything for money. In such extreme poverty these people barely have enough to eat, living in shacks and sleeping on dirt floors. Eager to pay off debts, they line up at hospitals, willing to sell a kidney for about $1,000. The money will go towards food and clothing, or perhaps to pay for a family member's medical operation (Goyal et al. 1590–1). Whatever the case, these people need the money.

There is certainly a risk in donating a kidney, but this risk is not great enough to be outlawed. Millions of people take risks to their health every day for money, or simply for enjoyment. As explained in *The Lancet*, "If the rich are free to engage in dangerous sports for pleasure, or dangerous jobs for high pay, it is difficult to see why the poor who take the lesser risk of kidney selling for greater rewards . . . should be thought so misguided as to need saving from themselves" (Radcliffe-Richards et al. 1951). Studies have shown that a person can live a healthy life with only one kidney. While these studies might not apply to the poor living under strenuous conditions in unsanitary environments, the risk is still theirs to take. These people have decided that their best hope for money is to sell a kidney. How can we deny them the best opportunity they have?

Some agree with Pope John Paul II that the selling of organs is morally wrong and violates "the dignity of the human person" (qtd. in Finkel 26), but this is a belief professed by healthy and affluent individuals. Are we sure that the peasants of third world countries agree? The morals we hold are not absolute truths. We have the responsibility to protect and help those less fortunate, but we cannot let our own ideals cloud the issues at hand.

In a legal kidney transplant, everybody gains except the donor. The doctors and nurses are paid for the operation, the patient receives a new kidney, but the donor receives nothing. Sure, the donor will have the warm, uplifting feeling associated with helping a fellow human being, but this is not enough reward for most people to part with a piece of themselves. In an ideal world, the average person would be altruistic

10

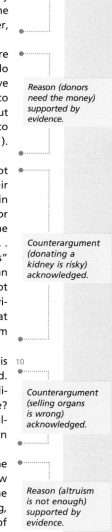

Reason (donors need the money) supported by evidence.

Counterargument (donating a kidney is risky) acknowledged.

Counterargument (selling organs is wrong) acknowledged.

Reason (altruism is not enough) supported by evidence.

enough to donate a kidney with nothing expected in return. The real world, however, is run by money. We pay men for donating sperm, and we pay women for donating ova, yet we expect others to give away an entire organ for no compensation. If the sale of organs were allowed, people would have a greater incentive to help save the life of a stranger.

While many argue that legalizing the sale of organs will exploit the poorer people of third world countries, the truth of the matter is that this is already the case. Even with the threat of a $50,000 fine and five years in prison (Finkel 26), the current ban has not been successful in preventing illegal kidney transplants. The kidneys of the poor are still benefiting only the rich. While the sellers do receive most of the money promised, the sum is too small to have any real impact on their financial situation. A study in India discovered that in the long run, organ sellers suffer. In the illegal kidney trade, nobody has the interests of the seller at heart. After selling a kidney, their state of living actually worsens. While the $1,000 pays off one debt, it is not enough to relieve the donor of the extreme poverty that placed him in debt in the first place (Goyal et al. 1591).

Counterargument (poor people are exploited) acknowledged.

These impoverished people do not need stricter and harsher penalties against organ selling to protect them, but quite the opposite. If the sale of organs were made legal, it could be regulated and closely monitored by the government and other responsible organizations. Under a regulated system, education would be incorporated into the application process. Before deciding to donate a kidney, the seller should know the details of the operation and any hazards involved. Only with an understanding of the long-term physical health risks can a person make an informed decision (Radcliffe-Richards et al. 1951).

Reason (regulating organ sales would lead to better decisions).

Regulation would ensure that the seller is fairly compensated. In the illegal kidney trade, surgeons collect most of the buyer's money in return for putting their careers on the line. The brokers arranging the procedure also receive a modest cut, typically around ten percent. If the entire practice were legalized, more of the money could be directed towards the person who needs it most, the seller. By eliminating the middleman and allowing the doctors to settle for lower prices, a regulated system would benefit all those in need of a kidney, both rich and poor. According to Finkel, the money that would otherwise be spent on dialysis treatment could not only cover the charge of a kidney

Reason (fairness to sellers) followed by evidence.

transplant at no cost to the recipient, but also reward the donor with as much as $25,000 (32). This money could go a long way for people living in the poverty of third world countries.

Critics fear that controlling the lawful sale of organs would be too difficult, but could it be any more difficult than controlling the unlawful sale of organs? Governments have tried to eradicate the kidney market for decades to no avail. Maybe it is time to try something else. When "desperately wanted goods" are made illegal, history has shown that there is more opportunity for corruption and exploitation than if those goods were allowed (Radcliffe-Richards et al. 1951). (Just look at the effects of the prohibition of alcohol, for example.) Legalization of organ sales would give governments the authority and the opportunity to closely monitor these live kidney operations.

Regulation would also protect the buyers. Because of the need for secrecy, the current illegal method of obtaining a kidney has no contracts and, therefore, no guarantees. Since what they are doing is illegal, the buyers have nobody to turn to if something goes wrong. There is nobody to point the finger at, nobody to sue. While those participating in the kidney market are breaking the law, they have no other choice. Without a new kidney, end-stage renal disease will soon kill them. Desperate to survive, they are forced to take the only offer available. It seems immoral to first deny them the opportunity of a new kidney and then to leave them stranded at the mercy of the black market. Without laws regulating live kidney transplants, these people are subject to possibly hazardous procedures. Instead of turning our backs, we have the power to ensure that these operations are done safely and efficiently for both the recipient and the donor.

Those suffering from end-stage renal disease would do anything for the chance at a new kidney, take any risk or pay any price. There are other people so poor that the sale of a kidney is worth the profit. Try to tell someone that he has to die from kidney failure because selling a kidney is morally wrong. Then turn around and try to tell another person that he has to remain in poverty for that same reason. In matters of life and death, our stances on moral issues must be reevaluated. If legalized and regulated, the sale of human organs would save lives. Is it moral to sentence thousands to unnecessary deaths?

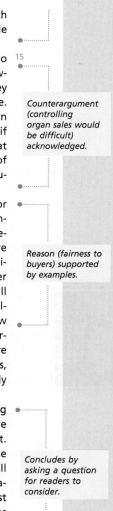

15

Counterargument (controlling organ sales would be difficult) acknowledged.

Reason (fairness to buyers) supported by examples.

Concludes by asking a question for readers to consider.

Works Cited

Finkel, Michael. "This Little Kidney Went to Market." *New York Times Magazine* 27 May 2001: 26–33, 40, 52, 59. Print.

Goyal, Madhav, et al. "Economic and Health Consequences of Selling a Kidney in India." *Journal of the American Medical Association* 288 (2002): 1589–92. Print.

McDonnell, Michael B., and William K. Mallon. "Kidney Transplant." *eMedicine Health*. WebMD, 18 Aug. 2008. Web. 30 Nov. 2008.

Radcliffe-Richards, J., et al. "The Case for Allowing Kidney Sales." *Lancet* 351.9120 (1998): 1950–52. Print.

MacKay clearly states her position at the beginning of her text: "Governments should not ban the sale of human organs; they should regulate it." Her argument appeals to her readers' sense of fairness; when kidney sales are legalized and regulated, both sellers and buyers will benefit from the transaction. She uses MLA style to document her sources.

HEATHER E. DOUGLAS

The Dark Side of Science

In this text, philosopher of science Heather E. Douglas argues that scientists are responsible for the effects of their research. It first appeared in November 2011 in The Scientist, *a magazine dedicated to "exploring life, inspiring innovation."*

Within the burgeoning field of synthetic biology, teams of biologists and engineers are making great strides in understanding the cell and its functioning. . . . However, there is more that should be discussed than the triumphs. There are also the dark purposes to which science (and synthetic biology in particular) can be put. Worries range from the development of pathogenic bioweapons to the potential contamination of native gene pools in our environment. The question is, are scientists responsible for the potentially negative impacts of their work?

Some have argued that the answer to this question is no — that it is not researchers' responsibility how science gets used in society. But that is sophistry. Scientists are responsible for both the impacts they

Albert Einstein sits with J. Robert Oppenheimer, who went on to develop the atomic bomb.

intend and some of the impacts they do not intend, if they are readily foreseeable in specific detail. These are the standards to which we are all held as moral agents. If I were to negligently throw a used match into a dry field (merely because I wanted to dispose of it), for example, I would be responsible for the resulting wild fire. In contrast, Einstein was not responsible for the use of his $E=mc^2$ equation to build an atomic bomb and its use in wartime, though the scientists at Los Alamos were.

Of course, impacts (whether harmful or beneficial) are not solely scientists' responsibility — others involved will also bear responsibility for their actions. If scientific knowledge is used in a biological attack, the terrorists are first and foremost responsible for their heinous act. But the researchers who generated the knowledge may be also partly responsible. Consider, for example, the knowledge of how to build a virus like smallpox from the ground up or how to create other pathogenic, tailored organisms — targeted either to humans or the foods on which we depend. If it is readily foreseeable that such knowledge could be used for nefarious purposes, the scientists who introduce such new technological capacities are partially responsible for an attack that could ultimately cause millions of deaths.

Scientists can no longer hope naively that people will only use science for the public good. The world will always have the mentally unbalanced, the delusional, the vicious, and the sociopathic members of society, some of whom will also be intelligent enough to use the results of science. Recognizing this should be part of the everyday backdrop of science, the assessment of its potential, and the desirability of the pursuit of a particular project.

As scientists plumb the depths of the cell, they must be particularly cognizant of the potentially harmful uses of their work, in addition to all its intended benefits. For example, knowledge of how to generate specific strings of nucleotides with high precision greatly aids research by providing particular and accurate DNA sequences with which scientists can assess cell functioning and design new living systems. But such knowledge can also produce the raw materials for building known pathogens from scratch, as has already been done (for research purposes) with the polio virus and the Spanish flu virus. As scientists develop ways to generate sequences of base-pairs ever more cheaply and efficiently, the opportunity for the malicious or the simply unreflective to play with pathogens to see what kind of traits arise looms larger. And it is not just technological know-how that can be problematic. The detailed knowledge of cellular or genetic functioning can have worrisome implications as well. Knowledge of what makes a virus more transmissible can assist us in detecting when a virus might be more prone to producing an epidemic, but it could also be used to make viruses more virulent. 5

In sum, scientists are responsible for both what they intend to achieve and that which is readily foreseeable, as we all are. There is nothing inherent in becoming a scientist that removes this burden of responsibility. The burden can be shared — scientists can come together to decide how to proceed, or ask for input from ethicists, social scientists, even the broader public. Alternatively, scientists could decide (and it has been proposed) that some forms of regulation — either in the selection of projects or in the control and dissemination of results — be imposed on the field of synthetic biology, to reduce the risks. The more oversight scientists submit to, the less responsibility they bear, but it comes at the cost of the freedom to choose the type of work they can do and how they do it. This is the essential tension: as long as there is freedom of research, there is the responsibility that comes with it.

rhetorical situations | genres | processes | strategies | research MLA / APA | media / design | readings

As a philosopher, Douglas supports her claim primarily with logical arguments, but her choice of examples also appeals to readers' emotions.

LAWRENCE LESSIG

Some Like It Hot

OK, P2P Is "Piracy." But So Was the Birth of Hollywood, Radio, Cable TV, and (Yes) the Music Industry.

This essay on electronic piracy appeared in Wired *magazine in March 2004. Lawrence Lessig is an authority on copyright law. He is a professor at Harvard Law School.*

If piracy means using the creative property of others without their permission, then the history of the content industry is a history of piracy. Every important sector of big media today — film, music, radio, and cable TV — was born of a kind of piracy. The consistent story is how each generation welcomes the pirates from the last. Each generation — until now.

The Hollywood film industry was built by fleeing pirates. Creators and directors migrated from the East Coast to California in the early twentieth century in part to escape controls that film patents granted the inventor Thomas Edison. These controls were exercised through the Motion Pictures Patents Company, a monopoly "trust" based on Edison's creative property and formed to vigorously protect his patent rights.

California was remote enough from Edison's reach that filmmakers like Fox and Paramount could move there and, without fear of the law, pirate his inventions. Hollywood grew quickly, and enforcement of federal law eventually spread west. But because patents granted their holders a truly "limited" monopoly of just seventeen years (at that time), the patents had expired by the time enough federal marshals appeared. A new industry had been founded, in part from the piracy of Edison's creative property.

Meanwhile, the record industry grew out of another kind of piracy. At the time that Edison and Henri Fourneaux invented machines for reproducing music (Edison the phonograph; Fourneaux the player piano), the law gave composers the exclusive right to control copies and public performances of their music. Thus, in 1900, if I wanted a copy of Phil Russel's 1899 hit, "Happy Mose," the law said I would have to pay for the right to get a copy of the score, and I would also have to pay for the right to perform it publicly.

But what if I wanted to record "Happy Mose" using Edison's phono- 5 graph or Fourneaux's player piano? Here the law stumbled. If I simply sang the piece into a recording device in my home, it wasn't clear that I owed the composer anything. And more important, it wasn't clear whether I owed the composer anything if I then made copies of those recordings. Because of this gap in the law, I could effectively use some-one else's song without paying the composer anything. The composers (and publishers) were none too happy about this capacity to pirate.

In 1909, Congress closed the gap in favor of the composer and the recording artist, amending copyright law to make sure that composers would be paid for "mechanical reproductions" of their music. But rather than simply granting the composer complete control over the right to make such reproductions, Congress gave recording artists a right to record the music, at a price set by Congress, after the com-poser allowed it to be recorded once. This is the part of copyright law that makes cover songs possible. Once a composer authorizes a record-ing of his song, others are free to record the same song, so long as they pay the original composer a fee set by the law. So, by limiting musicians' rights — by partially pirating their creative work — record producers and the public benefit.

A similar story can be told about radio. When a station plays a composer's work on the air, that constitutes a "public performance." Copyright law gives the composer (or copyright holder) an exclusive right to public performances of his work. The radio station thus owes the composer money.

But when the station plays a record, it is not only performing a copy of the *composer's* work. The station is also performing a copy of the *recording artist's* work. It's one thing to air a recording of "Happy Birthday" by the local children's choir; it's quite another to air a record-ing of it by the Rolling Stones or Lyle Lovett. The recording artist is adding to the value of the composition played on the radio station. And if the law were perfectly consistent, the station would have to pay the artist for his work, just as it pays the composer.

But it doesn't. This difference can be huge. Imagine you compose a piece of music. You own the exclusive right to authorize public

A "pirated" image combines photographs of Marilyn Monroe and Cyril Ritchard (as Captain Hook) to poke fun at overly controlling copyright laws.

performances of that music. So if Madonna wants to sing your song in public, she has to get your permission.

Imagine she does sing your song, and imagine she likes it a lot. 10 She then decides to make a recording of your song, and it becomes a top hit. Under today's law, every time a radio station plays your song, you get some money. But Madonna gets nothing, save the indirect effect on the sale of her CDs. The public performance of her recording is not a "protected" right. The radio station thus gets to pirate the value of Madonna's work without paying her a dime.

No doubt, one might argue, the promotion artists get is worth more than the performance rights they give up. Maybe. But even if that's the case, this is a choice that the law ordinarily gives to the creator. Instead, the law gives the radio station the right to take something for nothing.

Cable TV, too: When entrepreneurs first started installing cable in 1948, most refused to pay the networks for the content that they hijacked and delivered to their customers—even though they were basically selling access to otherwise free television broadcasts. Cable companies were thus Napsterizing broadcasters' content, but more egregiously than anything Napster ever did—Napster never charged for the content it enabled others to give away.

Broadcasters and copyright owners were quick to attack this theft. As then Screen Actors Guild president Charlton Heston put it, the cable outfits were "free riders" who were "depriving actors of compensation."

Copyright owners took the cable companies to court. Twice the Supreme Court held that the cable companies owed the copyright owners nothing. The debate shifted to Congress, where almost thirty years later it resolved the question in the same way it had dealt with phonographs and player pianos. Yes, cable companies would have to pay for the content that they broadcast, but the price they would have to pay was not set by the copyright owner. Instead, lawmakers set the price so that the broadcasters couldn't veto the emerging technologies of cable. The companies thus built their empire in part upon a piracy of the value created by broadcasters' content.

As the history of film, music, radio, and cable TV suggest, even if 15 some piracy is plainly wrong, not all piracy is. Or at least not in the sense that the term is increasingly being used today. Many kinds of piracy are useful and productive, either to create new content or foster new ways of doing business. Neither our tradition, nor any tradition, has ever banned all piracy.

This doesn't mean that there are no questions raised by the latest piracy concern—peer-to-peer file sharing. But it does mean that we need to understand the harm in P2P sharing a bit more before we condemn it to the gallows.

Like the original Hollywood, P2P sharing seeks to escape an overly controlling industry. And like the original recording and radio industries, it is simply exploiting a new way of distributing content. But unlike cable TV, no one is selling the content that gets shared on P2P services. This difference distinguishes P2P sharing. We should find a way to protect artists while permitting this sharing to survive.

Much of the "piracy" that file sharing enables is plainly legal and good. It provides access to content that is technically still under copyright but that is no longer commercially available—in the case of music, some four million tracks. More important, P2P networks enable sharing of content that copyright owners want shared, as well as work already in the public domain. This clearly benefits authors and society.

Moreover, much of the sharing—which is referred to by many as piracy—is motivated by a new way of spreading content made possible

rhetorical situations

genres

processes

strategies

research MLA / APA

media / design

readings

by changes in the technology of distribution. Thus, consistent with the tradition that gave us Hollywood, radio, the music industry, and cable TV, the question we should be asking about file sharing is how best to preserve its benefits while minimizing (to the extent possible) the wrongful harm it causes artists.

The question is one of balance, weighing the protection of the law 20 against the strong public interest in continued innovation. The law should seek that balance, and that balance will be found only with time.

Lessig argues that the "piracy" that Napster and other peer-to-peer music-sharing services are accused of is similar to that practiced by every other electronic medium in the last one hundred years. He offers a clear definition of piracy and carefully supports his assertions with historical evidence for each one.

ANDREW LEONARD

Black Friday: Consumerism Minus Civilization

This essay arguing that advertising for day-after-Thanksgiving sales has gone too far first appeared on Salon, *where it includes several videos and links to other websites, which are underlined in this text. The online version may be accessed via* wwnorton.com/write/fieldguidelinks.

Here's a Thanksgiving recipe guaranteed to deliver a nervous breakdown impervious to even the most bleeding-edge psychopharmaceutical wonder drug. Go to YouTube, search for "Black Friday commercials," start watching, and then, once you've sated yourself on grown men screaming at Justin Bieber, remakes of Rebecca Black's "Friday," and, most distressingly, the continuing adventures of the Crazy Target Lady, ask yourself this question:

What does it all mean?

I stared into this heart of retail panic darkness, and the more I clicked and pondered, the more confused — (mind-boggled? fascinated? flabbergasted?) — I became. The Crazy Target Lady, so proud of her OCD — obsessive Christmas disorder — is not funny. She's scary. She's why people trample each other to death. She is wrong.

Grown men scream at Justin Bieber in the Macy's Black Friday ad.

There is a point in our culture beyond which camp and kitsch no longer make the least ironic sense, where consumerism loses its last mooring to civilization, where even seemingly legitimate protest devolves into farce. That point is Black Friday.

Let me be clear. I am not opposed to vigorous sprees of retail 5 spending. For the sake of the U.S. economy, I would love to see a robust Christmas shopping season and I plan to do my part. I find the notion that we should "occupy Black Friday" and withhold our consumer dollars as a way of hitting back at the 1 percent just nutty. Voluntarily subtracting demand from the economy hurts *us*. A general consumer strike would result in more layoffs and pay cuts and bankruptcies and foreclosures. Sure, Wal-Mart would take a hit, but so would Wal-Mart employees.

But there's also a point where healthy consumerism becomes out-of-control marketing-driven commodity fetishism, and when we find ourselves checking our smartphones for last minute online deals while

standing in line for a chain store opening at midnight on Thanksgiving, we are clearly too far gone. That's insanity.

And corporate America knows this. The retail moguls are counting on it. They are outright encouraging it — and role-modeling the appropriate behavior for us. The Crazy Target Lady is not a joke. Watch her cannibalize her gingerbread man, or strategize her reverse psychology shopping techniques, or show off her shopping utility belt: You cannot avoid the dual conclusion that a) she is not a healthy woman, and b) she is *America*. She might be a lunatic, but it's a culturally approved lunacy — the kind that keeps the American engine of capitalism all stoked up. The message that keeps getting blasted across my TV is that we should all be more like her — doing our patriotic duty to boost fourth-quarter retail sales. Sure, you can laugh at her. But then get in line and keep your credit card handy.

But, of course, the big story of this year's Black Friday has been the welcome news that at least some subsection of the population of the United States has come to the realization that it's time to step back from the brink. The budding protests against the decision by some of the country's biggest retailers — Target, Macy's, Best Buy, Kohl's — to move the start of their Black Friday sales to midnight Thanksgiving, or even earlier, is laudable.

The Crazy Target Lady models her shopping utility belt.

The nearly 200,000 signatures on part-time Target employee Anthony Hardwick's petition to "Save Thanksgiving" is proof that both employees and customers of Target are beginning to see this endless race by retailers to one-up each other as dehumanizing and ridiculous. What does a Target employee forced to go to work at 11 p.m. on Thanksgiving have to give thanks for?

(Although, even here, in the protest arena, it's hard to know what to make of the "Respect the Bird" campaign hosted at AllRecipes.com that mixes pledges to "take back Thanksgiving" with KitchenAid mixer promotions and ads for pop-up turkey timers. Even the *protests* are inseparable from consumerist mania.)   10

The chains are lamely defending their move as a response to forces beyond their control:

"As that is the busiest shopping day of the year, it is imperative that we be competitive," said Anahita Cameron, a Target human resources director, in a statement quoted by the *L.A. Times*. "Our guests have expressed that they would prefer to kick off their holiday shopping by heading out after their holiday celebrations rather than getting up in the middle of the night."

The "Friday" parody used in the Kohl's campaign.

Guests? Pre-programmed automatons would be more accurate. I am undoubtedly reading too much into the "Black Friday" parody of Rebecca Black's "Friday" currently touting the midnight Thanksgiving sale at Kohl's, but there is an awfully revealing moment at the very end of the ad.

After the perky Stepford-wife shopper sings joyfully about how she's "been in line since yesterday" and how everybody's going to Kohl's at "midnight, midnight" the ad ends with her observing, with a mild air of perturbance, that she "can't get this darn song out of my head."

Ladies and gentlemen, there's your winner of the 2011 award for honesty in advertising. A commercial attempting to brainwash consumers into lining up for a midnight sale manages also to explicitly reference the difficulty of shaking free from mindless jingles.   15

That's kind of brilliant. But also very wrong. Which makes it the perfect commercial for summing up the culture-wide psychotic spasm that is Black Friday. Stay home Thanksgiving night. Go shopping after getting a full night's rest. Sure, you might miss a sale or two. But you'll be a better human being.

Leonard's claim, that Black Friday represents "out-of-control marketing-driven commodity fetishism" or, more concisely, "insanity," is vividly illustrated by several videos of commercials that provide both background information and evidence for his argument. He acknowledges the need for "vigorous sprees of retail spending" while decrying the "psychotic spasm that is Black Friday."

For five more arguments, see CHAPTER 60.

Key Features / Arguments

A clear and arguable position.   At the heart of every argument is a claim with which people may reasonably disagree. Some claims are not arguable because they're completely subjective, matters of taste or opinion ("I hate sauerkraut"), because they are a matter of fact ("The first *Star Wars* movie came out in 1977"), or because they are based on belief or faith ("There is life after death"). To be arguable, a position must reflect one of at least two points of view, making reasoned argument necessary: Internet file sharing should (or should not) be considered fair use; selling human organs should be legal (or illegal). In college writing, you will often argue not that a position is correct but that it is plausible — that it is reasonable, supportable, and worthy of being taken seriously.

Necessary background information. Sometimes we need to provide some background on a topic we are arguing so that readers can understand what is being argued. MacKay establishes the need for kidney donors before launching her argument for legalizing the selling of organs; Douglas describes scientific progress in synthetic biology.

Good reasons. By itself, a position does not make an argument; the argument comes when a writer offers reasons to back the position up. There are many kinds of good reasons. Lessig makes his argument by comparing, showing many examples of so-called piracy in other media. Douglas reasons that scientists must recognize that their research may be used for destructive purposes. MacKay bases her argument in favor of legalizing the sale of human organs on the grounds that doing so would save more lives, that impoverished people should be able to make risky choices, and that regulation would protect such people who currently sell their organs on the black market as well as desperate buyers.

Convincing evidence. Once you're given reasons for your position, you then need to offer evidence for your reasons: facts, statistics, expert testimony, anecdotal evidence, case studies, textual evidence. All four arguments use a mix of these types of evidence. MacKay cites statistics about Americans who die from renal failure to support her argument for legalizing organ sales; Lessig offers facts from the history of the broadcast media to support his argument for file sharing. Douglas outlines the positive and negative uses to which cell research has been put. Leonard

rhetorical situations

genres

processes

strategies

research MLA / APA

media / design

readings

presents several videos to demonstrate how excessive Black Friday advertising has become.

Appeals to readers' values.   Effective arguers try to appeal to readers' values and emotions. Both MacKay and Lessig appeal to basic values — MacKay to the value of compassion, both writers to the value of fairness. These are deeply held values that we may not think about very much and as a result may see as common ground we share with the writers. And some of MacKay's evidence appeals to emotion — her descriptions of people dying from kidney disease and of poor people selling their organs are likely to evoke an emotional response in many readers.

A trustworthy tone.   Arguments can stand or fall on the way readers perceive the writer. Very simply, readers need to trust the person who's making the argument. One way of winning this trust is by demonstrating that you know what you're talking about. Lessig offers plenty of facts to show his knowledge of copyright history — and he does so in a self-assured tone. There are many other ways of establishing yourself (and your argument) as trustworthy — by showing that you have some experience with your subject, that you're fair, and of course that you're honest. Occasionally, an outraged tone such as Leonard's is appropriate, especially when it is tempered by good reasons and qualified as he does in noting that he is "undoubtedly reading too much into the Kohl's . . . parody."

Careful consideration of other positions.   No matter how reasonable and careful we are in arguing our positions, others may disagree or offer counterarguments. We need to consider those other views and to acknowledge and, if possible, refute them in our written arguments. MacKay, for example, acknowledges that some believe that selling organs is unethical, but she counters that it's usually healthy, affluent people who say this — not people who need either an organ or the money they could get by selling one.

A GUIDE TO WRITING ARGUMENTS

Choosing a Topic

A fully developed argument requires significant work and time, so choosing a topic in which you're interested is very important. Students often find that widely debated topics such as "animal rights" or "gun control" can be difficult to write on because they don't feel any personal connection to them. Better topics include those that

- interest you right now
- are focused but not too narrowly
- have some personal connection to your life

259–65 ◉

One good way to **GENERATE IDEAS** for a topic that meets those three criteria is to explore your own roles in life.

260–61 ◉

Start with your roles in life.   Make four columns with the headings "Personal," "Family," "Public," and "School." Then **LIST** the roles you play that relate to it. Here is a list one student wrote:

Personal	Family	Public	School
gamer	son	voter	college student
dog owner	younger	homeless-shelter	work-study
old-car owner	brother	volunteer	employee
male	grandson	American	dorm resident
white		resident	primary-education
middle class		of Ohio	major

Identify issues that interest you.   Think, then, about issues or controversies that may concern you as a member of one or more of those groups. For instance, as a primary-education major, this student cares about the controversy over whether teachers' jobs should be focused on preparing

kids for high-stakes standardized tests. As a college student, he cares about the costs of a college education. Issues that stem from these subjects could include the following: Should student progress be measured by standardized tests? Should college cost less than it does?

Pick four or five of the roles you list. In five or ten minutes, identify issues that concern or affect you as a member of each of those roles. It might help to word each issue as a question starting with *Should*.

Frame your topic as a problem.   Most position papers address issues that are subjects of ongoing debate — their solutions aren't easy, and people disagree on which ones are best. Posing your topic as a problem can help you think about the topic, find an issue that's suitable to write about, and find a clear focus for your essay.

For example, if you wanted to write an argument on the lack of student parking at your school, you could frame your topic as one of several problems: What causes the parking shortage? Why are the university's parking garages and lots limited in their capacity? What might alleviate the shortage?

Choose one issue to write about.   Remember that the issue should be interesting to you and have some connection to your life. It is a tentative choice; if you find later that you have trouble writing about it, simply go back to your list of roles or issues and choose another.

Considering the Rhetorical Situation

PURPOSE	Do you want to persuade your audience to do something? Change their minds? Consider alternative views? Accept your position as plausible — see that you have thought carefully about an issue and researched it appropriately?	3–4
AUDIENCE	Who is your intended audience? What do they likely know and believe about this issue? How personal is it for them? To what extent are they likely to agree or disagree with you? Why? What common ground can you find with them?	5–8

12–15 ■ **STANCE** What's your attitude toward your topic, and why? How do you want your audience to perceive your attitude? How do you want your audience to perceive you? As an authority on your topic? As someone much like them? As calm? reasonable? impassioned or angry? something else?

16–18 ■ **MEDIA / DESIGN** What media will you use, and how do your media affect your argument? Does your print or online argument call for photos or charts? If you're giving an oral presentation, should you put your reasons and support on slides? If you're writing online, should you include audio or video evidence or links to counterarguments?

Generating Ideas and Text

Most essays that successfully argue a position share certain features that make them interesting and persuasive. Remember that your goal is to stake out a position and convince your readers that it is plausible.

Explore what you already know about the issue.   Write out whatever 259–61 ○ you know about the issue by **FREEWRITING** or as a **LIST** or **OUTLINE.** Why are 263–64 you interested in this topic? What is your position on it at this point, and why? What aspect do you think you'd like to focus on? Where do you need to focus your research efforts? This activity can help you discover what more you need to learn. Chances are you'll need to learn a lot more about the issue before you even decide what position to take.

Do some research.   At this point, try to get an overview. Start with one 439–40 ● **GENERAL SOURCE** of information that will give you a sense of the ins and outs of your issue, one that isn't overtly biased. *The Daily Beast, Time,* and other online newsmagazines can be good starting points on current issues. 448–49 ● For some issues, you may need to **INTERVIEW** an expert. For example, one student who wanted to write about chemical abuse of animals at 4H competitions interviewed an experienced show competitor. Use your overview source to find out the main questions raised about your issue and to get some idea about the various ways in which you might argue it.

Explore the issue strategically. Most issues may be argued from many different perspectives. You'll probably have some sense of the different views that exist on your issue, but you should explore multiple perspectives before deciding on your position. The following methods are good ways of exploring issues:

- As a matter of **DEFINITION**. What is it? How should it be defined? How can *organic* or *genetically modified food* be defined? How do proponents of *organic food* define it — and how do they define *genetically modified food*? How do advocates of *genetically modified food* define it — and how do they define *organic food*? Considering such definitions is one way to identify different perspectives on the topic. 356–66

- As a matter of **CLASSIFICATION**. Can the issue be divided into categories? Are there different kinds of, or different ways of, producing organic foods and genetically modified foods? Do different categories suggest particular positions or perhaps a way of supporting a certain position? Are there other ways of categorizing foods? 342–47

- As a matter of **COMPARISON**. Is one subject being considered better than another? Is organic food healthier or safer than genetically modified food? Is genetically modified food healthier or safer than organic? Is the answer somewhere in the middle? 348–55

- As a matter of **PROCESS**. Should somebody do something? What? Should people buy and eat more organic food? More genetically modified food? Should they buy and eat some of each? 382–86

Reconsider whether the issue can be argued. Is this issue worth discussing? Why is it important to you and to others? What difference will it make if one position or another prevails? Is it **ARGUABLE**? At this point, you want to be sure that your topic is worth arguing about. 323–41

Draft a thesis. Having explored the possibilities, decide your position, and write it out as a complete sentence. For example:

> Barry Bonds should not be eligible for the Hall of Fame.
>
> Reading should be taught using a mix of whole language and phonics.
>
> Genetically modified foods should be permitted in the United States.

Qualify your thesis. Rather than taking a strict pro or con position, in most cases you'll want to QUALIFY YOUR POSITION—in certain circumstances, with certain conditions, with these limitations, and so on. This is not to say that we should settle, give in, sell out; rather, it is to say that our position may not be the only "correct" one and that other positions may be valid as well. QUALIFYING YOUR THESIS also makes your topic manageable by limiting it. For example:

325

314–15

> Barry Bonds should not be eligible for the Hall of Fame, though he should be permitted to contribute to major league baseball in other ways.
>
> Reading should be taught using a mix of phonics and whole language, but the needs of individual students, not a philosophy, should be the primary focus.
>
> Genetically modified foods should be permitted in the United States if they are clearly labeled as such.

Come up with good reasons. Once you have a thesis, you need to come up with good REASONS to convince your readers that it's plausible. Write out your position, and then list several reasons. For instance, if your thesis is that Barry Bonds should not be eligible for the Hall of Fame, two of your reasons might be:

326–27

> He almost certainly used steroids in the later part of his career.
>
> Using steroids gives athletes unfair advantages and must be considered cheating.

Think about which reasons are best for your purposes: Which seem the most persuasive? Which are most likely to be accepted by your audience? Which seem to matter the most now? If your list of reasons is short or you think you'll have trouble developing them enough to write an appropriate essay, this is a good time to rethink your topic — before you've invested too much time in it.

 rhetorical situations
 genres
 processes
 strategies
 research MLA / APA
 media / design
readings

Develop support for your reasons.   Next, you have to come up with
EVIDENCE to support your reasons: facts, statistics, examples, testimony
by authorities and experts, anecdotal evidence, scenarios, case studies
and observation, and textual evidence. For some topics, you may want or
need to use evidence in visual form like photos, graphs, and charts; online,
you could also use video or audio evidence and links to evidence in other
websites.

327–35

What counts as evidence varies across audiences. Statistical evidence may be required in certain disciplines but not in others; anecdotes
may be accepted as evidence in some courses but not in engineering.
Some audiences will be persuaded by emotional appeals while others
will not. For example, if you argue that Barry Bonds should be eligible for
the National Baseball Hall of Fame because he's one of the greatest baseball players of all time, you could support that reason with *facts*: he was
named Major League Player of the Year three times. Or you could support
it with *statistics*: Bonds holds Major League records for the most career
home runs, walks, and intentional walks. *Expert testimony* might include
Sports Illustrated columnist Jon Heyman, who writes, "A baseball Hall of
Fame would be empty without Bonds."

Identify other positions.   Now, think about positions that differ from
yours and about the reasons people are likely to give for those positions.
Be careful to represent their points of view as accurately and fairly as you
can. Then decide whether you need to acknowledge or to refute each
position.

Acknowledging other positions.   Some positions can't be refuted but are
too important to ignore, so you need to **ACKNOWLEDGE** concerns and objections they raise to show that you've considered other perspectives. For
example, in an essay arguing that vacations are necessary to maintain
good health, medical writer Alina Tugend acknowledges that "in some
cases, these trips — particularly with entire families in tow — can be stressful in their own way. The joys of a holiday can also include lugging around
a ridiculous amount of paraphernalia, jet-lagged children sobbing on air-
planes, hotels that looked wonderful on the Web but are in reality next to

336

a construction site." Tugend's acknowledgment moderates her position and makes her argument appear more reasonable.

Refuting other positions.   State the position as clearly and as fairly as

337

you can, and then **REFUTE** it by showing why you believe it is wrong. Perhaps the reasoning is faulty or the supporting evidence inadequate. Acknowledge the merits of the position, if any, but emphasize its short-

338–40

comings. Avoid the **FALLACY** of attacking the person holding the position or bringing up a competing position that no one seriously entertains.

Ways of Organizing an Argument

Readers need to be able to follow the reasoning of your argument from beginning to end; your task is to lead them from point to point as you build your case. Sometimes you'll want to give all the reasons for your argument first, followed by discussion of any other positions. Alternatively, you might discuss each reason and any opposing arguments together.

[Reasons to support your argument, followed by opposing arguments]

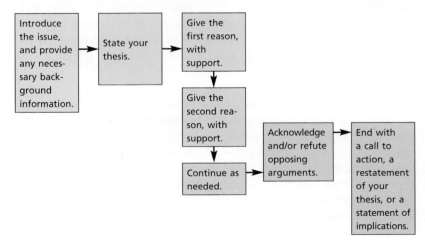

[Reason / opposing argument, reason/opposing argument]

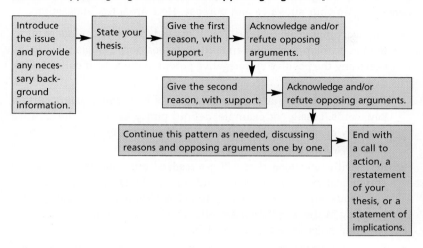

Consider carefully the order in which you discuss your reasons. Usually what comes last makes the strongest impression on readers and what comes in the middle the least impression, so you might want to put your most important or strongest reasons first and last.

Writing Out a Draft

Once you have generated ideas, done some research, and thought about how you want to organize your argument, it's time to start **DRAFTING.** Your goal in the initial draft is to develop your argument—you can fill in support and transitions as you revise. You may want to write your first draft in one sitting, so that you can develop your reasoning from beginning to end. Or you may write the main argument first and the introduction and conclusion after you've drafted the body of the essay; many writers find that beginning and ending an essay are the hardest tasks they face. Here is some advice on how you might **BEGIN AND END** your argument:

266–68

299–311

Draft a beginning. There are various ways to begin an argument essay, depending on your audience and purpose. Here are a few suggestions.

- *Offer background information.* You may need to give your readers information to help them understand your position. Douglas begins by sketching the positive and negative potential impacts of current work in synthetic biology.

- *Define a key term.* You may need to show how you're using certain key words. Lessig, for example, defines piracy as "using the creative property of others without their permission" in his first sentence, a **DEFINITION** that is central to his argument.

356–66

- *Begin with something that will get readers' attention.* MacKay begins emphatically: "There are thousands of people dying to buy a kidney and thousands of people dying to sell a kidney . . . So why are we standing in the way?" Leonard offers still photos from two commercials and links to two more available online.

- *Explain the context for your position.* All arguments are part of a larger, ongoing conversation, so you might begin by showing how your position fits into the arguments others have made. Lessig provides a history of piracy in four different electronic media.

Draft an ending. Your conclusion is the chance to wrap up your argument in such a way that readers will remember what you've said. Here are a few ways of concluding an argument essay.

- *Summarize your main points.* Especially when you've presented a complex argument, it can help readers to **SUMMARIZE** your main point. MacKay sums up her argument with the sentence "If legalized and regulated, the sale of human organs would save lives."

470–71

- *Call for action.* Lessig does this when he concludes by saying the law should seek a balance between copyright law and the need for continued innovation. Leonard presents an alternative to Black Friday's excesses: "Stay home Thanksgiving night. Go shopping after getting a full night's rest."

- *Frame your argument by referring to the introduction.* MacKay does this when she ends by reiterating that selling organs benefits both seller and buyer.

Come up with a title.   Most often you'll want your title to tell readers something about your topic—and to make them want to read on. MacKay's "Organ Sales Will Save Lives" tells us both her topic and position. Douglas's title, "The Dark Side of Science," entices us with melodrama. See the chapter on **GUIDING YOUR READER** for more advice on composing a good title.

312–17

Considering Matters of Design

You'll probably write the main text of your argument in paragraph form, but think about what kind of information you're presenting and how you can design it to make your argument as easy as possible for your readers to understand. Think also about whether any visual or audio elements would be more persuasive than written words.

- What would be an appropriate **FONT**? Something serious like Times Roman? Something traditional like Courier? Something else?

585–86

- Would it help your readers if you divided your argument into shorter sections and added **HEADINGS**?

588–89

- If you're making several points, would they be easier to follow if you set them off in a **LIST**?

587

- Do you have any supporting evidence that would be easier to understand in the form of a bar **GRAPH**, line graph, or pie chart?

593–95

- Would **ILLUSTRATIONS**—photos, diagrams, or drawings—add support for your argument? Online, would video, audio, or links help?

591–99

Getting Response and Revising

At this point you need to look at your draft closely, and if possible **GET RESPONSE** from others as well. Following are some questions for looking at an argument with a critical eye.

275–76

- Is there sufficient background or context?
- Is the thesis clear and appropriately qualified?
- Are the reasons plausible?
- Is there enough evidence to support these reasons? Is that evidence appropriate?
- Can readers follow the steps in your reasoning?
- Have you considered potential objections or other positions? Are there any others that should be addressed?
- Have you cited enough sources, and are these sources credible?
- Are source materials documented carefully and completely, with in-text citations and a works cited or references section?
- Are any visuals or links that are included used effectively and integrated smoothly with the rest of the text? If there are no visuals or links, would using some strengthen the argument?

276–79 Next it's time to **REVISE,** to make sure your argument offers convincing evidence, appeals to readers' values, and achieves your purpose.

Editing and Proofreading

Readers equate correctness with competence. Once you've revised your draft, follow these guidelines for **EDITING** an argument:

283–85

- Check to see that your tone is appropriate and consistent throughout, 12–15 reflects your **STANCE** accurately, and enhances the argument you're making.
- Be sure readers will be able to follow the argument; check to see you've 317 provided **TRANSITIONS** and summary statements where necessary.
- 462–74 480–83 Make sure you've smoothly integrated **QUOTATIONS, PARAPHRASES,** and **SUMMARIES** from source material into your writing and **DOCUMENTED** them accurately.
- Look for phrases such as "I think" or "I feel" and delete them; your essay itself expresses your opinion.

rhetorical situations
genres
processes
strategies
research MLA / APA
media / design
readings

- Make sure that **ILLUSTRATIONS** have captions and that charts and graphs have headings—and that all are referred to in the main text.
- **PROOFREAD** and spell-check your essay carefully.

591–99
285–86

Taking Stock of Your Work

Take stock of what you've written by writing out answers to these questions:

- What did you do well in this piece?
- What could still be improved?
- How did you go about researching your topic?
- How did others' responses influence your writing?
- How did you go about drafting this piece?
- Did you use visual elements (tables, graphs, diagrams, photographs), audio elements, or links effectively? If not, would they have helped?
- What would you do differently next time?
- What have you learned about your writing ability from writing this piece? What do you need to work on in the future?

> **IF YOU NEED MORE HELP**
>
> See Chapter 29 if you are required to submit your argument as part of a writing **PORTFOLIO.** See also Chapter 8 on **ANALYZING A TEXT,** Chapter 13 on **EVALUA-TIONS,** and Chapter 17 on **PROPOSALS** for advice on writing those specific types of arguments.

287–96
52–86
164–72
205–13

11 Abstracts

Abstracts are summaries written to give readers the gist of a report or presentation. Sometimes they are published in conference proceedings or databases. In some academic fields, you may be required to include an abstract in a **REPORT** or as a preview of a presentation you plan to give at an academic or professional conference. Abstracts are brief, typically 100–200 words, sometimes even shorter. Three common kinds are *informative abstracts*, *descriptive abstracts*, and *proposal abstracts*.

87–118 ▲

INFORMATIVE ABSTRACTS

Informative abstracts state in one paragraph the essence of a whole paper about a study or a research project. That one paragraph must mention all the main points or parts of the paper: a description of the study or project, its methods, the results, and the conclusions. Here is an example of the abstract accompanying a seven-page essay that appeared in the *Journal of Clinical Psychology*:

> The relationship between boredom proneness and health-symptom reporting was examined. Undergraduate students ($N = 200$) completed the Boredom Proneness Scale and the Hopkins Symptom Checklist. A multiple analysis of covariance indicated that individuals with high boredom-proneness total scores reported significantly higher ratings on all five subscales of the Hopkins Symptom Checklist (Obsessive–Compulsive, Somatization, Anxiety, Interpersonal Sensitivity, and Depression). The results suggest that boredom proneness may be an important element to consider when assessing symptom reporting. Implications for determining the effects of boredom proneness on psychological- and physical-health symptoms, as well as the application in clinical settings, are discussed.
>
> —Jennifer Sommers and Stephen J. Vodanovich,
> "Boredom Proneness"

rhetorical situations · genres · processes · strategies · research MLA / APA · media / design · readings

The first sentence states the nature of the study being reported. The next summarizes the method used to investigate the problem, and the following one gives the results: students who, according to specific tests, are more likely to be bored are also more likely to have certain medical or psychological symptoms. The last two sentences indicate that the paper discusses those results and examines the conclusion and its implications.

DESCRIPTIVE ABSTRACTS

Descriptive abstracts are usually much briefer than informative abstracts and provide much less information. Rather than summarizing the entire paper, a descriptive abstract functions more as a teaser, providing a quick overview that invites the reader to read the whole. Descriptive abstracts usually do not give or discuss results or set out the conclusion or its implications. A descriptive abstract of the boredom-proneness essay might simply include the first sentence from the informative abstract plus a final sentence of its own:

> The relationship between boredom proneness and health-symptom reporting was examined. The findings and their application in clinical settings are discussed.

PROPOSAL ABSTRACTS

Proposal abstracts contain the same basic information as informative abstracts, but their purpose is very different. You prepare proposal abstracts to persuade someone to let you write on a topic, pursue a project, conduct an experiment, or present a paper at a scholarly conference. This kind of abstract is not written to introduce a longer piece but rather to stand alone, and often the abstract is written before the paper itself. Titles and other aspects of the proposal deliberately reflect the theme of the proposed work, and you may use the future tense, rather than the past, to describe work not yet completed. Here is a possible proposal for doing research on boredom:

Undergraduate students will complete the Boredom Proneness Scale and the Hopkins Symptom Checklist. A multiple analysis of covariance will be performed to determine the relationship between boredom-proneness total scores and ratings on the five subscales of the Hopkins Symptom Checklist (Obsessive–Compulsive, Somatization, Anxiety, Interpersonal Sensitivity, and Depression).

Key Features / Abstracts

A summary of basic information. An informative abstract includes enough information to substitute for the report itself, a descriptive abstract offers only enough information to let the audience decide whether to read further, and a proposal abstract gives an overview of the planned work.

Objective description. Abstracts present information on the contents of a report or a proposed study; they do not present arguments about or personal perspectives on those contents. The informative abstract on boredom proneness, for example, offers only a tentative conclusion: "The results *suggest* that boredom proneness *may* be an important element to consider."

Brevity. Although the length of abstracts may vary, journals and organizations often restrict them to 120–200 words — meaning you must carefully select and edit your words.

A BRIEF GUIDE TO WRITING ABSTRACTS

Considering the Rhetorical Situation

3–4 ■	**PURPOSE**	Are you giving a brief but thorough overview of a completed study? Only enough information to create interest? Or a proposal for a planned study or presentation?
5–8 ■	**AUDIENCE**	For whom are you writing this abstract? What information about your project will your readers need?

STANCE   Whatever your stance in the longer work, your abstract
must be objective.

12–15

MEDIA / DESIGN   How will you set your abstract off from the rest of the
text? If you are publishing it online, should it be on a
separate page? What format do your readers expect?

16–18

Generating Ideas and Text

Write the paper first, the abstract last.   You can then use the finished
work as the guide for the abstract, which should follow the same basic
structure. *Exception:* You may need to write a proposal abstract months
before the work it describes will be complete.

Copy and paste key statements.   If you've already written the work,
highlight your THESIS, objective, or purpose; basic information on your
methods; your results; and your conclusion. Copy and paste those sentences into a new document to create a rough version of your abstract.

313–15

Pare down the rough abstract.   SUMMARIZE the key ideas in the document, editing out any nonessential words and details. In your first sentence, introduce the overall scope of your study. Also include any other
information that seems crucial to understanding your paper. Avoid
phrases that add unnecessary words, such as "It is concluded that." In
general, you probably won't want to use "I"; an abstract should cover
ideas, not say what you think or will do.

470–71

Conform to any requirements.   In general, an informative abstract
should be at most 10 percent as long as the original and no longer than
the maximum length allowed. Descriptive abstracts should be shorter still,
and proposal abstracts should conform to the requirements of the organization calling for the proposal.

Ways of Organizing an Abstract

[An informative abstract]

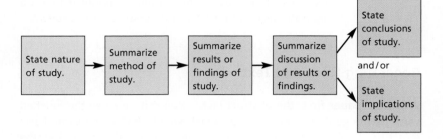

State nature of study. → Summarize method of study. → Summarize results or findings of study. → Summarize discussion of results or findings. → State conclusions of study. and/or State implications of study.

[A descriptive abstract]

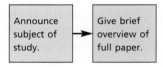

Announce subject of study. → Give brief overview of full paper.

[A proposal abstract]

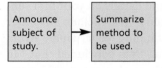

Announce subject of study. → Summarize method to be used.

266–68 ○
269–74
282–86

IF YOU NEED MORE HELP

See Chapter 25 for guidelines on **DRAFTING,** Chapter 26 on **ASSESSING YOUR OWN WRITING,** Chapter 27 on **GETTING RESPONSE AND REVISING,** and Chapter 28 on **EDITING AND PROOFREADING.**

rhetorical situations   genres   processes   strategies   research MLA / APA   media / design   readings

Annotated Bibliographies **12**

Annotated bibliographies describe, give publication information for, and sometimes evaluate each work on a list of sources. When we do research, we may consult annotated bibliographies to evaluate potential sources. You may also be assigned to create annotated bibliographies to weigh the potential usefulness of sources and to document your search efforts so that teachers can assess your ability to find, describe, and evaluate sources. There are two kinds of annotations, *descriptive* and *evaluative*; both may be brief, consisting only of phrases, or more formal, consisting of sentences and paragraphs. Sometimes an annotated bibliography is introduced by a short statement explaining its scope.

Descriptive annotations simply summarize the contents of each work, without comment or evaluation. They may be very short, just long enough to capture the flavor of the work, like the examples in the following excerpt from a bibliography of books and articles on teen films, published in the *Journal of Popular Film and Television*.

MICHAEL BENTON, MARK DOLAN, AND REBECCA ZISCH

Teen Film$

In the introduction to his book *The Road to Romance and Ruin*, Jon Lewis points out that over half of the world's population is currently under the age of twenty. This rather startling fact should be enough to make most Hollywood producers drool when they think of the potential profits from a target movie audience. Attracting the largest demographic group is, after all, the quickest way to box-office success.

155

In fact, almost from its beginning, the film industry has recognized the importance of the teenaged audience, with characters such as Andy Hardy and locales such as Ridgemont High and the 'hood.

Beyond the assumption that teen films are geared exclusively toward teenagers, however, film researchers should keep in mind that people of all ages have attended and still attend teen films. Popular films about adolescents are also expressions of larger cultural currents. Studying the films is important for understanding an era's common beliefs about its teenaged population within a broader pattern of general cultural preoccupations.

This selected bibliography is intended both to serve and to stimulate interest in the teen film genre. It provides a research tool for those who are studying teen films and their cultural implications. Unfortunately, however, in the process of compiling this list we quickly realized that it was impossible to be genuinely comprehensive or to satisfy every interest.

Doherty, Thomas. *Teenagers and Teenpics: The Juvenilization of American Movies in the 1950s*. Boston: Unwin Hyman, 1988. Print. Historical discussion of the identification of teenagers as a targeted film market.

Foster, Harold M. "Film in the Classroom: Coping with Teen Pics." *English Journal* 76.3 (1987): 86–88. Print. Evaluation of the potential of using teen films such as *Sixteen Candles*, *The Karate Kid*, *Risky Business*, *The Flamingo Kid*, and *The Breakfast Club* to instruct adolescents on the difference between film as communication and film as exploitation.

Washington, Michael, and Marvin J. Berlowitz."Blaxploitation Films and High School Youth: Swat Superfly." *Jump Cut* 9 (1975): 23–24. Print. Marxist reaction to the trend of youth-oriented black action films. Article seeks to illuminate the negative influences the films have on high school students by pointing out the false ideas about education, morality, and the black family espoused by the heroes in the films.

These annotations are purely descriptive; the authors express none of their own opinions. They describe works as "historical" or "Marxist" but do not indicate whether they're "good." The bibliography entries are documented in MLA style.

rhetorical situations   genres   processes   strategies   research MLA / APA   media / design   readings

Evaluative annotations offer opinions on a source as well as describe it. They are often helpful in assessing how useful a source will be for your own writing. The following evaluative annotations are from a bibliography by Jessica Ann Olson, a student at Wright State University.

JESSICA ANN OLSON

Global Warming

Gore, Al. *An Inconvenient Truth: The Planetary Emergency of Global Warming and What We Can Do about It*. New York: Rodale, 2006. Print.
This publication, which is based on Gore's slide show on global warming, stresses the urgency of the global warming crisis. It centers on how the atmosphere is very thin and how greenhouse gases such as carbon dioxide are making it thicker. The thicker atmosphere traps more infrared radiation, causing warming of the Earth. Gore argues that carbon dioxide, which is created by burning fossil fuels, cutting down forests, and producing cement, accounts for eighty percent of greenhouse gas emissions. He includes several examples of problems caused by global warming. Penguins and polar bears are at risk because the glaciers they call home are quickly melting. Coral reefs are being bleached and destroyed when their inhabitants overheat and leave. Global warming is now affecting people's lives as well. For example, the highways in Alaska are only frozen enough to be driven on fewer than eighty days of the year. In China and elsewhere, record-setting floods and droughts are taking place. Hurricanes are on the rise. This source's goal is to inform its audience about the ongoing global warming crisis and to inspire change across the world. It is useful because it relies on scientific data that can be referred to easily and it provides a solid foundation for me to build on. For example, it explains how carbon dioxide is produced and how it is currently affecting plants and animals. This evidence could potentially help my research on how humans are biologically affected by global warming. It will also help me structure my essay, using its general information to lead into the specifics of my topic. For example, I could introduce the issue by explaining the thinness of the atmosphere and the effect of greenhouse gases, then focus on carbon dioxide and its effects on organisms.

Parmesan, Camille, and Hector Galbraith. "Executive Summary." *Observed Impacts of Global Climate Change in the U.S.* Pew Center on Global Climate Change, Nov. 2004. Web. 17 Jan. 2007.

This report summarizes recent scientific findings that document the impact changes in the climate have had on the distribution of plants and animals in the United States and on how they interact within their communities. For example, it explains how a shift has taken place in the blooming period for plants and the breeding period for animals caused by global warming. Because of changes in their geographic range, species may interact differently, possibly resulting in population declines. For example, the red fox is now found in areas dominated by the arctic fox and is threatening its survival. The report stresses that such shifts can harm the world's biodiversity. Plants and animals that are rare now face extinction. The annual cycle of carbon dioxide levels in the atmosphere has also changed, largely due to the lengthening of the growing season, affecting basic ecosystem processes. I did not find this report as helpful as other sources because its information is based only on observations made in the United States. The information appears reliable, though, because it is based on scientific evidence. This essay will be helpful to my essay because it focuses on how plants and animals are currently affected, such as their shifting communities and how they are clashing. I could use this to explain human changes by providing evidence of what is happening to other species. This source will not be as helpful in explaining the climate's effects on human biological function in particular, but it will provide some framework. For example, I could explain how the plants that help convert carbon dioxide into oxygen are being harmed and relate that to how the humans will suffer the consequences.

These annotations not only describe the sources in detail, but also evaluate their usefulness for the writer's own project. They show that the writer understands the content of the sources and can relate it to her own anticipated needs as a researcher and writer.

Key Features / Annotated Bibliographies

A statement of scope.   Sometimes you need or are asked to provide a brief introductory statement to explain what you're covering. The authors

rhetorical situations   genres   processes   strategies   research MLA / APA   media / design   readings

of the bibliography on teen films introduce their bibliography with three paragraphs establishing a context for the bibliography and announcing their purpose for compiling it.

Complete bibliographic information. Provide all the information about each source using one documentation system (MLA, APA, or another one) so that your readers or other researchers will be able to find the source easily.

A concise description of the work. A good annotation describes each item as carefully and objectively as possible, giving accurate information and showing that you understand the source. These qualities will help to build authority—for you as a writer and for your annotations.

Relevant commentary. If you write an evaluative bibliography, your comments should be relevant to your purpose and audience. The best way to achieve relevance is to consider what questions a potential reader might have about the sources. Your evaluation might also focus on the text's suitability as a source for your writing, as Olson's evaluative annotations do.

Consistent presentation. All annotations should follow a consistent pattern: if one is written in complete sentences, they should all be. Each annotation in the teen films bibliography, for example, begins with a phrase (not a complete sentence) characterizing the work.

A BRIEF GUIDE TO WRITING ANNOTATED BIBLIOGRAPHIES

Considering the Rhetorical Situation

PURPOSE   Will your bibliography need to demonstrate the depth or breadth of your research? Will your readers actually track down and use your sources? Do you need or want to convince readers that your sources are good?   3–4

5–8 **AUDIENCE** For whom are you compiling this bibliography? What does your audience need to know about each source?

12–15 **STANCE** Are you presenting yourself as an objective describer or evaluator? Or are you expressing a particular point of view toward the sources you evaluate?

16–18 **MEDIA / DESIGN** If you are publishing the bibliography online, will you provide links from each annotation to the source itself? Online or off, do you need to distinguish the bibliographic information from the annotation by using a different font?

Generating Ideas and Text

Decide what sources to include.   You may be tempted to include in a bibliography every source you find or look at. A better strategy is to include only those sources that you or your readers may find potentially useful in researching your topic. For an academic bibliography, you need to consider the qualities in the list below. Some of these questions are not ones whose answers should rule a source in or out; they simply raise issues you need to think about.

- *Appropriateness.* Is this source relevant to your topic? Is it a primary source or a secondary source? Is it aimed at an appropriate audience? General or specialized? Elementary, advanced, or somewhere in between?

- *Credibility.* Is the author reputable? Is the publication, publishing company, or sponsor of the site reputable? Do the ideas more or less agree with those in other sources you've read?

- *Balance.* Does the source present enough evidence for its assertions? Does it show any particular bias? Does it present countering arguments fairly?

- *Timeliness.* Is the source recent enough? Does it reflect current thinking or research about the subject?

432–52 If you need help **FINDING SOURCES**, see Chapter 45.

■ rhetorical situations   ▲ genres   ○ processes   ◆ strategies   ● research MLA / APA   □ media / design   ▌ readings

Compile a list of works to annotate.   Give the sources themselves in whatever documentation style is required; see the guidelines for **MLA** and **APA** styles in Chapters 51 and 52.

● MLA 484–532
APA 533–74

Determine what kind of bibliography you need to write.   Descriptive or evaluative? Will your annotations be in the form of phrases? Complete sentences? Paragraphs? The form will shape your reading and note taking. If you're writing a descriptive bibliography, your reading goal will be just to understand and capture the writer's message as clearly as possible. If you're writing an evaluative bibliography, you will also need to assess the source as you read in order to include your own opinions of it.

Read carefully.   To write an annotation, you must understand the source's argument, but when you are writing an annotated bibliography as part of a **PROPOSAL,** you may have neither the time nor the need to read the whole text. Here's a way of quickly determining whether a source is likely to serve your needs:

▲ 205–13

- Check the publisher or sponsor (university press? scholarly journal? popular magazine? website sponsored by a reputable organization?).

- Read the preface (of a book), abstract (of a scholarly article), introduction (of an article in a nonscholarly magazine or a website).

- Skim the table of contents or the headings.

- Read the parts that relate specifically to your topic.

Research the writer, if necessary.   If you are required to indicate the writer's credentials, you may need to do additional research. You may find information by typing the writer's name into a search engine or looking up the writer in *Contemporary Authors*. In any case, information about the writer should take up no more than one sentence in your annotation.

Summarize the work in a sentence or two.   **DESCRIBE** it as objectively as possible: even if you are writing an evaluative annotation, you can evaluate the central point of a work better by stating it clearly first. *If you're writing a descriptive annotation, you're done.*

◆ 367–75

164–72 ▲

12–15 ■

Establish criteria for evaluating sources.   If you're **EVALUATING** sources for a project, you'll need to evaluate them in terms of their usefulness for your project, their **STANCE,** and their overall credibility.

Write a brief evaluation of the source.   If you can generalize about the worth of the entire work, fine. You may find, however, that some parts are useful while others are not, and what you write should reflect that mix.

Be consistent—in content, sentence structure, and format.

- *Content.* Try to provide about the same amount of information for each entry. If you're evaluating, don't evaluate some sources and just describe others.

- *Sentence structure.* Use the same style throughout—complete sentences, brief phrases, or a mix.

585–86 ☐

- *Format.* Use one documentation style throughout; use a consistent **FONT** for each element in each entry—for example, italicize or underline all book titles.

Ways of Organizing an Annotated Bibliography

Depending on their purpose, annotated bibliographies may or may not include an introduction. Most annotated bibliographies cover a single topic and so are organized alphabetically by author's or editor's last name. When a work lacks a named author, alphabetize it by the first important word in its title. Consult the documentation system you're using for additional details about alphabetizing works appropriately.

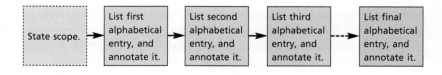

State scope. → List first alphabetical entry, and annotate it. → List second alphabetical entry, and annotate it. → List third alphabetical entry, and annotate it. ⇢ List final alphabetical entry, and annotate it.

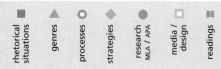

rhetorical situations

genres

processes

strategies

research MLA / APA

media / design

readings

Sometimes an annotated bibliography needs to be organized into several subject areas (or genres, periods, or some other category); if so, the entries are listed alphabetically within each category. For example, a bibliography about terrorism breaks down into subjects such as "Global Terrorism" and "Weapons of Mass Destruction."

[Multicategory bibliography]

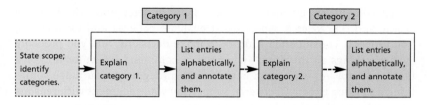

IF YOU NEED MORE HELP

See Chapter 25 for guidelines on **DRAFTING,** Chapter 26 on **ASSESSING YOUR OWN WRITING,** Chapter 27 on **GETTING RESPONSE AND REVISING,** and Chapter 28 on **EDITING AND PROOFREADING.** See Chapter 29 if you are required to submit your bibliography in a writing **PORTFOLIO.**

266–68
269–74
275–81
282–86
287–98

13 Evaluations

ConsumerReports.org evaluates cars and laundry detergents. The *Princeton Review* and *U.S. News & World Report* evaluate colleges and universities. You probably consult such sources to make decisions, and you probably evaluate things all the time—when you recommend a film (or not) or a teacher (ditto). An evaluation is at bottom a judgment; you judge something according to certain criteria, supporting your judgment with reasons and evidence. You need to give your reasons for evaluating it as you do because often your evaluation will affect your audience's actions: they must see this movie, needn't bother with this book, should be sure to have the Caesar salad at this restaurant, and so on. In a review on the following page, written for a first-year writing class at Wright State University, Ali Heinekamp offers her evaluation of the film *Juno*.

ConsumerReports.org *uses lab testing to support the evaluations it publishes.*

rhetorical situations

genres

processes

strategies

research MLA / APA

media / design

readings

ALI HEINEKAMP

Juno: *Not Just Another Teen Movie*

It all starts with a chair, where Juno (Ellen Page) has unprotected sex with her best friend Bleeker (Michael Cera). Several weeks later, she's at a convenience store, buying a pregnancy test. Only sixteen, Juno faces the terrifying task of telling her parents that she is pregnant. With their support, Juno moves forward in her decision to give birth and give the child to Mark (Jason Bateman) and Vanessa (Jennifer Garner), a wealthy and seemingly perfect married couple looking to adopt. Although the situations *Juno*'s characters find themselves in and their dialogue may be criticized as unrealistic, the film, written by Diablo Cody and directed by Jason Reitman, successfully portrays the emotions of a teen being shoved into maturity way too fast.

Much of the time, *Juno* seems unrealistic because it seems to treat the impact of teen pregnancy so lightly. The consequences of Juno's pregnancy are sugar-coated to such an extent that in many cases, they are barely apparent. The film downplays the emotional struggle that a pregnant woman would feel in deciding to give birth and then put that child up for adoption, and it ignores the discomforts of pregnancy, such as mood swings and nausea.

Likewise, *Juno*'s dialogue is too good to be true — funny and clever, but unrealistic. For example, Juno tells Mark and Vanessa "If I could just have the thing and give it to you now, I totally would. But I'm guessing it looks probably like a sea monkey right now, and we should let it get a little cuter." At another point, talking about her absent mother, Juno says, "Oh, and she inexplicably mails me a cactus every Valentine's Day. And I'm like, 'Thanks a heap, coyote ugly. This cactus-gram stings even worse than your abandonment.'" As funny as they are, the creatively quirky one-liners often go a bit too far, detracting from both the gravity of Juno's situation and the film's believability.

But although the situations and dialogue are unrealistic, the emotional heart of the movie is believable — and moving. Despite the movie's lack of realism in portraying her pregnancy, Juno's vulnerability transforms her character and situation into something much more believable. Juno mentions at various times that her classmates stare at her stomach and talk about her behind her back, but initially she seems

Ellen Page as Juno.

unconcerned with the negative attention. This façade falls apart, how-ever, when Juno accuses Bleeker, the baby's father, of being ashamed of the fact that he and Juno have had sex. The strong front she is put-ting up drops when she bursts out, "At least you don't have to have the evidence under your sweater." This break in Juno's strength reveals her vulnerability and makes her character relatable and believable.

The juxtaposition of Juno's teenage quirks and the adult situation 5 she's in also reminds us of her youth and vulnerability. As a result of the adult situation Juno finds herself in and her generally stoic demeanor, it's easy to see her as a young adult. But the film fills each scene with visual reminders that Juno is just a kid being forced into sit-uations beyond her maturity level. At a convenience store, Juno buys a pregnancy test along with a licorice rope. She calls Women Now, an abortion clinic, on a phone that looks like a hamburger. And while she is giving birth, she wears long, brightly striped socks. These subtle visual cues help us remember the reality of Juno's position as both physically an adult and emotionally an adolescent.

While the dialogue is too clever to be realistic, in the end it's car-ried by the movie's heart. Scott Tobias from the entertainment website

rhetorical situations

genres

processes

strategies

research MLA / APA

media / design

readings

The A.V. Club says it best when he writes that the colorful dialogue is often "too ostentatious for its own good, but the film's sincerity is what ultimately carries it across." In fact, intensely emotional scenes are marked by their *lack* of witty dialogue. For example, when Juno runs into Vanessa at the mall, Vanessa, reluctantly at first, kneels down to talk to the baby through Juno's stomach. Vanessa's diction while talking to the baby is so simple, so expected. She simply starts with, "Hi baby, it's me. It's Vanessa," and then continues, "I can't wait to meet you." This simple, everyday statement stands out in comparison to the rest of the well-crafted, humorous script. For her part, Juno simply stares admiringly at Vanessa. She doesn't have to say anything to transform the scene into a powerful one. Another scene in which the dialogue stops being clever is the one in which Juno and Bleeker lie side by side in a hospital bed after Juno has given birth, Juno in tears and Bleeker lost in thought. They don't need to say anything for us to feel their pain at the realization that although the pregnancy is over, it will never truly be in the past. The absence of dialogue in scenes such as these actually contributes to their power. We finally see more than stoicism and sarcasm from Juno: we see caring and fear, which are feelings most would expect of a pregnant teen.

There has been much concern among critics that as a pregnant teenager, Juno doesn't present a good role model for teen girls. Worrying that teens may look up to Juno so much that being pregnant becomes "cool," Dana Stevens writes in *Slate*, "Let's hope that the teenage girls of America don't cast their condoms to the wind in hopes of becoming as cool as 16-year-old Juno MacGuff." But it is not Juno's pregnancy that makes her cool: it is her ability to overcome the difficult obstacles thrown at her, and that strength does make her a good role model. Another critic, Lisa Schwarzbaum from *Entertainment Weekly*, feels that the movie might have been more realistic had Juno chosen to go through with an abortion. It's true that Juno may have chosen the more difficult answer to a teen pregnancy, but she is far from alone in her decision. Perhaps Schwarzbaum underestimates teens in thinking that they would not be able to cope with the emotionally difficult situation Juno chooses. Again, in her strength, Juno is a role model for young women.

Although *Juno* is a comedy filled with improbable situations, exaggerations, and wit, its genuine emotion allows us to connect with and relate to the film. The reality of the characters' emotions in controversial and serious situations allows *Juno* to transcend its own genre. It reaches depths of emotion that are unusual for teenage comedies, proving that *Juno* is not just another teen movie.

Works Cited

Cody, Diablo, scr. *Juno.* Dir. Jason Reitman. Perf. Ellen Page, Michael Cera, Jennifer Garner, Jason Bateman. Fox Searchlight, 2007. Film.

Schwarzbaum, Lisa. Rev. of *Juno*, dir. Jason Reitman. *EW.com*. Entertainment Weekly, 28 Nov. 2007. Web. 14 Apr. 2008.

Stevens, Dana. "Superpregnant: How *Juno* Is *Knocked Up* from the Girl's Point of View." Rev. of *Juno*, dir. Jason Reitman. *Slate.com*. Slate, 5 Dec. 2007. Web. 12 Apr. 2008.

Tobias, Scott. Rev. of *Juno*, dir. Jason Reitman. *The A.V. Club*. The Onion, 6 Dec. 2007. Web. 13 Apr. 2008.

For five more evaluations, see CHAPTER 61.

Heinekamp quickly summarizes Juno's plot and then evaluates the film according to clearly stated criteria. In the process, she responds to several reviewers' comments, joining the critical conversation about the film. She documents her sources according to MLA style.

Key Features / Evaluations

A concise description of the subject. You should include just enough information to let readers who may not be familiar with your subject understand what it is; the goal is to evaluate, not summarize. Depending on your topic and medium, some of this information may be in visual or audio form. Heinekamp briefly describes *Juno*'s main plot points in her first paragraph, only providing what readers need to understand the context of her evaluation.

Clearly defined criteria. You need to determine clear criteria as the basis for your judgment. In reviews or other evaluations written for a broad audience, you can integrate the criteria into the discussion as reasons for

rhetorical situations   genres   processes   strategies   research MLA / APA   media / design   readings

your assessment, as Heinekamp does in her evaluation of *Juno*. In more formal evaluations, you may need to announce your criteria explicitly. Heinekamp evaluates the film based on the power of its emotion and the realism of its situations, characters, and dialogue.

A knowledgeable discussion of the subject.   To evaluate something credibly, you need to show that you know it yourself and that you've researched what other authoritative sources say. Heinekamp cites many examples from *Juno*, showing her knowledge of the film. She also cites reviews from three internet sources, showing that she's researched others' views as well.

A balanced and fair assessment.   An evaluation is centered on a judgment. Heinekamp concedes that *Juno*'s situations and dialogue are unrealistic, but she says it nevertheless "reaches depths of emotion that are unusual for teenage comedies." It is important that any judgment be balanced and fair. Seldom is something all good or all bad. A fair evaluation need not be all positive or all negative; it may acknowledge both strengths and weaknesses. For example, a movie's soundtrack may be wonderful while the plot is not. Heinekamp criticizes *Juno*'s too-witty dialogue and unrealistic situations, even as she appreciates its heart.

Well-supported reasons.   You need to argue for your judgment, providing reasons and evidence that might include visual and audio as well as verbal material. Heinekamp gives several reasons for her positive assessment of *Juno*—the believability of its characters, the intensely emotional scenes, the strength of the main character as a role model—and she supports these reasons with many quotations and examples from the film.

A BRIEF GUIDE TO WRITING EVALUATIONS

Choosing Something to Evaluate

You can more effectively evaluate a limited subject than a broad one: review certain dishes at a local restaurant rather than the entire menu; review one film or episode rather than all the films by Alfred Hitchcock or all eighty *Star Trek* episodes. The more specific and focused your subject, the better you can write about it.

Considering the Rhetorical Situation

3–4
PURPOSE　Are you writing to affect your audience's opinion of a subject? to help others decide what to see, do, or buy? to demonstrate your expertise in a field?

5–8
AUDIENCE　To whom are you writing? What will your audience already know about the subject? What will they expect to learn from your evaluation of it? Are they likely to agree with you or not?

12–15
STANCE　What is your attitude toward the subject, and how will you show that you have evaluated it fairly and appropriately? Think about the tone you want to use: should it be reasonable? Passionate? Critical?

16–18
MEDIA / DESIGN　How will you deliver your evaluation? In print? Online? As a speech? Can you show images or audio or video clips? If you're submitting your text for publication, are there any format requirements?

Generating Ideas and Text

259–60
Explore what you already know.　**FREEWRITE** to answer the following questions: What do you know about this subject or subjects like it? What are your initial or gut feelings, and why do you feel as you do? How does this subject reflect or affect your basic values or beliefs? How have others evaluated subjects like this?

Identify criteria.　Make a list of criteria you think should be used to evaluate your subject. Think about which criteria will likely be important
5–8
262–63
to your **AUDIENCE.** You might find **CUBING** and **QUESTIONING** to be useful processes for thinking about your criteria.

rhetorical situations　genres　processes　strategies　research MLA / APA　media / design　readings

Evaluate your subject. Study your subject closely to determine to what extent it meets each of your criteria. You may want to list your criteria and take notes related to each one, or you may develop a rating scale for each criterion to help stay focused on it. Come up with a tentative judgment.

Compare your subject with others. Often, evaluating something involves **COMPARING AND CONTRASTING** it with similar things. We judge movies in comparison with the other movies we've seen and french fries with the other fries we've tasted. Sometimes those comparisons can be made informally. For other evaluations, you may have to do research — to try on several pairs of jeans before buying any, for example — to see how your subject compares.

348–55

State your judgment as a tentative thesis statement. Your **THESIS STATEMENT** should be one that addresses both pros and cons. "*Covert Affairs* is fun to watch despite its stilted dialogue." "Of the five sport-utility vehicles tested, the Toyota 4Runner emerged as the best in comfort, power, and durability, though not in styling or cargo capacity." Both of these examples offer a judgment but qualify it according to the writer's criteria.

313–15

Anticipate other opinions. I think Will Ferrell is a comic genius whose movies are first-rate. You think Will Ferrell is a terrible actor who makes awful movies. How can I write a review of his latest film that you will at least consider? One way is by **ACKNOWLEDGING** other opinions — and **REFUTING** those opinions as best I can. I may not persuade you to see Ferrell's next film, but I can at least demonstrate that by certain criteria he should be appreciated. You may need to **RESEARCH** how others have evaluated your subject.

336

337

419

Identify and support your reasons. Write out all the **REASONS** you can think of that will convince your audience to accept your judgment. Review your list to identify the most convincing or important reasons. Then review how well your subject meets your criteria and decide how best to **SUPPORT** your reasons: through examples, authoritative opinions, statistics, visual or audio evidence, or something else.

326–27

327–35

Ways of Organizing an Evaluation

Evaluations are usually organized in one of two ways. One way is to introduce what's being evaluated, followed by your judgment, discussing your criteria along the way. This is a useful strategy if your audience may not be familiar with your subject.

[Start with your subject]

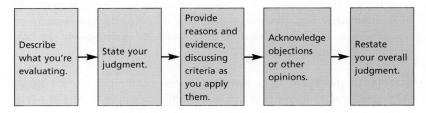

You might also start by identifying your criteria and then follow with a discussion of how well your subject meets those criteria. This strategy foregrounds the process by which you reached your conclusions.

[Start with your criteria]

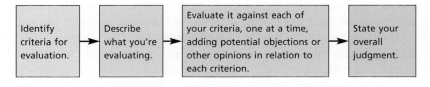

IF YOU NEED MORE HELP

266–68
269–74
275–81
282–86
287–98

See Chapter 25 for guidelines on **DRAFTING,** Chapter 26 on **ASSESSING YOUR DRAFT,** Chapter 27 on **GETTING RESPONSE AND REVISING,** and Chapter 28 on **EDITING AND PROOFREADING.** See Chapter 29 if you are required to submit your report in a writing **PORTFOLIO.**

Lab Reports **14**

Lab reports describe the procedures and results of experiments in the natural sciences, the social sciences, and engineering. We write reports of lab work in school to show instructors that we have followed certain procedures, achieved appropriate results, and drawn accurate conclusions. On the job, lab reports not only describe what we did and what we learned; they may also present data and interpretations to attempt to persuade others to accept our hypotheses, and they become a record that others may refer to in the future. As an example, here is a lab report written by a student for a psychology class at Wittenberg University.

SARAH THOMAS

The Effect of Biofeedback Training on Muscle Tension and Skin Temperature

Purpose

The purpose of this lab was for subjects to train themselves to increase their skin temperature, measured on the index finger of their non-dominant hand, and to decrease their muscle tension, measured over the frontalis muscle, by using biofeedback training. This study is based on the research of Miller and Brucker (1979), which demonstrated that smooth muscles could experience operant conditioning.

Methods

Subjects

Seven subjects were used in this study: five female and two male. The subjects were the undergraduate students of Dr. Jo Wilson in her honors

173

psychophysiology class at Wittenberg University in Springfield, Ohio. All subjects were in their early 20s.

Apparatus

Equipment used in this lab included an Apple Microlab system configured to measure (a) skin temperature through a thermode taped with paper surgical tape onto the index finger of the subjects' nondominant hand and (b) frontalis muscle tension via three electrodes placed over the frontalis. When subjects' skin temperatures were more than the means for the previous 90-second intervals, the computer emitted a tone. It also emitted a tone when muscle tension in the frontalis was less than the mean of the previous interval. See the Procedure section for exact electrode placement specifications.

Materials

Materials used in this lab included paper surgical tape, alcohol to clean off the forehead, conducting gel, wire, electrode collars, and a chair.

Procedure

Upon arriving at the lab, the researchers turned on the Apple Microlab computer. With the aid of Dr. Wilson, subjects had either electrodes attached to their forehead or a thermode attached to the nondominant hand's index finger. The treatment order was random for each subject, and it was reversed for his or her second biofeedback session. The forehead was swiped with alcohol to clean the skin. Electrodes with conducting gel were placed over the frontalis muscle by putting the ground electrode in the center of the forehead and the white electrodes two inches on either side of the center of the forehead. Premeasured electrode collars allowed the researchers to place the conducting gel on the electrodes, peel off the backing on the collar, and place it on the subjects' forehead. The researchers still made sure the electrodes were placed properly. The wire running from the electrodes to the computer was then taped to the subjects' back so it would be out of the way. Subjects were then seated in a comfortable chair with their back to the computer.

Depending on the experimental condition, subjects were told to reduce their frontalis muscle tension by relaxing and even thinking of holding something warm in their hands. They were told that they

would know they were meeting the goal when they heard a tone emitted by the computer.

Each session began with a 90-second baseline period, followed by fifteen 90-second trial periods. During each trial period, a tone was emitted by the computer each time the subjects' frontalis muscle tension was below their mean tension for the previous trial; the tone served as the rewarding stimulus in the operant conditioning paradigm.

When skin temperature was to be measured, a thermode was attached to the index finger of the subjects' nondominant hand with surgical tape. The wire running from the thermode to the computer was taped to the back of their hand so it would be out of their way. Then a 90-second baseline period occurred, followed by fifteen 90-second trial periods. During each trial period, a tone was emitted by the computer each time the subjects' skin temperature was above their mean temperature for the previous trial; once again, the tone served as the rewarding stimulus in the operant conditioning paradigm.

Results

The results of this lab were generally similar (Tables 1 and 2). All subjects demonstrated the ability to increase their skin temperature and decrease the tension in their frontalis muscle in at least one of their sessions. Five subjects were able to increase their skin temperature in both sessions; the same number decreased their muscle tension in both trials.

The majority of subjects (five) were able to both increase the skin temperature of the index finger of their nondominant hand and decrease the tension of their frontalis muscle more during the second trial than the first.

Specifically, Subject 7 had atypical results. This subject's overall average skin temperature was less than the baseline value; the subject's overall average muscle tension was more than the baseline value.

Discussion

The bulk of the data collected in this study validated the research of Neal Miller; the subjects appeared to undergo operant conditioning of their smooth muscles in order to relax their frontalis muscles and increase their skin temperatures. Subjects 3 and 6 each failed to do this in one session; Subject 7 failed to do this several times. This finding is difficult to explain precisely. It is possible that for Subjects 3 and 6, this

Table 1

Skin Temperature in Degrees Fahrenheit During Sessions 1 and 2

	Subject 1	Subject 2	Subject 3	Subject 4	Subject 5	Subject 6	Subject 7
Baseline, Session 1	75.2	77.3	78.5	74.3	78.0	67.7	75.1
Mean skin temp, Session 1	79.3	85.6	78.5	74.4	83.2	73.5	72.6
Mean minus baseline, Session 1	4.1	8.3	0.0	0.1	5.2	5.8	−2.5
Baseline, Session 2	77.9	80.1	69.5	80.9	67.2	73.7	88.0
Mean skin temp, Session 2	79.9	86.3	70.7	84.6	76.8	79.7	88.8
Mean minus baseline, Session 2	2.0	6.2	1.2	3.7	9.6	6.0	0.8
Overall average of mean skin temp minus baseline	3.1	7.3	0.6	1.9	7.4	5.9	−0.85

data was a fluke. For Subject 7, it is likely that the subject was simply stressed due to outside factors before arriving for the first trials of EMG and skin temperature, and this stress skewed the data.

The effect of biofeedback training was generally greater as the operant conditioning became better learned. Learning was indicated by the finding that the majority of the subjects performed better on the second trials than on the first trials. This finding shows the effectiveness of

Table 2

EMG of the Frontalis Muscle in Microvolts for Sessions 1 and 2

	Subject 1	Subject 2	Subject 3	Subject 4	Subject 5	Subject 6	Subject 7
Baseline, Session 1	4.4	4.5	2.8	3.8	7.9	3.1	2.4
Mean EMG, Session 1	2.1	1.4	1.7	3.2	2.0	3.7	3.2
Baseline minus mean, Session 1	2.3	3.1	1.1	0.6	5.9	−0.6	−0.8
Baseline, Session 2	4.1	2.3	3.0	2.9	11.1	6.5	1.9
Mean EMG, Session 2	1.3	1.3	1.4	2.3	2.5	3.2	1.4
Baseline minus mean, Session 2	2.8	1.0	1.6	0.6	8.6	3.3	0.5
Overall average of mean EMG minus baseline	2.6	2.1	1.4	0.6	7.3	1.4	−0.15

biofeedback on reducing factors associated with stress, like muscle tension and low skin temperature; biofeedback's impact is even greater when it is administered over time. The implications of this information are without limits, especially for the treatment of a variety of medical disorders.

There were a few problems with this lab. The subjects all were at different levels of relaxation to begin with. It is impossible to determine the effects of outside events, like exams or other stresses, on their EMG and skin temperature levels. Skin temperature itself could have been altered by cold outside temperatures. Being in a lab may have altered the stress level of some subjects, and noises from outside the lab may have had an effect as well.

If this study were repeated, it would be a good idea to let sub- 15 jects simply be in the lab for a period of time before measures are taken. This would allow the effect of outside temperature to be minimized. It would also reduce the effect of getting used to the lab, decreasing the orienting response. Finally, it would also be good to do the experiment in a soundproof room.

Reference

Miller, N. E., & Brucker, B. S. (1979). A learned visceral response apparently independent of skeletal ones in patients paralyzed by spinal lesions. In N. Birnbaumer & H. D. Kimmel (Eds.), *Biofeedback and self-regulation* (pp. 287–304). Hillsdale, NJ: Erlbaum.

This report includes sections commonly part of lab reports in the natural and social sciences: purpose, method, results, discussion, and references. Some reports keep results and discussion in one section; some reports include an abstract; and some reports include one or more appendices containing tables, calculations, and other supplemental material, depending on the audience and publication. In this example, the author assumes that her audience understands basic terms used in the report, such as frontalis muscle and biofeedback. The report is formatted and documented according to APA style.

Key Features / Lab Reports

An explicit title.   Lab report titles should describe the report factually and explicitly to let readers know exactly what the report is about and to provide keywords for indexes and search engines. Avoid phrases like "an Investigation into" or "a Study of" and titles that are clever or cute. Thomas's title, "The Effect of Biofeedback Training on Muscle Tension and Skin Temperature," clearly describes the report's subject and includes the keywords needed for indexing (*biofeedback training, muscle tension, skin temperature*).

rhetorical situations — genres — processes — strategies — research MLA / APA — media / design — readings

Abstract. Some lab reports include a one-paragraph, 100–200-word abstract, a summary of the report's purpose, method, and discussion.

Purpose. Sometimes called an "Introduction," this section describes the reason for conducting the study: Why is this research important, and why are you doing it? What has been done by others, and how does your work relate to previous work? What will your research tell your audience?

Methods. Here you describe how you conducted the study, including the materials and equipment you used and the procedures you followed. This section is usually written as a narrative, explaining the process you followed in order to allow others to repeat your study, step-by-step. Your explanation should thoroughly describe the following:

- subjects studied and any necessary contextual information
- apparatus — equipment used, by brand and model number
- materials used
- procedures — including reference to the published work that describes any procedures you used that someone else had already followed; the techniques you used and any modifications you made to them; any statistical methods you used

Results and discussion. Here you analyze the results and present their implications, explain your logic in accepting or rejecting your initial hypotheses, relate your work to previous work in the field, and discuss the experiment's design and techniques and how they may have affected the results: what did you find out, and what does it mean? In longer reports, you may have two separate sections. "Results" should focus on the factual data you collected by doing the study; "Discussion" should speculate about what the study means: why the results turned out as they did, and what the implications for future studies may be.

References.   List works cited in your report, alphabetized by author's last name and using the appropriate documentation style.

Appendices.   Appendices are optional, presenting information that is too detailed for the body of the report.

Appropriate format.   The design conventions for lab reports vary from discipline to discipline, so you'll need to check to see that yours meets the appropriate requirements. Find out whether any sections need to start their own page, whether you need to include a list of figures, whether you need to include a separate title page — and whether there are any other conventions you need to follow.

A BRIEF GUIDE TO WRITING LAB REPORTS

Considering the Rhetorical Situation

3–4 ■	**PURPOSE**	Why are you writing? To demonstrate your ability to follow the appropriate methods and make logical inferences? To persuade others that your hypotheses are sound and your conclusions believable? To provide a record of the experiment for others?
5–8 ■	**AUDIENCE**	Can you assume that your audience is familiar with the field's basic procedures? How routine were your procedures? Which procedures need to be explained in greater detail so your audience can repeat them?
12–15 ■	**STANCE**	Whatever your attitude toward the topic, lab reports need to have an impersonal, analytical tone. Take care not to be too informal, and don't try to be cute.
16–18 ■	**MEDIA / DESIGN**	Are you planning to deliver your report in print or online? All lab reports have headings; choose a typeface that includes bold or italics so your headings will show clearly.

Generating Ideas and Text

Research your subject.   Researchers do not work in isolation; rather, each study contributes to an ever-growing body of information, and you need to situate your work in that context. **RESEARCH** what studies others have done on the same subject and what procedures they followed.

● 419

Take careful notes as you perform your study.   A lab report must be repeatable. Another researcher should be able to duplicate your study exactly, using only your report as a guide, so you must document every method, material, apparatus, and procedure carefully. Break down proce- dures and activities into discrete parts, and record them in the order in which they occurred. **ANALYZE CAUSES AND EFFECTS**; think about whether you should **COMPARE** your findings with other studies. Take careful notes so that you'll be able to **EXPLAIN PROCESSES** you followed.

◆ 318–22
348–55
382–86

Draft the report a section at a time.   You may find it easiest to start with the "Methods" or "Results" section first, then **DRAFT** the "Discussion," followed by the "Purpose." Do the "Abstract" last.

◐ 266–68

- Write in complete sentences and paragraphs.
- Avoid using the first person *I* or *we*; keep the focus on the study and the actions taken.
- Use the active voice as much as possible ("the rats pushed the lever" rather than "the lever was pushed by the rats").
- Use the past tense throughout the report.
- Place subjects and verbs close together to make your sentences easy to follow.
- Use precise terms consistently throughout the report; don't alternate among synonyms.
- Be sure that each pronoun refers clearly to one noun.

Organizing a Lab Report

Lab reports vary in their details but generally include these sections:

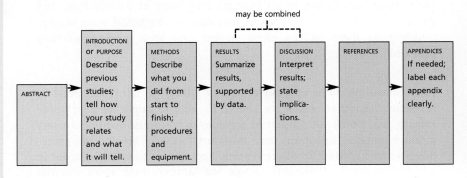

269–74
275–81
282–86
287–98

IF YOU NEED MORE HELP

See Chapter 26 on **ASSESSING YOUR OWN WRITING,** Chapter 27 on **GETTING RESPONSE AND REVISING,** and Chapter 28 on **EDITING AND PROOFREADING.** See Chapter 29 if you are required to submit your report in a writing **PORTFOLIO.**

We write memoirs to explore our past—about shopping for a party dress with Grandma, or driving a car for the first time, or breaking up with our first love. Memoirs focus on events and people and places that are important to us. We usually have two goals when we write a memoir: to capture an important moment and to convey something about its significance for us. The following example is from Pulitzer Prize–winning journalist Rick Bragg's autobiography, *All Over but the Shoutin'*. Bragg grew up in Alabama, and in this memoir he recalls when, as a teenager, he paid a final visit to his dying father.

RICK BRAGG

All Over but the Shoutin'

He was living in a little house in Jacksonville, Alabama, a college and mill town that was the closest urban center—with its stoplights and a high school and two supermarkets—to the country roads we roamed in our raggedy cars. He lived in the mill village, in one of those houses the mills subsidized for their workers, back when companies still did things like that. It was not much of a place, but better than anything we had ever lived in as a family. I knocked and a voice like an old woman's, punctuated with a cough that sounded like it came from deep in the guts, told me to come on in, it ain't locked.

It was dark inside, but light enough to see what looked like a bundle of quilts on the corner of a sofa. Deep inside them was a ghost of a man, his hair and beard long and going dirty gray, his face pale and cut with deep grooves. I knew I was in the right house because my daddy's only real possessions, a velvet-covered board pinned with medals, sat inside a glass cabinet on a table. But this couldn't be him.

He coughed again, spit into a can and struggled to his feet, but stopped somewhere short of standing straight up, as if a stoop was all he could manage. "Hey, Cotton Top," he said, and then I knew. My daddy, who was supposed to be a still-young man, looked like the walking dead, not just old but damaged, poisoned, used up, crumpled up and thrown in a corner to die. I thought that the man I would see would be the trim, swaggering, high-toned little rooster of a man who stared back at me from the pages of my mother's photo album, the young soldier clowning around in Korea, the arrow-straight, good-looking boy who posed beside my mother back before the fields and mop handle and the rest of it took her looks. The man I remembered had always dressed nice even when there was no cornmeal left, whose black hair always shone with oil, whose chin, even when it wobbled from the beer, was always angled up, high.

I thought he would greet me with that strong voice that sounded so fine when he laughed and so evil when, slurred by a quart of corn likker, he whirled through the house and cried and shrieked, tormented by things we could not see or even imagine. I thought he would be the man and monster of my childhood. But that man was as dead as a man could be, and this was what remained, like when a snake sheds its skin and leaves a dry and brittle husk of itself hanging in the Johnson grass.

"It's all over but the shoutin' now, ain't it, boy," he said, and when he let the quilt slide from his shoulders I saw how he had wasted away, how the bones seemed to poke out of his clothes, and I could see how it killed his pride to look this way, unclean, and he looked away from me for a moment, ashamed.

He made a halfhearted try to shake my hand but had a coughing fit again that lasted a minute, coughing up his life, his lungs, and after that I did not want to touch him. I stared at the tops of my sneakers, ashamed to look at his face. He had a dark streak in his beard below his lip, and I wondered why, because he had never liked snuff. Now I know it was blood.

I remember much of what he had to say that day. When you don't see someone for eight, nine years, when you see that person's life red on their lips and know that you will never see them beyond this day, you listen close, even if what you want most of all is to run away.

"Your momma, she alright?" he said.

I said I reckon so.

"The other boys? They alright?"

I said I reckon so.

Then he was quiet for a minute, as if trying to find the words to a question to which he did not really want an answer.

"They ain't never come to see me. How come?"

I remember thinking, fool, why do you think? But I just choked down my words, and in doing so I gave up the only real chance I would ever have to accuse him, to attack him with the facts of his own sorry nature and the price it had cost us all. The opportunity hung perfectly still in the air in front of my face and fists, and I held my temper and let it float on by. I could have no more challenged him, berated him, hurt him, than I could have kicked some three-legged dog. Life had kicked his ass pretty good.

"How come?"

I just shrugged.

For the next few hours—unless I was mistaken, having never had one before—he tried to be my father. Between coughing and long pauses when he fought for air to generate his words, he asked me if I liked school, if I had ever gotten any better at math, the one thing that just flat evaded me. He asked me if I ever got even with the boy who blacked my eye ten years ago, and nodded his head, approvingly, as I described how I followed him into the boys' bathroom and knocked his dick string up to his watch pocket, and would have dunked his head in the urinal if the aging principal, Mr. Hand, had not had to pee and caught me dragging him across the concrete floor.

He asked me about basketball and baseball, said he had heard I had a good game against Cedar Springs, and I said pretty good, but it was two years ago, anyway. He asked if I had a girlfriend and I said, "One," and he said, "Just one?" For the slimmest of seconds he almost grinned and the young, swaggering man peeked through, but disappeared again in the disease that cloaked him. He talked and talked and never said a word, at least not the words I wanted.

He never said he was sorry.

He never said he wished things had turned out different.

He never acted like he did anything wrong.

Part of it, I know, was culture. Men did not talk about their feelings in his hard world. I did not expect, even for a second, that he would bare his soul. All I wanted was a simple acknowledgment that he was wrong, or at least too drunk to notice that he left his pretty wife and sons alone again and again, with no food, no money, no way to get any, short of begging, because when she tried to find work he yelled, screamed, refused. No, I didn't expect much.

After a while he motioned for me to follow him into a back room where he had my present, and I planned to take it and run. He handed me a long, thin box, and inside was a brand-new, well-oiled Remington .22 rifle. He said he had bought it some time back, just kept forgetting to give it to me. It was a fine gun, and for a moment we were just like anybody else in the culture of that place, where a father's gift of a gun to his son is a rite. He said, with absolute seriousness, not to shoot my brothers.

I thanked him and made to leave, but he stopped me with a hand on my arm and said wait, that ain't all, that he had some other things for me. He motioned to three big cardboard egg cartons stacked against one wall.

Inside was the only treasure I truly have ever known.   25

I had grown up in a house in which there were only two books, the King James Bible and the spring seed catalog. But here, in these boxes, were dozens of hardback copies of everything from Mark Twain to Sir Arthur Conan Doyle. There was a water-damaged Faulkner, and the nearly complete set of Edgar Rice Burroughs's *Tarzan*. There was poetry and trash, Zane Grey's *Riders of the Purple Sage,* and a paperback with two naked women on the cover. There was a tiny, old copy of *Arabian Nights,* threadbare Hardy Boys, and one Hemingway. He had bought most of them at a yard sale, by the box or pound, and some at a flea market. He did not even know what he was giving me, did not recognize most of the writers. "Your momma said you still liked to read," he said.

There was Shakespeare. My father did not know who he was, exactly, but he had heard the name. He wanted them because they were pretty, because they were wrapped in fake leather, because they looked like rich folks' books. I do not love Shakespeare, but I still have those books. I would not trade them for a gold monkey.

"They's maybe some dirty books in there, by mistake, but I know you ain't interested in them, so just throw 'em away," he said. "Or at least, throw 'em away before your momma sees 'em." And then I swear to God he winked.

I guess my heart should have broken then, and maybe it did, a little. I guess I should have done something, anything, besides mumble

"Thank you, Daddy." I guess that would have been fine, would not have betrayed in some way my mother, my brothers, myself. But I just stood there, trapped somewhere between my long-standing, comfortable hatred, and what might have been forgiveness. I am trapped there still.

Bragg's memoir illustrates all the features that make a memoir good: how the son and father react to each other creates the kind of suspense that keeps us reading; vivid details and rich dialogue bring the scene to life. His later reflections make the significance of that final meeting very clear.

For five more memoirs, see CHAPTER 62.

Key Features / Memoirs

A good story.   Your memoir should be interesting, to yourself and others. It need not be about a world-shaking event, but your topic — and how you write about it — should interest your readers. At the center of most good stories stands a conflict or question to be resolved. The most compelling memoirs feature some sort of situation or problem that needs resolution. That need for resolution is another name for suspense. It's what makes us want to keep reading.

Vivid details.   Details bring a memoir to life by giving readers mental images of the sights, sounds, smells, tastes, and textures of the world in which your story takes place. The goal is to show as well as tell, to take readers there. When Bragg describes a "voice like an old woman's, punctuated with a cough that sounded like it came from deep in the guts," we can hear his dying father ourselves. A memoir is more than simply a report of what happened; it uses vivid details and dialogue to bring the events of the past to life, much as good fiction brings to life events that the writer makes up or embellishes. Depending on your topic and medium, you may want to provide some of the details in audio or visual form.

Clear significance.   Memories of the past are filtered through our view from the present: we pick out some moments in our lives as significant, some as more important or vivid than others. Over time, our interpretations change, and our memories themselves change.

A good memoir conveys something about the significance of its subject. As a writer, you need to reveal something about what the incident means to you. You don't, however, want to simply announce the significance as if you're tacking on the moral of the story. Bragg tells us that he's "trapped between [his] long-standing, comfortable hatred, and what might have been forgiveness," but he doesn't come right out and say that's why the incident is so important to him.

A BRIEF GUIDE TO WRITING MEMOIRS

Choosing an Event to Write About

260–61 ○

LIST several events or incidents from your past that you consider significant in some way. They do not have to be earthshaking; indeed, they may involve a quiet moment that only you see as important — a brief encounter with a remarkable person, a visit to a special place, a memorable achievement (or failure), something that makes you laugh whenever you think about it. Writing about events that happened at least a few years ago is often easier than writing about recent events because you can more easily step back and see those events with a clear perspective. To choose the event that you will write about, consider how well you can recall what happened, how interesting it will be to readers, and whether you want to share it with an audience.

Considering the Rhetorical Situation

3–4 ■

PURPOSE What is the importance of the memory you are trying to convey? How will this story help your readers (and you yourself) understand you, as you were then and as you are now?

5–8 ■

AUDIENCE Who are your readers? What do you want them to think of you after reading your memoir? How can you help them understand your experience?

STANCE   What impression do you want to give, and how can your words contribute to that impression? What tone do you want to project? Sincere? Serious? Humorous? Detached? Self-critical?

12–15

MEDIA / DESIGN   Will your memoir be a print document? A speech? Will it be posted on a website? Can you include photographs, audio or video clips, or other visual texts?

16–18

Generating Ideas and Text

Think about what happened.   Take a few minutes to write out an account of the incident: **WHAT** happened, **WHERE** it took place, **WHO** else was involved, what was said, how you feel about it, and so on. Can you identify any tension or conflict that will make for a compelling story? If not, you might want to rethink your topic.

262–63

Consider its significance.   Why do you still remember this event? What effect has it had on your life? What makes you want to tell someone else about it? Does it say anything about you? What about it might interest someone else? If you have trouble answering these questions, you should probably find another topic. But in general, once you have defined the significance of the incident, you can be sure you have a story to tell—and a reason for telling it.

Think about the details.   The best memoirs connect with readers by giving them a sense of what it was like to be there, leading them to experience in words and images what the writer experienced in life. Spend some time **DESCRIBING** the incident, writing what you see, hear, smell, touch, and taste when you envision it. Do you have any photos or memorabilia or other **VISUAL** materials you might include in your memoir? Try writing out **DIALOGUE,** things that were said (or, if you can't recall exactly, things that might have been said). Look at what you come up with—is there detail enough to bring the scene to life? Anything that might be called vivid? If you don't have enough detail, you might reconsider whether you recall

367–75

591–99

376–81

259–61 ◯

enough about the incident to write about it. If you have trouble coming up with plenty of detail, try **FREEWRITING**, **LISTING**, or **LOOPING**.

Ways of Organizing Memoirs

[Tell about the event from beginning to end]

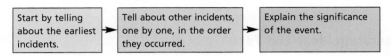

Start by telling about the earliest incidents. → Tell about other incidents, one by one, in the order they occurred. → Explain the significance of the event.

[Start at the end and tell how the event came about]

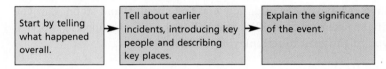

Start by telling what happened overall. → Tell about earlier incidents, introducing key people and describing key places. → Explain the significance of the event.

IF YOU NEED MORE HELP

See Chapter 25 for guidelines on **DRAFTING**, Chapter 26 on **ASSESSING YOUR OWN WRITING**, Chapter 27 on **GETTING RESPONSE AND REVISING**, and Chapter 28 on **EDITING AND PROOFREADING**. See Chapter 29 if you are required to submit your memoir in a writing **PORTFOLIO**.

266–68 ◯
269–74
275–81
282–86
287–98

Profiles are written portraits — of people, places, events, or other things. We find profiles of celebrities, travel destinations, and offbeat festivals in magazines and newspapers, on radio and TV. A profile presents a subject in an entertaining way that conveys its significance, showing us something or someone that we may not have known existed or that we see every day but don't know much about. Here, for example, is a profile of one student's quest to break a Guinness world record. It originally appeared in *Prized Writing*, an anthology of writing done by students at the University of California at Davis.

CHRISTIAN DANIELSEN

Paperclip Man

Radhakant Bajpai of India currently has the longest bunch of ear hair in the world, measuring just over 5 inches. In 1997, Davis Huxly of Australia pulled a Boeing 747 weighing 184 tons a distance of 91 meters. And in 1993, the Italian clothing firm Benetton constructed what is still the largest condom ever made: a 72-foot monster that covered an obelisk in Paris to mark World AIDS Day. Such is the world of world records, where the physically amazing, the painfully stupid, and the laughably bizarre are meticulously recorded in *Guinness World Records*, the ultimate authority on superlative feats.

Some records are truly pointless. Enter Daniel Meyer, a 22-year-old student at the University of California at Davis. Dan has wanted a world record since high school, but always knew that his title would have to be something, well, obscure. And after a lot of consideration, Dan decided to challenge the world record for the longest chain of paper-clips put together in a 24-hour period. This is the story of Dan. The Paper-clip Man.

A week before his attempt took place on May 23, Dan spoke to me about his world-record dream. Dan is basketball-player tall and thin with short brown hair. He laughed frequently and answered my questions with a dry and slightly self-mocking sense of humor. "I've always wanted a record. The ones requiring strength and agility, anything studly really, were immediately out," he said. "It was really a process of elimination, going through the book and crossing out records that definitely weren't me. And when I came across the paperclip record, I thought, 'Yes. I can do this.'" The current record was set in 2000 and stands at 895 yards, or just shy of nine football fields. That chain contained 22,025 paperclips.

Ms. Jeanine Van der Meiren of Belgium is the owner of that record. Dan didn't try to contact Meiren about his attempt to dethrone her and said he would have no remorse about claiming the title for himself: "At first, I was very concerned about breaking her record. Very concerned. But then I found out that she actually has more than one record. So I'm not taking this little old lady's reason for living away from her." He also deadpanned, "I do harvest a secret paranoia that she's going to find out where I'm doing this and she'll come and try to disrupt it, but I proba-bly give myself too much credit."

Setting a world record is a complex process. Dan was required to   5
videotape the entire 24-hour period. He had to have some kind of local media coverage. He also had to furnish color photographs and have two witnesses with "some standing in the community" watch the entire event. Finding two people to watch him assemble paperclips for 24 hours was a challenge. Dan offered perks to anyone willing to help him out, including an Internet connection, food, and a television with DVD and video hookups, but even so, the response was underwhelming.

By May 17, only one week before his attempt, Dan had only secured the help of his friend Troy Sammons, a vet student and a friend of Dan's through their church. Troy wasn't terribly excited about his assignment, but was glad he could help out his friend: "It's kind of humorous, and I really admire Dan for setting a goal and going for it." With only a week to go before "D-Day," as Dan called it, he was getting a little nervous about finding another witness. His publicity effort included an open call for witnesses on his website at www.paperclipchallenge.com and

This image of Daniel Meyer by John Burgess won first prize in the 31st annual San Francisco Bay Area Press Photographers Association contest.

conducting an interview for the UC Davis newspaper, the *California Aggie*, in the hopes of catching someone's attention. "People seem to be very attracted to the weirdness of it, so I'm hoping that will help," he said. The website also has a message board. Various notes offer Dan encouragement, sarcastic advice, and one marriage proposal. Dan's website even reached one fan in Leipzig, Germany, who invited him to join the International Record Breakers' Club (www.recordholders.org) if he were to succeed.

Dan is a mathematics major and hopes to teach eventually. As he described his vision for how the 24 hours would play out, he spoke logically, with attention to every detail. He spent months preparing. Along with accounting for Guinness requirements, Dan had to find a corporate sponsor willing to donate 50,000 paperclips (about $200 worth), more than enough to break the record. He clearly wanted to make sure his effort would remain standing for a while, "I definitely want to smash the old record," he said. "I've done practice rounds with a spreadsheet that makes projections; and right now I would probably go about 1,000 feet (about 12,000 clips) over." Dan sent out four letters to various office supply companies. He got two polite declines and one no-answer. But then, Dan said, "Office Depot called and wanted to know if it was legit. At first their representative was suspicious that it was some kind of prank. I was so happy that someone had replied. Eventually I convinced him and they sent me 50,000 paperclips and some t-shirts."

That brought up another problem. What does one do with a chain of paperclips that would stretch out almost a mile long? Borrowing an idea from Jeanine van der Meiren's strategy, Dan constructed a giant wooden spool that an assistant would use to wind up the chain as Dan would work through the night. Unfortunately, according to Guinness rules, Dan was required to verify the chain's length by stretching it out fully when finished, all within the 24-hour period. Dan didn't work out all the details of this annoying requirement before the attempt, but he imagined going out to one of Davis's many country roads and unraveling it, praying for no tangles. As for what he wanted to do with the chain when everything was done? "I have no idea."

I showed up at Dan's apartment on May 23 at 2:50 p.m., ten minutes early. A van from the local NBC news affiliate was parked outside. Apparently Dan had gotten his media coverage. A typed sign on his front door was the only other indication that a world record attempt was being

made here. It read, "Record Breaking in Progress. Come in!" I walked in out of the heat to see an elaborate setup. The couches had been moved into an arc facing the giant spool and a small card table with several chairs. A television displayed the video feed of the room and a digital clock of the current time. The little dining room had an iMac set up with Dan's spreadsheet and AOL's instant messenger, allowing Dan to get detailed statistics on his pace as he worked and also the ability to give dictated updates to friends online. In one corner were two giant stacks of small boxes, each containing exactly 100 paperclips. Each stack had a sign above it reading "For the Tie" and "For the Win," respectively. Dan greeted me as I walked in the door and then quickly went back to checking last-minute details, nervously giving orders to his support staff of friends while the clock clicked ahead to 3:00:00 p.m. He was wearing his bright red Office Depot t-shirt.

Standing next to the card table were a cameraman and Sacramento reporter John Alston. John was testing his microphone. The expression on his face alternated between amusement and the look of a reporter who was seeing a slow news day. Troy Sammons was sitting on one of the couches, along with Dan's second witness, David Fillingame. Another student and friend from Dan's church, David had known about the project for a long time and was holding out as a possible emergency witness. "There are worse things you could do with your day," he laughed. "Like going to class." 10

Other friends scurried into position as the final seconds approached. Dan had a total of four assistants: one spooler, two people to unload and untangle paperclips from boxes and finally, one person to pass Dan paperclips in the right orientation to allow for maximum speed. All legal under Guinness rules.

3:00 p.m. Everyone let out a cheer as Dan began to clip away. His technique was flawless, fingers racing like an intricate machine while he talked and made jokes, only rarely taking his eyes off of his hands. At one point he had to ask his assistants to speed up. The spool was being held in place by a stack of books on either side, specifically, Dan's math textbooks. "The irony is not lost on me," he quipped cheerfully.

Most of Dan's friends were excited about the prospect of being on TV as Alston prepared to broadcast a teaser segment for the six o'clock news. "I need some Vaseline for my teeth!" cracked Dan, clipping furiously. All of a sudden, Alston went into broadcast mode, locked onto the camera and speaking with the anchors back in the studio in a pro-nounced and practiced voice. "Dave and Lois, I'm standing here with UC Davis student Dan Meyer who is attempting to break the world record for longest paperclip chain. It's not as dull as watching paint dry . . . but it's close. How are you feeling, champ?"

Dan's reply, "I'm great, John. No cramping here!" Laughter broke out behind the camera.

12:31 a.m. A small crisis broke out at around midnight. With the spool containing three tightly wound layers of almost 10,000 clips, David asked the uncomfortable question of whether they would really come off of the spool like that without tangling. Realizing the terrible possibility that nine hours of work might have gone to waste, Dan took only his second break to come up with a plan. Several of Dan's engineering friends were present, and they eagerly threw out suggestions. Eventually, someone came up with the clever idea of separating each layer with Saran Wrap and duct tape. Immediately Dan went back to work. He was clearly annoyed, furious with himself that he could have overlooked such an important detail, and frightened by the thought that now he would now have to race just to break the old record, instead of obliterating it. 15

4:15 a.m. A small cheer went up as the latest spreadsheet numbers informed Dan that he had broken the old record, as far as total number of clips put together. His pace had slowed a little, but he was determined to make his margin of victory as large as possible. He also wanted to account for the possibility that the first 10,000 clips would be essentially useless. His friends, meanwhile, had succumbed to fatigue. Dave and Troy slouched on the sofa, eyes drooping as they watched a movie to fight off sleep and boredom. "Watching Dan is kind of hypnotizing," Dave yawned. "Otherwise I'm sure I would have dropped off a long time ago."

Sleep deprivation also produced some strange commentary. Dan's friend Miranda asked him, "You know what you should do with all these paperclips Dan, when this is all done?"

"What?"

"You should . . . you should fill up a swimming pool and jump in!"

"What a weird, non sequitur thing to say, Miranda," Dan replied, laughing. 20

1:30 p.m. A small army of friends came out to a remote farming road to help Dan stretch the chain out to full length. A KCRA cameraman was present for a follow-up, and Dan's parents had also come out to help. Dan's mom walked next to the crew, looking proud and amused at the same time. "Dan's always had a lot of initiative and leadership skills, and he's wanted to do something like this for a long time," she said. "Of all the things he could be doing in college, this is OK by me."

The unspooling process was slow, frustrating work. Dan soon discovered how flimsy paperclips are as they broke under the slightest tug from the spool. As the crew walked slowly down the road, Dan had to continually order halts to fix broken links as well as tangles and snags, all eating up precious time. The Saran Wrap turned out to have worked reasonably well, but the duct tape was a mistake. It tore the wrap as Dan yanked it off, exposing underlying layers and causing more tangles. At this point, Dan hadn't slept for close to 36 hours, and the frustration of this rather banal detail derailing all his work was starting to take its toll. His friends offered well-intentioned advice and tried to take charge, but this usually made matters worse. Dan's mom wanted him to drink more water. The cameraman asked him distracting interview questions. As a particularly bad tangle halted them, with only about a quarter of the spool unrolled, Dan let out a yell of frustration. With less than an hour to go, he could only unroll as much as possible and hope the people at Guinness would understand.

One week after Dan's attempt at immortality, his website posts the disappointing news: despite having put together almost 40,000 paperclips, he was unable to measure out enough of them in a straight line to officially break the record. Dan is pinning his hopes on the video that he will send to Guinness, over twenty hours of paperclip assembly footage. He is not optimistic: "The rules are fairly strict, so I would say there's probably only a twenty percent chance they'll accept it." But despite what would seem like a total failure, he speaks cheerfully about his favorite moments of the experience. What started out as one small dream to be the best in the world at something snowballed into a massive undertaking. It came to involve Dan's friends, his family, his school and the local community, and thanks to the Internet, randomly interested people around the globe. A note on his website claims even people in Hawaii saw him on the news. "I think my favorite part was at around 11 p.m. on Friday," he says. "There were almost twenty-five people crammed in my living room and the lights from the news camera were on me. I just never expected it to get that big. I had a lot of fun."

But of course, the million-dollar question is, after losing on a technicality, will he try it again some day? "Well," he laughs, "this paperclip thing is my Mt. Everest. And you don't quit climbing Mt Everest because one of your sherpas dies. But it won't be for a while."

▌▌ For five more profiles, see CHAPTER 63.

This profile focuses on Daniel Meyer and his quest for a world record. The writer engages our interest first by admitting the pointlessness of Meyer's attempt and then by meticulously chronicling his preparation and eventual failure.

Key Features / Profiles

An interesting subject. The subject may be something unusual, or it may be something ordinary shown in an intriguing way. You might profile an interesting person (like Daniel Meyer), a place (like the site of a world record attempt), or an event (like the attempt to break a record).

Any necessary background. A profile usually includes just enough information to let readers know something about the subject's larger context. Danielson lets us know that Meyer is a mathematics major at UC Davis and wants to teach but focuses on his activities involving paperclips.

An interesting angle. A good profile captures its subject from a particular angle. Sometimes finding an angle will be fairly easy because your topic — like trying to build a record-breaking paperclip chain — is offbeat enough to be interesting in and of itself. Other topics, though, may require you to find a particular aspect that you can focus on. For example, a profile of a person might focus on the important work the person does or a challenging hobby he or she pursues; it would likely ignore aspects of the person's life that don't relate to that angle.

A firsthand account.   Whether you are writing about a person, place, or event, you need to spend time observing and interacting with your subject. With a person, interacting means watching and conversing. Journalists tell us that "following the guy around," getting your subject to do something and talk about it at the same time, yields excellent material for a profile. When one writer met Theodor Geisel (Dr. Seuss) before profiling him, she asked him not only to talk about his characters but also to draw one — resulting in an illustration for her profile. With a place or event, interacting may mean visiting and participating, although sometimes you may gather even more information by playing the role of the silent observer.

Engaging details.   You need to include details that bring your subject to life. These may include *specific information* ("The current record was set in 2000 and stands at 895 yards, or just shy of nine football fields"); *sensory images* ("As the crew walked slowly down the road, Dan had to continually order halts to fix broken links as well as tangles and snags"); *figurative language* (Meyer's fingers were "racing like an intricate machine"); *dialogue* (" 'I need some Vaseline for my teeth!' cracked Dan"); and *anecdotes* ("All of a sudden, Alston went into broadcast mode . . ."). Choose details that show rather than tell — that let your audience see and hear your subject rather than merely read an abstract description of it. Sometimes you may let them see and hear it literally, by including *photographs* or *video and audio clips.* And be sure all the details create some *dominant impression* of your subject: the impression that we get out of this profile, for example, is of a good-natured, bright, and energetic young man willing to go all out for an ultimately meaningless goal.

A BRIEF GUIDE TO WRITING PROFILES

Choosing a Suitable Subject

A person, a place, an event — whatever you choose, make sure it's something that arouses your curiosity and that you're not too familiar with. Knowing your subject too well can blind you to interesting details. **LIST**

○ 260–61

five to ten interesting subjects that you can experience firsthand. Obviously, you can't profile a person who won't be interviewed or a place or activity that can't be observed. So before you commit to a topic, make sure you'll be able to carry out firsthand research and not find out too late that the people you need to interview aren't willing or that places you need to visit are off-limits.

Considering the Rhetorical Situation

3–4 **PURPOSE**   Why are you writing the profile? What angle will best achieve your purpose? How can you inform *and engage* your audience?

5–8 **AUDIENCE**   Who is your audience? How familiar are they with your subject? What expectations of your profile might they have? What background information or definitions do you need to provide? How interested will they be—and how can you get their interest?

12–15 **STANCE**   What view of your subject do you expect to present? Sympathetic? Critical? Sarcastic? Will you strive for a carefully balanced perspective?

16–18 **MEDIA / DESIGN**   Will your profile be a print document? Will it be published on the web? Will it be an oral presentation? Can (and should) you include images or any other visuals? Will it be recorded as an audio file or multimodal text?

Generating Ideas and Text

Explore what you already know about your subject.   Why do you find this subject interesting? What do you know about it now? What do you

expect to find out about it from your research? What preconceived ideas about or emotional reactions to this subject do you have? Why do you have them? It may be helpful to try some of the activities in the chapter on GENERATING IDEAS AND TEXT.

259–65

Visit your subject.   If you're writing about an amusement park, go there; if you're profiling the man who runs the carousel, make an appointment to meet and interview him. Get to know your subject — if you profile Ben and Jerry, sample the ice cream! Take along a camera if there's anything you might want to show visually in your profile. Find helpful hints for OBSERVING and INTERVIEWING in the chapter on finding sources.

448–50

If you're planning to interview someone, prepare questions. Danielsen likely asked Daniel Meyer questions like, "What made you want to break the record? Why *this* record? What are the rules for Guinness record attempts?"

Do additional research.   You may be able to write a profile based entirely on your field research. You may, though, need to do some library or web RESEARCH as well, to deepen your understanding, get a different perspective, or fill in gaps. Often the people you interview can help you find sources of additional information; so can the sponsors of events and those in charge of places. To learn more about a city park, for instance, contact the government office that maintains it. Download any good photos of your subject that you find online (such as the one of Daniel Meyer on the following page), both to refer to as you write and to illustrate your profile.

419

Analyze your findings.   Look for patterns, images, recurring ideas or phrases, and engaging details. Look for contrasts or discrepancies: between a subject's words and actions, between the appearance of a place and what goes on there, between your expectations and your research findings. Danielsen may have expected Meyer to take his attempt seriously — but may not have been prepared to see him stay awake for thirty-six hours

Research can lead you to more than just text sources. This photo of Daniel Meyer and the supplies he used in his attempt to break the record was found with a Google search that used his name and "paper clip" as keywords.

352–66 straight. You may find the advice in the **READING STRATEGIES** chapter helpful here.

Come up with an angle. What's most memorable about your subject? What most interests you? What will interest your audience? Danielsen focuses on a college student who, in a unique quest to be the best at something, chooses to try to break a silly world record. Sometimes you'll know your angle from the start; other times you'll need to look further 259–62 into your topic. You might try **CLUSTERING**, **CUBING**, **FREEWRITING**, and **LOOPING**, activities that will help you look at your topic from many different angles.

Note details that support your angle.   Use your angle to focus your
research and generate text. Try **DESCRIBING** your subject as clearly as you
can, **COMPARING** your subject with other subjects of its sort, writing
DIALOGUE that captures your subject. Danielsen, for instance, offers
details, like Daniel Meyer's "bright red Office Depot t-shirt," that help
us see his subject, and he quotes Meyer to give a sense of his attitude
toward his attempt: "You don't quit climbing Mt. Everest because one
of your sherpas dies." Engaging details will bring your subject to life for
your audience. Together, these details should create a dominant impression of your subject.

367–75
348–55
376–81

Ways of Organizing a Profile

[As a narrative]

One common way to organize a profile is by **NARRATING.** For example, if
you are profiling a chess championship, you may write about it chronologically, creating suspense as you move from start to finish. The profile
of Daniel Meyer's record attempt is organized this way.

387–95

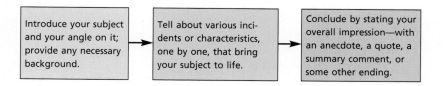

Introduce your subject and your angle on it; provide any necessary background. → Tell about various incidents or characteristics, one by one, that bring your subject to life. → Conclude by stating your overall impression—with an anecdote, a quote, a summary comment, or some other ending.

[As a description]

Sometimes you may organize a profile by **DESCRIBING** — a person or a place,
for instance.

367–75

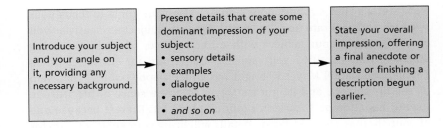

Introduce your subject and your angle on it, providing any necessary background.

Present details that create some dominant impression of your subject:
• sensory details
• examples
• dialogue
• anecdotes
• *and so on*

State your overall impression, offering a final anecdote or quote or finishing a description begun earlier.

266–68
269–74
275–81
282–86
287–98

IF YOU NEED MORE HELP

See Chapter 25 for guidelines on **DRAFTING,** Chapter 26 on **ASSESSING YOUR OWN WRITING,** Chapter 27 on **GETTING RESPONSE AND REVISING,** and Chapter 28 on **EDITING AND PROOFREADING.** See Chapter 29 if you are required to submit your analysis in a writing **PORTFOLIO.**

■ rhetorical situations
▲ genres
○ processes
◆ strategies
● research MLA / APA
□ media / design
▮ readings

Proposals 17

Contractors bid on building projects. Musicians and educators apply for grants. Researchers seek funding. Student leaders call for lights on bike paths. You offer to pay half the cost of a car and insurance if your parents will pay the other half. Lovers propose marriage; friends propose sharing dinner and a movie. These are all examples of proposals: ideas put forward for consideration that say, "Here is a solution to a problem" or "This is what ought to be done." All proposals are arguments: when you propose something, you are trying to persuade others to see a problem in a particular way and to accept your solution to the problem. For example, here is a proposal for reducing the costs of college textbooks, written by an accounting professor at the University of Texas who is chairman of the university's Co-op Bookstore and himself a textbook author.

MICHAEL GRANOF

Course Requirement: Extortion

By now, entering college students and their parents have been warned: textbooks are outrageously expensive. Few textbooks for semester-long courses retail for less than $120, and those for science and math courses typically approach $180. Contrast this with the $20 to $30 cost of most hardcover best sellers and other trade books.

Perhaps these students and their parents can take comfort in knowing that the federal government empathizes with them, and in an attempt to ease their pain Congress asked its Advisory Committee on Student Financial Assistance to suggest a cure for the problem. Unfortunately, though, the committee has proposed a remedy that would only worsen the problem.

The committee's report, released in May, mainly proposes strengthening the market for used textbooks — by encouraging college bookstores to guarantee that they will buy back textbooks, establishing online book swaps among students, and urging faculty to avoid switching textbooks from one semester to the next. The fatal flaw in that proposal (and similar ones made by many state legislatures) is that used books are the cause of, not the cure for, high textbook prices.

Yet there is a way to lighten the load for students in their budgets, if not their backpacks. With small modifications to the institutional arrangements between universities, publishers, and students, textbook costs could be reduced — and these changes could be made without government intervention.

Today the used-book market is exceedingly well organized and 5 efficient. Campus bookstores buy back not only the books that will be used at their university the next semester but also those that will not. Those that are no longer on their lists of required books they resell to national wholesalers, which in turn sell them to college bookstores on campuses where they will be required. This means that even if a text is being adopted for the first time at a particular college, there is almost certain to be an ample supply of used copies.

As a result, publishers have the chance to sell a book to only one of the multiple students who eventually use it. Hence, publishers must cover their costs and make their profit in the first semester their books are sold — before used copies swamp the market. That's why the prices are so high.

As might be expected, publishers do what they can to undermine the used-book market, principally by coming out with new editions every three or four years. To be sure, in rapidly changing fields like biology and physics, the new editions may be academically defensible. But in areas like algebra and calculus, they are nothing more than a transparent attempt to ensure premature textbook obsolescence. Publishers also try to discourage students from buying used books by bundling the text with extra materials like workbooks and CDs that are not reusable and therefore cannot be passed from one student to another.

The system could be much improved if, first of all, colleges and publishers would acknowledge that textbooks are more akin to computer software than to trade books. A textbook's value, like that of a software program, is not in its physical form, but rather in its intellectual content. Therefore, just as software companies typically "site license" to colleges, so should textbook publishers.

rhetorical situations   genres   processes   strategies   research MLA / APA   media / design   readings

Here's how it would work: A teacher would pick a textbook, and the college would pay a negotiated fee to the publisher based on the number of students enrolled in the class. If there were 50 students in the class, for example, the fee might be $15 per student, or $750 for the semester. If the text were used for ten semesters, the publisher would ultimately receive a total of $150 ($15 × 10) for each student enrolled in the course, or as much as $7,500.

In other words, the publisher would have a stream of revenue for as long as the text was in use. Presumably, the university would pass on this fee to the students, just as it does the cost of laboratory supplies and computer software. But the students would pay much less than the $900 a semester they now typically pay for textbooks.

Once the university had paid the license fee, each student would have the option of using the text in electronic format or paying more to purchase a hard copy through the usual channels. The publisher could set the price of hard copies low enough to cover only its production and distribution costs plus a small profit, because it would be covering most of its costs and making most of its profit by way of the license fees. The hard copies could then be resold to other students or back to the bookstore, but that would be of little concern to the publisher.

A further benefit of this approach is that it would not affect the way courses are taught. The same cannot be said for other recommendations from the Congressional committee and from state legislatures, like placing teaching materials on electronic reserve, urging faculty to adopt cheaper "no frills" textbooks, and assigning mainly electronic textbooks. While each of these suggestions may have merit, they force faculty to weigh students' academic interests against their fiscal concerns and encourage them to rely less on new textbooks.

Neither colleges nor publishers are known for their cutting-edge innovations. But if they could slightly change the way they do business, they would make a substantial dent in the cost of higher education and provide a real benefit to students and their parents.

This proposal clearly defines the problem — some textbooks cost a lot — and explains why. It proposes a solution to the problem of high textbook prices and offers reasons why this solution will work better than others. Its tone is reasonable and measured, yet decisive.

For five more proposals, see CHAPTER 64.

Key Features / Proposals

A well-defined problem.   Some problems are self-evident and relatively simple, and you would not need much persuasive power to make people act — as with the problem "This university discards too much paper." While some people might see nothing wrong with throwing paper away, most are likely to agree that recycling is a good thing. Other issues are controversial: some people see them as problems while others do not, such as this one: "Motorcycle riders who do not wear helmets risk serious injury and raise healthcare costs for everyone." Some motorcyclists believe that wearing or not wearing a helmet should be a personal choice; you would have to present arguments to convince your readers that not wearing a helmet is indeed a problem needing a solution. Any written proposal must establish at the outset that there is a problem — and that it's serious enough to require a solution. For some topics, visual or audio evidence of the problem may be helpful.

A recommended solution.   Once you have defined the problem, you need to describe the solution you are suggesting and to explain it in enough detail for readers to understand what you are proposing. Again, photographs, diagrams, or other visuals may help. Sometimes you might suggest several solutions, weigh their merits, and choose the best one.

A convincing argument for your proposed solution.   You need to convince readers that your solution is feasible — and that it is the best way to solve the problem. Sometimes you'll want to explain in detail how your proposed solution would work. See, for example, how the textbook proposal details the way a licensing system would operate. Visuals may strengthen this part of your argument as well.

A response to anticipated questions.   You may need to consider any questions readers may have about your proposal — and to show how its advantages outweigh any disadvantages. Had the textbook proposal been written for college budget officers, it would have needed to anticipate and answer questions about the costs of implementing the proposed solution.

A call to action.   The goal of a proposal is to persuade readers to accept your proposed solution. This solution may include asking readers to take action.

rhetorical situations   genres   processes   strategies   research MLA / APA   media / design   readings

Granof's proposal for reducing textbook prices via licensing fees might benefit from a photograph like this one, which provides a comparison of other approaches to the problem.

An appropriate tone. Since you're trying to persuade readers to act, your tone is important—readers will always react better to a reasonable, respectful presentation than to anger or self-righteousness.

A BRIEF GUIDE TO WRITING PROPOSALS

Deciding on a Topic

Choose a problem that can be solved. Complex, large problems, such as poverty, hunger, or terrorism, usually require complex, large solutions. Most of the time, focusing on a smaller problem or a limited aspect of a large problem will yield a more manageable proposal. Rather than tackling the problem of world poverty, for example, think about the problem faced by people in your community who have lost jobs and need help until they find employment.

Considering the Rhetorical Situation

3–4 **PURPOSE**   Do you have a vested interest in a particular solution, or do you simply want to eliminate the problem by whatever solution might be adopted?

5–8 **AUDIENCE**   Do you know if readers share your view of the problem or how receptive or resistant to trying to solve it they are likely to be? Do they have the authority to carry out a proposed solution?

12–15 **STANCE**   How can you show your audience that your proposal is reasonable and should be taken seriously? How can you demonstrate your own authority and credibility?

16–18 **MEDIA / DESIGN**   How will you deliver your proposal? In print? Online? As a speech? Would visuals, or video or audio clips help support your proposal?

Generating Ideas and Text

Explore potential solutions to the problem.   Many problems can be solved in more than one way, and you need to show your readers that you've examined several potential solutions. You may develop solutions on your own; more often, though, you'll need to do **RESEARCH** to see how others have solved—or tried to solve—similar problems. Don't settle on a single solution too quickly—you'll need to **COMPARE** the advantages and disadvantages of several solutions in order to argue convincingly for one.

419
348–55

Decide on the most desirable solution(s).   One solution may be head and shoulders above others—but be open to rejecting all the possible solutions on your list and starting over if you need to, or to combining two or more potential solutions in order to come up with an acceptable fix.

rhetorical situations   genres   processes   strategies   research MLA / APA   media / design   readings

Think about why your solution is the best one. Why did you choose your solution? Why will it work better than others? What has to be done to enact it? What will it cost? What makes you think it can be done? Writing out answers to these questions will help you argue for your solution: to show that you have carefully and objectively outlined a problem, analyzed the potential solutions, weighed their merits, and determined the reasons the solution you propose is the best.

Ways of Organizing a Proposal

You can organize a proposal in various ways, but always you will begin by establishing that there is a problem. You may then identify several possible solutions before recommending one of them or a combination of several. Sometimes, however, you might discuss only a single solution.

[Several possible solutions]

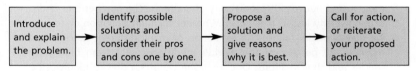

[A single solution]

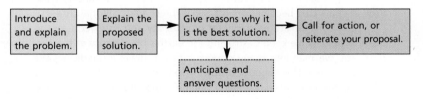

TOPIC PROPOSALS

Instructors often ask students to write topic proposals to ensure that their topics are appropriate or manageable. Some instructors may also ask for an **ANNOTATED BIBLIOGRAPHY** showing that appropriate sources of information are available—more evidence that the project can be carried out. Here a

▲ 155–63

first-year student proposes a topic for an assignment in a writing course in which she has been asked to take a position on a global issue.

JENNIFER CHURCH

Biodiversity Loss and Its Effect on Medicine

The loss of biodiversity—the variety of organisms found in the world—is affecting the world every day. Some scientists estimate that we are losing approximately one hundred species per day and that more than a quarter of all species may vanish within fifty years. I recently had the issue of biodiversity loss brought to my attention in a biological sciences course that I am taking this quarter. I have found myself interested in and intrigued by the subject and have found an abundance of information both in books and on the Internet.

In this paper, I will argue that it is crucial for people to stop this rapid loss of our world's biodiversity. Humans are the number-one cause of biodiversity loss in the world. Whether through pollution or toxins, we play a crucial role in the extinction of many different species. For example, 80 percent of the world's medicine comes from biological species and their habitats. One medicine vanishing due to biodiversity loss is TAXOL. Found in the Wollemi pine tree, TAXOL is one of the most promising drugs for the treatment of ovarian and breast cancer. If the Wollemi pine tree becomes extinct, we will lose this potential cure.

I will concentrate primarily on biodiversity and its effects on the medical field. If we keep destroying the earth's biodiversity at the current rate, we may lose many opportunities to develop medicines we need to survive. The majority of my information will be found on the Internet, because there are many reliable Web sites from all around the world that address the issue of biodiversity loss and medicine.

Church defines and narrows her topic (from biodiversity loss to the impact of that loss on medicine), discusses her interest, outlines her argument, and discusses her research strategy. Her goal is to convince her instructor that she has a realistic writing project and a clear plan.

Key Features / Topic Proposals

You'll need to explain what you want to write about, why you want to explore it, and what you'll do with your topic. Unless your instructor has additional requirements, here are the features to include:

A concise discussion of the subject. Topic proposals generally open with a brief discussion of the subject, outlining any important areas of controversy or debate associated with it and clarifying the extent of the writer's current knowledge of it. In its first two paragraphs, Church's proposal includes a concise statement of the topic she wishes to address.

A clear statement of your intended focus. State what aspect of the topic you intend to write on as clearly as you can, narrowing your focus appropriately. Church does so by stating her intended topic—loss of biodiversity—and then showing how she will focus on the importance of biodiversity to the medical field.

A rationale for choosing the topic. Tell your instructor why this topic interests you and why you want to write about it. Church both states what made her interested in her topic and hints at a practical reason for choosing it: plenty of information is available.

Mention of resources. To show your instructor that you can achieve your goal, you need to identify the available research materials.

IF YOU NEED MORE HELP

See Chapter 25 for guidelines on **DRAFTING,** Chapter 26 on **ASSESSING YOUR OWN WRITING,** Chapter 27 on **GETTING RESPONSE AND REVISING,** and Chapter 28 on **EDITING AND PROOFREADING.** See Chapter 29 if you are required to submit your proposal in a writing **PORTFOLIO.**

266–68
269–74
275–81
282–86
287–98

---

18 Reflections

Sometimes we write essays just to think about something—to speculate, ponder, probe; to play with an idea, develop a thought; or simply to share something. Reflective essays are our attempt to think something through by writing about it and to share our thinking with others. If such essays make an argument, it is about things we care or think about more than about what we believe to be "true." Have a look at one example by Jonathan Safran Foer, a novelist who lives in Brooklyn. This essay originally appeared on the Op-Ed page of the *New York Times* in 2006.

JONATHAN SAFRAN FOER

My Life as a Dog

For the last twenty years, New York City parks without designated dog runs have permitted dogs to be off-leash from 9 p.m. to 9 a.m. Because of recent complaints from the Juniper Park Civic Association in Queens, the issue has been revisited. On December 5, the Board of Health will vote on the future of off-leash hours.

Retrievers in elevators, Pomeranians on No. 6 trains, bull mastiffs crossing the Brooklyn Bridge . . . it is easy to forget just how strange it is that dogs live in New York in the first place. It is about as unlikely a place for dogs as one could imagine, and yet 1.4 million of them are among us. Why do we keep them in our apartments and houses, always at some expense and inconvenience? Is it even possible, in a city, to provide a good life for a dog, and what is a "good life"? Does the health board's vote matter in ways other than the most obvious?

I adopted George (a Great Dane/Lab/pit/greyhound/ridgeback/ whatever mix—a.k.a. Brooklyn shorthair) because I thought it would be fun. As it turns out, she is a major pain an awful lot of the time.

rhetorical situations

genres

processes

strategies

research MLA / APA

media / design

readings

She mounts guests, eats my son's toys (and occasionally tries to eat my son), is obsessed with squirrels, lunges at skateboarders and Hasids,* has the savant-like ability to find her way between the camera lens and subject of every photo taken in her vicinity, backs her tush into the least interested person in the room, digs up the freshly planted, scratches the newly bought, licks the about-to-be-served, and occasionally relieves herself on the wrong side of the front door. Her head is resting on my foot as I type this. I love her.

Our various struggles — to communicate, to recognize and accommodate each other's desires, simply to coexist — force me to interact with something, or rather someone, entirely "other." George can respond to a handful of words, but our relationship takes place almost entirely outside of language. She seems to have thoughts and emotions, desires and fears. Sometimes I think I understand them; often I don't. She is a mystery to me. And I must be one to her.

Of course our relationship is not always a struggle. My morning walk with George is very often the highlight of my day — when I have my best thoughts, when I most appreciate both nature and the city, and in a deeper sense, life itself. Our hour together is a bit of compensation for the burdens of civilization: business attire, email, money, etiquette, walls, and artificial lighting. It is even a kind of compensation for language. Why does watching a dog be a dog fill one with happiness? And why does it make one feel, in the best sense of the word, human?

It is children, very often, who want dogs. In a recent study, when asked to name the ten most important "individuals" in their lives, 7- and 10-year-olds included two pets on average. In another study, 42 percent of 5-year-olds spontaneously mentioned their pets when asked, "Whom do you turn to when you are feeling, sad, angry, happy, or wanting to share a secret?" Just about every children's book in my local bookstore has an animal for its hero. But then, only a few feet away in the cookbook section, just about every cookbook includes recipes for cooking animals. Is there a more illuminating illustration of our paradoxical relationship with the nonhuman world?

In the course of our lives, we move from a warm and benevolent relationship with animals (learning responsibility through caring for

Hasids: a Jewish sect whose members dress distinctively. [Editor's note]

our pets, stroking and confiding in them) to a cruel one (virtually all animals raised for meat in this country are factory farmed — they spend their lives in confinement, dosed with antibiotics and other drugs).

How do you explain this? Is our kindness replaced with cruelty? I don't think so. I think in part it's because the older we get, the less exposure we have to animals. And nothing facilitates indifference or forgetfulness so much as distance. In this sense, dogs and cats have been very lucky: they are the only animals we are intimately exposed to daily.

Folk parental wisdom and behavioral studies alike generally view 10 the relationships children have with companion animals as beneficial. But one does not have to be a child to learn from a pet. It is precisely my frustrations with George, and the inconveniences she creates, that reinforce in me how much compromise is necessary to share space with other beings.

The practical arguments against off-leash hours are easily refuted. One doesn't have to be an animal scientist to know that the more a dog is able to exercise its "dogness" — to run and play, to socialize with other dogs — the happier it will be. Happy dogs, like happy people, tend not to be aggressive. In the years that dogs have been allowed to run free in city parks, dog bites have decreased 90 percent. But there is another argument that is not so easy to respond to: some people just don't want to be inconvenienced by dogs. Giving dogs space necessarily takes away space from humans.

We have been having this latter debate, in different forms, for ages. Again and again we are confronted with the reality — some might say the problem — of sharing our space with other living things, be they dogs, trees, fish, or penguins. Dogs in the park are a present example of something that is often too abstracted or far away to gain our consideration.

The very existence of parks is a response to this debate: earlier New Yorkers had the foresight to recognize that if we did not carve out places for nature in our cities, there would be no nature. It was recently estimated that Central Park's real estate would be worth more than $500 billion. Which is to say we are half a trillion dollars inconvenienced by trees and grass. But we do not think of it as an inconvenience. We think of it as balance.

rhetorical situations

genres

processes

strategies

research MLA / APA

media / design

readings

Living on a planet of fixed size requires compromise, and while we are the only party capable of negotiating, we are not the only party at the table. We've never claimed more, and we've never had less. There has never been less clean air or water, fewer fish or mature trees. If we are not simply ignoring the situation, we keep hoping for (and expecting) a technological solution that will erase our destruction, while allowing us to continue to live without compromise. Maybe zoos will be an adequate replacement for wild animals in natural habitats. Maybe we will be able to recreate the Amazon somewhere else. Maybe one day we will be able to genetically engineer dogs that do not wish to run free. Maybe. But will those futures make us feel, in the best sense of the word, human?

I have been taking George to Prospect Park twice a day for more 15 than three years, but her running is still a revelation to me. Effortlessly, joyfully, she runs quite a bit faster than the fastest human on the planet. And faster, I've come to realize, than the other dogs in the park. George might well be the fastest land animal in Brooklyn. Once or twice every morning, for no obvious reason, she'll tear into a full sprint. Other dog owners can't help but watch her. Every now and then someone will cheer her on. It is something to behold.

A vote regarding off-leash hours for dogs sparks Foer's reflection on the relationship between dogs and humans. He begins by thinking about his relationship with his own dog, then goes on to consider the paradoxical nature of our treatment of animals in general. From there, he moves into a larger discussion of the compromises we make to "share space with other beings." Finally, he brings his reflection back to the personal, describing the joy of watching his dog be herself, off-leash.

█ For five more reflections, see CHAPTER 65.

Key Features / Reflections

A topic that intrigues you. A reflective essay has a dual purpose: to ponder something you find interesting or puzzling and to share your thoughts with an audience. Your topic may be anything that interests you.

You might write about someone you have never met and are curious about, an object or occurrence that makes you think, a place where you feel comfortable or safe. Your goal is to explore the meaning that the person, object, event, or place has for you in a way that will interest others. One way to do that is by making connections between your personal experience and more general ones that readers may share. Foer writes about his experience with his dog, but in so doing he raises questions and offers insights about the way everyone relates to others, human and nonhuman alike.

Some kind of structure.   A reflective essay can be structured in many ways, but it needs to *be* structured. It may seem to wander, but all its paths and ideas should relate, one way or another. The challenge is to keep your readers' interest as you explore your topic and to leave readers satisfied that the journey was pleasurable, interesting, and profitable. Foer brings his essay full-circle, introducing the vote on the off-leash law in his opening, then considering our complex relationship with dogs, and, after suggesting some of the compromises we make to share our world with other nonhuman living things, closing with an indelible image of the joy that freedom from a leash brings.

Specific details.   You'll need to provide specific details to help readers understand and connect with your subject, especially if it's an abstract or unfamiliar one. Foer offers a wealth of details about his dog: "She mounts guests, eats my son's toys (and occasionally tries to eat my son), is obsessed by squirrels, lunges at skateboarders and Hasids." Anecdotes can bring your subject to life: "Once or twice every morning, for no obvious reason, she'll tear into a full sprint. Other dog owners can't help but watch her. Every now and then someone will cheer her on." Reflections may be about causes, such as why dogs make us feel more human; comparisons, such as when Foer compares animals as pets and as food; and examples: "virtually all animals raised for meat in this country are factory farmed." Photographs or other visuals may help provide details as well as set a certain tone for a reflection, as discussed below.

A questioning, speculative tone.   In a reflective essay, you are working toward answers, not providing them neatly organized and ready for

consumption. So your tone is usually tentative and open, demonstrating a willingness to entertain, accept, and reject various ideas as your essay progresses from beginning to end. Foer achieves this tone by looking at people's relationships with dogs from several different perspectives as well as by asking questions for which he provides no direct answers.

A BRIEF GUIDE TO WRITING REFLECTIONS

Deciding on a Topic

Choose a subject you want to explore. Write a list of things that you think about, wonder about, find puzzling or annoying. They may be big things—life, relationships—or little things—quirks of certain people's behavior, curious objects, everyday events. Try **CLUSTERING** one or more of those things, or begin by **FREEWRITING** to see what comes to mind as you write.

261–62
259–60

Considering the Rhetorical Situation

PURPOSE What's your goal in writing this essay? To introduce a topic that interests you? Entertain? Provoke readers to think about something? What aspects of your subject do you want to ponder and reflect on?

3–4

AUDIENCE Who is the audience? How familiar are they with your subject? How will you introduce it in a way that will interest them?

5–8

STANCE What is your attitude toward the topic you plan to explore? Questioning? Playful? Critical? Curious? Something else?

12–15

MEDIA / DESIGN Will your essay be a print document? An oral presentation? Will it be posted on a website? Would it help to include any visuals or video or audio files?

16–18

Generating Ideas and Text

Explore your subject in detail.   Reflections often include descriptive details. Foer, for example, **DESCRIBES** the many ways he encounters dogs in New York: "Retrievers in elevators, Pomeranians on No. 6 trains, bull mastiffs crossing the Brooklyn Bridge." Those details provide a base for the speculations to come. You may also make your point by **DEFINING**, **COMPARING**, even **CLASSIFYING**. Virtually any organizing pattern will help you explore your subject.

367–75
356–66
348–55
342–47

Back away.   Ask yourself why your subject matters: why is it important or intriguing or significant? You may try **LISTING** or **OUTLINING** possibilities, or you may want to start **DRAFTING** to see where the writing takes your thinking. Your goal is to think on screen (or paper) about your subject, to play with its possibilities.

260–61
263–64
266–68

Think about how to keep readers with you.   Reflections may seem loose or unstructured, but they must be carefully crafted so that readers can follow your train of thought. It's a good idea to sketch out a rough **THESIS** to help focus your thoughts. You may not include the thesis in the essay itself, but every part of the essay should in some way relate to it.

313–15

Ways of Organizing a Reflective Essay

Reflective essays may be organized in many ways because they mimic the way we think, associating one idea with another in ways that make sense but do not necessarily form a "logical" progression. In general, you might consider organizing a reflection using this overall strategy:

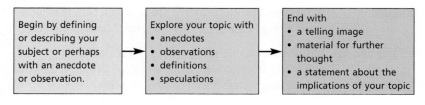

Begin by defining or describing your subject or perhaps with an anecdote or observation.	Explore your topic with • anecdotes • observations • definitions • speculations	End with • a telling image • material for further thought • a statement about the implications of your topic

Another way to organize this type of essay is as a series of brief reflections that together create an overall impression:

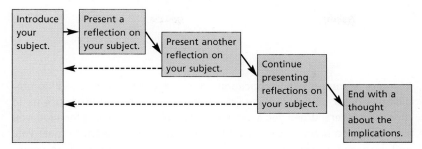

IF YOU NEED MORE HELP

See Chapter 25 for guidelines on **DRAFTING,** Chapter 26 on **ASSESSING YOUR OWN WRITING,** Chapter 27 on **GETTING RESPONSE AND REVISING,** and Chapter 28 on **EDITING AND PROOFREADING.** See Chapter 29 if you are required to submit your reflection in a writing **PORTFOLIO.**

266–68
269–74
275–81
282–86
287–98

19 Résumés and Job Letters

Résumés summarize our education, work experience, and other accomplishments for prospective employers. Application letters introduce us to those employers. When you send a letter and résumé applying for a job, you are making an argument for why that employer should want to meet you, and perhaps hire you. In a way, the two texts together serve as an advertisement selling your talents and abilities to someone who likely has to sift through many applications to decide whom to invite for an interview. That's why résumés and application letters require a level of care that few other documents do. In the same way, sending a thank-you letter following an interview completes your presentation of yourself to potential employers. Résumés, application letters, and thank-you letters are obviously very different genres—yet they share one common purpose and are done for the same audience. Thus, they are presented together in this chapter.

RÉSUMÉS

This chapter covers two kinds of résumés, print ones and scannable ones. *Print résumés* are presented on paper to be read by people. You usually design a print résumé to highlight key information typographically, using italic or bold type for headings, for instance. *Scannable résumés* can be delivered on paper or via email, but they are formatted to be read by a computer. Therefore, you need to use a single sans serif font without any bold or italics or even indents, and you need to write the résumé using keywords that you hope will match words found in the computer's job description database.

    Following are two résumés—the first one print and the second one scannable—both written by a college student applying for an internship before his senior year.

rhetorical situations

genres

processes

strategies

research MLA / APA

media / design

readings

Print Résumé

Samuel Praeger
28 Murphy Lane
Springfield, OH 45399
937-555-2640
spraeger22@webmail.com

OBJECTIVE	To obtain an internship with a public relations firm
EDUCATION Fall 2009–present	Wittenberg University, Springfield, OH • B.A. in Psychology expected in May 2013 • Minor in East Asian Studies
EXPERIENCE 2011–present	Department of Psychology, Wittenberg University *Research Assistant* • Collect and analyze data • Interview research participants
Summer 2011	Landis and Landis Public Relations, Springfield, OH *Events Coordinator* • Organized local charity events • Coordinated database of potential donors • Produced two radio spots for event promotion
Summers 2009, 2010	Springfield Aquatic Club, Springfield, OH *Assistant Swim Coach* • Instructed children ages 5–18 in competitive swimming
HONORS 2012	Psi Chi National Honor Society in Psychology
2010–2012	Community Service Scholarship, Wittenberg University
ACTIVITIES	Varsity Swim Team; Ronald McDonald House Fund-raiser
SKILLS	Microsoft Office; SPSS for Windows; Prezi; fluent in Japanese
REFERENCES	Available upon request

name in boldface

objective tailored to specific job sought

work experience in reverse chronological order

format to fill entire page

Scannable Résumé

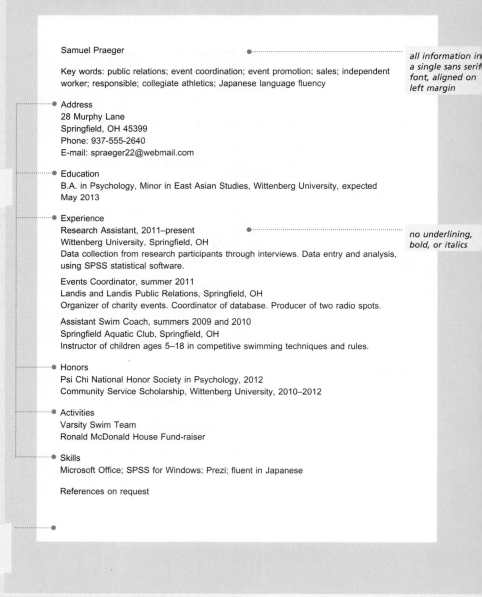

Samuel Praeger

Key words: public relations; event coordination; event promotion; sales; independent worker; responsible; collegiate athletics; Japanese language fluency

Address
28 Murphy Lane
Springfield, OH 45399
Phone: 937-555-2640
E-mail: spraeger22@webmail.com

Education
B.A. in Psychology, Minor in East Asian Studies, Wittenberg University, expected May 2013

Experience
Research Assistant, 2011–present
Wittenberg University, Springfield, OH
Data collection from research participants through interviews. Data entry and analysis, using SPSS statistical software.

Events Coordinator, summer 2011
Landis and Landis Public Relations, Springfield, OH
Organizer of charity events. Coordinator of database. Producer of two radio spots.

Assistant Swim Coach, summers 2009 and 2010
Springfield Aquatic Club, Springfield, OH
Instructor of children ages 5–18 in competitive swimming techniques and rules.

Honors
Psi Chi National Honor Society in Psychology, 2012
Community Service Scholarship, Wittenberg University, 2010–2012

Activities
Varsity Swim Team
Ronald McDonald House Fund-raiser

Skills
Microsoft Office; SPSS for Windows; Prezi; fluent in Japanese

References on request

all information in a single sans serif font, aligned on left margin

key words to aid computer searching

no underlining, bold, or italics

printed on white paper; not folded or stapled

Samuel Praeger's résumé is arranged chronologically, and because he was look-ing for work in a certain field, the résumé is targeted, focusing on his related work and skills and leaving out any references to high school (that he is in college allows readers to assume graduation from high school) or his past job as a house painter, which is not relevant. The print version describes his work responsibilities using action verbs to highlight what he actually did — produced, instructed, *and so on — whereas the scannable version converts the verbs to nouns —* producer, instructor. *The scannable version is format-ted in a single standard font, with no italics, boldfacing, or other typographic variation.*

Key Features / Résumés

An organization that suits your goals and experience.   There are con-ventional ways of organizing a résumé but no one right way. You can organize a résumé chronologically or functionally, and it can be targeted or not. A *chronological résumé* is the most general, listing pretty much all your academic and work experience from the most recent to the earliest. A *targeted résumé* will generally announce the specific goal up top, just beneath your name, and will offer information selectively, showing only the experience and skills relevant to your goal. A *functional résumé* is organized around various kinds of experience and is not chronological. You might write a functional résumé if you wish to demonstrate a lot of experience in more than one area and perhaps if you wish to downplay dates.

Succinct.   A résumé should almost always be short — one page if at all possible. Entries should be parallel but do not need to be written in com-plete sentences — "Produced two radio spots," for instance, rather than "I produced two radio spots." *Print résumés* often use action verbs ("instructed," "produced") to emphasize what you accomplished; *scannable résumés* use nouns instead ("instructor," "producer").

A design that highlights key information.   It's important for a résumé to look good and to be easy to scan. *On a print résumé,* typography, white space, and alignment matter. Your name should be bold at the top. Major sections should be labeled with headings, all of which should be in one slightly larger or bolder font. And you need to surround each section and the text as a whole with adequate white space to make the parts easy to read—and to make the entire document look professional. *On a scannable résumé,* you should use one standard font throughout and *not* use any italics, boldface, bullets, or indents.

A BRIEF GUIDE TO WRITING RÉSUMÉS

Considering the Rhetorical Situation

3–4 ■ **PURPOSE**   Are you seeking a job? An internship? Some other position? How will the position for which you're applying affect what you include on your résumé?

5–8 ■ **AUDIENCE**   What sort of employee is the company or organization seeking? What experience and qualities will the person doing the hiring be looking for?

12–15 ■ **STANCE**   What personal and professional qualities do you want to convey? Think about how you want to come across—as eager? polite? serious? ambitious?—and choose your words accordingly.

16–18 ■ **MEDIA / DESIGN**   Are you planning to send your résumé and letter on paper? As an email attachment? In a scannable format? Whatever your medium, be sure both documents are formatted appropriately and proofread carefully.

Generating Ideas and Text for a Résumé

Define your objective. Are you looking for a particular job for which you should create a targeted résumé? Are you preparing a generic chronological résumé to use in a search for work of any kind? Defining your objective as specifically as possible helps you decide on the form the résumé will take and the information it will include.

Consider how you want to present yourself. Begin by gathering the information you will need to include. As you work through the steps of putting your résumé together, think about the method of organization that works best for your purpose—chronological, targeted, or functional.

- *Contact information.* At the top of your résumé, list your full name, a permanent address (rather than your school address), a permanent telephone number with area code, and your email address (which should sound professional; addresses like hotbabe334@gmail.com do not make a good first impression on potential employers).

- *Your education.* Start with the most recent: degree, major, college attended, and minor (if any). You may want to list your GPA (if it's over 3.0) and any academic honors you've received. If you don't have much work experience, list education first.

- *Your work experience.* As with education, list your most recent job first and work backward. Include job title, organization name, city and state, start and end dates, and responsibilities. Describe them in terms of your duties and accomplishments. If you have extensive work experience in the area in which you're applying, list that first.

- *Community service, volunteer, and charitable activities.* Many high school students are required to perform community service, and many students participate in various volunteer activities that benefit others. List what you've done, and think about the skills and aptitudes that participation helped you develop or demonstrate.

- *Other activities, interests, and abilities.* What do you do for fun? What skills do your leisure activities require? (For example, if you play a sport, you probably have a good grasp of the value of teamwork. You should describe your skills in a way that an employer might find useful.)

Choose references.   Whether you list references on your résumé or offer to provide them on request, ask people to serve as references for you before you send out a résumé. It's a good idea to provide each reference with a one-page summary of relevant information about you (for example, give professors a list of courses you took with them, including the grades you earned and the titles of papers you wrote).

Choose your words carefully.   Remember, your résumé is a sales document—you're trying to present yourself as someone worth a second look. Focus on your achievements, using action verbs that say what you've done. If, however, you're composing a scannable résumé, use nouns rather than verbs, and use terms that will function as keywords. Keywords help the computer match your qualifications to the organization's needs. People in charge of hiring search the database of résumés by entering keywords relating to the job for which they are seeking applicants. Keywords for a lab technician, for example, might include *laboratory, technician, procedures, subjects, experiment*—among many others. To determine what key words to list on your résumé, read job ads carefully, and use the same words the ads do—as long as they accurately reflect your experience. Be honest—employers expect truthfulness, and embellishing the truth can cause you to lose a job later.

Consider key design elements.   Make sure your résumé is centered on the page and that it looks clean and clear. It's usually best to use a single, simple **FONT** (serif for print, sans serif for scannable) throughout and to print on white or off-white paper. Limit paper résumés to no more—and no less—than one full page. If you plan to send a scannable résumé or post one on a website, it should *not* contain bullets, boldface, indents, italics, or underlining.

585–86 ▢

rhetorical situations

genres

processes

strategies

research MLA / APA

media / design

readings

Edit and proofread carefully. Your résumé must be perfect. Show it to others, and proofread again. You don't want even one typo.

Ways of Organizing a Résumé

If you don't have much work experience or if you've just gone back to school to train for a new career, put education before work experience; if you have extensive work experience in the area in which you're applying, list work before education.

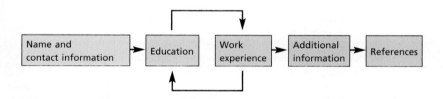

APPLICATION AND THANK YOU LETTERS

The application letter argues that the writer should be taken seriously as a candidate for a job or some other opportunity. Generally, it is sent together with a résumé, so it doesn't need to give that much information. It does, however, have to make a favorable impression: the way it's written and presented can get you in for an interview — or not. On the following page is an application letter that Samuel Praeger wrote seeking a position at the end of his junior year. Praeger tailored his letter to one specific reader at a specific organization. The letter cites details, showing that it is not a generic application letter being sent to many possible employers. Rather, it identifies a particular position — the public relations internship — and stresses the fit between Praeger's credentials and the position. Praeger also states his availability.

Application Letter

equal space at top and bottom of page, all text aligning at left margin

street address
city, state ZIP
date

28 Murphy Lane
Springfield, OH 45399
May 19, 2011

line space

recipient's name and title, organization, address

Barbara Jeremiah, President
Jeremiah Enterprises
44322 Commerce Way
Worthington, OH 45322

line space

salutation, with a colon

Dear Ms. Jeremiah:

position identified

I am writing to apply for the public relations internship advertised in the Sunday, May 15, *Columbus Dispatch*. The success of your company makes me eager to work with you and learn from you.

match between experience and job description

My grasp of public relations goes beyond the theories I have learned in the classroom. I worked last summer at Landis and Landis, the Springfield public relations firm, where I was responsible for organizing two charity events that drew over two hundred potential donors each. Since your internship focuses on public relations, my experience in the field should allow me to make a contribution to your company.

line space between paragraphs

availability

I will be available to begin any time after May 23, when the spring term at Wittenberg ends. I enclose my résumé, which provides detailed information about my background. I will phone this week to see if I might arrange an interview.

line space

closing

Sincerely,

4 lines space for signature

Samuel Praeger

sender's name, typed

Samuel Praeger

Thank You Letter

equal space at top and bottom of page, all text aligning at left margin

28 Murphy Lane
Springfield, OH 45399
June 1, 2011

street address
city, state ZIP
date

one space

Barbara Jeremiah, President
Jeremiah Enterprises
44322 Commerce Way
Worthington, OH 45322

recipient's name and title, organization, address

one space

Dear Ms. Jeremiah:

salutation, with a colon

Thank you for the opportunity to meet with you yesterday. I enjoyed talking with you and meeting the people who work with you, and I continue to be very interested in becoming an intern with Jeremiah Enterprises.

thanks and confirmation of interest

one space between paragraphs

As we discussed, I worked with a public relations firm last summer, and since then I have completed three courses in marketing and public relations that relate directly to the work I would be doing as an intern.

brief review of qualifications

I enclose a list of references, as you requested.

enclosures

Thank you again for your time. I hope to hear from you soon.

repeat thanks

one space

Sincerely,

closing

Samuel Praeger

4 lines space for signature

Samuel Praeger

sender's name, typed

Sending a thank you letter within a day or two of your interview is a way of showing appreciation for the interview and restating your interest in the position. It also shows that you have good manners and understand proper business etiquette. On the previous page is a letter Samuel Praeger sent to the person who interviewed him for an internship, thanking the interviewer for her time and the opportunity to meet her, indicating his interest in the position, and reiterating his qualifications.

Key Features / Application and Thank You Letters

A succinct indication of your qualifications. In an application letter, you need to make clear why you're interested in the position or the organization—and at the same time give some sense of why the person you're writing to should at least want to meet you. In a thank you letter, you should remind the interviewer of your qualifications.

A reasonable and pleasing tone. When writing application and thank you letters, you need to go beyond simply stating your accomplishments or saying thank you. Through your words, you need to demonstrate that you will be the kind of employee the organization wants. Presentation is also important—your letter should be neat and error-free.

A conventional, businesslike format. Application and thank you letters typically follow a prescribed format. The most common is the block format shown in the examples. It includes the writer's address, the date, the recipient's name and address, a salutation, the message, a closing, and a signature.

A BRIEF GUIDE TO WRITING JOB LETTERS

Generating Ideas and Text for Application and Thank You Letters

Focus. Application and thank-you letters are not personal and should not be chatty. Keep them focused: when you're applying for a position,

include only information relevant to the position. Don't make your audience wade through irrelevant side issues. Stay on topic.

State the reason for the letter.   Unlike essays, which develop a thesis over several paragraphs, or emails, which announce their topic in a subject line, letters need to explicitly introduce their reason for being written, usually in the first paragraph. When you're applying for something or thanking someone, say so in the first sentence: "I am writing to apply for the Margaret Branscomb Peabody Scholarship for students majoring in veterinary science." "Thank you for meeting with me."

Think of your letter as an argument.   When you're asking for a job, you're making an **ARGUMENT.** You're making a claim — that you're qualified for a certain position — and you need to support your claim with reasons and evidence. Praeger, for example, cites his education and his work experience — and he offers to supply references who will support his application.

◆ 323–41

Choose an appropriate salutation.   If you know the person's name and title, use it: "Dear Professor Turnigan." If you don't know the person's title, one good solution is to address him or her by first and last name: "Dear Julia Turnigan." If, as sometimes happens, you must write to an unknown reader, your options include "To Whom It May Concern" and the more old fashioned "Dear Sir or Madam." Another option in such situations might be to omit the salutation completely and instead use a subject line, for example: "Subject: Public Relations Internship Application." Whenever possible, though, write to a specific person; call the organization and ask whom to write to. Once you've had an interview, write to your interviewer.

Proofread.   Few writing situations demand greater perfection than professional letters — especially job letters. Employers receive dozens, sometimes hundreds, of applications, and often can't look at them all. Typos, grammar errors, and other forms of sloppiness prejudice readers against applicants: they're likely to think that if this applicant can't take the time and care to **PROOFREAD,** how badly does he or she want this position? To compete, strive for perfection.

 285–86

Ways of Organizing an Application or Thank You Letter

Application and thank you letters should both follow a conventional organization, though you might vary the details somewhat. Here are two standard organizations.

[Application letter]

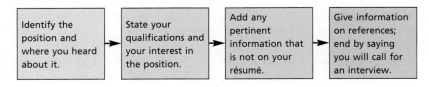

Identify the position and where you heard about it. → State your qualifications and your interest in the position. → Add any pertinent information that is not on your résumé. → Give information on references; end by saying you will call for an interview.

[Thank you letter]

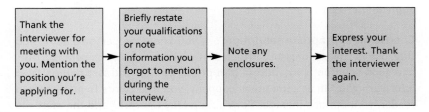

Thank the interviewer for meeting with you. Mention the position you're applying for. → Briefly restate your qualifications or note information you forgot to mention during the interview. → Note any enclosures. → Express your interest. Thank the interviewer again.

IF YOU NEED MORE HELP

266–68
269–74
275–81
282–86

See Chapter 25 for guidelines on **DRAFTING**, Chapter 26 on **ASSESSING YOUR OWN WRITING**, Chapter 27 on **GETTING RESPONSE AND REVISING**, and Chapter 28 on **EDITING AND PROOFREADING.**

rhetorical situations   genres   processes   strategies   research MLA / APA   media / design   readings

Mixing Genres **20**

Musicians regularly mix genres, blending, for instance, reggae, hip-hop, and jazz to create a unique sound. Like musicians, writers often combine different genres in a single text. An **EVALUATION** of mining practices might include a **PROFILE** of a coal company CEO. A **PROPOSAL** to start a neighborhood watch might begin with a **REPORT** on crime in the area. Here's a column that mixes genres written by Anna Quindlen for *Newsweek* magazine in 2007.

164–72
191–204
205–13
87–118

ANNA QUINDLEN
Write for Your Life

The new movie *Freedom Writers* isn't entirely about the themes the trailers suggest. It isn't only about gang warfare and racial tensions and tolerance. It isn't only about the difference one good teacher can make in the life of one messed-up kid. *Freedom Writers* is about the power of writing in the lives of ordinary people. That's a lesson everyone needs. The movie, and the book from which it was taken, track the education of a young teacher named Erin Gruwell, who shows up shiny-new to face a class of what are called, in pedagogical jargon, "at risk" students. It's a mixed bag of Latino, Asian, and black teenagers with one feckless white kid thrown in. They ignore, belittle, and dismiss her as she proffers lesson plans and reading materials seriously out of step with the homelessness, drug use, and violence that are the stuff of their precarious existences.

   And then one day, she gives them all marbled composition books and the assignment to write their lives, ungraded, unjudged, and the world breaks open.

Textual analysis

235

"My probation officer thinks he's slick; he swears he's an expert on gangs."

"Sorry, diary, I was going to try not to do it tonight, but the little baggy of white powder is calling my name."

"If you pull up my shirtsleeves and look at my arms, you will see   5
black and blue marks."

"The words 'Eviction Notice' stopped me dead in my tracks."

"When I was younger, they would lock me up in the closet because they wanted to get high and beat up on each other."

Ms. G, as the kids called her, embraced a concept that has been lost in modern life: writing can make pain tolerable, confusion clearer and the self stronger.

How is it, at a time when clarity and strength go begging, that we have moved so far from everyday prose? Social critics might trace this back to the demise of letter writing. The details of housekeeping and child rearing, the rigors of war and work, advice to friends and family: none was slated for publication. They were communications that gave shape to life by describing it for others.

Report

But as the letter fell out of favor and education became profes-   10
sionalized, with its goal less the expansion of the mind than the acquisition of a job, writing began to be seen largely as the purview of writers. Writing at work also became so stylistically removed from the story of our lives that the two seemed to have nothing in common. Corporate prose conformed to an equation: information × polysyllabic words + tortured syntax = aren't you impressed?

And in the age of the telephone most communication became evanescent, gone into thin air no matter how important or heartfelt. Think of all those people inside the World Trade Center saying goodbye by phone. If only, in the blizzard of paper that followed the col-

Reflection

lapse of the buildings, a letter had fallen from the sky for every family member and friend, something to hold on to, something to read and reread. Something real. Words on paper confer a kind of immortality. Wouldn't all of us love to have a journal, a memoir, a letter, from those we have loved and lost? Shouldn't all of us leave a bit of that behind?

The age of technology has both revived the use of writing and provided ever more reasons for its spiritual solace. Emails are letters, after all, more lasting than phone calls, even if many of them r 2 cursory 4 u. And the physical isolation they and other arms-length cyber-advances create makes talking to yourself more important than ever. That's also what writing is: not just a legacy, but therapy. As the novelist Don DeLillo once said, "Writing is a form of personal freedom. It frees us from the mass identity we see in the making all around us. In the end, writers will write not to be outlaw heroes of some under-culture but mainly to save themselves, to survive as individuals."

That's exactly what Gruwell was after when she got the kids in her class writing, in a program that's since been duplicated at other schools. Salvation and survival for teenagers whose chances of either seemed negligible. "Growing up, I always assumed I would either drop out of school or get pregnant," one student wrote. "So when Ms. G started talking about college, it was like a foreign language to me." Maybe that's the moment when that Latina girl began to speak that foreign language, when she wrote those words down. Today she has a college degree.

Argument

One of the texts Erin Gruwell assigned was *The Diary of a Young Girl* by Anne Frank. A student who balked at reading a book about someone so different, so remote, went on to write: "At the end of the book, I was so mad that Anne died, because as she was dying, a part of me was dying with her." Of course Anne never dreamed her diary would be published, much less read by millions of people after her death at the hands of the Nazis. She wrote it for the same reason the kids who called themselves Freedom Writers wrote in those composition books: to make sense of themselves. That's not just for writers. That's for people.

Quindlen argues that writing helps us understand ourselves and our world. She uses several genres to help advance her argument — textual analysis of the film Freedom Writers, *a brief report on the decline of letter writing, and a reflection on the technologies we use to write. Together, these genres help her develop her argument that writing helps us "make sense of [our]selves."*

For five more multi-genre texts, see CHAPTER 66.

Key Features / Texts That Mix Genres

One primary genre. Your writing situation will often call for a certain genre that is appropriate for your purpose — an argument, a proposal, a report, a textual analysis, and so forth. Additional genres then play supporting roles. Quindlen's essay, for example, primarily argues a position and mixes in other genres, including report and reflection, to elaborate her argument and bring it to life.

A clear focus.   A text that mixes genres approaches the topic several different ways, but each genre must contribute to your main point. One genre may serve as the introduction, and others may be woven throughout the text in other ways, but all must address some aspect of the topic and support the central claim. Quindlen's analysis of the film *Freedom Writers*, for example, supports her claim that writing is one way we learn about ourselves.

Careful organization.   A text that combines several genres requires careful organization — the various genres must fit together neatly and clearly. Quindlen opens by analyzing the theme of *Freedom Writers*, noting that it's about "the power of writing in the lives of ordinary people." She then switches genres, reporting on how "we have moved so far from everyday prose" and then reflecting on the consequences of that move.

Clear transitions.   When a text includes several genres, those genres need to be connected in some way. Transitions do that, and in so doing, they help readers make their way through the text. Transitions may include words such as "in addition" and "however," and they may also consist of phrases that sum up an idea and move it forward. See, for example, how Quindlen ends one paragraph by quoting Don DeLillo as saying that writers write "to save themselves, to survive as individuals" and then begins the next paragraph by referring to DeLillo's words, saying "That's exactly what Gruwell was after."

Some Typical Ways of Mixing Genres

It's possible to mix almost any genres together. Following are some of the most commonly mixed genres and how they combine with other genres.

rhetorical situations   genres   processes   strategies   research MLA / APA   media / design   readings

Memoirs.   Sometimes a personal anecdote can help support an **ARGUMENT** or enhance a **REPORT.** Stories from your personal experience can help readers understand your motivations for arguing a certain position and can enhance your credibility as a writer.

▲ 119–49
87–118

Profiles.   One way to bring a **REPORT** on an abstract topic to life is to include a profile of a person, place, or event. For example, if you were writing a report for your boss on the need to hire more sales representatives, including a profile of one salesperson's typical day might drive home the point that your sales force is stretched too thin.

▲ 87–118

Textual analyses.   You might need to analyze a speech or other document as part of an **ARGUMENT,** especially on a historical or political topic. For instance, you might analyze speeches by Abraham Lincoln and Jefferson Davis if you're writing about the causes of the Civil War, or an advertisement for cigarettes if you're making an argument about teen smoking.

▲ 119–49

Evaluations.   You might include an evaluation of something when you write a **PROPOSAL** about it. For example, if you were writing a proposal for additional student parking on your campus, you would need to evaluate the current parking facilities to discuss their inadequacy.

▲ 205–13

A BRIEF GUIDE TO WRITING TEXTS THAT MIX GENRES

Considering the Rhetorical Situation

PURPOSE   Why are you writing this text? To inform? persuade? entertain? explore an idea? something else? What genres will help you achieve your purpose?

■ 3–4

AUDIENCE   Who are your readers? Which genres will help these readers understand your point? Will starting with a memoir or profile draw them in? Will some analysis help them

■ 5–8

understand the topic? Will a profile make the topic less abstract or make them more sympathetic to your claim?

9–11 **GENRE**　What is your primary genre? What other genres might support that primary genre?

12–15 **STANCE**　What is your stance on your topic—objective? opinionated? something else? Will including a textual analysis or report help you establish an objective or analytical tone? Will some reflection or a brief memoir show your personal connection to your topic?

16–18 **MEDIA / DESIGN**　Will your text be a print document? An oral presentation? Will it be published on the web? Should you include illustrations? Audio or video clips? Do you need to present any information that would be best shown in a chart or graph?

Generating Ideas and Text

Identify your primary genre.　If you're writing in response to an assignment, does it specify a particular genre? Look for key verbs that name specific genres — for example, *analyze*, *argue*, *evaluate*, and so on. Be aware that other verbs imply certain genres: *explain*, *summarize*, *review*, and *describe* ask for a report; *argue*, *prove*, and *justify* signal that you need to argue a position; and *evaluate* and *propose* specify evaluations and proposals.

3–4
5–8
　　　If the choice of genre is up to you, consider your **PURPOSE** and **AUDIENCE** carefully to determine what genre is most appropriate. Consult the appropriate genre chapter to identify the key features of your primary genre and to generate ideas and text.

Determine if other genres would be helpful.　As you write a draft, you may identify a need — for a beginning that grabs readers' attention, for a satisfying ending, for ways to make an abstract concept more concrete or to help in analyzing something. At this point, you may want to try mixing

one or more genres within your draft. Determine what genre will help you achieve your purpose and consult the appropriate genre chapter for advice on writing in that genre. Remember, however, that you're mixing genres into your draft to support and enhance it — so your supporting genres may not be as developed as complete texts in that genre would be and may not include all the key features. For example, if you include a brief memoir as part of an argument, it should include a good story and vivid details — but its significance may well be stated as part of the argument rather than revealed through the storytelling itself.

Integrate the genres.   Your goal is to create a focused, unified, coherent text. So you need to make sure that your genres work together to achieve that goal. Make sure that each genre fulfills a purpose within the text — for example, that a textual analysis within an argument provides evidence to support your claim, or that the profile you include in a report provides a clear illustration of the larger subject. Also, use **TRANSITIONS** to help readers move from section to section in your text.

317

Multigenre Projects

Sometimes a collection of texts can together represent an experience or advance an argument. For example, you might document a trip to the Grand Canyon in an album that contains journal entries written during the trip, photographs, a map of northern Arizona showing the canyon, postcards, an essay on the geology of the canyon, and a souvenir coin stamped with an image of the canyon. Each represents a different way of experiencing the Grand Canyon, and together they offer a multifaceted way to understand your trip.

You might also write in several different genres on the same topic. If you begin by **ARGUING** that the government should provide universal health care, for example, writing a **MEMOIR** about a time you were ill could help you explore a personal connection to the topic. Composing a **PROFILE** of a doctor might give you new insights into the issue, and writing a **PROPOSAL** for how universal health care could work might direct you to potential

323–41
183–90
191–204
205–13

solutions. You could assemble all these texts in a folder, with a title page and table of contents so that readers can see how it all fits together — or you could create an online multimodal text, combining text, images, video, sound, and links to other sites.

266–68
269–74
299–311
312–17

IF YOU NEED MORE HELP

See Chapter 25 for guidelines on DRAFTING, Chapter 26 on ASSESSING YOUR OWN WRITING, Chapter 31 on BEGINNING AND ENDING, and Chapter 32 on GUIDING YOUR READER.

rhetorical situations　genres　processes　strategies　research MLA / APA　media / design　readings

Choosing Genres 21

Write an essay responding to one of the course readings. Show how James Joyce uses financial and economic imagery in "Araby." Explore the various policies adopted toward the use of marijuana. Much of the time, your college writing assignments will specify a particular genre, but sometimes — as these examples suggest — they won't. Vague verbs like *discuss* or *explore* may leave you wondering exactly what your instructor expects. This chapter will help you decide what genre(s) to use when an assignment doesn't tell you what to do.

Recognizing Which Genres Are Required

LITERACY NARRATIVE   A personal account of how you learned to read or write or to make meaning through words, pictures, music, or other means. If you're assigned to explore your development as a writer or reader or to describe how you came to be interested in a particular subject or career, you'll likely need to write a literacy narrative. Some terms that might signal a literacy narrative: *describe a learning experience, tell how you learned, trace your development, write a story.*

▲ 27–51

TEXTUAL ANALYSIS   A careful examination of a text both for what it says and for how it says it, with the goal of demonstrating the ways the text achieves certain effects. If your assignment calls on you to look at a text to see not only what it says but how it works, you likely need to write a textual analysis. Some terms that might signal that a textual analysis is being asked for: *analyze, examine, explicate, read closely, interpret.*

▲ 52–86

87–118 ◢ **REPORT**   A presentation of information as objectively as possible to inform readers about a subject. If your task is to research a topic and then tell your audience in a balanced, neutral way what you know about it, your goal is probably to write a report. Some terms that might signal that a report is being asked for: *define, describe, explain, inform, observe, record, report, show.*

119–49 ◢ **POSITION PAPER** or **ARGUMENT**   Writing that asserts a belief or claim about an issue — usually stated as a thesis — and supports it with reasons and various kinds of evidence. Some terms that might signal that your instructor wants you to take a position or argue for or against something: *agree or disagree, argue, claim, criticize, defend, justify, position paper, prove.*

150–54 ◢
470–71 ● **ABSTRACT** or **SUMMARY**   A condensation of a text into a briefer version that conveys the main points of the original. If your assignment is to reduce a text, either someone else's or your own, into a single paragraph or so, one of these genres is called for. A summary usually either stands on its own or is inserted within a larger text you're writing; an abstract is a condensation of a text you've written yourself, and you write it either to submit the text for publication or to serve as an introduction to the text. Some terms that might signal that an abstract or summary is expected: *abridge, boil down, compress, condense, recap, summarize.*

155–63 ◢ **ANNOTATED BIBLIOGRAPHY**   A genre that includes an overview of published research and scholarship on a topic. Assignments asking you to list potential sources on a topic with complete publication information for and descriptions or evaluations of each one are likely asking for annotated bibliographies. Some terms that might signal that an annotated bibliography is expected: *an annotated list, list and comment on, list and describe, list and evaluate, list sources.*

164–72 ◢ **EVALUATION**   Writing that makes a judgment about something — a source, poem, film, restaurant, whatever — based on certain criteria. If your instructor asks you to say whether or not you like something or whether it's a good or bad example of a category or better or worse than something else, an evaluation is likely being called for. Some terms that might signal that an evaluation is expected: *assess, critique, evaluate, judge, recommend, review.*

LAB REPORT   Writing that covers the process of conducting an experiment in a controlled setting. Lab reports commonly include specific information presented in a particular order, but they vary from discipline to discipline: those in some disciplines include Materials and Data sections, while others may require sections on Participants or Procedures. Some terms that might signal that a lab report is wanted: *describe, discuss, present results, write up.*

▲ 173–82

MEMOIR   A genre of writing that focuses on something significant in your past. If you're asked to explore an important moment or event in your life, you're probably being asked to write a memoir. Some terms that likely signal that a memoir is desired: *autobiography, chronicle, narrate, a significant personal memory, a story drawn from your experience.*

▲ 183–90

PROFILE   A type of writing that presents a person, place, or event from an interesting angle in an engaging way and is based on first-hand field research. If your instructor assigns you the task of portraying a subject in a way that is both informative and entertaining, you're likely being asked to write a profile. Some terms that might indicate that a profile is being asked for: *angle, describe, dominant impression, interview, observe, report on.*

▲ 191–204

PROPOSAL   Writing that argues for a particular solution to a problem or suggests some action — or that makes a case for pursuing a certain project. Some terms that might indicate a proposal: *argue for [a solution or action], propose, put forward, recommend.*

▲ 205–13

REFLECTION   A genre of writing that presents a writer's thoughtful, personal exploration of a subject. If your assignment calls on you to think in writing about something or to play with ideas, you are likely being asked to write a reflection. Some terms that may mean that a reflection is called for: *consider, explore, ponder, probe, reflect, speculate.*

▲ 214–21

Dealing with Ambiguous Assignments

Sometimes even the key term in an assignment doesn't indicate clearly which genre is wanted, so you need to read such an assignment especially carefully. A first step might be to consider whether it's asking for a report or an argument. For example, here are two sample assignments:

> Discuss ways in which the invention of gas and incandescent lighting significantly changed people's daily lives in the nineteenth century.
>
> Discuss why Willy Loman in *Death of a Salesman* is, or is not, a tragic hero.

Both assignments use the word *discuss*, but in very different ways. The first may be simply be requesting an informative, researched report: the thesis — new forms of lighting significantly changed people's daily lives in various ways — is already given, and you may be simply expected to research and explain what some of these changes were. It's also possible, though, that this assignment is asking you to make an argument about which of these changes were the most significant ones.

In contrast, *discuss* in the second assignment is much more open-ended. It does not lead to a particular thesis but is more clearly asking you to present an argument: to choose a position (Willy Loman *is* a tragic hero; Willy Loman is *not* a tragic hero; even, possibly, Willy Loman both *is and is not* a tragic hero) and to marshall reasons and evidence from the play to support your position. A clue that an argument is being asked for lies in the way the assignment offers a choice of paths.

Other potentially ambiguous words in assignments are *show* and *explore*, both of which could lead in many directions. If after a careful reading of the entire assignment you still aren't sure what it's asking for, ask your instructor to clarify the appropriate genre or genres.

Mixing Genres

Genres are seldom "pure" — a pure argument, a pure memoir, a pure literary analysis. Most of the writing we read and produce mixes genres to

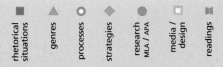

meet the needs of the writer's purpose and audience. For example, writing that **TAKES A POSITION** rarely jumps into the argument immediately. Instead, it may include several paragraphs in which the context for the disputed position is explained or information crucial to the audience's understanding is reported. Sometimes that **REPORT** will be introduced by a brief **MEMOIR** that makes the topic personal to the writer and so less abstract. And the argument itself may well do much more than simply take a position — it may **EVALUATE** alternatives and end with a **PROPOSAL,** and even include genres in other media, such as a video clip **PROFILING** the subject of the argument.

▲ 119–49

▲ 87–118
183–90
164–72
205–13
191–204

A decision about whether to mix genres or not should depend primarily on your purpose and audience. If doing so would help you achieve your goal, and you are not restricted to a particular genre, then combining genres is appropriate. Be creative — but not to the extent that you confuse or annoy readers who expect, say, a straightforward academic report. And if you are required to write using a single genre, then you must find ways of making it suit your purpose.

Considering the Rhetorical Situation

If you're still unsure which genre or combination of genres you should use, try exploring your rhetorical situation by answering some or all of the following questions:

PURPOSE   Why are you writing? What do you hope to achieve? What genre(s) do writers typically use to achieve this purpose? Where might you find examples of these genres? What alternatives to these genres are available?

■ 3–4

AUDIENCE   To whom are you writing? How do members of this audience typically communicate with one another? What information do they typically include, and what do they omit? How much information or explanation will they need? Will they expect you to cite the work of others?

■ 5–8

9–11 ■ **GENRE** What will your audience expect? Which ones do they use themselves in similar situations?

12–15 ■ **STANCE** What stance do you wish to project — and what stances are acceptable for your audience and purpose? What is your relationship with your audience? Are you writing as an equal, a student, an interested or concerned outsider, something else? What tone is appropriate — objective, impassioned, respectful, informal, something else? What genre(s) will allow you to express that tone?

16–18 ■ **MEDIA / DESIGN** What media are typically used to communicate in this situation, and do these media suggest or encourage a particular genre? If so, does the genre require a particular design or format? Are charts, graphs, photos, or other visual elements typically included?

rhetorical situations

genres

processes

strategies

research MLA / APA

media / design

readings

part 3

Processes

To create anything, we generally break the work down into a series of steps. We follow a recipe (or the directions on a box) to bake a cake; we break a song down into different parts and the music into various chords to arrange a piece of music. So it is when we write. We rely on various processes to get from a blank screen or page to a finished product. The chapters that follow offer advice on some of these processes — from WRITING AS INQUIRY and GENERATING IDEAS to DRAFTING to GETTING RESPONSE to EDITING to COMPILING A PORTFOLIO, and more.

Processes

Writing as Inquiry 22

Sometimes we write to say what we think. Other times, however, we write in order to figure out what we think. Much of the writing you do in college will be the latter. Even as you learn to write, you will be writing to learn. This chapter is about writing with a spirit of inquiry — approaching writing projects with curiosity, moving beyond the familiar, keeping your eyes open, tackling issues that don't have easy answers. It's about starting with questions and going from there — and taking risks. As Mark Twain once said, "Sail away from the safe harbor. . . . Explore. Dream. Discover." This chapter offers strategies for doing just that with your writing.

Starting with Questions

The most important thing is to start with questions — with what you don't know rather than with what you do know. Your goal is to learn about your subject and then to learn more. If you're writing about a topic you know well, you want to expand on what you already know. In academic writing, good topics arise from important questions, issues, and problems that are already being discussed. As a writer, you need to find out what's being said about your topic and then see your writing as a way of entering that larger conversation.

So start with questions, and don't expect to find easy answers. If there were easy answers, there would be no reason for discussion — or for you to write. For purposes of inquiry, the best questions can't be answered by looking in a reference book. Instead, they are ones that help you explore what you think — and why. As it happens, many of the strategies in this book can help you ask questions of this kind. Following are some questions to get you started.

rhetorical situations

genres

processes

strategies

research MLA / APA

media / design

readings

356–66 **How can it be DEFINED?**   What is it, and what does it do? Look it up in a dictionary; check *Wikipedia*. Remember, though, that these are only starting points. How *else* can it be defined? What more is there to know about it? If your topic is being debated, chances are that its very definition is subject to debate. If, for instance, you're writing about gay marriage, how you define marriage will affect how you approach the topic.

367–75 **How can it be DESCRIBED?**   What details should you include? From what vantage point should you describe your topic? If, for example, your topic were the physiological effects of running a marathon, what would those effects be — on the lungs, heart muscles, nerves, brain, and so on? How would you describe the physical experience of running over twenty-six miles from the runner's point of view?

382–86 **How can it be EXPLAINED?**   What does it do? How does it work? If you were investigating the use of performance-enhancing drugs by athletes, for example, what exactly is the effect of these drugs? What makes them dangerous — and are they always dangerous or only in certain conditions? Why are they illegal — and should they be illegal?

348–55 **What can it be COMPARED with?**   Again with the use of performance-enhancing drugs by athletes as an example, how does taking such supplements compare with wearing high-tech footwear or uniforms? Does such a comparison make you see taking steroids or other performance-enhancing drugs in a new light?

318–22 **What may have CAUSED it? What might be its EFFECTS?**   Who or what does it affect? What causes cerebral palsy in children, for example? What are its symptoms? If children with cerebral palsy are not treated, what might be the consequences?

342–47 **How can it be CLASSIFIED?**   Is it a topic or issue that can be placed into categories of similar topics or issues? What categories can it be placed into? Are there legal and illegal performance-enhancing supplements (human growth hormone and steroids, for instance), and what's the difference? Are some safe and others less safe? Classifying your topic in this way can help you consider its complexities.

rhetorical situations   genres   processes   strategies   research MLA / APA   media / design   readings

How can it be ANALYZED?   What parts can the topic be divided into? For example, if you were exploring the health effects of cell phone use, you might ask what evidence suggests that cell phone radiation causes cancer? What cancers are associated with cell phone use? What do medical experts and phone manufacturers say? How can cell phone users reduce their risk?

◆ 412

How can it be INTERPRETED?   What does it really mean? How do you interpret it, and how does your interpretation differ from others? What evidence supports your interpretation, and what argues against it? Imagine you were exploring the topic of sports injuries among young women. Do these injuries reflect a larger cultural preoccupation with competition? a desire to win college scholarships? something else?

▲ 52–86

What expectations does it raise?   What will happen next? What makes you think so? If this happens, how will it affect those involved? For instance, will the governing bodies of professional sports require more testing of athletes' blood, urine, and hair than they do now? Will such tests be unfair to athletes taking drugs for legitimate medical needs?

What are the different POSITIONS on it?   What controversies or disagreements exist, and what evidence is offered for the various positions? What else might be said? Are there any groups or individuals who seem especially authoritative? If so, you might want to explore what they have said.

▲ 119–49

What are your own feelings about it?   What interests you about the topic? How much do you already know about it? For example, if you're an athlete, how do you feel about competing against others who may have taken supplements? If a friend has problems with drugs, do those problems affect your thinking about drugs in sports? How do you react to what others say about the topic? What else do you want to find out?

Are there other ways to think about it?   Is what seems true in this case also true in others? How can you apply this subject in another situation? Will what works in another situation also work here? What do you have to do to adapt it? Imagine you were writing about traffic fatalities. If replacing stop signs with roundabouts or traffic circles reduced traffic fatalities in England, could doing so also reduce accidents in the United States?

262–63 ⊙
You can also start with the journalist's **QUESTIONS**: *Who? What? When? Where? Why? How?* Asking questions from these various perspectives can help you deepen your understanding of your topic by leading you to see it from many angles.

Keeping a Journal

One way to get into the habit of using writing as a tool for inquiry is to keep a journal. You can use a journal to record your observations, reactions, whatever you wish. Some writers find journals especially useful places to articulate questions or speculations. You may be assigned by teachers to do certain work in a journal, but in general, you can use a journal to write for yourself. Note your ideas, speculate, digress — go wherever your thoughts lead you.

Keeping a Blog

602–3 ▢
You may also wish to explore issues or other ideas online in the form of a **BLOG**. Most blogs have a comments section that allows others to read and respond to what you write, leading to potentially fruitful discussions. You can also include links to other websites, helping you connect various strands of thought and research. The blogs of others, along with online discussion forums and groups, may also be useful sources of opinion on your topic, but keep in mind that they probably aren't authoritative research sources. There are a number of search engines that can help you find blog posts related to specific topics, including *Google Blog Search, Ask,* and *IceRocket.* You can create your own blog on sites such as *Blogger, Tumblr,* or *WordPress.*

■ rhetorical situations
▲ genres
○ processes
◆ strategies
● research MLA / APA
▢ media / design
▨ readings

Collaborating 23

Whether you're working in a face-to-face group, posting on an online discussion board or wiki, or exchanging drafts with a classmate for peer review, you likely spend a lot of time collaborating with others on writing tasks. Even if you do much of your writing sitting alone at a computer, you probably get help from others at various stages in the writing process—and provide help as well. The fact is that two heads can be better than one—and learning to work well with a team is as important as anything else you'll learn in college. This chapter offers some guidelines for collaborating successfully with other writers.

Some Ground Rules for Face-to-Face Group Work

- Make sure everyone is facing everyone else and is physically part of the group. Doing that makes a real difference in the quality of the interactions—think how much better conversation works when you're sitting around a table than it does when you're sitting in a row.

- Thoughtfulness, respect, and tact are key, since most writers (as you know) are sensitive and need to be able to trust those commenting on their work. Respond to the contributions of others as you would like others to respond to yours.

- Each meeting needs an agenda—and careful attention paid to time. Appoint one person as timekeeper to make sure all necessary work gets done in the available time.

- Appoint another person to be group leader or facilitator. That person needs to make sure everyone gets a chance to speak, no one dominates the discussion, and the group stays on task.

- Appoint a third member of the group to keep a record of the group's discussion. He or she should jot down the major points as they come up and afterward write a **SUMMARY** of the discussion that the group members approve.

470–71

Online Collaboration

Sometimes you'll need or want to work with one or more people online. Working together online offers many advantages, including the ability to collaborate without being in the same place at the same time. Nonetheless, it also presents some challenges that differ from those of face-to-face group work. When sharing writing or collaborating with others online in other ways, consider the following suggestions:

- As with all online communication, remember that you need to choose your words carefully to avoid inadvertently hurting someone's feelings. Without facial expressions, gestures, and other forms of body language and without tone of voice, your words carry all the weight.

5–8

- Remember that the **AUDIENCE** for what you write may well extend beyond your group—your work might be forwarded to others, so there is no telling who else might read it.

- Decide as a group how best to deal with the logistics of exchanging drafts and comments. You can cut and paste text directly into email, send it as an attachment to a message, or post it to your class course management system site. You may need to use a combination of methods, depending on each group member's access to equipment and software. In any case, name your files carefully so that everyone knows which version to use.

Group Writing Projects

Creating a document with a team is common in business and professional work and in some academic fields as well. Here are some tips for making collaboration of this kind work well:

rhetorical situations   genres   processes   strategies   research MLA / APA   media / design   readings

- *Define the task as clearly as possible,* and make sure everyone understands and agrees with the stated goals.
- *Divide the task into parts.* Decide which parts can be done by individuals, which can be done by a subgroup, and which need to be done by everyone together.
- *Assign each group member certain tasks.* Try to match tasks to each person's skills and interests and to divide the work equally.
- *Establish a deadline for each task.* Allow time for unforeseen problems before the project deadline.
- *Try to accommodate everyone's style of working.* Some people value discussion; others want to get right down to the writing. There's no best way to get work done; everyone needs to be conscious that his or her way is not the only way.
- *Work for consensus — not necessarily total agreement.* Everyone needs to agree that the plan to get the writing accomplished is doable and appropriate — if not exactly the way you would do the project if you were working alone.
- *Make sure everyone performs.* In some situations, your instructor may help, but in others the group itself may have to develop a way to make sure that the work gets done well and fairly. During the course of the project, it's sometimes helpful for each group member to write an assessment both of the group's work and of individual members' contributions.

Writing Conferences

Conferences with instructors or writing tutors can be an especially helpful kind of collaboration. These one-on-one sessions often offer the most strongly focused assistance you can get — and truly valuable instruction. Here are some tips for making the most of conference time:

- *Come prepared.* Bring all necessary materials, including the draft you'll be discussing, your notes, any outlines — and, of course, any questions.

- **Be prompt.** Your instructor or tutor has set aside a block of time for you, and once that time is up, there's likely to be another student writer waiting.

- **Listen carefully, discuss your work seriously, and try not to be defensive.** Your instructor or tutor is only trying to help you produce the best piece possible. If you sense that your work is being misunderstood, explain what you're trying to say. Don't get angry! If a sympathetic reader who's trying to help can't understand what you mean, maybe you haven't conveyed your meaning well enough.

- **Take notes.** During the conference, jot down key words and suggestions. Immediately afterward, flesh out your notes so you'll have a complete record of what was said.

- **Reflect on the conference.** Afterward, think about what you learned. What do you have to do now? Create a plan for revising or doing further work, and write out questions you will ask at your next conference.

rhetorical
situations

genres

processes

strategies

research
MLA / APA

media /
design

readings

Generating Ideas and Text

All good writing revolves around ideas. Whether you're writing a job-application letter, a sonnet, or an essay, you'll always spend time and effort generating ideas. Some writers can come up with a topic, put their thoughts in order, and flesh out their arguments in their heads; but most of us need to write out our ideas, play with them, tease them out, and examine them from some distance and from multiple perspectives. This chapter offers activities that can help you do just that. *Freewriting, looping, listing,* and *clustering* can help you explore what you know about a subject; *cubing* and *questioning* nudge you to consider a subject in new ways; and *outlining, letter writing, journal keeping,* and *discovery drafting* offer ways to generate a text.

Freewriting

An informal method of exploring a subject by writing about it, freewriting ("writing freely") can help you generate ideas and come up with materials for your draft. Here's how to do it:

1. Write as quickly as you can without stopping for 5 to 10 minutes (or until you fill a screen or page).

2. If you have a subject to explore, write it at the top and then start writing about it, but if you stray, don't worry—just keep writing. If you don't have a subject yet, just start writing and don't stop until the time is up. If you can't think of anything to say, write that ("I can't think of anything to say") again and again until you do—and you will!

3. Once the time is up, read over what you've written, and underline or highlight passages that interest you.

4. Then write some more, starting with one of those underlined or high-lighted passages as your new topic. Repeat the process until you've come up with a usable topic.

Looping

Looping is a more focused version of freewriting; it can help you explore what you know about a subject. You stop, reflect on what you've written, and then write again, developing your understanding in the process. It's good for clarifying your knowledge and understanding of a subject and finding a focus. Here's what you do:

1. Write for 5 to 10 minutes on whatever you know about your subject. This is your first loop.

2. Read over what you wrote, and then write a single sentence summa-rizing the most important or interesting idea. You might try completing one of these sentences: "I guess what I was trying to say was . . . " or "What surprises me most in reading what I wrote is . . . ." This will be the start of another loop.

3. Write again for 5 to 10 minutes, using your summary sentence as your beginning and your focus. Again, read what you've written, and then write a sentence capturing the most important idea—in a third loop.

Keep going until you have enough understanding of your topic to be able to decide on a tentative focus—something you can write about.

Listing

Some writers find it useful to keep lists of ideas that occur to them while they are thinking about a topic. Follow these steps:

1. Write a list of potential ideas about a topic. Don't try to limit your list—include anything that interests you.

rhetorical situations   genres   processes   strategies   research MLA / APA   media / design   readings

2. Look for relationships among the items on your list: what patterns do you see? If other ideas occur to you, add them to the list.

3. Finally, arrange the items in an order that makes sense for your purpose and can serve as the beginning of an outline for your writing.

Clustering

Clustering is a way of generating and connecting ideas visually. It's useful for seeing how various ideas relate to one another and for developing subtopics. The technique is simple:

1. Write your topic in the middle of a sheet of paper and circle it.

2. Write ideas relating to that topic around it, circle them, and connect them to the central circle.

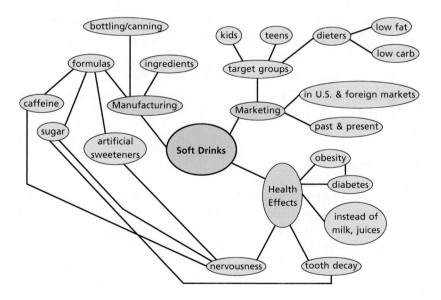

3. Write down examples, facts, or other details relating to each idea, and join them to the appropriate circles.

4. Keep going until you can't think of anything else relating to your topic.

You should end up with various ideas about your topic, and the clusters will allow you to see how they relate to one another. In the example cluster on the topic of "soft drinks" from page 261, note how some ideas link not only to the main topic or related topics but also to other ideas.

Cubing

A cube has six sides. You can examine a topic as you might a cube, looking at it in these six ways:

367–75
- **DESCRIBE** it. What's its color? shape? age? size? What's it made of?

348–55
- **COMPARE** it to something else. What is it similar to or different from?

342–47
- Associate it with other things. What does it remind you of? What connections does it have to other things? How would you **CLASSIFY** it?

- Analyze it. How is it made? Where did it come from? Where is it going? How are its parts related?

- Apply it. What is it used for? What can be done with it?

119–49
- **ARGUE** for or against it. Choose a position relating to your subject, and defend it.

Questioning

251–54
It's always useful to ask **QUESTIONS**. One way is to start with *What? Who? When? Where? How?* and *Why?* A particular method of exploring a topic is to ask questions as if the topic were a play. This method is especially useful for exploring literature, history, the arts, and the social sciences. Start with these questions:

rhetorical situations

genres

processes

strategies

research
MLA / APA

media / design

readings

- **What?** What happens? How is it similar to or different from other actions?

- **Who?** Who are the actors? Who are the participants, and who are the spectators? How do the actors affect the action, and how are they affected by it?

- **When?** When does the action take place? How often does it happen? What happens before, after, or at the same time? Would it be different at another time? Does the time have historical significance?

- **Where?** What is the setting? What is the situation, and what makes it significant?

- **How?** How does the action occur? What are the steps in the process? What techniques are required? What equipment is needed?

- **Why?** Why did this happen? What are the actors' motives? What end does the action serve?

Outlining

You may create an *informal outline* by simply listing your ideas and numbering them in the order in which you want to write about them. You might prefer to make a *working outline*, to show the hierarchy of relationships among your ideas. While still informal, a working outline distinguishes your main ideas and your support, often through simple indentation:

First main idea
    Supporting evidence or detail
    Supporting evidence or detail
Second main idea
    Supporting evidence or detail
    Supporting evidence or detail

A *formal outline* shows the hierarchy of your ideas through a system of indenting, numbering, and lettering. Remember that when you divide a point into more specific subpoints, you should have at least two of them — you can't divide something into only one part. Also, try to keep items at each level parallel in structure. Formal outlines work this way:

Thesis statement
I. First reason
   A. Supporting evidence
      1. Detail of evidence
      2. Detail of evidence
   B. Supporting evidence
II. Another reason

Writing out a formal outline can be helpful when you're dealing with a complex subject; as you revise your drafts, though, be flexible and ready to change your outline as your understanding of your topic develops.

Letter Writing

Sometimes the prospect of writing a report or essay can be intimidating. You may find that simply explaining your topic to someone will help you get started. In that case, write a letter to someone you know — your best friend, a parent or grandparent, a sibling — in which you discuss your subject. Explain it in terms that your reader can understand. Use the unsent letter to rehearse your topic; make it a kind of rough draft that you can then revise and develop to suit your actual audience.

Keeping a Journal

Some writers find that writing in a journal helps them generate ideas. Making note of your ideas, thoughts, feelings, or the events of your day can provide a wealth of topics, and a journal can also be a good place to explore what you think and why you think as you do.

Discovery Drafting

Some writers do best by jumping in and writing. Here are the steps to take if you're ready to write a preliminary **DRAFT:**

⊙ 266–68

1. Write your draft quickly, in one sitting if possible.

2. Assume that you are writing to discover what you want to say and how you need to say it—and that you will make substantial revisions in a later part of the process.

3. Don't worry about grammatical or factual correctness—if you can't think of a word, leave a blank space to fill in later. If you're unsure of a date or spelling, put a question mark in parentheses as a reminder to check it later. Just write.

> **IF YOU NEED MORE HELP**
>
> See each of the **GENRE** chapters for specific strategies for generating text in each genre.

▲ 25

25 Drafting

At some point, you need to write out a draft. By the time you begin drafting, you've probably written quite a bit — in the form of notes, lists, outlines, and other kinds of informal writing. This chapter offers some hints on how to write a draft — and reminds you that as you draft, you may well need to get more information, rethink some aspect of your work, or follow new ideas that occur to you as you write.

Establishing a Schedule with Deadlines

421–22

Don't wait until the last minute to write. Computers crash, printers jam. Life intervenes in unpredictable ways. You increase your chances of success immensely by setting and meeting **DEADLINES**: Research done by ____; rough draft done by ____; revisions done by ____; final draft edited, proofread, and submitted by ____. How much time you need varies with each writing task — but trying to compress everything into twenty-four or forty-eight hours before the deadline is asking for trouble.

Getting Comfortable

When are you at your best? When do you have your best ideas? For major writing projects, consider establishing a schedule that lets you write when you stand the best chance of doing good work. Schedule breaks for exercise and snacks. Find a good place to write, a place where you've got a good surface on which to spread out your materials, good lighting, a comfortable chair, and the right tools (computer, pen, paper) for the job. Often, however, we must make do: you may have to do your drafting in a busy computer lab or classroom. The trick is to make yourself as comfortable as you can manage. Sort out what you *need* from what you *prefer*.

rhetorical situations

genres

processes

strategies

research MLA / APA

media / design

readings

Starting to Write

All of the above advice notwithstanding, don't worry so much about the trappings of your writing situation that you don't get around to writing. Write. Start by **FREEWRITING**, start with a first sentence, start with awful writing that you know you'll discard later—but write. That's what gets you warmed up and going.

⊙ 259–60

Write quickly in spurts.   Write quickly with the goal of writing a complete draft, or a complete section of a longer draft, in one sitting. If you need to stop in the middle, make some notes about where you were headed when you stopped so that you can easily pick up your train of thought when you begin again.

Break down your writing task into small segments.   Big projects can be intimidating. But you can always write one section or, if need be, one paragraph or even a single sentence—and then another and another. It's a little like dieting. If I think I need to lose twenty pounds, I get discouraged and head for the doughnuts; but if I decide that I'll lose one pound and I lose it, well, I'll lose another—*that* I can do.

Expect surprises.   Writing is a form of thinking; the words you write lead you down certain roads and away from others. You may end up somewhere you didn't anticipate. Sometimes that can be a good thing—but sometimes you can write yourself into a dead end or out onto a tangent. Just know that this is natural, part of every writer's experience, and it's okay to double back or follow a new path that opens up before you.

Expect to write more than one draft.   A first sentence, first page, or first draft represents your attempt to organize into words your thoughts, ideas, feelings, research findings, and more. It's likely that some of that first try will not achieve your goals. That's okay—having writing on screen or on paper that you can change, add to, and cut means you're part of the way there. As you revise, you can fill in gaps and improve your writing and thinking.

Dealing with Writer's Block

You may sit down to write but find that you can't—nothing occurs to you; your mind is blank. Don't panic; here are some ways to get started writing again:

- Think of the assignment as a problem to be solved. Try to capture that problem in a single sentence: "How do I explain the context for my topic?" "What is the best way to organize my argument?" "What am I trying to do in the conclusion?" Think of a solution to the problem, and then stop thinking about it. If you can't solve it, do something else; give yourself time. Many of us find the solution in the shower, after a good night's sleep.

- Stop trying: take a walk, take a shower, do something else. Come back in a half hour, refreshed.

259–61
- Open a new document on your computer or get a fresh piece of paper and **FREEWRITE**, or try **LOOPING** or **LISTING**. What are you trying to say? Just let whatever comes come—you may write yourself out of your box.

- If you usually write on your computer, turn it off, get out paper and pencil, and write by hand.

262–63
- Try a graphic approach: try **CLUSTERING,** or draw a chart of what you want to say; draw a picture; doodle.

419
- Do some **RESEARCH** on your topic to see what others have said about it.

275–76
- Talk to someone about what you are trying to do. If there's a writing center at your school, talk to a tutor: **GET RESPONSE**. If there's no one to talk to, talk to yourself. It's the act of talking—using your mouth instead of your hands—that can free you up.

IF YOU NEED MORE HELP

259–65
269–74
275–81

See the chapter on **GENERATING IDEAS AND TEXT** if you find you need more material. And once you have a draft, see the chapters on **ASSESSING YOUR OWN WRITING** and **GETTING RESPONSE AND REVISING** for help evaluating your draft.

rhetorical situations   genres   processes   strategies   research MLA / APA   media / design   readings

Assessing Your Own Writing

In school and out, our work is continually assessed by others. Teachers determine whether our writing is strong or weak; supervisors decide whether we merit raises or promotions; even friends and relatives size up in various ways the things we do. As writers, we need to assess our own work—to step back and see it with a critical eye. By developing standards of our own and being conscious of the standards others use, we can assess—and shape—our writing, making sure it does what we want it to do. This chapter will help you assess your own written work.

Assessing the Writing You Do for Yourself

We sometimes write not for an audience but for ourselves—to generate ideas, reflect, make sense of things. The best advice on assessing such writing is *don't*. If you're writing to explore your thoughts, understand a subject, record the events of your day, or just for the pleasure of expressing yourself in words, shut off your internal evaluator. Let the words flow without worrying about them. Let yourself wander without censoring yourself or fretting that what you're writing is incorrect or incomplete or incoherent. That's okay.

One measure of the success of personal writing is its length. FREEWRITING, LISTING, CUBING, JOURNAL KEEPING, and other types of informal writing are like warm-up exercises to limber you up and get you thinking. If you don't give those writing exercises enough time and space, they may not do what you want them to. Often, students' best insights appear at the end of their journal entries. Had they stopped before that point, they never would have had those good ideas.

259–65

A way to study the ideas in your personal writing is to highlight useful patterns in different colors. For example, journal entries usually involve some questioning and speculating, as well as summarizing and para-phrasing. Try color coding each of these, sentence by sentence, phrase by phrase: yellow for summaries or paraphrases, green for questions, blue for speculations. Do any colors dominate? If, for example, your text is mostly yellow, you may be restating the course content too much and perhaps need to ask more questions. If you're generating ideas for an essay, you might assign colors to ideas or themes to see which ones are most promising.

Assessing the Writing You Do for Others

What we write for others must stand on its own because we usually aren't present when it is read—we rarely get to explain to readers why we did what we did and what it means. So we need to make our writing as clear as we can before we submit, post, display, or publish it. It's a good idea to assess your writing in two stages, first considering how well it meets the needs of your particular rhetorical situation, then studying the text itself to check its focus, argument, and organization. Sometimes some simple questions can get you started:

> What works?
> What still needs work?
> Where do I need to say more (or less)?

Considering the Rhetorical Situation

3–4 **PURPOSE** What is your purpose for writing? If you have multiple purposes, list them, and then note which ones are the most important. How well does your draft achieve your purpose(s)? If you're writing for an assignment, what are the requirements of the assignment, and does your draft meet those requirements?

rhetorical situations genres processes strategies research MLA / APA media / design readings

AUDIENCE To whom are you writing? What do those readers need and expect, as far as you can tell? Does your draft answer their needs? Do you define any terms and explain any concepts they won't know?

5–8

GENRE What is the genre, and what are the key features of that genre? Does your draft include each of those features?

9–11

STANCE Is it clear where you stand on your topic? Does your writing project the personality, voice, and tone that you want? Look at the words you use—how do they represent you as a person?

12–15

MEDIA / DESIGN What medium (print? spoken? electronic?) or combination of media is your text intended for, and how well does your writing suit it? How well does the design of the text suit your purpose and audience? Does it meet any requirements of the genre or of the assignment, if you're writing for one?

16–18

Examining the Text Itself

Look carefully at your text to see how well it says what you want it to say. Start with its focus, and then examine its reasons and evidence, organization, and clarity, in that order. If your writing lacks focus, the revising you'll do to sharpen the focus is likely to change everything else; if it needs more reasons and evidence, the organization may well change.

Consider your focus. Your writing should have a clear point, and every part of the writing should support that point. Here are some questions that can help you see if your draft is adequately focused:

- What is your **THESIS?** Even if it is not stated directly, you should be able to summarize it for yourself in a single sentence.

313–15

- Is your thesis narrow or broad enough to suit the needs and expectations of your audience?

- How does the **BEGINNING** focus attention on your thesis or main point?

299–306

- Does each paragraph support or develop that point? Do any paragraphs or sentences stray from your focus?

306–10
- Does the **ENDING** leave readers thinking about your main point? Is there another way of concluding the essay that would sharpen your focus?

Consider the support you provide for your argument. Your writing needs to give readers enough information to understand your points, follow your argument, and see the logic of your thinking. How much information is enough will vary according to your audience. If they already know a lot about your subject or are likely to agree with your point of view, you may need to give less detail. If, however, they are unfamiliar with your topic or are skeptical about your views, you will probably need to provide much more.

326–34
- What **REASONS** and **EVIDENCE** do you give to support your thesis? Where might more information be helpful? If you're writing online, could you provide links to it?

356–66
- What key terms and concepts do you **DEFINE?** Are there any other terms your readers might need to have explained? Could you do so by providing links?

367–75
- Where might you include more **DESCRIPTION** or other detail?

348–55
- Do you make any **COMPARISONS?** Especially if your readers will not be familiar with your topic, it can help to compare it with something more familiar.

387–95
- If you include **NARRATIVE,** how is it relevant to your point?

297
- See Part 4 for other useful **STRATEGIES**.

Consider the organization. As a writer, you need to lead readers through your text, carefully structuring your material so that they will be able to follow your argument.

263–64 ◎
- Analyze the structure by **OUTLINING** it. An informal outline will do since you mainly need to see the parts, not the details.

rhetorical situations | genres | processes | strategies | research MLA / APA | media / design | readings

- Is your text complete? Does your genre require an abstract, a works-cited list, or any other elements?

- What **TRANSITIONS** help readers move from idea to idea and paragraph to paragraph? Do you need more?   ◆ 317

- If there are no **HEADINGS,** would adding them help orient readers?   ▢ 588–89

Check for clarity.   Nothing else matters if readers can't understand what you write. Following are some questions that can help you see whether your meaning is clear and your text is easy to read:

- Does your **TITLE** announce the subject of your text and give some sense of what you have to say? If not, would a more direct title strengthen your argument?   ◆ 312–13

- Do you state your **THESIS** directly? If not, will readers easily understand what your main point is? Try stating your thesis outright, and see if it makes your argument easier to follow.   ◆ 313–15

- Does your **BEGINNING** tell readers what they need to understand your text, and does your **ENDING** help them make sense of what they've just read?   ◆ 299–311

- How does each paragraph relate to the ones before and after? Are those relationships clear—or do you need to add **TRANSITIONS**?   ◆ 317

- Do you vary your sentences? If all the sentences are roughly the same length or follow the same subject-verb-object pattern, your text probably lacks any clear emphasis and might even be difficult to read.

- Are **VISUALS** clearly labeled, positioned near the text they relate to, and referred to clearly in the text?   ▢ 591–99

- If you introduce materials from other sources, have you clearly distinguished **QUOTED, PARAPHRASED,** or **SUMMARIZED** ideas from your own?   ● 462–74

- Do you **DEFINE** all the words that your readers may not know?   ◆ 356–66

- Does your punctuation make your writing more clear or less? Incorrect punctuation can make writing difficult to follow or, worse, change the meaning from what you intended. As a best-selling punctuation manual reminds us, there's a considerable difference between "eats, shoots, and leaves" and "eats shoots and leaves."

Thinking about Your Process

Your growth as a writer depends on how well you understand what you do when you write, so that you can build on good habits. After you finish a writing project, considering the following questions can help you see the process that led to its creation — and find ways to improve the process next time.

- How would you tell the story of your thinking? Try writing these sentences: "When I first began with my topic, I thought _____. But as I did some thinking, writing, and research about the topic, my ideas changed and I thought _____."

- At some point in your writing, did you have to choose between two or more alternatives? What were they, and how did you choose?

- What was the most difficult problem you faced while writing? How did you go about trying to solve it?

- Whose advice did you seek while researching, organizing, drafting, revising, and editing? What advice did you take, and what did you ignore? Why?

Getting Response and Revising

If we want to learn to play a song on the guitar, we play it over and over again until we get it right. If we play basketball or baseball, we likely spend hours shooting foul shots or practicing a swing. Writing works the same way. Making our meaning clear can be tricky, and you should plan on revising and, if need be, rewriting in order to get it right. When we speak with someone face-to-face or on the phone or text a friend, we can get immediate response and restate or adjust our message if we've been misunderstood. In most other situations when we write, that immediate response is missing, so we need to seek out responses from readers to help us revise. This chapter includes a list of things for those readers to consider, along with various strategies for subsequent revising and rewriting.

Getting Response

Sometimes the most helpful eyes belong to others: readers you trust, including trained writing-center tutors. They can often point out problems (and strengths) that you simply cannot see in your own work. Ask your readers to consider the specific elements in the list below, but don't restrict them to those elements. Caution: If a reader says nothing about any of these elements, don't be too quick to assume that you needn't think about them yourself.

- What did you think when you first saw the TITLE? Is it interesting? informative? appropriate? Will it attract other readers' attention? 312–13

- Does the BEGINNING grab your attention? If so, how does it do so? Does it give enough information about the topic? offer necessary background information? How else might the piece begin? 299–306

- Is there a clear THESIS? What is it? 313–15

324–34
480–83
- Is there sufficient **SUPPORT** for the thesis? Is there anywhere you'd like to have more detail? Is the supporting material sufficiently **DOCUMENTED?**

- Does the text have a clear pattern of organization? Does each part relate to the thesis? Does each part follow from the one preceding it? Was the text easy to follow? How might the organization be improved?

306–10
- Is the **ENDING** satisfying? What did it leave you thinking? How else might the piece end?

- Can you tell the writer's attitude toward the subject and audience? What words convey that attitude? Is it consistent throughout?

5–8
3–4
9–11
- How well does the text meet the needs and expectations of its **AUDIENCE?** Where might readers need more information, guidance, or clarification? How well does it achieve its **PURPOSE?** Does every part of the text help achieve the purpose? Could anything be cut? Should anything be added? Does the text meet the requirements of its **GENRE?** Should anything be added, deleted, or changed to meet those requirements?

Revising

Once you have studied your draft with a critical eye and, if possible, gotten responses from other readers, it's time to revise. Major changes may be necessary, and you may need to generate new material or do some rewriting. But assume that your draft is good raw material that you can revise to achieve your purposes. Revision should take place on several levels, from global (whole-text issues) to particular (the details). Work on your draft in that order, starting with the elements that are global in nature and gradually moving to smaller, more particular aspects. This allows you to use your time most efficiently and take care of bigger issues first. In fact, as you deal with the larger aspects of your writing, many of the smaller ones will be taken care of along the way.

Give yourself time to revise.   When you have a due date, set deadlines for yourself that will give you time — preferably several days but as much as your schedule permits — to work on the text before it has to be delivered.

■ rhetorical situations　　▲ genres　　○ processes　　◆ strategies　　● research MLA / APA　　□ media / design　　❙❙ readings

Also, get some distance. Often when you're immersed in a project, you can't see the big picture because you're so busy creating it. If you can, get away from your writing for a while and think about something else. When you return to it, you're more likely to see it freshly. If there's not time to put a draft away for several days or more, even letting it sit overnight or for a few hours can help.

As you revise, assume that nothing is sacred. Bring a critical eye to all parts of a draft, not only to those parts pointed out by your reviewers. Content, organization, sentence patterns, individual words — all are subject to improvement. Be aware that a change in one part of the text may require changes in other parts.

At the same time, don't waste energy struggling with writing that simply doesn't work; you can always discard it. Look for the parts of your draft that do work — the parts that match your purpose and say what you want to say. Focus your efforts on those bright spots, expanding and developing them.

Revise to sharpen your focus. Examine your **THESIS** to make sure it matches your **PURPOSE** as you now understand it. Read each paragraph to ensure that it contributes to your main point; you may find it helpful to **OUTLINE** your draft to help you see all the parts. One way to do this is to highlight one sentence in each paragraph that expresses the paragraph's main idea. Then, copy and paste the highlighted sentences into a new document. Does one state the thesis of the entire essay? Do the rest relate to the thesis? Are they in the best order? If not, you need to either modify the parts of the draft that don't advance your thesis or revise your thesis to reflect your draft's focus and to rearrange your points so they advance your discussion more effectively.

313–15
3–4
263–64

Read your **BEGINNING AND ENDING** carefully; make sure that the first paragraphs introduce your topic and provide any needed contextual information and that the final paragraphs provide a satisfying conclusion.

299–311

Revise to strengthen the argument. If readers find some of your claims unconvincing, you need to provide more information or more support. You may need to define terms you've assumed they will understand, offer additional examples, or provide more detail by describing, explaining processes, adding dialogue, or using some other **STRATEGIES**. Make sure you show as well as tell — and don't forget that you might need to do so literally, with visuals like photos, graphs, or charts. You might try freewriting, clustering, or other ways of **GENERATING IDEAS AND TEXT**. If you need to provide additional evidence, you might need to do additional **RESEARCH**.

Revise to improve the organization.   If you've outlined your draft, number each paragraph, and make sure each one follows from the one before. If anything seems out of place, move it, or if necessary, cut it completely.

Check to see if you've included appropriate **TRANSITIONS** or **HEADINGS** to help readers move through the text, and add them as needed. Check to make sure your text meets the requirements of the **GENRE** you're writing in.

Revise for clarity.   Be sure readers will be able to understand what you're saying. Look closely at your **TITLE** to be sure it gives a sense of what

the text is about and at your **THESIS** to be sure readers will recognize your main point. If you don't state a thesis directly, consider whether you should. Be sure you provide any necessary background information

and **DEFINE** any key terms. Make sure you've integrated any **QUOTATIONS, PARAPHRASES,** or **SUMMARIES** into your text smoothly. Be sure all paragraphs are focused around one main point and that the sentences in each paragraph contribute to that point. Finally, consider whether there are any

data that would be more clearly presented in a **CHART**, **TABLE**, or **GRAPH**.

One way to test whether your text is clear is to switch audiences: write what you're trying to express as if you were talking to an eight-year-old. Your final draft probably won't be written that way, but the act of explaining your ideas to a young audience or readers who know nothing about your topic can help you discover any points that may be unclear.

Read and reread — and reread.   Take some advice from writing theorist Donald Murray:

> Nonwriters confront a writing problem and look away from the text to rules and principles and textbooks and handbooks and models. Writers look at the text, knowing that the text itself will reveal what needs to be done and what should not yet be done or may never be done.

rhetorical situations · genres · processes · strategies · research MLA / APA · media / design · readings

The writer reads and rereads and rereads, standing far back and reading quickly from a distance, moving in close and reading slowly line by line, reading again and again, knowing that the answers to all writing problems lie within the evolving text.

—Donald Murray, *A Writer Teaches Writing*

Rewriting

Some writers find it useful to try rewriting a draft in various ways or from various perspectives just to explore possibilities. Try it! If you find that your original plan works best for your purpose, fine. But you may find that another way will work better. Especially if you're not completely satisfied with your draft, consider the following ways of rewriting. Experiment with your rhetorical situation:

- Rewrite your draft from different points of view, through the eyes of different people perhaps or through the eyes of an animal or even from the perspective of an object. See how the text changes (in the information it presents, its perspective, its voice).

- Rewrite for a different AUDIENCE. How might an email detailing a recent car accident be written to a friend, an insurance agent, a parent? 5–8

- Rewrite in a different TONE. If the first draft was temperate and judicious, be extreme; if it was polite, be more direct. If the first draft was in standard English, rewrite it more informally. 12–15

- Rewrite the draft in a different GENRE or MEDIUM. Rewrite an essay as a letter, story, poem, speech. Which genre and medium work best to reach your intended audience and achieve your purpose? 9–11 16–18

Ways of rewriting a narrative

- Rewrite one scene completely in DIALOGUE. 376–81
- Start at the end of the story and work back to the beginning, or start in the middle and fill in the beginning as you work toward the end.

Ways of rewriting a textual analysis

348–55

- **COMPARE** the text you're analyzing with another text (which may be in a completely different genre — film, TV, song lyrics, computer games, poetry, fiction, whatever).

- Write a parody of the text you're analyzing. Be as silly and as funny as you can while maintaining the structure of the original text. Alternatively, write a parody of your analysis, using evidence from the text to support an outrageous analysis.

Ways of rewriting a report

5–8

- Rewrite for a different **AUDIENCE.** For example, explain a concept to your grandparents; describe the subject of a profile to a visitor from another planet.

- Be silly. Rewrite the draft as if for *The Daily Show* or the *Onion*, or rewrite it as if it were written by Bart Simpson.

Ways of rewriting an argument

119–49

- Rewrite taking another **POSITION.** Argue as forcefully for that position as you did for your actual one, acknowledging and refuting your original position. Alternatively, write a rebuttal to your first draft from the perspective of someone with different beliefs.

387–95

- Rewrite your draft as a **STORY** — make it real in the lives of specific individuals. (For example, if you were writing about abortion rights, you could write a story about a young pregnant woman trying to decide what she believes and what to do.) Or rewrite the argument as a fable or parable.

- Rewrite the draft as a letter responding to a hostile reader, trying at least to make him or her understand what you have to say.

- Rewrite the draft as an angry letter to someone, or as a table-thumping dinner-with-the-relatives discussion. Write from the most extreme position possible.

- Write an **ANALYSIS** of the topic of your argument in which you iden- ▲ 74–75
tify, as carefully and as neutrally as you can, the various positions
people hold on the issue.

Once you've rewritten a draft in any of these ways, see whether there's
anything you can use. Read each draft, considering how it might help you
achieve your purpose, reach your audience, convey your stance. Revise
your actual draft to incorporate anything you think will make your text
more effective, whether it's other genres or a different perspective.

28 Editing and Proofreading

Your ability to produce clear, error-free writing shows something about your ability as a writer and also leads readers to make assumptions about your intellect, your work habits, even your character. Readers of job-application letters and résumés, for example, may reject applications if they contain a single error, for no other reason than it's an easy way to narrow the field of potential candidates. In addition, they may well assume that applicants who present themselves sloppily in an application will do sloppy work on the job. This is all to say that you should edit and proofread your work carefully.

Editing

Editing is the stage when you work on the details of your paragraphs, sentences, words, and punctuation to make your writing as clear, precise, correct—and effective—as possible. Your goal is not to achieve "perfection" (whatever that may be) so much as to make your writing as effective as possible for your particular purpose and audience. Check a good writing handbook for detailed advice, but the following guidelines can help you check your drafts systematically for some common errors with paragraphs, sentences, and words.

Editing paragraphs

315–16

- Does each paragraph focus on one point? Does it have a **TOPIC SENTENCE** that announces that point, and if so, where is it located? If it's not the first sentence, should it be? If there's no clear topic sentence, should there be one?

- Does every sentence relate to the main point of the paragraph? If any sentences do not, should they be deleted, moved, or revised?

- Is there enough detail to develop the paragraph's main point? How is the point developed — with narrative? definition? some other **STRATEGY**?   297

- Where have you placed the most important information — at the beginning? the end? in the middle? The most emphatic spot is at the end, so in general that's where to put information you want readers to remember. The second most emphatic spot is at the beginning.

- Are any paragraphs especially long or short? Consider breaking long paragraphs if there's a logical place to do so — maybe an extended example should be in its own paragraph, for instance. If you have paragraphs of only a sentence or two, see if you can add to them or combine them with another paragraph.

- Check the way your paragraphs fit together. Does each one follow smoothly from the one before? Do you need to add any **TRANSITIONS**?   317

- Does the **BEGINNING** paragraph catch readers' attention? In what other ways might you begin your text?   299–306

- Does the final paragraph provide a satisfactory **ENDING**? How else might you conclude your text?   306–10

Editing sentences

- Is each sentence complete? Does it have someone or something (the subject) performing some sort of action or expressing a state of being (the verb)? Does each sentence begin with a capital letter and end with a period, question mark, or exclamation point?

- Check your use of the passive voice. Although there are some rhetorical situations in which the passive voice ("The emperor was assassinated by an anarchist") is more appropriate than the active voice ("An anarchist assassinated the emperor") because you want to emphasize an action rather than who performed it, you'll do well to edit it out unless you have a good reason for using it.

- Check for parallelism. Items in a list or series should be parallel in form—all nouns (lions, tigers, bears), all verbs (hopped, skipped, jumped), all clauses (he came, he saw, he conquered), and so on.

- Do many of your sentences begin with *it* or *there*? Too often these words make your writing wordy and vague or even conceal needed information. Why write "There are reasons we voted for him" when you can say "We had reasons to vote for him"?

317

- Are your sentences varied? If they all start with the subject or are the same length, your writing might be dull and maybe even hard to read. Try varying your sentence openings by adding **TRANSITIONS**, introductory phrases or clauses. Vary sentence lengths by adding detail to some or combining some sentences.

- Make sure you've used commas correctly. Is there a comma after each introductory element? ("After the lead singer quit, the group nearly disbanded. However, they then produced a string of hits.") Do commas set off nonrestrictive elements — parts that aren't needed to understand the sentence? ("The books I read in middle school, like the Harry Potter series, became longer and more challenging.") Are compound sentences connected with a comma? ("I'll eat broccoli steamed, but I prefer it roasted.")

Editing words

- Are you sure of the meaning of every word? Use a dictionary; be sure to look up words whose meanings you're not sure about. And remember your audience—do you use any terms they'll need to have defined?

- Is any of your language too general or vague? Why write that you competed in a race, for example, if you could say you ran the 4 × 200 relay?

13

- What about the **TONE?** If your stance is serious (or humorous or critical or something else), make sure that your words all convey that attitude.

- Do any pronouns have vague or unclear antecedents? If you use "he" or "they" or "it" or "these," will readers know whom or what the words refer to?

- Have you used any clichés — expressions that are used so frequently that they are no longer fresh? "Live and let live," avoiding something

"like the plague," and similar expressions are so predictable that your writing will almost always be better off without them.

- Be careful with language that refers to others. Make sure that your words do not stereotype any individual or group. Mention age, gender, race, religion, sexual orientation, and so on only if they are relevant to your subject. When referring to an ethnic group, make every effort to use the terms members of the group prefer.

- Edit out language that might be considered sexist. Do you say "he" when you mean "he and she"? Have you used words like *manpower* or *policeman* to refer to people who may be female? If so, substitute less gendered words such as *personnel* or *police officer*. Do your words reflect any gender stereotypes — for example, that all engineers are male, or all nurses female? If you mention someone's gender, is it even necessary? If not, eliminate the unneeded words.

- How many of your verbs are forms of *be* and *do*? If you rely too much on these words, try replacing them with more specific verbs. Why write "She did a proposal for" when you could say "She proposed"?

- Do you ever confuse *its* and *it's*? Use *it's* when you mean *it is* or *it has*. Use *its* when you mean *belonging to it*.

Proofreading

Proofreading is the final stage of the writing process, the point where you clean up your work to present it to your readers. Proofreading is like checking your appearance in a mirror before going into a job interview: being neat and well groomed looms large in creating a good first impression, and the same principle applies to writing. Misspelled words, missing pages, mixed-up fonts, and other lapses send a negative message about your work — and about you. Most readers excuse an occasional error, but by and large readers are an intolerant bunch: too many errors will lead them to declare your writing — and maybe your thinking — flawed. There goes your credibility. So proofread your final draft with care to ensure that your message is taken as seriously as you want it to be.

Up to this point, you've been told *not* to read individual words on the page and instead to read for meaning. Proofreading demands the opposite: you must slow down your reading so that you can see every word, every punctuation mark.

- Use your computer's grammar checker and spelling checker, but only as a first step, and know that they're not very reliable. Computer programs don't read writing; instead, they rely on formulas and banks of words, so what they flag (or don't flag) as mistakes may or may not be accurate. If you were to write, "I hope to sea you soon," *sea* would not be flagged as misspelled because it is a word, even though it's the wrong word in that sentence.

- To keep your eyes from jumping ahead, place a ruler or piece of paper under each line as you read. Use your finger or a pencil as a pointer.

- Some writers find it helpful to read the text one sentence at a time, beginning with the last sentence and working backward.

- Read your text out loud to yourself — or better, to others, who may *hear* problems you can't see. Alternatively, have someone else read your text aloud to you while you follow along on the screen or page.

- Ask someone else to read your text. The more important the writing is, the more important this step.

- If you find a mistake after you've printed out your text and are unable to print out a corrected version, make the change as neatly as possible in pencil or pen.

Compiling a Portfolio **29**

Artists maintain portfolios of their work to show gallery owners, collectors, and other potential buyers. Money managers work with investment portfolios of stocks, bonds, and various mutual funds. And often as part of a writing class, student writers compile portfolios of their work. As with a portfolio of paintings or drawings, a portfolio of writing includes a writer's best work and, sometimes, preliminary and revised drafts of that work, along with a statement by the writer articulating why he or she considers it good. The *why* is as important as the work, for it provides you with an occasion for assessing your overall strengths and weaknesses as a writer. This chapter offers guidelines to help you compile both a *writing portfolio* and a *literacy portfolio*, a project that writing students are sometimes asked to complete as part of a literacy narrative.

Considering the Rhetorical Situation

As with the writing you put in a portfolio, the portfolio itself is generally intended for a particular audience but could serve a number of different purposes. It's a good idea, then, to consider these and the other elements of your rhetorical situation when you begin to compile a portfolio.

PURPOSE   Why are you creating this portfolio? To create a record of your writing? As the basis for a grade in a course? To organize your research? To explore your literacy? For something else?   3–4

AUDIENCE   Who will read your portfolio? What will your readers expect it to contain? How can you help them understand the context or occasion for each piece of writing you include?   5–8

9-11　**GENRE** — What genres of writing should the portfolio contain? Do you want to demonstrate your ability to write one particular type of writing or in a variety of genres? Will your statement about the portfolio be in the form of a letter or an essay?

12-15　**STANCE** — How do you want to portray yourself in this portfolio? What items should you include to create this impression? What stance do you want to take in your written assessment of its contents? Thoughtful? Enthusiastic? Something else?

16-18　**MEDIA / DESIGN** — Will your portfolio be in print? Or will it be electronic? Whichever medium you use, how can you help readers navigate its contents? What design elements will be most appropriate to your purpose and medium?

A WRITING PORTFOLIO

What to Include in a Writing Portfolio

A portfolio developed for a writing course typically contains examples of your best work in that course, including any notes, outlines, preliminary drafts, and so on, along with your own assessment of your performance in the course. You might include any of the following items:

- freewriting, outlines, and other work you did to generate ideas
- drafts, rough and revised
- in-class writing assignments
- source material—copies of articles and online sources, observation notes, interview transcripts, and other evidence of your research
- tests and quizzes

rhetorical situations　genres　processes　strategies　research MLA / APA　media / design　readings

- responses to your drafts
- conference notes, error logs, lecture notes, other course materials
- reflections on your work

What you include will vary depending on what your instructor asks for. You may be asked to include three or four of your best papers or everything you've written. You may also be asked to show work in several different genres. In any case, you will usually need to choose, and to do that you will need to have criteria for making your choices. Don't base your decision solely on grades (unless grades are one criterion); your portfolio should reflect *your* assessment of your work, not your instructor's. What do you think is your best work? your most interesting work? your most ambitious work? Whatever criteria you use, you are the judge.

Organizing a Portfolio

Your instructor may provide explicit guidelines for organizing your portfolio. If not, here are some guidelines. If you set up a way to organize your writing at the start of the course, you'll be able to keep track of it throughout the course, making your job at term's end much easier. Remember that your portfolio presents you as a writer, presumably at your best. It should be neat, well organized, and easy to navigate.

Paper portfolios. Choose something in which to gather your work. You might use a two-pocket folder, a three-ring binder, or a file folder, or you may need a box, basket, or some other container to accommodate bulky or odd-shaped items.

Label everything. Label each piece at the top of the first page, specifying the assignment, the draft, and the date: "Proposal, Draft 1, 9/12/12"; "Text Analysis, Final Draft, 10/10/12"; "Portfolio Self-Assessment, Final Draft, 12/11/12" — and so on. Write this information neatly on the page, or

put it on a Post-it note. For each assignment, arrange your materials chronologically, with your earliest material (freewriting, for example) on the bottom, and each successive item (source materials, say, then your outline, then your first draft, and so on) on top of the last, ending with your final draft on top. That way readers can see how your writing changed from draft to draft.

Electronic portfolios. You might also create an electronic portfolio, or e-portfolio, that includes a homepage with links to your portfolio's contents. There are several tools that can help you create an e-portfolio:

- *Online tools.* Several websites offer free tools to help you create a pre-formatted e-portfolio. For example, *GoogleSites* provides templates you can use to build an e-portfolio, uploading documents, images, and videos from your computer.

- *Blogging tools.* You can create an e-portfolio using a blogging platform, like *Tumblr*, *WordPress* or *Weebly*, which allows you to upload files and create a network of linked pages. Readers can then comment on your e-portfolio, just as they might on your blog entries.

- *Wikis.* Wiki-based e-portfolios differ from blog-based ones in the level of interactivity they allow. In addition to commenting, readers may — if you allow them — make changes and add information. *PBworks* is one free provider, as is *WikiSpaces*.

- *Courseware.* Your school may use a learning platform, such as *Blackboard* or *Moodle*, that allows you to create a portfolio of your work.

It's also possible to create an electronic portfolio using word processing, spreadsheet, or presentation software. The programs available for your use and the requirements for publishing your portfolio vary from school to school and instructor to instructor; ask your instructor or your school's help desk for assistance (and see Chapter 55 on **WRITING ONLINE** for general guidance).

600–608

rhetorical situations | genres | processes | strategies | research MLA / APA | media / design | readings

Reflecting on Your Writing Portfolio

The most important part of your portfolio is your written statement reflecting on your work. This is an opportunity to assess your work with a critical eye and to think about what you're most proud of, what you most enjoyed doing, what you want to improve. It's your chance to think about and say what you've learned. Some instructors may ask you to write out your assessment in essay form; others will want you to put it in letter form, which usually allows for a more relaxed and personal tone. Whatever form it takes, your statement should cover the following ground:

- *An evaluation of each piece of writing in the portfolio.* Consider both strengths and weaknesses, and give examples from your writing to support what you say. What would you change if you had more time? Which is your favorite piece, and why? your least favorite?

- *An assessment of your overall writing performance.* What do you do well? What still needs improvement? What do you *want* your work to say about you? What *does* your work say about you?

- *A discussion of how the writing you did in this course has affected your development as a writer.* How does the writing in your portfolio compare with writing you did in the past? What do you know now that you didn't know before? What can you do that you couldn't do before?

- *A description of your writing habits and process.* What do you usually do? How well does it work? What techniques seem to help you most, and why? Which seem less helpful? Cite passages from your drafts that support your conclusions.

- *An analysis of your performance in the course.* How did you spend your time? Did you collaborate with others? Did you have any conferences with your instructor? Did you visit the writing center? Consider how these or any other activities contributed to your success.

A Sample Self-Assessment

Here is a letter written by Nathaniel Cooney as part of his portfolio for his first-year writing class at Wright State University.

2 June 2013

Dear Reader,

It is my hope that in reading this letter, you will gain an understanding of the projects contained in this portfolio. I enclose three works that I have submitted for an introductory writing class at Wright State University, English 102, Writing in Academic Discourse: an informative report, an argument paper, and a genre project based largely on the content of the argument paper. I selected the topics of these works for two reasons: First, they address issues that I believe to be relevant in terms of both the intended audience (peers and instructors of the course) and the times when they were published. Second, they speak to issues that are important to me personally. Below I present general descriptions of the works, along with my review of their strengths and weaknesses.

My purpose in writing the informative report "Higher Standards in Education Are Taking Their Toll on Students" was to present a subject in a factual manner and to support it with well-documented research. My intent was not to argue a point. However, because I chose a narrowly focused topic and chose information to support a thesis, the report tends to favor one side of the issue over the other. Because as a student I have a personal stake in the changing standards in the formal education system, I chose to research recent changes in higher education and their effects on students. Specifically, I examine students' struggles to reach a standard that seems to be moving further and further beyond their grasp.

I believe that this paper could be improved in two areas. The first is a bias that I think exists because I am a student presenting information from the point of view of a student. It is my hope, however, that my inclusion of unbiased sources lessens this problem somewhat and, furthermore, that it presents the reader

rhetorical situations   genres   processes   strategies   research MLA / APA   media / design   readings

with a fair and accurate collection of facts and examples that supports the thesis. My second area of concern is the overall balance in the paper between outside sources supporting my own thoughts and outside sources supporting opposing points of view. Rereading the paper, I notice many places where I may have worked too hard to include sources that support my ideas.

The second paper, "Protecting Animals That Serve," is an argument intended not only to take a clear position on an issue but also to argue for that position and convince the reader that it is a valid one. That issue is the need for legislation guaranteeing that certain rights of service animals be protected. I am blind and use a guide dog. Thus, this issue is especially important to me. During the few months that I have had him, my guide dog has already encountered a number of situations where intentional or negligent treatment by others has put him in danger. At the time I was writing the paper, a bill was being written in the Ohio House of Representatives that, if passed, would protect service animals and establish consequences for those who violated the law. The purpose of the paper, therefore, was to present the reader with information about service animals, establish the need for the legislation in Ohio and nationwide, and argue for passage of such legislation.

I think that the best parts of my argument are the introduction and the conclusion. In particular, I think that the conclusion does a good job of not only bringing together the various points but also conveying the significance of the issue for me and for others. In contrast, I think that the area most in need of further attention is the body of the paper. While I think the content is strong, I believe the overall organization could be improved. The connections between ideas are unclear in places, particularly in the section that acknowledges opposing viewpoints. This may be due in part to the fact that I had difficulty understanding the reasoning behind the opposing argument.

The argument paper served as a starting point for the genre project, for which the assignment was to revise one paper written for this class in a different genre. My genre project consists of a poster and a brochure. As it was for the argument paper, my primary goal was to convince my audience of the importance of a particular issue and viewpoint — specifically, to convince my audience to support House Bill 369, the bill being introduced in the Ohio legislature that would create laws to protect the rights of service animals in the state.

Perhaps both the greatest strength and the greatest weakness of the genre project is my use of graphics. Because of my blindness, I was limited in my use of some graphics. Nevertheless, the pictures were carefully selected to capture the attention of readers and, in part, to appeal to their emotions as they viewed and reflected on the material.

I put a great deal of time, effort, and personal reflection into each project. While I am hesitant to say that they are finished and while I am dissatisfied with some of the finer points, I am satisfied with the overall outcome of this collection of works. Viewing it as a collection, I am also reminded that writing is an evolving process and that even if these works never become exactly what I envisioned them to be, they stand as reflections of my thoughts at a particular time in my life. In that respect, they need not be anything but what they already are, because what they are is a product of who I was when I wrote them. I hope that you find the papers interesting and informative and that as you read them, you, too, may realize their significance.

Respectfully,

Nathaniel J. Cooney

Nathaniel J. Cooney

Enclosures (3)

Cooney describes each of the works he includes and considers their strengths and weaknesses, citing examples from his texts to support his assessment.

A LITERACY PORTFOLIO

As a writing student, you may be asked to think back to the time when you first learned to read and write or to remember significant books or other texts you've read and perhaps to put together a portfolio that chronicles your development as a reader and writer. You may also be asked to put together a literacy portfolio as part of a written narrative assignment.

What you include in such a portfolio will vary depending on what you've kept over the years and what your family has kept. You may have all of your favorite books, stories you dictated to a preschool teacher, notebooks in which you practiced writing the alphabet. Or you may have almost nothing. What you have or don't have is unimportant in the end: what's important is that you gather what you can and arrange it in a way that shows how you think about your development and growth as a literate person. What has been your experience with reading and writing? What's your earliest memory of learning to write? If you love to read, what led you to love it? Who was most responsible for shaping your writing ability? Those are some of the questions you'll ask if you write a **LITERACY NARRATIVE.** You might also compile a literacy portfolio as a good way to generate ideas and text for that assignment.

▲ 27–51

What to Include in a Literacy Portfolio

- school papers
- drawings and doodles from preschool
- favorite books
- photographs you've taken
- drawings
- poems
- letters
- journals and diaries
- lists
- reading records or logs

- marriage vows
- speeches you've given
- awards you've received

Organizing a Literacy Portfolio

You may wish to organize your material chronologically, but there are other methods of organization to consider as well. For example, you might group items according to where they were written (at home, at school, at work), by genre (stories, poems, essays, letters, notes), or even by purpose (pleasure, school, work, church, and so on). Arrange your portfolio in the way that best conveys who you are as a literate person. Label each item you include, perhaps with a Post-it note, to identify what it is, when it was written or read, and why you've included it in your portfolio.

Reflecting on Your Literacy Portfolio

- Why did you choose each item?
- Is anything missing? Are there any other important materials that should be here?
- Why is the portfolio organized as it is?
- What does the portfolio show about your development as a reader and writer?
- What patterns do you see? Are there any common themes you've read or written about? Any techniques you rely on? Any notable changes over time?
- What are the most significant items, and why?

rhetorical situations

genres

processes

strategies

research MLA / APA

media / design

readings

part 4

Strategies

Whenever we write, we draw on many different strategies to articulate what we have to say. We may DEFINE key terms, DESCRIBE people or places, and EXPLAIN how something is done. We may COMPARE one thing to another. Sometimes we may choose a pertinent story to NARRATE, and we may even want to include some DIALOGUE. The chapters that follow offer advice on how to use these AND OTHER BASIC STRATEGIES for developing and organizing the texts you write.

Strategies

Beginning and Ending

Whenever we pick up something to read, we generally start by looking at the first few words or sentences to see if they grab our attention, and based on them we decide whether to keep reading. Beginnings, then, are important, both attracting readers and giving them some information about what's to come. When we get to the end of a text, we expect to be left with a sense of closure, of satisfaction — that the story is complete, our questions have been answered, the argument has been made. So endings are important, too. This chapter offers advice on how to write beginnings and endings.

Beginning

How you begin depends on your RHETORICAL SITUATION, especially your purpose and audience. Academic audiences generally expect your introduction to establish context, explaining how the text fits into some larger conversation, addresses certain questions, or explores an aspect of the subject. Most introductions also offer a brief description of the text's content, often in the form of a thesis statement. The following opening of an essay on the effect of texting on student writing does all of this:

> It's taking over our lives. We can do it almost anywhere — walking to class, waiting in line at the grocery store, or hanging out at home. It's quick, easy, and convenient. It has become a concern of doctors, parents, and teachers alike. What it is? It's texting!
>
> Text messaging — or texting, as it's more commonly called — is the process of sending and receiving typed messages via a cellular phone. It is a common means of communication among teenagers and is even becoming popular in the business world because it allows quick messages

to be sent without people having to commit to a telephone conversation. A person is able to say what is needed, and the other person will receive the information and respond when it's convenient to do so.

In order to more quickly type what they are trying to say, many people use abbreviations instead of words. The language created by these abbreviations is called textspeak. Some people believe that using these abbreviations is hindering the writing abilities of students, and others argue that texting is actually having a positive effect on writing. In fact, it seems likely that texting has no significant effect on student writing.

—Michaela Cullington, "Does Texting Affect Writing?"

If you're writing for a nonacademic audience or genre—for a newspaper or a website, for example—your introduction may need to entice your readers to read on by connecting your text to their interests through shared experiences, anecdotes, or some other attention-getting device. Cynthia Bass, writing a newspaper article about the Gettysburg Address on its 135th anniversary, connects that date—the day her audience would read it—to Lincoln's address. She then develops the rationale for thinking about the speech and introduces her specific topic: debates about the writing and delivery of the Gettysburg Address:

November 19 is the 135th anniversary of the Gettysburg Address. On that day in 1863, with the Civil War only half over and the worst yet to come, Abraham Lincoln delivered a speech now universally regarded as both the most important oration in U.S. history and the best explanation—"government of the people, by the people, for the people"—of why this nation exists.

We would expect the history of an event so monumental as the Gettysburg Address to be well established. The truth is just the opposite. The only thing scholars agree on is that the speech is short—only ten sentences—and that it took Lincoln under five minutes to stand up, deliver it, and sit back down.

Everything else—when Lincoln wrote it, where he wrote it, how quickly he wrote it, how he was invited, how the audience reacted—has been open to debate since the moment the words left his mouth.

—Cynthia Bass, "Gettysburg Address: Two Versions"

rhetorical situations

genres

processes

strategies

research MLA / APA

media / design

readings

Ways of Beginning

Explain the larger context of your topic.   Most essays are part of an ongoing conversation, so you might begin by outlining the context of the subject to which your writing responds. An essay exploring the "emotional climate" of the United States after Barack Obama became president begins by describing the national moods during some of his predecessors' administrations:

> Every president plays a symbolic, almost mythological role that's hard to talk about, much less quantify — it's like trying to grab a ball of mercury. I'm not referring to using the bully pulpit to shape the national agenda but to the way that the president, as America's most inescapably powerful figure, colors the emotional climate of the country. John Kennedy and Ronald Reagan did this affirmatively, expressing ideals that shaped the whole culture. Setting a buoyant tone, they didn't just change movies, music, and television; they changed attitudes. Other presidents did the same, only unpleasantly. Richard Nixon created a mood of angry paranoia, Jimmy Carter one of dreary defeatism, and George W. Bush, especially in that seemingly endless second term, managed to do both at once.
>
> —John Powers, "Dreams from My President"

State your thesis.   Sometimes the best beginning is a clear **THESIS** stating your position, like the following statement in an essay arguing that fairy tales and nursery rhymes introduce us to "the rudiments and the humanness of engineering":

313–15

> We are all engineers of sorts, for we all have the principles of machines and structures in our bones. We have learned to hold our bodies against the forces of nature as surely as we have learned to walk. We calculate the paths of our arms and legs with the computer of our brain, and we catch baseballs and footballs with more dependability than the most advanced weapons systems intercept missiles. We may wonder if human evolution may not have been the greatest engineering feat of all time. And though many of us forget how much we once knew about the principles and practices of engineering, the nursery rhymes and fairy tales of our youth preserve the evidence that we did know quite a bit.
>
> —Henry Petroski, "Falling Down Is Part of Growing Up"

Forecast your organization.   You might begin by briefly outlining the way in which you will organize your text. The following example from a scholarly paper on the role of immigrants in the U.S. labor market offers background on the subject and describes the points that the writer's analysis will discuss:

> Debates about illegal immigration, border security, skill levels of workers, unemployment, job growth and competition, and entrepreneurship all rely, to some extent, on perceptions of immigrants' role in the U.S. labor market. These views are often shaped as much by politics and emotion as by facts.
>
> To better frame these debates, this short analysis provides data on immigrants in the labor force at the current time of slowed immigration, high unemployment, and low job growth and highlights eight industries where immigrants are especially vital. How large a share of the labor force are they and how does that vary by particular industry? How do immigrants compare to native-born workers in their educational attainment and occupational profiles?
>
> The answers matter because our economy is dependent on immigrant labor now and for the future. The U.S. population is aging rapidly as the baby boom cohort enters old age and retirement. As a result, the labor force will increasingly depend upon immigrants and their children to replace current workers and fill new jobs. This analysis puts a spotlight on immigrant workers to examine their basic trends in the labor force and how these workers fit into specific industries and occupations of interest.
>
> —Audrey Singer, "Immigrant Workers in the U.S. Labor Force"

Offer background information.   If your readers may not know as much as you do about your topic, giving them information to help them understand your position can be important, as David Guterson does in an essay on the Mall of America:

> Last April, on a visit to the new Mall of America near Minneapolis, I carried with me the public-relations press kit provided for the benefit of reporters. It included an assortment of "fun facts" about the mall: 140,000 hot dogs sold each week, 10,000 permanent jobs, 44 escalators and 17 elevators, 12,750 parking places, 13,300 short tons of steel, $1 million in cash disbursed weekly from 8 automatic-teller machines.

rhetorical situations / genres / processes / strategies / research MLA / APA / media / design / readings

The rotunda of the Mall of America.

Opened in the summer of 1992, the mall was built on the 78-acre site of the former Metropolitan Stadium, a five-minute drive from the Minneapolis–St. Paul International Airport. With 4.2 million square feet of floor space—including twenty-two times the retail footage of the average American shopping center—the Mall of America was "the largest fully enclosed combination retail and family entertainment complex in the United States."

—David Guterson, "Enclosed. Encyclopedic. Endured.
One Week at the Mall of America"

Visuals can also help provide context. For example, this essay on the Mall of America might have included a photo like the one on the preceding page to convey the size of the structure.

Define key terms or concepts.   The success of an argument often hinges on how key terms are DEFINED. You may wish to provide definitions up front, as an advocacy website, *Health Care without Harm*, does in a report on the hazards of fragrances in health-care facilities:

356–66

To many people, the word "fragrance" means something that smells nice, such as perfume. We don't often stop to think that scents are chemicals. Fragrance chemicals are organic compounds that volatilize, or vaporize into the air—that's why we can smell them. They are added to products to give them a scent or to mask the odor of other ingredients. The volatile organic chemicals (VOCs) emitted by fragrance products can contribute to poor indoor air quality (IAQ) and are associated with a variety of adverse health effects.

— "Fragrances," *Health Care without Harm*

Connect your subject to your readers' interests or values.   You'll always want to establish common ground with your readers, and sometimes you may wish to do so immediately, in your introduction, as in this example:

We all want to feel safe. Most Americans lock their doors at night, lock their cars in parking lots, try to park near buildings or under lights, and wear seat belts. Many invest in expensive security systems, carry pepper spray or a stun gun, keep guns in their homes, or take self-defense classes. Obviously, safety and security are important issues in American life.

—Andy McDonie, "Airport Security: What Price Safety?"

Start with something that will provoke readers' interest. Anna Quindlen opens an essay on feminism with the following eye-opening assertion:

> Let's use the F word here. People say it's inappropriate, offensive, that it puts people off. But it seems to me it's the best way to begin, when it's simultaneously devalued and invaluable.
> Feminist. Feminist, feminist, feminist.
>
> —Anna Quindlen, "Still Needing the F Word"

Start with an anecdote. Sometimes a brief **NARRATIVE** helps bring a topic to life for readers. See, for example, how an essay on the dozens, a type of verbal contest played by some African Americans, begins:

387–95

> Alfred Wright, a nineteen-year-old whose manhood was at stake on Longwood Avenue in the South Bronx, looked fairly calm as another teenager called him Chicken Head and compared his mother to Shamu the whale.
> He fingered the gold chain around his thin neck while listening to a detailed complaint about his sister's sexual abilities. Then he slowly took the toothpick out of his mouth; the jeering crowd of young men quieted as he pointed at his accuser.
> "He was so ugly when he was born," Wright said, "the doctor smacked his mom instead of him."
>
> —John Tierney, "Playing the Dozens"

Ask a question. Instead of a thesis statement, you might open with a question about the topic your text will explore, as this study of the status of women in science does:

> Are women's minds different from men's minds? In spite of the women's movement, the age-old debate centering around this question continues. We are surrounded by evidence of de facto differences between men's and women's intellects—in the problems that interest them, in the ways they try to solve those problems, and in the professions they choose. Even though it has become fashionable to view such differences as environmental in origin, the temptation to seek an explanation in terms of innate differences remains a powerful one.
>
> —Evelyn Fox Keller, "Women in Science: A Social Analysis"

Jump right in.   Occasionally you may wish to start as close to the key action as possible. See how one writer jumps right into his profile of a blues concert:

> Long Tongue, the Blues Merchant, strolls onstage. His guitar rides side-saddle against his hip. The drummer slides onto the tripod seat behind the drums, adjusts the high-hat cymbal, and runs a quick, off-beat tattoo on the tom-tom, then relaxes. The bass player plugs into the amplifier, checks the settings on the control panel, and nods his okay. Three horn players stand off to one side, clustered, lurking like brilliant sorcerer-wizards waiting to do magic with their musical instruments.
>
> —Jerome Washington, "The Blues Merchant"

Ending

Endings are important because they're the last words readers read. How you end a text will depend in part on your RHETORICAL SITUATION. You may end by wrapping up loose ends, or you may wish to give readers something to think about. Some endings do both, as Cynthia Bass does in a report on the debate over the Gettysburg Address. In her two final paragraphs, she first summarizes the debate and then shows its implications:

> What's most interesting about the Lincoln-as-loser and Lincoln-as-winner versions is how they marshal the same facts to prove different points. The invitation asks Lincoln to deliver "a few appropriate remarks." Whether this is a putdown or a reflection of the protocol of the time depends on the "spin" —an expression the highly politicized Lincoln would have readily understood—which the scholar places on it.
>
> These diverse histories should not in any way diminish the power or beauty of Lincoln's words. However, they should remind us that history, even the history of something as deeply respected as the Gettysburg Address, is seldom simple or clear. This reminder is especially useful today as we watch expert witnesses, in an effort to divine what the founders meant by "high crimes and misdemeanors," club one another with conflicting interpretations of the same events, the same words, the same precedents, and the same laws.
>
> —Cynthia Bass, "Gettysburg Address: Two Versions"

Bass summarizes the dispute about Lincoln's Address and then moves on to discuss the role of scholars in interpreting historical events. Writing during the Clinton impeachment hearings, she concludes by pointing out the way in which expert government witnesses often offer conflicting interpretations of events to suit their own needs. The ending combines several strategies to bring various strands of her essay together, leaving readers to interpret her final words themselves.

Ways of Ending

Restate your main point. Sometimes you'll simply SUMMARIZE your central idea, as in this example from an essay arguing that we have no "inner" self and that we should be judged by our actions alone:

470–71

> The inner man is a fantasy. If it helps you to identify with one, by all means, do so; preserve it, cherish it, embrace it, but do not present it to others for evaluation or consideration, for excuse or exculpation, or, for that matter, for punishment or disapproval.
>
> Like any fantasy, it serves your purposes alone. It has no standing in the real world which we share with each other. Those character traits, those attitudes, that behavior—that strange and alien stuff sticking out all over you—*that's the real you!*
>
> —Willard Gaylin, "What You See Is the Real You"

Discuss the implications of your argument. The following conclusion of an essay on the development of Post-it notes leads readers to consider how failure sometimes leads to innovation:

> Post-it notes provide but one example of a technological artifact that has evolved from a perceived failure of existing artifacts to function without frustrating. Again, it is not that form follows function but, rather, that the form of one thing follows from the failure of another thing to function as we would like. Whether it be bookmarks that fail to stay in place or taped-on notes that fail to leave a once-nice surface clean and intact, their failure and perceived failure is what leads to the true evolution of artifacts. That the perception of failure may take

centuries to develop, as in the case of loose bookmarks, does not reduce the importance of the principle in shaping our world.

—Henry Petroski, "Little Things Can Mean a Lot"

387–95

End with an anecdote, maybe finishing a **NARRATIVE** that was begun earlier in your text or adding one that illustrates the point you are making. See how Sarah Vowell uses a story to end an essay on students' need to examine news reporting critically:

> I looked at Joanne McGlynn's syllabus for her media studies course, the one she handed out at the beginning of the year, stating the goals of the class. By the end of the year, she hoped her students would be better able to challenge everything from novels to newscasts, that they would come to identify just who is telling a story and how that person's point of view affects the story being told. I'm going to go out on a limb here and say that this lesson has been learned. In fact, just recently, a student came up to McGlynn and told her something all teachers dream of hearing. The girl told the teacher that she was listening to the radio, singing along with her favorite song, and halfway through the sing-along she stopped and asked herself, "What am I singing? What do these words mean? What are they trying to tell me?" And then, this young citizen of the republic jokingly complained, "I can't even turn on the radio without thinking anymore."
>
> —Sarah Vowell, "Democracy and Things Like That"

Refer to the beginning.　One way to bring closure to a text is to bring up something discussed in the beginning; often the reference adds to or even changes the original meaning. For example, Amy Tan opens an essay on her Chinese mother's English by establishing herself as a writer and lover of language who uses many versions of English in her writing:

> I am not a scholar of English or literature. I cannot give you much more than personal opinions on the English language and its variations in this country or others.
>
> I am a writer. And by that definition, I am someone who has always loved language. I am fascinated by language in daily life. I spend a

rhetorical situations

genres

processes

strategies

research MLA / APA

media / design

readings

great deal of my time thinking about the power of language — the way it can evoke an emotion, a visual image, a complex idea, or a simple truth. Language is the tool of my trade. And I use them all — all the Englishes I grew up with.

At the end of her essay, Tan repeats this phrase, but now she describes language not in terms of its power to evoke emotions, images, and ideas, but in its power to evoke "the essence" of her mother. When she began to write fiction, she says,

> [I] decided I should envision a reader for the stories I would write. And the reader I decided upon was my mother, because these were stories about mothers. So with this reader in mind — and in fact she did read my early drafts — I began to write stories using all the Englishes I grew up with: the English I spoke to my mother, which for lack of a better term might be described as "simple"; the English she used with me, which for lack of a better term might be described as "broken"; my translation of her Chinese, which could certainly be described as "watered down"; and what I imagined to be her translation of her Chinese if she could speak in perfect English, her internal language, and for that I sought to preserve the essence, but neither an English nor a Chinese structure. I wanted to capture what language ability tests can never reveal: her intent, her passion, her imagery, the rhythms of her speech and the nature of her thoughts.
>
> — Amy Tan, "Mother Tongue"

Note how Tan not only repeats "all the Englishes I grew up with," but also provides parallel lists of what those Englishes can do for her: "evoke an emotion, a visual image, a complex idea, or a simple truth," on the one hand, and, on the other, capture her mother's "intent, her passion, her imagery, the rhythms of her speech and the nature of her thoughts."

Propose some action, as in the following conclusion of a report on the consequences of binge drinking among college students:

> The scope of the problem makes immediate results of any interventions highly unlikely. Colleges need to be committed to large-scale and long-term behavior-change strategies, including referral of alcohol abusers to

appropriate treatment. Frequent binge drinkers on college campuses are similar to other alcohol abusers elsewhere in their tendency to deny that they have a problem. Indeed, their youth, the visibility of others who drink the same way, and the shelter of the college community may make them less likely to recognize the problem. In addition to addressing the health problems of alcohol abusers, a major effort should address the large group of students who are not binge drinkers on campus who are adversely affected by the alcohol-related behavior of binge drinkers.

—Henry Wechsler et al., "Health and Behavioral Consequences of Binge Drinking in College: A National Survey of Students at 140 Campuses"

Considering the Rhetorical Situation

As a writer or speaker, think about the message that you want to articulate, the audience you want to reach, and the larger context you are writing in.

3–4	**PURPOSE**	Your purpose will affect the way you begin and end. If you're trying to persuade readers to do something, you may want to open by clearly stating your thesis and end by calling for a specific action.
5–8	**AUDIENCE**	Who do you want to reach, and how does that affect the way you begin and end? You may want to open with an intriguing fact or anecdote to entice your audience to read a profile, for instance, whereas readers of a report may expect it to conclude with a summary of your findings.
9–11	**GENRE**	Does your genre require a certain type of beginning or ending? Arguments, for example, often provide a statement of the thesis near the beginning; proposals typically end with a call for some solution.
12–15	**STANCE**	What is your stance, and can your beginning and ending help you convey that stance? For example, beginning an argument on the distribution of AIDS medications to underdeveloped countries with an anecdote may demonstrate

concern for the human costs of the disease, whereas starting with a statistical analysis may suggest the stance of a
careful researcher. Ending a proposal by weighing the
advantages and disadvantages of the solution you propose
may make you seem reasonable.

MEDIA / DESIGN   Your medium may affect the way you begin and end. A   16–18
web text, for instance, may open with a home page list-
ing a menu of the site—and giving readers a choice of
where they will begin. With a print text, you get to decide
how it will begin and end.

IF YOU NEED MORE HELP

See also the guides to writing in Chapters 7–10 for ways of beginning and ending   48
a **LITERACY NARRATIVE,** an essay **ANALYZING TEXT,** a **REPORT,** or an **ARGU-**   77–78
MENT.   114–15

146

31 Guiding Your Reader

Traffic lights, street signs, and lines on the road help drivers find their way. Readers need similar guidance—to know, for example, whether they're reading a report or an argument, an evaluation or a proposal. They also need to know what to expect: What will the report be about? What perspective will it offer? What will this paragraph cover? What about the next one? How do the two paragraphs relate to each other?

When you write, then, you need to provide cues to help your readers navigate your text and understand the points you're trying to make. This chapter offers advice on guiding your reader and, specifically, on using *titles, thesis statements, topic sentences,* and *transitions.*

Titles

A title serves various purposes, naming a text and providing clues to the content. It also helps readers decide whether they want to read further, so it's worth your while to come up with a title that attracts interest. Some titles include subtitles. You generally have considerable freedom in choosing a title, but always you'll want to consider the **RHETORICAL SITUATION** to be sure your title serves your purpose and appeals to the audience you want to reach.

Some titles simply announce the subject of the text:

"Black Men and Public Space"
The Pencil
"Why Colleges Shower Their Students with A's"
"Does Texting Affect Writing?"

Some titles provoke readers or otherwise entice them to read:

"Kill 'Em! Crush 'Em! Eat 'Em Raw!"
"Thank God for the Atom Bomb"
"What Are Homosexuals For?"

Sometimes writers add a subtitle to explain or illuminate the title:

Aria: Memoir of a Bilingual Childhood
"It's in Our Genes: The Biological Basis of Human Mating Behavior"
"From Realism to Virtual Reality: Images of America's Wars"

Sometimes when you're starting to write, you'll think of a title that helps you generate ideas and write. More often, though, a title is one of the last things you'll write, when you know what you've written and can craft a suitable name for your text.

Thesis Statements

A thesis identifies the topic of your text along with the claim you are making about it. A good thesis helps readers understand an essay. Working to create a sharp thesis can help you focus both your thinking and your writing. Here are three steps for moving from a topic to a thesis statement:

1. State your topic as a question.   You may have an idea for a topic, such as "gasoline prices," "analysis of 'real women' ad campaigns," or "famine." Those may be good topics, but they're not thesis statements, primarily because none of them actually makes a statement. A good way to begin moving from topic to thesis statement is to turn your topic into a question:

What causes fluctuations in gasoline prices?

Are ads picturing "real women" who aren't models effective?

What can be done to prevent famine in Africa?

2. Then turn your question into a position. A thesis statement is an assertion—it takes a stand or makes a claim. Whether you're writing a report or an argument, you are saying, "This is the way I see . . ." "My research shows . . . ," or "This is what I believe about . . ." Your thesis statement announces your position on the question you are raising about your topic, so a relatively easy way of establishing a thesis is to answer your own question:

> Gasoline prices fluctuate for several reasons.
>
> Ads picturing "real women" instead of models are effective because women can easily identify with them.
>
> The most recent famine in Somalia could have been avoided if certain measures had been taken.

3. Narrow your thesis. A good thesis is specific, guiding you as you write and showing your audience exactly what your essay will cover. The preceding thesis statements need to be qualified and focused—they need to be made more specific. For example:

> Gasoline prices fluctuate because of production procedures, consumer demand, international politics, and oil companies' policies.
>
> Dove's "Campaign for Self-Esteem" and Cover Girl's ads featuring Queen Latifah work because consumers can identify with the women's bodies and admire their confidence in displaying them.
>
> The 2012 famine in Somalia could have been avoided if farmers had received training in more effective methods and had had access to certain technology and if other nations had provided more aid more quickly.

251–54 A good way to narrow a thesis is to ask **QUESTIONS** about it: *Why* do gasoline prices fluctuate? *How* could the Somalia famine have been avoided? The answers will help you craft a narrow, focused thesis.

4. Qualify your thesis. Sometimes you want to make a strong argument and to state your thesis bluntly. Often, however, you need to acknowledge that your assertions may be challenged or may not be unconditionally true. In those cases, consider limiting the scope of your thesis by adding to it such terms as *may, probably, apparently, very likely, sometimes,* and *often.*

Gasoline prices *very likely* fluctuate because of production procedures, consumer demand, international politics, and oil companies' policies.

Dove's and Cover Girl's ad campaigns featuring "real women" *may* work because consumers can identify with the women's bodies and admire their confidence in displaying them.

The 2012 famine in Somalia could *probably* have been avoided if farmers had received training in more effective methods and had had access to certain technology and if other nations had provided more aid more quickly.

Thesis statements are typically positioned at or near the end of a text's introduction, to let readers know at the outset what is being claimed and what the text will be aiming to prove. A thesis doesn't necessarily forecast your organization, which may be more complex than the thesis itself. For example, Carolyn Stonehill's research paper, "It's in Our Genes: The Biological Basis of Human Mating Behavior," contains this thesis statement:

> While cultural values and messages clearly play a part in the process of mate selection, the genetic and psychological predispositions developed by our ancestors play the biggest role in determining to whom we are attracted.

However, the paper that follows includes sections on "Women's Need to Find a Capable Mate" and "Men's Need to Find a Healthy Mate," in which the "genetic and psychological predispositions" are discussed, followed by sections titled "The Influence of the Media on Mate Selection" and "If Not Media, Then What?" discussing "cultural values and messages." The paper delivers what the thesis includes without following the order in which the thesis presents the topics.

Topic Sentences

Just as a thesis statement announces the topic and position of an essay, a topic sentence states the subject and focus of a paragraph. Good paragraphs focus on a single point, which is summarized in a topic sentence. Usually, but not always, the topic sentence begins the paragraph:

Graduating from high school or college is an exciting, occasionally even traumatic event. Your identity changes as you move from being a high school teenager to a university student or a worker; your connection to home loosens as you attend school elsewhere, move to a place of your own, or simply exercise your right to stay out later. You suddenly find yourself doing different things, thinking different thoughts, fretting about different matters. As recent high school graduate T. J. Devoe puts it, "I wasn't really scared, but having this vast range of opportunity made me uneasy. I didn't know *what* was gonna happen." Jenny Petrow, in describing her first year out of college, observes, "It's a tough year. It was for all my friends."

—Sydney Lewis, *Help Wanted: Tales from the First Job Front*

Sometimes the topic sentence may come at the end of the paragraph or even at the end of the preceding paragraph, depending on the way the paragraphs relate to one another. Other times a topic sentence will summarize or restate a point made in the previous paragraph, helping readers understand what they've just read as they move on to the next point. See how the linguist Deborah Tannen does this in the first paragraphs of an article on differences in men's and women's conversational styles:

I was addressing a small gathering in a suburban Virginia living room — a women's group that had invited men to join them. Throughout the evening, one man had been particularly talkative, frequently offering ideas and anecdotes, while his wife sat silently beside him on the couch. Toward the end of the evening, I commented that women frequently complain that their husbands don't talk to them. This man quickly concurred. He gestured toward his wife and said, "She's the talker in our family." The room burst into laughter; the man looked puzzled and hurt. "It's true," he explained. "When I come home from work I have nothing to say. If she didn't keep the conversation going, we'd spend the whole evening in silence."

This episode crystallizes the irony that although American men tend to talk more than women in public situations, they often talk less at home. And this pattern is wreaking havoc with marriage.

—Deborah Tannen, "Sex, Lies, and Conversation:
Why Is It So Hard for Men and Women to Talk to Each Other?"

Transitions

Transitions help readers move from thought to thought—from sentence to sentence, paragraph to paragraph. You are likely to use a number of transitions as you draft; when you're **EDITING,** you should make a point of checking transitions. Here are some common ones:

282–85

- *To signal causes and effects:* accordingly, as a result, because, consequently, hence, so, then, therefore, thus
- *To signal comparisons:* also, in the same way, like, likewise, similarly
- *To signal changes in direction or exceptions:* although, but, even though, however, in contrast, instead, nevertheless, nonetheless, on the contrary, on the one hand . . . on the other hand, still, yet
- *To signal examples:* for example, for instance, indeed, in fact, such as
- *To signal sequences or similarities:* again, also, and, and then, besides, finally, furthermore, last, moreover, next, too
- *To signal time relations:* after, as soon as, at first, at the same time, before, eventually, finally, immediately, later, meanwhile, next, simultaneously, so far, soon, then, thereafter
- *To signal a summary or conclusion:* as a result, as we have seen, finally, in a word, in any event, in brief, in conclusion, in other words, in short, in the end, in the final analysis, on the whole, therefore, thus, to summarize

---

IF YOU NEED MORE HELP

See also Chapter 54 on **USING VISUALS, INCORPORATING SOUND** for ways of creating visual signals for your readers.

591–99

32 Analyzing Causes and Effects

Analyzing causes helps us think about why something happened, whereas thinking about effects helps us consider what might happen. When we hear a noise in the night, we want to know what caused it. Children poke sticks into holes to see what will happen. Researchers try to understand the causes of diseases. Writers often have occasion to consider causes or effects as part of a larger topic or sometimes as a main focus: in a **PROPOSAL,** we might consider the effects of reducing tuition or the causes of recent tuition increases; in a **MEMOIR,** we might explore why the person we had a date with failed to show up.

205–13

183–90

323–41

Usually we can only speculate about *probable* causes or *likely* effects. In writing about causes and effects, then, we are generally **ARGUING** for those we consider plausible, not proven. This chapter will help you analyze causes and effects in writing—and to do so in a way that suits your rhetorical situation.

Determining Plausible Causes and Effects

What causes ozone depletion? Sleeplessness? Obesity? And what are their effects? Those are of course large, complex topics, but whenever you have reason to ask why something happened or what could happen, there will likely be several possible causes and just as many predictable effects. There may be obvious causes, though often they will be less important than others that are harder to recognize. (Eating too much may be an obvious cause of being overweight, but *why* people eat too much has several less obvious causes: portion size, advertising, lifestyle, and physiological disorders are only a few possibilities.) Similarly, short-term effects are often less important than long-term ones. (A stomachache may be an

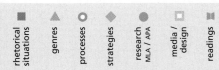

effect of eating too much candy, but the chemical imbalance that can result from consuming too much sugar is a much more serious effect.)

LISTING, CLUSTERING, and **OUTLINING** are useful processes for analyzing causes. And at times you might need to do some **RESEARCH** to identify possible causes or effects and to find evidence to support your analysis. When you've identified potential causes and effects, you need to analyze them. Which causes and effects are primary? Which seem to be secondary? Which are most relevant to your **PURPOSE** and are likely to convince your **AUDIENCE?** You will probably have to choose from several possible causes and effects for your analysis because you won't want or need to include all of them.

260–64
419

3–4
5–8

Arguing for Causes or Effects

Once you've identified several possible causes or predictable effects, you need to **ARGUE** that some are more plausible than others. You must provide convincing support for your argument because you usually cannot *prove* that x causes y or that y will be caused by z; you can show only, with good reasons and appropriate evidence, that x is *likely* to cause y or that y will *likely* follow from z. See, for example, how an essay on the psychological basis for risk taking speculates about two potential causes for the popularity of extreme sports:

323–41

> Studies now indicate that the inclination to take high risks may be hardwired into the brain, intimately linked to arousal and pleasure mechanisms, and may offer such a thrill that it functions like an addiction. The tendency probably affects one in five people, mostly young males, and declines with age. It may ensure our survival, even spur our evolution as individuals and as a species. Risk taking probably bestowed a crucial evolutionary advantage, inciting the fighting and foraging of the hunter-gatherer. . . .
>
> As psychologist Salvadore Maddi, PhD, of the University of California at Davis warns, "High-risk takers may have a hard time deriving meaning and purpose from everyday life." Indeed, this peculiar form of dissatisfaction could help explain the explosion of high-risk sports in America and other postindustrial Western nations. In unstable cultures, such as those at war or suffering poverty, people rarely seek

out additional thrills. But in a rich and safety-obsessed country like America, land of guardrails, seat belts, and personal-injury lawsuits, everyday life may have become too safe, predictable, and boring for those programmed for risk taking. —Paul Roberts, "Risk"

Roberts suggests that genetics is one likely cause of extreme sports and that an American obsession with safety is perhaps a cause of their growing popularity. Notice, however, that he presents these as likely or possible, not certain, by choosing his words carefully: "studies now *indicate*"; "the inclination to take high risks *may* be hardwired"; "[r]isk taking *probably* bestowed a crucial evolutionary advantage"; "this . . . dissatisfaction *could help* explain." Like Roberts, you will almost always need to qualify what you say about causes and effects—to say that something *could explain* (rather than saying it "explains") or that it *suggests* (rather than "shows"). Causes and effects can seldom be proved definitively, so you need to acknowledge that your argument is not the last word on the subject.

Ways of Organizing an Analysis of Causes and Effects

Your analysis of causes and effects may be part of a proposal or some other genre of writing, or you may write a text whose central purpose is to analyze causes or speculate about effects. While there are many ways to organize an analysis of causes and effects, three common ways are to state a cause and then discuss its effects, to state an effect and then discuss its causes, and to identify a chain of causes and effects.

Identify a cause and then discuss its effects. If you were writing about global warming, you might first show that many scientists fear it will have several effects, including drastic climate changes, the extinction of various kinds of plants, and elevated sea levels.

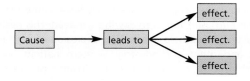

Identify an effect and then trace its causes.   If you were writing about school violence, for example, you might argue that it is a result of sloppy dress, informal teacher-student relationships, low academic standards, and disregard for rules.

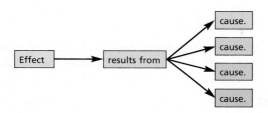

Identify a chain of causes and effects.   You may sometimes discuss a chain of causes and effects. If you were writing about the right to privacy, for example, you might consider the case of Megan's law. A convicted child molester raped and murdered a girl named Megan; the crime caused New Jersey legislators to pass the so-called Megan's law (an effect), which requires that convicted sex offenders be publicly identified. As more states enact versions of Megan's law, concern for the rights of those who are identified is developing—the effect is becoming a cause of further effects.

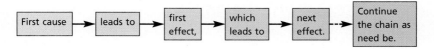

Considering the Rhetorical Situation

As a writer or speaker, you need to think about the message that you want to articulate, the audience you want to reach, and the larger context you are writing in.

PURPOSE   Your main purpose may be to analyze the causes and effects of something. But sometimes you'll have another goal that calls for such analysis—a business report, for example, might need to explain what caused a decline in sales.

3–4

5–8 ■   **AUDIENCE**   Who is your intended audience, and how will analyzing causes help you reach them? Do you need to tell them why some event happened or what effects resulted?

9–11 ■   **GENRE**   Does your genre require you to analyze causes? Proposals, for example, often need to consider the effects of a proposed solution.

12–15 ■   **STANCE**   What is your stance, and could analyzing causes or effects show that stance? Could it help demonstrate your seriousness or show that your conclusions are reasonable?

16–18 ■   **MEDIA / DESIGN**   You can rely on words to analyze causes, but sometimes a drawing will help readers *see* how causes lead to effects.

---

249 ○

IF YOU NEED MORE HELP

See also the **PROCESSES** chapters for help generating ideas, drafting, and so on if you need to write an entire text whose purpose is to analyze causes or speculate about effects.

Arguing 33

Football fans argue about who's better, Eli or Peyton Manning. Political candidates argue that they have the most experience or best judgment. A toilet paper ad argues that "you deserve a little luxury in your life, and so does your bottom." As you likely realize, we are surrounded by arguments, and much of the work you do as a college student requires you to read and write arguments. When you write a **LITERARY ANALYSIS**, for instance, you argue for a particular interpretation. In a **PROPOSAL**, you argue for a particular solution to a problem. Even a **PROFILE** argues that a subject should be seen in a certain way. This chapter offers advice on some of the key elements of making an argument, from developing an arguable thesis and identifying good reasons and evidence that supports those reasons to building common ground and dealing with viewpoints other than your own.

81–86
205–13
191–204

Reasons for Arguing

We argue for many reasons, and they often overlap: to convince others that our position on a subject is reasonable, to influence the way they think about a subject, to persuade them to change their point of view or to take some sort of action. In fact, many composition scholars and teachers believe that all writing makes an argument.

As a student, you'll be called upon to make arguments continually: when you participate in class discussions, when you take an essay exam, when you post a comment to an online discussion or a blog. In all these instances, you are adding your opinions to some larger conversation, arguing for what you believe—and why.

Arguing Logically: Claims, Reasons, and Evidence

The basic building blocks of argument are claims, reasons, and evidence that supports those reasons. Using these building blocks, we can construct a strong logical argument.

Claims. Good arguments are based on arguable claims — statements that reasonable people may disagree about. Certain kinds of statements cannot be argued:

- *Verifiable statements of fact.* Most of the time, there's no point in arguing about facts like "The earth is round" or "George H. W. Bush was America's forty-first president." Such statements contain no controversy, no potential opposition — and so no interest for an audience. However, you might argue about the basis of a fact. For example, until recently it was a fact that our solar system had nine planets, but when further discoveries led to a change in the definition of *planet*, Pluto no longer qualified.

- *Issues of faith or belief.* By definition, matters of faith cannot be proven or refuted. If you believe in reincarnation or don't believe there is an afterlife, there's no way I can convince you otherwise. However, in a philosophy or religion course you may be asked to argue, for example, whether or not the universe must have a cause.

- *Matters of simple opinion or personal taste.* If you think cargo pants are ugly, no amount of arguing will convince you to think otherwise. If you own every Pink CD and think she's the greatest singer ever, you won't convince your Beatles-loving parents to like her, too. If matters of taste are based on identifiable criteria, though, they may be argued in an **EVALUATION,** where "Tom Cruise is a terrible actor" is more than just your opinion — it's an assertion you can support with evidence.

164–72

You may begin with an opinion: "I think wearing a helmet makes riding a bike more dangerous, not less." As it stands, that statement can't be considered a claim — it needs to be made more reasonable and informed. To do that, you might reframe it as a question — "Do bike riders who wear helmets get injured more often than those who don't?" — that may be answered as you do research and start to write. Your opinion or question should lead

you to an arguable claim, however, one that could be challenged by another thoughtful person. In this case, for example, your research might lead you to a focused, qualified claim: *Contrary to common sense, wearing a helmet while riding a bicycle increases the chances of injury, at least to adult riders.*

Qualifying a claim.　According to an old saying, there are two sides to every story. Much of the time, though, arguments don't sort themselves neatly into two sides, pro and con. No matter what your topic, your argument will rarely be a simple matter of being for or against; in most cases, you'll want to qualify your claim — that it is true in certain circumstances, with certain conditions, with these limitations, and so on. Qualifying your claim shows that you're reasonable and also makes your topic more manageable by limiting it. The following questions can help you qualify your claim.

- *Can it be true in some circumstances or at some times but not others?* For example, freedom of speech should generally be unrestricted, but individuals can sue for slander or libel.
- *Can it be true only with certain conditions?* For instance, cell phones and computer monitors should be recycled, but only by licensed, domestic recyclers.
- *Can it be true for some groups or individuals but not others?* For example, nearly everyone should follow a low-carb diet, but some people, such as diabetics, should avoid it.

SOME WORDS FOR QUALIFYING A CLAIM

sometimes	nearly	it seems/seemingly
rarely	usually	some
in some cases	more or less	perhaps
often	for the most part	possibly
routinely	in many cases	in most cases

Drafting a thesis statement.　Once your claim is focused and appropriately qualified, it can form the core of your essay's **THESIS STATEMENT**, which announces your position and forecasts the path your argument will

 313–15

follow. For example, here is the opening paragraph of an essay by the executive director of the National Congress of American Indians arguing that the remains of Native Americans should be treated with the same respect given to others. The author outlines the context of her argument and then presents her thesis (here, in italics):

> What if museums, universities and government agencies could put your dead relatives on display or keep them in boxes to be cut up and otherwise studied? What if you believed that the spirits of the dead could not rest until their human remains were placed in a sacred area? The ordinary American would say there ought to be a law — and there is, for ordinary Americans. *The problem for American Indians is that there are too many laws of the kind that make us the archeological property of the United States and too few of the kind that protect us from such insults.* —Susan Shown Harjo, "Last Rites for Indian Dead: Treating Remains Like Artifacts Is Intolerable"

Reasons. Your claim must be supported by reasons that your audience will accept. A reason can usually be linked to a claim with the word *because*:

CLAIM	+	*BECAUSE*	+	REASON
iPods and other MP3 players harm society		*because*		they isolate users from other people.

Keep in mind that you likely have a further reason, a rule or principle that underlies the reason you link directly to your claim. In this argument, the underlying reason is that isolation from other people is bad. If your audience doesn't accept that principle, you may have to back it up with further reasons or evidence.

To come up with good reasons, start by stating your position and then answering the question *why?*

CLAIM: iPods and other MP3 players harm society. *Why?*

REASON: (Because) They isolate users from other people. *Why?*

UNDERLYING REASON: Isolation from other people is bad.

rhetorical situations   genres   processes   strategies   research MLA / APA   media / design   readings

As you can see, this exercise can continue indefinitely as the underlying reasons grow more and more general and abstract. You can do the same with other positions:

CLAIM: Smoking should be banned. *Why?*

REASON: (Because) It is harmful to smokers and also to nonsmokers.

UNDERLYING REASON: People should be protected from harmful substances.

Evidence. Evidence to support your reasons can come from various sources. In fact, you may need to use several kinds of evidence to persuade your audience that your claim is true. Some of the most common types of evidence include facts, statistics, examples, authorities, anecdotes, scenarios, case studies, textual evidence, and visuals.

Facts are ideas that are proven to be true. Facts can include observations or scholarly research (your own or someone else's), but they need to be accepted as true. If your audience accepts the facts you present, they can be powerful means of persuasion. For example, an essay on junk email offers these facts to demonstrate the seasonal nature of spam:

> The flow of spam is often seasonal. It slows in the spring, and then, in the month that technology specialists call "black September"—when hundreds of thousands of students return to college, many armed with new computers and access to fast Internet connections—the levels rise sharply.
>
> —Michael Specter, "Damn Spam"

Specter offers this fact with only a general reference to its origin ("technology specialists"), but given what most people know—or think they know—about college students, it rings true. A citation from a study published by a "technology specialist" would offer even greater credibility.

Statistics are numerical data, usually produced through research, surveys, or polls. Statistics should be relevant to your argument, as current as possible, accurate, and from a reliable source. An argument advocating that Americans should eat less meat presents these data to support the writer's contention that we eat far too much of it:

Americans are downing close to 200 pounds of meat, poultry, and fish per capita per year (dairy and eggs are separate, and hardly insignificant), an increase of 50 pounds per person from 50 years ago. We each consume something like 110 grams of protein a day, about twice the federal government's recommended allowance; of that, about 75 grams come from animal protein. (The recommended level is itself considered by many dietary experts to be higher than it needs to be.) It's likely that most of us would do just fine on around 30 grams of protein a day, virtually all of it from plant sources.

—Mark Bittman, "Rethinking the Meat-Guzzler"

Bittman's statistics demonstrate the extent to which Americans have increased their meat consumption over the last half century, the proportion of our diets that comes from meat, and, by comparison, how much protein our bodies require—and summarize the heart of his argument in stark numeric terms.

Examples are specific instances that illustrate general statements. In a book on life after dark in Europe, a historian offers several examples to demonstrate his point that three hundred years ago, night—without artificial lighting—was treacherous:

Even sure-footed natives on a dark night could misjudge the lay of the land, stumbling into a ditch or off a precipice. In Aberdeenshire, a fifteen-year-old girl died in 1739 after straying from her customary path through a churchyard and tumbling into a newly dug grave. The Yorkshireman Arthur Jessop, returning from a neighbor's home on a cold December evening, fell into a stone pit after losing his bearings.

—A. Roger Ekirch, *At Day's Close: Night in Times Past*

Ekirch illustrates his point and makes it come alive for readers by citing two specific individuals' fates.

Authorities are experts on your subject. To be useful, authorities must be reputable, trustworthy, and qualified to address the subject. You should **EVALUATE** any authorities you consult carefully to be sure they have the credentials necessary for readers to take them seriously. When you cite

453–56 ●

experts, you should clearly identify them and the origins of their authority in a **SIGNAL PHRASE**, as does the author of an argument that deforested
land can be reclaimed:

471–74

> Reed Funk, professor of plant biology at Rutgers University, believes
> that the vast areas of deforested land can be used to grow millions of
> genetically improved trees for food, mostly nuts, and for fuel. Funk
> sees nuts used to supplement meat as a source of high-quality protein
> in developing-country diets.
>
> —Lester R. Brown, *Plan B 2.0: Rescuing a Planet
> under Stress and a Civilization in Trouble*

Brown cites Funk, an expert on plant biology, to support his argument that
humans need to rethink the global economy in order to create a sustainable world. Without the information on Funk's credentials, though, readers would have no reason to take his proposal seriously.

Anecdotes are brief **NARRATIVES** that your audience will find believable and
that contribute directly to your argument. Anecdotes may come from
your personal experience or the experiences of others. In an essay arguing
that it's understandable when athletes give in to the temptation to use
performance-enhancing drugs, sports blogger William Moller uses an
anecdote to show that the need to perform can outweigh the potential negative consequences of using drugs:

387–95

> I spent my high school years at a boarding school hidden among the
> apple orchards of Massachusetts. Known for a spartan philosophy
> regarding the adolescent need for sleep, the school worked us to the
> bone, regularly slamming us with six hours of homework. I pulled a lot
> more all-nighters (of the scholastic sort) in my years there than I ever
> did in college. When we weren't in class, the library, study hall, or for-
> mal sit-down meals, we were likely found on a sports field. We also
> had school on Saturday, beginning at 8 a.m. just like every other non-
> Sunday morning.
>   Adding kindling to the fire, the students were not your laid-back
> types; everyone wanted that spot at the top of the class, and social life
> was rife with competition. The type A's that fill the investment banking,

legal, and political worlds — those are the kids I spent my high school years with.

And so it was that midway through my sophomore year, I found myself on my third all-nighter in a row, attempting to memorize historically significant pieces of art out of E. H. Gombrich's *The Story of Art*. I had finished a calculus exam the day before, and the day before that had been devoted to world history. And on that one cold night in February, I had had enough. I had hit that point where you've had so little sleep over such a long time that you start seeing spots, as if you'd been staring at a bright light for too long. The grade I would compete for the next day suddenly slipped in importance, and I began daydreaming about how easy the real world would be compared to the hell I was going through.

But there was hope. A friend who I was taking occasional study breaks with read the story in the bags beneath my eyes, in the slump of my shoulders, the nervous drumming of my fingers on the chair as we sipped flat, warm Coke in the common room. My personal *deus ex machina*,* he handed me a small white pill.

I was very innocent. I matured way after most of my peers, and was probably best known for being the kid who took all the soprano solos away from the girls in the choir as a first-year student. I don't think I had ever been buzzed, much less drunk. I'd certainly never smoked a cigarette. And knowing full well that what I was doing could be nothing better than against the rules (and less importantly, illegal) I did what I felt I needed to do, to accomplish what was demanded of me. And it worked. I woke up and regained focus like nothing I'd ever experienced. Unfortunately, it also came with serious side effects: I was a hypersensitized, stuffed-up, sweaty, wide-eyed mess, but I studied until the birds started chirping. And I aced my test.

Later I found out the pill was Ritalin, and it was classified as a class 3 drug.[†] I did it again, too — only a handful of times, as the side effects were so awful. But every time it was still illegal, still against the rules.

---

*Deus ex machina: In ancient Greek and Roman drama, a god introduced to resolve plot difficulties.

[†]*Class 3 drug*: Drug that is illegal to possess without a prescription.

And as emphasized above, I was much more worried about the scholastic consequences if I were discovered abusing a prescription drug than the fact that I was breaking the law. Though I was using it in a far different manner than the baseball players who would later get caught with it in their systems, it was still very clearly a "performance-enhancing drug."

Just like every other person on this planet, I was giving in to the incentive scheme that was presented to me. The negative of doing poorly on the test was far greater than the negative of getting caught, discounted by the anesthetic of low probability.

—William Moller, "We, the Public,
Place the Best Athletes on Pedestals"

Moller uses this anecdote to demonstrate the truth of his argument, that given the choice between "breaking the rules and breaking my grades" or "getting an edge" in professional sports, just about everyone will choose to break the rules.

Scenarios are hypothetical situations. Like anecdotes, "what if" scenarios can help you describe the possible effects of particular actions or offer new ways of looking at a particular state of affairs. For example, a mathematician presents this lighthearted scenario about Santa Claus in a tongue-in-cheek argument that Christmas is (almost) pure magic:

Let's assume that Santa only visits those who are children in the eyes of the law, that is, those under the age of 18. There are roughly 2 billion such individuals in the world. However, Santa started his annual activities long before diversity and equal opportunity became issues, and as a result he doesn't handle Muslim, Hindu, Jewish and Buddhist children. That reduces his workload significantly to a mere 15% of the total, namely 378 million. However, the crucial figure is not the number of children but the number of homes Santa has to visit. According to the most recent census data, the average size of a family in the world is 3.5 children per household. Thus, Santa has to visit 108,000,000 individual homes. (Of course, as everyone knows,

Santa only visits good children, but we can surely assume that, on an average, at least one child of the 3.5 in each home meets that criterion.)

—Keith Devlin, "The Mathematics of Christmas"

Devlin uses this scenario, as part of his mathematical analysis of Santa's yearly task, to help demonstrate that Christmas is indeed magical—because if you do the math, it's clear that Santa's task is physically impossible.

Case studies and observations feature detailed reporting about a subject. Case studies are in-depth, systematic examinations of an occasion, a person, or a group. For example, in arguing that class differences exist in the United States, sociologist Gregory Mantsios presents studies of three "typical" Americans to show "enormous class differences" in their lifestyles.

Observations offer detailed descriptions of a subject. Here's an observation of the emergence of a desert stream that flows only at night:

At about 5:30 water came out of the ground. It did not spew up, but slowly escaped into the surrounding sand and small rocks. The wet circle grew until water became visible. Then it bubbled out like a small fountain and the creek began.

—Craig Childs, *The Secret Knowledge of Water*

Childs presents this and other observations in a book that argues (among other things) that even in harsh, arid deserts, water exists, and knowing where to find it can mean the difference between life and death.

462–74   **Textual evidence** includes QUOTATIONS, PARAPHRASES, and SUMMARIES. Usually, the relevance of textual evidence must be stated directly, as excerpts from a text may carry several potential meanings. For example, here is an excerpt from a student essay analyzing the function of the raft in *Huckleberry Finn* as "a platform on which the resolution of conflicts is made possible":

[T]he scenes where Jim and Huck are in consensus on the raft contain the moments in which they are most relaxed. For instance, in chapter twelve of the novel, Huck, after escaping capture from Jackson's Island, calls the rafting life "solemn" and articulates their experience as living

rhetorical situations   genres   processes   strategies   research MLA / APA   media / design   readings

"pretty high" (Twain 75–76). Likewise, subsequent to escaping the unresolved feud between the Grangerfords and Shepherdsons in chapter eighteen, Huck is unquestionably at ease on the raft: "I was powerful glad to get away from the feuds. . . . We said there warn't no home like a raft, after all. Other places do seem so cramped up and smothery, but a raft don't. You feel mighty free and easy and comfortable on a raft" (Twain 134).

—Dave Nichols, " 'Less All Be Friends': Rafts as
Negotiating Platforms in Twain's *Huckleberry Finn*"

Huck's own words support Nichols's claim that he can relax on a raft. Nichols strengthens his claim by quoting evidence from two separate pages, suggesting that Huck's opinion of rafts pervades the novel.

Visuals can be a useful way of presenting evidence. Remember, though, that charts, graphs, photos, drawings, and other VISUAL TEXTS seldom speak for themselves and thus must be explained in your text. Below, for example, is a photograph of a poster carried by demonstrators at the 2008 Beijing Summer Olympics, protesting China's treatment of Tibetans. If you

591–99

were to use this photo in an essay, you would need to explain that the poster combines the image of a protester standing before a tank during the 1989 Tiananmen Square uprising with the Olympic logo, making clear to your readers that the protesters are likening China's treatment of Tibetans to its brutal actions in the past. Similarly, the poster for a recycling campaign below uses an American flag made from household waste to argue that recycling is patriotic.

Choosing appropriate evidence. The kinds of evidence you provide to support your argument depends on your RHETORICAL SITUATION. If your purpose is, for example, to convince readers to accept the need for a proposed solution, you'd be likely to include facts, statistics, and anecdotes. If you're writing for an academic audience, you'd be less likely to rely on anecdotes, preferring authorities, textual evidence, statistics, and case studies instead. And even within academic communities different disciplines and genres may focus primarily on different kinds of evidence. If you're not sure what counts as appropriate evidence, ask your instructor for guidance.

Convincing Readers You're Trustworthy

For your argument to be convincing, you need to establish your own credibility with readers — to demonstrate your knowledge about your topic, to show that you and your readers share some common ground, and to show yourself to be evenhanded in the way you present your argument.

Building common ground.

One important element of gaining readers' trust is to identify some common ground, some values you and your audience share. For example, to introduce a book arguing for the compatibility of science and religion, author Chet Raymo offers some common memories:

> Like most children, I was raised on miracles. Cows that jump over the moon; a jolly fat man that visits every house in the world in a single night; mice and ducks that talk; little engines that huff and puff and say, "I think I can"; geese that lay golden eggs. This lively exercise of credulity on the part of children is good practice for what follows — for believing in the miracle stories of traditional religion, yes, but also for the practice of poetry or science.
>
> —Chet Raymo, *Skeptics and True Believers: The Exhilarating Connection between Science and Religion*

Raymo presents childhood stories and myths that are part of many people's shared experiences to help readers find a connection between two realms that are often seen as opposed.

Incorporating other viewpoints.   To show that you have carefully considered the viewpoints of others, including those who may agree or disagree with you, you should incorporate those viewpoints into your argument by acknowledging, accommodating, or refuting them.

Acknowledging other viewpoints. One essential part of establishing your credibility is to acknowledge that there are viewpoints different from yours and to represent them fairly and accurately. Rather than weakening your argument, acknowledging possible objections to your position shows that you've thought about and researched your topic thoroughly. For example, in an essay about his experience growing up homosexual, writer Andrew Sullivan admits that not every young gay man or woman has the same experience:

> I should add that many young lesbians and homosexuals seem to have had a much easier time of it. For many, the question of sexual identity was not a critical factor in their life choices or vocation, or even a factor at all.   —Andrew Sullivan, "What Is a Homosexual?"

In response to a reasonable objection, Sullivan qualifies his assertions, making his own stance appear to be reasonable.

Accommodating other viewpoints. You may be tempted to ignore views you don't agree with, but in fact it's important to demonstrate that you are aware of them and have considered them carefully. You may find yourself conceding that opposing views have some merit and qualifying your claim or even making them part of your own argument. See, for example, how a philosopher arguing that torture is sometimes "not merely permissible but morally mandatory" addresses a major objection to his position:

> The most powerful argument against using torture as a punishment or to secure confessions is that such practices disregard the rights of the individual. Well, if the individual is all that important—and he is—it is correspondingly important to protect the rights of individuals threatened by terrorists. If life is so valuable that it must never be taken,

the lives of the innocents must be saved even at the price of hurting the one who endangers them.

—Michael Levin, "The Case for Torture"

Levin acknowledges his critics' argument that the individual is indeed important but then asserts that if the life of one person is important, the lives of many people must be even more important. In effect, he uses an opposing argument to advance his own.

Refuting other viewpoints.   Often you may need to refute other arguments and make a case for why you believe they are wrong. Are the values underlying the argument questionable? Is the reasoning flawed? Is the evidence inadequate or faulty? For example, an essay arguing for the elimination of college athletics scholarships includes this refutation:

> Some argue that eliminating athletics scholarships would deny opportunity and limit access for many students, most notably black athletes. The question is, access to what? The fields of competition or an opportunity to earn a meaningful degree? With the six-year graduation rates of black basketball players hovering in the high 30-percent range, and black football players in the high 40-percent range, despite years of "academic reform," earning an athletics scholarship under the current system is little more than a chance to play sports.
>
> —John R. Gerdy, "For True Reform, Athletics Scholarships Must Go"

Gerdy bases his refutation on statistics showing that for more than half of African American college athletes, the opportunity to earn a degree by playing a sport is an illusion.

When you incorporate differing viewpoints, be careful to avoid the FALLACIES of attacking the person making the argument or refuting a competing position that no one seriously entertains. It is also important that you not distort or exaggerate opposing viewpoints. If *your* argument is to be persuasive, other arguments should be represented fairly.

◆ 338–40

Appealing to Readers' Emotions

Logic and facts, even when presented by someone who seems reasonable and trustworthy, may not be enough to persuade readers. Many successful arguments include an emotional component that appeals to readers' hearts as well as to their minds. Advertising often works by appealing to its audience's emotions, as in this paragraph from a Volvo ad:

> Choosing a car is about the comfort and safety of your passengers, most especially your children. That's why we ensure Volvo's safety research examines how we can make our cars safer for everyone who travels in them—from adults to teenagers, children to babies. Even those who aren't even born yet. —*Volvo.com*

This ad plays on the fear that children—or a pregnant mother—may be injured or killed in an automobile accident.

Keep in mind that emotional appeals can make readers feel as though they are being manipulated and, consequently, less likely to accept an argument. For most kinds of academic writing, use emotional appeals sparingly.

Checking for Fallacies

Fallacies are arguments that involve faulty reasoning. It's important to avoid fallacies in your writing because they often seem plausible but are usually unfair or inaccurate and make reasonable discussion difficult. Here are some of the most common fallacies:

- **Ad hominem** arguments attack someone's character rather than address the issues. (*Ad hominem* is Latin for "to the man.") It is an especially common fallacy in political discourse and elsewhere: "Jack Turner has no business talking about the way we run things in this city. He's just another flaky liberal." Whether or not Turner is a "flaky liberal" has no bearing on the worth of his argument about "the way we run things in this city"; insulting one's opponents isn't an argument against their positions.

- *Bandwagon appeals* argue that because others think or do something, we should, too. For example, an advertisement for a rifle association suggests that "67 percent of voters support laws permitting concealed weapons. You should, too." It assumes that readers want to be part of the group and implies that an opinion that is popular must be correct.

- *Begging the question* is a circular argument. It assumes as a given what is trying to be proved, essentially supporting an assertion with the assertion itself. Consider this statement: "Affirmative action can never be fair or just because you cannot remedy one injustice by committing another." This statement begs the question because to prove that affirmative action is unjust, it assumes that it is an injustice.

- *Either-or* arguments, also called *false dilemmas*, are oversimplifications that assert there can be only two possible positions on a complex issue. For example, "Those who oppose our actions in this war are enemies of freedom" inaccurately assumes that if someone opposes the war in question, he or she opposes freedom. In fact, people might have many other reasons for opposing the war.

- *False analogies* compare things that resemble each other in some ways but not in the most important respects — for example, "Trees pollute the air just as much as cars and trucks do." Although it's true that plants emit hydrocarbons, and hydrocarbons are a component of smog, they also produce oxygen, whereas motor vehicles emit gases that combine with hydrocarbons to form smog. Vehicles pollute the air; trees provide the air that vehicles' emissions pollute.

- *Faulty causality,* also known as *post hoc, ergo propter hoc* (Latin for "after this, therefore because of this"), assumes that because one event followed another, the first event caused the second — for example, "Legalizing same-sex marriage in Sweden led to a decline in the marriage rate of opposite-sex couples." The statement contains no evidence to show that the first event caused the second.

- *Straw man* arguments misrepresent an opposing position to make it ridiculous or extreme and thus easy to refute, rather than dealing with the actual position. For example, if someone argues that funding for food stamps should be cut, a straw man response would be, "You want the poor to starve," transforming a proposal to cut a specific program into an exaggerated argument that the proposer hasn't made.

- *Hasty generalizations* are conclusions based on insufficient or inappropriately qualified evidence. This summary of a research study is a good example: "Twenty randomly chosen residents of Brooklyn, New York, were asked whether they found graffiti tags offensive; fourteen said yes, five said no, and one had no opinion. Therefore, 70 percent of Brooklyn residents find tagging offensive." In Brooklyn, a part of New York City with a population of over two million, twenty residents is far too small a group from which to draw meaningful conclusions. To be able to generalize, the researcher would have had to survey a much greater percentage of Brooklyn's population.

- *Slippery slope* arguments assert that one event will inevitably lead to another, often cataclysmic event without presenting evidence that such a chain of causes and effects will in fact take place. Here's an example: "If the state legislature passes this 2 percent tax increase, it won't be long before all the corporations in the state move to other states and leave thousands unemployed." According to this argument, if taxes are raised, the state's economy will be ruined—not a likely scenario, given the size of the proposed increase.

Considering the Rhetorical Situation

To argue effectively, you need to think about the message that you want to articulate, the audience you want to persuade, the effect of your stance, and the larger context you are writing in.

3–4

PURPOSE   What do you want your audience to do? To think a certain way? To take a certain action? To change their minds? To consider alternative views to their current ones? To accept your position as plausible? To see that you have thought carefully about an issue and researched it appropriately?

rhetorical situations | genres | processes | strategies | research MLA / APA | media / design | readings

AUDIENCE
Who is your intended audience? What do they likely know and believe about your topic? How personal is it for them? To what extent are they likely to agree or disagree with you? Why? What common ground can you find with them? How should you incorporate other viewpoints they have? What kind of evidence are they likely to accept?

5–8

GENRE
What genre will help you achieve your purpose? A position paper? An evaluation? A review? A proposal? An analysis?

9–11

STANCE
What's your attitude toward your topic, and why? What strategies will help you to convey that stance? How do you want your audience to perceive you? As an authority on your topic? As someone much like them? As calm? reasonable? impassioned or angry? something else?

12–15

MEDIA / DESIGN
What media will you use, and how do your media affect your argument? If you're writing on paper, does your argument call for photos or charts? If you're giving an oral presentation, should you put your reasons and support on slides? If you're writing online, should you add links to sites representing other positions or containing evidence that supports your position?

16–18

34 Classifying and Dividing

Classification and division are ways of organizing information: various items may be classified according to their similarities, or a single topic may be divided into parts. We might classify different kinds of flowers as annuals or perennials, for example, and classify the perennials further as dahlias, daisies, roses, and peonies. We might also divide a flower garden into distinct areas: for herbs, flowers, and vegetables.

Writers often use classification and division as ways of developing and organizing material. This book, for instance, classifies comparison, definition, description, and several other common ways of thinking and writing as strategies. It divides the information it provides about writing into seven parts: "Rhetorical Situations," "Genres," "Processes," and so on. Each part further divides its material into various chapters. Even if you never write a book, you will have occasion to classify and divide material

155–63
52–86

in ANNOTATED BIBLIOGRAPHIES and essays ANALYZING TEXTS and other kinds of writing. This chapter offers advice for classifying and dividing information for various writing purposes—and in a way that suits your own rhetorical situation.

Classifying

When we classify something, we group it with similar things. A linguist would classify French and Spanish and Italian as Romance languages, for example—and Russian, Polish, and Bulgarian as Slavic languages. In a hilarious (if totally phony) news story from the *Onion* about a church bake

rhetorical situations ▲ genres ○ processes ◆ strategies ● research MLA / APA □ media / design ▨ readings sale, the writer classifies the activities observed there as examples of the seven deadly sins:

> GADSDEN, AL—The seven deadly sins—avarice, sloth, envy, lust, gluttony, pride, and wrath—were all committed Sunday during the twice-annual bake sale at St. Mary's of the Immaculate Conception Church.
>
> —"All Seven Deadly Sins Committed at Church Bake Sale," *The Onion*

The article goes on to categorize the participants' behavior in terms of the sins, describing one parishioner who commits the sin of pride by bragging about her cookies and others who commit the sin of envy by envying the popularity of the prideful parishioner's baked goods (the consumption of which leads to the sin of gluttony). In all, the article notes, "347 individual acts of sin were committed at the bake sale," and every one of them can be classified as one of the seven deadly sins.

Dividing

As a writing strategy, division is a way of breaking something into parts—and a way of making the information easy for readers to follow and understand. See how this example about children's ways of nagging divides their tactics into seven categories:

> James U. McNeal, a professor of marketing at Texas A&M University, is considered America's leading authority on marketing to children. In his book *Kids as Customers* (1992), McNeal provides marketers with a thorough analysis of "children's requesting styles and appeals." He [divides] juvenile nagging tactics into seven major categories. A *pleading* nag is one accompanied by repetitions of words like "please" or "mom, mom, mom." A *persistent* nag involves constant requests for the coveted product and may include the phrase "I'm gonna ask just one more time." *Forceful* nags are extremely pushy and may include subtle threats, like "Well, then, I'll go and ask Dad." *Demonstrative* nags are the most high risk, often characterized by full-blown tantrums in public places, breath holding, tears, a refusal to leave the store. *Sugar-coated* nags promise affection in

return for a purchase and may rely on seemingly heartfelt declarations, like "You're the best dad in the world." *Threatening* nags are youthful forms of blackmail, vows of eternal hatred and of running away if something isn't bought. *Pity* nags claim the child will be heartbroken, teased, or socially stunted if the parent refuses to buy a certain item. "All of these appeals and styles may be used in combination," McNeal's research has discovered, "but kids tend to stick to one or two of each that prove most effective . . . for their own parents."

> —Eric Schlosser, *Fast Food Nation:*
> *The Dark Side of the All-American Meal*

Here the writer announces the division scheme of "seven major categories." Then he names each tactic and describes how it works. And notice the italics: each nagging tactic is italicized, making it easy to recognize and follow. Take away the italics, and the divisions would be less visible.

Creating Clear and Distinct Categories

When you classify or divide, you need to create clear and distinct categories. If you're writing about music, you might divide it on the basis of the genre (hip-hop, rock, classical, gospel), artist (male or female, group or solo), or instruments (violins, trumpets, bongos, guitars). These categories must be distinct, so that no information overlaps or fits into more than one category, and they must include every member of the group you're discussing. The simpler the criteria for selecting the categories, the better. The nagging categories in the example from *Fast Food Nation* are based on only one criterion: a child's verbal behavior.

Sometimes you may want to highlight your categories visually to make them easier to follow. Eric Schlosser does that by italicizing each category: the *pleading* nag, the *persistent* nag, the *forceful* nag, and so on. Other DESIGN elements—bulleted lists, pie charts, tables, images—might also prove useful.

See, for instance, how *The World of Caffeine* authors Bennett Alan Weinberg and Bonnie K. Bealer use a two-column list to show what they say are the differing cultural connotations of coffee and tea:

581–90

Coffee Aspect	Tea Aspect
Male	Female
Boisterous	Decorous
Indulgence	Temperance
Hardheaded	Romantic
Topology	Geometry
Heidegger	Carnap
Beethoven	Mozart
Libertarian	Statist
Promiscuous	Pure

—Bennett Alan Weinberg and Bonnie K. Bealer,
The World of Caffeine

Sometimes you might show categories visually, as in this website promoting Michigan apples. Each of the sixteen varieties grown in Michigan is pictured and its taste, uses, and texture described.

The photographs allow us to see the differences among the varieties at a glance. The varieties are arranged alphabetically, but could have been arranged by color, flavor (sweet or tart), or whether they are best for baking or eating raw.

Considering the Rhetorical Situation

As a writer or speaker, you need to think about the message that you want to articulate, the audience you want to reach, and the larger context you are writing in.

3–4 **PURPOSE** Your purpose for writing will affect how you classify or divide information. Weinberg and Bealer classify coffee as "boisterous" and tea as "decorous" to help readers understand the cultural styles the two beverages represent, whereas J. Crew might divide sweaters into cashmere, wool, and cotton to help shoppers find and buy things from their website.

5–8 **AUDIENCE** What audience do you want to reach, and will classifying or dividing your material help them follow your discussion?

9–11 **GENRE** Does your genre call for you to categorize or divide information? A long report might need to be divided into sections, for instance.

12–15 **STANCE** Your stance may affect the way you classify information. Weinberg and Bealer's classification of coffee as "Beethoven" and tea as "Mozart" reflects a stance that focuses on cultural analysis (and assumes an audience familiar with the difference between the two composers). If the authors were botanists, they might categorize the two beverages in terms of their biological origins ("seed based" and "leaf based").

rhetorical situations   genres   processes   strategies   research MLA / APA   media / design   readings

MEDIA / DESIGN   You can classify or divide in paragraph form, but sometimes a pie chart or list will show the categories better.

16–18

IF YOU NEED MORE HELP

See also **CLUSTERING, CUBING,** and **LOOPING,** three methods of generating ideas that can be especially helpful for classifying material. And see all the **PROCESSES** chapters for guidelines on drafting, revising, and so on if you need to write a classification essay.

260–62

249

35 Comparing and Contrasting

Comparing things looks at their similarities; contrasting them focuses on their differences. It's a kind of thinking that comes naturally and that we do constantly—for example, comparing Houston with Dallas, iPhones with Androids, or three paintings by Renoir. And once we start comparing, we generally find ourselves contrasting—Houston and Dallas have differences as well as similarities.

As a student, you'll often be asked to compare and contrast paintings or poems or other things. As a writer, you'll have cause to compare and contrast in most kinds of writing. In a **PROPOSAL,** for instance, you will need to compare your solution with other possible solutions; or in an **EVALUATION,** such as a movie review, you might contrast the film you're reviewing with some other film. This chapter offers advice on ways of comparing and contrasting things for various writing purposes and for your own rhetorical situations.

205–13
164–72

Most of the time, we compare obviously similar things: cars we might purchase, three competing political candidates, two versions of a film. Occasionally, however, we might compare things that are less obviously similar. See how John McMurtry, an ex–football player, compares football with war in an essay arguing that the attraction football holds for spectators is based in part on its potential for violence and injury:

> The family resemblance between football and war is, indeed, striking. Their languages are similar: "field general," "long bomb," "blitz," "take a shot," "front line," "pursuit," "good hit," "the draft," and so on. Their principles and practices are alike: mass hysteria, the art of intimidation, absolute command and total obedience, territorial aggression, censorship, inflated insignia and propaganda, blackboard maneuvers and strategies, drills, uniforms, marching bands, and training

camps. And the virtues they celebrate are almost identical: hyper-aggressiveness, coolness under fire, and suicidal bravery.

> —John McMurtry, "Kill 'Em! Crush 'Em! Eat 'Em Raw!"

McMurtry's comparison helps focus readers' attention on what he's arguing about football in part because it's somewhat unexpected. But the more unlikely the comparison, the more you might be accused of comparing apples and oranges. It's important, therefore, that the things we compare be legitimately compared—as is the case in the following comparison of the health of the world's richest and poorest people:

> World Health Organization (WHO) data indicate that roughly 1.2 billion people are undernourished, underweight, and often hungry. At the same time, roughly 1.2 billion people are overnourished and over-weight, most of them suffering from excessive caloric intake and exercise deprivation. So while 1 billion people worry whether they will eat, another billion should worry about eating too much.
>
> Disease patterns also reflect the widening gap. The billion poorest suffer mostly from infectious diseases—malaria, tuberculosis, dysentery, and AIDS. Malnutrition leaves infants and small children even more vulnerable to such infectious diseases. Unsafe drinking water takes a heavier toll on those with hunger-weakened immune systems, resulting in millions of fatalities each year. In contrast, among the billion at the top of the global economic scale, it is diseases related to aging and lifestyle excesses, including obesity, smoking, diets rich in fat and sugar, and exercise deprivation, that cause most deaths.
>
> —Lester R. Brown, *Plan B 2.0: Rescuing a Planet*
> *under Stress and a Civilization in Trouble*

While the two groups of roughly a billion people each undoubtedly have similarities, this selection from a book arguing for global action on the environment focuses on the stark contrasts.

Two Ways of Comparing and Contrasting

Comparisons and contrasts may be organized in two basic ways: block and point by point.

The block method. One way is to discuss separately each item you're comparing, giving all the information about one item and then all the information about the next item. A report on Seattle and Vancouver, for example, compares the firearm regulations in each city using a paragraph about Seattle and then a paragraph about Vancouver:

> Although similar in many ways, Seattle and Vancouver differ markedly in their approaches to the regulation of firearms. In Seattle, handguns may be purchased legally for self-defense in the street or at home. After a thirty-day waiting period, a permit can be obtained to carry a handgun as a concealed weapon. The recreational use of handguns is minimally restricted.
>
> In Vancouver, self-defense is not considered a valid or legal reason to purchase a handgun. Concealed weapons are not permitted. Recreational uses of handguns (such as target shooting and collecting) are regulated by the province, and the purchase of a handgun requires a restricted-weapons permit. A permit to carry a weapon must also be obtained in order to transport a handgun, and these weapons can be discharged only at a licensed shooting club. Handguns can be transported by car, but only if they are stored in the trunk in a locked box.
>
> —John Henry Sloan et al., "Handgun Regulations, Crime, Assaults, and Homicide: A Tale of Two Cities"

The point-by-point method. The other way to compare things is to focus on specific points of comparison. In this paragraph, humorist David Sedaris compares his childhood with his partner's, discussing corresponding aspects of the childhoods one at a time:

> Certain events are parallel, but compared with Hugh's, my childhood was unspeakably dull. When I was seven years old, my family moved to North Carolina. When he was seven years old, Hugh's family moved to the Congo. We had a collie and a house cat. They had a monkey and two horses named Charlie Brown and Satan. I threw stones at stop signs. Hugh threw stones at crocodiles. The verbs are the same, but he definitely wins the prize when it comes to nouns and objects. An eventful day for my mother might have involved a trip to the dry cleaner or a conversation with the potato-chip deliveryman. Asked one ordinary

rhetorical situations   genres   processes   strategies   research MLA / APA   media / design   readings

Congo afternoon what she'd done with her day, Hugh's mother answered that she and a fellow member of the Ladies' Club had visited a leper colony on the outskirts of Kinshasa.

—David Sedaris, "Remembering My Childhood on the Continent of Africa"

Using Graphs and Images to Present Comparisons

Some comparisons can be easier to understand if they're presented visually, as a **CHART**, **GRAPH**, or **ILLUSTRATION**. For example, this excerpt from a chart from the *Huffington Post* shows the results of various opinion polls about Americans' identification with a political party in April and May 2012; it allows readers to compare not only percentages of Republicans, Democrats, and Independents but also differences in results among the polls. (In the third column, pop-up links explain that "Pop." means "Population," "A" means "adults," "RV" means "registered voters," and "LV" means "likely voters.")

591–99

Pollster	Dates	Pop.	Democrat	Independent	Republican	Undecided
AP-GfK	5/3–5/7	1,004 A	31	46	22	1
DailyKos/SEIU/ PPP (D)	5/3–5/6	1,000 RV	38	26	35	—
NBC/WSJ	4/13–4/17	800 A	30	42	24	4
CBS/Times	4/13–4/17	957 A	34	36	30	—
Ipsos/Reuters	4/12–4/15	1,044 A	29	49	22	—

—*The Huffington Post*

The following bar graph, from an economics textbook, compares the incomes of various professions in the United States, both with one another and with the average U.S. income (defined as 100 percent). Again, it would be possible to write out this information in a paragraph—but it is much easier to understand it this way:

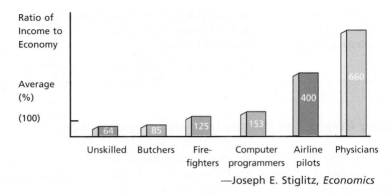

—Joseph E. Stiglitz, *Economics*

Sometimes photographs can make a comparison. The two photos below show areas of Japan before and after the 2011 tsunami.

Ishinomaki Prefecture before the 2011 tsunami (top) and after the storm (bottom).

Using Figurative Language to Make Comparisons

Another way we make comparisons is with figurative language: words and phrases used in a nonliteral way to help readers see a point. Three kinds of figurative language that make comparisons are similes, metaphors, and analogies. When Robert Burns wrote that his love was "like a red, red rose," he was comparing his love with a rose and evoking an image—in this case, a simile—that helps us understand his feelings for her. A simile makes a comparison using *like* or *as*. In the following example, from an article in the food section of the *New York Times*, a restaurant critic uses several similes (underlined) to help us visualize an unusual food dish:

> Once upon a time, possibly at a lodge in Wyoming, possibly at a butcher shop in Maurice, Louisiana, or maybe even at a plantation in South Carolina, an enterprising cook decided to take a boned chicken, a boned duck, and a boned turkey, stuff them one inside the other <u>like Russian dolls</u>, and roast them. He called his masterpiece turducken. . . .
>
> A well-prepared turducken is a marvelous treat, a free-form poultry terrine layered with flavorful stuffing and moistened with duck fat. When it's assembled, it looks <u>like a turkey</u> and it roasts <u>like a turkey</u>, but when you go to carve it, you can slice through it <u>like a loaf of bread</u>. In each slice you get a little bit of everything: white meat from the breast; dark meat from the legs, duck, carrots, bits of sausage, bread, herbs, juices, and chicken, too.
>
> —Amanda Hesser, "Turkey Finds Its Inner Duck (and Chicken)"

Metaphors make comparisons without such connecting words as *like* or *as*. See how desert ecologist Craig Childs uses a metaphor to help us understand the nature of water during a flood in the Grand Canyon:

> Water splashed off the desert and ran all over the surface, looking for the quickest way down. It was too swift for the ground to absorb. When water flows like this, it will not be clean tap water. It will be <u>a gravy of debris</u>, snatching everything it finds.
>
> —Craig Childs, *The Secret Knowledge of Water*

Calling the water "a gravy of debris" allows us to see the murky liquid as it streams through the canyon.

Analogies are extended similes or metaphors that compare something unfamiliar with something more familiar. Arguing that corporations should not patent parts of DNA whose function isn't yet clear, a genetics professor uses the familiar image of a library to explain an unfamiliar concept:

> It's like having a library of books and randomly tearing pages out. You may know which books the pages came from but that doesn't tell you much about them.
>
> —Peter Goodfellow, quoted in John Vidal and
> John Carvel, "Lambs to the Gene Market"

Sometimes analogies are used for humorous effect as well as to make a point, as in this passage from a critique of history textbooks:

> Another history text—this one for fifth grade—begins with the story of how Henry B. Gonzalez, who is a member of Congress from Texas, learned about his own nationality. When he was ten years old, his teacher told him he was an American because he was born in the United States. His grandmother, however, said, "The cat was born in the oven. Does that make him bread?"
>
> —Frances FitzGerald, America Revised:
> History Schoolbooks in the Twentieth Century

The grandmother's question shows how an intentionally ridiculous analogy can be a source of humor—and can make a point memorably.

Considering the Rhetorical Situation

As a writer or speaker, you need to think about the message that you want to articulate, the audience you want to reach, and the larger context you are writing in.

3–4 ■   **PURPOSE**   Sometimes your main purpose for writing will be to compare two or more things. Other times, you may want to compare several things for some other purpose—to compare your views with those of others in an argument essay or to compare one text with another as you analyze them.

AUDIENCE Who is your audience, and will comparing your topic with a more familiar one help them to follow your discussion?

5–8

GENRE Does your genre require you to compare something? Evaluations often include comparisons — one book to another in a review, or ten different cell phones in *Consumer Reports*.

9–11

STANCE Your stance may affect any comparisons you make. How you compare two things — evenhandedly, or clearly favoring one over the other, for example — will reflect your stance.

12–15

MEDIA / DESIGN Some things you will want to compare with words alone (lines from two poems, for instance), but sometimes you may wish to make comparisons visually (two images juxtaposed on a page, or several numbers plotted on a line graph).

16–18

IF YOU NEED MORE HELP

See **LOOPING** and **CUBING,** two methods of generating ideas that can be especially helpful for comparing and contrasting. If you're writing an essay whose purpose is to compare two or more things, see also the **PROCESSES** chapters for help drafting, revising, and so on.

260–62
249

36 Defining

Defining something says what it is — and what it is not. A terrier, for example, is a kind of dog. A fox terrier is a small dog now generally kept as a pet but once used by hunters to dig for foxes. Happiness is a jelly donut, at least according to Homer Simpson. All of those are definitions. As writers, we need to define any terms our readers may not know. And sometimes you'll want to stipulate your own definition of a word in order to set the terms of an ARGUMENT — as Homer Simpson does with a definition that's not found in any dictionary. This chapter details strategies for using definitions in your writing to suit your own rhetorical situations.

323–41

Formal Definitions

Sometimes to make sure readers understand you, you will need to provide a formal definition. If you are using a technical term that readers are unlikely to know or if you are using a term in a specific way, you need to say then and there what the word means. The word *mutual*, for example, has several dictionary meanings:

> **mu•tu•al** . . .
>
> **1a:** directed by each toward the other or the others <*mutual* affection> **b:** having the same feelings one for the other <they had long been *mutual* enemies> **c:** shared in common <enjoying their *mutual* hobby> **d:** joint
> **2:** characterized by intimacy
> **3:** of or relating to a plan whereby the members of an organization share in the profits and expenses; *specifically*: of, relating to, or taking the form of an insurance method in which the policyholders constitute the members of the insuring company
>
> — *Merriam-Webster.com*

rhetorical situations genres processes strategies research MLA / APA media / design readings

The first two meanings are commonly understood and probably require no definition. But if you were to use *mutual* in the third sense, it might—depending on your audience. A general audience would probably need the definition; an audience from the insurance industry would not. A website that gives basic financial advice to an audience of non-specialists, for instance, offers a specific definition of the term *mutual fund*:

> *Mutual funds* are financial intermediaries. They are companies set up to receive your money and then, having received it, to make investments with the money.
>
> —Bill Barker, "A Grand, Comprehensive
> Overview to Mutual Funds Investing"

But even writers in specialized fields routinely provide formal definitions to make sure their readers understand the way they are using certain words. See how two writers define the word *stock* as it pertains to their respective (and very different) fields:

> Stocks are the basis for sauces and soups and important flavoring agents for braises. Admittedly, stock making is time consuming, but the extra effort yields great dividends.
>
> —Tom Colicchio, *Think Like a Chef*

> Want to own part of a business without having to show up at its office every day? Or ever? Stock is the vehicle of choice for those who do. Dating back to the Dutch mutual stock corporations of the sixteenth century, the modern stock market exists as a way for entrepreneurs to finance businesses using money collected from investors. In return for ponying up the dough to finance the company, the investor becomes a part owner of the company. That ownership is represented by stock— specialized financial "securities," or financial instruments, that are "secured" by a claim on the assets and profits of a company.
>
> — "Investing Basics: Stocks," *The Motley Fool*

To write a formal definition

- Use words that readers are likely to be familiar with.
- Don't use the word being defined in the definition.

- Begin with the word being defined; include the general category to which the term belongs and the attributes that make it different from the others in that category.

For example:

Term	General Category	Distinguishing Attributes
Stock is	a specialized financial "security"	that is "secured" by a claim.
Photosynthesis is	a process	by which plants use sunlight to create energy.
Astronomers are	scientists	who study celestial objects and phenomena.
Sacha Baron Cohen,	a comedian,	has acted in several films, including *Brüno* and *The Dictator.*

Note that the category and distinguishing attributes cannot be stated too broadly; if they were, the definition would be too vague to be useful. It wouldn't be helpful in most circumstances, for example, to say, "Sacha Baron Cohen is a man who has acted" or "Photosynthesis is something having to do with plants."

Extended Definitions

Sometimes you need to provide a more detailed definition. Extended definitions may be several sentences long or several paragraphs long and may include pictures or diagrams. Sometimes an entire essay is devoted to defining a difficult or important concept. Here is one writer's extended definition of *meme*:

> Richard Dawkins first came up with the idea of a meme in his 1976 book *The Selfish Gene*. Essentially, memes are ideas that evolve according to the same principles that govern biological evolution. Think about all the ideas that you have in your head right now. They are all memes, and they all came from somewhere. Some of them will have come from friends and some will have come from the internet or television.

Examples of memes are musical tunes, jokes, trends, fashions, catch phrases, and car designs. Now, the memes that inhabit your mind are in competition with all the other memes in the *memepool* (the collection of all existing memes). This means that they are all competing to get themselves copied into other people's minds. Some of these memes do quite well. Every time you whistle your favorite tune or utter a useful catch phrase, you are facilitating the spread of those memes. Every time you wear something that is "in fashion" you are helping the idea of that fashion enter other people's minds. Consider the first four notes of Beethoven's 5th symphony, or the "Happy Birthday" song. These are ideas that inhabit our minds and have been very successful at replicating. Not only have these memes found their way into literally millions of minds, they have also managed to leave copies of themselves on paper, in books, on audiotape, on compact disks, and in computer hard-drives.

There is a limited amount of memetic storage space on this planet, so only the best memes manage to implant themselves. Memes that are good at replicating tend to leave more copies of themselves in minds and in other mediums such as books. Memes that are not so good at replicating tend to die out. We can imagine what sorts of memes have become extinct. Ancient songs that were once sung and never written down are one example. Another example is the many stories that were once told but have since slipped into oblivion.

—Brent Silby, "What Is a Meme?"

That definition includes a description of the basic features and behavior of memes, examples of them, and the origin of the term. We can assume that it's written for a general audience, one that doesn't know anything about memes.

Abstract concepts often require extended definitions because by nature they are more complicated to define. There are many ways of writing an extended definition, depending in part on the term being defined and on your audience and purpose. The following examples show some of the methods that can be used for composing extended definitions of *democracy*.

Explore the word's origins. Where did the word come from? When did it first come into use? In the following example, from an essay considering what democracy means in the twenty-first century, the writer started by looking at the word's first known use in English. Though it's from an essay written for a first-year writing course and thus for a fairly general audience, it's a definition that might pique any audience's interest:

> According to the *Oxford English Dictionary*, the term *democracy* first appeared in English in a thirteenth-century translation of Aristotle's works — specifically, in his *Politics*, where he stated that the "underlying principle of democracy is freedom" and that "it is customary to say that only in democracies do men have a share in freedom, for that is what every democracy makes its aim." By the sixteenth century, the word was used much as it is now. One writer in 1586, for instance, defined it in this way: "where free and poore men being the greater number, are lords of the estate."
>
> — Susanna Mejía, "What Does Democracy Mean Now?"

Here's another example, this one written for a scholarly audience, from an essay about women, participation, democracy, and the information age:

> The very word *citizenship* carries with it a connotation of place, a "citizen" being, literally, the inhabitant of a city. Over the years the word has, of course, accumulated a number of associated meanings . . . and the word has come to stand in for such concepts as participation, equality, and democracy. The fact that the concept of locality is deeply embedded in the word *citizen* suggests that it is also fundamental to our current understanding of these other, more apparently abstract words.
>
> In Western thought, the concepts of citizenship, equality, and democracy are closely interlinked and can be traced back to a common source, in Athens in the fifth century B.C. Perhaps it is no accident that it was the same culture which also gave us, in its theater, the concept of the unity of time and space. The Greek city-state has been represented for centuries as the ideal model of democracy, with free and equal access for all citizens to decision making. Leaving aside, for the moment, the question of who was included, and who excluded from this notion of citizenship, we can see that the sense of place is fundamental to this model. Entitlement to participate in the democratic process is circumscribed by geography; it is the inhabitants of the geographical entity of the city-state, precisely defined and bounded, who have the rights to citizenship. Those who are not defined as inhabitants

Norman Rockwell's 1943 painting Freedom of Speech *presents a visual defini-tion of democracy: a citizen stands to speak at a public meeting while his fellow citizens listen attentively.*

of that specific city-state are explicitly excluded, although, of course, they may have the right to citizenship elsewhere.

—Ursula Huws, "Women, Participation, and
Democracy in the Information Society"

Provide details. What are its characteristics? What is it made of? See how a historian explores the basic characteristics of democracy in a book written for an audience of historians:

> As a historian I am naturally disposed to be satisfied with the meaning which, in the history of politics, men have commonly attributed to the word—a meaning, needless to say, which derives partly from the experience and partly from the aspirations of mankind. So regarded, the term *democracy* refers primarily to a form of government, and it has always meant government by the many as opposed to government by the one—government by the people as opposed to government by a tyrant, a dictator, or an absolute monarch. . . . Since the Greeks first used the term, the essential test of democratic government has always been this: the source of political authority must be and remain in the people and not in the ruler. A democratic government has always meant one in which the citizens, or a sufficient number of them to represent more or less effectively the common will, freely act from time to time, and according to established forms, to appoint or recall the magistrates and to enact or revoke the laws by which the community is governed.

—Carl Becker, *Modern Democracy*

Compare it with other words. How is this concept like other similar things? How does it differ? What is it *not* like? **COMPARE AND CONTRAST** it.

348–55

See how a political science textbook defines a *majoritarian democracy* by comparing its characteristics with those of a *consensual democracy*:

> A majoritarian democracy is one
>
> 1. having only two major political parties, not many
> 2. having an electoral system that requires a bare majority to elect one clear winner in an election, as opposed to a proportional

rhetorical situations   genres   processes   strategies   research MLA / APA   media / design   readings

electoral system that distributes seats to political parties according to the rough share of votes received in the election

3. a strong executive (president or prime minister) and cabinet that together are largely independent of the legislature when it comes to exercising the executive's constitutional duties, in contrast to an executive and cabinet that are politically controlled by the parties in the legislature and therefore unable to exercise much influence when proposing policy initiatives.

> —Benjamin Ginsberg, Theodore J. Lowi, and Margaret Weir,
> *We the People: An Introduction to American Politics*

And here's an example in which democracy is contrasted with various other forms of governments of the past:

> Caesar's power derived from a popular mandate, conveyed through established republican forms, but that did not make his government any the less a dictatorship. Napoleon called his government a democratic republic, but no one, least of all Napoleon himself, doubted that he had destroyed the last vestiges of the democratic republic.

> —Carl Becker, *Modern Democracy*

Give examples. See how the essayist E. B. White defines democracy by giving some everyday examples of considerate behavior, humility, and civic participation—all things he suggests constitute democracy:

> It is the line that forms on the right. It is the don't in "don't shove." It is the hole in the stuffed shirt through which the sawdust slowly trickles; it is the dent in the high hat. Democracy is the recurrent suspicion that more than half of the people are right more than half of the time. . . . Democracy is a letter to the editor.

> —E. B. White, "Democracy"

White's definition is elegant because he uses examples that his readers will know. His characteristics—metaphors, really—define democracy not as a conceptual way of governing but as an everyday part of American life.

342–47

Classify it.   Often it is useful to divide or **CLASSIFY** a term. The ways in which democracy unfolds are complex enough to warrant entire textbooks, of course, but the following definition, from a political science textbook, divides democracy into two kinds, representative and direct:

> A system of government that gives citizens a regular opportunity to elect the top government officials is usually called a representative democracy or republic. A system that permits citizens to vote directly on laws and policies is often called a direct democracy. At the national level, America is a representative democracy in which citizens select government officials but do not vote on legislation. Some states, however, have provisions for direct legislation through popular referendum. For example, California voters in 1995 decided to bar undocumented immigrants from receiving some state services.
>
> —Benjamin Ginsberg, Theodore J. Lowi, and Margaret Weir,
> *We the People: An Introduction to American Politics*

Stipulative Definitions

Sometimes a writer will stipulate a certain definition, essentially saying, "This is how I'm defining x." Such definitions are not usually found in a dictionary—and at the same time are central to the argument the writer is making. Here is one example, from an essay by Toni Morrison. Describing a scene from a film in which a newly arrived Greek immigrant, working as a shoe shiner in Grand Central Terminal, chases away an African American competitor, Morrison calls the scene an example of "race talk," a concept she then goes on to define:

> This is race talk, the explicit insertion into everyday life of racial signs and symbols that have no meaning other than pressing African Americans to the lowest level of the racial hierarchy. Popular culture, shaped by film, theater, advertising, the press, television, and literature, is heavily engaged in race talk. It participates freely in this most enduring and efficient rite of passage into American culture: negative appraisals of the native-born black population. Only when the lesson of racial estrangement is learned is assimilation complete. Whatever

rhetorical situations   genres   processes   strategies   research MLA / APA   media / design   readings

the lived experience of immigrants with African Americans—pleasant, beneficial, or bruising—the rhetorical experience renders blacks as noncitizens, already discredited outlaws.

All immigrants fight for jobs and space, and who is there to fight but those who have both? As in the fishing ground struggle between Texas and Vietnamese shrimpers, they displace what and whom they can. Although U.S. history is awash in labor battles, political fights and property wars among all religious and ethnic groups, their struggles are persistently framed as struggles between recent arrivals and blacks. In race talk the move into mainstream America always means buying into the notion of American blacks as the real aliens. Whatever the ethnicity or nationality of the immigrant, his nemesis is understood to be African American.

—Toni Morrison, "On the Backs of Blacks"

The following example is from a book review of Nancy L. Rosenblum's *Membership and Morals: The Personal Uses of Pluralism in America*, published in the *American Prospect*, a magazine for readers interested in political analysis. In it a Stanford law professor outlines a definition of "the democracy of everyday life":

Democracy, in this understanding of it, means simply treating people as equals, disregarding social standing, avoiding attitudes of either deference or superiority, making allowances for others' weaknesses, and resisting the temptation to respond to perceived slights. It also means protesting everyday instances of arbitrariness and unfairness—from the rudeness of the bakery clerk to the sexism of the car dealer or the racism of those who vandalize the home of the first black neighbors on the block.

—Kathleen M. Sullivan, "Defining Democracy Down"

Considering the Rhetorical Situation

As a writer or speaker, you need to think about the message that you want to articulate, the audience you want to reach, and the larger context you are writing in.

PURPOSE   Your purpose for writing will affect any definitions you include. Would writing an extended definition help you explain something? Would stipulating definitions of key terms help you shape an argument? Could an offbeat definition help you entertain your readers?

AUDIENCE   What audience do you want to reach, and are there any terms your readers are unlikely to know (and therefore need to be defined)? Are there terms they might understand differently from the way you're defining them?

GENRE   Does your genre require you to define terms? Chances are that if you're reporting information you'll need to define some terms, and some arguments rest on the way you define key terms.

STANCE   What is your stance, and do you need to define key terms to show that stance clearly? How you define *fetus*, for example, is likely to reveal your stance on abortion.

MEDIA / DESIGN   Your medium will affect the form your definitions take. In a print text, you will need to define terms in your text; if you're giving a speech or presentation, you might also provide images of important terms and their definitions. In an electronic text, you may be able to define terms by linking to an online dictionary definition.

IF YOU NEED MORE HELP

See also the **PROCESSES** chapters for help generating ideas, drafting, revising, and so on if you are writing a whole essay dedicated to defining a term or concept.

Describing 37

When we describe something, we indicate what it looks like—and sometimes how it sounds, feels, smells, and tastes. Descriptive details are a way of showing rather than telling, of helping readers see (or hear, smell, and so on) what we're writing about—that the sky is blue, that Miss Havisham is wearing an old yellowed wedding gown, that the chemicals in the beaker have reacted and smell like rotten eggs. You'll have occasion to describe things in most of the writing you do—from describing a favorite hat in a **MEMOIR** to detailing a chemical reaction in a **LAB REPORT**. This chapter will help you work with description—and, in particular, help you think about the use of *detail*, about *objectivity and subjectivity*, about *vantage point*, about creating a clear *dominant impression*, and about using description to fit your rhetorical situation.

183–90

173–82

Detail

The goal of using details is to be as specific as possible, providing information that will help your audience imagine the subject or make sense of it. See, for example, how Nancy Mairs, an author with multiple sclerosis, describes the disease in clear, specific terms:

> During its course, which is unpredictable and uncontrollable, one may lose vision, hearing, speech, the ability to walk, control of bladder and/or bowels, strength in any or all extremities, sensitivity to touch, vibration, and/or pain, potency, coordination of movements—the list of possibilities is lengthy and, yes, horrifying. One may also lose one's sense of humor. That's the easiest to lose and the hardest to survive without.
>
> In the past ten years, I have sustained some of these losses. Characteristic of MS are sudden attacks, called exacerbations, followed by remissions, and these I have not had. Instead, my disease has been

slowly progressive. My left leg is now so weak that I walk with the aid of a brace and a cane, and for distances I use an Amigo, a variation on the electric wheelchair that looks rather like an electrified kiddie car. I no longer have much use of my left hand. Now my right side is weakening as well. I still have the blurred spot in my right eye. Overall, though, I've been lucky so far.

—Nancy Mairs, "On Being a Cripple"

Mairs's gruesome list demonstrates, through *specific details*, how the disease affects sufferers generally and her in particular. We know far more after reading this text than we do from the following more general description, from a National Multiple Sclerosis Society brochure:

Multiple sclerosis is a chronic, unpredictable disease of the central nervous system (the brain, optic nerves, and spinal cord). It is thought to be an autoimmune disorder. This means the immune system incorrectly attacks the person's healthy tissue.

MS can cause blurred vision, loss of balance, poor coordination, slurred speech, tremors, numbness, extreme fatigue, problems with memory and concentration, paralysis, and blindness. These problems may be permanent, or they may come and go.

—National Multiple Sclerosis Society, *Just the Facts*

Specific details are also more effective than labels, which give little meaningful information. Instead of saying that someone is a "moron" or "really smart," it's better to give details so that readers can understand the reasons behind the label: what does this person *do* or *say* that makes him or her deserve this label? See, for example, how the writer of a news story about shopping on the day after Thanksgiving opens with a description of a happy shopper:

Last Friday afternoon, the day ritualized consumerism is traditionally at its most frenetic, Alexx Balcuns twirled in front of a full-length mirror at the Ritz Thrift Shop on West Fifty-seventh Street as if inhabited by the soul of Eva Gabor in *Green Acres*. Ms. Balcuns was languishing in a $795 dyed-mink parka her grandmother had just bought her. Ms. Balcuns is six.

—Ginia Bellafante, "Staying Warm and Fuzzy during Uncertain Times"

rhetorical situations   genres   processes   strategies   research MLA / APA   media / design   readings

The writer might simply have said, "A spoiled child admired herself in the mirror." Instead, she shows her subject twirling and "languishing" in a "$795 dyed-mink parka" and seemingly possessed by the soul of the actress Eva Gabor—all details that create a far more vivid description.

Sensory details help readers imagine sounds, odors, tastes, and physical sensations in addition to sights. In the following example, writer Scott Russell Sanders recalls sawing wood as a child. Note how visual details, odors, and even the physical sense of being picked up by his father mingle to form a vivid scene:

> As the saw teeth bit down, the wood released its smell, each kind with its own fragrance, oak or walnut or cherry or pine—usually pine because it was the softest, easiest for a child to work. No matter how weathered and gray the board, no matter how warped and cracked, inside there was this smell waiting, as of something freshly baked. I gathered every smidgen of sawdust and stored it away in coffee cans, which I kept in a drawer of the workbench. When I did not feel like hammering nails I would dump my sawdust on the concrete floor of the garage and landscape it into highways and farms and towns, running miniature cars and trucks along miniature roads. Looming as huge as a colossus, my father worked over and around me, now and again bending down to inspect my work, careful not to trample my creations. It was a landscape that smelled dizzyingly of wood. Even after a bath my skin would carry the smell, and so would my father's hair, when he lifted me for a bedtime hug.
>
> —Scott Russell Sanders, *The Paradise of Bombs*

Whenever you describe something, you'll select from many possible details you might use. Simply put, to exhaust all the details available to describe something is impossible—and would exhaust your readers as well. To focus your description, you'll need to determine the kinds of details appropriate for your subject. They will vary, depending on your **PURPOSE.** See, for example, how the details might differ in three different genres:

3–4

- For a **MEMOIR** *about an event*, you might choose details that are significant for you, that evoke the sights, sounds, and other sensations that give meaning to your event.

183–90

191–204 ▲

- For a **PROFILE,** you're likely to select details that will reinforce the dominant impression you want to give, that portray the event from the perspective you want readers to see.

173–82 ▲

- For a **LAB REPORT,** you need to give certain specifics — what equipment was used, what procedures were followed, what exactly were the results.

Deciding on a focus for your description can help you see it better, as you'll look for details that contribute to that focus.

Objectivity and Subjectivity

Descriptions can be written with objectivity, with subjectivity, or with a mixture of both. Objective descriptions attempt to be uncolored by personal opinion or emotion. Police reports and much news writing aim to describe events objectively; scientific writing strives for objectivity in describing laboratory procedures and results. See, for example, the following objective account of what happened at the World Trade Center on September 11, 2001:

> **World Trade Center Disaster — Tuesday, September 11, 2001**
>
> On Tuesday, September 11, 2001, at 8:45 a.m. New York local time, One World Trade Center, the north tower, was hit by a hijacked 767 commercial jet airplane loaded with fuel for a transcontinental flight. Two World Trade Center, the south tower, was hit by a similar hijacked jet eighteen minutes later, at 9:03 a.m. (In separate but related attacks, the Pentagon building near Washington, D.C., was hit by a hijacked 757 at 9:43 a.m., and at 10:10 a.m. a fourth hijacked jetliner crashed in Pennsylvania.) The south tower, WTC 2, which had been hit second, was the first to suffer a complete structural collapse, at 10:05 a.m., 62 minutes after being hit itself, 80 minutes after the first impact. The north tower, WTC 1, then also collapsed, at 10:29 a.m., 104 minutes after being hit. WTC 7, a substantial forty-seven-story office building in its own right, built in 1987, was damaged by the collapsing towers, caught fire, and later in the afternoon also totally collapsed.
>
> — "World Trade Center," *GreatBuildings.com*

Subjective descriptions, on the other hand, allow the writer's opinions and emotions to come through. A house can be described as comfortable, with a lived-in look, or as rundown and in need of a paint job and a new roof. Here's a subjective description of the planes striking the World Trade Center, as told by a woman watching from a nearby building:

> Incredulously, while looking out [the] window at the damage and carnage the first plane had inflicted, I saw the second plane abruptly come into my right field of vision and deliberately, with shimmering intention, thunder full-force into the south tower. It was so close, so low, so huge and fast, so intent on its target that I swear to you, I swear to you, I felt the vengeance and rage emanating from the plane.
>
> —Debra Fontaine, "Witnessing"

Vantage Point

Sometimes you'll want or need to describe something from a certain vantage point. Where you locate yourself in relation to what you're describing will determine what you can perceive (and so describe) and what you can't. You may describe your subject from a *stationary vantage point*, from which you (and your readers) see your subject from one angle only, as if you were a camera. This description of one of three photographs that captured a woman's death records only what the camera saw from one angle at one particular moment:

> The first showed some people on a fire escape—a fireman, a woman and a child. The fireman had a nice strong jaw and looked very brave. The woman was holding the child. Smoke was pouring from the building behind them. A rescue ladder was approaching, just a few feet away, and the fireman had one arm around the woman and one arm reaching out toward the ladder.
>
> —Nora Ephron, "The Boston Photographs"

By contrast, this description of a drive to an Italian villa uses a *moving vantage point*; the writer recounts what he saw as he passed through a gate in a city wall, moving from city to country:

La Pietra — "the stone" — is situated one mile from the Porta San Gallo, an entry to the Old City of Florence. You drive there along the Via Bolognese, twisting past modern apartment blocks, until you come to a gate, which swings open — and there you are, at the upper end of a long lane of cypresses facing a great ocher palazzo; with olive groves spreading out on both sides over an expanse of fifty-seven acres. There's something almost comically wonderful about the effect: here, the city, with its winding avenue; there, on the other side of a wall, the country, fertile and gray green.

—James Traub, "Italian Hours"

The description of quarries in the following section uses *multiple vantage points* to capture the quarries from many perspectives.

This ad for Adidas uses a stationary vantage point (looking down on the basketball court or grassy court from above the backboard) to make a point about the universality of the game — and hence the need for Adidas.

rhetorical situations

genres

processes

strategies

research
MLA / APA

media / design

readings

The vast expanse of sky and desert in this Harley-Davidson ad creates a dominant impression of spaciousness and freedom that's underscored by the image the text evokes — one of cramped confinement.

Dominant Impression

With any description, your aim is to create some dominant impression — the overall feeling that the individual details add up to. The dominant impression may be implied, growing out of the details themselves. For example, Scott Russell Sanders's memory of the smell of sawdust creates a dominant impression of warmth and comfort: the "fragrance . . . as of something freshly baked," sawdust "stored . . . away in coffee cans," a young boy "lifted . . . for a bedtime hug." Sometimes, though, a writer will state the dominant impression directly, in addition to creating it with details. In an essay about Indiana limestone quarries, Sanders makes the dominant impression clear from the start: "they are battlefields."

> The quarries will not be domesticated. They are not backyard pools; they are battlefields. Each quarry is an arena where violent struggles have taken place between machines and planet, between human ingenuity and brute

resisting stone, between mind and matter. Waste rock litters the floor and brim like rubble in a bombed city. The ragged pits might have been the basements of vanished skyscrapers. Stones weighing tens of tons lean against one another at precarious angles, as if they have been thrown there by some gigantic strength and have not yet finished falling. Wrecked machinery hulks in the weeds, grimly rusting, the cogs and wheels, twisted rails, battered engine housings, trackless bulldozers and burst boilers like junk from an armored regiment. Everywhere the ledges are scarred from drills, as if from an artillery barrage or machine-gun strafing. Stumbling onto one of these abandoned quarries and gazing at the ruins, you might be left wondering who had won the battle, men or stone.

—Scott Russell Sanders, *The Paradise of Bombs*

The rest of his description, full of more figurative language ("like rubble in a bombed city," "like junk from an armored regiment," "as if from an artillery barrage or machine-gun strafing") reinforces the direct "they are battlefields" statement.

Organizing Descriptions

You can organize descriptions in many ways. When your description is primarily visual, you will probably organize it spatially: from left to right, top to bottom, outside to inside. One variation on this approach is to begin with the most significant or noteworthy feature and move outward from that center, as Ephron does. Or you may create a chronological description of objects as you move past or through them in space, as Traub does in his description of his drive. You might even pile up details to create a dominant impression, as Sanders and Mairs do, especially if your description draws on senses besides vision.

Considering the Rhetorical Situation

As a writer or speaker, you need to think about the message that you want to articulate, the audience you want to reach, and the larger context you are writing in.

PURPOSE   Your purpose may affect the way you use description. If you're arguing that a government should intervene in another country's civil war, for example, describing the anguish of refugees from that war could make your argument more persuasive. If you're analyzing a painting, you will likely need to describe it.   ▪ 3–4

AUDIENCE   Who is your audience, and will they need detailed description to understand the points you wish to make?   ▪ 5–8

GENRE   Does your genre require description? A lab report generally calls for you to describe materials and results; a memoir about grandma should probably describe her — her smile, her dress, her apple pie.   ▪ 9–11

STANCE   The way you describe things can help you convey your stance. For example, the details you choose can show you to be objective (or not), careful or casual.   ▪ 12–15

MEDIA / DESIGN   Your medium will affect the form your description can take. In a print or spoken text, you will likely rely on words, though you may also include visuals. In an electronic text, you can easily provide links to visuals as well as audio clips and so may need fewer words of your own.   ▪ 16–18

IF YOU NEED MORE HELP

See also **FREEWRITING, CUBING,** and **LISTING,** three methods of generating ideas that can be especially helpful for developing detailed descriptions. Sometimes you may be assigned to write a whole essay describing something: see the **PROCESSES** chapters for help drafting, revising, and so on.   ○ 259–62
249

38 Dialogue

183–90
191–204
81–86
119–49

Dialogue is a way of including people's own words in a text, letting readers hear those people's voices—not just what you say about them. **MEMOIRS** and **PROFILES** often include dialogue, and many other genres do as well: **LITERARY ANALYSES** often quote dialogue from the texts they analyze, and essays **ARGUING A POSITION** might quote an authoritative source as support for a claim. This chapter provides brief guidelines for the conventions of paragraphing and punctuating dialogue and offers some good examples of how you can use dialogue most effectively to suit your own rhetorical situations.

Why Add Dialogue?

Dialogue is a way of bringing in voices other than your own, of showing people and scenes rather than just telling about them. It can add color and texture to your writing, making it memorable. Most important, however, dialogue should be more than just colorful or interesting. It needs to contribute to your rhetorical purpose, to support the point you're making. See how dialogue is used in the following excerpt from a magazine profile of the Mall of America, how it gives us a sense of the place that the journalist's own words could not provide:

> Two pubescent girls in retainers and braces sat beside me sipping coffees topped with whipped cream and chocolate sprinkles, their shopping bags gathered tightly around their legs, their eyes fixed on the passing crowds. They came, they said, from Shakopee—"It's nowhere," one of them explained. The megamall, she added, was "a buzz at first, but now it seems pretty normal. 'Cept my parents are like Twenty Questions every time I want to come here. 'Specially since the shooting."

rhetorical situations

genres

processes

strategies

research MLA / APA

media / design

readings

On a Sunday night, she elaborated, three people had been wounded when shots were fired in a dispute over a San Jose Sharks jacket. "In the *mall*," her friend reminded me. "Right here at megamall. A shooting."
"It's like nowhere's safe," the first added.

> —David Guterson, "Enclosed. Encyclopedic. Endured.
> One Week at the Mall of America"

Of course it was the writer who decided whom and what to quote, and Guterson deliberately chose words that capture the young shoppers' speech patterns, quoting fragments ("In the *mall*. . . . Right here at megamall. A shooting"), slang ("a buzz at first," "my parents are like Twenty Questions"), even contractions ("'cept," "'specially").

Integrating Dialogue into Your Writing

There are certain conventions for punctuating and paragraphing dialogue:

- **Punctuating.** Enclose each speaker's words in quotation marks, and put any end punctuation—periods, question marks, and exclamation marks—inside the closing quotation mark. Whether you're transcribing words you heard or making them up, you will sometimes need to add punctuation to reflect the rhythm and sound of the speech. In the last sentence of the example below, see how Chang-Rae Lee adds a comma after *well* and italicizes *practice* to show intonation—and attitude.

- **Paragraphing.** When you're writing dialogue that includes more than one speaker, start a new paragraph each time the speaker changes.

- **Signal phrases.** Sometimes you'll need to introduce dialogue with SIGNAL PHRASES—"I said," "she asked," and so on—to make clear who is speaking. At times, however, the speaker will be clear enough, and you won't need any signal phrases.

471–74

Here is a conversation between a mother and her son that illustrates each of the conventions for punctuating and paragraphing dialogue:

> "Whom do I talk to?" she said. She would mostly speak to me in Korean, and I would answer back in English.

"The bank manager, who else?"

"What do I say?"

"Whatever you want to say."

"Don't speak to me like that!" she cried.

"It's just that you should be able to do it yourself," I said.

"You know how I feel about this!"

"Well, maybe then you should consider it *practice*," I answered lightly, using the Korean word to make sure she understood.

—Chang-Rae Lee, "Coming Home Again"

Interviews

Interviews are a kind of dialogue, with different conventions for punctuation. When you're transcribing an interview, give each speaker's name each time he or she speaks, starting a new line but not indenting, and do not use quotation marks. Here is an excerpt from a National Public Radio interview that Audie Cornish conducted with writer Susan Cain:

> **Audie Cornish:** In the 1940s and '50s, the message to most Americans was, don't be shy. And in the era of reality television, Twitter and relentless self-promotion, it seems that cultural mandate is in overdrive.
>
> A new book tells the story of how things came to be this way, and it's called *Quiet: The Power of Introverts in a World that Can't Stop Talking*. The author is Susan Cain, and she joins us from the NPR studios in New York to talk more about it. Welcome, Susan.
>
> **Susan Cain:** Thank you. It's such a pleasure to be here, Audie.
>
> **Cornish:** Well, we're happy to have you. And to start out — I think we should get this on the record — do you consider yourself an introvert or an extrovert?
>
> **Cain:** Oh, I definitely consider myself an introvert, and that was part of the fuel for me to write the book.
>
> **Cornish:** And what's the difference between being an introvert versus being shy? I mean, what's your definition?
>
> **Cain:** So introversion is really about having a preference for lower-stimulation environments — so just a preference for quiet, for less noise, for less action — whereas extroverts really crave more stimulation in

order to feel at their best. And what's important to understand about this is that many people believe that introversion is about being anti-social. And that's really a misperception because actually, it's just that introverts are differently social. So they would prefer to have, you know, a glass of wine with a close friend as opposed to going to a loud party full of strangers.

Now shyness, on the other hand, is about a fear of negative social judgment. So you can be introverted without having that particular fear at all, and you can be shy but also be an extrovert.

Cornish: And in the book, you say that there's a spectrum. So if some people are listening and they think, well, I, too, like a glass of wine and a party. It's like we all have these tendencies.

Cain: Yeah, yeah. That's an important thing. And, in fact, Carl Jung, the psychologist who first popularized these terms all the way back in the 1920s — even he said there's no such thing as a pure introvert or a pure extrovert, and he said such a man would be in a lunatic asylum.

Cornish: That makes me worry because I took your test in the book and I'm like, 90 percent extroverted, basically.

[*soundbite of laughter*]

Cornish: Now, you mentioned going back into the history. And I want to talk more about that because I was really fascinated by how you showed how this extrovert ideal — you call it — came to be. When did being introverted move from being a character trait to being looked at as a problem?

Cain: Yeah. What I found is, to some extent, we've always had an admi-ration for extroversion in our culture. But the extrovert ideal really came to play at the turn of the 20th century, when we had the rise of big business. And so suddenly, people were flocking to the cities, and they were needing to prove themselves in big corporations — at job interviews and on sales calls.

And so at that moment in time, we moved from what cultural his-torians call a culture of character to a culture of personality. So during the culture of character, what was important was the good deeds that you performed when nobody was looking. You know, Abraham Lincoln is the embodiment of the culture of character, and people celebrated him back then for being a man who did not offend by superiority.

But at the turn of the century, when we moved into this culture of personality, suddenly, what was admired was to be magnetic and charismatic. And then at the same time, we suddenly had the rise of movies and movie stars. And movie stars, of course, were the embodiment of what it meant to be a charismatic figure. And so part of people's fascination with these movie stars was for what they could learn from them, and bring with them to their own jobs.

—"Quiet, Please: Unleashing 'The Power of Introverts' "

In preparing the interview transcript for publication, NPR had to add punctuation, which of course was not part of the oral conversation, and probably deleted pauses and verbal expressions such as *um* and *uh*. At the same time, the editor kept informal constructions, such as incomplete sentences, which are typical answers to questions ("Yeah.") to maintain the oral flavor of the interview and to reflect Cain's voice.

Considering the Rhetorical Situation

As a writer or speaker, you need to think about the message that you want to articulate, the audience you want to reach, and the larger context of your writing.

3–4 ▪ **PURPOSE** Your purpose will affect any use of dialogue. Dialogue can help bring a profile to life and make it memorable. Interviews with experts or firsthand witnesses can add credibility to a report or argument.

5–8 ▪ **AUDIENCE** Whom do you want to reach, and will dialogue help? Sometimes actual dialogue can help readers hear human voices behind facts or reason.

9–11 ▪ **GENRE** Does your genre require dialogue? If you're evaluating or analyzing a literary work, for instance, you may wish to include dialogue from that work. If you're writing a profile of a person or event, dialogue can help you bring your subject to life. Similarly, an interview with an expert can add credibility to a report or argument.

rhetorical situations   genres   processes   strategies   research MLA / APA   media / design   readings

STANCE   What is your stance, and can dialogue help you communicate that stance? For example, excerpts of an interview may allow you to challenge someone's views and make your own views clear.

12–15

MEDIA / DESIGN   Your medium will affect the way you present dialogue. In a print text, you will present dialogue through written words. In an oral or electronic text, you might include actual recorded dialogue.

16–18

IF YOU NEED MORE HELP

See also the guidelines on **INTERVIEWING EXPERTS** for advice on setting up and recording interviews and those on **QUOTING, PARAPHRASING,** and **SUMMARIZING** for help deciding how to integrate dialogue into your text.

448–49
462–74

39 Explaining Processes

When you explain a process, you tell how something is (or was) done—how a bill becomes a law, how an embryo develops—or you tell someone how to do something—how to throw a curve ball, how to write a memoir. This chapter focuses on those two kinds of explanations, offering examples and guidelines for explaining a process in a way that works for your rhetorical situation.

Explaining a Process Clearly

Whether the process is simple or complex, you'll need to identify its key stages or steps and explain them one by one, in order. The sequence matters because it allows readers to follow your explanation; it is especially important when you're explaining a process that others are going to follow. Most often you'll explain a process chronologically, from start to finish. **TRANSITIONS**—words like *first*, *next*, *then*, and so on—are often necessary, therefore, to show readers how the stages of a process relate to one another and to indicate time sequences. Finally, you'll find that verbs matter; they indicate the actions that take place at each stage of the process.

317 ◆

Explaining How Something Is Done

All processes consist of steps, and when you explain how something is done, you describe each step, generally in order, from first to last. Here, for example, is an explanation of how French fries are made, from an essay published in the *New Yorker:*

> Fast-food French fries are made from a baking potato like an Idaho russet, or any other variety that is mealy, or starchy, rather than waxy. The potatoes are harvested, cured, washed, peeled, sliced, and then blanched—cooked enough so that the insides have a fluffy texture but not so much that the fry gets soft and breaks. Blanching is followed by drying, and drying by a thirty-second deep fry, to give the potatoes a crisp shell. Then the fries are frozen until the moment of service, when they are deep-fried again, this time for somewhere around three minutes. Depending on the fast-food chain involved, there are other steps interspersed in this process. McDonald's fries, for example, are briefly dipped in a sugar solution, which gives them their golden-brown color; Burger King fries are dipped in a starch batter, which is what gives those fries their distinctive hard shell and audible crunch. But the result is similar. The potato that is first harvested in the field is roughly 80 percent water. The process of creating a French fry consists, essentially, of removing as much of that water as possible—through blanching, drying, and deep-frying—and replacing it with fat.
>
> —Malcolm Gladwell, "The Trouble with Fries"

Gladwell clearly explains the process of making French fries, showing us the specific steps—how the potatoes "are harvested, cured, washed, peeled, sliced," and so on—and using clear transitions—"followed by," "then," "until," "when"—and action verbs to show the sequence. His last sentence makes his stance clear, pointing out that the process of creating a French fry consists of removing as much of a potato's water as possible "and replacing it with fat."

Explaining How to Do Something

In explaining how to do something, you are giving instruction so that others can follow the process themselves. See how Martha Stewart explains the process of making French fries. She starts by listing the ingredients and then describes the steps:

4 medium baking potatoes
2 tablespoons olive oil
1½ teaspoons salt
¼ teaspoon freshly ground pepper
malt vinegar (optional)

1. Heat oven to 400 degrees. Place a heavy baking sheet in the oven. Scrub and rinse the potatoes well, and then cut them lengthwise into ½-inch-wide batons. Place the potato batons in a medium bowl, and toss them with the olive oil, salt, and pepper.

2. When baking sheet is hot, about 15 minutes, remove from the oven. Place prepared potatoes on the baking sheet in a single layer. Return to oven, and bake until potatoes are golden on the bottom, about 30 minutes. Turn potatoes over, and continue cooking until golden all over, about 15 minutes more. Serve immediately.

—Martha Stewart, *Favorite Comfort Food*

Coming from Martha Stewart, the explanation leaves out no details, giving a clear sequence of steps and descriptive verbs that tell us exactly what to do: "heat," "place," "scrub and rinse," and so on. After she gives the recipe, she even goes on to explain the process of *serving* the fries—"Serve these French fries with a bowl of malt vinegar"—and reminds us that "they are also delicious dipped in spicy mustard, mayonnaise, and, of course, ketchup."

Explaining a Process Visually

591–99

Some processes are best explained **VISUALLY**, with diagrams or photographs. See, for example, how a blogger explains one process of shaping dough into a bagel—giving the details in words and then showing us in photos how to do it:

rhetorical situations ▲ genres ○ processes ◆ strategies ● research MLA / APA □ media / design ▨ readings

Roll each portion into a ball and place on prepared baking sheet. Cover with a damp towel and let rest for 20 minutes.

Wrap the dough around your palm and the back of your hand, overlapping the ends by an inch or two.

Roll balls into 6- to 7-inch ropes. If the dough resists, just let it rest for a few minutes and try rolling it again.

Press the overlapping edges against the countertop, rolling the bagel back and forth to seal the seam.

Place bagels back on baking sheet and cover with plastic wrap that has been coated with cooking spray.

—Maggie Lauer, *The Other Side of Fifty*

Considering the Rhetorical Situation

As always, you need to think about the message that you want to articulate, the audience you want to reach, and the larger context you are writing in.

3–4 **PURPOSE** Your purpose for writing will affect the way you explain a process. If you're arguing that we should avoid eating fast food, you might explain the process by which chicken nuggets are made. But to give information about how to fry chicken, you would explain the process quite differently.

5–8 **AUDIENCE** Whom are you trying to reach, and will you need to provide any special background information or to interest them in the process before you explain it?

9–11 **GENRE** Does your genre require you to explain a process? In a lab report, for example, you'll need to explain processes used in the experiment. You might want to explain a process in a profile of an activity or a proposal for a solution.

12–15 **STANCE** If you're giving practical directions for doing something, you'll want to take a straightforward "do this, then do that" perspective. If you're writing to entertain, you need to take a clever or amusing stance.

16–18 **MEDIA / DESIGN** Your medium will affect the way you explain a process. In a print text, you can use both words and images. On the web, you may have the option of showing an animation of the process as well.

IF YOU NEED MORE HELP

173–82
191–204
387–95
249 See also **LAB REPORTS** if you need to explain the process by which an experiment is carried out; and **PROFILES** if you are writing about an activity that needs to be explained. See **NARRATING** for more advice on organizing an explanation chronologically. Sometimes you may be assigned to write a whole essay or report that explains a process; see **PROCESSES** for help drafting, revising, and so on.

rhetorical situations | genres | processes | strategies | research MLA / APA | media / design | readings

Narrating 40

Narratives are stories. As a writing strategy, a good narrative can lend support to most kinds of writing—in a **POSITION PAPER** arguing for Title IX compliance, for example, you might include a brief narrative about an Olympic sprinter who might never have learned to run without Title IX. Or you can bring a **PROFILE** of a favorite coach to life with an anecdote about a pep talk he or she once gave before a championship track meet. Whatever your larger writing purpose, you need to make sure that any narratives you add support that purpose—they should not be inserted simply to tell an interesting story. You'll also need to compose them carefully—to put them in a clear *sequence*, include *pertinent detail*, and make sure they are appropriate to your particular rhetorical situation.

▲ 119–49

▲ 191–204

Sequencing

When we write a narrative, we arrange events in a particular sequence. Writers typically sequence narratives in chronological order, reverse chronological order, or as a flashback.

Use chronological order. Often you may tell the story chronologically, starting at the beginning of an event and working through to the end, as Maya Angelou does in this brief narrative from an essay about her high school graduation:

> The school band struck up a march and all classes filed in as had been rehearsed. We stood in front of our seats, as assigned, and on a signal from the choir director, we sat. No sooner had this been accomplished than the band started to play the national anthem. We rose again and sang the song, after which we recited the pledge of allegiance. We

remained standing for a brief minute before the choir director and the principal signaled to us, rather desperately I thought, to take our seats.

—Maya Angelou, "Graduation"

Use reverse chronological order. You may also begin with the final action and work back to the first, as Aldo Leopold does in this narrative about cutting down a tree:

Now our saw bites into the 1890s, called gay by those whose eyes turn cityward rather than landward. We cut 1899, when the last passenger pigeon collided with a charge of shot near Babcock, two counties to the north; we cut 1898, when a dry fall, followed by a snowless winter, froze the soil seven feet deep and killed the apple trees; 1897, another drouth year, when another forestry commission came into being; 1896, when 25,000 prairie chickens were shipped to market from the village of Spooner alone; 1895, another year of fires; 1894, another drouth year; and 1893, the year of "the Bluebird Storm," when a March blizzard reduced the migrating bluebirds to near zero.

—Aldo Leopold, *A Sand County Almanac*

222–29 ▲

RÉSUMÉS are one genre where we generally use reverse chronological order, listing the most recent jobs or degrees first and then working backward. Notice, too, that we usually write these as narratives—telling what we have done rather than just naming positions we have held:

Sept. 2011–present	*Student worker*, Department of Information Management, Central State University, Wilberforce, OH. Compile data and format reports using Excel, Word, and university database programs.
June–Sept. 2011	*Intern*, QuestPro Corporation, West Louisville, KY. Assisted in development of software programs.
Sept. 2010–June 2011	*Bagger*, Ace Groceries, Elba, KY. Bagged customers' purchases.

rhetorical situations   genres   processes   strategies   research MLA / APA   media / design   readings

Use a flashback. You can sometimes put a flashback in the middle of a narrative, to tell about an incident that illuminates the larger narrative. Terry Tempest Williams does this in an essay about the startling incidence of breast cancer in her family: she recalls a dinnertime conversation with her father right after her mother's death from cancer, when she learned for the first time what caused all of the cancer in her family:

> Over dessert, I shared a recurring dream of mine. I told my father that for years, as long as I could remember, I saw this flash of light in the night in the desert. That this image had so permeated my being, I could not venture south without seeing it again, on the horizon, illuminating buttes and mesas.
>
> "You did see it," he said.
>
> "Saw what?" I asked, a bit tentative.
>
> "The bomb. The cloud. We were driving home from Riverside, California. You were sitting on your mother's lap. She was pregnant. In fact, I remember the date, September 7, 1957. We had just gotten out of the Service. We were driving north, past Las Vegas. It was an hour or so before dawn, when this explosion went off. We not only heard it, but felt it. I thought the oil tanker in front of us had blown up. We pulled over and suddenly, rising from the desert floor, we saw it, clearly, this golden-stemmed cloud, the mushroom. The sky seemed to vibrate with an eerie pink glow. Within a few minutes, a light ash was raining on the car."
>
> I stared at my father. This was new information to me.
>
> —Terry Tempest Williams, "The Clan of the One-Breasted Women"

Williams could have simply announced this information as a fact—but see how much more powerful it is when told in narrative form.

Use time markers. Time markers help readers follow a sequence of events. The most obvious time markers are those that simply label the time, as the narrative entries in a diary, journal, or log might. For example, here is the final part of the narrative kept in a diary by a doomed Antarctic explorer:

> WEDNESDAY, MARCH 21: Got within eleven miles of depot. Monday night; had to lay up all yesterday in severe blizzard. Today forlorn hope, Wilson and Bowers going to depot for fuel.

MARCH 22 and 23: Blizzard bad as ever—Wilson and Bowers unable to start—tomorrow last chance—no fuel and only one or two [days] of food left—must be near the end. Have decided it shall be natural—we shall march for the depot with or without our effects and die in our tracks.

THURSDAY, MARCH 29: Since the 21st we have had a continuous gale from W.S.W. and S.W. We had fuel to make two cups of tea apiece and bare food for two days on the 20th. Every day we have been ready to start for our depot eleven miles away, but outside the door of the tent it remains a scene of whirling drift. I do not think we can hope for any better things now. We shall stick it out to the end, but we are getting weaker, of course, and the end cannot be far. It seems a pity, but I do not think I can write more. . . .

Last Entry: For God's sake look after our people.

—Robert F. Scott, *Scott's Last Expedition: The Journals*

More often you will integrate time markers into the prose itself, as is done in this narrative about a woman preparing and delivering meals to workers at a cotton gin:

She made her plans meticulously and in secret. <u>One early evening</u> to see if she was ready, she placed stones in two five-gallon pails and carried them three miles to the cotton gin. She rested a little, and then, discarding some rocks, she walked in the darkness to the sawmill five miles farther along the dirt road. <u>On her way back</u> to her little house and her babies, she dumped the remaining rocks along the path.

<u>That same night</u> she worked into the early hours boiling chicken and frying ham. She made dough and filled the rolled-out pastry with meat. At last she went to sleep.

<u>The next morning</u> she left her house carrying the meat pies, lard, an iron brazier, and coals for a fire. <u>Just before lunch</u> she appeared in an empty lot behind the cotton gin. <u>As the dinner noon bell rang</u>, she dropped the savors into boiling fat, and the aroma rose and floated over to the workers who spilled out of the gin, covered with white lint, looking like specters.

—Maya Angelou, *Wouldn't Take Nothing for My Journey Now*

rhetorical situations   genres   processes   strategies   research MLA / APA   media / design   readings

Use transitions.   Another way to help readers follow a narrative is with
TRANSITIONS, words like *first, then, meanwhile, at last,* and so on. See how
the following paragraphs from Langston Hughes's classic essay about
meeting Jesus use transitions (and time markers) to advance the action:

◆ 317

> <u>Suddenly</u> the whole room broke into a sea of shouting, <u>as</u> they saw
> me rise. Waves of rejoicing swept the place. Women leaped in the air.
> My aunt threw her arms around me. The minister took me by the hand
> and led me to the platform.
>   <u>When</u> things quieted down, in a hushed silence, punctuated by a
> few ecstatic "Amens," all the new young lambs were blessed in the
> name of God. <u>Then</u> joyous singing filled the room. <u>That night,</u> for the
> last time in my life but one — for I was a big boy twelve years old — I
> cried.
>
> —Langston Hughes, "Salvation"

Including Pertinent Detail

When you include a narrative in your writing, you must decide which
details you need — and which ones you don't need. For example, you don't
want to include so much detail that the narrative distracts the reader from
the larger text. You must also decide whether you need to include any
background, to set the stage for the narrative. The amount of detail you
include depends on your audience and purpose: How much detail does
your audience need? How much detail do you need to make your meaning clear? In an essay on the suspicion African American men often face
when walking at night, a journalist deliberately presents a story without
setting the stage at all:

> My first victim was a woman — white, well dressed, probably in her late
> twenties. I came upon her late one evening on a deserted street in
> Hyde Park, a relatively affluent neighborhood in an otherwise mean,
> impoverished section of Chicago. As I swung onto the avenue behind
> her, there seemed to be a discreet, uninflammatory distance between
> us. Not so. She cast back a worried glance. To her, the youngish black

man—a broad six feet two inches with a beard and billowing hair, both hands shoved into the pockets of a bulky military jacket—seemed menacingly close. After a few more quick glimpses, she picked up her pace and was soon running in earnest. Within seconds she disappeared into a cross street.

—Brent Staples, "Black Men and Public Space"

Words like *victim* and phrases like "came upon her" lead us to assume the narrator is scary and perhaps dangerous. We don't know why he is walking on the deserted street because he hasn't told us: he simply begins with the moment he and the woman encounter each other. For his purposes, that's all the audience needs to know at first, and details of his physical appearance that explain the woman's response come later, after he tells us about the encounter. Had he given us those details at the outset, the narrative would not have been nearly so effective. In a way, Staples lets the story sneak up on us, as the woman apparently felt he had on her.

Other times you'll need to provide more background information, as an MIT professor does when she uses an anecdote to introduce an essay about young children's experiences with electronic toys. First the writer tells us a little about Merlin, the computer tic-tac-toe game that the children in her anecdote play with. As you'll see, the anecdote would be hard to follow without the introduction:

Among the first generation of computational objects was Merlin, which challenged children to games of tic-tac-toe. For children who had only played games with human opponents, reaction to this object was intense. For example, while Merlin followed an optimal strategy for winning tic-tac-toe most of the time, it was programmed to make a slip every once in a while. So when children discovered strategies that allowed them to win and then tried these strategies a second time, they usually would not work. The machine gave the impression of not being "dumb enough" to let down its defenses twice. Robert, seven, playing with his friends on the beach, watched his friend Craig perform the "winning trick," but when he tried it, Merlin did not slip up and the game ended in a draw. Robert, confused and frustrated, threw Merlin into the sand and said, "Cheater. I hope your brains break." He was overheard by Craig and Greg, aged six and eight, who salvaged

the by-now very sandy toy and took it upon themselves to set Robert straight. "Merlin doesn't know if it cheats," says Craig. "It doesn't know if you break it, Robert. It's not alive." Greg adds, "It's smart enough to make the right kinds of noises. But it doesn't really know if it loses. And when it cheats, it don't even know it's cheating." Jenny, six, interrupts with disdain: "Greg, to cheat you have to know you are cheating. Knowing is part of cheating."

—Sherry Turkle, "Cuddling Up to Cyborg Babies"

Opening and Closing with Narratives

Narratives are often useful as **BEGINNINGS** to essays and other kinds of writing. Everyone likes a good story, so an interesting or pithy narrative can be a good way to get your audience's attention. In the following introductory paragraph, a historian tells a gruesome but gripping story to attract our attention to a subject that might not otherwise merit our interest, bubonic plague:

◆ 299–306

> In October 1347, two months after the fall of Calais, Genoese trading ships put into the harbor of Messina in Sicily with dead and dying men at the oars. The ships had come from the Black Sea port of Caffa (now Feodosiya) in the Crimea, where the Genoese maintained a trading post. The diseased sailors showed strange black swellings about the size of an egg or an apple in the armpits and groin. The swellings oozed blood and pus and were followed by spreading boils and black blotches on the skin from internal bleeding. The sick suffered severe pain and died quickly, within five days of the first symptoms. As the disease spread, other symptoms of continuous fever and spitting of blood appeared instead of the swellings or buboes. These victims coughed and sweated heavily and died even more quickly, within three days or less, sometimes in twenty-four hours. In both types everything that issued from the body—breath, sweat, blood from the buboes and lungs, bloody urine, and blood-blackened excrement—smelled foul. Depression and despair accompanied the physical symptoms, and before the end "death is seen seated on the face."
>
> —Barbara Tuchman, "This Is the End of the World: The Black Death"

Imagine how different the preceding paragraph would be if it weren't in the form of a narrative. Imagine, for example, that Tuchman began by defining bubonic plague. Would that have gotten your interest? The piece was written for a general audience; how might it have been different if it had been written for scientists? Would they need (or appreciate) the story told here?

306–10

Narrative can be a good way of **ENDING** a text, too, by winding up a discussion with an illustration of the main point. Here, for instance, is a concluding paragraph from an essay on American values and Las Vegas weddings.

> I sat next to one . . . wedding party in a Strip restaurant the last time I was in Las Vegas. The marriage had just taken place; the bride still wore her dress, the mother her corsage. A bored waiter poured out a few swallows of pink champagne ("on the house") for everyone but the bride, who was too young to be served. "You'll need something with more kick than that," the bride's father said with heavy jocularity to his new son-in-law; the ritual jokes about the wedding night had a certain Panglossian character, since the bride was clearly several months pregnant. Another round of pink champagne, this time not on the house, and the bride began to cry. "It was just as nice," she sobbed, "as I hoped and dreamed it would be."
>
> —Joan Didion, "Marrying Absurd"

No doubt Didion makes her points about American values clearly and cogently in the essay. But concluding with this story lets us *see* (and hear) what she is saying about Las Vegas wedding chapels, which sell " 'niceness,' the facsimile of proper ritual, to children who do not know how else to find it, how to make the arrangements, how to do it 'right.' "

Considering the Rhetorical Situation

As a writer or speaker, you need to think about the message that you want to articulate, the audience you want to reach, and the larger context you are writing in.

PURPOSE
Your purpose will affect the way you use narrative. For example, in an essay about seat belt laws, you might tell about the painful rehabilitation of a teenager who was not wearing a seat belt and was injured in an accident in order to persuade readers that seat belt use should be mandatory.

3–4

AUDIENCE
Whom do you want to reach, and do you have an anecdote or other narrative that will help them understand your topic or persuade them that your argument has merit?

5–8

GENRE
Does your genre require you to include narrative? A memoir about an important event might be primarily narrative, whereas a reflection about an event might focus more on the significance of the event than on what happened.

9–11

STANCE
What is your stance, and do you have any stories that would help you convey that stance? A funny story, for example, can help create a humorous stance.

12–15

MEDIA / DESIGN
In a print or spoken text, you will likely be limited to brief narratives, perhaps illustrated with photos or other images. In an electronic text, you might have the option of linking to full-length narratives or visuals available on the web.

16–18

IF YOU NEED MORE HELP

See also the **PROCESSES** chapters if you are assigned to write a narrative essay and need help drafting, revising, and so on. Two special kinds of narratives are **LAB REPORTS** (which use narrative to describe the steps in an experiment from beginning to end) and **RÉSUMÉS** (which essentially tell the story of the work we've done, at school and on the job).

249
173–82

222–29

41 Reading Strategies

We read newspapers and websites to learn about the events of the day. We read cookbooks to find out how to make brownies and textbooks to learn about history, chemistry, and other academic topics. We read short stories for pleasure — and, in literature classes, to analyze plot, setting, character, and theme. And as writers, we read our own drafts to make sure they say what we mean and to make sure they're correct. In other words, we read in various ways for many different purposes. But almost all of us could benefit from learning to read more effectively.

Taking Stock of Your Reading

One way to become a better reader is to understand your reading process; if you know what you do when you read, you're in a better position to decide what you need to change or improve. Consider the answers to the following questions:

- What do you read — for pleasure? for work? for school? for something else? Consider all the sorts of reading you do: books, magazines, newspapers, websites, *Facebook*, texting, blogs, instructions.

- When you're facing a reading assignment, what do you do? Do you do certain things to get comfortable? Do you play music or seek quiet? Do you plan your reading time or set reading goals for yourself? Do you flip through or skim the text before settling down to read it or just start at the beginning and work through it?

- When you begin to read something for an assignment, do you make sure you understand the purpose of the assignment — why you must read this text? Do you ever ask your instructor (or whoever else assigned the reading) what its purpose is?

- How do you motivate yourself to read material you don't have any interest in? How do you deal with boredom while reading?

- Does your mind wander? If you realize that you haven't been paying attention and don't know what you just read, what do you do?

- Do you ever highlight, underline, or annotate text as you read? Do you take notes? If so, what do you mark or write down? Why?

- When you read text you don't understand, what do you do?

- As you anticipate and read an assigned text, what attitudes or feelings do you typically have? If they differ from reading to reading, why do they?

- What do you do when you've finished reading an assigned text? Write out notes? Think about what you've just read? Move on to the next task? Something else?

- How well do your reading processes work for you, both in school and otherwise? What would you like to change?

The rest of this chapter offers advice and strategies that you may find helpful as you work to improve your reading skills.

Reading Strategically

Academic reading is challenging because it makes several demands on you at once. Textbooks present new vocabulary and concepts, and picking out the main ideas can be difficult. Scholarly articles present content and arguments you need to understand, but they often assume readers already know key concepts and vocabulary and so don't generally provide background information. As you read more texts in an academic field and participate in its conversations, the reading will become easier, but in the meantime you can develop strategies that will help you to read carefully and critically.

Different texts require different kinds of effort. Some texts can be read fairly quickly, if you're reading to get a general overview. Most of the time, though, you need to read carefully, matching the pace of your reading to the difficulty of the text. To read with a critical eye, you can't be in too much of a hurry. You'll likely need to skim the text for an overview of the basic ideas and then go back to read carefully. And then you may read the text again. That is true for visual as well as verbal texts—you'll often need to get an overview of a text and then reread to pay close attention to its details.

Preparing to Read

To learn, we need to place new information into a context of what we already know. For example, to understand photosynthesis, we need to already know something about plants, energy, and air, among other things. To learn a new language, we draw on similarities and differences between it and any other languages we know. A method of bringing to conscious attention our current knowledge on a topic and of helping us articulate our purposes for reading is a list-making process called KWL+. To use it, create a table with three columns:

K: What I Know	W: What I Want to Know	L: What I Learned

Before you begin reading a text, list in the "K" column what you already know about the topic. Brainstorm ideas, and list terms or phrases that come to mind. Then group them into categories. Also before reading, or after reading the first few paragraphs, list in the "W" column questions you have that you expect, want, or hope to be answered as you read. Number or reorder the questions by their importance to you.

Then read the text. As you read or afterward, list in the "L" column what you learned from the text. Compare your "L" list with your "W" list to see what you still want or need to know (the "+") — and what you learned that you didn't expect.

rhetorical situations | genres | processes | strategies | research MLA / APA | media / design | readings

Previewing a Text

It's usually a good idea to start by skimming a text: read the title and subtitle, any headings, the first and last paragraphs, the first sentences of all the other paragraphs. Study any illustrations and other visuals. Your goal is to get a sense of where the text is heading. At this point, don't stop to look up unfamiliar words; just mark them somehow (such as with underlining, highlighting, or electronic annotations), and look them up later.

Considering the Rhetorical Situation

As a reader, you need to think about the message that the writer wants to articulate, the intended audience, and the larger context in which the text was created.

PURPOSE   What is the writer's purpose? To entertain? inform? persuade readers to think something or take some action? What is *your* purpose for reading this text?

3–4

AUDIENCE   Who is the intended audience? Are you a member of that group? If not, should you expect that you'll need to look up unfamiliar terms or concepts or that you'll run into assumptions you don't necessarily share?

5–8

GENRE   What is the genre? Is it a report? an argument? an analysis? something else? Knowing the genre can help you anticipate certain key features.

9–11

STANCE   Who is the writer, and what is his or her stance? Critical? Curious? Opinionated? Objective? Passionate? Indifferent? Something else? Knowing the stance affects the way you understand a text, whether you're inclined to agree or disagree, to take it seriously, and so on.

12–14

MEDIA / DESIGN   What is the medium, and how does it affect the way you read? If it's a print text, what do you know about the publisher? If it's on the web, who sponsors the site, and when was it last updated? Are there any headings, summaries, color, or boxes that highlight key parts of the text?

15–18

Thinking about Your Initial Response

It's usually good to read a text first just to get a sense of it. Some readers find it helps to make brief notes about their first response to a text, noting their reaction and thinking a little about why they reacted as they did:

- **What are your initial reactions?** Describe both your intellectual reaction and any emotional reaction. Identify places in the text that caused you to react as you did. If you had no particular reaction, note that.

- **What accounts for your reaction?** Do you agree or disagree with the writer or have a different perspective? Why? Are your reactions rooted in personal experiences? positions you hold? As much as possible, you want to keep your opinions from coloring your analysis, so it's important to try to identify those opinions up front.

Annotating

Many readers find it helps to annotate as they read: highlighting key words, phrases, sentences; connecting ideas with lines or symbols; writing comments or questions in the margin or on sticky notes; circling new words so you can look up the definitions later; noting anything that seems noteworthy or questionable. Annotating forces you to read for more than just the surface meaning. Especially when you are going to be writing about or responding to a text, annotating creates a record of things you may want to refer to.

Annotate as if you're having a conversation with the author, someone you take seriously but whose words you do not accept without question. Put your part of the conversation in the margin, asking questions, talking back: "What's this mean?" "So what?" "Says who?" "Where's evidence?" "Yes!" "Whoa!" or even ☺ or ☹ or texting shorthand like LOL or INTRSTN. If you're using online sources, you may be able to copy them and annotate them electronically. If so, make your annotations a different color from the text itself.

What you annotate depends on your **PURPOSE** or what you're most interested in. If you're analyzing an argument, you would probably underline any **THESIS STATEMENT** and then the **REASONS AND EVIDENCE** that support the statement. It might help to restate those ideas in your own words, in the margins—in order to put them in your own words, you need to understand them! If you are trying to **IDENTIFY PATTERNS**, you might highlight each pattern in a different color or mark it with a sticky note and write any questions or notes about it in that color.

3–4

313–15
326–34

408–9

There are some texts that you cannot annotate, of course: library books, some materials you read on the web, and so on. Then you will need to use sticky notes or make notes elsewhere, and you might find it useful to keep a reading log for that purpose.

Coding

You may also find it useful to record your responses to your reading as you go through a text by using a coding system — for example, using "X" or "?" to indicate passages that contradict your assumptions or puzzle you. You can make up your own coding system, of course, but you could start with this one*:

✔ Confirms what you thought

X Contradicts what you thought

? Puzzles you

?? Confuses you

☆ Strikes you as important

→ Is new or interesting to you

You might also circle new words that you'll want to look up later and highlight or underline key phrases.

_____

*Adapted from *Subjects Matter: Every Teacher's Guide to Content-Area Reading* by Harvey Daniels and Steven Zemelman.

A Sample Annotated Text

Here is an annotated passage from Lawrence Lessig's essay "Some Like It Hot."
These annotations rephrase key definitions, identify the essay's thesis and main
ideas, ask questions, and comment on issues raised in the essay. Annotating
the entire essay, which appears on pages 127–31, would provide a look at
Lessig's ideas and a record of the experience of reading the essay—useful for
both understanding it and analyzing it.

Piracy—
unauthorized use
of the artistic
work of others.

"Content
industry"—new
term. Film, music,
and so on?
Doesn't include
books and
magazines?

Thesis: "Big
media" are all
based on piracy.

Hollywood film
industry started
in order to avoid
Edison's patents.
What were they
for? Cameras and
projectors? Is this
true?

Record-industry
piracy.

Player pianos?

If <u>piracy</u> means using the creative property of others without their permission, then the history of the <u>content industry</u> is a history of piracy. <u>Every important sector of big media today — film, music, radio, and cable TV — was born of a kind of piracy</u>. The consistent story is how each generation welcomes the pirates from the last. Each generation — until now.

<u>The Hollywood film industry was built by fleeing pirates.</u> Creators and directors migrated from the East Coast to California in the early twentieth century in part to escape controls that film patents granted the inventor Thomas Edison. These controls were exercised through the Motion Pictures Patents Company, a monopoly "trust" based on Edison's creative property and formed to vigorously protect his patent rights.

California was remote enough from Edison's reach that filmmakers like Fox and Paramount could move there and, without fear of the law, pirate his inventions. Hollywood grew quickly, and enforcement of federal law eventually spread west. But because patents granted their holders a truly "limited" monopoly of just seventeen years (at that time), the patents had expired by the time enough federal marshals appeared. A new industry had been founded, in part from the piracy of Edison's creative property.

<u>Meanwhile, the record industry grew out of another kind of piracy.</u> At the time that Edison and Henri Fourneaux invented machines for reproducing music (Edison the phonograph; Fourneaux the <u>player piano</u>), the law gave composers the exclusive right to

control copies and public performances of their music. Thus, in 1900, if I wanted a copy of Phil Russel's 1899 hit, "Happy Mose," the law said I would have to pay for the right to get a copy of the score, and I would also have to pay for the right to perform it publicly.

But what if I wanted to record "Happy Mose" using Edison's phonograph or Fourneaux's player piano? Here the law stumbled. If I simply sang the piece into a recording device in my home, it wasn't clear that I owed the composer anything. And more important, it wasn't clear whether I owed the composer anything if I then made copies of those recordings. Because of this gap in the law, I could effectively use someone else's song without paying the composer anything. The composers (and publishers) were none too happy about this capacity to pirate.

In 1909, Congress closed the gap in favor of the composer and the recording artist, amending <u>copyright law</u> to make sure that composers would be paid for "mechanical reproductions" of their music. But rather than simply granting the composer complete control over the right to make such reproductions, Congress gave recording artists a right to record the music, at a price set by Congress, after the composer allowed it to be recorded once. This is the part of copyright law that makes cover songs possible. Once a composer authorizes a recording of his song, others are free to record the same song, so long as they pay the original composer a fee set by the law. So, by limiting musicians' rights — by <u>partially pirating</u> their creative work — record producers and the public benefit.

—Lawrence Lessig, "Some Like It Hot"

> Is copyright law different for books and other printed matter?

> Partial piracy? Not sure about this — when artists use a song, they pay a fee but don't need permission. The composer doesn't have complete control. So it's piracy, but not completely?

Playing the Believing and Doubting Game

259–61 ○
One way to think about your response to a text is to **LIST** or **FREEWRITE** as many reasons as you can think of for believing what the writer says and then as many as you can for doubting it. First, write as if you agree with everything in the writer's argument; look at the world from his or her perspective, trying to understand the writer's premises and reasons for arguing as he or she does even if you strongly disagree. Then, write as if you doubt everything in the text: try to find every flaw in the argument, every possible way it can be refuted — even if you totally agree with it. Developed by writing theorist Peter Elbow, the believing and doubting game helps you consider new ideas and question ideas you already have — and at the same time see where you stand in relation to the ideas in the text you're reading.

Reflecting, Rereading, Persisting

Let's face it: Some texts are difficult. You may have no interest in the subject matter, or understanding the text requires knowledge you don't have, or you don't have a clear sense of why you have to read the text at all. Whatever the reason, reading such texts can be a challenge. Here are some tips for dealing with them:

Look for something familiar. Difficult texts are often difficult and seem boring because we don't know what we need to know in order to read them effectively. By skimming the headings, the abstract or introduction, and the conclusion, you may find something that relates to knowledge you already have — and being aware of that prior knowledge can help you see how this new material relates to it.

Reread. Reading a text the first time through is like driving to an unfamiliar destination on roads you've never traveled: you don't know where you're headed, you don't recognize anything along the way, and you're not sure how long getting there will take. As you drive the route again,

though, you see landmarks along the way; you know where you're going. When you must read a difficult text, sometimes you need to get through it once just to understand what it is saying. On the second reading, look for parts of the text that relate to other parts, to other texts or course information, or to other knowledge you have.

Be persistent.   Studies reveal that students who do not do well in school attempt to read a difficult text and respond, "I don't understand this text. I'm too dumb to get it." And they quit reading. Successful students, on the other hand, see difficult texts as challenges: "I'm going to keep working on this text until I make sense of it." Remember that reading is an active process, and the more you work to control your reading processes, the more successful you will be.

Thinking about How the Text Works: What It Says, What It Does

Sometimes you'll need to think about how a text works, how its parts fit together. You may be assigned to analyze a text, or you may just need to make sense of a difficult text, to think about how the ideas all relate to one another. Whatever your purpose, a good way to think about a text's structure is by OUTLINING it, paragraph by paragraph. If you're interested in analyzing its ideas, look at what each paragraph *says*; if, on the other hand, you're concerned with how the ideas are presented, pay attention to what each paragraph *does*.

263–64

What it says.   Write a sentence that identifies what each paragraph says. Once you've done that for the whole text, look for patterns in the topics the writer addresses. Pay attention to the order in which the topics are presented. Also look for gaps, ideas the writer has left unsaid. Such paragraph-by-paragraph outlining of the content can help you see how the writer has arranged ideas and how that arrangement builds an argument or develops a topic. Here, for example, is such an outline of Lawrence

Lessig's essay (the left column refers to paragraph numbering noted in the full version of the essay on pages 127–31):

1	Every major type of media bases its development on piracy, the unauthorized use of artists' work.
2–3	To escape patents that restricted the copying of innovations in filmmaking, the movie industry moved from the East Coast to California.
4–5	Copyright law gave composers control over the performance of their music—but because it didn't cover the recording of music and the sale of copies of the recordings, it allowed piracy in the record industry.
6	Congress eventually changed the law, allowing musicians to record a song without the composer's permission if they paid the composer a fee.
7–11	When a radio station plays a song, it pays the composer but not the recording artist, thus pirating the artist's work.
12, 13	Cable TV has pirated works, too, by paying networks nothing for their broadcasts—despite protests by broadcasters and copyright owners.
14	Congress eventually extended the copyright law to cable TV, forcing the cable companies to pay for their broadcasts at a price controlled by Congress in order to protect the innovations of the cable industry.
15	The history of the major media industries suggests that piracy is not necessarily "plainly wrong."
16, 17	Peer-to-peer file sharing, like the earlier media-industry innovations, is being used to share artistic content and avoid industry controls, but it differs from the early cable industry in that it is not selling any content.
18	P2P file sharing provides access to music that can no longer be purchased, music that copyright holders want to share, and music that is no longer copyrighted.
19	P2P file sharing, like the earlier innovations, is the result of new technology, and it raises a similar question: how can it best be used without penalizing the artists whose works are "pirated"?
20	Copyright law must balance the protection of artists' works with the innovation in technologies, a process that takes time.

rhetorical situations · genres · processes · strategies · research MLA / APA · media / design · readings

What it does.   Identify the function of each paragraph. Starting with the first paragraph, ask, What does this paragraph do? Does it introduce a topic? provide background for a topic to come? describe something? define something? entice me to read further? something else? What does the second paragraph do? the third? As you go through the text, you may identify groups of paragraphs that have a single purpose. For an example, look at this functional outline of Lessig's essay (again, the numbers on the left refer to the paragraphs):

1	Defines the key term, *piracy*, and illustrates the thesis using the history of four media industries in the United States.
2–3	Tells the history of the first medium, film, by focusing on piracy as a major factor in its development.
4–6	Tells the history of the second medium, the recording industry, again by focusing on the role of piracy in its development.
7–11	Tells the history of the third medium, radio, focusing on the role of piracy in its development.
12–14	Tells the history of the fourth medium, cable TV, focusing on the role of piracy in its development.
15	Offers conclusions about piracy based on the similar roles played by piracy in the histories of the four media.
16–17	Compares the current controversy over piracy in peer-to-peer file sharing on the internet with the role of piracy in the earlier media.
18	Describes the benefits of P2P file sharing.
19–20	Compares those benefits with those of the other media and offers a conclusion in the form of a problem to be solved.

Summarizing

Summarizing a text can help you both to see the relationships among its ideas and to understand what it's saying. When you SUMMARIZE, you restate a text's main ideas in your own words, leaving out most examples and other details. Here's a summary of Lawrence Lessig's essay:

470–71

> In his essay "Some Like It Hot," Lawrence Lessig argues that the development of every major media industry is based on piracy, the unauthorized

use of artists' or inventors' work. First, the film industry flourished by evading restrictions on the copying of innovations in filmmaking. Then, the recording industry benefited from copyright laws that gave composers control over the performance of their music but not over the recording of it or the sale of the recordings. A law passed in 1909 in effect allows musicians to record a song without the composer's permission if they pay the composer a fee. According to Lessig, radio broadcasters benefit from piracy, too, every time they play a song recorded by someone other than the composer: they pay the composer a fee but not the recording artist. Finally, when it first started operating, cable TV benefited from piracy—by paying the networks nothing for their broadcasts. Congress eventually extended the copyright law, forcing cable companies to pay for the content they broadcast—but at a price controlled by Congress so that the networks wouldn't be able to drive the cable companies out of business. Peer-to-peer file sharing, like the early media industries, is being used to share artistic content and avoid industry controls on that sharing. It benefits the public by allowing access to music that is out of print, that copyright holders want to share, and that is no longer copyrighted. Therefore, Lessig argues, the public needs to figure out how to make file-sharing work without penalizing musicians by pirating their songs. Copyright law must balance the protection of artists' work with the encouragement of technological innovation.

Identifying Patterns

Look for notable patterns in the text: recurring words and their synonyms, as well as repeated phrases, metaphors and other images, and types of sentences. Some readers find it helps to highlight patterns in various colors. Does the author repeatedly rely on any particular writing strategies:

387–95 ◈
348–55

NARRATION? COMPARISON? Something else?

It might be important to consider the kind of evidence offered: Is it more opinion than fact? Nothing but statistics? If many sources are cited, is the information presented in any predominant patterns: as **QUOTATIONS?**

462–74 ●

PARAPHRASES? SUMMARIES? Are there repeated references to certain experts or sources?

rhetorical situations | genres | processes | strategies | research MLA / APA | media / design | readings

In visual texts, look for patterns of color, shape, and line. What's in the foreground, and what's in the background? What's completely visible, partly visible, or invisible? In both verbal and visual texts, look for omissions and anomalies. What isn't there that you would expect to find? Is there anything that doesn't really fit in?

If you discover patterns, then you need to consider what, if anything, they mean in terms of what the writer is saying. What do they reveal about the writer's underlying premises and beliefs? What do they tell you about the writer's strategies for persuading readers to accept the truth of what he or she is saying?

See how color coding William Safire's essay on the Gettysburg Address reveals several patterns in the language Safire uses. In this excerpt from the essay, which appears in full in Chapter 8, religious references are colored yellow; references to a "national spirit," green; references to life, death, and rebirth, blue; and places where he directly addresses the reader, gray.

But the selection of this poetic political sermon as the oratorical centerpiece of our observance need not be only an exercise. . . . now, as then, a national spirit rose from the ashes of destruction.

Here is how to listen to Lincoln's all-too-familiar speech with new ears.

In those 266 words, you will hear the word *dedicate* five times. . . .

Those five pillars of dedication rested on a fundament of religious metaphor. From a president not known for his piety—indeed, often criticized for his supposed lack of faith—came a speech rooted in the theme of national resurrection. The speech is grounded in conception, birth, death, and rebirth.

Consider the barrage of images of birth in the opening sentence. . . .

Finally, the nation's spirit rises from this scene of death: "that this nation, under God, shall have a new birth of freedom." Conception, birth, death, rebirth. The nation, purified in this fiery trial of war, is resurrected. Through the sacrifice of its sons, the sundered nation would be reborn as one. . . .

Do not listen on Sept. 11 only to Lincoln's famous words and comforting cadences. Think about how Lincoln's message encompasses but goes beyond paying "fitting and proper" respect to the dead and the bereaved. His sermon at Gettysburg reminds "us the living" of our "unfinished work" and "the great task remaining before us"—to resolve that this generation's response to the deaths of thousands of our people leads to "a new birth of freedom."

The color coding helps us to see patterns in Safire's language, just as Safire reveals patterns in Lincoln's words. He offers an interpretation of Lincoln's address as a "poetic political sermon," and the words he uses throughout support that interpretation. At the end, he repeats the assertion that Lincoln's address is a sermon, inviting us to consider it differently. Safire's repeated commands ("Consider," "Do not listen," "Think about") offer additional insight into how he wishes to position himself in relation to his readers.

Count up the parts.   This is a two-step process. First, you count things: how many of this, how many of that. After you count, see what you can conclude about the writing. You may want to work with others, dividing up the counting.

- *Count words.* Count one-, two-, three-syllable words, repeated words, active and passive verbs, prepositions, jargon or specialized terms.

- *Count sentences.* Count the number of words in each sentence and the average number of words per sentence. Count the number of sentences in each paragraph. Count the number of simple sentences, compound sentences, complex sentences, and fragments. Count repeated phrases.

- *Count paragraphs.* Count the number of paragraphs, the average number of words and sentences per paragraph, the shortest and longest paragraphs. Consider the position of the longest and shortest paragraphs. Find parallel paragraph structures.

- *Count images.* List or mark images, similes, metaphors, and other figures of speech. Categorize them by meaning as well as type.

What do your findings tell you about the text? What generalizations can you make about it? Why did the author choose the words or images he or

she used and in those combinations? What do those words tell you about the writer—or about his or her stance? Do your findings suggest a strategy, a plan for your analysis? For instance, Safire counts the number of times Lincoln uses *dedicate* and images of birth, death, and rebirth to argue something about Lincoln's speech and what it should mean to Safire's audience on the anniversary of 9/11.

Analyzing the Argument

All texts make some kind of argument, claiming something and then offering reasons and evidence as support for the claim. As a critical reader, you need to look closely at the argument a text makes—to recognize all the claims it makes, consider the support it offers for those claims, and decide how you want to respond. What do you think, and why? Here are some questions to consider when analyzing the argument:

- *What claim is the text making?* What is the writer's main point? Is it stated as a THESIS or only implied? Is it qualified somehow? If not, should it have been?

  313–15

- *How is the claim supported?* What REASONS does the writer provide for the claim, and what EVIDENCE is given for the reasons? What kind of evidence is it: facts? statistics? examples? expert opinion? images? How convincing do you find the reasons and evidence? Is there enough evidence?

  326–27
327–34

- *What appeals besides* LOGICAL *ones are used?* Does the writer appeal to readers' EMOTIONS? Try to establish COMMON GROUND? Demonstrate his or her CREDIBILITY as trustworthy and knowledgeable? How successful are these appeals?

  324–34
338
334–35
334–37

- *Are any* COUNTERARGUMENTS *acknowledged?* If so, are they presented accurately and respectfully? Does the writer accommodate them or try to refute them? How successfully does he or she deal with them?

  336–37

- *What outside sources of information does the writer cite?* What kinds of sources are they, and how credible do they seem? Are they current and authoritative? How well do they support the argument?

12–14 ■

- *What* STANCE *does the writer take toward readers?* What attitudes does it assume they hold? Do you feel that you are part of the intended audience? How can you tell?

338–40 ◆

Check for fallacies. FALLACIES are arguments that involve faulty reasoning. Because they often seem plausible, they can be persuasive. It is important, therefore, that you question the legitimacy of such reasoning when you run across it.

Considering the Larger Context

All texts are part of ongoing conversations with other texts that have dealt with the same topic. An essay arguing for handgun trigger locks is part of an ongoing conversation about gun control, which is itself part of a conversation on individual rights and responsibilities. Academic texts document their sources in part to show their relationship to the ongoing scholarly conversations on a particular topic. Academic reading usually challenges you to become aware of those conversations. And, in fact, any time you're reading to learn, you're probably reading for some larger context. Whatever your reading goals, being aware of that larger context can help you better understand what you're reading. Here are some specific aspects of the text to pay attention to:

- *Who else cares about this topic?* Especially when you're reading in order to learn about a topic, the texts you read will often reveal which people or groups are part of the conversation — and might be sources of further reading. For example, an essay describing the formation of Mammoth Cave could be of interest to geologists, spelunkers, travel writers, or tourists. If you're reading such an essay while doing research on the cave, you should consider how the audience addressed determines the nature of the information provided — and its suitability as a source for your research.

- *Ideas.* Does the text refer to any concepts or ideas that give you some sense that it's part of a larger conversation? An argument on airport

security measures, for example, is part of larger conversations about government response to terrorism, the limits of freedom in a democracy, and the possibilities of using technology to detect weapons and explosives, among others.

- *Terms.* Is there any terminology or specialized language that reflects the writer's allegiance to a particular group or academic discipline? If you run across words like *false consciousness*, *ideology*, and *hegemony*, for example, you might guess the text was written by a Marxist scholar.

- *Citations.* Whom does the writer cite? Do the other writers have a particular academic specialty, belong to an identifiable intellectual school, share similar political leanings? If an article on politics cites Paul Krugman and Barbara Ehrenreich in support of its argument, you might assume the writer holds liberal opinions; if it cites Michelle Malkin and Sean Hannity, the writer is likely a conservative.

IF YOU NEED MORE HELP

See also the chapter on **EVALUATING SOURCES** for help analyzing the reliability of a text, and see the chapters on **ASSESSING YOUR OWN WRITING, GETTING RESPONSE AND REVISING,** and **EDITING AND PROOFREADING** for advice on reading your own writing.

453–56
269–74
275–81
282–86

42

Taking Essay Exams

Essay exams present writers with special challenges. You must write quickly, on a topic presented to you on the spot, to show your instructor what you know about a specific body of information. This chapter offers advice on how to take essay exams.

Considering the Rhetorical Situation

3–4 **PURPOSE**   In an essay exam, your purpose is to show that you have mastered certain material and that you can analyze and apply it in an essay. You may need to make an argument or simply to convey information on a topic.

5–8 **AUDIENCE**   Will your course instructor be reading your exam, or a TA? Sometimes standardized tests are read by groups of trained readers. What specific criteria will your audience use to evaluate your writing?

9–11 **GENRE**   Does the essay question specify or suggest a certain genre? In a literature course, you may need to write a compelling literary analysis of a passage. In a history course, you may need to write an argument for the significance of a key historical event. In an economics course, you may need to contrast the economies of the North and South before the Civil War. If the essay question doesn't specify a genre, look for key words such as *argue*, *evaluate*, or *explain*, which point to a certain genre.

12–15 **STANCE**   In an essay exam, your stance is usually unemotional, thoughtful, and critical.

414

MEDIA / DESIGN   Since essay exams are usually handwritten on lined paper or in an exam booklet, legible handwriting is a must.

16–18

Analyzing Essay Questions

Essay questions usually include key verbs that specify the kind of writing you'll need to do—argue a position, compare two texts, and so on. Following are some of the most common kinds of writing you'll be asked to do on an essay exam.

- *Analyze:* Break an idea, theory, text, or event into its parts and examine them. For example, a world history exam might ask you to **ANALYZE** European imperialism's effect on Africa in the late nineteenth century, and discuss how Africans responded.

52–86

- *Apply:* Consider how an idea or concept might work out in practice. For instance, a film studies exam might ask you to apply the concept of auteurism—a theory of film that sees the director as the primary creator, whose body of work reflects a distinct personal style—to two films by Clint Eastwood. An economics exam might ask you to apply the concept of opportunity costs to a certain supplied scenario.

- *Argue/prove/justify:* Offer reasons and evidence to support a position. A philosophy exam, for example, might ask you to **ARGUE** whether or not all stereotypes contain a "kernel of truth" and whether believing a stereotype is ever justified.

323–41

- *Classify:* Group something into categories. For example, a marketing exam might ask you to **CLASSIFY** shoppers in categories based on their purchasing behavior, motives, attitudes, or lifestyle patterns.

342–47

- *Compare/contrast:* Explore the similarities and/or differences between two or more things. An economics exam, for example, might ask you to **COMPARE** the effectiveness of patents and tax incentives in encouraging technological advances.

348–55

- *Critique:* **ANALYZE** and **EVALUATE** a text or argument, considering its strengths and weaknesses. For instance, an evolutionary biology exam might ask you to critique John Maynard Smith's assertion that "scientific theories say nothing about what is right but only about what is possible" in the context of the theory of evolution.

- *Define:* Explain what a word or phrase means. An art history exam, for example, might ask you to **DEFINE** negative space and discuss the way various artists use it in their work.

- *Describe:* Tell about the important characteristics or features of something. For example, a sociology exam might ask you to **DESCRIBE** Erving Goffman's theory of the presentation of self in ordinary life, focusing on roles, props, and setting.

- *Evaluate:* Determine something's significance or value. A drama exam, for example, might ask you to **EVALUATE** the setting, lighting, and costumes in a filmed production of *Macbeth*.

- *Explain:* Provide reasons and examples to clarify an idea, argument, or event. For instance, a rhetoric exam might ask you to explain the structure of the African American sermon and discuss its use in writings of Frederick Douglass and Martin Luther King Jr.

- *Summarize/review:* Give the major points of a text or idea. A political science exam, for example, might ask you to **SUMMARIZE** John Stuart Mill's concept of utilitarianism and its relation to freedom of speech.

- *Trace:* Explain a sequence of ideas or order of events. For instance, a geography exam might ask you to trace the patterns of international migration since 1970 and discuss how these patterns differ from those of the period between 1870 and World War I.

Some Guidelines for Taking Essay Exams

Before the exam

- *Read* over your class notes and course texts strategically, **ANNOTATING** them to keep track of details you'll want to remember.

- *Collaborate* by forming a **STUDY GROUP** to help one another master the course content. ◗ 255–56

- *Review* key ideas, events, terms, and themes. Look for common themes and **CONNECTIONS** in lecture notes, class discussions, and any read- ings — they'll lead you to important ideas. ● 457–59

- *Ask* your instructor about the form the exam will take: how long it will be, what kind of questions will be on it, how it will be evaluated, and so on. Working with a study group, write questions you think your instructor might ask, and then answer the questions together.

- *Warm up* just before the exam by **FREEWRITING** for ten minutes or so to gather your thoughts. ◗ 259–60

During the exam

- *Scan the questions* to determine how much each part of the test counts and how much time you should spend on it. For example, if one essay is worth 50 points and two others are worth 25 points each, you'll want to spend half your time on the 50-point question.

- *Read over* the entire test before answering any questions. Start with the question you feel most confident answering, which may or may not be the first question on the test.

- *Don't panic.* Sometimes when students first read an essay question, their minds go blank, but after a few moments they start to recall the information they need.

- *Plan.* Although you won't have much time for revising or editing, you still need to plan and allow yourself time to make some last-minute changes before you turn in the exam. So apportion your time. For a three-question essay test in a two-hour test period, you might divide your time like this:

Total Exam Time — 120 minutes
Generating ideas — 20 minutes (6–7 minutes per question)
Drafting — 85 minutes (45 for the 50-point question,
                     20 for each 25-point question)
Revising, editing, proofreading — 15 minutes

Knowing that you have built in time at the end of the exam period can help you remain calm as you write, as you can use that time to fill in gaps or reconsider answers you feel unsure about.

- *Jot down the main ideas* you need to cover in answering the question on scratch paper or on the cover of your exam book, number those ideas in the order you think makes sense—and you have an outline for your essay. If you're worried about time, plan to write the most important parts of your answers early on. If you don't complete your answer, refer your instructor to your outline to show where you were headed.

- *Turn the essay question into your introduction,* like this:

  Question: How did the outcomes of World War II differ from those of World War I?

  Introduction: The outcomes of World War II differed from those of World War I in three major ways: World War II affected more of the world and its people than World War I, distinctions between citizens and soldiers were eroded, and the war's brutality made it impossible for Europe to continue to claim cultural superiority over other cultures.

326–34

- *State your thesis explicitly,* provide REASONS and EVIDENCE to support your thesis, and use transitions to move logically from one idea to the next. Restate your main point in your conclusion. You don't want to give what one professor calls a "garbage truck answer," dumping everything you know into a blue book and expecting the instructor to sort it all out.

- *Write on every other line* and only on one side of each page so that you'll have room to make additions or corrections. If you're typing on a computer, double space.

- *If you have time left, go over your exam,* looking for ideas that need elaboration as well as for grammatical and punctuation errors.

After the exam.   If your instructor doesn't return your exam, consider asking for a conference to go over your work so you can learn what you did well and where you need to improve—important knowledge to take with you into your next exam.

part 5

Doing Research

We do research all the time, for many different reasons. We search the web for information about a new computer, ask friends about the best place to get coffee, try on several pairs of jeans before deciding which ones to buy. You have no doubt done your share of library research before now, and you probably have visited a number of schools' websites before deciding which college you wanted to attend. Research, in other words, is something you do every day. The following chapters offer advice on the kind of research you'll need to do for your academic work and, in particular, for research projects.

Doing Research

Developing a Research Plan **43**

When you need to do research, it's sometimes tempting to jump in and start looking for information right away. To do research well, however—to find appropriate sources and use them wisely—you need to work systematically. You need a research plan. This chapter will help you establish such a plan and then get started.

Establishing a Schedule

Doing research is complex and time-consuming, so it's good to establish a schedule for yourself. Research-based writing projects usually require you to come up with a topic (or to analyze the requirements of an assigned topic) and then come up with a research question to guide your research efforts. Once you do some serious, focused research to find the information you need, you'll be ready to turn your research question into a tentative thesis and sketch out a rough outline. After doing whatever additional research you need to fill in your outline, you'll write a draft—and get some response to that draft. Perhaps you'll need to do additional research before revising. Finally, you'll need to edit and proofread. And so you'll want to start by creating a timeline for getting all this work done, perhaps using the form on the next page.

Getting Started

Once you have a schedule, you can get started. The sections that follow offer advice on considering your rhetorical situation, coming up with a

rhetorical situations | genres | processes | strategies | research MLA / APA | media / design | readings

Scheduling a Research Project

	Complete by:
Analyze your rhetorical situation.	_____
Choose a possible topic or analyze the assignment.	_____
Plan a research strategy and do preliminary research.	_____
Come up with a research question.	_____
Schedule interviews and other field research.	_____
Find sources.	_____
Read sources and take notes.	_____
Do any field research.	_____
Come up with a tentative thesis and outline.	_____
Write a draft.	_____
Get response.	_____
Do any additional research.	_____
Revise.	_____
Prepare a list of works cited.	_____
Edit.	_____
Proofread the final draft.	_____
Submit the final draft.	_____

topic, and doing preliminary research; developing a research question, a tentative thesis, and a rough outline; and creating a working bibliography and keeping track of your sources. The chapters that follow offer guidelines for FINDING SOURCES, EVALUATING SOURCES, and SYNTHESIZING IDEAS.

432–52
453–56
457–61

Considering the Rhetorical Situation

As with any writing task, you need to start by considering your purpose, your audience, and the rest of your rhetorical situation:

rhetorical situations · genres · processes · strategies · research MLA / APA · media / design · readings

| PURPOSE | Is this project part of an assignment—and if so, does it specify any one purpose? If not, what is your broad purpose? To inform? argue? entertain? a combination? | 3–4 |

PURPOSE Is this project part of an assignment—and if so, does it specify any one purpose? If not, what is your broad purpose? To inform? argue? entertain? a combination? ■ 3–4

AUDIENCE To whom are you writing? What does your audience likely know about your topic, and is there any background information you'll need to provide? What opinions or attitudes do your readers likely hold? What kinds of evidence will they find persuasive? How do you want them to respond to your writing? ■ 5–8

GENRE Are you writing to report on something? To compose a profile? To make a proposal? An argument? What are the requirements of your genre in terms of the number and kind of sources you must use? ■ 9–11

STANCE What is your attitude toward your topic? What accounts for your attitude? How do you want to come across? Curious? Critical? Positive? Something else? ■ 12–15

MEDIA / DESIGN What medium or media will you use? Print? Spoken? Electronic? Will you need to create any charts, photographs, video, presentation software slides, or other visuals? ■ 16–18

Coming Up with a Topic

If you need to choose a topic, consider your interests as they relate to the course for which you're writing. What do you want to learn about? What do you have questions about? What topics from the course have you found intriguing? What community, national, or global issues do you care about?

If your topic is assigned, you need to make sure you understand exactly what it asks you to do. Read the assignment carefully, looking for keywords: does it ask you to ANALYZE, COMPARE, EVALUATE, SUMMARIZE, or ARGUE? If the assignment offers broad guidelines but allows you to choose within them, identify the requirements and the range of possible topics and define your topic within those constraints.

52–86
348–55
164–72
470–71
323–41

For example, in an American history course, your instructor might ask you to "discuss social effects of the Civil War." Potential but broad topics might include poverty among Confederate soldiers or former slaveholders, the migration of members of those groups to Mexico or Northern cities, the establishment of independent African American churches, or the spread of the Ku Klux Klan—to name only a few of the possibilities.

Narrow the topic.   As you consider possible topics, look for ways to narrow your topic's focus to make it specific enough to discuss in depths. For example:

> **Too general:** fracking
>
> **Still too general:** fracking and the environment
>
> **Better:** the potential environmental effects of extracting natural gas from under ground by hydraulic fracturing, or fracking

If you limit your topic, you can address it with specific information that you'll be more easily able to find and manage. In addition, a limited topic will be more likely to interest your audience than a broad topic that forces you to use abstract, general statements. For example, it's much harder to write well about "the environment" than it is to address a topic that covers a single environmental issue.

Think about what you know about your topic.   Chances are you already know something about your topic, and articulating that knowledge can help you see possible ways to focus your topic or come up with potential sources of information. **FREEWRITING, LISTING, CLUSTERING,** and **LOOPING** are all good ways of tapping your knowledge of your topic. Consider where you might find information about it: Have you read about it in a textbook? Heard stories about it on the news? Visited websites focused on it? Do you know anyone who knows about this topic?

259–62

Consulting with Librarians and Doing Preliminary Research

Consulting with a reference librarian at your school and doing some preliminary research in the library can save you time in the long run. Reference

rhetorical situations

genres

processes

strategies

research MLA / APA

media / design

readings

librarians can direct you to the best scholarly sources for your topic and help you focus your topic by determining appropriate search terms and keywords. They can also help you choose the most appropriate reference works, sources that provide general overviews of the scholarship in a field. General internet searches can be time-consuming, as they often result in thousands of possible sites — too many to weed out efficiently, either by revising your search terms or by going through the sites themselves, many of which are unreliable. Library databases, on the other hand, include only sources that already have been selected by experts, and searches in them usually present manageable numbers of results.

Wikipedia can often serve as a jumping-off point for preliminary research, but since its entries are written and edited by people who may not have expertise in the subject, it is not considered a reliable academic source. Specialized encyclopedias, however, usually present subjects in much greater depth and provide more scholarly references that might suggest starting points for your research. Even if you know a lot about a subject, doing preliminary research can open you to new ways of seeing and approaching it, increasing your options for developing and narrowing your topic.

At this stage, pay close attention to the terms used to discuss your topic. These terms could be keywords that you can use to search for information on your topic in library catalogs, in databases, and on the web.

Find Keywords Using Word Clouds

One way to find keywords to help you narrow and focus your topic is to create a word cloud, a visual representation of words used in a text; the more often a word is used, the larger it looks in the word cloud. Several websites, including *Tagxedo, Wordle,* and *TagCrowd,* let you create word clouds. Examining a word cloud created from an article in a reference work may help you see what terms are used to discuss your topic — and may help you see new possible ways to narrow it. Here, for example, is a word cloud derived from an article in *Scientific American* discussing fracking. Many of the terms — *fracking, water, gas, wells, drilling* — are just what you'd expect. However, some terms—*Ingraffea, Marcellus, cementing*—may be unfamiliar and lead to additional possibilities for research. For instance,

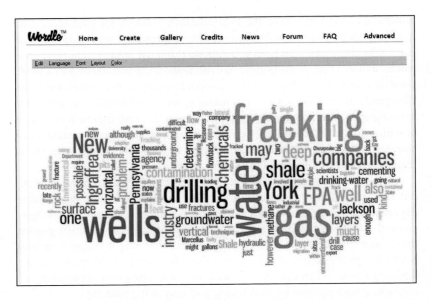

Ingraffea refers to an expert on fracking whose publications might be worth examining, while *cementing* refers to an important and controversial aspect of the hydraulic fracturing process.

Coming Up with a Research Question

Once you've surveyed the territory of your topic, you'll likely find that your understanding of your topic has become broader and deeper. You may find that your interests have changed and your research has led to surprises and additional research. That's okay: as a result of exploring avenues you hadn't anticipated, you may well come up with a better topic than the one you'd started with. At some point, though, you need to come up with a research question—a specific question that you will then work to answer through your research.

To write a research question, review your analysis of the RHETORICAL SITUATION, to remind yourself of any time constraints or length considerations. Generate a list of questions beginning with *What? When? Where? Who?*

1

rhetorical situations

genres

processes

strategies

research MLA / APA

media / design

readings

How? Why? Would? Could? and *Should?* Here, for example, are some questions about the tentative topic "the potential environmental effects of extracting natural gas through the process of hydraulic fracturing, or fracking":

What are the environmental effects of fracking?

When was fracking introduced as a way to produce natural gas?

Where is fracking done, and how does this affect the surrounding people and environment?

Who will benefit from increased fracking?

How much energy does fracking use?

Why do some environmental groups oppose fracking?

Would other methods of extracting natural gas be safer?

Could fracking cause earthquakes?

Should fracking be increased?

Select one question from your list that you find interesting and that suits your rhetorical situation. Use the question to guide your research.

Drafting a Tentative Thesis

Once your research has led you to a possible answer to your research question, try formulating that answer as a tentative **THESIS.** You need not be committed to the thesis; in fact, you should not be. The object of your research should be to learn about your topic, not to find information that simply supports what you already think you believe. Your tentative thesis may (and probably will) change as you learn more about your subject, consider the many points of view on it, and reconsider your topic and, perhaps, your goal: what you originally planned to be an argument for considering other points of view may become a call to action. However tentative, a thesis allows you to move forward by clarifying your purpose for doing research. Here are some tentative thesis statements on the topic of fracking:

313–15

Fracking is a likely cause of earthquakes in otherwise seismically stable regions of the country.

The federal government should strictly regulate the production of natural gas by fracking.

> Fracking can greatly increase our supplies of natural gas, but other methods of producing energy should still be pursued.

251–54 ◯

As with a research question, a tentative thesis should guide your research efforts — but be ready to revise it as you learn still more about your topic. Research should be a process of INQUIRY in which you approach your topic with an open mind, ready to learn and possibly change. If you hold too tightly to a tentative thesis, you risk focusing only on evidence that supports your view, making your writing biased and unconvincing.

Creating a Rough Outline

263–64 ◯

After you've created a tentative thesis, write out a rough OUTLINE for your research project. Your outline can be a simple list of topics you want to explore, something that will help you structure your research efforts and organize your notes and other materials. As you read your sources, you can use your outline to keep track of what you need to find and where the information you do find fits into your argument. Then you'll be able to see if you've covered all the ideas you intended to explore — or whether you need to rethink the categories on your outline.

Keeping a Working Bibliography

A working bibliography is a record of all the sources you consult. You should keep such a record so that you can find sources easily when you need them and then cite any that you use. Your library likely offers tools to store source information you find in its databases and catalog, and software such as *Zotero* can also help you save, manage, and cite your sources. You may find it useful to print out bibliographical data you find useful or to keep your working bibliography on index cards or in a notebook. However you decide to compile your working bibliography, include all the information you'll need later to document any sources you use; follow the

480–83 ⬤

DOCUMENTATION style you'll use when you write so that you won't need to

Information for a Working Bibliography

FOR A BOOK

Library call number
Author(s) or editor(s)
Title and subtitle
Publication information: city, publisher, year of publication
Other information: edition, volume number, translator, and so on
If your source is an essay in a collection, include its author, title, and page numbers.

FOR A SOURCE FROM A DATABASE

Publication information for the source, as listed above
Name of database
DOI (digital object identifier) or URL of original source, such as the periodical in which an article was published. (for APA style)
Stable URL or permalink for database
Date you accessed source

FOR AN ARTICLE IN A PRINT PERIODICAL

Author(s)
Title and subtitle
Name of periodical
Volume number, issue number, date
Page numbers

FOR A WEB SOURCE

URL
Author(s) or editor(s) if available
Name of site
Sponsor of site
Date site was first posted or last updated
Date you accessed site
If the source is an article or book reprinted on the web, include its title, the title and publication information of the periodical or book, where it was first published, and any page numbers.

go back to your sources to find the information. Some databases make this step easy by preparing citations in several styles that you can copy and paste.

On the previous page is most of the basic information you'll want to include for each source in your working bibliography. Go to wwnorton.com/write/fieldguide for templates you can use to keep track of this information.

Keeping Track of Your Sources

- *Staple together photocopies and printouts.* It's easy for individual pages to get shuffled or lost on a desk or in a backpack. Keep a stapler handy, and fasten pages together as soon as you copy them or print them out.

- *Bookmark web sources* or save them using a free bookmark management tool. For database sources, use the DOI or stable URL, permalink, or document URL (the terms used by databases vary) — not the URL in the "Address" or "Location" box in your browser, which will expire after you end your online session.

- *Label everything.* Label your copies with the source's author and title.

- *Highlight sections you plan to use.* When you sit down to draft, your goal will be to find what you need quickly, so as soon as you decide you might use a source, highlight the paragraphs or sentences that you think you'll use. If your instructor wants copies of your sources to see how you used them, you've got them ready.

- *Use your rough outline to keep track of what you've got.* In the margin of each highlighted section, write the number or letter of the outline division to which the section corresponds. (It's a good idea to write it in the same place consistently so you can flip through a stack of copies and easily see what you've got.) Alternatively, attach sticky notes to each copy, using a different color for each main heading in your outline.

rhetorical situations

genres

processes

strategies

research
MLA / APA

media / design

readings

- *Keep everything in an online folder, file folder, or box.* That way, even though your research material may not look organized, it will all be in one place—and if you highlight, number, and use sticky notes, your material will be organized and you'll be better prepared to write a draft. This folder or box will also serve you well if you are required to create a portfolio that includes your research notes, copies of sources, and drafts.

- *Use a reference management system.* Web-based reference or citation management systems allow you to create and organize a personal database of resources. You can import references from databases to a personal account, organize them, and draft citations in various formats. *RefWorks, EndNote, Mendeley, CiteULike,* and *Zotero* are five such systems; check with your librarian to see what system your library supports, or search online, as several of them are available for free.

IF YOU NEED MORE HELP

See the guidelines on **FINDING SOURCES** once you're ready to move on to in-depth research and those on **EVALUATING SOURCES** for help thinking critically about the sources you find.

432–52
453–56

44 Finding Sources

To analyze media coverage of the 2012 Democratic National Convention, you examine news stories and blogs published at the time. To write an essay interpreting a poem by Maya Angelou, you study the poem and read several critical interpretations in literary journals. To write a report on career opportunities in psychology, you interview a graduate of your university who is working in a psychology clinic. In each of these cases, you go beyond your own knowledge to consult additional sources of information.

This chapter offers guidelines for locating a range of sources — print and online, general and specialized, published and firsthand. Keep in mind that as you do research, finding and **EVALUATING SOURCES** are two activities that usually take place simultaneously. So this chapter and the next one go hand in hand.

453–56

Kinds of Sources

Primary and secondary sources.   Your research will likely lead you to both primary and secondary sources. *Primary sources* include historical documents, literary works, eyewitness accounts, field reports, diaries, letters, and lab studies, as well as any original research you do through interviews, observation, experiments, or surveys. *Secondary sources* include scholarly books and articles, reviews, biographies, textbooks, and other works that interpret or discuss primary sources. Novels and films are primary sources; articles interpreting them are secondary sources. The Declaration of Independence is a

rhetorical situations ▲ genres ○ processes ◆ strategies ● research MLA / APA □ media / design ▶ readings primary historical document; a historian's description of the events surrounding the Declaration's writing is secondary. A published report of scientific findings is primary; a critique of that report is secondary.

Whether a work is considered primary or secondary sometimes depends on your topic and purpose: if you're analyzing a poem, a critic's article interpreting the poem is a secondary source — but if you're investigating that critic's work, the article would be a primary source for your own study and interpretation.

Primary sources are useful because they offer subjects for firsthand study, whereas secondary sources can help you understand and evaluate primary source material.

Scholarly and popular sources.   Scholarly sources are written by academic experts or scholars in a particular discipline and are *peer-reviewed* — evaluated by other experts in the same discipline for their factual accuracy and lack of bias. They are also written largely *for* experts in a discipline, as a means of sharing research, insights, and in-depth analysis with one another; that's why they must meet high standards of accuracy and objectivity and adhere to the discipline's accepted research methods, including its style for documenting sources. Scholarly articles are usually published in academic journals; scholarly books may be published by university presses or by other academically focused publishers.

Popular sources include just about all other online and print publications, from websites to magazines to books written for nonspecialists. These sources generally explain or provide opinion on current events or topics of general interest; when they discuss scholarly research, they tend to simplify the concepts and facts, providing definitions, narratives, and examples to make them understandable to nonspecialist audiences. They are often written by journalists or other professional writers who may specialize in a particular area but who report or comment on the scholarship of others rather than doing any themselves. Their most important difference from scholarly sources is that popular sources are not reviewed by other experts in the field being discussed, although editors or fact-checkers review the writing before it's published.

In most of your college courses, you'll be expected to rely primarily on scholarly sources rather than popular ones. However, if you're writing about a very current topic or need to provide background information on a topic, a mix of scholarly and popular sources may be appropriate. Here's a guide to determining whether or not a potential source is scholarly.

IDENTIFYING SCHOLARLY SOURCES: WHAT TO LOOK FOR

- *Author.* Look for the author's scholarly credentials, including his or her affiliations with academic or other research-oriented institutions.

- *Peer review.* Look for a list of reviewers at the front of the journal or on the journal's or publisher's website. If you don't find one, the source is probably not peer-reviewed.

- *Source citations.* Look for a detailed list of works cited or references at the end of the source and citations either parenthetically within the text or in footnotes or endnotes. (Popular sources may include a reference list but seldom cite sources within the text, except in signal phrases.)

- *Publisher.* Look for publishers that are professional scholarly organizations, such as the Modern Language Association or the Organization of American Historians, that are affiliated with universities or colleges, or that have a stated academic mission.

- *Language and content.* Look for abstracts (one-paragraph summaries of the contents) at the beginning of articles and for technical or specialized language and concepts that readers are assumed to be familiar with.

- *Other clues.* Look for little or no advertising on websites or within the journal; for a plain design with few or no illustrations, especially in print sources; and for listing in academic databases when you limit your search to *academic, peer-reviewed,* or *scholarly sources.*

To see how scholarly and popular sources differ in appearance, look at the Documentation Maps for scholarly journals (pp. 504 and 554) and popular magazines (pp. 505 and 549) and at the illustrations on the next page.

Identifying Scholarly and Popular Periodicals

Scholarly journal

Plain cover and design suggest intellectual seriousness

KITAE SOHN

The Social Class Origins of U.S. Teachers, 1860–1920

1. Introduction

U.S. teachers have long been neglected in the history of education in spite of their important roles in education. Clifford calls this neglect a "virtual invisibility of teachers."[1] Hence, it is not surprising to encounter immense difficulty in tracing the social class origins of teachers in the late nineteenth and early twentieth centuries. This task is of great importance, however, because it allows one to understand the circumstances surrounding the individuals that entered the profession, to speculate on the quality of teaching, and to form an idea about class bias, intentional or not, inculcated by teachers in classrooms.

Research on the social class origins has been done for a century, as discussed in the next section. However, most of the research missed the broad picture of the profession. Some attention was paid to students in one college or normal school in one state even if few teachers attained such a high level of education at the time. In fact, a serious attempt was made to collect nationally representative data of teachers, but the data are severely biased. Of course, anecdotal evidence for the origins is scattered in qualitative historical materials such as diaries, letters, memoirs, and vacancy advertisements, but this evidence is highly selective. No one, to the best of my knowledge, has investigated the social class origins of U.S. teachers from 1860 to 1920 with nationally representative data, which would make one's understanding of the issue more comprehensive in terms of space and time.

This paper leads this line of study. In particular, this paper directly responds to the question raised by Perlmann and Margo, "Was teaching an engine of upward mobility into the middle class for relatively well-educated daughters of skilled workers and of low manual workers?" They propose using census data to answer this question because the data allow for a much wider perspective in terms of space and time. This paper closely follows their proposition and tries to answer the above question. Reaching further, OLS analyses are performed to

Formal documentation with endnotes

Author's note: This work was supported in part by the new faculty research program 2011 of Kookmin University in Korea. Address correspondence to Kitae Sohn, Department of Economics, Kookmin University, 861-1 Jeongneung-dong Seongbuk-gu Seoul 136-702, South Korea.

Journal of Social History vol. 45 no. 4 (2012), pp. 908–935
doi:10.1093/jsh/shr121

Author's institutional affiliation

Paginated by volume, not issue

Popular magazine

Eye-catching cover and design intended to attract readers

GROWTH

"The first and simplest emotion which we discover in the human mind is, Curiosity." *Edmund Burke*

A leading researcher in the field of cognitive development says when children pretend, they're not just being silly—they're doing science

WHY PLAY IS SERIOUS

BY ALISON GOPNIK

Documentation with signal phrases only

Page numbers begin at 1 for each issue

Print and online sources. Some sources are available only in print; some are available only online. But many print sources are also available on the web. You'll find print sources in your school's library, but chances are that many reference books in your library will also be available online. And when it comes to finding sources, it's likely that you'll search for most sources online. In general, for academic writing it's best to try to find most of your sources through the library's website rather than commercial search sites, which may lead you to unreliable sources and cause you to spend much more time sorting and narrowing search results. This chapter discusses four paths to finding sources you'll want to consult:

GENERAL REFERENCE WORKS, for encyclopedias, dictionaries, and the like

THE LIBRARY CATALOG, for books

INDEXES AND DATABASES, for periodicals

SEARCH SITES AND SUBJECT DIRECTORIES, for material on the web

Take a look at a sample search page from the catalog of one university library. This page offers several options for searching. The buttons on the left allow searches by type of publication and medium ("Books & more," "Articles & more," "eJournals & eBooks"), while additional buttons provide information about requesting material from Interlibrary Loan (for materials your library doesn't have); accessing library resources when you're off campus, and accessing various media, digital, and government document collections, among other options. The "Ask us" button can be very useful, as it permits email, texting, or phone conversations with reference librarians when you need help but aren't working in the library.

Typing a search term into "Research starting point" leads to a list of possible sources, as you'll see in the list of sources that came up when we searched for "fracking." As with most databases, the left-hand column allows searches to be further limited to sources whose full text is available online, to those in scholarly or other types of publications, and so on; this search result also offers related search terms that might help in refining your topic.

rhetorical
situations

genres

processes

strategies

research
MLA / APA

media /
design

readings

A library catalog homepage that allows searches by type of publication and medium.

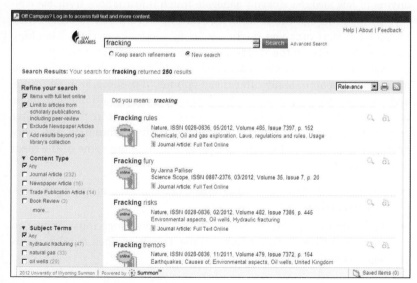

Results of a refined search for "fracking."

Searching Effectively

Whether you're searching for books, articles in periodicals, or material available on the web, chances are you'll conduct most of your search online. Most materials produced since the 1980s and most library catalogs are online, and most periodical articles can be found by searching electronic indexes and databases. In each case, you can search for authors, titles, or subjects.

When you're looking for books, articles, or web sources, you'll need to come up with *keywords*. Usually if you start with only one keyword, you'll end up with far too many results — tens of thousands of references when you're searching the web — so the key to searching efficiently is to come up with keywords and combinations of them that will focus your searches on the information you need. Be more general (*education Japan* instead of *secondary education Japan*) when you get too few sources; be more specific (*homeopathy* instead of *medicine*) when you get far too many sources. If you don't get results with one set of keywords, substitute synonyms (if *folk medicine* doesn't generate much information, try *home remedy*). Or look through the sources that turn up in response to other terms to see what keywords you might use in subsequent searches. Searching requires flexibility, in the words you use and the methods you try.

Most search sites have "advanced search" options that will help you focus your research. Many offer these options in preprogrammed forms, and some even allow you to ask questions in conversational language: *What did Thomas Jefferson write about slavery?* Others require that you enter certain commands to activate options. Specific commands will vary among search sites and within databases, but here are some of the most common ones:

- Type quotation marks around words to search for an exact phrase — "Thomas Jefferson."

- Type AND to specify that more than one keyword must appear in sources: Jefferson AND Adams. Some search engines require a plus sign instead: +Jefferson +Adams.

rhetorical situations genres processes strategies research MLA / APA media / design readings

- Type OR if you're looking for sources that include any of several terms: Jefferson OR Adams OR Madison.
- Type NOT to find sources *without* a certain word: Jefferson NOT Adams. Some search engines call for a minus sign (actually, a hyphen) instead: +Jefferson –Adams.
- Type an asterisk to search for words in different form. For example, teach* will yield sources containing *teacher* and *teaching*.

Reference Works

The reference section of your school's library is the place to find encyclopedias, dictionaries, atlases, almanacs, bibliographies, and other reference works in print. Many of these sources are also online and can be accessed from any computer that is connected to the Internet. Others are available only in the library. Remember, though, that whether in print or online, reference works are only a starting point, a place where you can get an overview of your topic.

General reference works. Consult encyclopedias for general background information on a subject, dictionaries for definitions of words, atlases for maps and geographic data, and almanacs for statistics and other data on current events. These are some works you might consult:

The New Encyclopaedia Britannica

The Columbia Encyclopedia

Webster's Third New International Dictionary

Oxford English Dictionary

National Geographic Atlas of the World

Statistical Abstract of the United States

The World Almanac and Book of Facts

Caution: *Wikipedia* is a popular online research tool, but since anyone can edit its entries, you can't be certain of its accuracy. Use it for general overviews, but look elsewhere — including *Wikipedia's* own references and citations — for authoritative sources.

Specialized reference works. You can also go to specialized reference works, which provide in-depth information on a single field or topic. These may also include authoritative bibliographies, leading you to more specific works. A reference librarian can refer you to specialized encyclopedias in particular fields, but good places to start are online collections of many topic-specific reference works that offer overviews of a topic, place it in a larger context, and sometimes provide links to potential academic sources. Collections that are available through libraries include the following:

> *CQ Researcher* offers in-depth reports on topics in education, health, the environment, criminal justice, international affairs, technology, the economy, and social trends. Each report gives an overview of a particular topic, outlines of the differing positions on it, and a bibliography of resources on it.
>
> *Credo Reference* provides access to more than 550 reference works, including several general reference encyclopedias and dictionaries, as well as subject-specific works. Users may search for specific topics, and *Credo* provides concept maps that show relationships among topics visually and offer immediate access to entries discussing those topics.
>
> *Gale Virtual Reference Library* offers thousands of full-text specialized encyclopedias, almanacs, articles, and ebooks.
>
> *Oxford Reference Online* contains almost 200 dictionaries, encyclopedias, and other reference works on a wide variety of subjects, as well as timelines with links to each item mentioned on each timeline.
>
> *SAGE Reference Online* includes over 250 encyclopedias and handbooks on topics in the social sciences.

Bibliographies. Bibliographies provide an overview of what has been published on a topic, listing published works along with the information you'll need to find each work. Some are annotated with brief summaries of each work's contents. You'll find bibliographies at the end of scholarly articles and books, and you can also find book-length bibliographies, both

rhetorical situations   genres   processes   strategies   research MLA / APA   media / design   readings

in the reference section of your library and online. Check with a reference librarian for bibliographies on your research topic.

Books / Searching the Library Catalog

The library catalog is your primary source for finding books. Almost all library catalogs are computerized and can be accessed through the library's website. You can search by author, title, subject, or keyword. The image below shows the result of a keyword search for material on art in Nazi Germany. This search of the library's catalog revealed forty items — print books, ebooks, and video recordings — on the topic; to access information on each one, the researcher must simply click on the title or thumbnail image. The image on the next page shows detailed information for one source: bibliographic data about author, title, and publication; related subject headings (which may lead to other useful materials in the library) — and more. Library catalogs also supply a call number, which identifies the book's location on the library's shelves.

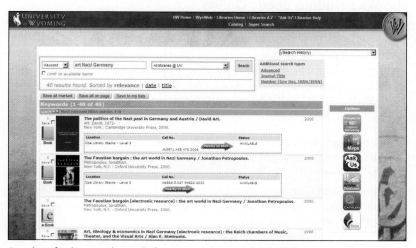

Results of a keyword search for material on art in Nazi Germany.

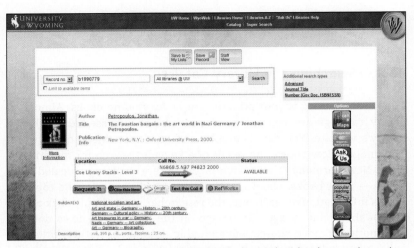

Detailed information about one of the books located with a keyword search.

Ebooks / Finding Books Online

Many books in the library catalog are available online. Some may be down-loaded to a tablet or mobile device. In addition, thousands of classic works that are in the public domain — no longer protected by copyright — may be read online. *Bartleby, Google Books, Open Library,* and *Project Gutenberg* are four collections of public-domain works. Here are some other sources of ebooks:

> *Hathi Trust Digital Library* offers access to over 5 million ebooks, about half still under copyright protection, contributed by over sixty university libraries.

> *Internet Archive* includes over 3 million ebooks, as well as audio, moving images, a live music archive, and the Way Back Machine, which archives historical webpages.

> The *Gale Virtual Reference Library, Oxford Scholarship Online,* and *SAGE Reference Online* all contain large ebook collections.

rhetorical situations | genres | processes | strategies | research MLA / APA | media / design | readings

Periodicals / Searching Indexes and Databases

To find journal, magazine, and newspaper articles, you will need to search periodical indexes and databases. Indexes provide listings of articles organized by topics; many databases provide the full texts. Some indexes are in print and can be found in the reference section of the library; most are online. Some databases are available for free; most of the more authoritative ones, however, are available only by subscription and so must be accessed through a library.

Many databases now include not only scholarly articles but also dissertations, theses, book chapters, book reviews, and conference proceedings. Dissertations and theses are formal works of scholarship done as requirements for graduate degrees; book reviews offer critical evaluations of scholarly and popular books; and conference proceedings are papers presented, usually orally, at scholarly meetings.

When you access a source through a database, the URL or link address is different each time you log in, so if you want to return to a source, look for a *stable URL, permalink,* or *document URL* option and choose it to copy and paste into your list of sources.

General indexes and databases. A reference librarian can help you determine which databases will be most helpful to you, but here are some useful ones:

Academic Search Complete is a multidisciplinary index and database containing the full text of articles in nearly 9,000 journals and indexing of almost 13,000 journals, with abstracts of their articles.

EBSCOhost provides interlinked databases of abstracts and full-text articles from a variety of periodicals.

FirstSearch offers access to millions of full-text, full-image articles in dozens of databases covering many disciplines.

InfoTrac offers over 20 million full-text articles in a broad spectrum of disciplines and on a wide variety of topics from nearly 6,000 scholarly and popular periodicals, including the *New York Times.*

JSTOR archives scanned copies of entire publication runs of scholarly journals in many disciplines, but it does not include current issues of the journals.

LexisNexis contains full-text publications and articles from a large number of sources — newspapers, business and legal resources, medical texts, and reference sources such as *The World Almanac* and the Roper public opinion polls.

ProQuest Central provides access to full-text articles from thousands of periodicals and newspapers from 1971 to the present, with many entries updated daily, and a large collection of dissertations and theses.

SIRS Issues Researcher contains records of articles from selected domestic and international newspapers, magazines, journals, and government publications.

Single-subject indexes and databases.   The following are just a sample of what's available; check with a reference librarian for indexes and databases in the subject you're researching.

America: History and Life indexes scholarly literature on the history of the United States and Canada.

BIOSIS Previews provides abstracts and indexes for more than 5,500 sources on biology, botany, zoology, environmental studies, and agriculture.

ERIC is the U.S. Department of Education's Educational Resource Information Center database.

Historical Abstracts includes abstracts of articles on the history of the world, excluding the United States and Canada, since 1450.

Humanities International Index contains bibliographic references to more than 2,300 journals dealing with the humanities.

MLA International Bibliography indexes scholarly articles on modern languages, literature, folklore, and linguistics.

PsycINFO indexes scholarly literature in a number of disciplines relating to psychology.

PubMed includes millions of citations for biomedical literature.

Print indexes.   You may need to consult print indexes to find articles published before the 1980s. Here are six useful ones:

The Readers' Guide to Periodical Literature (print, 1900–; online, 1983–)

Magazine Index (print, 1988–; online via InfoTrac, 1973–)

The New York Times Index (print and online, 1851–)

Humanities Index (print, 1974–; online, 1984–)

Social Sciences Index (print, 1974–; online, 1983–)

General Science Index (print, 1978–; online, 1984–)

Images, Sound, and More

Your library likely subscribes to various databases that allow you to find and download video, audio, and image files. Here is a sampling:

AP Images provides access to photographs taken for the Associated Press, the cooperative agency of more than 6.700 newspapers and radio and television stations worldwide.

ArtStor provides images in the arts, architecture, humanities, and sciences.

Dance in Video offers more than 600 videos of dance productions and documentaries on dance.

Education in Video includes more than 3,000 videos of teaching demonstrations, lectures, documentaries, and footage of students and teachers in their classrooms.

Naxos Music Library contains more than 60,000 classical, jazz, and world music recordings, as well as libretti and synopses of more and 700 operas and other background information.

Theatre in Video provides videos of more than 250 performances of plays and more than 100 film documentaries.

The following indexes and databases are freely available on the internet:

Infomine contains "useful Internet resources such as databases, electronic journals, electronic books, bulletin boards, mailing lists, online library card catalogs, articles, directories of researchers, and many other types of information."

ipl2 is a searchable, annotated subject directory of thousands of websites selected and evaluated by librarians for their usefulness to users of public libraries.

The WWW Virtual Library is a catalog of websites on a wide range of subjects, compiled by volunteers with expertise in particular subject areas.

CSA Discovery Guides provide comprehensive information on current issues in the arts and humanities, natural sciences, social sciences, and technology, with an overview of each subject, key citations with abstracts, and links to websites.

The Voice of the Shuttle: Web Site for Humanities Research offers information on subjects in the humanities, organized to mirror "the way the humanities are organized for research and teaching as well as the way they are adapting to social, cultural, and technological changes."

The Library of Congress offers online access to information on a wide range of subjects, including academic subjects, as well as prints, photographs, and government documents.

JURIST is a university-based online gateway to authoritative legal instruction, information, scholarship, and news.

Searching the Web

The web provides access to countless sites containing information posted by governments, educational institutions, organizations, businesses, and individuals. Such websites are different from other sources — including the kinds of online sources you access through indexes and databases — in two key ways: (1) their content varies greatly in its reliability and (2) they are not stable: what you see on a site today may be different (or gone) tomorrow. Anyone who wants to can post material on the web, so you need to evaluate carefully what you find there to eliminate sources that are not current, lack credibility, or are primarily advertisements or promotional in nature.

rhetorical situations | genres | processes | strategies | research MLA / APA | media / design | readings

Because it is so vast and dynamic, finding what you want on the web can be a challenge. The primary way of finding information on the web is with a search site. There are several ways of searching the web:

- **Keyword searches.** *Google, Yahoo!, Bing* and most other search sites all scan the web looking for keywords that you specify.

- **Subject directories.** *Google, Yahoo!,* and some other search sites offer directories that arrange information by topics, much like a library cataloging system. Such directories allow you to broaden or narrow your search if you need to — for example, a search for "birds" can be broadened to "animals" or narrowed to "blue-footed booby."

- **Metasearches.** *Yippy, Dogpile, Copernic Agent,* and *SurfWax* are metasearch sites that allow you to use several search engines simultaneously. They are best for searching broadly; use a single search site for the most precise results.

- **Academic searches.** You may find more suitable results for academic writing at *Google Scholar*, a search site that finds scholarly literature, including peer-reviewed papers, technical reports, and abstracts, or at *Scirus*, which finds peer-reviewed documents on scientific, technical, and medical topics. In general, though, use academic databases whenever possible.

- **Blog searches.** Several search sites can help you find blog posts, including *Google Blog Search, Technorati,* and *Icerocket*.

- **Twitter searches.** In addition to *Twitter* Search, you can find *Twitter* content through search sites such as *Twazzup, Collecta,* and *Scoopler*.

Each search site and metasearch site has its own protocols for searching; most have an "advanced search" option that will help you search more productively. Remember, though, that you need to be careful about EVALUATING SOURCES that you find on the web because the web is unregulated and no one independently verifies the information posted on its sites.

453–56

Doing Field Research

Sometimes you'll need to do your own research, to go beyond the information you find in published sources and gather data by doing field research. Three kinds of field research you might want to consider are interviews, observations, and questionnaires.

Interviewing experts. Some kinds of writing—a profile of a living person, for instance—almost require that you conduct an interview. And sometimes you may just need to find information that you haven't been able to find in published sources. To get firsthand information on the experience of serving as a soldier in Afghanistan, you might interview your cousin who served a tour of duty there; to find current research on pesticide residues in food, you might need to interview a toxicologist. Whatever your goal, you can conduct interviews in person, using video-calling software, by telephone, through email, or by mail. In general, you will want to use interviews to find information you can't find elsewhere. Below is some advice on planning and conducting an interview.

Before the interview

1. Once you identify someone you want to interview, email or phone to ask the person, stating your **PURPOSE** for the interview and what you hope to learn.

   3–4 ◼

2. Once you've set up an appointment, send a note or email confirming the time and place. If you wish to record the interview, be sure to ask for permission to do so. If you plan to conduct the interview by mail or email, state when you will send your questions.

3. Write out questions. Plan questions that invite extended response and supporting details: "What accounts for the recent spike in gasoline prices?" forces an explanation, whereas "Is the recent spike in gas prices a direct result of global politics?" is likely to elicit only a yes or a no.

At the interview

4. Record the full name of the person you interview, along with the date, time, and place of the interview; you'll need this information to cite and document the interview accurately.

5. Take notes, even if you are recording the interview.
6. Keep track of time: don't take more than you agreed to beforehand unless both of you agree to keep talking. End by saying "thank you" and offering to provide a copy of your final product.

After the interview

7. Flesh out your notes with details as soon as possible after the interview, while you still remember them. What did you learn? What surprised you? Summarize both the interviewee's words and your impressions.
8. Make sure you've reproduced quotations from the interview accurately and fairly. Avoid editing quotations in ways that distort the speaker's intended meaning.
9. Be sure to send a thank you note or email.

Observation.   Some writing projects are based on information you get by observing something. For a sociology report, you may observe how students behave in large lectures. For an education course, you may observe one child's progress as a writer over a period of time. The following advice can help you conduct observations.

Before observing

1. Think about your research PURPOSE: What are you looking for? What do you expect to find? How will your presence as an observer affect what you observe? What do you plan to do with what you find?
2. If necessary, set up an appointment. You may need to ask permission of the people you wish to observe and of your school as well. (Check with your instructor about your school's policy in this area.) Be honest and open about your goals and intentions; college students doing research assignments are often welcomed where others may not be.

■ 3–4

While observing

3. If you're taking notes on paper, you may want to divide each page down the middle vertically and write only on the left side of the page, reserving the right side for information you will fill in later. If you're using a laptop, you can set up two columns or a split screen.

4. Note descriptive details about the setting. What do you see? What do you hear? Do you smell anything? Get down details about color, shape, size, sound, and so on. Consider photographing or making a sketch of what you see.

367–75

5. Who is there, and what are they doing? **DESCRIBE** what they look like, and make notes about what they say. Note any significant demographic details — about gender, race, occupation, age, dress, and so on.

6. What is happening? Who's doing what? What's being said? Make note

387–95

of these kinds of **NARRATIVE** details.

After observing

7. As soon as possible after you complete your observations, use the right side of your notes to fill in gaps and include additional details.

52–86

8. **ANALYZE** your notes, looking for patterns. Did some things appear or happen more than once? Did anything stand out? surprise or puzzle you? What did you learn?

Questionnaires and surveys.   Various kinds of questionnaires and surveys can provide information or opinions from a large number of people. For a political science course, you might conduct a survey to ask students who they plan to vote for. Or, for a marketing course, you might distribute a questionnaire asking what they think about an advertising campaign. The advice in this section will help you create useful questionnaires and surveys.

Define your goal.   The goal of a questionnaire or survey should be limited and focused, so that every question will contribute to your research question. Also, people are more likely to respond to a brief, focused survey.

Define your sample.   A survey gets responses from a representative sample of the whole group. The answers to these questions will help you define that sample:

1. Who should answer the questions? The people you contact should represent the whole population. For example, if you want to survey undergraduate students at your school, your sample should reflect

rhetorical situations

genres

processes

strategies

research MLA / APA

media / design

readings

your school's enrollment in terms of gender, year, major, age, ethnicity, and so forth as closely as possible.

2. How many people make up a representative sample? In general, the larger your sample, the more the answers will reflect those of the whole group. But if your population is small—200 students in a history course, for example—your sample must include a large percentage of that group.

Decide on a medium.   Will you ask the questions face-to-face? over the phone? on a website such as *SurveyMonkey*? by mail? by email? Face-to-face questions work best for simple surveys or for gathering impersonal information. You're more likely to get responses to more personal questions with printed or online questionnaires, which should be neat and easy to read. Phone interviews may require well-thought-out scripts that anticipate possible answers and make it easy to record these answers.

Design good questions.   The way you ask questions will determine the usefulness of the answers you get, so take care to write questions that are clear and unambiguous. Here are some typical question types:

* *Multiple-choice*

  What is your current age?

  _____ 15–20   _____ 21–25   _____ 26–30   _____ 31–35   _____ Other

* *Rating scale*

  How would you rate the service at the campus bookstore?

  _____ Excellent   _____ Good   _____ Fair   _____ Poor

* *Agreement scale*

  How much do you agree with the following statements?

	Strongly Agree	Agree	Disagree	Strongly Disagree
The bookstore has sufficient numbers of textbooks available.	❐	❐	❐	❐

	Strongly Agree	Agree	Disagree	Strongly Disagree
Staff at the bookstore are knowledgeable.	❐	❐	❐	❐
Staff at the bookstore are courteous.	❐	❐	❐	❐

- *Open-ended*

  How often do you visit the campus bookstore?

  How can the campus bookstore improve its service?

Include all potential alternatives when phrasing questions to avoid biasing the answers. And make sure each question addresses only one issue — for example, "bookstore staff are knowledgeable and courteous" could lead to the response "knowledgeable, agree; courteous, disagree."

When arranging questions, place easier ones at the beginning and harder ones near the end (but if the questions seem to fall into a different natural order, follow it). Make sure each question asks for information you will need — if a question isn't absolutely necessary, omit it.

Include an introduction.   Start by stating your survey's purpose and how the results will be used. It's also a good idea to offer an estimate of the time needed to complete the questions. Remind participants of your deadline.

Test the survey or questionnaire.   Make sure your questions elicit the kinds of answers you need by asking three or four people who are part of your target population to answer them. They can help you find unclear instructions, questions that aren't clear or that lack sufficient alternatives, or other problems that you should correct to make sure your results are useful. But if you change the questionnaire as a result of their responses, don't include their answers in your total.

453–56
462–63

IF YOU NEED MORE HELP

See **EVALUATING SOURCES** for help determining their usefulness. See also Chapter 47 for help **TAKING NOTES** on your sources.

rhetorical situations   genres   processes   strategies   research MLA / APA   media / design   readings

Evaluating Sources **45**

Searching the *Health Source* database for information on the incidence of meningitis among college students, you find seventeen articles. A *Google* search on the same topic produces over 10,000 hits. How do you decide which sources to read? This chapter presents advice on evaluating sources — first to determine whether a source might be useful for your purposes and is worth looking at more closely and then to read with a critical eye the ones you choose.

Considering Whether a Source Might Be Useful

Think about your **PURPOSE.**   Are you trying to persuade readers to believe or do something? to inform them about something? If the former, it will be especially important to find sources representing various stances; if the latter, you may need sources that are more factual or informative. Reconsider your **AUDIENCE.** What kinds of sources will they find persuasive? If you're writing for readers in a particular field, what counts as evidence in that field? Following are some questions that can help you judge whether a possible source you've found deserves your time and attention:

3–4

5–8

- *Is it reliable?* Is it **SCHOLARLY?** peer-reviewed? published in a reputable journal or magazine, or by a reputable publisher? Did you find it in a library database? on the web? Evaluating web-based texts may require more work and scrutiny than results from library databases. But whatever kind of search you do, the results need to be scanned to quickly evaluate their reliability.

433–35

- *Is it relevant?* How does the source relate to your purpose? What will it add to your work? Look at the title and at any introductory material — a preface, abstract, or introduction — to see what it covers.

- *What are the author's credentials?* What are the author's qualifications to write on the subject? Is he or she associated with a particular position on the issue? See whether the source mentions other works this author has written. In any case, you might do a web search to see what else you can learn about him or her.

12–15 ◼

- *What is the* STANCE? Consider whether a source covers various points of view or advocates one particular point of view. Does its title suggest a certain slant? If it's online, you might check to see whether it includes links to other sites and if so, what their perspectives are. You'll want to consult sources with a variety of viewpoints.

- *Who is the publisher or sponsor?* If it's a book, what kind of company published it; if an article, what kind of periodical did it appear in? Books published by university presses and articles in scholarly journals are reviewed by experts before they are published. Books and articles written for the general public typically do not undergo rigorous review—and they may lack the kind of in-depth discussion that is useful for research. If it's online, is the site maintained by an organization? an interest group? a government agency? an individual? Look for clues in the URL: *edu* is used mostly by colleges and universities, *gov* by government agencies, *org* by nonprofit organizations, *mil* by the military, and *com* by commercial organizations. Evaluate the publisher's or sponsor's motives: to present information evenhandedly? To promote a certain point of view, belief, or position? To sell something?

- *What is the level?* Can you understand the material? Texts written for a general audience might be easier to understand but not authoritative enough for academic work. Texts written for scholars will be more authoritative but may be hard to comprehend.

- *When was it published?* See when books and articles were published. Check to see when online sources were created and last updated. (If the site lists no date, see if links to other sites still work.) Recent does not necessarily mean better — some topics may require very current information whereas others may call for older sources.

- *Is it available?* Is it a source you can get hold of? If it's a book and your school's library doesn't have it, can you get it through interlibrary loan?

- *Does it include other useful information?* Is there a bibliography that might lead you to other sources? How current are the sources it cites?

Once you've decided that a source should be examined more closely, use the following questions to give it critical scrutiny.

Reading Sources with a Critical Eye

- *What **ARGUMENTS** does the author make?* Does the author present a number of different positions, or does he or she argue for a particular position? Do you need to **ANALYZE THE ARGUMENT?**

- *How persuasive do you find the argument?* What reasons and evidence does the author provide in support of any position(s)? Are there citations or links — and if so, are they credible? Is any evidence presented without citations? Do you find any of the author's assumptions questionable? How thoroughly does he or she consider opposing arguments?

- *What is the author's **STANCE?*** Does the author strive for objectivity, or does the content or language reveal a particular bias? Does the author consider opposing views and treat them fairly?

- *Do you recognize ideas you've run across in other sources?* Does the source leave out any information or perspective that other sources include — or include any that other sources leave out?

- *Does this source support or challenge your own position — or does it do both?* Does it support your thesis? Offer a different argument altogether? Does it represent a position you may need to **ACKNOWLEDGE** or **REFUTE?** Don't reject a source just because it challenges your views; your sources should reflect a variety of views on your topic, showing that you've considered the subject thoroughly.

- *What can you tell about the intended **AUDIENCE** and **PURPOSE?*** Are you a member of the audience addressed — and if not, does that affect the

83–110

411–12

12–15

104

105

5–8
3–4

way you interpret what you read? Is the main purpose to inform readers about a topic or to argue a certain point?

462–74
475–79

IF YOU NEED MORE HELP

See QUOTING, PARAPHRASING, AND SUMMARIZING for help in taking notes on your sources and deciding how to use them in your writing. See also ACKNOWLEDGING SOURCES, AVOIDING PLAGIARISM for advice on giving credit to the sources you use.

---

rhetorical
situations

genres

processes

strategies

research
MLA / APA

media /
design

readings

Synthesizing Ideas **46**

To **ANALYZE** the works of a poet, you show how she uses similar images in three different poems to explore a recurring concept. To solve a crime, a detective studies several eyewitness accounts to figure out who did it. To trace the history of photojournalism, a professor **COMPARES** the uses of photography during the Civil War and during the Vietnam War. These are all cases where someone *synthesizes*—brings together material from two or more sources in order to generate new information or to support a new perspective. When you do research, you need to go beyond what your sources say; you need to use what they say to inspire and support *what you want to say*. This chapter focuses on how to synthesize ideas you find in other sources as the basis for your own ideas.

▲ 52–86

◆ 348–55

Reading for Patterns and Connections

Your task as a writer is to find as much information as you can on your topic—and then to sift through all that you have found to determine and support what you yourself will write. In other words, you'll need to synthesize ideas and information from the sources you've consulted to figure out first what arguments *you* want to make and then to provide support for those arguments.

When you synthesize, you group similar bits of information together, looking for patterns or themes or trends and trying to identify the key points. For example, researching the effectiveness of the SAT writing exam you find several sources showing that scores correlate directly with length and that a majority of U.S. colleges and universities have decided not to count the results of the test in their admission decisions. You can infer that the test is not yet seen as an effective measure of writing ability. Here are some tips for reading to identify patterns and connections:

- Read all your sources with an open mind. Withhold judgment, even of sources that seem wrong-headed or implausible. Don't jump to conclusions.

470–71
- Take notes and write a brief **SUMMARY** of each source to help you see relationships, patterns, and connections among your sources. Take notes on your own thoughts, too.

- Pay attention to your first reactions. You'll likely have many ideas to work with, but your first thoughts can often lead somewhere that you 259–62 will find interesting. Try **FREEWRITING**, **CLUSTERING**, or **LISTING** to see where they lead. How do these thoughts and ideas relate to your topic? Where 263–64 might they fit into your rough **OUTLINE?**

- Try to think creatively, and pay attention to thoughts that flicker at the edge of your consciousness, as they may well be productive.

- Be playful. Good ideas sometimes come when we let our guard down or take ideas to extremes just to see where they lead.

Ask yourself these questions about your sources:

- What sources make the strongest arguments? What makes them so strong?
- Do some arguments recur in several sources?
- Which arguments do you agree with? disagree with? Of those you disagree with, which ones seem strong enough that you need to 336 **ACKNOWLEDGE** them in your text?
- Are there any disagreements among your sources?
- Are there any themes you see in more than one source?
- Are any data—facts, statistics, examples—or experts cited in more than one source?

- Do several of your sources use the same terms? Do they use the terms similarly, or do they use them in different ways?

- What have you learned about your topic? How have your sources affected your thinking on your topic? Do you need to adjust your THESIS? If so, how?

313–15

- Have you discovered new questions you need to investigate?

- Keep in mind your RHETORICAL SITUATION — have you found the information you need that will achieve your purpose, appeal to your audience, and suit your genre and medium?

1

What is likely to emerge from this questioning is a combination of big ideas, including new ways of understanding your topic and insights into recent scholarship about it, and smaller ones, such as how two sources agree with each other but not completely and how the information in one source supports or undercuts the argument of another. These ideas and insights will become the basis for your own ideas and for what *you* have to say about the topic.

Synthesizing Ideas Using Notes

You may find that identifying connections among your sources is easier if you examine them together rather than reading them one by one. For example, taking notes on note cards and then laying the cards out on a desk or table (or on the floor) lets you see passages that seem related. Doing the same with photocopies or printouts of your sources can help you identify similarities as well.

In doing research for an essay arguing that the sale of assault weapons should be banned, you might find several sources that address the scope of U.S. citizens' right to bear arms. Here are notes taken on three such sources: Joe Klein, a journalist writing in *Time.com*; Antonin Scalia, a U.S. Supreme Court justice, quoted in an online news article; and Drew Westen, a professor of psychology writing in a blog sponsored by *The New York Times*. Though the writers hold very different views, juxtaposing these

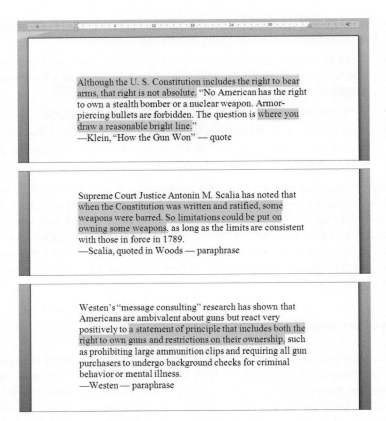

Although the U. S. Constitution includes the right to bear arms, that right is not absolute. "No American has the right to own a stealth bomber or a nuclear weapon. Armor-piercing bullets are forbidden. The question is where you draw a reasonable bright line."
—Klein, "How the Gun Won" — quote

Supreme Court Justice Antonin M. Scalia has noted that when the Constitution was written and ratified, some weapons were barred. So limitations could be put on owning some weapons, as long as the limits are consistent with those in force in 1789.
—Scalia, quoted in Woods — paraphrase

Westen's "message consulting" research has shown that Americans are ambivalent about guns but react very positively to a statement of principle that includes both the right to own guns and restrictions on their ownership, such as prohibiting large ammunition clips and requiring all gun purchasers to undergo background checks for criminal behavior or mental illness.
—Westen — paraphrase

notes and highlighting certain passages shows a common thread running through the sources. In this example, all three sources might be used to support the thesis that restrictions on the owning of weapons — but not an outright ban — are both constitutional and necessary.

Synthesizing Information to Support Your Own Ideas

87–118 ▲

If you're doing research to write a **REPORT**, your own ideas will be communicated primarily through which information you decide to include from the sources you cite and how you organize that information. If you're

rhetorical situations   genres   processes   strategies   research MLA / APA   media / design   readings

writing a TEXTUAL ANALYSIS, your synthesis may focus on the themes, techniques, or other patterns you find. If you're writing a research-based ARGUMENT, on the other hand, your synthesis of sources must support the position you take in that argument. No matter what your genre, the challenge is to synthesize information from your research to develop ideas about your topic and then to support those ideas.

52–86

119–49

Entering the Conversation

As you read and think about your topic, you will come to an understanding of the concepts, interpretations, and controversies relating to your topic — and you'll become aware that there's a larger conversation going on. When you begin to find connections among your sources, you will begin to see your own place in that conversation, to discover your own ideas, your own stance on your topic. This is the exciting part of a research project, for when you write out your own ideas on the topic, you will find yourself entering that conversation. Remember that your STANCE as an author needs to be clear: simply stringing together the words and ideas of others isn't enough. You need to show readers *how* your source materials relate to one another and to your thesis.

12–15

IF YOU NEED MORE HELP

See Chapter 47, QUOTING, PARAPHRASING, AND SUMMARIZING, for help in integrating source materials into your own text. See also Chapter 48 on ACKNOWL-EDGING SOURCES, AVOIDING PLAGIARISM for advice on giving credit to the sources you cite.

462–74
475–79

47 Quoting, Paraphrasing, and Summarizing

In an oral presentation about the rhetoric of Abraham Lincoln, you quote a memorable line from the Gettysburg Address. For an essay on the Tet Offensive in the Vietnam War, you paraphrase arguments made by several commentators and summarize some key debates about that war. Like all writers, when you work with the ideas and words of others, you need to clearly distinguish those ideas and words from your own and give credit to their authors. This chapter will help you with the specifics of quoting, paraphrasing, and summarizing source materials that you wish to use in your writing.

Taking Notes

When you find material you think will be useful, take careful notes. How do you determine how much or how little to record? You need to write down enough information so that when you refer to it later, you will be reminded of the main points and have a precise record of where the information comes from.

- *Use a computer file, note cards, or a notebook,* labeling each entry with the information that will allow you to keep track of where it comes from—author, title, and the pages or the URL (or DOI [digital object identifier]). You needn't write down full bibliographic information (you can abbreviate the author's name and title) since you'll include that information in your **WORKING BIBLIOGRAPHY**.

428–30

rhetorical situations

genres

processes

strategies

research MLA / APA

media / design

readings

- *Take notes in your own words, and use your own sentence patterns.* If you make a note that is a detailed **PARAPHRASE,** label it as such so that you'll know to provide appropriate **DOCUMENTATION** if you use it.

467–70
480–83

- *If you find wording that you'd like to quote,* be sure to enclose it in quotation marks to distinguish your source's words from your own. Double-check your notes to be sure any quoted material is accurately quoted—and that you haven't accidentally **PLAGIARIZED** your sources.

475–79

- *Label each note with a subject heading* to relate it to a subject, supporting point, or other element in your essay. This will help you to sort your sources and match them up with your rough outline. Restrict each note to a single subject, and briefly cite your source in each one.

Here are a few examples of one writer's notes on a source discussing synthetic dyes, bladder cancer, and the use of animals to determine what causes cancers. Each note includes a subject heading and brief source information and identifies whether the source is quoted or paraphrased.

<u>Synthetic dyes</u>

The first synthetic dye was mauve, invented in 1854 and derived from coal. Like other coal-derived dyes, it contained aromatic amines.

Steingraber, "Pesticides," 976 —paraphrase

<u>Synthetic dyes & cancer</u>

Bladder cancer was common among textile workers who used dyes. Steingraber: "By the beginning of the twentieth century, bladder cancer rates among this group of workers had skyrocketed."

Steingraber, "Pesticides," 976 — paraphrase and quote

<u>Synthetic dyes & cancer</u>

In 1938, Wilhelm Hueper exposed dogs to aromatic amines and showed that the chemical caused bladder cancer.

Steingraber, "Pesticides," 976 —paraphrase

Deciding Whether to Quote, Paraphrase, or Summarize

266–68 O
463–67 ●

When it comes time to **DRAFT,** you'll need to decide *how* to use the sources you've found — in other words, whether to quote, paraphrase, or summarize. You might follow this rule of thumb: **QUOTE** texts when the wording is worth repeating or makes a point so well that no rewording will do it justice, when you want to cite the exact words of a known authority on your topic, when an authority's opinions challenge or disagree with those of others, or when the source is one you want to emphasize. **PARAPHRASE** sources that are not worth quoting but contain details you need to include. **SUMMARIZE** longer passages whose main points are important but whose details are not.

467–70 ●
470–71 ●

Quoting

Quoting a source is a way of weaving someone else's exact words into your text. You need to reproduce the source exactly, though you can modify it to omit unnecessary details (with ellipses) or to make it fit smoothly into your text (with brackets). You also need to distinguish quoted material from your own by enclosing short quotations in quotation marks, setting off longer quotes as a block, and using appropriate **SIGNAL PHRASES.**

471–74 ●

Incorporate short quotations into your text, enclosed in quotation marks. If you are following **MLA STYLE,** this rule holds for four typed lines or fewer; if using **APA STYLE,** as below, short means fewer than forty words.

484–532 ●
533–74

> Gerald Graff (2003) has argued that colleges make the intellectual life seem more opaque than it needs to be, leaving many students with "the misconception that the life of the mind is a secret society for which only an elite few qualify" (p. 1).

If you are quoting three lines or fewer of poetry, run them in with your text, enclosed in quotation marks. Separate lines with slashes, leaving one space on each side of the slashes.

Emma Lazarus almost speaks for the Statue of Liberty with the words inscribed on its pedestal: "Give me your tired, your poor, / Your huddled masses yearning to breathe free, / The wretched refuse of your teeming shore" (58).

Set off long quotations block style.   If you are using MLA style, set off quotations of five or more typed lines by indenting the quote one inch (or ten spaces) from the left margin. If you are using APA style, indent quotes of forty or more words one-half inch (or five-to-seven spaces) from the left margin. In either case, do not use quotation marks, and put any parenthetical citation *after* any end punctuation.

> Nonprofit organizations such as Oxfam and Habitat for Humanity rely on visual representations of the poor. What better way to get our attention, asks rhetorician Diana George:
>
>> In a culture saturated by the image, how else do we convince Americans that—despite the prosperity they see all around them—there is real need out there? The solution for most nonprofits has been to show the despair. To do that they must represent poverty as something that can be seen and easily recognized: fallen down shacks and trashed out public housing, broken windows, dilapidated porches, barefoot kids with stringy hair, emaciated old women and men staring out at the camera with empty eyes. (210)

If you are quoting four or more lines of poetry, they need to be set off block style in the same way.

Indicate any omissions with ellipses.   You may sometimes delete words from a quotation that are unnecessary for your point. Insert three ellipsis marks (leaving a space before the first and after the last one) to indicate the deletion. If you omit a sentence or more in the middle of a quotation, put a period before the three ellipsis dots. Be careful not to distort the source's meaning, however.

Faigley points out that Gore's "Information Superhighway" metaphor "associated the economic prosperity of the 1950s and . . . 1960s facilitated by new highways with the potential for vast . . . commerce to be conducted over the Internet" (253).

According to Welch, "Television is more acoustic than visual. . . . One can turn one's gaze away from the television, but one cannot turn one's ears from it without leaving the area where the monitor leaks its aural signals into every corner" (102).

Indicate additions or changes with brackets.   Sometimes you'll need to change or add words in a quote—to make the quote fit grammatically within your sentence, for example, or to add a comment. In the following example, the writer changes the passage "one of our goals" to fit the grammar of her sentences:

Writing about the dwindling attention among some composition scholars to the actual teaching of writing, Susan Miller notes that "few discussions of writing pedagogy take it for granted that one of [their] goals is to teach how to write" (480).

Here's an example of brackets used to add explanatory words to a quotation:

Barbosa observes that even Buarque's lyrics have long included "many a metaphor of *saudades* [yearning] so characteristic of *fado* music" (207).

Use punctuation correctly with quotations.   When you incorporate a quotation into your text, you have to think about the end punctuation in the quoted material and also about any punctuation you need to add when you insert the quote into your own sentence.

Periods and commas. With brief quotations, put periods or commas *inside* the quotation marks, except when you have a parenthetical citation at the end, in which case you put the period after the parentheses.

"Country music," Tichi says, "is a crucial and vital part of the American identity" (23).

With long quotes set off block style, however, there are no quotation marks, so the period goes *before* the citation, as shown in the example on page 465.

Question marks and exclamation points. These go *inside* closing quotation marks if they are part of the quoted material but *outside* when they are not. If there's a parenthetical citation at the end, it follows the closing quotation mark, and any punctuation that's part of your sentence comes after.

> Speaking at a Fourth of July celebration in 1852, Frederick Douglass asked, "What have I, or those I represent, to do with your national independence?" (35).

> Who can argue with W. Charisse Goodman's observation that media images persuade women that "thinness equals happiness and fulfillment" (53)?

Colons and semicolons. These always go *outside* closing quotation marks.

> It's hard to argue with W. Charisse Goodman's observation that media images persuade women that "thinness equals happiness and fulfillment"; nevertheless, American women today are more overweight than ever (53).

Paraphrasing

When you paraphrase, you restate information from a source in your own words, using your own sentence structures. Paraphrase when the source material is important but the original wording is not. Because it includes all the main points of the source, a paraphrase is usually about the same length as the original.

Here is a paragraph about synthetic dyes and cancer, followed by three example paraphrases. The first two demonstrate some of the challenges of paraphrasing:

ORIGINAL SOURCE

In 1938, in a series of now-classic experiments, exposure to synthetic dyes derived from coal and belonging to a class of chemicals called aromatic amines was shown to cause bladder cancer in dogs. These results helped explain why bladder cancers had become so prevalent among dyestuffs workers. With the invention of mauve in 1854, synthetic dyes began replacing natural plant-based dyes in the coloring of cloth and leather. By the beginning of the twentieth century, bladder cancer rates among this group of workers had skyrocketed, and the dog experiments helped unravel this mystery. The International Labor Organization did not wait for the results of these animal tests, however, and in 1921 declared certain aromatic amines to be human carcinogens. Decades later, these dogs provided a lead in understanding why tire-industry workers, as well as machinists and metalworkers, also began falling victim to bladder cancer: aromatic amines had been added to rubbers and cutting oils to serve as accelerants and antirust agents.

— Sandra Steingraber, "Pesticides, Animals, and Humans"

This paraphrase borrows too much of the language of the original or changes it only slightly, as the underlined words and phrases show.

UNACCEPTABLE PARAPHRASE: WORDING TOO CLOSE

<u>Now-classic experiments</u> in 1938 showed that when dogs were exposed to aromatic amines, chemicals used in <u>synthetic dyes derived from coal</u>, they developed bladder cancer. Similar cancers were <u>prevalent among dyestuffs workers</u>, and <u>these</u> experiments <u>helped</u> to <u>explain why</u>. Mauve, a synthetic dye, was invented in 1854, after which <u>cloth and leather</u> manufacturers replaced most of the natural plant-based dyes with synthetic dyes. <u>By the</u> early <u>twentieth century</u>, <u>this group of workers had skyrocketing</u> rates of bladder cancer, a <u>mystery the dog experiments helped to unravel</u>. As early as 1921, though, before the test results proved the connection, the International Labor Organization had labeled <u>certain aromatic amines</u> carcinogenic. Even so, <u>decades later</u> many metalworkers, machinists, and tire-industry workers began developing bladder cancer. The animal tests helped researchers understand that <u>rubbers and cutting oils</u> contained aromatic amines <u>as accelerants and antirust agents</u> (Steingraber 976).

This paraphrase uses original language but follows the sentence structure of Steingraber's text too closely.

UNACCEPTABLE PARAPHRASE: SENTENCE STRUCTURE TOO CLOSE

In 1938, several pathbreaking experiments showed that being exposed to synthetic dyes that are made from coal and belong to a type of chemicals called aromatic amines caused dogs to get bladder cancer.

These results helped researchers identify why cancers of the bladder had become so common among textile workers who worked with dyes. With the development of mauve in 1854, synthetic dyes began to be used instead of dyes based on plants in the dyeing of leather and cloth. By the end of the nineteenth century, rates of bladder cancer among these workers had increased dramatically, and the experiments using dogs helped clear up this oddity. The International Labor Organization anticipated the results of these tests on animals, though, and in 1921 labeled some aromatic amines carcinogenic. Years later these experiments with dogs helped researchers explain why workers in the tire industry, as well as metalworkers and machinists, also started dying of bladder cancer: aromatic amines had been put into rubbers and cutting oils as rust inhibitors and accelerants (Steingraber 976).

Patchwriting, a third form of unacceptable paraphrase, combines the other two. Composition researcher Rebecca Moore Howard defines it as "copying from a source text and then deleting some words, altering grammatical structures, or plugging in one-for-one synonym-substitutes." Even though the student in the example below cites the source, most of the language and structure are taken directly from the source without being identified through the use of quotation marks. (The source's exact words are shaded in yellow; paraphrases are in blue).

ORIGINAL SOURCE

In 1938, in a series of now-classic experiments, exposure to synthetic dyes derived from coal and belonging to a class of chemicals called aromatic amines was shown to cause bladder cancer in dogs. These results explain why bladder cancers had become so prevalent among dyestuffs workers.

PATCHWRITE

Scientists have known for a long time that chemicals in the environment can cause cancer. For example, in 1938, in a series of important experiments, being exposed to synthetic dyes made out of coal and belonging to a kind of chemicals called aromatic amines was shown to cause dogs to develop bladder cancer. These experiments explain why this type of cancer had become so common among workers who handled dyes.

Here is an acceptable paraphrase of the entire passage.

ACCEPTABLE PARAPHRASE

Biologist Sandra Steingraber explains that pathbreaking experiments in 1938 demonstrated that dogs exposed to aromatic amines (chemicals used in coal-derived synthetic dyes) developed cancers of the bladder that were similar to cancers common among dyers in the textile industry. After mauve, the first synthetic dye, was invented in 1854, leather and cloth manufacturers replaced most natural dyes made from plants with synthetic dyes, and by the early 1900s textile workers had very high rates of bladder cancer. The experiments with dogs proved the connection, but years before, in 1921, the International Labor Organization had labeled some aromatic amines carcinogenic. Even so, years later many metalworkers, machinists, and workers in the tire industry started to develop unusually high rates of bladder cancer. The experiments with dogs helped researchers understand that the cancers were caused by aromatic amines used in cutting oils to inhibit rust and in rubbers as accelerants (976).

Some guidelines for paraphrasing

- *Use your own words and sentence structure.* It is acceptable to use some words from the original, but as much as possible, the phrasing and sentence structures should be your own.

- *Put in quotation marks any of the source's original phrasing that you use.*

- *Indicate the source of your paraphrase.*   Although the wording may be yours, the ideas and information come from another source; be sure to name the author and include an **IN-TEXT CITATION** to avoid the possibility of **PLAGIARISM.**

488–93 MLA
536–40 APA
475–79

Summarizing

A summary states the main ideas in a source concisely and in your own words. Unlike a paraphrase, a summary does *not* present all the details, and it is generally as brief as possible. Summaries may boil down an entire book or essay into a single sentence, or they may take a paragraph or more to present the main ideas. Here, for example, is a summary of the Steingraber paragraph:

rhetorical situations genres processes strategies research MLA / APA media / design readings

> Steingraber explains that experiments with dogs demonstrated that aromatic amines, chemicals used in synthetic dyes, cutting oils, and rubber, cause bladder cancer (976).

In the context of an essay, the summary might take this form:

> Medical researchers have long relied on experiments using animals to expand understanding of the causes of disease. For example, biologist and ecologist Sandra Steingraber notes that in the second half of the nineteenth century, the rate of bladder cancer soared among textile workers. According to Steingraber, experiments with dogs demonstrated that synthetic chemicals in dyes used to color the textiles caused the cancer (976).

Some guidelines for summarizing

- *Include only the main ideas; leave out the details.* A summary should include just enough information to give the reader the gist of the original. It is always much shorter than the original, sometimes even as brief as one sentence.

- *Use your own words.* If you quote phrasing from the original, enclose the phrase in quotation marks.

- *Indicate the source.* Although the wording may be yours, the ideas and information come from another source. Name the author, either in a signal phrase or parentheses, and include an appropriate **IN-TEXT CITATION** to avoid the possibility of **PLAGIARISM**.

488–93 MLA
536–40 APA
475–79

Introducing Source Materials Using Signal Phrases

You need to introduce quotations, paraphrases, and summaries clearly, usually letting readers know who the author is—and, if need be, something about his or her credentials. Consider this sentence:

> Professor and textbook author Elaine Tyler May argues that many high school history books are too bland to interest young readers (531).

The beginning ("Professor and textbook author Elaine Tyler May argues") functions as a *signal phrase*, telling readers who is making the assertion and why she has the authority to speak on the topic—and making clear that everything between the signal phrase and the parenthetical citation comes from that source. Since the signal phrase names the author, the parenthetical citation includes only the page number; had the author not been identified in the signal phrase, she would have been named in the parentheses:

> Even some textbook authors believe that many high school history books are too bland to interest young readers (May 531).

MLA and APA have different conventions for constructing signal phrases. In MLA, the language you use in a signal phrase can be neutral — like X *says* or Y *thinks* or *according to* Z. Or it can suggest something about the **STANCE** — the source's or your own. The example above referring to the textbook author uses the verb *argues*, suggesting that what she says is open to dispute (or that the writer believes it is). How would it change your understanding if the signal verb were *observes* or *suggests*?

In addition to the names of sources' authors, signal phrases often give readers information about institutional affiliations and positions authors have, their academic or professional specialties, and any other information that lets readers judge the credibility of the sources. You should craft each signal phrase you use so as to highlight the credentials of the author. Here are some examples:

> A study done by Anthony M. Armocida, professor of psychology at Duke University, showed that . . .

The signal phrase identifies the source's author, his professional position, and his university affiliation, emphasizing his title.

> Science writer Isaac McDougal argues that . . .

This phrase acknowledges that the source's author may not have scholarly credentials but is a published writer; it's a useful construction if the source doesn't provide much information about the writer.

> Writing in *Psychology Today*, Amanda Chao-Fitz notes that . . .

This is the sort of signal phrase you use if you have no information on the author; you establish credibility on the basis of the publication in which the source appears.

12–15 ▪

If you're writing using APA style, signal phrases are typically briefer, giving only the author's last name and the date of publication:

According to Benzinger (2010), . . .

Quartucci (2011) observed that . . .

SOME COMMON SIGNAL VERBS

acknowledges	claims	disagrees	observes
admits	comments	disputes	points out
advises	concludes	emphasizes	reasons
agrees	concurs	grants	rejects
argues	confirms	illustrates	reports
asserts	contends	implies	responds
believes	declares	insists	suggests
charges	denies	notes	thinks

Verb tenses.   MLA and APA also have different conventions regarding the tenses of verbs in signal phrases. MLA requires present-tense verbs (*writes, asserts, notes*) in signal phrases to introduce a work you are quoting, paraphrasing, or summarizing.

In *Poor Richard's Almanack*, Benjamin Franklin <u>notes</u>, "He that cannot obey, cannot command" (739).

If, however, you are referring to the act of writing or saying something rather than simply quoting someone's words, you might not use the present tense. The writer of the following sentence focuses on the year in which the source was written — therefore, the verb is necessarily in the past tense:

Back in 1941, Kenneth Burke <u>wrote</u> that "the ethical values of work are in its application of the competitive equipment to cooperative ends" (316).

If you are following APA style, use the past tense or present-perfect tense to introduce sources composed in the past.

Dowdall, Crawford, and Wechsler (1998) <u>observed</u> that women attending women's colleges are less likely to engage in binge drinking than are women who attend coeducational colleges (p. 713).

APA requires the present tense, however, to discuss the results of an experiment or to explain conclusions that are generally agreed on.

The findings of this study <u>suggest</u> that excessive drinking has serious consequences for college students and their institutions.

The authors of numerous studies <u>agree</u> that smoking and drinking among adolescents are associated with lower academic achievement.

IF YOU NEED MORE HELP

See **ACKNOWLEDGING SOURCES, AVOIDING PLAGIARISM** for help in giving credit to the sources you use. See also the **SAMPLE RESEARCH PAPERS** to see how sources are cited in MLA and APA styles.

475–79
522–32 MLA
563–74 APA

Acknowledging Sources, 48
Avoiding Plagiarism

Whenever you do research-based writing, you find yourself entering a conversation—reading what many others have had to say about your topic, figuring out what you yourself think, and then putting what you think in writing—"putting in your oar," as the rhetorician Kenneth Burke once wrote. As a writer, you need to *acknowledge* any words and ideas that come from others—to give credit where credit is due, to recognize the various authorities and many perspectives you have considered, to show readers where they can find your sources, and to situate your own arguments in the ongoing conversation. Using other people's words and ideas without acknowledgment is *plagiarism,* a serious academic and ethical offense. This chapter will show you how to acknowledge the materials you use and avoid plagiarism.

Acknowledging Sources

When you insert in your text information that you've obtained from others, your reader needs to know where your source's words or ideas begin and end. Therefore, you should introduce a source by naming the author in a **SIGNAL PHRASE,** and follow it with a brief parenthetical **IN-TEXT CITATION** or by naming the source in a parenthetical citation. (You need only a brief citation here, since your readers will find full bibliographic information in your list of **WORKS CITED** or **REFERENCES.)**

471–74
488–93 MLA
536–40 APA
494–521 MLA
541–61 APA

Sources that need acknowledgment. You almost always need to acknowledge any information that you get from a specific source. Material you should acknowledge includes the following:

- *Direct quotations.* Unless they are well known (see p. 478 for some examples), any quotations from another source must be enclosed in quotation marks, cited with brief bibliographic information in parentheses, and usually introduced with a signal phrase that tells who wrote or said it and provides necessary contextual information, as in the following sentence:

> In a dissenting opinion on the issue of racial preferences in college admissions, Supreme Court justice Ruth Bader Ginsburg argues, "The stain of generations of racial oppression is still visible in our society, and the determination to hasten its removal remains vital" (*Gratz v. Bollinger*).

- *Arguable statements and information that may not be common knowledge.* If you state something about which there is disagreement or for which arguments can be made, cite the source of your statement. If in doubt about whether you need to give the source of an assertion, provide it. As part of an essay on "fake news" programs like *The Daily Show*, for example, you might make the following assertion:

> The satire of *The Daily Show* complements the conservative bias of FOX News, since both have abandoned the stance of objectivity maintained by mainstream news sources, contends Michael Hoyt, executive editor of the *Columbia Journalism Review* (43).

Others might argue with the contention that the FOX News Channel offers biased reports of the news, so the source of this assertion needs to be acknowledged. In the same essay, you might present information that should be cited because it's not widely known, as in this example:

> According to a report by the Pew Research Center, 21 percent of Americans under thirty got information about the 2004 presidential campaign primarily from "fake news" and comedy shows like *The Daily Show* and *Saturday Night Live* (2).

- *The opinions and assertions of others.* When you present the ideas, opinions, and assertions of others, cite the source. You may have rewritten

rhetorical situations　　genres　　processes　　strategies　　research MLA / APA　　media / design　　readings

the concept in your own words, but the ideas were generated by someone else and must be acknowledged, as they are here:

> David Boonin, writing in the *Journal of Social Philosophy,* asserts
> that, logically, laws banning marriage between people of different
> races are not discriminatory since everyone of each race is affected
> equally by them. Laws banning same-sex unions are discriminatory,
> however, since they apply only to people with a certain sexual
> orientation (256).

- *Any information that you didn't generate yourself.* If you did not do the
  research or compile the data yourself, cite your source. This goes for
  interviews, statistics, graphs, charts, visuals, photographs—anything
  you use that you did not create. If you create a chart using data from
  another source, you need to cite that source.

- *Collaboration with and help from others.* In many of your courses and
  in work situations, you'll be called on to work with others. You may
  get help with your writing at your school's writing center or from fellow students in your writing courses. Acknowledging such collaboration or assistance, in a brief informational note, is a way of giving
  credit—and saying thank you. See guidelines for writing notes in the
  MLA and APA sections of this book.

494

541

Sources that don't need acknowledgment.   Widely available information and common knowledge do not require acknowledgment. What constitutes common knowledge may not be clear, however. When in doubt,
provide a citation, or ask your instructor whether the information needs
to be cited. You generally do not need to cite the following:

- *Information that most readers are likely to know.* You don't need to
  acknowledge information that is widely known or commonly accepted
  as fact. For example, in a literary analysis, you wouldn't cite a source
  saying that Harriet Beecher Stowe wrote *Uncle Tom's Cabin;* you can
  assume your readers already know that. On the other hand, you should
  cite the source from which you got the information that the book was
  first published in installments in a magazine and then, with revisions,
  in book form, because that information isn't common knowledge. As

you do research in areas you're not familiar with, be aware that what constitutes common knowledge isn't always clear; the history of the novel's publication would be known to Stowe scholars and would likely need no acknowledgment in an essay written for them. In this case, too, if you aren't sure whether to acknowledge information, do so.

- *Information and documents that are widely available.* If a piece of information appears in several sources or reference works or if a document has been published widely, you needn't cite a source for it. For example, the date when astronauts Neil Armstrong and Buzz Aldrin landed a spacecraft on the moon can be found in any number of reference works. Similarly, the Declaration of Independence and the Gettysburg Address are reprinted in thousands of sources, so the ones where you found them need no citation.

- *Well-known quotations.* These include such famous quotations as Lady Macbeth's "Out, damned spot!" and John F. Kennedy's "Ask not what your country can do for you; ask what you can do for your country." Be sure, however, that the quotation is correct; Winston Churchill is said to have told a class of schoolchildren, "Never, ever, ever, ever, ever, ever, ever give up. Never give up. Never give up. Never give up." His actual words, however, taken from a longer speech, are much different and begin "Never give in."

- *Material that you created or gathered yourself.* You need not cite photographs that you took, graphs that you composed based on your own findings, or data from an experiment or survey that you conducted—though you should make sure readers know that the work is yours.

A good rule of thumb: *when in doubt, cite your source.* You're unlikely to be criticized for citing too much—but you may invite charges of plagiarism by citing too little.

Avoiding Plagiarism

When you use the words or ideas of others, you need to acknowledge who and where the material came from; if you don't credit those sources, you

rhetorical situations

genres

processes

strategies

research MLA / APA

media / design

readings

are guilty of plagiarism. Plagiarism is often committed unintentionally—as when a writer paraphrases someone else's ideas in language that is close to the original. It is essential, therefore, to know what constitutes plagiarism: (1) using another writer's words or ideas without in-text citation and documentation, (2) using another writer's exact words without quotation marks, and (3) paraphrasing or summarizing someone else's ideas using language or sentence structures that are too close to theirs.

To avoid plagiarizing, take careful **NOTES** as you do your research, clearly labeling as quotations any words you quote directly and being careful to use your own phrasing and sentence structures in paraphrases and summaries. Be sure you know what source material you must **DOCUMENT**, and give credit to your sources, both in the text and in a list of **REFERENCES** or **WORKS CITED.**

459–60
480–83
541–61 APA
494–521 MLA

Be aware that it's easy to inadvertently plagiarize when you're working with online sources, such as full-text articles, that you've downloaded or cut and pasted into your notes. Keep careful track of these materials, since saving copies of your sources is so easy. Later, be sure to check your draft against the original sources to make sure your quotations are accurately worded — and take care, too, to include quotation marks and cite the source correctly. Copying online material right into a document you are writing and forgetting to put quotation marks around it or to cite it (or both) is all too easy to do. You must acknowledge information you find on the web just as you must acknowledge all other source materials.

And you must recognize that plagiarism has consequences. Scholars' work will be discredited if it too closely resembles another's. Journalists found to have plagiarized lose their jobs, and students routinely fail courses or are dismissed from their school when they are caught cheating—all too often by submitting as their own essays that they have purchased from online "research" sites. If you're having trouble completing an assignment, seek assistance. Talk with your instructor, or if your school has a writing center, go there for advice on all aspects of your writing, including acknowledging sources and avoiding plagiarism.

49 Documentation

In everyday life, we are generally aware of our sources: "I read it on Andrew Sullivan's blog." "Amber told me it's your birthday." "If you don't believe me, ask Mom." Saying how we know what we know and where we got our information is part of establishing our credibility and persuading others to take what we say seriously.

The goal of a research project is to study a topic, combining what we learn from sources with our own thinking and then composing a written text. When we write up the results of a research project, we cite the sources we use, usually by quoting, paraphrasing, or summarizing, and we acknowledge those sources, telling readers where the ideas came from. The information we give about sources is called documentation, and we provide it not only to establish our credibility as researchers and writers but also so that our readers, if they wish to, can find the sources themselves.

Understanding Documentation Styles

The Norton Field Guide covers the documentation styles of the Modern Language Association (MLA) and the American Psychological Association (APA). MLA style is used chiefly in the humanities; APA is used mainly in the social sciences. Both are two-part systems, consisting of (1) brief in-text parenthetical documentation for quotations, paraphrases, or summaries and (2) more-detailed documentation in a list of sources at the end of the text. MLA and APA require that the end-of-text documentation provide the following basic information about each source you cite:

- author, editor, or creator of the source
- title of source (and of publication or site where it appears)
- place of publication
- name of publisher
- date of publication
- medium of publication (MLA only)
- retrieval information (for online sources; APA only)

MLA and APA are by no means the only documentation styles. Many other publishers and organizations have their own style, among them the University of Chicago Press and the Council of Science Editors. We focus on MLA and APA here because those are styles that college students are often required to use. On the following page are examples of how the two parts—the brief parenthetical documentation in your text and the more detailed information at the end—correspond in each of these systems.

The examples here and throughout this book are color-coded to help you see the crucial parts of each citation: tan for author and editor, yellow for title, and gray for publication information: place of publication, name of publisher, date of publication, page number(s), medium of publication, and so on.

As the examples of in-text documentation show, in either MLA or APA style you should name the author either in a signal phrase or in parentheses following the source information. But there are several differences between the two styles in the details of the citation. In MLA, the author's full name is used in a signal phrase; in APA, only the last name is used. In APA, the abbreviation *p.* is used with the page number, which is provided only for a direct quotation; in MLA, a page number (if there is one) is always given, but with no abbreviation before it. Finally, in APA the date of publication always appears just after the author's name. Comparing the MLA and APA styles of listing works cited or references also reveals some differences: MLA includes an author's first name while APA gives only initials; MLA puts the date near the end while APA places it right after the author's name; MLA requires the medium of publication while APA usually does not; MLA capitalizes most of the words in a book's title and subtitle while APA capitalizes only the first words and proper nouns and proper adjectives in each.

Some of these differences are related to the nature of the academic fields in which the two styles are used. In humanities disciplines, the authorship of a text is emphasized, so both first and last names are included in MLA citations. Scholarship in those fields may be several years old but still current, so the publication date doesn't appear in the in-text citation. In APA style, as in many citation styles used in the sciences, education, and engineering, emphasis is placed on the date of publication because in these fields, more recent research is usually preferred over older studies. However, although the elements are arranged differently, both MLA and APA — and other documentation styles as well — require similar information about author, title, and publication.

MLA Style

IN-TEXT DOCUMENTATION

As Lester Faigley puts it, "The world has become a bazaar from which to shop for an individual 'lifestyle' " (12).

As one observer suggests, "The world has become a bazaar from which to shop for an individual 'lifestyle' " (Faigley 12).

WORKS-CITED DOCUMENTATION

Faigley, Lester. *Fragments of Rationality: Postmodernity and the Subject of Composition*. Pittsburgh: U of Pittsburgh P, 1992. Print.

author   title   publication

APA Style

IN-TEXT DOCUMENTATION

As Faigley (1992) suggested, "The world has become a bazaar from which to shop for an individual 'lifestyle'" (p. 12).

As one observer has noted, "The world has become a bazaar from which to shop for an individual 'lifestyle'" (Faigley, 1992, p. 12).

REFERENCE-LIST DOCUMENTATION

Faigley, L. (1992). *Fragments of rationality: Postmodernity and the subject of composition.* Pittsburgh, PA: University of Pittsburgh Press.

50 MLA Style

Modern Language Association style calls for (1) brief in-text documentation and (2) complete documentation in a list of works cited at the end of your text. The models in this chapter draw on the *MLA Handbook for Writers of Research Papers*, 7th edition (2009). Additional information is available at www.mla.org.

A DIRECTORY TO MLA STYLE

Throughout this chapter, you'll find models and examples that are color-coded to help you see how writers include source information in their texts and list of works cited: tan for author or editor, yellow for title, gray for publication information: place of publication, publisher, date of publication, page number(s), and so on.

IN-TEXT DOCUMENTATION

Brief documentation in your text makes clear to your reader what you took from a source and where in the source you found the information.

462–74

In your text, you have three options for citing a source: QUOTING, PARAPHRASING, and SUMMARIZING. As you cite each source, you will need to decide whether or not to name the author in a signal phrase — "as Toni Morrison writes" — or in parentheses — "(Morrison 24)."

The first examples in this chapter show basic in-text citations of a work by one author. Variations on those examples follow. The examples illustrate the MLA style of using quotation marks around titles of short works and italicizing titles of long works.

1. AUTHOR NAMED IN A SIGNAL PHRASE

If you mention the author in a signal phrase, put only the page number(s) in parentheses. Do not write *page* or *p.*

> McCullough describes John Adams's hands as those of someone used to manual labor (18).

2. AUTHOR NAMED IN PARENTHESES

If you do not mention the author in a signal phrase, put his or her last name in parentheses along with the page number(s). Do not use punctuation between the name and the page number(s).

> Adams is said to have had "the hands of a man accustomed to pruning his own trees, cutting his own hay, and splitting his own firewood" (McCullough 18).

Whether you use a signal phrase and parentheses or parentheses only, try to put the parenthetical citation at the end of the sentence or as close as possible to the material you've cited without awkwardly interrupting the sentence. Notice that in the example above, the parenthetical reference comes after the closing quotation marks but before the period at the end of the sentence.

3. TWO OR MORE WORKS BY THE SAME AUTHOR

If you cite multiple works by one author, include the title of the work you are citing either in the signal phrase or in parentheses. Give the full title if it's brief; otherwise, give a short version.

> Kaplan insists that understanding power in the Near East requires "Western leaders who know when to intervene, and do so without illusions" (*Eastward* 330).

Include a comma between author and title if you include both in the parentheses.

> Understanding power in the Near East requires "Western leaders who know when to intervene, and do so without illusions" (Kaplan, *Eastward* 330).

4. AUTHORS WITH THE SAME LAST NAME

Give the author's first name in any signal phrase or the author's first initial in the parenthetical reference.

> *Imaginative* applies not only to modern literature (E. Wilson) but also to writing of all periods, whereas *magical* is often used in writing about Arthurian romances (A. Wilson).

5. TWO OR MORE AUTHORS

For a work by two or three authors, name all the authors, either in a signal phrase or in the parentheses.

> Carlson and Ventura's stated goal is to introduce Julio Cortázar, Marjorie Agosín, and other Latin American writers to an audience of English-speaking adolescents (v).

For a work with four or more authors, either mention all their names or include just the name of the first author followed by *et al.*, Latin for "and others."

One popular survey of American literature breaks the contents into sixteen thematic groupings (Anderson et al. A19–24).

6. ORGANIZATION OR GOVERNMENT AS AUTHOR

Cite the organization either in a signal phrase or in parentheses. It's acceptable to shorten long names.

The U.S. government can be direct when it wants to be. For example, it sternly warns, "If you are overpaid, we will recover any payments not due you" (Social Security Administration 12).

7. AUTHOR UNKNOWN

If you don't know the author, use the work's title or a shortened version of the title in the parentheses.

A powerful editorial in last week's paper asserts that healthy liver donor Mike Hurewitz died because of "frightening" faulty postoperative care ("Every Patient's Nightmare").

8. LITERARY WORKS

When referring to literary works that are available in many different editions, cite the page numbers from the edition you are using, followed by information that will let readers of any edition locate the text you are citing.

NOVELS. Give the page and chapter number.

In *Pride and Prejudice,* Mrs. Bennett shows no warmth toward Jane and Elizabeth when they return from Netherfield (105; ch. 12).

VERSE PLAYS. Give the act, scene, and line numbers; separate them with periods.

Macbeth continues the vision theme when he addresses the Ghost with "Thou hast no speculation in those eyes / Which thou dost glare with" (3.3.96–97).

POEMS. Give the part and the line numbers (separated by periods). If a poem has only line numbers, use the word *line(s)* in the first reference.

> Whitman sets up not only opposing adjectives but also opposing nouns in "Song of Myself" when he says, "I am of old and young, of the foolish as much as the wise, / . . . a child as well as a man" (16.330–32).

> One description of the mere in *Beowulf* is "not a pleasant place!" (line 1372). Later, the label is "the awful place" (1378).

9. WORK IN AN ANTHOLOGY

Name the author(s) of the work, not the editor of the anthology—either in a signal phrase or in parentheses.

> "It is the teapots that truly shock," according to Cynthia Ozick in her essay on teapots as metaphor (70).

> In *In Short: A Collection of Creative Nonfiction,* readers will find both an essay on Scottish tea (Hiestand) and a piece on teapots as metaphors (Ozick).

10. ENCYCLOPEDIA OR DICTIONARY

Cite an entry in an encyclopedia or dictionary using the author's name, if available. For an entry in a reference work without an author, give the entry's title in parentheses. If entries are arranged alphabetically, no page number is needed.

> According to *Funk & Wagnall's New World Encyclopedia,* early in his career, Kubrick's main source of income came from "hustling chess games in Washington Square Park" ("Kubrick, Stanley").

11. LEGAL AND HISTORICAL DOCUMENTS

For legal cases and acts of law, name the case or act in a signal phrase or in parentheses. Italicize the name of a legal case.

> In 2005, the Supreme Court confirmed in *MGM Studios, Inc. v. Grokster, Ltd.* that peer-to-peer file sharing is illegal copyright infringement.

Do not italicize the titles of laws, acts, or well-known historical documents such as the Declaration of Independence. Give the title and any relevant articles and sections in parentheses. It's okay to use common abbreviations such as *art.* or *sec.* and to abbreviate well-known titles.

> The president is also granted the right to make recess appointments (US Const., art. 2, sec. 2).

12. SACRED TEXT

When citing sacred texts such as the Bible or the Qur'an, give the title of the edition used, and in parentheses give the book, chapter, and verse (or their equivalent), separated by periods. MLA style recommends that you abbreviate the names of the books of the Bible in parenthetical references.

> The wording from *The New English Bible* follows: "In the beginning of creation, when God made heaven and earth, the earth was without form and void, with darkness over the face of the abyss, and a mighty wind that swept over the surface of the waters" (Gen. 1.1–2).

13. MULTIVOLUME WORK

If you cite more than one volume of a multivolume work, each time you cite one of the volumes, give the volume *and* the page number(s) in parentheses, separated by a colon.

> Sandburg concludes with the following sentence about those paying last respects to Lincoln: "All day long and through the night the unbroken line moved, the home town having its farewell" (4: 413).

If your works-cited list includes only a single volume of a multivolume work, give just the page number in parentheses.

14. TWO OR MORE WORKS CITED TOGETHER

If you're citing two or more works closely together, you will sometimes need to provide a parenthetical citation for each one.

author　　　　title　　　publication

Tanner (7) and Smith (viii) have looked at works from a cultural perspective.

If you include both in the same parentheses, separate the references with a semicolon.

Critics have looked at both *Pride and Prejudice* and *Frankenstein* from a cultural perspective (Tanner 7; Smith viii).

15. SOURCE QUOTED IN ANOTHER SOURCE

When you are quoting text that you found quoted in another source, use the abbreviation *qtd. in* in the parenthetical reference.

Charlotte Brontë wrote to G. H. Lewes: "Why do you like Miss Austen so very much? I am puzzled on that point" (qtd. in Tanner 7).

16. WORK WITHOUT PAGE NUMBERS

For works without page numbers, including many online sources, identify the source using the author or other information either in a signal phrase or in parentheses.

Studies reported in *Scientific American* and elsewhere show that music training helps children to be better at multitasking later in life ("Hearing the Music").

If the source has paragraph or section numbers, use them with the abbreviation *par.* or *sec.*: ("Hearing the Music," par. 2). If an online work is available as a PDF with page numbers, cite the number(s) in parentheses.

17. AN ENTIRE WORK OR ONE-PAGE ARTICLE

If you cite an entire work rather than a part of it, or if you cite a single-page article, identify the author in a signal phrase or in parentheses. There's no need to include page numbers.

At least one observer considers Turkey and Central Asia explosive (Kaplan).

NOTES

Sometimes you may need to give information that doesn't fit into the text itself—to thank people who helped you, to provide additional details, to refer readers to other sources, or to add comments about sources. Such information can be given in a *footnote* (at the bottom of the page) or an *endnote* (on a separate page with the heading *Notes* just before your works-cited list). Put a superscript number at the appropriate point in your text, signaling to readers to look for the note with the corresponding number. If you have multiple notes, number them consecutively throughout your paper.

TEXT

This essay will argue that small liberal arts colleges should not recruit athletes and, more specifically, that giving student athletes preferential treatment undermines the larger educational goals.[1]

NOTE

[1] I want to thank all those who have contributed to my thinking on this topic, especially my classmates and my teachers Marian Johnson and Diane O'Connor.

LIST OF WORKS CITED

A works-cited list provides full bibliographic information for every source cited in your text. See page 523 for guidelines on preparing this list; for a sample work-cited list, see page 531.

Print Books

For most books, you'll need to provide information about the author; the title and any subtitle; and the place of publication, publisher, and date. At the end of the citation provide the medium—Print.

author   title   publication

IMPORTANT DETAILS FOR CITING PRINT BOOKS

- **AUTHORS**: Include the author's middle name or initials, if any.
- **TITLES**: Capitalize all principal words in titles and subtitles. Do not capitalize *a, an, the, to,* or any prepositions or coordinating conjunctions unless they are the first or last word of a title or subtitle.
- **PUBLICATION PLACE**: If there's more than one city, use the first.
- **PUBLISHER**: Use a short form of the publisher's name (Norton for W. W. Norton & Company, Yale UP for Yale University Press).
- **DATES**: If more than one year is given, use the most recent one.

1. ONE AUTHOR

Author's Last Name, First Name. *Title*. Publication City: Publisher, Year of publication. Medium.

Anderson, Curtis. *The Long Tail: Why the Future of Business Is Selling Less of More*. New York: Hyperion, 2006. Print.

2. TWO OR MORE WORKS BY THE SAME AUTHOR(S)

Give the author's name in the first entry, and then use three hyphens in the author slot for each of the subsequent works, listing them alphabetically by the first important word of each title.

Author's Last Name, First Name. *Title That Comes First Alphabetically*. Publication City: Publisher, Year of publication. Medium.

—. *Title That Comes Next Alphabetically*. Publication City: Publisher, Year of publication. Medium.

Kaplan, Robert D. *The Coming Anarchy: Shattering the Dreams of the Post Cold War*. New York: Random, 2000. Print.

—. *Eastward to Tartary: Travels in the Balkans, the Middle East, and the Caucasus*. New York: Random, 2000. Print.

Documentation Map (MLA)
Print Book

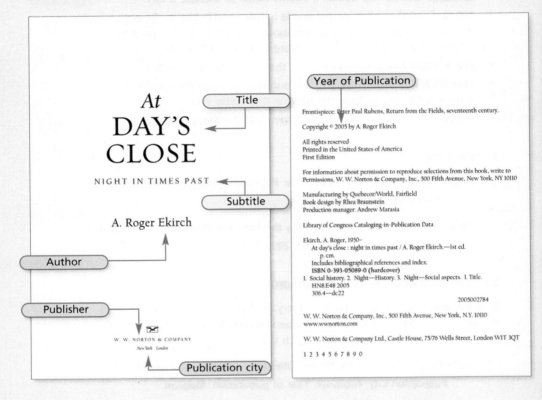

494–502
for more on
citing books
MLA style

Ekirch, A. Roger. *At Day's Close: Night in Times Past*. New York: Norton, 2005. Print.

author   title   publication

3. TWO OR THREE AUTHORS

First Author's Last Name, First Name, Second Author's First and Last
    Names, and Third Author's First and Last Names. *Title*. Publication
    City: Publisher, Year of publication. Medium.

Malless, Stanley, and Jeffrey McQuain. *Coined by God: Words and
    Phrases That First Appear in the English Translations of the Bible*.
    New York: Norton, 2003. Print.

Sebranek, Patrick, Verne Meyer, and Dave Kemper. *Writers INC: A Guide
    to Writing, Thinking, and Learning*. Burlington: Write Source,
    1990. Print.

4. FOUR OR MORE AUTHORS

You may give each author's name or the name of the first author only,
followed by *et al.*, Latin for "and others."

First Author's Last Name, First Name, Second Author's First and Last
    Names, Third Author's First and Last Names, and Final Author's First
    and Last Names. *Title*. Publication City: Publisher, Year of publication.
    Medium.

Anderson, Robert, John Malcolm Brinnin, John Leggett, Gary Q. Arpin,
    and Susan Allen Toth. *Elements of Literature: Literature of the
    United States*. Austin: Holt, 1993. Print.

Anderson, Robert, et al. *Elements of Literature: Literature of the United
    States*. Austin: Holt, 1993. Print.

5. ORGANIZATION OR GOVERNMENT AS AUTHOR

Organization Name. *Title*. Publication City: Publisher, Year of
    publication. Medium.

Diagram Group. *The Macmillan Visual Desk Reference*. New York:
    Macmillan, 1993. Print.

For a government publication, give the name of the government first, followed by the names of any department and agency.

> United States. Dept. of Health and Human Services. Natl. Inst. of Mental
> Health. *Autism Spectrum Disorders*. Washington: GPO, 2004. Print.

6. ANTHOLOGY

> Editor's Last Name, First Name, ed. *Title*. Publication City: Publisher, Year
> of publication. Medium.

> Hall, Donald, ed. *The Oxford Book of Children's Verse in America*. New
> York: Oxford UP, 1985. Print.

If there is more than one editor, list the first editor last-name-first and the others first-name-first.

> Kitchen, Judith, and Mary Paumier Jones, eds. *In Short: A Collection of
> Brief Creative Nonfiction*. New York: Norton, 1996. Print.

7. WORK(S) IN AN ANTHOLOGY

> Author's Last Name, First Name. "Title of Work." *Title of Anthology*.
> Ed. Editor's First and Last Names. Publication City: Publisher, Year of
> publication. Pages. Medium.

> Achebe, Chinua. "Uncle Ben's Choice." *The Seagull Reader: Literature*.
> Ed. Joseph Kelly. New York: Norton, 2005. 23–27. Print.

To document two or more selections from one anthology, list each selection by author and title, followed by the names of the anthology editor(s) and the pages of the selection. Then include an entry for the anthology itself (see no. 6).

> Author's Last Name, First Name. "Title of Work." Anthology Editor's Last
> Name Pages.

> Hiestand, Emily. "Afternoon Tea." Kitchen and Jones 65–67.

> Ozick, Cynthia. "The Shock of Teapots." Kitchen and Jones 68–71.

Do not list the anthology separately if you're citing only one selection.

author   title   publication

8. AUTHOR AND EDITOR

Start with the author if you've cited the text itself.

> Author's Last Name, First Name. *Title*. Ed. Editor's First and Last Names.
> Publication City: Publisher, Year of publication. Medium.

> Austen, Jane. *Emma*. Ed. Stephen M. Parrish. New York: Norton, 2000. Print.

Start with the editor to cite his or her contribution rather than the author's.

> Editor's Last Name, First Name, ed. *Title*. By Author's First and Last Names.
> Publication City: Publisher, Year of publication. Medium.

> Parrish, Stephen M., ed. *Emma*. By Jane Austen. New York: Norton, 2000. Print.

9. NO AUTHOR OR EDITOR

> *Title*. Publication City: Publisher, Year of publication. Medium.

> *2008 New York City Restaurants*. New York: Zagat, 2008. Print.

10. TRANSLATION

Start with the author to emphasize the work itself.

> Author's Last Name, First Name. *Title*. Trans. Translator's First and Last
> Names. Publication City: Publisher, Year of publication. Medium.

> Dostoevsky, Fyodor. *Crime and Punishment*. Trans. Richard Pevear and
> Larissa Volokhonsky. New York: Vintage, 1993. Print.

Start with the translator to emphasize the translation.

> Pevear, Richard, and Larissa Volokhonsky, trans. *Crime and Punishment*.
> By Fyodor Dostoevsky. New York: Vintage, 1993. Print.

11. GRAPHIC NARRATIVE

Start with the name of the person whose work is most relevant to your
research, and include labels to indicate each collaborator's role.

> Pekar, Harvey, writer. *American Splendor*. Illus. R. Crumb. New York: Four
> Walls, 1996. Print.

Crumb, R., illus. *American Splendor*. By Harvey Pekar. New York: Four
Walls, 1996. Print.

If the work was written and illustrated by the same person, format the
entry like that of any other book.

12. FOREWORD, INTRODUCTION, PREFACE, OR AFTERWORD

Part Author's Last Name, First Name. Name of Part. *Title of Book*.
By Author's First and Last Names. Publication City: Publisher, Year
of publication. Pages. Medium.

Tanner, Tony. Introduction. *Pride and Prejudice*. By Jane Austen.
London: Penguin, 1972. 7–46. Print.

13. MULTIVOLUME WORK

If you cite more than one volume of a multivolume work, give the total
number of volumes after the title.

Author's Last Name, First Name. *Title of Complete Work*. Number of vols.
Publication City: Publisher, Year of publication. Medium.

Sandburg, Carl. *Abraham Lincoln: The War Years*. 4 vols. New York:
Harcourt, 1939. Print.

If you cite only one volume, give the volume number after the title.

Sandburg, Carl. *Abraham Lincoln: The War Years*. Vol. 2. New York:
Harcourt, 1939. Print.

14. ARTICLE IN A REFERENCE BOOK

Provide the author's name if the article is signed. If the reference work is
well known, give only the edition and year of publication.

Author's Last Name, First Name. "Title of Article." *Title of Reference
Book*. Edition number. Year of publication. Medium.

"Kiwi." *Merriam-Webster's Collegiate Dictionary*. 11th ed. 2003. Print.

If the reference work is less familiar or more specialized, give full publication information. If it has only one volume or is in its first edition, omit that information.

> Author's Last Name, First Name. "Title of Article." *Title of Reference*
> *Book*. Ed. Editor's First and Last Name. Edition number. Number of
> vols. Publication City: Publisher, Year of publication. Medium.

> Campbell, James. "The Harlem Renaissance." *The Oxford Companion to*
> *Twentieth-Century Poetry.* Ed. Ian Hamilton. Oxford: Oxford UP,
> 1994. Print.

15. BOOK IN A SERIES

> Editor's Last Name, First Name, ed. *Title of Book*. By Author's First and
> Last Names. Publication City: Publisher, Year of publication. Medium.
> Series Title abbreviated.

> Wall, Cynthia, ed. *The Pilgrim's Progress*. By John Bunyan. New York:
> Norton, 2007. Print. Norton Critical Ed.

16. SACRED TEXT

If you have cited a specific edition of a religious text, you need to include it in your works-cited list.

> *The New English Bible with the Apocrypha*. New York: Oxford UP, 1971.
> Print.

> *The Torah: A Modern Commentary*. Ed. W. Gunther Plaut. New York:
> Union of Amer. Hebrew Congregations, 1981. Print.

17. BOOK WITH TITLE WITHIN THE TITLE

When the title of a book contains the title of another long work, do not italicize that title. (See next page for examples.)

Walker, Roy. *Time Is Free: A Study of* Macbeth. London: Dakers, 1949.
Print.

When the book title contains the title of a short work, put the short work
in quotation marks, and italicize the entire title.

Thompson, Lawrance Roger. *"Fire and Ice": The Art and Thought of
Robert Frost*. New York: Holt, 1942. Print.

18. EDITION OTHER THAN THE FIRST

Author's Last Name, First Name. *Title*. Name or number of ed. Publication
City: Publisher, Year of publication. Medium.

Hirsch, E. D., Jr., ed. *What Your Second Grader Needs to Know:
Fundamentals of a Good Second-Grade Education*. Rev. ed. New
York: Doubleday, 1998. Print.

19. REPUBLISHED WORK

Give the original publication date after the title, followed by the publication information of the republished edition.

Author's Last Name, First Name. *Title*. Year of original edition.
Publication City: Current Publisher, Year of republication. Medium.

Bierce, Ambrose. *Civil War Stories*. 1909. New York: Dover, 1994. Print.

20. PUBLISHER AND IMPRINT

Some sources may provide both a publisher's name and an imprint on the
title page; if so, include both, with a hyphen between the imprint and the
publisher.

Author's Last Name, First Name. *Title*. Publication City: Imprint-Publisher,
Year of publication. Medium.

Maguire, Gregory. Wicked: *The Life and Times of the Wicked Witch of
the West*. New York: ReganBooks-HarperCollins, 1995. Print.

Print Periodicals

For most articles, you'll need to provide information about the author, the article title and any subtitle, the periodical title, any volume or issue number, the date, inclusive page numbers, and the medium—Print.

IMPORTANT DETAILS FOR CITING PRINT PERIODICALS

- **AUTHORS**: If there is more than one author, list the first author last-name-first and the others first-name-first.
- **TITLES**: Capitalize titles and subtitles as you would for a book. For periodical titles, omit any initial *A*, *An*, or *The*.
- **DATES**: Abbreviate the names of months except for May, June, or July: Jan., Feb., Mar., Apr., Aug., Sept., Oct., Nov., Dec. Journals paginated by volume or issue need only the year (in parentheses).
- **PAGES**: If an article does not fall on consecutive pages, give the first page with a plus sign (55+).

21. ARTICLE IN A JOURNAL

Author's Last Name, First Name. "Title of Article." *Title of Journal*
   Volume.Issue (Year): Pages. Medium.

Cooney, Brian C. "Considering *Robinson Crusoe*'s 'Liberty of Conscience'
   in an Age of Terror." *College English* 69.3 (2007): 197–215. Print.

22. ARTICLE IN A JOURNAL NUMBERED BY ISSUE

Author's Last Name, First Name. "Title of Article." *Title of Journal*
   Issue (Year): Pages. Medium.

Flynn, Kevin. "The Railway in Canadian Poetry." *Canadian Literature* 174
   (2002): 70–95. Print.

23. ARTICLE IN A MAGAZINE

Author's Last Name, First Name. "Title of Article." *Title of Magazine*
   Day Month Year: Pages. Medium.

Walsh, Bryan. "Not a Watt to Be Wasted." *Time* 17 Mar. 2008: 46–47. Print.

Documentation Map (MLA)
Article in a Print Journal

Title of article →

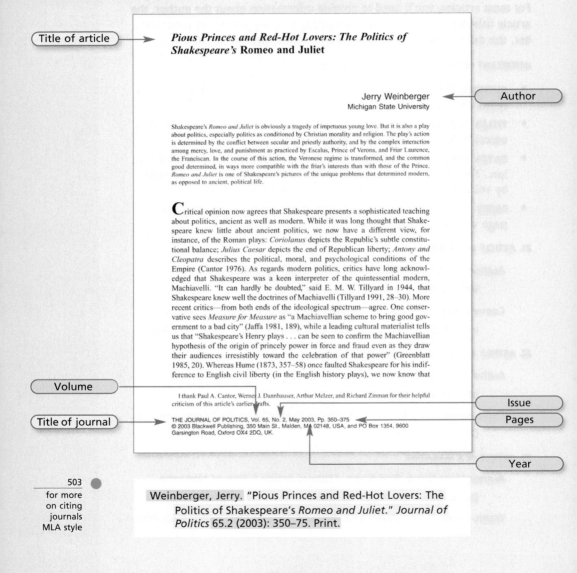

Pious Princes and Red-Hot Lovers: The Politics of Shakespeare's Romeo and Juliet

Jerry Weinberger
Michigan State University

← Author

Shakespeare's *Romeo and Juliet* is obviously a tragedy of impetuous young love. But it is also a play about politics, especially politics as conditioned by Christian morality and religion. The play's action is determined by the conflict between secular and priestly authority, and by the complex interaction among mercy, love, and punishment as practiced by Escalus, Prince of Verona, and Friar Laurence, the Franciscan. In the course of this action, the Veronese regime is transformed, and the common good determined, in ways more compatible with the friar's interests than with those of the Prince. *Romeo and Juliet* is one of Shakespeare's pictures of the unique problems that determined modern, as opposed to ancient, political life.

Critical opinion now agrees that Shakespeare presents a sophisticated teaching about politics, ancient as well as modern. While it was long thought that Shakespeare knew little about ancient politics, we now have a different view, for instance, of the Roman plays: *Coriolanus* depicts the Republic's subtle constitutional balance; *Julius Caesar* depicts the end of Republican liberty; *Antony and Cleopatra* describes the political, moral, and psychological conditions of the Empire (Cantor 1976). As regards modern politics, critics have long acknowledged that Shakespeare was a keen interpreter of the quintessential modern, Machiavelli. "It can hardly be doubted," said E. M. W. Tillyard in 1944, that Shakespeare knew well the doctrines of Machiavelli (Tillyard 1991, 28–30). More recent critics—from both ends of the ideological spectrum—agree. One conservative sees *Measure for Measure* as "a Machiavellian scheme to bring good government to a bad city" (Jaffa 1981, 189), while a leading cultural materialist tells us that "Shakespeare's Henry plays . . . can be seen to confirm the Machiavellian hypothesis of the origin of princely power in force and fraud even as they draw their audiences irresistibly toward the celebration of that power" (Greenblatt 1985, 20). Whereas Hume (1873, 357–58) once faulted Shakespeare for his indifference to English civil liberty (in the English history plays), we now know that

I thank Paul A. Cantor, Werner J. Dannhauser, Arthur Melzer, and Richard Zinman for their helpful criticism of this article's earlier drafts.

THE JOURNAL OF POLITICS, Vol. 65, No. 2, May 2003, Pp. 350–375
© 2003 Blackwell Publishing, 350 Main St., Malden, MA 02148, USA, and PO Box 1354, 9600
Garsington Road, Oxford OX4 2DQ, UK.

Volume

Title of journal →

Issue

Pages

Year

503
for more
on citing
journals
MLA style

Weinberger, Jerry. "Pious Princes and Red-Hot Lovers: The Politics of Shakespeare's *Romeo and Juliet*." *Journal of Politics* 65.2 (2003): 350–75. Print.

author   title   publication

Documentation Map (MLA)
Article in a Print Magazine

Title of article →

PERSPECTIVES
Essays by leading thinkers
in celebration of the dog

The Wolf in Your Dog

Author → By Michael W. Fox, DVM, PhD

Though in their deep heart's core, there is a commonality of origin, spirit, emotional intelligence and empathetic sensibility, the wild wolf looks through us, while the dog looks to us.

OF ALL THE MYRIAD MEMBERS OF THE ANIMAL KINGDOM, the domesticated dog (*Canis lupus familiaris*) is closest to us. With individual exceptions in other species, this canine species is the most understanding, if not also the most observant, of human behavior—of our actions and intentions. This is why dogs are so responsive to us, even mirroring or mimicking our behavior. And it is why dogs are so trainable.

Fear in unsocialized and abused dogs interferes with their attentiveness to and interpretation of human behavior and intentions. This is one reason wild species like the coyote and wolf, even when born and raised in captivity, are difficult to train. The wolf "Tiny," whom I bottle-raised and intensely socialized during her formative early days, never really lost her fear and distrust of strangers.

Tiny did not start mirroring human behavior until she was close to nine years old. At this point, she began to mimic the human-to-human greeting grin, revealing her front teeth as she curled her lips into a snarly smile. In my experience, dogs

who can do this do so at a much earlier age, even as early as four to six months.

In comparing socialized (human-bonded) wolves and dogs in terms of how they have related to me as well as to my family members, friends and strangers, I would say that the main difference between the two species is the fear factor. Differences in trainability hinge on this; as I theorize in my new book (*Dog Body, Dog Mind*), domestication has altered the tuning of the dog's adrenal and autonomic nervous systems. This tuning (which dampens adrenal fright, flight and fight reactions and possibly alters brain serotonin levels), is accomplished through selective breeding for docility, and by gentle handling during the critical period for socialization. According to the earlier research of my mentors—Drs. John Paul Scott and John L. Fuller of the Jackson Laboratory in Bar Harbor, Maine—pups with no human contact during this critical socialization period (which ends around 12 to 16 weeks of age) are wild and unapproachable.

Title of magazine →
Page →
Month and year → Mar/Apr 2008 | **Bark** 85

503, 506
for more
on citing
magazines
MLA style

Fox, Michael W. "The Wolf in Your Dog." *Bark* Mar.–Apr. 2008: 85–87. Print.

For a monthly magazine, include only the month and year.

> Fellman, Bruce. "Leading the Libraries." *Yale Alumni Magazine* Feb.
> 2002: 26–31. Print.

24. ARTICLE IN A DAILY NEWSPAPER

> Author's Last Name, First Name. "Title of Article." *Name of Newspaper*
> Day Month Year: Pages. Medium.

> Springer, Shira. "Celtics Reserves Are Whizzes vs. Wizards." *Boston Globe*
> 14 Mar. 2005: D4+. Print.

If you are citing a particular edition of a newspaper, list the edition (late ed., natl. ed., etc.) after the date. If a section is not identified by a letter or number, put the name of the section after the edition information.

> Burns, John F., and Miguel Helft. "Under Pressure, YouTube Withdraws
> Muslim Cleric's Videos." *New York Times* 4 Nov. 2010, late ed., sec.
> 1: 13. Print.

25. UNSIGNED ARTICLE

> "Title of Article." *Name of Publication* Day Month Year: Pages Medium.

> "Being Invisible Closer to Reality." *Atlanta Journal-Constitution* 11 Aug.
> 2008: A3. Print.

26. EDITORIAL

> "Title." Editorial. *Name of Publication* Day Month Year: Page. Medium.

> "Gas, Cigarettes Are Safe to Tax." Editorial. *Lakeville Journal* 17 Feb.
> 2005: A10. Print.

27. LETTER TO THE EDITOR

> Author's Last Name, First Name. "Title (if any)." Letter. *Name of*
> *Publication* Day Month Year: Page. Medium.

> Festa, Roger. "Social Security: Another Phony Crisis." Letter. *Lakeville*
> *Journal* 17 Feb. 2005: A10. Print.

author   title   publication

28. REVIEW

> Reviewer's Last Name, First Name. "Title (if any) of Review." Rev. of *Title of Work*, by Author's First and Last Names. *Title of Periodical* Day Month Year: Pages. Medium.

Frank, Jeffrey. "Body Count." Rev. of *The Exception*, by Christian Jungersen. *New Yorker* 30 July 2007: 86–87. Print.

Online Sources

Not every online source gives you all the data that MLA would like to see in a works-cited entry. Ideally, you will be able to list the author's name, the title, information about any print publication, information about electronic publication (title of site, editor, date of first electronic publication and/or most recent revision, name of the publisher or sponsoring institution), the publication medium, the date of access, and, if necessary, a URL.

IMPORTANT DETAILS FOR CITING ONLINE SOURCES

- **AUTHORS OR EDITORS AND TITLES**: Format authors and titles as you would for a print book or periodical.
- **PUBLISHER**: If the name of the publisher or sponsoring institution is unavailable, use *N.p.*
- **DATES**: Abbreviate the months as you would for a print periodical. Although MLA asks for the date when materials were first posted or most recently updated, you won't always be able to find that information; if it's unavailable, use *n.d.* Be sure to include the date on which you accessed the source.
- **PAGES**: If the citation calls for page numbers but the source is unpaginated, use *n. pag.* in place of page numbers.
- **MEDIUM**: Indicate the medium—Web, Email, Tweet, and so on.

- **URL:** MLA assumes that readers can locate most sources on the Web by searching for the author, title, or other identifying information, so they don't require a URL for most online sources. When users can't locate the source without a URL, give the address of the website in angle brackets. When a URL won't fit on one line, break it only after a slash (and do not add a hyphen). If a URL is very long, consider giving the URL of the site's home or search page instead.

29. ENTIRE WEBSITE

For websites with an editor, compiler, director, narrator, or translator, follow the name with the appropriate abbreviation (*ed.*, *comp.*).

> Author's Last Name, First Name. *Title of Site*. Publisher or Sponsoring
>> Institution, Date posted or last updated. Medium. Day Month Year
>> of access.

> Zalta, Edward N., ed. *Stanford Encyclopedia of Philosophy*. Metaphysics
>> Research Lab, Center for the Study of Language and Information,
>> Stanford U, 2007. Web. 14 Nov. 2012.

PERSONAL WEBSITE

> Author's Last Name, First Name. Home page. Sponsor, Date posted or last
>> updated. Medium. Day Month Year of access.

> Nunberg, Geoffrey. Home page. School of Information, U of California,
>> Berkeley, 2009. Web. 13 Apr. 2012.

30. WORK FROM A WEBSITE

> Author's Last Name, First Name. "Title of Work." *Title of Site.*
>> Ed. Editor's First and Last Names. Sponsor, Date posted or last
>> updated. Medium. Day Month Year of access.

> Buff, Rachel Ida. "Becoming American." *Immigration History Research
>> Center*. U of Minnesota, 24 Mar. 2008. Web. 4 Apr. 2012.

Documentation Map (MLA)
Work from a Website

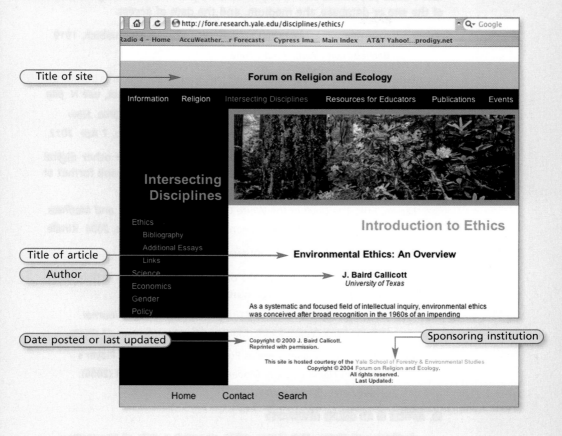

Title of site → Forum on Religion and Ecology

Title of article → Environmental Ethics: An Overview

Author → J. Baird Callicott

Date posted or last updated →

Sponsoring institution →

507–8
for more
on citing
websites
MLA style

Callicott, J. Baird. "Environmental Ethics: An Overview." *Forum on Religion and Ecology*. Yale School of Forestry & Environmental Studies, 2000. Web. 17 Sept. 2012.

31. ONLINE BOOK OR PART OF A BOOK

Cite a book you access online as you would a print book, adding the name of the site or database, the medium, and the date of access.

> Anderson, Sherwood. *Winesburg, Ohio*. New York: B. W. Huebsch, 1919. *Bartleby.com*. Web. 7 Apr. 2012.

If you are citing a part of a book, put the part in quotation marks before the book title. If the online book is paginated, give the pages; if not, use *N. pag*.

> Anderson, Sherwood. "The Strength of God." *Winesburg, Ohio*. New York: B. W. Huebsch, 1919. N. pag. *Bartleby.com*. Web. 7 Apr. 2012.

To cite a book you've downloaded onto a Kindle, Nook, or other digital device, follow the setup for a print book, but indicate the ebook format at the end of your citation.

> Larson, Erik. *The Devil in the White City: Murder, Mayhem, and Madness at the Fair That Changed America*. New York: Vintage, 2004. Kindle.

32. ARTICLE IN AN ONLINE SCHOLARLY JOURNAL

If a journal does not number pages or if it numbers each article separately, use *n. pag.* in place of page numbers.

> Author's Last Name, First Name. "Title of Article." *Title of Journal* Volume.Issue (Year): Pages. Medium. Day Month Year of access.

> Gleckman, Jason. "Shakespeare as Poet or Playwright? The Player's Speech in *Hamlet*." *Early Modern Literary Studies* 11.3 (2006): n. pag. Web. 24 June 2012.

33. ARTICLE IN AN ONLINE NEWSPAPER

> Author's Last Name, First Name. "Title of Article." *Title of Newspaper*. Publisher, Day Month Year. Medium. Day Month Year of access.

> Banerjee, Neela. "Proposed Religion-Based Program for Federal Inmates Is Canceled." *New York Times*. New York Times, 28 Oct. 2006. Web. 24 June 2012.

author   title   publication

34. ARTICLE IN AN ONLINE MAGAZINE

Author's Last Name, First Name. "Title of Article." *Title of Magazine*.
Publisher, Date of publication. Medium. Day Month Year of access.

Lithwick, Dahlia. "Privacy Rights Inc." *Slate*. Washington Post–Newsweek
Interactive, 14 Oct. 2010. Web. 25 Oct. 2012.

35. BLOG ENTRY

Author's Last Name, First Name. "Title of Entry." *Title of Blog*. Sponsor,
Day Month Year posted. Medium. Day Month Year of access.

Gladwell, Malcolm. "Enron and Newspapers." *Gladwell.com*. N.p., 4 Jan.
2007. Web. 26 Aug. 2012.

If the entry has no title, use "Blog entry" without quotation marks. Cite a
whole blog as you would an entire website (see no. 29). If the publisher or
sponsor is unavailable, use *N.p.*

36. ARTICLE ACCESSED THROUGH A DATABASE

For articles accessed through a library's subscription services, such as Info-
Trac and EBSCOhost, cite the publication information for the source, followed by the name of the database.

Author's Last Name, First Name. "Title of Article." *Title of Periodical* Date
or Volume.Issue (Year): Pages. *Database*. Medium. Day Month Year
of access.

Stalter, Sunny. "Subway Ride and Subway System in Hart Crane's
'The Tunnel.'" *Journal of Modern Literature* 33.2 (2010): 70–91.
Academic Search Complete. Web. 28 May 2012.

37. ONLINE EDITORIAL

"Title of Editorial." Editorial. *Title of Site*. Publisher, Day Month Year of
publication. Medium. Day Month Year of access.

"Keep Drinking Age at 21." Editorial. *ChicagoTribune.com*. Chicago
Tribune, 26 Aug. 2008. Web. 28 Aug. 2012.

Documentation Map (MLA)
Article Accessed through a Database

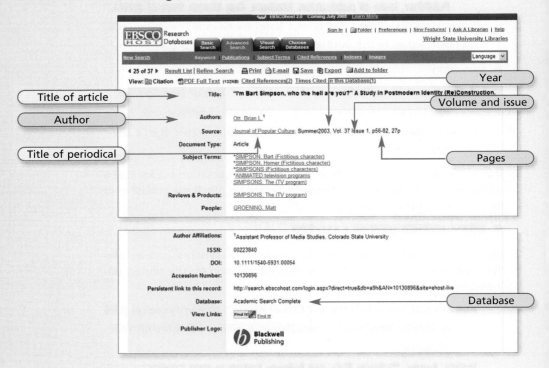

511
for more
on citing an
article in a
database
MLA style

Ott, Brian L. "'I'm Bart Simpson, Who the Hell Are You?' A Study in
Postmodern Identity (Re)Construction." *Journal of Popular Culture*
37.1 (2003): 56–82. *Academic Search Complete*. Web. 24 Mar. 2012.

author   title   publication

38. ONLINE FILM REVIEW

Reviewer's Last Name, First Name. "Title of Review." Rev. of *Title of Work*, dir. First and Last Names. *Title of Site*. Publisher, Day Month Year posted. Medium. Day Month Year of access.

Edelstein, David. "Best Served Cold." Rev. of *The Social Network*, dir. David Fincher. *New York Magazine*. New York Media, 1 Oct. 2010. Web. 3 Nov. 2012.

39. EMAIL

Writer's Last Name, First Name. "Subject Line." Message to the author. Day Month Year of message. Medium.

Smith, William. "Teaching Grammar—Some Thoughts." Message to the author. 19 Nov. 2012. Email.

40. POSTING TO AN ONLINE FORUM

Writer's Last Name, First Name. "Title of Posting." *Name of Forum*. Sponsor, Day Month Year of posting. Medium. Day Month Year of access.

Mintz, Stephen H. "Manumission During the Revolution." *H-Net List on Slavery*. Michigan State U, 14 Sept. 2006. Web. 18 Apr. 2012.

41. ARTICLE IN AN ONLINE REFERENCE WORK

"Title of Article." *Title of Reference Work*. Sponsor, Date of work. Medium. Day Month Year of access.

"Dubai." *MSN Encarta*. Microsoft Corporation, 2008. Web. 20 June 2012.

42. WIKI ENTRY

"Title of Entry." *Title of Wiki*. Sponsor, Day Month Year updated. Medium. Day Month Year of access.

"Pi." *Wikipedia*. Wikimedia Foundation, 28 Aug. 2008. Web. 2 Sept. 2012.

43. PODCAST

Performer or Host's Last Name, First Name. "Title of Podcast." Host Host's First and Last Name. *Title of Program*. Sponsor, Day Month Year posted. Medium. Day Month Year of access.

Blumberg, Alex, and Adam Davidson. "The Giant Pool of Money." Host Ira Glass. *This American Life*. Chicago Public Radio, 9 May 2008. Web. 18 Sept. 2012.

44. TWEET

Author's Last Name, First Name (User Name). "Full text of tweet." Day Month Year, Time. Medium.

Stern, Michael (Roadfood123). "Ice creamorama: Dr. Mike's is now open weekdays." 21 Mar. 2012, 5:21 p.m. Tweet.

Other Kinds of Sources

Many of the sources in this section can be found online, and you'll find examples here for how to cite them. If there is no Web model here, start with the guidelines most appropriate for the source you need to cite, omit the original medium, and end your citation with the title of the website, italicized; the medium (Web); and the day, month, and year of access.

45. ADVERTISEMENT

Product or Company. Advertisement. *Title of Periodical* Date or Volume.Issue (Year): Page. Medium.

Empire BlueCross BlueShield. Advertisement. *Fortune* 8 Dec. 2012: 208. Print.

ADVERTISEMENT ON THE WEB

Rolex. Advertisement. *Time*. Time, n.d. Web. 1 Apr. 2012.

46. ART

> Artist's Last Name, First Name. *Title of Art*. Medium. Year. Institution, City.

Van Gogh, Vincent. *The Potato Eaters*. Oil on canvas. 1885. Van Gogh
  Museum, Amsterdam.

ART ON THE WEB

Warhol, Andy. *Self-Portrait*. 1979. J. Paul Getty Museum, Los Angeles.
  The Getty. Web. 29 Mar. 2012.

Cite photographs you find online by giving the photographer, title, and
date of the image, if available. If the date is unavailable, use *n.d.* For photographs you take yourself, see no. 65.

Donnell, Ryan. At a *Pre-Civil War Railroad Construction Site Outside of
  Philadelphia*. 2010. Smithsonian Institution. Smithsonian.com. Web.
  3 Nov. 2012.

47. CARTOON

> Artist's Last Name, First Name. "Title of Cartoon (if titled)." Cartoon. *Title
> of Periodical* Date or Volume.Issue (Year): Page. Medium.

Chast, Roz. "The Three Wise Men of Thanksgiving." Cartoon. *New Yorker*
  1 Dec. 2003: 174. Print.

CARTOON ON THE WEB

Horsey, David. Cartoon. *Seattle Post-Intelligencer*. Seattle Post-Intelligencer,
  20 Apr. 2012. Web. 21 Apr. 2012.

48. DISSERTATION

Treat a published dissertation as you would a book, but after its title, add
the abbreviation *Diss.*, the institution, and the date of the dissertation.

> Author's Last Name, First Name. *Title*. Diss. Institution, Year.
>   Publication City: Publisher, Year. Medium.

Goggin, Peter N. *A New Literacy Map of Research and Scholarship in Computers and Writing*. Diss. Indiana U of Pennsylvania, 2000. Ann Arbor: UMI, 2001. Print.

For unpublished dissertations, put the title in quotation marks and end with the degree-granting institution and the year.

Kim, Loel. "Students Respond to Teacher Comments: A Comparison of Online Written and Voice Modalities." Diss. Carnegie Mellon U, 1998. Print.

49. CD-ROM OR DVD-ROM

Title. Any pertinent information about the edition, release, or version. Publication City: Publisher, Year of publication. Medium.

Othello. Princeton: Films for the Humanities and Sciences, 1998. CD-ROM.

If you are citing only part of the CD-ROM or DVD-ROM, name the part as you would a part of a book.

"Snow Leopard." *Encarta Encyclopedia 2007*. Seattle: Microsoft, 2007. CD-ROM.

50. FILM, DVD, OR VIDEO CLIP

Title. Dir. Director's First and Last Names. Perf. Lead Actors' First and Last Names. Distributor, Year of release. Medium.

Casablanca. Dir. Michael Curtiz. Perf. Humphrey Bogart, Ingrid Bergman, and Claude Rains. Warner, 1942. Film.

To cite a particular person's work, start with that name.

Cody, Diablo, scr. *Juno*. Dir. Jason Reitman. Perf. Ellen Page, Michael Cera, Jennifer Garner, and Jason Bateman. Fox Searchlight, 2007. DVD.

author　　　　title　　　publication

Cite a video clip as you would a short work from a website.

> Director's Last Name, First Name, dir. "Title of Video." *Title of Site.*
> Sponsor, Day Month Year of release. Medium. Day Month
> Year of access.

> PivotMasterDX, dir. "Bounce!" *YouTube*. YouTube, 14 June 2008. Web.
> 21 June 2012.

51. BROADCAST INTERVIEW

> Subject's Last Name, First Name. Interview. *Title of Program*. Network.
> Station, City. Day Month Year. Medium.

> Gates, Henry Louis, Jr. Interview. *Fresh Air*. NPR. WNYC, New York.
> 9 Apr. 2002. Radio.

52. PUBLISHED INTERVIEW

> Subject's Last Name, First Name. Interview, or "Title of Interview." *Title
> of Periodical* Date or Volume.Issue (Year): Pages. Medium.

> Stone, Oliver. Interview. *Esquire* Nov. 2004: 170. Print.

53. PERSONAL INTERVIEW

> Subject's Last Name, First Name. Personal interview. Day Month Year.

> Roddick, Andy. Personal interview. 17 Aug. 2012.

54. UNPUBLISHED LETTER

For medium, use MS for a hand-written letter and TS for a typed one.

> Author's Last Name, First Name. Letter to the author. Day Month Year.
> Medium.

> Quindlen, Anna. Letter to the author. 11 Apr. 2012. MS.

55. PUBLISHED LETTER

Letter Writer's Last Name, First Name. Letter to First and Last Names.
Day Month Year of letter. *Title of Book*. Ed. Editor's First and
Last Names. City: Publisher, Year of publication. Pages. Medium.

White, E. B. Letter to Carol Angell. 28 May 1970. *Letters of E. B. White*.
Ed. Dorothy Lobarno Guth. New York: Harper, 1976. 600. Print.

56. MAP OR CHART

Title of Map. Map. City: Publisher, Year of publication. Medium.

Toscana. Map. Milan: Touring Club Italiano, 1987. Print.

MAP ON THE WEB

"Portland, Oregon." Map. *Google Maps*. Google, 25 Apr. 2012. Web.
25 Apr. 2012.

57. MUSICAL SCORE

Composer's Last Name, First Name. *Title of Composition*. Year of
composition. Publication City: Publisher, Year of publication.
Medium. Series Information (if any).

Beethoven, Ludwig van. *String Quartet No. 13 in B Flat, Op. 130*. 1825.
New York: Dover, 1970. Print.

58. SOUND RECORDING

Artist's Last Name, First Name. *Title of Long Work*. Other pertinent
details about the artists. Manufacturer, Year of release. Medium.

Beethoven, Ludwig van. *Missa Solemnis*. Perf. Westminster Choir and
New York Philharmonic. Cond. Leonard Bernstein. Sony, 1992. CD.

Whether you list the composer, conductor, or performer first depends on where you want to place the emphasis. If you are citing a specific song, put it in quotation marks before the name of the recording.

> Brown, Greg. "Canned Goods." *The Live One*. Red House, 1995. MP3 file.

For a spoken-word recording, you may begin with the writer, speaker, or producer, depending on your emphasis.

> Dale, Jim, narr. *Harry Potter and the Deathly Hallows*. By J. K. Rowling. Random House Audio, 2007. CD.

59. ORAL PRESENTATION

> Speaker's Last Name, First Name. "Title of Presentation." Sponsoring Institution. Site, City. Day Month Year. Medium.

> Cassin, Michael. "Nature in the Raw—The Art of Landscape Painting." Berkshire Institute for Lifetime Learning. Clark Art Institute, Williamstown. 24 Mar. 2005. Lecture.

60. PAPER FROM PROCEEDINGS OF A CONFERENCE

> Author's Last Name, First Name. "Title of Paper." *Title of Conference Proceedings*. Date, City. Ed. Editor's First and Last Names. Publication City: Publisher, Year. Pages. Medium.

> Zolotow, Charlotte. "Passion in Publishing." *A Sea of Upturned Faces: Proceedings of the Third Pacific Rim Conference on Children's Literature*. 1986, Los Angeles. Ed. Winifred Ragsdale. Metuchen: Scarecrow P, 1989. 236–49. Print.

61. PERFORMANCE

> *Title*. By Author's First and Last Names. Other appropriate details about the performance. Site, City. Day Month Year. Medium.

Take Me Out. By Richard Greenberg. Dir. Scott Plate. Perf. Caleb Sekeres. Dobama Theatre, Cleveland. 17 Aug. 2007. Performance.

62. TELEVISION OR RADIO PROGRAM

"Title of Episode." *Title of Program*. Other appropriate information about the writer, director, actors, etc. Network. Station, City, Day Month Year of broadcast. Medium.

"The Silencer." *Criminal Minds*. Writ. Erica Messer. Dir. Glenn Kershaw. NBC. WCNC, Charlotte, 26 Sept. 2012. Television.

TELEVISION OR RADIO ON THE WEB

"Bush's War." *Frontline*. Writ. and Dir. Michael Kirk. PBS, 24 Mar. 2008. *PBS.org*. Web. 10 May 2012.

63. PAMPHLET, BROCHURE, OR PRESS RELEASE

Author's Last Name, First Name. *Title of Publication*. Publication City: Publisher, Year. Medium.

Bowers, Catherine. *Can We Find a Home Here? Answering Questions of Interfaith Couples*. Boston: UUA Publications, n.d. Print.

To cite a press release, include the day and month before the year.

64. LEGAL SOURCE

The name of a court case is not italicized in a works-cited entry.

Names of the First Plaintiff v. First Defendant. Volume Name Page numbers of law report. Name of Court. Year of decision. Source information for medium consulted.

District of Columbia v. Heller. 540 US 290. Supreme Court of the US. 2008. *Supreme Court Collection*. Legal Information Inst., Cornell U Law School, n.d. Web. 18 Mar. 2012.

For acts of law, include both the Public Law number and the Statutes at Large volume and page numbers.

> Name of Law. Public law number. Statutes at Large Volume Stat. Pages. Day Month Year enacted. Medium.

> Military Commissions Act. Pub. L. 109-366. 120 Stat. 2083–2521. 17 Oct. 2006. Print.

65. MP3, JPEG, PDF, OR OTHER DIGITAL FILE

For downloaded songs, photographs, PDFs, and other documents stored on your computer or another digital device, follow the guidelines for the type of work you are citing (art, journal article, and so on) and give the file type as the medium.

> Talking Heads. "Burning Down the House." *Speaking in Tongues*. Sire, 1983. Digital file.

> Taylor, Aaron. "Twilight of the Idols: Performance, Melodramatic Villainy, and *Sunset Boulevard*." *Journal of Film and Video* 59 (2007): 13–31. PDF file.

Citing Sources Not Covered by MLA

To cite a source for which MLA does not provide guidelines, look for models similar to the source you are citing. Give any information readers will need in order to find your source themselves — author; title, subtitle; publisher and / or sponsor; medium; dates; and any other pertinent information. You might want to try out your citation yourself, to be sure it will lead others to your source.

FORMATTING A PAPER

Name, course, title.   MLA does not require a separate title page. In the upper left-hand corner of your first page, include your name, your professor's name, the name of the course, and the date. Center the title of your paper on the line after the date; capitalize it as you would a book title.

Page numbers. In the upper right-hand corner of each page, one-half inch below the top of the page, include your last name and the page number. Number pages consecutively throughout your paper.

Font, spacing, margins, and indents. Choose a font that is easy to read (such as Times New Roman) and provides a clear contrast between regular and italic text. Double-space the entire paper, including your works-cited list. Set one-inch margins at the top, bottom, and sides of your text; do not justify your text. The first line of each paragraph should be indented one-half inch from the left margin.

Long quotations. When quoting more than three lines of poetry, more than four lines of prose, or dialogue between characters in a drama, set off the quotation in the rest of your text, indenting it one inch (or ten spaces) from the left margin. Do not use quotation marks, and put any parenthetical documentation *after* the final punctuation.

> In *Eastward to Tartary*, Kaplan captures ancient and contemporary Antioch for us:
>
> > At the height of its glory in the Roman-Byzantine age, when it had an amphitheater, public baths, aqueducts, and sewage pipes, half a million people lived in Antioch. Today the population is only 125,000. With sour relations between Turkey and Syria, and unstable politics throughout the Middle East, Antioch is now a backwater—seedy and tumbledown, with relatively few tourists. I found it altogether charming. (123)

> In the first stanza of Arnold's "Dover Beach," the exclamations make clear that the speaker is addressing someone who is also present in the scene:
>
> > Come to the window, sweet is the night air!
> > Only, from the long line of spray
> > Where the sea meets the moon-blanched land,
> > Listen! You hear the grating roar
> > Of pebbles which the waves draw back, and fling. (6–10)

Illustrations.   Insert illustrations in your paper close to the text that discusses them. For tables, provide a number (Table 1) and a title on separate lines above the table. Below the table, include a caption and provide information about the source. For figures (graphs, charts, photos, and so on), provide a figure number (Fig. 1), caption, and source information below the figure. If you give only brief information about the source (such as a parenthetical citation), or if the source is cited elsewhere in your text, include it in your list of works cited. Be sure to discuss any illustrations, and make it clear how they relate to the rest of your text.

List of Works Cited.   Start your list on a new page, following any notes. Center the title and double-space the entire list. Each entry should begin at the left margin, and subsequent lines should be indented one-half inch (or five spaces). Alphabetize the list by authors' last names (or by editors' or translators' names, if appropriate). Alphabetize works that have no identifiable author or editor by title, disregarding A, An, and The. If you cite more than one work by a single author, list them all alphabetically by title, and use three hyphens in place of the author's name after the first entry (see no. 2 on p. 495).

SAMPLE RESEARCH PAPER

Dylan Borchers wrote the following report for a first-year writing course. It is formatted according to the guidelines of the *MLA Handbook for Writers of Research Papers,* 7th edition (2009). While the MLA guidelines are used widely in literature and other disciplines in the humanities, exact documentation requirements may vary across disciplines and courses. If you're unsure about what your instructor wants, ask for clarification.

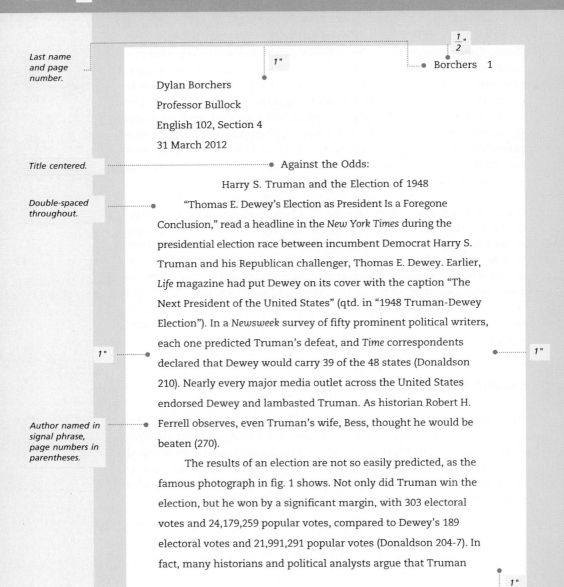

Last name and page number.

½"

Borchers   1

1"

Dylan Borchers

Professor Bullock

English 102, Section 4

31 March 2012

Title centered.

Against the Odds:

Harry S. Truman and the Election of 1948

Double-spaced throughout.

"Thomas E. Dewey's Election as President Is a Foregone

Conclusion," read a headline in the *New York Times* during the

presidential election race between incumbent Democrat Harry S.

Truman and his Republican challenger, Thomas E. Dewey. Earlier,

Life magazine had put Dewey on its cover with the caption "The

Next President of the United States" (qtd. in "1948 Truman-Dewey

Election"). In a *Newsweek* survey of fifty prominent political writers,

each one predicted Truman's defeat, and *Time* correspondents

1"   1"

declared that Dewey would carry 39 of the 48 states (Donaldson

210). Nearly every major media outlet across the United States

endorsed Dewey and lambasted Truman. As historian Robert H.

Author named in signal phrase, page numbers in parentheses.

Ferrell observes, even Truman's wife, Bess, thought he would be

beaten (270).

The results of an election are not so easily predicted, as the

famous photograph in fig. 1 shows. Not only did Truman win the

election, but he won by a significant margin, with 303 electoral

votes and 24,179,259 popular votes, compared to Dewey's 189

electoral votes and 21,991,291 popular votes (Donaldson 204-7). In

fact, many historians and political analysts argue that Truman

1"

Borchers   2

Fig. 1. President Harry S. Truman holds up an Election Day edition of the *Chicago Daily Tribune*, which mistakenly announced "Dewey Defeats Truman." St. Louis, 4 Nov. 1948 (Rollins).

Illustration close to the text to which it relates. Figure number, caption, and parenthetical source citation included.

would have won by an even greater margin had third-party Progressive candidate Henry A. Wallace not split the Democratic vote in New York State and Dixiecrat Strom Thurmond not won four states in the South (McCullough 711). Although Truman's defeat was heavily predicted, those predictions themselves, Dewey's passiveness as a campaigner, and Truman's zeal turned the tide for a Truman victory.

    In the months preceding the election, public opinion polls predicted that Dewey would win by a large margin. Pollster Elmo Roper stopped polling in September, believing there was no reason to continue, given a seemingly inevitable Dewey landslide. Although the margin narrowed as the election drew near, the other

Paragraphs indent $\frac{1}{2}$ inch or 5 spaces.

No signal phrase; author and page number in parentheses.

pollsters predicted a Dewey win by at least 5 percent (Donaldson 209). Many historians believe that these predictions aided the president in the long run. First, surveys showing Dewey in the lead may have prompted some of Dewey's supporters to feel overconfident about their candidate's chances and therefore to stay home from the polls on Election Day. Second, these same surveys may have energized Democrats to mount late get-out-the-vote efforts ("1948 Truman-Dewey Election"). Other analysts believe that the overwhelming predictions of a Truman loss also kept at home some Democrats who approved of Truman's policies but saw a Truman loss as inevitable. According to political analyst Samuel Lubell, those Democrats may have saved Dewey from an even greater

Text quoted in another source.

defeat (qtd. in Hamby, *Man of the People* 465). Whatever the impact on the voters, the polling numbers had a decided effect on Dewey.

Historians and political analysts alike cite Dewey's overly cautious campaign as one of the main reasons Truman was able to achieve victory. Dewey firmly believed in public opinion polls. With all indications pointing to an easy victory, Dewey and his staff believed that all he had to do was bide his time and make no foolish mistakes. Dewey himself said, "When you're leading, don't talk" (qtd. in McCullough 672). Each of Dewey's speeches was well-crafted and well-rehearsed. As the leader in the race, he kept his remarks faultlessly positive, with the result that he failed to deliver a solid message or even mention Truman or any of Truman's policies. Eventually, Dewey began to be perceived as aloof and stuffy. One

Borchers   4

observer compared him to the plastic groom on top of a wedding cake (Hamby, "Harry S. Truman"), and others noted his stiff, cold demeanor (McCullough 671–74).

Two or more works cited closely together.

As his campaign continued, observers noted that Dewey seemed uncomfortable in crowds, unable to connect with ordinary people. And he made a number of blunders. One took place at a train stop when the candidate, commenting on the number of children in the crowd, said he was glad they had been let out of school for his arrival. Unfortunately for Dewey, it was a Saturday ("1948: The Great Truman Surprise"). Such gaffes gave voters the feeling that Dewey was out of touch with the public.

Again and again through the autumn of 1948, Dewey's campaign speeches failed to address the issues, with the candidate declaring that he did not want to "get down in the gutter" (qtd. in McCullough 701). When told by fellow Republicans that he was losing ground, Dewey insisted that his campaign not alter its course. Even *Time* magazine, though it endorsed and praised him, conceded that his speeches were dull (McCullough 696). According to historian Zachary Karabell, they were "notable only for taking place, not for any specific message" (244). Dewey's numbers in the polls slipped in the weeks before the election, but he still held a comfortable lead over Truman. It would take Truman's famous whistle-stop campaign to make the difference.

Few candidates in U.S. history have campaigned for the presidency with more passion and faith than Harry Truman. In the autumn of 1948, he wrote to his sister, "It will be the greatest campaign any President ever made. Win, lose, or draw, people will know where I stand" (91). For thirty-three days, Truman traveled the nation, giving hundreds of speeches from the back of the *Ferdinand Magellan* railroad car. In the same letter, he described the pace: "We made about 140 stops and I spoke over 147 times, shook hands with at least 30,000 and am in good condition to start out again tomorrow for Wilmington, Philadelphia, Jersey City, Newark, Albany and Buffalo" (91). McCullough writes of Truman's campaign:

Quotations of 4 or more lines indented 1 inch (10 spaces).

> No President in history had ever gone so far in quest of support from the people, or with less cause for the effort, to judge by informed opinion. . . . As a test of his skills and judgment as a professional politician, not to say his stamina and disposition at age sixty-four, it would be like no other experience in his long, often difficult career, as he himself understood perfectly. More than any other event in his public life, or in his presidency thus far, it would reveal the kind of man he was. (655)

Parenthetical reference after final punctuation.

He spoke in large cities and small towns, defending his policies and attacking Republicans. As a former farmer and relatively late bloomer, Truman was able to connect with the public. He developed an energetic style, usually speaking from notes rather than from a prepared speech, and often mingled with the crowds that met his train. These crowds grew larger as the campaign progressed. In Chicago, over half a million people lined the streets as he passed, and in St. Paul the crowd numbered over 25,000. When Dewey entered St. Paul two days later, he was greeted by only 7,000 supporters ("1948 Truman-Dewey Election"). Reporters brushed off the large crowds as mere curiosity seekers wanting to see a president (McCullough 682). Yet Truman persisted, even if he often seemed to be the only one who thought he could win. By going directly to the American people and connecting with them, Truman built the momentum needed to surpass Dewey and win the election.

Use the title if no author is given.

The legacy and lessons of Truman's whistle-stop campaign continue to be studied by political analysts, and politicians today often mimic his campaign methods by scheduling multiple visits to key states, as Truman did. He visited California, Illinois, and Ohio 48 times, compared with 6 visits to those states by Dewey. Political scientist Thomas M. Holbrook concludes that his strategic campaigning in those states and others gave Truman the electoral votes he needed to win (61, 65).

The 1948 election also had an effect on pollsters, who, as Elmo Roper admitted, "couldn't have been more wrong" (qtd. in Karabell 255). *Life* magazine's editors concluded that pollsters as well as reporters and commentators were too convinced of a Dewey victory to analyze the polls seriously, especially the opinions of undecided voters (Karabell 256). Pollsters assumed that undecided voters would vote in the same proportion as decided voters—and that turned out to be a false assumption (Karabell 258). In fact, the lopsidedness of the polls might have led voters who supported Truman to call themselves undecided out of an unwillingness to associate themselves with the losing side, further skewing the polls' results (McDonald, Glynn, Kim, and Ostman 152). Such errors led pollsters to change their methods significantly after the 1948 election.

Work by 4
authors.

After the election, many political analysts, journalists, and historians concluded that the Truman upset was in fact a victory for the American people, who, the *New Republic* noted, "couldn't be ticketed by the polls, knew its own mind and had picked the rather unlikely but courageous figure of Truman to carry its banner" (qtd. in McCullough 715). How "unlikely" is unclear, however; Truman biographer Alonzo Hamby notes that "polls of scholars consistently rank Truman among the top eight presidents in American history" (*Man of the People* 641). But despite Truman's high standing, and despite the fact that the whistle-stop campaign is now part of our political landscape, politicians have increasingly imitated the style of the Dewey campaign, with its "packaged candidate who ran so as not to lose, who steered clear of controversy, and who made a good show of appearing presidential" (Karabell 266). The election of 1948 shows that voters are not necessarily swayed by polls, but it may have presaged the packaging of candidates by public relations experts, to the detriment of public debate on the issues in future presidential elections.

1"   Borchers   8

Works Cited

Donaldson, Gary A. *Truman Defeats Dewey.* Lexington: UP of
    Kentucky, 1999. Print.

Ferrell, Robert H. *Harry S. Truman: A Life.* Columbia: U of Missouri P,
    1994. Print.

Hamby, Alonzo L., ed. "Harry S. Truman (1945–1953)." *American*
    President: A Reference Resource. Miller Center, U of Virginia,
    11 Jan. 2012. Web. 17 Mar. 2012.

—. *Man of the People: A Life of Harry S. Truman.* New York: Oxford UP,
    1995. Print.

Holbrook, Thomas M. "Did the Whistle-Stop Campaign Matter?" *PS:*
    Political Science and Politics 35.1 (2002): 59–66. Print.

Karabell, Zachary. *The Last Campaign: How Harry Truman Won the*
    1948 Election. New York: Knopf, 2000. Print.

McCullough, David. *Truman.* New York: Simon, 1992. Print.

McDonald, Daniel G., Carroll J. Glynn, Sei-Hill Kim, and Ronald E.
    Ostman. "The Spiral of Silence in the 1948 Presidential
    Election." *Communication Research* 28.2 (2001): 139–55. Print.

"1948: The Great Truman Surprise." *The Press and the Presidency.*
    Dept. of Political Science and International Affairs, Kennesaw
    State U, 29 Oct. 2003. Web. 20 Mar. 2012.

"1948 Truman-Dewey Election." *American Political History.* Eagleton
    Inst. of Politics, Rutgers, State U of New Jersey, 2012. Web. 19
    Mar. 2012.

Heading centered.

Double-spaced.

Alphabetized by authors' last names.

Each entry begins at the left margin; subsequent lines are indented.

Multiple works by a single author listed alphabetically by title.

Borchers   9

Rollins, Byron. Untitled photograph. "The First 150 Years: 1948." *AP History*. Associated Press, n.d. Web. 23 Mar. 2012.

Truman, Harry S. "Campaigning, Letter, October 5, 1948." *Harry S. Truman*. Ed. Robert H. Ferrell. Washington: CQ P, 2003. 91. Print.

Every source used is in the list of works cited.

APA Style 51

American Psychological Association (APA) style calls for (1) brief documentation in parentheses near each in-text citation and (2) complete documentation in a list of references at the end of your text. The models in this chapter draw on the *Publication Manual of the American Psychological Association*, 6th edition (2009). Additional information is available at <u>www.apastyle.org</u>.

A DIRECTORY TO APA STYLE

author   title   publication

Throughout this chapter, you'll find models and examples that are color-coded to help you see how writers include source information in their texts and reference lists: tan for author or editor, yellow for title, gray for pub-lication information: place of publication, publisher, date of publication, page number(s), and so on.

IN-TEXT DOCUMENTATION

Brief documentation in your text makes clear to your reader precisely what you took from a source and, in the case of a quotation, precisely where (usually, on which page) in the source you found the text you are quoting.

462–74 PARAPHRASES and SUMMARIES are more common than QUOTATIONS in APA-style projects. As you cite each source, you will need to decide whether to name the author in a signal phrase—"as McCullough (2001) wrote"—or in parentheses—"(McCullough, 2001)." Note that APA requires you to 471–74 use the past tense or present perfect tense for verbs in SIGNAL PHRASES: "Moss (2003) argued," "Moss (2003) has argued."

1. AUTHOR NAMED IN A SIGNAL PHRASE

If you are quoting, you must give the page number(s). You are not required to give the page number(s) with a paraphrase or a summary, but APA encourages you to do so, especially if you are citing a long or complex work; most of the models in this chapter do include page numbers.

AUTHOR QUOTED

Put the date in parentheses right after the author's name; put the page in parentheses as close to the quotation as possible.

> McCullough (2001) described John Adams as having "the hands of a man accustomed to pruning his own trees, cutting his own hay, and splitting his own firewood" (p. 18).

Notice that in this example, the parenthetical reference with the page number comes *after* the closing quotation marks but *before* the period at the end of the sentence.

AUTHOR PARAPHRASED OR SUMMARIZED

Put the date in parentheses right after the author's name; follow the date with the page.

John Adams's hands were those of a laborer, according to McCullough (2001, p. 18).

2. AUTHOR NAMED IN PARENTHESES

If you do not mention an author in a signal phrase, put his or her name, a comma, and the year of publication in parentheses as close as possible to the quotation, paraphrase, or summary.

AUTHOR QUOTED

Give the author, date, and page in one parenthesis, or split the information between two parentheses.

> One biographer (McCullough, 2001) has said John Adams had "the hands of a man accustomed to pruning his own trees, cutting his own hay, and splitting his own firewood" (p. 18).

AUTHOR PARAPHRASED OR SUMMARIZED

Give the author, date, and page in one parenthesis toward the beginning or the end of the paraphrase or summary.

> John Adams's hands were those of a laborer (McCullough, 2001, p. 18).

3. AUTHORS WITH THE SAME LAST NAME

If your reference list includes more than one person with the same last name, include initials in all documentation to distinguish the authors from one another.

> Eclecticism is common in contemporary criticism (J. M. Smith, 1992, p. vii).

4. TWO AUTHORS

Always mention both authors. Use *and* in a signal phrase, but use an ampersand (&) in parentheses. (See next page for examples.)

> Carlson and Ventura (1990) wanted to introduce Julio Cortázar, Marjorie Agosín, and other Latin American writers to an audience of English-speaking adolescents (p. v).

> According to the Peter Principle, "In a hierarchy, every employee tends to rise to his level of incompetence" (Peter & Hull, 1969, p. 26).

5. THREE OR MORE AUTHORS

In the first reference to a work by three to five persons, name all contributors. In subsequent references, name the first author followed by *et al.*, Latin for "and others." Whenever you refer to a work by six or more contributors, name only the first author, followed by *et al.* Use *and* in a signal phrase, but use an ampersand (&) in parentheses.

> Faigley, George, Palchik, and Selfe (2004) have argued that where there used to be a concept called *literacy*, today's multitude of new kinds of texts has given us *literacies* (p. xii).

> Peilen et al. (1990) supported their claims about corporate corruption with startling anecdotal evidence (p. 75).

6. ORGANIZATION OR GOVERNMENT AS AUTHOR

If an organization has a long name that is recognizable by its abbreviation, give the full name and the abbreviation the first time you cite the source. In subsequent citations, use only the abbreviation. If the organization does not have a familiar abbreviation, always use its full name.

FIRST CITATION

> (American Psychological Association [APA], 2008)

SUBSEQUENT CITATIONS

> (APA, 2008)

7. AUTHOR UNKNOWN

Use the complete title if it is short; if it is long, use the first few words of the title under which the work appears in the reference list.

> *Webster's New Biographical Dictionary* (1988) identifies William James as "American psychologist and philosopher" (p. 520).

> A powerful editorial asserted that healthy liver donor Mike Hurewitz died because of "frightening" faulty postoperative care ("Every Patient's Nightmare," 2007).

8. TWO OR MORE WORKS CITED TOGETHER

If you cite multiple works in the same parenthesis, place them in the order that they appear in your reference list, separated by semicolons.

> Many researchers have argued that what counts as "literacy" is not necessarily learned at school (Heath, 1983; Moss, 2003).

9. TWO OR MORE WORKS BY AN AUTHOR IN THE SAME YEAR

If your list of references includes more than one work by the same author published in the same year, order them alphabetically by title, adding lowercase letters ("a," "b," and so on) to the year.

> Kaplan (2000a) described orderly shantytowns in Turkey that did not resemble the other slums he visited.

10. SOURCE QUOTED IN ANOTHER SOURCE

When you cite a source that was quoted in another source, let the reader know that you used a secondary source by adding the words *as cited in*.

> During the meeting with the psychologist, the patient stated repeatedly that he "didn't want to be too paranoid" (as cited in Oberfield & Yasik, 2004, p. 294).

11. WORK WITHOUT PAGE NUMBERS

Instead of page numbers, some electronic works have paragraph numbers, which you should include (preceded by the abbreviation *para.*) if you are referring to a specific part of such a source. In sources with neither page nor paragraph numbers, refer readers to a particular part of the source if possible, perhaps indicating a heading and the paragraph under the heading.

> Russell's dismissals from Trinity College at Cambridge and from City College in New York City have been seen as examples of the controversy that marked his life (Irvine, 2006, para. 2).

12. AN ENTIRE WORK

You do not need to give a page number if you are directing readers' attention to an entire work.

> Kaplan (2000) considered Turkey and Central Asia explosive.

When you are citing an entire website, give the URL in the text. You do not need to include the website in your reference list. To cite part of a website, see no. 20 on page 000.

> Beyond providing diagnostic information, the website for the Alzheimer's Association includes a variety of resources for family and community support of patients suffering from Alzheimer's (http://www.alz.org).

13. PERSONAL COMMUNICATION

Document email, telephone conversations, interviews, personal letters, messages from nonarchived discussion sources, and other personal texts as *personal communication*, along with the person's initial(s), last name, and the date. You do not need to include such personal communications in your reference list.

> L. Strauss (personal communication, December 6, 2012) told about visiting Yogi Berra when they both lived in Montclair, New Jersey.

NOTES

You may need to use content notes to give an explanation or information that doesn't fit into your text. To signal a content note, place a superscript numeral at the appropriate point in your text. Include this information as a footnote or put the notes on a separate page with the heading *Notes*, after your reference list. If you have multiple notes, number them consecutively throughout your text. Here is an example from *In Search of Solutions: A New Direction in Psychotherapy* (2003).

TEXT WITH SUPERSCRIPT

An important part of working with teams and one-way mirrors is taking the consultation break, as at Milan, BFTC, and MRI.[1]

CONTENT NOTE

[1]It is crucial to note here that, while working within a team is fun, stimulating, and revitalizing, it is not necessary for successful outcomes. Solution-oriented therapy works equally well when working solo.

REFERENCE LIST

A reference list provides full bibliographic information for every source cited in your text with the exception of entire websites and personal communications. See page 563 for guidelines on preparing such a list; for a sample reference list see pages 573–74.

Print Books

For most books, you'll need to provide the author, the publication date, the title and any subtitle, and the place of publication and publisher.

IMPORTANT DETAILS FOR CITING PRINT BOOKS

- **AUTHORS**: Use the author's last name but replace the first and middle names with initials (D. Kinder for Donald Kinder).

- **DATES**: If more than one year is given, use the most recent one.

- **TITLES**: Capitalize only the first word and proper nouns and proper adjectives in titles and subtitles.

- **PUBLICATION PLACE**: Give city followed by state (abbreviated) or country, if outside the United States (for example, Boston, MA; London, England; Toronto, Ontario, Canada). If more than one city is given, use the first. Do not include the state or country if the publisher is a university whose name includes that information.

- **PUBLISHER**: Use a shortened form of the publisher's name (Little, Brown for Little, Brown and Company), but retain *Association*, *Books*, and *Press* (American Psychological Association, Princeton University Press).

1. ONE AUTHOR

> Author's Last Name, Initials. (Year of publication). *Title*. Publication City, State or Country: Publisher.

> Louis, M. (2003). *Moneyball: The art of winning an unfair game*. New York, NY: Norton.

2. TWO OR MORE WORKS BY THE SAME AUTHOR

If the works were published in different years, list them chronologically.

> Lewis, B. (1995). *The Middle East: A brief history of the last 2,000 years*. New York, NY: Scribner.

> Lewis, B. (2003). *The crisis of Islam: Holy war and unholy terror*. New York, NY: Modern Library.

If the works were published in the same year, list them alphabetically by title, adding "a," "b," and so on to the year (see p. 544).

author   title   publication

Documentation Map (APA)

Print Book

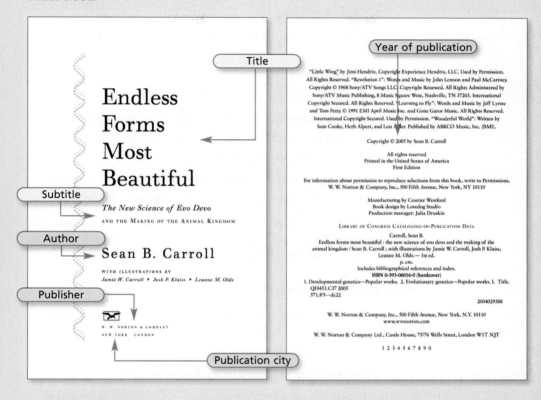

Title → Endless Forms Most Beautiful

Subtitle → *The New Science of Evo Devo* AND THE MAKING OF THE ANIMAL KINGDOM

Author → Sean B. Carroll

Publisher → W. W. NORTON & COMPANY NEW YORK LONDON

Year of publication

Publication city

541–47
for more on
citing books
APA style

Carroll, S. B. (2005). *Endless forms most beautiful: The new science of evo devo and the making of the animal kingdom.* New York, NY: Norton.

Kaplan, R. D. (2000a). *The coming anarchy: Shattering the dreams of the post cold war.* New York, NY: Random House.

Kaplan, R. D. (2000b). *Eastward to Tartary: Travels in the Balkans, the Middle East, and the Caucasus.* New York, NY: Random House.

3. TWO OR MORE AUTHORS

For two to seven authors, include all names.

First Author's Last Name, Initials, Next Author's Last Name, Initials, & Final Author's Last Name, Initials. (Year of publication). *Title.* Publication City, State or Country: Publisher.

Leavitt, S. D., & Dubner, S. J. (2005). *Freakonomics: A rogue economist explores the hidden side of everything.* New York, NY: Morrow.

For a work by eight or more authors, name just the first six authors, followed by three ellipses, and end with the final author (see no. 21 for an example from a magazine article).

4. ORGANIZATION OR GOVERNMENT AS AUTHOR

Sometimes an organization or government agency is both author and publisher. If so, use the word *Author* as the publisher.

Organization Name or Government Agency. (Year of publication). *Title.* Publication City, State or Country: Publisher.

Catholic News Service. (2002). *Stylebook on religion 2000: A reference guide and usage manual.* Washington, DC: Author.

5. AUTHOR AND EDITOR

Author's Last Name, Initials. (Year of edited edition). *Title.* (Editor's Initials Last Name, Ed.). Publication City, State or Country: Publisher. (Original work[s] published year[s])

author   title   publication

Dick, P. F. (2008). *Five novels of the 1960s and 70s.* (J. Lethem, Ed.). New York, NY: Library of America. (Original works published 1964–1977)

6. EDITED COLLECTION

First Editor's Last Name, Initials, Next Editor's Last Name, Initials, & Final Editor's Last Name, Initials. (Eds.). (Year of edited edition). *Title.* Publication City, State or Country: Publisher.

Raviv, A., Oppenheimer, L., & Bar-Tal, D. (Eds.). (1999). *How children understand war and peace: A call for international peace education.* San Francisco, CA: Jossey-Bass.

7. WORK IN AN EDITED COLLECTION

Author's Last Name, Initials. (Year of publication). Title of article or chapter. In Initials Last Name (Ed.), *Title* (pp. pages). Publication City, State or Country: Publisher.

Harris, I. M. (1999). Types of peace education. In A. Raviv, L. Oppenheimer, & D. Bar-Tal (Eds.), *How children understand war and peace: A call for international peace education* (pp. 46–70). San Francisco, CA: Jossey-Bass.

8. UNKNOWN AUTHOR

Title. (Year of publication). Publication City, State or Country: Publisher.

Webster's new biographical dictionary. (1988). Springfield, MA: Merriam-Webster.

If the title page of a work lists the author as *Anonymous*, treat the reference-list entry as if the author's name were Anonymous, and alphabetize it accordingly.

9. EDITION OTHER THAN THE FIRST

Author's Last Name, Initials. (Year). *Title* (name or number ed.). Publication City, State or Country: Publisher.

Burch, D. (2008). *Emergency navigation: Find your position and shape your course at sea even if your instruments fail* (2nd ed.). Camden, ME: International Marine/McGraw-Hill.

10. TRANSLATION

Author's Last Name, Initials. (Year of publication). *Title* (Translator's Initials Last Name, Trans.). Publication City, State or Country: Publisher. (Original work published Year)

Hugo, V. (2008). *Les misérables* (J. Rose, Trans.). New York, NY: Modern Library. (Original work published 1862)

11. MULTIVOLUME WORK

Author's Last Name, Initials. (Year). *Title* (Vols. numbers). Publication City, State or Country: Publisher.

Nastali, D. P., & Boardman, P. C. (2004). *The Arthurian annals: The tradition in English from 1250 to 2000* (Vols. 1–2). New York, NY: Oxford University Press USA.

ONE VOLUME OF A MULTIVOLUME WORK

Author's Last Name, Initials. (Year). *Title of whole work (Vol. number)*. Publication City, State or Country: Publisher.

Spiegelman, A. (1986). *Maus (Vol. 1)*. New York, NY: Random House.

12. ARTICLE IN A REFERENCE BOOK

UNSIGNED

Title of entry. (Year). In *Title of reference book* (Name or number ed., Vol. number, pp. pages). Publication City, State or Country: Publisher.

Macrophage. (2003). In *Merriam-Webster's collegiate dictionary* (10th ed., p. 698). Springfield, MA: Merriam-Webster.

SIGNED

Author's Last Name, Initials. (Year). Title of entry. In *Title of reference book* (Vol. number, pp. pages). Publication City, State or Country: Publisher.

Wasserman, D. E. (2006). Human exposure to vibration. In *International encyclopedia of ergonomics and human factors* (Vol. 2, pp. 1800–1801). Boca Raton, FL: CRC.

Print Periodicals

For most articles, you'll need to provide information about the author; the date; the article title and any subtitle; the periodical title; and any volume or issue number and inclusive page numbers.

IMPORTANT DETAILS FOR CITING PRINT PERIODICALS

- **AUTHORS**: List authors as you would for a book.
- **DATES**: For journals, give year only. For magazines and newspapers, give year followed by a comma and then month or month and day.
- **TITLES**: Capitalize article titles as you would for a book. Capitalize the first and last words and all principal words of periodical titles. Do not capitalize *a*, *an*, *the*, or any prepositions or coordinating conjunctions unless they begin the title of the periodical.
- **VOLUME AND ISSUE**: For journals and magazines, give volume or volume and issue, depending on the journal's pagination method. For newspapers, do not give volume or issue.
- **PAGES**: Use *p.* or *pp.* for a newspaper article but not for a journal or magazine article. If an article does not fall on consecutive pages, give all the page numbers (for example, 45, 75–77 for a journal or magazine; pp. C1, C3, C5–C7 for a newspaper).

13. ARTICLE IN A JOURNAL PAGINATED BY VOLUME

> Author's Last Name, Initials. (Year). Title of article. *Title of Journal,*
> *volume*, pages.

> Gremer, J. R., Sala, A., & Crone, E. E. (2010). Disappearing plants: Why
> they hide and how they return. *Ecology, 91*, 3407–3413.

14. ARTICLE IN A JOURNAL PAGINATED BY ISSUE

> Author's Last Name, Initials. (Year). Title of article. *Title of Journal*,
> *volume*(issue), pages.

> Weaver, C., McNally, C., & Moerman, S. (2001). To grammar or not to
> grammar: That is *not* the question! *Voices from the Middle, 8*(3),
> 17–33.

15. ARTICLE IN A MAGAZINE

If a magazine is published weekly, include the day and the month. If there
are a volume number and an issue number, include them after the magazine title.

> Author's Last Name, Initials. (Year, Month Day). Title of article. *Title of*
> *Magazine, volume*(issue), page(s).

> Gregory, S. (2008, June 30). Crash course: Why golf carts are more
> hazardous than they look. *Time, 171*(26), 53.

If a magazine is published monthly, include the month(s) only.

16. ARTICLE IN A NEWSPAPER

If page numbers are consecutive, separate them with a dash. If not, separate them with a comma.

> Author's Last Name, Initials. (Year, Month Day). Title of article. *Title of*
> *Newspaper*, p(p). page(s).

> Schneider, G. (2005, March 13). Fashion sense on wheels. *The Washington*
> *Post*, pp. F1, F6.

author　　　　title　　　　publication

Documentation Map (APA)

Article in a Print Magazine

Title of article

Author

Volume and issue

Title of magazine

Month, day, and year

Page(s)

547–48
for more
on citing
magazines
APA style

Cullen, L. T. (2008, March 24). Freshen up your drink: Reusing water bottles is good ecologically, but is it bad for your health? How to drink smart. *Time, 171*(12), 65.

17. ARTICLE BY AN UNKNOWN AUTHOR

> Title of article. (Year, Month Day). *Title of Periodical, volume*(issue), page(s) or p(p). page(s).

> Hot property: From carriage house to family compound. (2004, December). *Berkshire Living, 1*(1), 99.

> Clues in salmonella outbreak. (2008, June 21). *New York Times*, p. A13.

18. BOOK REVIEW

> Reviewer's Last Name, Initials. (Date of publication). Title of review [Review of by the book *Title of Work*, by Author's Initials Last Name]. *Title of Periodical, volume*(issue), page(s).

> Brandt, A. (2003, October). Animal planet [Review of the book *Intelligence of apes and other rational beings*, by D. R. Rumb & D. A. Washburn]. *National Geographic Adventure, 5*(10), 47.

If the review does not have a title, include the bracketed information about the work being reviewed, immediately afer the date of publication.

19. LETTER TO THE EDITOR

> Author's Last Name, Initials. (Date of publication). Title of letter [Letter to the editor]. *Title of Periodical, volume*(issue), page(s) or p(p). page(s).

> Hitchcock, G. (2008, August 3). Save our species [Letter to the editor]. *San Francisco Chronicle*, p. P-3.

Online Sources

Not every online source gives you all the data that APA would like to see in a reference entry. Ideally, you will be able to list author's or editor's name; date of first electronic publication or most recent revision; title of document; information about print publication if any; and retrieval information: DOI (Digital Object Identifier, a string of letters and numbers that

author   title   publication

identifies an online document) or URL. In some cases, additional information about electronic publication may be required (title of site, retrieval date, name of sponsoring institution).

IMPORTANT DETAILS FOR CITING ONLINE SOURCES

- **AUTHORS**: List authors as you would for a print book or periodical.

- **TITLES**: For websites and electronic documents, articles, or books, capitalize titles and subtitles as you would for a book; capitalize periodical titles as you would for a print periodical.

- **DATES**: After the author, give the year of the document's original publication on the Web or of its most recent revision. If neither of those years is clear, use *n.d.* to mean "no date." For undated content or content that may change (for example, a wiki entry), include the month, day, and year that you retrieved the document. You don't need to include the retrieval date for content that's unlikely to change.

- **DOI OR URL:** Include the DOI instead of the URL in the reference whenever one is available. If no DOI is available, provide the URL of the home page or menu page. If you do not identify the sponsoring institution, you do not need a colon before the URL or DOI. Don't include any punctuation at the end of the URL or DOI. When a URL won't fit on the line, break the URL before most punctuation, but do not break *http://*.

20. WORK FROM A NONPERIODICAL WEBSITE

Author's Last Name, Initials. (Date of publication). Title of work. *Title of site*. DOI or Retrieved Month Day, Year [if necessary], from URL

Cruikshank, D. (2009, June 15). Unlocking the secrets and powers of the brain. *National Science Foundation*. Retrieved from http://www.nsf.gov /discoveries/disc_summ.jsp?cntn_id=114979&org=NSF

To cite an entire website, include the URL in parentheses in an in-text citation. Do not list the website in your list of references.

Documentation Map (APA)
Work from a Website

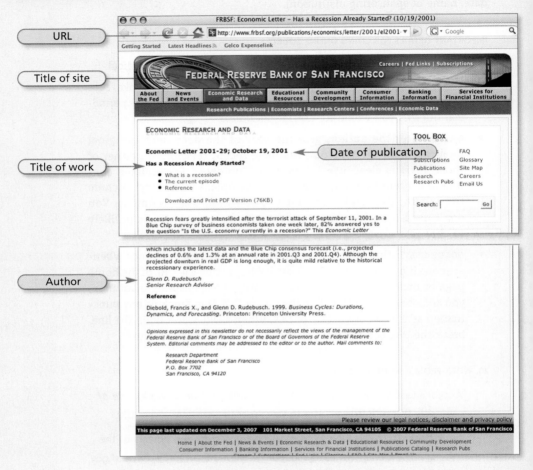

URL

Title of site

Title of work

Author

FRBSF: Economic Letter - Has a Recession Already Started? (10/19/2001)

http://www.frbsf.org/publications/economics/letter/2001/el2001 ▼

Getting Started   Latest Headlines   Gelco Expenselink

Careers | Fed Links | Subscriptions

FEDERAL RESERVE BANK OF SAN FRANCISCO

About the Fed | News and Events | Economic Research and Data | Educational Resources | Community Development | Consumer Information | Banking Information | Services for Financial Institutions

Research Publications | Economists | Research Centers | Conferences | Economic Data

ECONOMIC RESEARCH AND DATA

Economic Letter 2001-29; October 19, 2001   ← Date of publication

Has a Recession Already Started?

- What is a recession?
- The current episode
- Reference

Download and Print PDF Version (76KB)

Recession fears greatly intensified after the terrorist attack of September 11, 2001. In a Blue Chip survey of business economists taken one week later, 82% answered yes to the question "Is the U.S. economy currently in a recession?" This *Economic Letter*

TOOL BOX

Subscriptions
Publications
Search
Research Pubs

FAQ
Glossary
Site Map
Careers
Email Us

Search: [   ] Go

which includes the latest data and the Blue Chip consensus forecast (i.e., projected declines of 0.6% and 1.3% at an annual rate in 2001.Q3 and 2001.Q4). Although the projected downturn in real GDP is long enough, it is quite mild relative to the historical recessionary experience.

Glenn D. Rudebusch
Senior Research Advisor

Reference

Diebold, Francis X., and Glenn D. Rudebusch. 1999. *Business Cycles: Durations, Dynamics, and Forecasting*. Princeton: Princeton University Press.

Opinions expressed in this newsletter do not necessarily reflect the views of the management of the Federal Reserve Bank of San Francisco or of the Board of Governors of the Federal Reserve System. Editorial comments may be addressed to the editor or to the author. Mail comments to:

Research Department
Federal Reserve Bank of San Francisco
P.O. Box 7702
San Francisco, CA 94120

Please review our legal notices, disclaimer and privacy policy

This page last updated on December 3, 2007   101 Market Street, San Francisco, California 94105   © 2007 Federal Reserve Bank of San Francisco

Home | About the Fed | News & Events | Economic Research & Data | Educational Resources | Community Development
Consumer Information | Banking Information | Services for Financial Institutions | Publications Catalog | Research Pubs

550–51
for more
on citing
websites
APA style

Rudebusch, G. D. (2001, October 19). Has a recession already started? *Federal Reserve Bank of San Francisco*. Retrieved April 3, 2012, from http://www.frbsf.org/publications/economics/letter/2001/el2001-29.html

author   title   publication

21. ARTICLE IN AN ONLINE PERIODICAL

When available, include the volume number and issue number as you would for a print source. If no DOI has been assigned, provide the URL of the home page or menu page of the journal or magazine, even for articles that you access through a database.

ARTICLE IN AN ONLINE JOURNAL

Author's Last Name, Initials. (Year). Title of article. *Title of Journal, volume*(issue), pages. DOI or Retrieved from URL

Corbett, C. (2007). Vehicle-related crime and the gender gap. *Psychology, Crime & Law, 13*, 245–263. doi:10.1080/10683160600822022

ARTICLE IN AN ONLINE MAGAZINE

Author's Last Name, Initials. (Year, Month Day). Title of article. *Title of Magazine, volume*(issue). DOI or Retrieved from URL

Barreda, V. D., Palazzesi, L., Tellería, M. C., Katinas, L., Crisci, J. N., Bromer, K., . . . Bechis, F. (2010, September 24). Eocene Patagonia fossils of the daisy family. *Science, 329*, 1621. doi:10.1126/science .1193108

ARTICLE IN AN ONLINE NEWSPAPER

If the article can be found by searching the site, give the URL of the home page or menu page.

Author's Last Name, Initials. (Year, Month Day). Title of article. *Title of Newspaper*. Retrieved from URL

Collins, G. (2012, September 12). Game time. *The New York Times*. Retrieved from http://www.nytimes.com

22. ARTICLE AVAILABLE ONLY THROUGH A DATABASE

Some sources, such as an out-of-print journal or rare book, can be accessed only through a database. When no DOI is provided, give either the name of the database or its URL. (See p. 556 for a template and example.)

Documentation Map (APA)

Article in a Journal with DOI

Title of journal

Year

DOI

Volume

Pages

Title of article

Authors

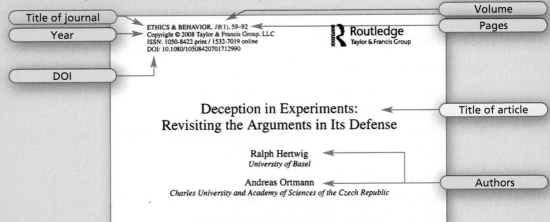

ETHICS & BEHAVIOR, *18*(1), 59–92
Copyright © 2008 Taylor & Francis Group, LLC
ISSN: 1050-8422 print / 1532-7019 online
DOI: 10.1080/10508420701712990

Routledge
Taylor & Francis Group

Deception in Experiments:
Revisiting the Arguments in Its Defense

Ralph Hertwig
University of Basel

Andreas Ortmann
Charles University and Academy of Sciences of the Czech Republic

In psychology, deception is commonly used to increase experimental control. Yet, its use has provoked concerns that it raises participants' suspicions, prompts second-guessing of experimenters' true intentions, and ultimately distorts behavior and endangers the control it is meant to achieve. Over time, these concerns regarding the methodological costs of the use of deception have been subjected to empirical analysis. We review the evidence stemming from these studies.

Keywords: deception, research ethics, experimental control, suspicion

The use of deception [in experiments] has become more and more extensive. ... It is easy to view this problem with alarm, but it is much more difficult to formulate an unambiguous position on the problem. ... I am too well aware of the fact that there are good reasons for using deception in many experiments. There are many significant problems that probably cannot be investigated without the use of deception, at least not at the present level of development of our experimental methodology. (Kelman, 1967, p. 2)

In his well-known article "Human Use of Human Subjects: The Problem of Deception in Social Psychological Experiments," Herbert Kelman (1967) described his dilemma as a social scientist as that of being caught between the Scylla of the use of deception to study important social behaviors and the Charybdis of ethical

Correspondence should be addressed to Ralph Hertwig, University of Basel, Department of Psychology, Missionsstrasse 60/62, 4055 Basel, Switzerland. E-mail: ralph.hertwig@unibas.ch

547–48, 553
for more
on citing
journals
APA style

551
for more
on DOIs

Hertwig, R., & Ortmann, A. (2008). Deception in experiments: Revisiting the arguments in its defense. *Ethics & Behavior, 18*, 59–92. doi:10.1080/10508420701712990

author   title   publication

Documentation Map (APA)
Article Accessed through a Database with DOI

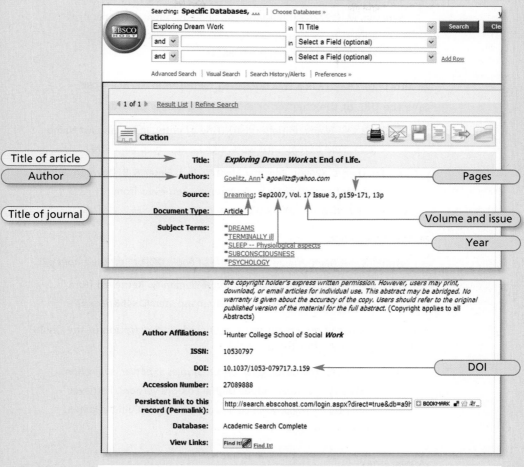

Title of article → Title: *Exploring Dream Work* at End of Life.

Author → Authors: Goelitz, Ann[1] agoelitz@yahoo.com

Pages →

Source: Dreaming; Sep2007, Vol. 17 Issue 3, p159-171, 13p

Document Type: Article

Title of journal →

Volume and issue →

Year →

Subject Terms: *DREAMS
*TERMINALLY ill
*SLEEP -- Physiological aspects
*SUBCONSCIOUSNESS
*PSYCHOLOGY

the copyright holder's express written permission. However, users may print, download, or email articles for individual use. This abstract may be abridged. No warranty is given about the accuracy of the copy. Users should refer to the original published version of the material for the full abstract. (Copyright applies to all Abstracts)

Author Affiliations: [1]Hunter College School of Social *Work*

ISSN: 10530797

DOI: 10.1037/1053-079717.3.159 ← DOI

Accession Number: 27089888

Persistent link to this record (Permalink): http://search.ebscohost.com/login.aspx?direct=true&db=a9h ○ BOOKMARK

Database: Academic Search Complete

View Links: Find It! Find It!

553, 556 for more on citing an article in a database APA style

Goerlitz, A. (2007). Exploring dream work at end of life. *Dreaming, 17*(3), 159–171. doi:10.1037/1053-0797.17.3.159

> Author's Last Name, Initials. (Year). Title of article. *Title of Journal,*
> *volume*(issue), pages. DOI or Retrieved from Name of database
> or URL

Simpson, M. (1972). Authoritarianism and education: A comparative
approach. *Sociometry, 35*(2), 223–234. Retrieved from
http://www.jstor.org/stable/2786619

23. ARTICLE OR CHAPTER IN A WEB DOCUMENT OR ONLINE REFERENCE WORK

Give the URL of the chapter or article if no DOI is provided.

> Author's Last Name, Initials. (Year). Title of entry. In Initials Last Name
> (Ed.), *Title of reference work*. DOI or Retrieved from URL

Korfmacher, C. (2006). Personal identity. In J. Fieser & B. Dowden (Eds.),
Internet encyclopedia of philosophy. Retrieved from
http://www.iep.utm.edu/person-i/

24. ELECTRONIC BOOK

> Author's Last Name, Initials. (Year). *Title of book*. DOI or Retrieved from URL

TenDam, H. (n.d.). *Politics, civilization & humanity*. Retrieved from
http://onlineoriginals.com/showitem.asp?itemID=46&page=2

For an ebook based on a print version, include a description of the digital
format in brackets after the book title.

Blain, M. (2009). *The sociology of terror: Studies in power, subjection,*
and victimage ritual [Adobe Digital Editions version]. Retrieved
from http://www.powells.com/sub/AdobeDigitalEditionsPolitics
.html?sec_big_link=1

25. WIKI ENTRY

Give the entry title and the date of posting, or *n.d.* if there is no date. Then
include the retrieval date, the name of the wiki, and the URL for the entry.

author   title   publication

Title of entry. (Year, Month Day). Retrieved Month Day, Year, from Title
of wiki: URL

Discourse. (n.d.). Retrieved November 8, 2012, from Psychology Wiki:
http://psychology.wikia.com/wiki/Discourse

26. ONLINE DISCUSSION SOURCE

If the name of the list to which to the message was posted is not part of
the URL, include it after *Retrieved from*. The URL you provide should be for
the archived version of the message or post.

Author's Last Name, Initials. (Year, Month Day). Subject line of message
[Descriptive label]. Retrieved from URL

Baker, J. (2005, February 15). Re: Huffing and puffing [Electronic
mailing list message]. Retrieved from American Dialect Society
electronic mailing list: http://listserv.linguistlist.org/cgi-bin
/wa?A2=ind0502C&L=ADS-L&P=R44

Do not include email or other nonarchived discussions in your list of
references. Simply cite the sender's name in your text. See no. 13 on
page 540 for guidelines on identifying such sources in your text.

27. BLOG ENTRY

Author's Last Name, Initials. (Year, Month Day). Title of post [Blog post].
Retrieved from URL

Collins, C. (2009, August 19). Butterfly benefits from warmer springs?
[Blog post]. Retrieved from http://www.intute.ac.uk/blog
/2009/08/19/butterfly-benefits-from-warmer-springs/

28. ONLINE VIDEO

Last Name, Initials (Writer), & Last Name, Initials (Producer). (Year, Month
Day posted). *Title* [Descriptive label]. Retrieved from URL

Coulter, J. (Songwriter & Performer), & Booth, M. S. (Producer). (2006, September 23). *Code Monkey* [Video file]. Retrieved from http://www.youtube.com/watch?v=v4Wy7gRGgeA

29. PODCAST

Writer's Last Name, Initials. (Writer), & Producer's Last Name, Initials. (Producer). (Year, Month Day). Title of podcast. *Title of site or program* [Audio podcast]. Retrieved from URL

Britt, M. A. (Writer & Producer). (2009, June 7). Episode 97: Stanley Milgram study finally replicated. *The Psych Files Podcast* [Audio podcast]. Retrieved from http://www.thepsychfiles.com/

Other Kinds of Sources

30. FILM, VIDEO, OR DVD

Last Name, Initials (Producer), & Last Name, Initials (Director). (Year). *Title* [Motion picture]. Country: Studio.

Wallis, H. B. (Producer), & Curtiz, M. (Director). (1942). *Casablanca* [Motion picture]. United States: Warner.

31. MUSIC RECORDING

Composer's Last Name, Initials. (Year of copyright). Title of song. On *Title of album* [Medium]. City, State or Country: Label.

Veloso, C. (1997). Na baixado sapateiro. On *Livros* [CD]. Los Angeles, CA: Nonesuch.

32. PROCEEDINGS OF A CONFERENCE

Author's Last Name, Initials. (Year of publication). Title of paper. In *Proceedings Title* (pp. pages). Publication City, State or Country: Publisher.

Heath, S. B. (1997). Talking work: Language among teens. In *Symposium about Language and Society–Austin* (pp. 27–45). Austin: Department of Linguistics at the University of Texas.

33. TELEVISION PROGRAM

Last Name, Initials (Writer), & Last Name, Initials (Director). (Year). Title of episode [Descriptive label]. In Initials Last Name (Producer), *Series title*. City, State or Country: Network.

Dunkle, R. (Writer), & Lange, M. (Director). (2012). Hit [Television series episode]. In E. A. Bernero (Executive Producer), *Criminal minds*. New York, NY: NBC.

34. SOFTWARE OR COMPUTER PROGRAM

Title and version number [Computer software]. (Year). Publication City, State or Country: Publisher.

Elder Scrolls V: Skyrim [Computer software]. (2011). Rockwood, MD: Bethesda.

35. GOVERNMENT DOCUMENT

Government Agency. (Year of publication). *Title*. Publication City, State or Country: Publisher.

U.S Department of Health and Human Services, Centers for Disease Control and Prevention. (2009). *Fourth national report on human exposure to environmental chemicals*. Washington, DC: Government Printing Office.

ONLINE GOVERNMENT DOCUMENT

Government Agency. (Year of publication). *Title* (Publication No. [if any]). Retrieved from URL

U.S Department of Health and Human Services, National Institutes of
Health, National Institute of Mental Health. (2006). *Bipolar disorder*
(NIH Publication No. 06-3679). Retrieved from http://www.nimh.nih
.gov/health/publications/bipolar-disorder/nimh-bipolar-adults.pdf

36. DISSERTATION

Include the database name and accession number for dissertations that
you retrieve from a database.

Author's Last Name, Initials. (Year). *Title of dissertation* (Doctoral
dissertation). Retrieved from Name of database. (accession number)

Knapik, M. (2008). *Adolescent online trouble-talk: Help-seeking in
cyberspace* (Doctoral dissertation). Retrieved from ProQuest
Dissertation and Theses database. (AAT NR38024)

For a dissertation that you access on the Web, include the name of institution after *Doctoral dissertation*. For example: (Doctoral dissertation, University of North Carolina). End your citation with *Retrieved from* and the URL.

37. TECHNICAL OR RESEARCH REPORT

Author's Last Name, Initials. (Year). *Title of report* (Report number).
Publication City, State or Country: Publisher.

Elsayed, T., Namata, G., Getoor, L., & Oard., D. W. (2008). *Personal name
resolution in email: A heuristic approach* (Report No. LAMP-TR-150).
College Park: University of Maryland.

Citing Sources Not Covered by APA

To cite a source for which APA does not provide guidelines, look at models similar to the source you are citing. Give any information readers will
need in order to find it themselves — author; date of publication; title;
publisher; information about electronic retrieval (DOI or URL); and any other
pertinent information. You might want to try your citation yourself, to be
sure it will lead others to your source.

author   title   publication

FORMATTING A PAPER

Title page.   APA generally requires a title page. At the upper left-hand corner of the page, include "Running head:" and a shortened version of your title in uppercase letters. The page number (1) should go in the upper right-hand corner. Center the full title of the paper, your name, and the name of your school on separate lines about halfway down the page. You may add an "Author Note" at the bottom of the page to provide course information, acknowledgments, or contact information.

Page numbers.   Use a shortened title in uppercase letters in the upper left-hand corner of each page; place the page number in the upper right-hand corner. Number pages consecutively throughout your paper.

Fonts, spacing, margins, and indents.   Use a serif font (such as Times New Roman or Cambria) for the text, and a sans serif font (such as Calibri or Arial) for figure labels. Double-space the entire paper, including any notes and your list of references. Leave one-inch margins at the top, bottom, and sides of your text; do not justify the text. Paragraphs should be indented one-half inch (or five-to-seven spaces) from the left margin. APA recommends using two spaces after end-of-sentence punctuation.

Headings.   Though they are not required in APA style, headings can help readers follow your organization. The first level of heading should be bold, centered, and capitalized as you would any other title; the second level of heading should be bold and flush with the left margin; the third level should be bold and indented, with only the first letter and proper nouns capitalized and with a period at the end of the heading, with the text following on the same line.

First Level Heading

Second Level Heading

    Third level heading.

Abstract.　An abstract is a concise summary of your paper that briefly introduces readers to your topic and main points. Most scholarly journals require an abstract; check with your instructor about his or her preference. Put your abstract on the second page, with the word Abstract centered at the top. Unless your instructor specifies a length, limit your abstract to 250 words or fewer.

Long quotations.　Indent quotations of more than forty words to one-half inch (or five-to-seven spaces) from the left margin. Do not use quotation marks, and place page number(s) in parentheses after the end punctuation.

> Kaplan (2000) captured ancient and contemporary Antioch for us:
>> At the height of its glory in the Roman-Byzantine age, when it had an amphitheater, public baths, aqueducts, and sewage pipes, half a million people lived in Antioch. Today the population is only 125,000. With sour relations between Turkey and Syria, and unstable politics throughout the Middle East, Antioch is now a backwater—seedy and tumbledown, with relatively few tourists. (p. 123)
>
> Antioch's decline serves as a reminder that the fortunes of cities can change drastically over time.

Illustrations.　For each table, provide a number (*Table* 1) and a descriptive title on separate lines above the table; below the table, include a note with information about the source. For figures — charts, diagrams, graphs, photos, and so on — include a figure number (*Figure* 1) and information about the source in a note below the figure. Number tables and figures separately, and be sure to refer to any illustrations in your text and clarify how they relate to the rest of your text.

Table 1

Hours of Instruction Delivered per Week

	American classrooms	Japanese classrooms	Chinese classrooms
First grade			
Language arts	10.5	8.7	10.4
Mathematics	2.7	5.8	4.0
Fifth grade			
Language arts	7.9	8.0	11.1
Mathematics	3.4	7.8	11.7

Note. Adapted from "Peeking Out from Under the Blinders: Some Factors We Shouldn't Forget in Studying Writing," by J. R. Hayes, 1991, National Center for the Study of Writing and Literacy (Occasional Paper No. 25). Retrieved from National Writing Project website: http://www.nwp.org/

List of references. Start your list on a new page after the text but before any endnotes. Center the title and double-space the entire list. Each entry should begin at the left margin, and subsequent lines should be indented one-half inch (or five-to-seven spaces). Alphabetize the list by authors' last names (or by editors' names, if appropriate). Alphabetize works that have no author or editor by title, disregarding *A, An,* and *The.* Be sure every source listed is cited in the text; don't include sources that you consulted but didn't cite.

SAMPLE RESEARCH PAPER

Carolyn Stonehill wrote the following paper for a first-year writing course. It is formatted according to the guidelines of the *Publication Manual of the American Psychological Association,* 6th edition (2009). While APA guidelines are used widely in linguistics and the social sciences, exact requirements may vary from discipline to discipline and course to course. If you're unsure about what your instructor wants, ask for clarification.

"Running head:" and shortened title.

Running head: IT'S IN OUR GENES

1

Page number.

It's in Our Genes:

Title, name, and school name.

The Biological Basis of Human Mating Behavior

Carolyn Stonehill

Wright State University

IT'S IN OUR GENES   2

Abstract

While cultural values and messages certainly play a part in the process of mate selection, the genetic and psychological predispositions developed by our ancestors play the biggest role in determining to whom we are attracted. Women are attracted to strong, capable men with access to resources to help rear children. Men find women attractive based on visual signs of youth, health, and, by implication, fertility. While perceptions of attractiveness are influenced by cultural norms and reinforced by advertisements and popular media, the persistence of mating behaviors that have no relationship to societal realities suggests that they are part of our biological heritage.

Heading centered.

Limited to 250 words or fewer.

Two spaces after end punctuation.

IT'S IN OUR GENES   3

Title centered.
It's in Our Genes:

Double-spaced throughout.
The Biological Basis of Human Mating Behavior

Consider the following scenario: It's a sunny afternoon on campus, and Jenny is walking to her next class. Out of the corner of her eye, she catches sight of her lab partner, Joey, parking his car. She stops to admire how tall, muscular, and stylishly dressed he is, and she does not take her eyes off him as he walks away from his shiny new BMW. As he flashes her a pearly white smile, Jenny melts, then quickly adjusts her skirt and smooths her hair.

Paragraphs indent 5 to 7 spaces ($\frac{1}{2}$ inch).
This scenario, while generalized, is familiar: Our attraction to people—or lack of it—often depends on their physical traits. But why this attraction? Why does Jenny respond the way she does to her handsome lab partner? Why does she deem him handsome at all? Certainly Joey embodies the stereotypes of physical attractiveness prevalent in contemporary American society. Advertisements, television shows, and magazine articles all provide Jenny with signals telling her what constitutes the ideal American man. Yet she is also attracted to Joey's new sports car even though she has a new car herself. Does Jenny find this man striking because of the influence of her culture, or does her attraction lie in a more fundamental part of her constitution? Evolutionary psychologists, who apply principles of evolutionary biology to research on the human mind, would say that Jenny's responses in this situation are due largely to mating strategies developed by her prehistoric ancestors. Driven by the need to reproduce and

1"   1"   1"

IT'S IN OUR GENES   4

propagate the species, these ancestors of ours formed patterns of
mate selection so effective in providing for their needs and those of
their offspring that they are mimicked even in today's society.
While cultural values and messages clearly play a part in the
process of mate selection, the genetic and psychological
predispositions developed by our ancestors play the biggest role in
determining to whom we are attracted.

Women's Need to Find a Capable Mate

Pioneering evolutionary psychologist Trivers (as cited in Allman,
1993) observed that having and rearing children requires women to
invest far more resources than men because of the length of
pregnancy, the dangers of childbirth, and the duration of infants'
dependence on their mothers (p. 56). According to Fisher (as cited in
Frank, 2001), one of the leading advocates of this theory, finding a
capable mate was a huge preoccupation of all prehistoric reproductive
women, and for good reason: "A female couldn't carry a baby in one
arm and sticks and stones in the other arm and still feed and protect
herself on the very dangerous open grasslands, so she began to need a
mate to help her rear her young" (p. 85). So because of this it became
advantageous for the woman to find a strong, capable man with
access to resources, and it became suitable for the man to find a
healthy, reproductively sound woman to bear and care for his
offspring. According to evolutionary psychologists, these are the
bases upon which modern mate selection is founded, and there are
many examples of this phenomenon to be found in our own society.

First-level headings boldface, centered.

Authors referred to by last name.

Source quoted in another source; secondary source and date in first parentheses, page number in second parentheses.

IT'S IN OUR GENES   5

One can see now why Jenny might be attracted by Joey's display of resources—his BMW. In our society, men with good job prospects, a respected social position, friends in high places, or any combination thereof have generally been viewed as more desirable mates than those without these things because they signal to women that the men have resources (Buss & Schmitt, 1993, p. 226). Compared with males, females invest more energy in bearing and raising children, so it is most advantageous for females to choose mates with easy access to resources, the better to provide for their children.

Author names in parentheses when no signal phrase is used.

Men's Need to Find a Healthy Mate

For men, reproductive success depends mainly on the reproductive fitness of their female counterpart: No amount of available resources can save a baby miscarried in the first month of gestation. Because of this need for a healthy mate, men have evolved a particular attraction "radar" that focuses on signs of a woman's health and youth, markers that are primarily visual (Weiten, 2001, p. 399). Present-day attractiveness ratings are based significantly on this primitive standard: "Some researchers have suggested that cross-cultural standards of beauty reflect an evolved preference for physical traits that are generally associated with youth, such as smooth skin, good muscle tone, and shiny hair" (Boyd & Silk, 2000, p. 625). This observation would explain why women of our time are preoccupied with plastic surgery, makeup, and—in Jenny's case—a quick hair check as a potential date

Ampersands used in parenthetical references, and used in signal phrases.

IT'S IN OUR GENES   6

approaches. As Cunningham, Roberts, Barbee, Druen, and Wu (1995)

noted, "A focus on outer beauty may have stemmed from a need for

desirable inner qualities," such as health, strength, and fertility, and

"culture may build on evolutionary dynamics by specifying grooming

attributes that signal successful adaptation" (pp. 262–263).

Author named in a signal phrase, publication date in parentheses after the name.

The Influence of the Media on Mate Selection

There is, however, a good deal of opposition to evolutionary

theory. Some critics say that the messages fed to us by the media

are a larger influence on the criteria of present-day mate selection

than any sort of ancestral behavior. Advertisements and popular

media have long shown Americans what constitutes a physically

ideal mate: In general, youthful, well-toned, symmetrical features

are considered more attractive than aging, flabby, or lopsided ones.

Evolutionary psychologists argue that research has not determined

what is cause and what is effect. Cosmides and Tooby (1997)

offered the following analogy to show the danger of assigning

culture too powerful a causal role:

> For example, people think that if they can show that there is
> information in the culture that mirrors how people behave,
> then *that* is the cause of their behavior. So if they see that men
> on TV have trouble crying, they assume that their example is
> *causing* boys to be afraid to cry. But which is cause and which
> effect? Does the fact that men don't cry much on TV *teach* boys
> to not cry, or does it merely *reflect* the way boys normally
> develop? In the absence of research on the particular topic,

Quotations of 40+ words indented 5 to 7 spaces.

Major heading and paragraph number cited for quote from unpaginated work from a website.

there is no way of knowing. ("Nature and Nurture: An Adaptationist Perspective," para. 16)

We can hypothesize, then, that rather than media messages determining our mating habits, our mating habits determine the media messages. Advertisers rely on classical conditioning to interest consumers in their products. For instance, by showing an image of a beautiful woman while advertising a beauty product, advertisers hope that consumers will associate attractiveness with the use of that particular product (Weiten, 2001). In order for this method to be effective, however, the images depicted in conjunction with the beauty product must be ones the general public already finds attractive, and an image of a youthful, clear-skinned woman would, according to evolutionary psychologists, be attractive for reasons of reproductive fitness. In short, what some call media influence is not an influence at all but merely a mirror in which we see evidence of our ancestral predispositions.

If Not Media, Then What?

Tattersall (2001), a paleoanthropologist at the American Museum of Natural History, offered another counterargument to the evolutionary theory of mate selection. First, he argued that the behavior of organisms is influenced not only by genetics, but also by economics and ecology working together (p. 663). Second, he argued that no comparisons can be made between modern human behavior and that of our evolutionary predecessors because the appearance of *Homo sapiens* presented a sudden, qualitative change

IT'S IN OUR GENES   8

from the Neanderthals—not a gradual evolution of behavioral

traits:

> As a cognitive and behavioral entity, our species is truly
> unprecedented. Our consciousness is an emergent quality,
> not the result of eons of fine-tuning of a single instrument.
> And, if so, it is to this recently acquired quality of uniqueness,
> not to the hypothetical "ancestral environments," that we
> must look in the effort to understand our often unfathomable
> behaviors. (p. 665)

End punctuation before parentheses in block quotations.

The key to Tattersall's argument is this "emergent quality" of

symbolic thought; according to his theories, the ability to think

symbolically is what separates modern humans from their

ancestors and shows the impossibility of sexual selection behaviors

having been passed down over millions of years. Our sexual

preferences, Tattersall said, are a result of our own recent and

species-specific development and have nothing whatsoever to do

with our ancestors.

Opponents of the evolutionary theory, though, fail to explain

how "unfathomable" mating behaviors can exist in our present

society for no apparent or logical reason. Though medicine has

advanced to the point where fertility can be medically enhanced,

Singh (1993) observed that curvy women are still viewed as

especially attractive because they are perceived to possess greater

fertility—a perception that is borne out by several studies of female

fertility, hormone levels, and waist-to-hip ratio (p. 304). Though more and more women are attending college and achieving high-paying positions, women are still "more likely than men to consider economic prospects a high priority in a mate" (Sapolsky, 2001–2002, p. 18). While cultural norms and economic conditions influence our taste in mates, as Singh (1993) showed in observing that "the degree of affluence of a society or of an ethnic group within a society may, to a large extent, determine the prevalence and admiration of fatness [of women]" (pp. 304–305), we still react to potential mates in ways determined in Paleolithic times. The key to understanding our mating behavior does not lie only in an emergent modern quality, nor does it lie solely in the messages relayed to us by society; rather, it involves as well the complex mating strategies developed by our ancestors.

IT'S IN OUR GENES 10

References

Allman, W. F. (1993, July 19). The mating game. *U.S. News & World Report, 115*(3), 56–63.

Boyd, R., & Silk, J. B. (2000). *How humans evolved* (2nd ed.). New York, NY: Norton.

Buss, D. M., & Schmitt, D. P. (1993). Sexual strategies theory: An evolutionary perspective on human mating. *Psychological Review, 100*(2), 204–232.

Cosmides, L., & Tooby, J. (1997). *Evolutionary psychology: A primer.* Retrieved February 2, 2012, from http://www.psych.ucsb.edu /research/cep/primer.html

Cunningham, M. R., Roberts, A. R., Barbee, A. P., Druen, P. B., & Wu, C.-H. (1995). "Their ideas of beauty are, on the whole, the same as ours": Consistency and variability in the cross-cultural perception of female physical attractiveness. *Journal of Personality and Social Psychology, 68,* 261–279.

Frank, C. (2001, February). Why do we fall in — and out of — love? Dr. Helen Fisher unravels the mystery. *Biography,* 85–87, 112.

Sapolsky, R. M. (2001–2002, December–January). What do females want? *Natural History,* 18–21.

Singh, D. (1993). Adaptive significance of female physical attractiveness: Role of waist-to-hip ratio. *Journal of Personality and Social Behavior, 65,* 293–307.

Heading centered.

Alphabetized by authors' last names.

All lines after the first line of each entry indented.

IT'S IN OUR GENES   11

Tattersall, I. (2001). Evolution, genes, and behavior. *Zygon: Journal of Religion & Science, 36,* 657–666. Retrieved from the Psychology and Behavioral Sciences Collection database.

Weiten, W. (2001). *Psychology: Themes & variations* (5th ed.). San Bernardino, CA: Wadsworth.

All sources cited in the text are listed.

part 6

Media / Design

Consciously or not, we design all the texts we write, choosing typefaces, setting up text as lists or charts, deciding whether to add headings—and then whether to center them or align them on the left. Sometimes our genre calls for certain design elements—essays begin with titles, letters begin with salutations ("Dear Auntie Em"). Other times we design texts to meet the demands of particular audiences, formatting documentation in MLA or APA or some other style, setting type larger for young children, and so on. And our designs always depend upon our medium. A memoir might take the form of an essay in a book, be turned into a bulleted list for a slide presentation, or include links to images or other pages if presented on a website. The chapters in this part offer advice for CHOOSING MEDIA; working with DESIGN, IMAGES, and SOUND; WRITING ONLINE; and GIVING PRESENTATIONS.

Media / Design

Choosing Media **52**

USA Today reports on contract negotiations between automakers and autoworkers with an article that includes a large photo and a colorful graph; the article on the same story on *nytimes.com* includes a video of striking workers. In your economics class, you give a presentation about the issue that includes *Prezi* slides.

These examples show how information about the same events can be delivered using three different media: print (*USA Today*), electronic (*nytimes.com*), and spoken (the main medium for your class presentation). They also show how different media offer writers different modes of expressing meaning, ranging from words to images to sounds and hyperlinks. A print text can include written words and still visuals; online, the same text can also incorporate links to moving images and sound as well as to other written materials. A presentation with slides can include both spoken and written words, can incorporate video and audio elements — and can also include print handouts.

In college writing, the choice of medium often isn't up to you: your instructor may require a printed essay or a classroom talk, a website, or some combination of media. Sometimes, though, you'll be the one deciding. Because your medium will play a big part in the way your audience receives and reacts to your message, you'll need to think hard about what media best suits your audience, purpose, and message. This chapter will help you choose media when the choice is yours.

rhetorical situations   genres   processes   strategies   research MLA / APA   media / design   readings

Print

When you have a choice of medium, print has certain advantages over spoken and electronic text in that it's more permanent and doesn't depend on audience access to technology. Depending on your own access to technology, you can usually insert photos or other visuals and can present data and other information as graphs or charts. Obviously, though, print documents are more work than electronic ones to update or change, and they don't allow for sound, moving images, or hyperlinks to other materials.

Electronic

Online writing is everywhere: on course learning platforms and class websites; in virtual discussion groups and wikis; in emails, text messages, tweets, and social media. And when you're taking an online course, you are, by definition, always using an electronic medium. Remember that this medium has advantages as well as limitations and potential pitfalls. You can add audio, video, and hyperlinks — but your audience may not have the same access to technology that you do. These are just some of the things you'll need to keep in mind when deciding, say, whether to include or to link to videos or a site that has restricted access.

Spoken

If you deliver your text orally, as a speech or presentation, you have the opportunity to use your tone of voice, gestures, and physical bearing to establish credibility. But you must write your text so that it's easy to understand when it is heard rather than read. The spoken medium can be used alone with a live, face-to-face audience, but it's often combined with print, in the form of handouts, or with electronics, in the form of presentation software like *PowerPoint* or *Prezi*, or designed for remote audiences in formats like webcasts, webinars, podcasts, or video-calling services such as *Skype*.

Multimedia

It's increasingly likely that you'll be assigned to create a multimedia text, one that includes some combination of print, oral, and electronic elements. It's also possible that you'll have occasion to write a multimodal text, one that uses more than one mode of expression: words, images, audio, video, hyperlinks, and so on. The words *multimedia* and *multimodal* are often used interchangeably, but *multimodal* is the term that's used most often in composition classes, whereas *multimedia* is the one used in other disciplines and in industry. In composition classes, the word generally refers to writing that includes more than just words.

For example, let's say that in a U.S. history class you're assigned to do a project about the effects of the Vietnam War on American society. You might write an essay using words alone to discuss such effects as increased hostility toward the military and government, generational conflict within families and society at large, and increased use of recreational drugs. But you could in addition weave such a text together with many other materials to create a multimodal composition.

If you're using print, for example, you could include famous photographs from the Vietnam era, such as of antiwar protests or military funerals. Another possibility might be a time line that puts developments in the war in the context of events going on simultaneously elsewhere in American life, such as in fashion and entertainment or in the feminist and civil rights movements. If you're posting your project online, you might also incorporate video clips of TV news coverage of the war and clips from films focusing on it or its social effects, such as *Apocalypse Now* or *Easy Rider*. Audio elements could include recorded interviews with veterans who fought in the war, people who protested against it, or government officials who were involved in planning or overseeing it. Many of these elements could be inserted into your document as hyperlinks.

If your assignment specifies that you give an oral presentation, you could play some of the music of the Vietnam era, show videos of government officials defending the war and demonstrators protesting it, maybe hang some psychedelic posters from the era.

Considering the Rhetorical Situation

3–4 **PURPOSE** What's your purpose, and what media will best suit that purpose? A text or email may be appropriate for inviting a friend to lunch, but neither would be ideal for demonstrating to a professor that you understand a complex historical event; for that, you'd likely write a report, either in print or online — and you might include photos or maps or other such texts to provide visual context.

5–8 **AUDIENCE** What media are your audience likely to expect — and be able to access? A blog may be a good way to reach people who share your interest in basketball or cupcakes, but to reach your grandparents, you may want to put a handwritten note in the mail. Some employers require applicants to submit résumés and applications online, while others prefer to receive them in print form.

9–11 **GENRE** Does your genre require a particular medium? If you're giving an oral presentation, you'll often be expected to include slides. Academic essays are usually formatted to be printed out, even if they are submitted electronically. An online essay based on field research might include audio files of those you've interviewed, but if your essay were in print, you'd need to quote (or paraphrase or summarize) what they said.

12–15 **STANCE** If you have a choice of media, think about whether a particular medium will help you convey your stance. A print document in MLA format, for instance, will make you seem scholarly and serious. Tweeting or blogging, however, might work better for a more informal stance. Presenting data in charts will sometimes help you establish your credibility as a knowledgeable researcher.

Once you decide on the media and modes of expression you're using, you'll need to design your text to take advantage of their possibilities and to deal with their limitations. The next chapters will help you do that.

Designing Text **53**

You're trying to figure out why a magazine ad you're looking at is so funny, and you realize that the font used for the text is deliberately intended to make you laugh. In giving an assignment for a research paper, your psychology professor specifies that you are to follow APA format. Your classmates complain that the *PowerPoint* slides you use for a presentation are hard to read, and one of them suggests that it's because there's not enough contrast between the colors of the words and the background. Whether you're putting together your résumé, creating a website for your intramural soccer league, or writing a research essay for a class, you need to think about how you design what you write.

Sometimes you can rely on established conventions: in academic writing using MLA and APA style, for example, there are specific guidelines for margins, headings, and the use of single-, double-, or triple-spaced lines of text. But often you'll have to make design decisions on your own — and not just about words and spacing. If what you're writing includes photos, charts, tables, graphs, or other visuals, you'll need to figure out how to integrate these with your written text in the most attractive and effective way; online, you may also need to decide where and how to include video clips and hyperlinks. You might even use scissors, glue, and staples to attach objects to a poster or create pop-ups in a brochure.

No matter what your text includes, its design will influence how your audience responds to it and therefore how well it achieves your purpose. This chapter offers general advice on designing print and online texts to suit your purpose, audience, genre, and stance.

Considering the Rhetorical Situation

As with all writing tasks, your rhetorical situation should affect the way you design a text. Here are some points to consider.

3–4 **PURPOSE** How can you design your text to help achieve your purpose? If you're reporting information, for instance, you may want to present statistical data in a chart or table rather than in the main text to help readers grasp it more quickly. If you're trying to get readers to care about an issue, a photo or pull quote — a brief selection of text "pulled out" and reprinted in a larger font — might help you do so.

5–8 **AUDIENCE** How can you make your design appeal to your intended audience? By using a certain font style or size to make your text look hip, serious, or easy to read? What kind of headings — big and bold, simple and restrained? — would your readers expect or find helpful? What colors would appeal to them?

9–11 **GENRE** Are you writing in a genre that has design conventions, such as an annotated bibliography, a lab report, or a résumé? Do you need to follow a format such as those prescribed in MLA or APA style?

12–15 **STANCE** How can your design reflect your attitude toward your audience and subject? Do you need a businesslike font or a playful one? Would tables and graphs help you establish your credibility? How can illustrations help you convey a certain tone?

Some Basic Principles of Design

Be consistent.   To keep readers oriented while reading documents or browsing multiple webpages, any design elements should be used consistently. In a print academic essay, that task may be as simple as using the same font throughout for your main text and using boldface or italics for headings. If you're writing for the web, navigation buttons and other major elements should be in the same place on every page. In a presentation, each slide should use the same background and the same font unless there's a good reason to introduce differences.

Keep it simple. One of your main design goals should be to help readers see quickly — even intuitively — what's in your text and how to find specific information. Adding headings to help readers see the parts, using consistent colors and fonts to help them recognize key elements, setting off steps in lists, using white space to set off blocks of text or to call attention to certain elements, and (especially) resisting the temptation to fill pages with fancy graphics or unnecessary animations: these are all ways of making your text simple to read.

Look, for example, at a furniture store's simple, easy-to-understand webpage design on page 584. This webpage contains considerable information: a row of links across the top, directing readers to various products; a search option; a column down the right side that provides details about the chair shown in the wide left-hand column; thumbnail photos below the chair, showing its various options; and suggestions across the bottom for furniture to go with it. Despite the wealth of content, the site's design is both easy to figure out and, with the generous amount of white space, easy on the eyes.

Aim for balance. On the webpage on page 584, the photo takes up about a quarter of the screen and is balanced by a narrower column of text, and the "Matching Products" and "More POÄNG series" sections across the page bottom balance the company logo and links bar across the top. For a page without images, balance can be created through the use of margins, headings, and spacing. MLA and APA styles have specific design guidelines for academic research papers that cover these elements. A magazine page might create a sense of balance by using pull quotes and illustrations to break up dense vertical columns of text. In the magazine page shown on

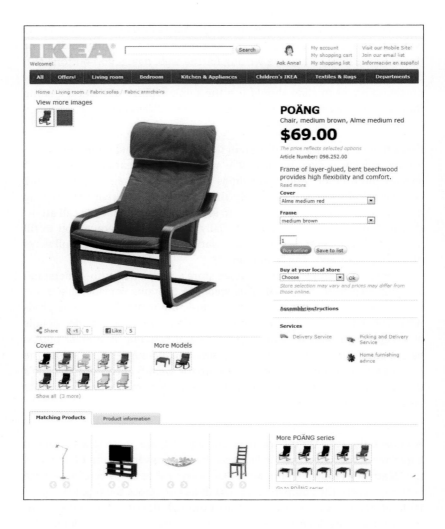

page 505, for example, the large title at the top left is broken into two short lines, leaving a large blank space on the right. Below, two photos in the left column and a brief summary of the article in large italic type on the

rhetorical situations

genres

processes

strategies

research MLA / APA

media / design

readings

right, surrounded by more blank space, provide additional visual relief from the two columns of solid text at the bottom.

Use color and contrast carefully. Academic readers usually expect black text on a white background, with perhaps one other color for headings. Presentation slides and webpages are most readable with a plain, light-colored background and dark text that provides contrast. Remember that not everyone can see all colors and that an online text that includes several colors might be printed out and read in black and white; make sure your audience will be able to distinguish any color variations well enough to grasp your meaning. Colored lines on a graph, for example, should be distinguishable even if readers cannot see the colors. Red-green contrasts are especially hard to see and should be avoided.

Use available templates. Good design takes time, and most of us do not have training as designers. If you're pressed for time or don't feel up to the challenge of designing your own text, take advantage of the many templates available. In *Microsoft Word*, for example, you can customize "styles" to specify the font, including its size and color; single- or double-spacing; paragraph indentations; and several other features that will then automatically apply to your document. Websites that host personal webpages and blogs offer dozens of templates that you can use or modify to suit your needs. And presentation software offers many templates that can simplify creating slides.

Some Elements of Design

Fonts. You can usually choose from among many fonts, and the one you choose will affect how well the audience can read your text and how they will perceive your TONE. Times Roman will make a text look businesslike or academic; Comic Sans will make it look playful. For most academic writing,

13

you'll want to use a font size between 10 and 12 points and a serif font (such as Times Roman or Bookman) rather than a sans serif font (such as Arial, Verdana, or Century Gothic) because serif fonts are generally easier to read. Reserve sans serif for headings and parts of the text that you want to highlight. Decorative fonts (such as *Magneto*, *Amaze*, *Chiller*, and *Jokerman*) should be used sparingly and only when they're appropriate for your audience, purpose, and the rest of your RHETORICAL SITUATION. If you use more than one font in a text, use each one consistently: one for HEADINGS, one for captions, one for the main body of your text. And don't go over-board—you won't often have reason to use more than two or, at most, three fonts in any one text.

Every font has regular, **bold**, and *italic* forms. In general, choose regular for the main text and lower-level headings, bold for major headings, and italic within the main text to indicate titles of books and other long works and, occasionally, to emphasize words or brief phrases. Avoid italicizing or boldfacing entire sentences or paragraphs, especially in academic writing. If you are following MLA, APA, or some other style format, be sure your use of fonts conforms to its requirements.

Finally, consider the line spacing of your text. Generally, academic writing is double-spaced, whereas JOB LETTERS and RÉSUMÉS are usually single-spaced. Some kinds of REPORTS may call for single-spacing; check with your instructor if you're not sure. You'll often need to add extra space to set off parts of a text—items in a list, for instance, or headings.

Layout.   Layout is the way text is arranged on a page. An academic essay, for example, will usually have a title centered at the top, one-inch margins all around, and double-spacing. A text can be presented in paragraphs—or in the form of LISTS, TABLES, CHARTS, GRAPHS, and so on. Sometimes you'll need to include other elements as well: headings, images and other graphics, captions, lists of works cited.

Paragraphs.   Dividing text into paragraphs focuses information for readers and helps them process the information by dividing it into manageable chunks. If you're writing a story for a print newspaper with narrow columns, for example, you'll divide your text into shorter paragraphs

1
588–89

484–532
533–74

222–34
87–118

593–95

than you would if you were writing an academic essay. In general, indent paragraphs five to seven spaces (one-half inch) when your text is double-spaced; either indent or skip a line between paragraphs that are single-spaced.

Lists.   Put information into list form that you want to set off and make easily accessible. Number the items in a list when the sequence matters (in instructions, for example); use bullets when the order is not important. Set off lists with an extra line of space above and below, and add extra space between the items on a list if necessary for legibility. Here's an example:

> Darwin's theory of how species change through time derives from three postulates, each of which builds on the previous one:
>
> 1. The ability of a population to expand is infinite, but the ability of any environment to support populations is always finite.
> 2. Organisms within populations vary, and this variation affects the ability of individuals to survive and reproduce.
> 3. The variations are transmitted from parents to offspring.
>
> —Robert Boyd and Joan B. Silk, *How Humans Evolved*

Do not set off text as a list unless there's a good reason to do so, however. Some lists are more appropriately presented in paragraph form, especially when they give information that is not meant to be referred to more than once. In the following example, there is no reason to highlight the information by setting it off in a list—and bad news is softened by putting it in paragraph form:

> I regret to inform you that the Scholarship Review Committee did not approve your application for a Board of Rectors scholarship for the following reasons: your grade-point average did not meet the minimum requirements; your major is not among those eligible for consideration; and the required letter of recommendation was not received before the deadline.

Presented as a list, that information would be needlessly emphatic.

150–54 ▲

523 ●

87–118 ▲

Headings. Headings make the structure of a text easier to follow and help readers find specific information. Some genres require standard headings — announcing an ABSTRACT, for example, or a list of WORKS CITED. Other times you will want to use headings to provide an overview of a section of text. You may not need any headings in brief texts, but when you do, you'll probably want to use one level at most, just to announce major topics. Longer texts, information-rich genres such as brochures or detailed REPORTS, and websites may require several levels of headings. If you decide to include headings, you will need to decide how to phrase them, what fonts to use, and where to position them.

Phrase headings concisely. Make your headings succinct and parallel in structure. You might make all the headings nouns (**Mushrooms**), noun phrases (**Kinds of Mushrooms**), gerund phrases (**Recognizing Kinds of Mushrooms**), or questions (**How Do I Identify Mushrooms?**). Whatever form you decide on, use it consistently for each heading. Sometimes your phrasing will depend on your purpose. If you're simply helping readers find information, use brief phrases:

HEAD *Forms of Social Groups among Primates*
SUBHEAD *Solitary Social Groups*
SUBHEAD *Monogamous Social Groups*

If you want to address your readers directly with the information in your text, consider writing your headings as questions:

How can you identify morels?
Where can you find morels?
How can you cook morels?

Make headings visible. Headings need to be visible, so if you aren't following an academic style like MLA or APA, consider making them larger than the regular text, putting them in **bold** or *italics*, or using underlining — or a different font. For example, you could make your main text a serif font like Times Roman and your headings in a sans serif font like Arial. On the web, consider making headings a different color from the body text.

When you have several levels of headings, use capitalization, bold, and italics to distinguish among the various levels:

First-Level Head
Second-Level Head
Third-level head

APA format requires that each level of heading appear in a specific style: centered bold uppercase and lowercase for the first level, flush-left bold uppercase and lowercase for the second level, and so on.

Position headings appropriately.   If you're following APA format, center first-level headings. If you're following MLA format, first-level headings should be typed to align with the left-hand margin. If you are not following a prescribed format, you get to decide where to position your headings: centered, flush with the left margin, or even alongside the text in a wide left-hand margin. Position each level of head consistently throughout your text. Generally, online headings are positioned flush left.

561–63
522–23

White space.   Use white space to separate the various parts of a text. In general, use one-inch margins for the text of an essay or report. Unless you're following MLA or APA format, include space above headings, above and below lists, and around photos, graphs, and other visuals. See the two SAMPLE RESEARCH PAPERS in this book for examples of the formats required by MLA and APA.

MLA 523–32
APA 563–74

Evaluating a Design

Does the design suit your PURPOSE?   Does the overall look of the design help convey the text's message, support its argument, or present information?

3–4

How well does the design meet the needs of your AUDIENCE?   Will the overall appearance of the text appeal to the intended readers? Is the font large enough for them to read? Are there headings to help them find their

5–8

way through the text? Does the design help readers find the information they need?

9–11 **How well does the text meet any GENRE requirements?** Can you tell by looking at the text that it is an academic essay, a lab report, a résumé, a blog? Do its fonts, margins, headings, and page layout meet the require- 484–532
533–74 ments of **MLA**, **APA**, or whatever style is being followed?

12–15 **How well does the design reflect your STANCE?** Do the page layout and fonts convey the appropriate tone—serious, playful, adventuresome, con- servative, or whatever other tone you intended?

■ rhetorical situations

▲ genres

○ processes

◆ strategies

● research MLA / APA

□ media / design

◗ readings

Using Visuals, Incorporating Sound 54

For an art history class, you write an essay comparing two paintings by Willem de Kooning. For an engineering class project, you design a model of a bridge and give an in-class presentation explaining the structures and forces involved, which you illustrate with slides. For a psychology assignment, you interview several people who've suffered foreclosures on their homes in recent years about how the experience affected them and how they've tried to cope with the resulting stress — and then create an online text weaving together a slideshow of photos of the people outside their former homes, a graph of foreclosure rates, video and audio clips from the interviews, and your own insights.

All of these writing tasks require you to incorporate and sometimes to create visuals and sound. Many kinds of visuals can be included in print documents: photos, diagrams, graphs, charts, and more. And with writing that's delivered online or as a spoken presentation, your choices expand to include audio and video, voice-over narration, and links to other materials.

Visuals and sound aren't always appropriate, however, or even possible—so think carefully before you set out to include them. But they can help you make a point in ways that words alone cannot. Election polling results are easier to see in a bar graph than the same information would be in a paragraph; an audio clip can make a written analysis of an opera easier to understand. This chapter provides some tips for using visuals and incorporating sound in your writing.

Considering the Rhetorical Situation

Use visuals that are appropriate for your audience, purpose, and the rest of your **RHETORICAL SITUATION**. If you're trying to persuade voters in your

■ 1

591

town to back a proposal on an issue they don't know or care much about, for example, you might use dramatic pictures just to get their attention. But when it's important to come across as thoughtful and objective, maybe you need a more subdued look — or to make your points with written words alone. A newspaper article on housing prices might include a bar graph or line graph and also some photos. A report on the same topic for an economics class would probably have graphs with no photos; a community website might have graphs, links to related sites, and a video interview with a homeowner.

In your academic writing, especially, be careful that any visuals you use support your main point — and don't just serve to decorate the text. (Therefore, avoid clip art, which is primarily intended as decoration.) Images should support what you say elsewhere with written words and add information that words alone can't provide as clearly or easily.

Using Visuals

Photos, videos, tables, pie charts, bar graphs: these are many kinds of visuals you could use.

An essay discussing the work of Willem de Kooning might contrast one of his more representational works (such as the one on the left) with one that's more abstract (right).

rhetorical situations

genres

processes

strategies

research MLA / APA

media / design

readings

Photographs can support an **ARGUMENT,** illustrate **NARRATIVES** and **PROCESSES,** present other points of view, and help readers "place" your information in time and space. You may use photos you take yourself, or you can download photos and other images from the internet — within limits. Most downloadable photos are copyrighted, meaning that you can use them without obtaining permission from the copyright owner only if you are doing so for academic purposes, to fulfill an assignment. If you are going to publish your text, either in print or on the web, you must have permission. Consider, too, the file size of digital images; large files can clog readers' email in-boxes, take a long time to display on their screens, or be hard for you to upload in the first place, so you may have to compress an image or reduce its resolution (which can diminish its sharpness).

323–41
387–95
382–86

Videos   If you're writing online, you can include video clips for readers to play. If you're using a video already available online, such as on *YouTube*, you can show the opening image with an arrow for readers to click on to start the video, or you can simply copy the video's URL and paste it into your text as a **LINK**. In either case, you need to introduce the video in your text with a **SIGNAL PHRASE**. As with any other source, you need to provide an in-text citation and full documentation.

597
471–73

If you want to include a video you made yourself, you can edit it using such programs as *iMovie* or *Windows Movie Maker*. Once you're ready to insert it into your document, the easiest way is to first upload it to *YouTube*, choosing the Private setting so only those you authorize may view it, and then create a link in your document.

Graphs, charts, and tables   are excellent ways to present statistical and other numerical information. If you can't find the right one for your purpose, you can create your own, as long as it's based on sound data from reliable sources. To do so, you can use various spreadsheet programs or online chart and graph generators.

In any case, remember to follow basic design principles: be **CONSISTENT,** label all parts clearly, and **KEEP THE DESIGN SIMPLE,** so readers can focus on the information and, not be a distracted by a needlessly complex design. In particular, use color and contrast wisely to emphasize what's

582–83

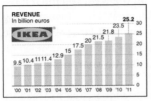

Line graphs are a good way of showing changes in data over time. Each line here represents a different social networking site. Plotting the lines together allows readers to compare the data at different points in time. Be sure to label the x and y axes and limit the number of lines to four at the most.

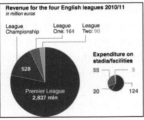

Bar graphs are useful for comparing quantitative data, measurements of how much or how many. The bars can be horizontal or vertical. This graph shows IKEA's earnings between 2000 and 2011. Some software offers 3-D and other special effects, but simple graphs are often easier to read.

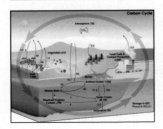

Pie charts can be used to show how a whole is divided into parts or how parts of a whole relate to one another. The segments in a pie should always add up to 100 percent, and each segment should be clearly labeled.

Tables are useful for displaying numerical information concisely, especially when several items are being compared. Presenting information in columns and rows permits readers to find data and identify relationships among them.

Diagrams and flowcharts are ways of showing relationships and processes. This diagram shows how carbon moves between the Earth and its atmosphere. Flowcharts can be made using widely available templates; diagrams, on the other hand, can range from simple drawings to works of art. Some simple flowcharts may be found in the Genre chapters (for example, p. 221).

rhetorical situations   genres   processes   strategies   research MLA / APA   media / design   readings

most significant. Choose **COLORS** that are easy to distinguish from one
— and that remain so if the graph or chart is printed out in black and
white. (Using gradations of color from light to dark will show in black
and white.) Some common kinds of graphs, charts, and tables are shown
on the facing page.

585

SOME TIPS FOR USING VISUALS

- Position images as close as possible to the discussion to which they
  relate. In *Microsoft Word*, simply position your cursor where you want
  to insert an image; click Picture on the Insert tab; choose the appropriate image from your files; and click Insert. You may then need to
  adjust the way the text flows or wraps around the image: in the Page
  Layout tab, choose the appropriate option in Wrap Text.

- In academic writing, number all images, using separate sequences of
  numbers for figures (photos, graphs, diagrams, video clips, and drawings) and tables: Fig. 1, Fig. 2; Table 1, Table 2.

- Explain in your written text whatever information you present in an
  image — don't expect it to speak for itself. Refer to the image before it
  appears, identifying it and summarizing its point. For example: "As Table
  1 shows, Italy's economic growth rate has been declining for thirty years."

- Provide a title or caption for each image to identify it and explain its
  significance for your text. For example: "Table 1: Italy's Economic
  Growth Rate, 1980–2010."

- Label the parts of visuals clearly to ensure that your audience will
  understand what they show. For example, label each section of a pie
  chart to show what it represents.

- Cite the source of any images you don't create yourself. You need not
  document visuals you create, based on data from your own experimental or field research, but if you use data from a source to create
  a graph or chart, **CITE THE SOURCE** of the data.

475–78

- In general, you may use visuals created by someone else in your academic writing as long as you include full **DOCUMENTATION**. If you post
  your writing online, however, you must first obtain permission from
  the copyright owner.

480–83

Incorporating Sound

Audio clips, podcasts, and other sound files can serve various useful purposes in online writing. Music, for example, can create a mood for your text, giving your audience hints about how to interpret the meaning of your words and images or what emotional response you're evoking. Other types of sound effects — such as background conversations, passing traffic, birdsongs, crowd noise at sports events — can provide a sense of immediacy, of being part of the scene or event you're describing. Spoken words can serve as the primary way you present an online text or as an enhancement of or even a counterpoint to a written text. (And if your audience includes visually impaired people, an audio track can allow or help them to follow the text.)

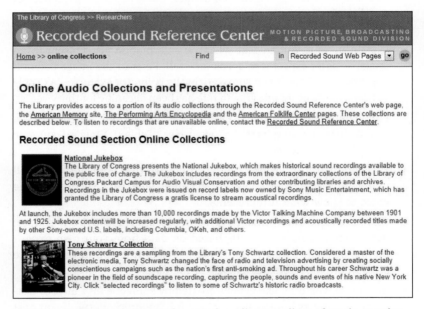

The Library of Congress is a good source for online recordings of music, speeches, and radio broadcasts.

You can download or link to various spoken texts online, or you can record voice and music as podcasts using programs such as *GarageBand* and *Audacity*. Remember to provide an **IN-TEXT CITATION** and full **DOCUMENTATION** of any sound material you obtain from another source.

● 480–83

Adding Links

If you're writing an online text in which you want to include images, video, or sound material available on the web, it's often easier and more effective to create links to them within the text than to embed them by copying and pasting. Such links allow readers to see the materials' original context and to explore it if they wish.

The example below shows a blog post from the Archives of American Art with links to additional detail and documentation.

John Singer Sargent

This lively caricature from the Francis Davis Millet and Millet family papers features an artist fervently painting his subject, just in the background. Most likely it is John Singer Sargent at work on his painting *Carnation, Lily, Lily, Rose*. His posture and the expression on his face suggest an exuberance that matches the action of the paint dripping and splashing as it prepares to meet the canvas with energetic strokes.

Caricature of an artist painting vigorously, ca. 1885-1886. Francis Davis Millet and Millet family papers, Archives of American Art, Smithsonian Institution.

471–73 ●

SOME TIPS FOR CREATING LINKS

- Indicate links with underlining and color (most often blue), and introduce them with a **SIGNAL PHRASE.**

- Don't include your own punctuation in a link. In the example on page 597, the period is not part of the link.

- Try to avoid having a link open in a new browser window. Readers expect links to open in the same window.

Editing Carefully — and Ethically

You may want to edit a photograph, cropping to show only part of it or using *Photoshop* or similar programs to enhance the colors or otherwise alter it. Similarly, you may want to edit a video, podcast, or other audio file to shorten it or remove irrelevant parts. If you are considering making a change of this kind, however, be sure not to do so in a way that misrepresents the content. If you alter a photo, be sure the image still represents the subject accurately; if you alter a recording of a speech or interview, be sure the edited version maintains the speaker's intent. Whenever you alter an image, a video, or a sound recording, tell your readers how you have changed it.

The same goes of editing charts and graphs. Changing the scale on a bar graph, for example, can change the effect of the comparison, making the quantities being compared seem very similar or very different, as shown in the two bar graphs of identical data in figures 1 and 2.

Because of the different fund-raising goals implied by the graphs ($800 or $5,000) and the different increments of the dollars raised ($200 or $1,000), the graphs send very different messages, though the dollars raised by each fund-raiser remain the same. Just as you shouldn't edit a quotation or a photograph in a way that might misrepresent its meaning, you should not present statistical data in a way that could mislead readers.

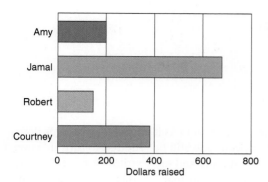

Fig. 1. Fundraising results for the class gift.

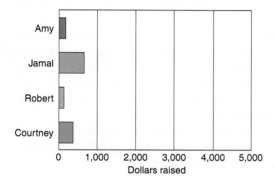

Fig. 2. Fundraising results for the class gift.

55 Writing Online

Email. *Facebook*. Texts. Tweets. It may seem as if almost all writing is done online now. In college courses, you may still be required to turn in some writing assignments on paper, but more and more writing is not only done online but submitted that way too. And many classes are being taught online, with little or no face-to-face communication between instructors and students.

Online, your instructor and classmates usually cannot see or hear you — and that matters more than you might think. A puzzled look or a smile of recognition can start an important conversation in a face-to-face class, but in an online environment, your audience usually has only your written words to respond to. Therefore, you need to express your thoughts and feelings as clearly as you can *in writing*.

So it's useful to think about how the electronic medium affects the way we write — and how we can express ourselves most effectively when we write online. This chapter provides some advice.

Online Genres

For most of us, email, texting, and social networking sites like *Facebook* are already parts of everyday life. But using them for academic purposes may require some careful attention. Following are some guidelines.

Email. When emailing faculty members and school administrators, you are writing in an academic context, so your messages should reflect it: use an appropriate salutation ("Dear Professor Hagzanian"); write clearly and concisely in complete sentences; use standard capitalization and punctuation; proofread; and sign your full name. If you're writing about a specific

rhetorical situations

genres

processes

strategies

research
MLA / APA

media / design

readings

course or group work, identify the course or group explicitly. Also, craft a specific subject line; instead of writing "Question about paper," be specific: "Profile organization question." If you change topics, change your subject line as well rather than simply replying to an old email. And be careful before you hit Send — you want to be good and sure that your email neither says something you'll regret later (don't send an email when you're angry!) nor includes anything you don't want the whole world reading (don't put confidential or sensitive information in email).

Texting   is a way of sending and receiving brief text messages on a phone. Texting is inherently informal and often serves as an alternative to a phone call. Since texting often takes place as a conversation in real time (and phone keyboards can be hard to use), those who write texts often use acronyms, shorthand, and emoticons — ROTFL (rolling on the floor laughing), OST (on second thought), 2nite (tonight), 10Q (thank you), :) (happy) — to get their meaning across quickly and efficiently. If you use these abbreviations, though, be sure your readers will understand them!

Social media.   You may take a course that involves using *Facebook* or another social media site as a way for class members to communicate or as part of a **LEARNING MANAGEMENT SYSTEM.** If so, you need to consider your rhetorical situation to make sure your course postings represent you as a respectful (and respectable) member of the class. Also, remember that many employers routinely check job applicants' social media pages, so don't post writing or photos that you wouldn't want a potential employer to see.

□ 606–8

Websites   are groups of webpages organized around a homepage and connected to one another (and to other websites) through hyperlinks, which take users automatically from one page to another. While it's possible to create your own websites from scratch, free website builders such as *Weebly, Google Sites,* or *Wix* make it easy to create a site by providing templates for homepages, page designs, and navigation systems.

One key element in a website is the use of links to bring material from other sources into your text. You can link to the definition of a key term,

The homepage of Discover History, the National Park Service cultural resource program, provides a navigation menu on the left that leads to various sections of the site. Links embedded within the introductory text connect to Park Service pages outside the program.

for instance, rather than defining it yourself, or you can summarize a source and link to the full text rather than quoting or paraphrasing it. Providing links lets readers decide whether they need or want to see more detailed information — or not.

Blogs   are websites that generally focus on a single topic — politics, celebrities, gaming, baseball, you name it. They're maintained and updated regularly by individuals or groups who post opinions, reflections, information, and more — with writing, photos, video and audio files, and links to other sites. Blogs are an easy way to share your writing with others — and to invite response. Free blog hosting sites such as *WordPress* or *Blogger* offer templates that let you create a blog and post to it easily, and some learning management systems include blogging capability as well.

This blog, hosted by the Smithsonian Institution, focuses on marine biology and includes video, audio, slideshows and written narratives. Readers can interact with and respond to the text by clicking on icons for Facebook, Twitter, and other social networking sites.

If your blog is public, anyone can read it, including potential employers, so just as with *Facebook* and other social media, you'll want to be careful about how you present yourself and avoid posting anything that others could see as offensive. (Think twice before posting when you're angry or upset.) You may want to activate privacy settings that let you restrict access to some of the content or that make your blog unsearchable by *Google* and other search tools. Also, assume that what you post in a blog is permanent: your friends, family, employer — anyone — may read a posting years in the future, even if the blog is no longer active.

Wikis are websites that allow a group to work collaboratively, with all users free to add, edit, and delete content. *Wikipedia,* the online encyclopedia, is one of the most famous wikis: its content is posted and edited by people all over the world. You may be asked to contribute to a class wiki, such as the one below from a writing course at Sinclair Community College. Students post their work to the wiki, and everyone in the class has access to everyone else's writing and can comment on or revise it. When contributing to a wiki, you should be careful to write precisely, edit carefully, and make sure your research is accurate and appropriately cited — others may be quick to question and rewrite your work if it's sloppy or inaccurate.

A writing-course wiki from Sinclair Community College.

Managing Online Course Work

Because so much of your college work will be done online — at the very least, you'll do most of your writing on a computer and submit some assignments via email — it's important to set up some procedures for yourself. In a single writing course, for example, you may write three or four drafts of four essays — that's twelve to sixteen documents. To keep track of your files, you'll need to create folders, establish consistent file names, and back up your work.

Creating folders.   Create a folder for each course, and name it with the course title or number and the academic term: ENG 101 Fall 2013. Within each course folder, create a folder for each major assignment. Save your work in the appropriate folder, so you can always find it.

Saving files.   Your word processor likely saves documents to a specific format identified by a three- or four-letter ending automatically added to the file name: .doc, .docx, .txt, and so on. However, this default format may not be compatible with other programs. If you're not sure what format you'll need, use the Save As command to save each document in Rich Text Format, or .rtf, which most word processors can read.

Naming files.   If you are expected to submit files electronically, your instructor may ask you to name them in a certain way. If not, devise a system that will let you easily find the files, including multiple drafts of your writing. For example, you might name your files using *Your last name + Assignment + Draft number + Date*: Jones Evaluation Draft 2 10-5-2013.docx. You'll then be able to find a particular file by looking for the assignment, the draft number, or the date. Saving all your drafts as separate files will make it easy to include them in a portfolio; also, if you lose a draft, you'll be able to use the previous one to reconstruct it.

Backing up your work.   Hard drives fail, laptops get dropped, flash drives are left in public computers. Because files stored in computers can be damaged or lost, you should save your work in several places: on your computer, on a flash drive or portable hard drive, in space supplied by your school, or online. You can also ensure that an extra copy of your work exists by emailing a copy to yourself.

Finding Basic Course Information

You'll need to learn some essential information about any online courses you take:

606–8 □

- *The phone number for the campus help desk* or technology center. Check the hours of operation, and keep the number handy.

- *The syllabus,* list of assignments, and calendar with deadlines.

- *Where to find tutorials* for your school's LEARNING MANAGEMENT SYSTEM and other programs you may need help with.

- *How and when you can contact your instructor* — in person during office hours? by phone or email? — and how soon you can expect a response.

- *What file format you should use* to submit assignments — .doc, .docx, .rtf, .pdf, something else? — and how to submit them.

- *How to use the spellcheck function* on your word processor or learning management system.

- *How to participate in online discussions* — will you use a discussion board? a chat function in a learning management system? a blog? a social network? something else?

Using Learning Management Systems

Whether you're in a face-to-face, hybrid, or online class, you may be asked to do some or all of your classwork online using a learning management system (LMS) such as *Blackboard* or *Desire2Learn*. An LMS is a web-based educational tool that brings together all the course information your

A course homepage from Wright State's Pilot LMS.

instructor wants you to have, along with features that allow you to participate in the class in various ways. Your school's LMS likely includes the following features that you'll be expected to use:

A course homepage contains posts from your instructor; a calendar with due dates for assignments; and links to the course syllabus, other course content, and additional features available on the site.

A discussion board allows you to communicate with classmates even if everyone isn't logged in to the board at the same time. These conversations may be organized in "threads" so that posts on a particular topic appear together and may be read in order. When you contribute to a threaded discussion, treat it as an ongoing conversation: you need not introduce the topic but can simply add your comments.

A chat tool   allows you to engage in written conversations in real time, with all participants logged in simultaneously. In a classroom, doing this may be like texting with many others at once, so the rules for class discussion apply: be patient while waiting for a response; focus on the topic being discussed; avoid sarcasm or personal attacks.

A dropbox   is a place where you submit assignments online. If your course dropbox has folders for each assignment, be sure to upload your assignment into the correct folder. Keep in mind that systems go down, so don't wait until the last minute to submit a file. It's a good idea to double-check that the file you've submitted has been uploaded; often you can simply exit the dropbox and then return to it to see that your file is where it should be.

Online portfolios.   Many LMSs allow you to create an online portfolio where you may post your coursework as well as photos, personal information, and links to other websites.

Additional features.   An LMS may also include email; a space to keep a journal; a whiteboard for posting images, graphics, and presentations; a gradebook; a social network (sometimes called a Ning) for class members only; and other features that can help you keep track of your work in a class.

Giving Presentations 56

In a marketing class, you give a formal presentation that includes slides and handouts as part of a research project on developing brand loyalty to clothing labels among college students. As a candidate for student government, you deliver several speeches to various campus groups that are simultaneously broadcast over the web. At a good friend's wedding, after you make a toast to the married couple, another friend who couldn't attend in person toasts them remotely using *Skype*; a third guest records both toasts on his cell phone and uploads them to *Facebook*. Whether or not you include electronic and print media, whenever you are called on to give a spoken presentation, you need to make your points clear and memorable. This chapter offers guidelines to help you prepare and deliver effective presentations. We'll start with two good examples.

ABRAHAM LINCOLN

Gettysburg Address

Given by the sixteenth president of the United States, at the dedication of the Gettysburg battlefield as a memorial to those who died in the Civil War, this is one of the most famous speeches ever delivered in the United States.

> Four score and seven years ago our fathers brought forth on this continent, a new nation, conceived in Liberty, and dedicated to the proposition that all men are created equal.
> Now we are engaged in a great civil war, testing whether that nation, or any nation so conceived and so dedicated, can long endure.

We are met on a great battle-field of that war. We have come to dedicate a portion of that field, as a final resting place for those who here gave their lives that that nation might live. It is altogether fitting and proper that we should do this.

But, in a larger sense, we can not dedicate — we can not consecrate — we can not hallow — this ground. The brave men, living and dead, who struggled here, have consecrated it, far above our poor power to add or detract. The world will little note, nor long remember what we say here, but it can never forget what they did here. It is for us the living, rather, to be dedicated here to the unfinished work which they who fought here have thus far so nobly advanced. It is rather for us to be here dedicated to the great task remaining before us — that from these honored dead we take increased devotion to that cause for which they gave the last full measure of devotion — that we here highly resolve that these dead shall not have died in vain — that this nation, under God, shall have a new birth of freedom — and that government of the people, by the people, for the people, shall not perish from the earth.

You won't likely be called on to deliver such an address, but the techniques Lincoln used — brevity, rhythm, recurring themes — are ones you can use in your own spoken texts. The next example represents the type of spoken text we are sometimes called on to deliver at important occasions in the lives of our families.

JUDY DAVIS

Ours Was a Dad . . .

This short eulogy was given at the funeral of the writer's father, Walter Boock. Judy Davis lives in Davis, California, where she was for many years the principal of North Davis Elementary School.

Elsa, Peggy, David, and I were lucky to have such a dad. Ours was a dad who created the childhood for us that he did not have for himself.

The dad who sent us airborne on the soles of his feet, squealing with delight. The dad who built a platform in the peach tree so we could eat ourselves comfortably into peachy oblivion. The dad who assigned us chores and then did them with us. The dad who felt our pain when we skinned our knees.

Ours was the dad who took us camping, all over the U.S. and Canada, but most of all in our beloved Yosemite. The one who awed us with his ability to swing around a full pail of water without spilling a drop and let us hold sticks in the fire and draw designs in the night air with hot orange coals.

Our dad wanted us to feel safe and secure. On Elsa's eighth birthday, we acquired a small camping trailer. One very blustery night in Minnesota, Mom and Dad asleep in the main bed, David suspended in the hammock over them, Peggy and Elsa snuggled in the little dinette bed, and me on an air mattress on the floor, I remember the most incredible sense of well-being: our family all together, so snug, in that little trailer as the storm rocked us back and forth. It was only in the morning that I learned about the tornado warnings. Mom and Dad weren't sleeping: they were praying that when morning came we wouldn't find ourselves in the next state.

Ours was the dad who helped us with homework at the round oak table. He listened to our oral reports, taught us to add by looking for combinations of 10, quizzed us on spelling words, and when our written reports sounded a little too much like the *World Book* encyclopedia, he told us so.

Ours was a dad who believed our round oak table that seated twelve when fully extended should be full at Thanksgiving. Dad called the chaplain at the airbase, asked about homesick boys, and invited them to join our family. Or he'd call International House in Berkeley to see if someone from another country would like to experience an American Thanksgiving. We're still friends with the Swedish couple who came for turkey forty-five years ago. Many people became a part of our extended family around that table. And if twelve around the table was good, then certainly fourteen would be better. Just last fall, Dad commissioned our neighbor Randy to make yet another leaf for the table. There were fourteen around the table for Dad's last Thanksgiving.

Ours was a dad who had a lifelong desire to serve. He delivered Meals on Wheels until he was eighty-three. He delighted in picking up the day-old doughnuts from Mr. Rollen's shop to give those on his route an extra treat. We teased him that he should be receiving those meals himself! Even after walking became difficult for him, he continued to drive and took along an able friend to carry the meals to the door.

Our family, like most, had its ups and downs. But ours was a dad who forgave us our human failings as we forgave him his. He died in peace, surrounded by love. Elsa, Peggy, David, and I were so lucky to have such a dad.

This eulogy, in honor of the writer's father, provides concrete and memorable details that give the audience a clear image of the kind of man he was. The repetition of the phrase "ours was a dad" provides a rhythm and unity that moves the text forward, and the use of short, conventional sentences makes the text easy to understand — and deliver.

Key Features / Spoken Presentations

A clear structure. Spoken texts need to be clearly organized so that your audience can follow what you're saying. The **BEGINNING** needs to engage their interest, make clear what you will be talking about, and perhaps forecast the central parts of your talk. The main part of the text should focus on a few main points — only as many as your listeners can be expected to absorb and retain. (Remember, they can't go back to reread!) The **ENDING** is especially important: it should leave your audience with something, to remember, think about, or do. Davis ends as she begins, saying that she and her sisters and brother "were so lucky to have such a dad." Lincoln ends with a dramatic resolution: "that government of the people, by the people, for the people, shall not perish from the earth."

Signpost language to keep your audience on track. You may need to provide cues to help your listeners follow your text, especially **TRANSITIONS** that lead them from one point to the next. Sometimes you'll also want to stop and **SUMMARIZE** a complex point to help your audience keep track of your ideas and follow your development of them.

299–306 ◆

306–10 ◆

317 ◆

470–71 ●

rhetorical situations ■   genres ▲   processes ○   strategies ◆   research MLA / APA ●   media / design ▢   readings ▮

A tone to suit the occasion.   Lincoln spoke at a serious, formal event, the dedication of a national cemetery, and his address is formal and even solemn. Davis's eulogy is more informal in TONE, as befits a speech given for friends and loved ones. In a presentation to a panel of professors, you probably would want to take an academic tone, avoiding too much slang and speaking in complete sentences. If you had occasion to speak on the very same topic to a neighborhood group, however, you would likely want to speak more casually.

■ 13

Repetition and parallel structure.   Even if you're never called on to deliver a Gettysburg Address, you will find that repetition and parallel structure can lend power to a presentation, making it easier to follow — and more likely to be remembered. "We can not dedicate — we can not consecrate — we can not hallow": the repetition of "we can not" and the parallel forms of the three verbs are one reason these words stay with us more than 150 years after they were written and delivered. These are structures any writer can use. See how the repetition of "ours was a dad" in Davis's eulogy creates a rhythm that engages listeners and at the same time unifies the text.

Slides and other media.   Depending on the way you deliver your presentation, you will often want or need to use other media — *PowerPoint* or other presentation slides, video and audio clips, handouts, flip charts, whiteboards, and so on — to present certain information and to highlight key points.

Considering the Rhetorical Situation

As with any writing, you need to consider your rhetorical situation when preparing a presentation:

PURPOSE   Consider what your primary purpose is. To inform? persuade? entertain? evoke another kind of emotional response?

■ 3–4

5–8 ■
AUDIENCE Think about whom you'll be addressing and how well you know them. Will they be interested, or will you need to get them interested? Are they likely to be friendly? How can you get and maintain their attention, and how can you establish common ground with them? How much will they know about your subject — will you need to provide background or define any terms?

9–11 ■
GENRE The genre of your text will affect the way you structure and present it. If you're making an argument, for instance, you'll need to consider counterarguments — and, depending on the way you're giving the presentation, perhaps to allow for questions and comments from members of the audience who hold other opinions. If you're giving a report, you may have reasons to prepare handouts with detailed information you don't have time to cover in your spoken text, or links to online documents or websites.

12–15 ■
STANCE Consider the attitude you want to express. Is it serious? thoughtful? passionate? well-informed? humorous? something else? Choose your words and any other elements of your presentation accordingly. Whatever your attitude, your presentation will be received better by your listeners if they perceive you as comfortable and sincere.

A Brief Guide to Writing Presentations

Whether you're giving a poster presentation at a conference or an oral report in class, what you say will differ in important ways from what you might write for others to read. Here are some tips for composing an effective presentation.

Budget your time.   A five-minute presentation calls for about two and a half pages of writing, and ten minutes means only four or five pages. Your introduction and conclusion should each take about one-tenth of the total time available; time for questions (if the format allows for them) should take about one-fifth; and the body of the talk, the rest. In a ten-minute presentation, then, allot one minute for your introduction, one minute for your conclusion, and two minutes for questions, leaving six minutes for the body of your talk.

Organize and draft your presentation.   Readers can go back and reread if they don't understand or remember something the first time through a text. Listeners can't. Therefore, it's important that you structure your presentation so that your audience can follow your text — and remember what you say.

- *Craft an introduction* that engages your audience's interest and tells them what to expect. Depending on your rhetorical situation, you may want to **BEGIN** with humor, with an anecdote, or with something that reminds them of the occasion for your talk or helps them see the reason for it. In any case, you always need to summarize your main points, provide any needed background information, and outline how you'll proceed.

299–306

- *In the body of your presentation,* present your main points in more detail and support them with **REASONS** and **EVIDENCE.** As you draft, you may well find that you have more material than you can present in the time available, so you'll need to choose the most important points to focus on and leave out the rest.

326–35

- *Let your readers know you're concluding* (but try to avoid saying "in conclusion"), and then use your remaining time to restate your main points and to explain why they're important. End by saying "thank you" and offering to answer questions or take comments if the format allows for them.

Consider whether to use visuals.   You may want or need to include some visuals to help listeners follow what you're saying. Especially when you're presenting complex information, it helps to let them see it as well as hear it. Remember, though, that visuals should be a means of conveying information, not mere decoration.

DECIDING ON THE APPROPRIATE VISUALS

- *Slides* are useful for listing main points and for projecting illustrations, tables, and graphs.

- *Videos, animations, and sounds* can add additional information to your presentations.

- *Flip charts, whiteboards, or chalkboards* allow you to create visuals as you speak or to keep track of comments from your audience.

- *Posters* sometimes serve as the main part of a presentation, providing a summary of your points. You then offer only a brief introduction and answer any questions.

- *Handouts* can provide additional information, lists of works cited, or copies of any slides you show.

What visual tools (if any) you decide to use is partly determined by how your presentation will be delivered. Will you be speaking to a crowd or a class, delivering your presentation through a podcast, or creating an interactive presentation for a web conference? Make sure that any necessary equipment and programs are available — and that they work. If at all possible, check out any equipment in the place where you'll deliver your presentation before you go live. If you bring your own equipment for a live presentation, make sure you can connect to the internet if you need to and that electrical outlets are in reach of your power cords. Also, make sure that your visuals can be seen. You may have to rearrange the furniture or the screen to make sure everyone can see.

And finally, have a backup plan. Computers fail; projector bulbs burn out; marking pens run dry. Whatever your plan is, have an alternative in case any problems occur.

Presentation software.   *PowerPoint, Keynote,* and other presentation software can include images, video, and sound in addition to displaying written text. They are most useful for linear presentations that move audiences along one slide at a time. Cloud-based programs like *Prezi* also allow you to arrange words or slides in various designs, group related content together, and zoom in and out. Here are some tips for writing and designing slides:

- *Use* LISTS *or images, not paragraphs.* Use slides to emphasize your main points, not to reproduce your talk onscreen: keep your audience's attention focused on what you're saying. A list of brief points, presented one by one, reinforces your words. An image can provide additional information that your audience can take in quickly.

587

- *Make your text easy for your audience to read.* FONTS should be at least 18 points, and larger than that for headings. Projected slides are easier to read in sans serif fonts like Arial, Helvetica, and Tahoma than in serif fonts like Times New Roman. And avoid using all capital letters, which can be hard to read.

585–86

- *Choose colors carefully.* Your text and any illustrations must contrast with the background. Dark content on a light background is easier to read than the reverse. And remember that not everyone sees all colors; be sure your audience doesn't need to be able to see particular colors or contrasts in order to get your meaning. Red-green and blue-yellow contrasts are especially hard for some people to see and should be avoided.

- *Use bells and whistles sparingly, if at all.* Presentation software offers lots of decorative backgrounds, letters that fade in and out or dance across the screen, and sound effects. These features can be more distracting than helpful; use them only if they help to make your point.

- *Mark your text.* In your notes or prepared text, mark each place where you need to click a mouse to call up the next slide.

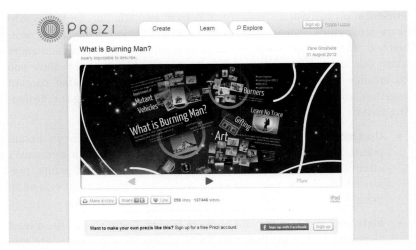

This Prezi *presentation rotates, includes audio and video, and zooms in and out to let viewers take a closer look.*

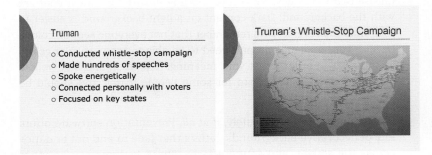

Two PowerPoint slides on the U.S. presidential election of 1948. The slide on the left outlines the main points; the one on the right shows a map of Truman's whistle-stop campaign, providing a graphic illustration of the miles he traveled as he campaigned to be president.

Handouts.   When you want to give your audience information they can refer to later — reproductions of your visuals, bibliographic information about your sources, printouts of your slides — do so in the form of handouts. Refer to the handouts in your presentation, but unless they include material your audience needs to consult before or as you talk, wait until you are finished to distribute them so as not to distract listeners. Clearly label everything you give out, including your name and the date and title of the presentation.

Delivering a Presentation

The success of a presentation often hinges on how you deliver it. As you work on your spoken texts, bear in mind the following points:

Practice.   Practice, practice, and then practice some more. The better you know your talk, the more confident you will be, and your audience will respond positively to that confidence. If you're reading a prepared text, try to write it as if you were talking. Then practice by recording it as you read it; listen for spots that sound as if you're reading, and work on your delivery to sound more relaxed. As you practice, pay attention to keeping within your time limit. If possible, rehearse your talk with a small group of friends to test their response and to get used to speaking in front of an audience.

Speak clearly.   When you're giving a spoken presentation, your first goal is to be understood by your audience. If listeners miss important words or phrases because you don't pronounce them distinctly, your talk will not succeed. Make sure, too, that your pace matches your audience's needs. Often you'll need to make yourself speak more slowly than usual to explain complex material (or to compensate for nerves); sometimes you may need to speed up to keep your audience's attention. In general, though, strive for a consistent pace throughout, one that ensures you don't have to rush at the end.

Pause for emphasis.   In writing, you have white space and punctuation to show readers where an idea or discussion ends. When speaking, you need to pause to signal the end of a thought, to give listeners a moment to consider something you've said, or to get them ready for a surprising or amusing statement.

Stand up (or sit up) straight and look at your audience.   If you're in the same physical space as your audience, try to maintain some eye contact with them. If that's uncomfortable, fake it: pick a spot on the wall just above the head of a person in the back of the room, and focus on it. You'll appear as if you're looking at your audience even if you're not looking them in the eye. And if you stand or sit up straight, you'll project the sense that you have confidence in what you're saying. If you appear to believe in your words, others will, too. If you're speaking via an online forum like *Skype,* look at the computer's camera — not at the screen. Also, make sure the camera is positioned at your eye level, so you aren't looking down at it (and showing your viewers the ceiling behind you!).

Use gestures for emphasis.   If you're not used to speaking in front of a group, you may let your nervousness show by holding yourself stiffly, elbows tucked in. To overcome some of that nervousness, take some deep breaths, try to relax, and move your arms and the rest of your body as you would if you were talking to a friend. Use your hands for emphasis: most public speakers use one hand to emphasize specific points and both hands to make larger gestures. Watch politicians on C-SPAN to see how people who speak on a regular basis use gestures as part of their overall delivery.

part 7

Readings

"Read, read, read. Read everything — trash, classics, good and bad, and see how they do it." So said the American writer William Faulkner, and on the following pages you will find an anthology of readings that show how Sojourner Truth, Malcolm X, David Sedaris, Nicholas Carr, Judith Ortiz Cofer, and many other writers "do it." Read on, and pay attention to how these writers use the KEY FEATURES and STRATEGIES that you yourself are learning to use. The anthology includes readings in nine GENRES and a chapter of readings that mix genres; you'll find a menu of readings in the back of the book.

Readings

Literacy Narratives 57

rhetorical situations · genres · processes · strategies · research MLA / APA · media / design · readings

DANIEL FELSENFELD

Rebel Music

Daniel Felsenfeld writes for the Opinionator, which provides "exclusive online commentary" from the New York Times, and which originally published this piece in March 2010. He also maintains a blog titled Daniel Felsenfeld News. As a composer, he has written in many different genres: orchestral music, opera, chamber music, solo music for piano and violin, and vocal music. He is author and coauthor of several books on music, including Benjamin Britten and Samuel Barber: Their Lives and Their Music (2005), and of several listening guides that accompany CDs. Felsenfeld teaches music at City College of New York. In this essay, he explores his journey of becoming literate in classical music.

MUSIC MAY BE THE UNIVERSAL LANGUAGE, but those of us who spend our lives with it are expected to know it in depth, from early on. Many composers, whether traditional or experimental, have been steeped in Western classical music from the cradle. That was not the case with me.

My primal time was the middle of the '80's in Orange County, Calif. I was 17 years old. The O.C. was billed as the ideal suburban community, but when you are raised in a palm-tree lined Shangri-La as I was, it is hard to grasp what's missing without that crucial glimpse beyond. Now I realize: even though we had enough water to keep the manicured lawns just so, I was experiencing a personal drought, an arid lack of culture of all kinds, especially music.

I was by no means unmusical, though any talent I have remains a mystery, coming as I do from perhaps the least musical of families (who would be the first to admit this). To her credit, my mother signed me up for the de rigueur piano lessons. Each week I dazzled poor Ms. Shimizu with either an astonishing performance of a Mozart sonata or a heretofore unseen level of ill-preparedness. I slogged my way through Chopin Preludes, culminating my high school piano study with a middling performance of Beethoven's "Pathétique" sonata. Probably not unlike most kids' first encounter with formal music study: uninspiring.

rhetorical situations · genres · processes · strategies · research MLA / APA · media / design · readings

Eventually I quit lessons, but had developed chops enough to work in both piano bars (an underage piano man, traveling with my own snifter) and community theater orchestra pits. The music was dull, or at least had a dulling effect on me — it didn't sparkle, or ask questions. I took a lot of gigs, but at 17 I was already pretty detached. I was attracted to music for some reason I lacked vocabulary to explain, and neither *Oklahoma!* nor *Annie* offered answers.

That might have been it — working my way through junior college 5 playing in pits or at Nordstrom's, settling into some career or other — a piano studio, weddings, writing songs for mild amusement. Thankfully, it was not.

Some afternoons I would go to my friend Mike's house at the end of my cul-de-sac to listen to tapes of bands a lot of my friends were listening to: General Public, Howard Jones, the Thompson Twins (or David Bowie, Bauhaus and The Clash in our edgier moments). One day, bored with the music, Mike flipped his double-decked cassette case over to reveal rows of hidden tapes in a concealed compartment.

"Want to hear something really wild?" he said.

"But of course."

At 17, rebellion was of course a staple in my life. The smartest kids I knew took the route of dolling themselves up in anti-establishment finery — goth, punk, straight edge — forming bands, going to clubs in Los Angeles, spouting manifestos. I had auditioned this mode, joining a band (whose name escapes me) and, in one of my great (mercifully unphotographed) late high school moments, taking a long, throbbing solo at a school assembly on one of those bygone over-the-shoulder keyboards.

It seems implausible now, but the "something really wild" Mike held 10 was not goth, metal, or punk. It was a neatly hand-labeled tape of Beethoven's Ninth Symphony. He put it on, and I listened. I think it was then I actually heard music for the first time.

Was this the same Beethoven to whose sonata I had done such violence? It unrolled from the small speakers, this big, gorgeous, unruly beast of a thing, contemporary, horrifying, a juggernaut that moved from the dark to unbearable brightness, soaring and spitting, malingering and dancing wildly, the Most Beautiful Thing I Ever Heard. This "symphony" by this Beethoven had a drug-like effect on me. At my insistence we listened again. And again. I wished it would just keep going.

Mike, who was just a kid in the neighborhood with odd — evolved? sophisticated?— taste, had dozens more tapes: Brahms, Mozart, Bach, Prokofiev, Tchaikovsky, Sibelius, Rachmaninoff, Strauss. I may have known that this kind of music was called classical, but I certainly did not understand that it was considered "great" or that it was revered as the foundation of musical culture in the West. I just loved it more than anything I'd heard before, and I must have sensed it was also miles away from Orange County, exactly as far as my adolescent self longed to be. I dubbed Mike's tapes, and listened to them in secret. Driving to school with Beethoven blaring, I'd switch to KROQ as I entered the parking lot, swerving into my spot believing I'd put one over on people again.

> The symphony unrolled from the small speakers — a big, gorgeous, unruly beast of a thing. Was this the same Beethoven to whose sonata I had done such violence?

My passion for this "other" kind of music felt like the height of rebellion: I was the lone Bolshevik in my army. I loved this new (to me) music, but loved my abstract role in it even more. Rebels sought to break the mold, to do something that was exclusively "theirs," to be weird by way of self-expression. And since I was the only one I knew listening to symphonies and concerti, operas and string quartets, I felt I was the weirdest of them all; it served my adolescent need to be misunderstood. And so I decided, with little prior experience or interest, to become a composer.

Little did I know, right?

All too soon, I came to understand what hard work this was. I studied scores, read biographies, got a serious piano teacher and logged hours a day practicing, traded up Mike's cassettes for the then-novel compact discs, and boarded the spaceship bound for planet New York once or twice (always returning, at least then, to warmer climes). After signing up for theory classes at Fullerton Junior College, I met my first living composers: Brent Pierce taught me counterpoint and harmony (one summer I wrote a daily fugue), and Lloyd Rodgers was my private teacher (who encouraged me to copy out the entire "Well Tempered

15

Clavier" by hand). In the meantime, I heard my first examples of what is called "New Music," that is, classical music written more recently than the 19th century.

Of course, some of my illusions vanished as soon as I realized there were composers I could actually meet. I was no longer a rebellion of one, but this halcyon innocence was traded for the ability to interact with artists who were always taking on the obscene challenge of creating music that was totally new, completely theirs.

Now I live far from the O.C., in New York, having long ago colonized this distant planet and gone native, an active member of a community I once admired from what seemed an impossible distance. And while there are moments I lament not having been raised in a musical family, or my late and clumsy start, I also strive to make my less-than-ideal origins an asset. I've learned I do my best work when I remove myself and try to return to that Age of Wonder when I first heard the gorgeous dissonances of pieces like Samuel Barber's *Hermit Songs* or *Prayers of Kierkegaard*, Elliott Carter's Second String Quartet, Michael Nyman's The Kiss, George Crumb's *Black Angels*, Arnold Schoenberg's *Pierrot Lunaire*, Benjamin Britten's *Turn of the Screw*, John Corigliano's First Symphony, and Stephen Sondheim's *Sweeney Todd*, and took them to be the *same* dissonances, not contrasting sides of a sometimes-contentious or politicized art world. When I am composing, I try to return to that time and place of inexperience when I was knocked sideways by dangerous sounds. Why else write? Why else listen?

Engaging with the Text

1. What is the SIGNIFICANCE of Daniel Felsenfeld's literacy narrative? Where in the essay does the author make the significance clear?   ▲ 43

2. What STANCE does Felsenfeld assume toward his stated topic of "rebel music?" Where does this stance become clear in the essay? By the end of the essay, what are we meant to understand about why he uses the phrase "rebel music"?   ■ 12–15

3. This essay details some of Felsenfeld's journey to becoming literate in music so that he could become a composer. How is music literacy similar to literacy in the sense of reading and writing? What does the latter prepare you to do in the world?

591–99 ▢

4. If you were asked to choose or design a **VISUAL** to accompany this essay, what would it show or look like? What point(s) about the essay would you want the visual to highlight?

5. *For Writing.* As this essay shows, there are many literacies people develop in life: math literacy, music literacy, art literacy, body building literacy, knitting literacy, and so on. In addition to the ability to read and write essays, what other literacies have you developed? Write a **NARRATIVE** about one of those literacies, including specific details about how you developed it.

387–95 ◆

TANYA MARIA BARRIENTOS
Se Habla Español

*Tanya Maria Barrientos is manager of internal communications for the
University of Pennsylvania and a former columnist and feature writer
for the* Philadelphia Inquirer. *The following essay appeared in* Latina,
*a bilingual magazine published by and for Latinas. It was adapted from
an essay of the same title that was published in* Border-Line Personalities: A New Generation of Latinas Dish on Sex, Sass, and Cultural
Shifting *(2004). In this piece, Barrientos recounts her struggles as a
Latina who is not fluent in Spanish. She takes her title from a phrase
often seen in store windows, announcing that "Spanish is spoken" there.*

THE MAN ON THE OTHER END of the phone line is telling me the classes
I've called about are first-rate: native speakers in charge, no more than
six students per group. I tell him that will be fine and yes, I've studied a
bit of Spanish in the past. He asks for my name and I supply it, rolling
the double "r" in "Barrientos" like a pro. That's when I hear the silent
snag, the momentary hesitation I've come to expect at this part of the
exchange. Should I go into it again? Should I explain, the way I have to
half a dozen others, that I am Guatemalan by birth but *pura gringa* by
circumstance?

This will be the sixth time I've signed up to learn the language my
parents speak to each other. It will be the sixth time I've bought workbooks and notebooks and textbooks listing 501 conjugated verbs in
alphabetical order, in hopes that the subjunctive tense will finally take
root in my mind. In class I will sit across a table from the "native
speaker," who will wonder what to make of me. "Look," I'll want to say
(but never do). "Forget the dark skin. Ignore the obsidian eyes. Pretend
I'm a pink-cheeked, blue-eyed blonde whose name tag says 'Shannon.'"
Because that is what a person who doesn't innately know the difference
between *corre, corra,* and *corrí* is supposed to look like, isn't it?

I came to the United States in 1963 at age 3 with my family and
immediately stopped speaking Spanish. College-educated and seamlessly

bilingual when they settled in west Texas, my parents (a psychology professor and an artist) wholeheartedly embraced the notion of the American melting pot. They declared that their two children would speak nothing but *inglés*. They'd read in English, write in English, and fit into Anglo society beautifully.

It sounds politically incorrect now. But America was not a hyphenated nation back then. People who called themselves Mexican Americans or Afro-Americans were considered dangerous radicals, while law-abiding citizens were expected to drop their cultural baggage at the border and erase any lingering ethnic traits.

To be honest, for most of my childhood I liked being the brown girl who defied expectations. When I was 7, my mother returned my older brother and me to elementary school one week after the school year had already begun. We'd been on vacation in Washington, D.C., visiting the Smithsonian, the Capitol, and the home of Edgar Allan Poe. In the Volkswagen on the way home, I'd memorized "The Raven," and I would recite it with melodramatic flair to any poor soul duped into sitting through my performance. At the school's office, the registrar frowned when we arrived.

"You people. Your children are always behind, and you have the nerve to bring them in late?"

"My children," my mother answered in a clear, curt tone, "will be at the top of their classes in two weeks."

The registrar filed our cards, shaking her head.

I did not live in a neighborhood with other Latinos, and the public school I attended attracted very few. I saw the world through the clear, cruel vision of a child. To me, speaking Spanish translated into being poor. It meant waiting tables and cleaning hotel rooms. It meant being left off the cheerleading squad and receiving a condescending smile from the guidance counselor when you said you planned on becoming a lawyer or a doctor. My best friends' names were Heidi and Leslie and Kim. They told me I didn't seem "Mexican" to them, and I took it as a compliment. I enjoyed looking into the faces of Latino store clerks and waitresses and, yes, even our maid and saying *"Yo no hablo español."* It made me feel superior. It made me feel American. It made me feel white. I thought if I stayed away from Spanish, stereotypes would stay away from me.

rhetorical situations

genres

processes

strategies

research MLA / APA

media / design

readings

Then came the backlash. During the two decades when I'd worked 10 hard to isolate myself from the stereotype I'd constructed in my own head, society shifted. The nation changed its views on ethnic identity. College professors started teaching history through African American and Native American eyes. Children were told to forget about the melting pot and picture America as a multicolored quilt instead. Hyphens suddenly had muscle, and I was left wondering where I fit in.

The Spanish language was supposedly the glue that held the new Latino community together. But in my case it was what kept me apart. I felt awkward among groups whose conversations flowed in and out of Spanish. I'd be asked a question in Spanish and I'd have to answer in English, knowing this raised a mountain of questions. I wanted to call myself Latina, to finally take pride, but it felt like a lie. So I set out to learn the language that people assumed I already knew.

If I stayed away from Spanish, stereotypes would stay away from me.

After my first set of lessons, I could function in the present tense. "*Hola, Paco. ¿Qué tal? ¿Qué color es tu cuaderno? El mío es azul.*" My vocabulary built quickly, but when I spoke, my tongue felt thick inside my mouth — and if I needed to deal with anything in the future or the past, I was sunk. I enrolled in a three-month submersion program in Mexico and emerged able to speak like a sixth-grader with a solid C average. I could read Gabriel García Márquez with a Spanish-English dictionary at my elbow, and I could follow 90 percent of the melodrama on any given telenovela. But true speakers discover my limitations the moment I stumble over a difficult construction, and that is when I get the look. The one that raises the wall between us. The one that makes me think I'll never really belong. Spanish has become a litmus test showing how far from your roots you've strayed.

My bilingual friends say I make too much of it. They tell me that my Guatemalan heritage and unmistakable Mayan features are enough to legitimize my membership in the Latin American club. After all, not all Poles speak Polish. Not all Italians speak Italian. And as this nation grows more and more Hispanic, not all Latinos will share one language. But I don't believe them.

There must be other Latinas like me. But I haven't met any. Or, I should say, I haven't met any who have fessed up. Maybe they are secretly struggling to fit in, the same way I am. Maybe they are hiring tutors and listening to tapes behind locked doors, just like me. I wish we all had the courage to come out of our hiding places and claim our rightful spot in the broad Latino spectrum. Without being called hopeless gringas. Without having to offer apologies or show remorse.

If it will help, I will go first.   15

Aquí estoy. Spanish-challenged and *pura* Latina.

Engaging with the Text

312–13 1. Tanya Maria Barrientos gives her article a Spanish TITLE. How does this prepare you for the subject of the article? What does this title lead you to believe about Barrientos's feelings about Spanish? Is that impression supported by the rest of the article? Why or why not?

299–306 2. Barrientos BEGINS her essay with an anecdote about signing up for a Spanish class. What is the effect of beginning with this anecdote? Does it attract your interest? How does it prepare you for the rest of the essay?

43 3. Barrientos tells of learning to read and write in Spanish. One key feature of a literacy narrative is an indication of the narrative's SIGNIFICANCE. For her, what is the significance of learning that language? Why is it so important to her?

12–15 4. Barrientos peppers her essay with Spanish words and phrases, without offering any English translation. What does this tell you about her STANCE? Would her stance seem different if she'd translated the Spanish? Why or why not?

5. *For Writing.* As Barrientos notes, language plays a big part in her identity. Think about the languages you speak. If you speak only English, think about what kind of accent you have. (If you think you don't have one, consider how you might sound to someone from a different region.) Does the language you speak or accent you have change according to the situation? Does it change according to how you perceive yourself? Write an essay REFLECTING on the way you speak and how it affects (or is affected by) your identity.

214–21

rhetorical situations   genres   processes   strategies   research MLA / APA   media / design   readings

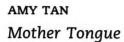

AMY TAN

Mother Tongue

Amy Tan is the author of novels, children's books, essays, and a memoir. Her work has appeared in McCall's, Atlantic Monthly, the New Yorker, and other magazines. She is best known for her novel The Joy Luck Club (1989), which examines the lives of and the relationships between four Chinese American daughters and their mothers. The following selection was first delivered as a talk at a symposium on language in San Francisco in 1989.

I AM NOT A SCHOLAR OF ENGLISH OR LITERATURE. I cannot give you much more than personal opinions on the English language and its variations in this country or others.

I am a writer. And by that definition, I am someone who has always loved language. I am fascinated by language in daily life. I spend a great deal of my time thinking about the power of language — the way it can evoke an emotion, a visual image, a complex idea, or a simple truth. Language is the tool of my trade. And I use them all — all the Englishes I grew up with.

Recently, I was made keenly aware of the different Englishes I do use. I was giving a talk to a large group of people, the same talk I had already given to half a dozen other groups. The nature of the talk was about my writing, my life, and my book, *The Joy Luck Club*. The talk was going along well enough, until I remembered one major difference that made the whole talk sound wrong. My mother was in the room. And it was perhaps the first time she had heard me give a lengthy speech, using the kind of English I have never used with her. I was saying things like, "The intersection of memory upon imagination" and "There is an aspect of my fiction that relates to thus-and-thus" — a speech filled with carefully wrought grammatical phrases, burdened, it suddenly seemed to me, with nominalized forms, past perfect tenses, conditional phrases, all the forms of standard English that I had learned in school and through books, the forms of English I did not use at home with my mother.

Just last week, I was walking down the street with my mother, and I again found myself conscious of the English I was using, the English I do use with her. We were talking about the price of new and used furniture and I heard myself saying this: "Not waste money that way." My husband was with us as well, and he didn't notice any switch in my English. And then I realized why. It's because over the twenty years we've been together I've often used the same kind of English with him, and sometimes he even uses it with me. It has become our language of intimacy, a different sort of English that relates to family talk, the language I grew up with.

So you'll have some idea of what this family talk I heard sounds like, I'll quote what my mother said during a recent conversation which I videotaped and then transcribed. During this conversation, my mother was talking about a political gangster in Shanghai who had the same last name as her family's, Du, and how the gangster in his early years wanted to be adopted by her family, which was rich by comparison. Later, the gangster became more powerful, far richer than my mother's family, and one day showed up at my mother's wedding to pay his respects. Here's what she said in part:

"Du Yusong having business like fruit stand. Like off the street kind. He is Du like Du Zong — but not Tsung-ming Island people. The local people call putong, the river east side, he belong to that side local people. That man want to ask Du Zong father take him in like become own family. Du Zong father wasn't look down on him, but didn't take seriously, until that man big like become a mafia. Now important person, very hard to inviting him. Chinese way, came only to show respect, don't stay for dinner. Respect for making big celebration, he shows up. Mean gives lots of respect. Chinese custom. Chinese social life that way. If too important won't have to stay too long. He come to my wedding. I didn't see, I heard it. I gone to boy's side, they have YMCA dinner. Chinese age I was nineteen."

You should know that my mother's expressive command of English belies how much she actually understands. She reads the *Forbes* report, listens to *Wall Street Week*, converses daily with her stockbroker, reads all of Shirley MacLaine's books with ease — all kinds of things I can't

begin to understand. Yet some of my friends tell me they understand 50 percent of what my mother says. Some say they understand 80 to 90 percent. Some say they understand none of it, as if she were speaking pure Chinese. But to me, my mother's English is perfectly clear, perfectly natural. It's my mother tongue. Her language, as I hear it, is vivid, direct, full of observation and imagery. That was the language that helped shape the way I saw things, expressed things, made sense of the world.

Lately, I've been giving more thought to the kind of English my mother speaks. Like others, I have described it to people as "broken" or "fractured" English. But I wince when I say that. It has always bothered me that I can think of no way to describe it other than "broken," as if it were damaged and needed to be fixed, as if it lacked a certain wholeness and soundness. I've heard other terms used, "limited English," for example. But they seem just as bad, as if everything is limited, including people's perceptions of the limited English speaker.

I know this for a fact, because when I was growing up, my mother's "limited" English limited *my* perception of her. I was ashamed of her English. I believed that her English reflected the quality of what she had to say. That is, because she expressed them imperfectly her thoughts were imperfect. And I had plenty of empirical evidence to support me: the fact that people in department stores, at banks, and at restaurants did not take her seriously, did not give her good service, pretended not to understand her, or even acted as if they did not hear her.

My mother has long realized the limitations of her English as well. 10 When I was fifteen, she used to have me call people on the phone to pretend I was she. In this guise, I was forced to ask for information or even to complain and yell at people who had been rude to her. One time it was a call to her stockbroker in New York. She had cashed out her small portfolio and it just so happened we were going to go to New York the next week, our very first trip outside California. I had to get on the phone and say in an adolescent voice that was not very convincing, "This is Mrs. Tan."

And my mother was standing in the back whispering loudly, "Why he don't send me check, already two weeks late. So mad he lie to me, losing me money."

And then I said in perfect English, "Yes, I'm getting rather concerned. You had agreed to send the check two weeks ago, but it hasn't arrived."

Then she began to talk more loudly. "What he want, I come to New York tell him front of his boss, you cheating me?" And I was trying to calm her down, make her be quiet, while telling the stockbroker, "I can't tolerate any more excuses. If I don't receive the check immediately, I am going to have to speak to your manager when I'm in New York next week." And sure enough, the following week there we were in front of this astonished stockbroker, and I was sitting there red-faced and quiet, and my mother, the real Mrs. Tan, was shouting at his boss in her impeccable broken English.

We used a similar routine just five days ago, for a situation that was far less humorous. My mother had gone to the hospital for an appointment, to find out about a benign brain tumor a CAT scan had revealed a month ago. She said she had spoken very good English, her best English, no mistakes. Still, she said, the hospital did not apologize when they said they had lost the CAT scan and she had come for nothing. She said they did not seem to have any sympathy when she told them she was anxious to know the exact diagnosis, since her husband and son had both died of brain tumors. She said they would not give her any more information until the next time and she would have to make another appointment for that. So she said she would not leave until the doctor called her daughter. She wouldn't budge. And when the doctor finally called her daughter, me, who spoke in perfect English — lo and behold — we had assurances the CAT scan would be found, promises that a conference call on Monday would be held, and apologies for any suffering my mother had gone through for a most regrettable mistake.

I think my mother's English almost had an effect on limiting my possibilities in life as well. Sociologists and linguists probably will tell you that a person's developing language skills are more influenced by peers. But I do think that the language spoken in the family, especially in immigrant families which are more insular, plays a large role in shaping the language of the child. And I believe that it affected my results on achievement tests, IQ tests, and the SAT. While my English skills were never judged as poor, compared to math, English could not be

15

rhetorical situations   genres   processes   strategies   research MLA / APA   media / design   readings

considered my strong suit. In grade school I did moderately well, getting perhaps B's, sometimes B-pluses, in English and scoring perhaps in the sixtieth or seventieth percentile on achievement tests. But those scores were not good enough to override the opinion that my true abilities lay in math and science, because in those areas I achieved A's and scored in the ninetieth percentile or higher.

This was understandable. Math is precise; there is only one correct answer. Whereas, for me at least, the answers on English tests were always a judgment call, a matter of opinion and personal experience. Those tests were constructed around items like fill-in-the-blank sentence completion, such as, "Even though Tom was _____, Mary thought he was _____." And the correct answer always seemed to be the most bland combinations of thoughts, for example, "Even though Tom was shy, Mary thought he was charming," with the grammatical structure "even though" limiting the correct answer to some sort of semantic opposites, so you wouldn't get answers like, "Even though Tom was foolish, Mary thought he was ridiculous." Well, according to my mother, there were very few limitations as to what Tom could have been and what Mary might have thought of him. So I never did well on tests like that.

The same was true with word analogies, pairs of words in which you were supposed to find some sort of logical, semantic relationship — for example, "*Sunset* is to *nightfall* as _____ is to _____." And here you would be presented with a list of four possible pairs, one of which showed the same kind of relationship: *red* is to *stoplight*, *bus* is to *arrival*, *chills* is to *fever*, *yawn* is to *boring*. Well, I could never think that way. I knew what the tests were asking, but I could not block out of my mind the images already created by the first pair, "*sunset* is to *nightfall*" — and I would see a burst of colors against a darkening sky, the moon rising, the lowering of a curtain of stars. And all the other pairs of words — red, bus, stoplight, boring — just threw up a mass of confusing images, making it impossible for me to sort out something as logical as saying: "A sunset precedes nightfall" is the same as "a chill precedes a fever." The only way I would have gotten that answer right would have been to imagine an associative situation, for example, my being disobedient and staying out past sunset, catching a chill at night, which turns into feverish pneumonia as punishment, which indeed did happen to me.

I have been thinking about all this lately, about my mother's English, about achievement tests. Because lately I've been asked, as a writer, why there are not more Asian Americans represented in American literature. Why are there few Asian Americans enrolled in creative writing programs? Why do so many Chinese students go into engineering? Well, these are broad sociological questions I can't begin to answer. But I have noticed in surveys — in fact, just last week — that Asian students, as a whole, always do significantly better on math achievement tests than in English. And this makes me think that there are other Asian-American students whose English spoken in the home might also be described as "broken" or "limited." And perhaps they also have teachers who are steering them away from writing and into math and science, which is what happened to me.

Fortunately, I happen to be rebellious in nature and enjoy the challenge of disproving assumptions made about me. I became an English major my first year in college, after being enrolled as pre-med. I started writing nonfiction as a freelancer the week after I was told by my former boss that writing was my worst skill and I should hone my talents toward account management.

But it wasn't until 1985 that I finally began to write fiction. And at 20 first I wrote using what I thought to be wittily crafted sentences, sentences that would finally prove I had mastery over the English language. Here's an example from the first draft of a story that later made its way into *The Joy Luck Club*, but without this line: "That was my mental quandary in its nascent state." A terrible line, which I can barely pronounce.

Fortunately, for reasons I won't get into today, I later decided I should envision a reader for the stories I would write. And the reader I decided upon was my mother, because these were stories about mothers. So with this reader in mind — and in fact she did read my early drafts — I began to write stories using all the Englishes I grew up with: the English I spoke to my mother, which for lack of a better term might be described as "simple"; the English she used with me, which for lack of a better term might be described as "broken"; my translation of her

Chinese, which could certainly be described as "watered down"; and what I imagined to be her translation of her Chinese if she could speak in perfect English, her internal language, and for that I sought to preserve the essence, but neither an English nor a Chinese structure. I wanted to capture what language ability tests can never reveal: her intent, her passion, her imagery, the rhythms of her speech and the nature of her thoughts.

Apart from what any critic had to say about my writing, I knew I had succeeded where it counted when my mother finished reading my book and gave me her verdict: "So easy to read."

Engaging with the Text

1. Amy Tan **BEGINS** by announcing, "I am not a scholar of English. . . . I cannot give you much more than personal opinions on the English language and its variations in this country or others." How does this opening set up your expectations for the rest of the essay? Why do you think she chose to begin by denying her own authority?

   ◆ 299–306

2. Tan writes about the different "Englishes" she speaks. What categories does she **DIVIDE** English into? Why are these divisions important to Tan? How does she say they affect her as a writer?

   ◆ 343–44

3. How does writing for a literary **AUDIENCE** affect the language Tan primarily uses in the essay? What kind of English do you think she believes her audience speaks? Why? Support your answer with quotations from the text.

   ■ 5–8

4. How does Tan's **TITLE** — "Mother Tongue" — affect the way you read her argument? What other titles might she have chosen?

   ◆ 312–13

5. *For Writing.* Explore the differences between the language you speak at home and the languages you use with friends, teachers, employers, and so on. Write an essay that **REFLECTS** on the various languages you speak. If you speak only one language, consider the variations in the ways you speak it — at home, at work, at school, at church, wherever.

   ▲ 214–21

MALCOLM X

Literacy behind Bars

Best known as a militant black nationalist leader who rose to global fame as an advocate for Pan-Africanism (a movement that aims to unite all people of African descent), Malcolm X was born Malcolm Little in 1925. He replaced the name Little, which he considered a slave name, with the letter X to represent his lost African tribal name. Founder of the Muslim Mosque Inc. and the Organization of Afro-American Unity, Malcolm X was assassinated by political rivals on February 21, 1965. The following narrative comes from his autobiography, The Auto-biography of Malcolm X (1965), which he wrote with Alex Haley.

MANY WHO TODAY HEAR ME somewhere in person, or on television, or those who read something I've said, will think I went to school far beyond the eighth grade. This impression is due entirely to my prison studies.

It had really begun back in the Charlestown Prison,* when Bimbi first made me feel envy of his stock of knowledge. Bimbi had always taken charge of any conversation he was in, and I had tried to emulate him. But every book I picked up had few sentences which didn't contain anywhere from one to nearly all of the words that might as well have been in Chinese. When I just skipped those words, of course, I really ended up with little idea of what the book said. So I had come to the Norfolk Prison Colony still going through only book-reading motions. Pretty soon, I would have quit even these motions, unless I had received the motivation that I did.

I saw that the best thing I could do was get hold of a dictionary — to study, to learn some words. I was lucky enough to reason also that I should try to improve my penmanship. It was sad. I couldn't even write in a straight line. It was both ideas together that moved me to request a dictionary along with some tablets and pencils from the Norfolk Prison Colony school.

---

*Charlestown Prison: a prison near Boston, Massachusetts. [Editor's note]

rhetorical situations   genres   processes   strategies   research MLA / APA   media / design   readings

I spent two days just riffling uncertainly through the dictionary's pages. I'd never realized so many words existed! I didn't know *which* words I needed to learn. Finally, just to start some kind of action, I began copying.

In my slow, painstaking, ragged handwriting, I copied into my tablet 5 everything printed on that first page, down to the punctuation marks.

I believe it took me a day. Then, aloud, I read back, to myself, everything I'd written on the tablet. Over and over, aloud, to myself, I read my own handwriting.

I woke up the next morning, thinking about those words — immensely proud to realize that not only had I written so much at one time, but I'd written words that I never knew were in the world. Moreover, with a little effort, I also could remember what many of these words meant. I reviewed the words whose meanings I didn't remember. Funny thing, from the dictionary first page right now, that "aardvark" springs to my mind. The dictionary had a picture of it, a long-tailed, long-eared, burrowing African mammal, which lives off termites caught by sticking out its tongue as an anteater does for ants.

I was so fascinated that I went on — I copied the dictionary's next page. And the same experience came when I studied that. With every succeeding page, I also learned of people and places and events from history. Actually the dictionary is like a miniature encyclopedia. Finally the dictionary's A section had filled a whole tablet — and I went on into the B's. That was the way I started copying what eventually became the entire dictionary. It went a lot faster after so much practice helped me to pick up handwriting speed. Between what I wrote in my tablet, and writing letters, during the rest of my time in prison I would guess I wrote a million words.

I suppose it was inevitable that as my word-base broadened, I could for the first time pick up a book and read and now begin to understand what the book was saying. Anyone who has read a great deal can imagine the new world that opened. Let me tell you something: from then until I left that prison, in every free moment I had, if I was not reading in the library, I was reading on my bunk. You couldn't have gotten me out of books with a wedge. Between Mr. Muhammad's teachings, my correspondence, my visitors — usually Ella and Reginald — and my reading of books, months passed without my even thinking about being imprisoned. In fact, up to then, I never had been so truly free in my life.

As you can imagine, especially in a prison where there was heavy emphasis on rehabilitation, an inmate was smiled upon if he demonstrated an unusually intense interest in books. There was a sizable number of well-read inmates, especially the popular debaters. Some were said by many to be practically walking encyclopedias. They were almost celebrities. No university would ask any student to devour literature as I did when this new world opened to me, of being able to read and *understand*.   10

I read more in my room than in the library itself. An inmate who was known to read a lot could check out more than the permitted maximum number of books. I preferred reading in the total isolation of my own room.

When I had progressed to really serious reading, every night at about ten P.M. I would be outraged with the "lights out." It always seemed to catch me right in the middle of something engrossing.

Fortunately, right outside my door was a corridor light that cast a glow into my room. The glow was enough to read by, once my eyes adjusted to it. So when "lights out" came, I would sit on the floor where I could continue reading in that glow.

At one-hour intervals the night guards paced past every room. Each time I heard the approaching footsteps, I jumped into bed and feigned sleep. And as soon as the guard passed, I got back out of bed onto the floor area of that light-glow, where I would read for another fifty-eight minutes — until the guard approached again. That went on until three or four every morning. Three or four hours of sleep a night was enough for me. Often in the years in the streets I had slept less than that. . . .

I have often reflected upon the new vistas that reading opened to me. I knew right there in prison that reading had changed forever the course of my life. As I see it today, the ability to read awoke inside me some long dormant craving to be mentally alive. I certainly wasn't seeking any degree, the way a college confers a status symbol upon its students. My homemade education gave me, with every additional book   15

that I read, a little bit more sensitivity to the deafness, dumbness, and blindness that was afflicting the black race in America. Not long ago, an English writer telephoned me from London, asking questions. One was, "What's your alma mater?" I told him, "Books." You will never catch me with a free fifteen minutes in which I'm not studying something I feel might be able to help the black man. . . .

Every time I catch a plane, I have with me a book that I want to read — and that's a lot of books these days. If I weren't out here every day battling the white man, I could spend the rest of my life reading, just satisfying my curiosity — because you can hardly mention anything I'm not curious about. I don't think anybody ever got more out of going to prison than I did. In fact, prison enabled me to study far more intensively than I would have if my life had gone differently and I had attended some college. I imagine that one of the biggest troubles with colleges is there are too many distractions, too much panty-raiding, fraternities, and boola-boola and all of that. Where else but in a prison could I have attacked my ignorance by being able to study intensely sometimes as much as fifteen hours a day.

Engaging with the Text

1. In **DESCRIBING** how he felt after learning to read and write more fluently, Malcolm X states that even though he was in prison, he "never had been so truly free in [his] life." There is a certain irony that anyone would feel free while incarcerated. What does his narrative suggest about the relationship between literacy and freedom?   367–75

2. How would you characterize Malcolm X's **STANCE?** Where in his narrative is this stance made most explicit? Point to specific words and phrases that convey his stance.   12–15

3. As he describes his efforts to learn to read and write, do you think Malcolm X is **OBJECTIVE, SUBJECTIVE,** or a mixture of both? Give examples from the text to support your answer. Why do you think he chose to write that way?   370–71

43 ▲

4. Discuss the **SIGNIFICANCE** of Malcolm X's narrative and, by implication, the significance of learning to read and write. What lessons does his experience teach us about the power of reading and writing?

5. *For Writing.* Malcolm X advocates reading as an excellent road to education, but a college education consists of far more than reading. Write a **LITERACY NARRATIVE** looking at the role that reading has played in your education so far. Consider the kinds of texts you've read — those you've been assigned to read, and also those you yourself have chosen to read. Consider also the other kinds of work you've done at school — lectures you've attended, exams you've taken, discussions you've participated in, essays you've written, blogs you've created. How important is reading compared with this other work?

27–51 ▲

■ rhetorical situations
▲ genres
○ processes
◆ strategies
● research MLA / APA
▢ media / design
❚❚ readings

AMBER WILTSE

How Do You Go from This . . . to This?

Amber Wiltse was a student at St. John Fisher College, majoring in bio-chemistry, when she was assigned to write a literacy narrative essay for a composition class and to create video version of the narrative for a paired Literacies and Justice class. She created all the text slides for the video using text from the essay, located family photos on Facebook as well as photos of the books and stills from the movies she wanted to show, and then looked for appropriate songs to accompany both the text and the pictures she used. (The hardest part, she said, was finding just the right parts of songs and editing them to fit into the video.) Finally, after putting all the elements together, she proofed the final product by "watching it too many times to count." Following are the transcript of the text of Wiltse's slides and a few of the slides themselves. To see the actual video, go to <u>wwnorton.com/write/fieldguidelinks</u>.

SO HOW DO YOU GO from this . . .   . . . to this?

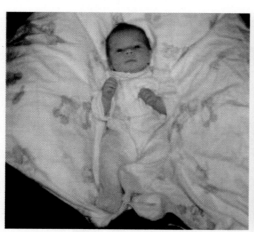

The answer is . . .

LITERACY.

Yeah, it sounds boring . . .

. . . but it's really not.   5

Books have always been a big part of who I am.
I have always loved the way a book can take you to a new dimension

There are genres I love!!!

Romance

And genres I can't stand.

Science Fiction   Manga

But just like everything else in life . . .   10

there are exceptions to my "rules."

The biggest exception is actually the reason I LOVE literacy.

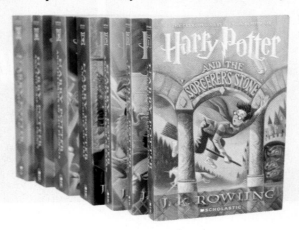

In my house, Harry Potter was more than a fad.
                    IT WAS A WAY OF LIFE.

This meant I had to share my reading time.   15
Mom always got to read the latest book whenever she wanted. . . .
And my brother, Stan, got to read whenever Mom wasn't. . . .
Which meant I got the worst reading "time slots."
Lucky for me, it was always summertime when the books came out. . . .
And I'm a night owl.   20

Next, came the movies . . .
My dad was never very interested in reading Harry Potter . . .
But he has always watched the movies along with Mom, Stan, and me.

For me, Harry Potter isn't just about being able to read something enter-
taining . . .
Or watch a movie just because I love the story it tells.   25
It's a special bond I share with my family.

Especially my brother.

The Harry Potter series is the way my brother and I stayed connected as we were starting new eras in our lives.
Even after the books were over, the movies remained.
Now Stan and I use the movies as an excuse to have time for just the 30 two of us.

Since Harry Potter, my brother and I have found other series of books to read as a way to stay connected.
Harry Potter was just the gateway to teach us that things were never going to have to change between us.

So you see, literacy isn't boring at all.
It can be a useful tool for making and solidifying relationships.

rhetorical situations · genres · processes · strategies · research MLA / APA · media / design · readings

Engaging with the Text

1. This literacy narrative begins with a question: "So how do you go from this . . . to this?" How effective is this **BEGINNING?** How does it relate to the **ENDING?** Amber Wiltse begins with a picture of herself alone as a baby and one of her alone now. She ends with a picture of herself and her brother embracing. How do these visuals support her narrative?

299–300

2. How does Wiltse use music — **AUDIO** — in her narrative? What songs does she use, and how effective are they? What ambience does the music create? What other songs might she have used?

591–99

3. Wiltse writes: "In my house, Harry Potter was more than a fad." What does she mean? What role did books in general play in her life? What role did the Potter series play in her life?

4. What does the text Wiltse uses in the video contribute to her narrative? What would be lost if she had written the narrative only in text form?

5. *For Writing.* Create a **LITERACY NARRATIVE** that details one event in your process of learning to read and/or write, either in general or in a particular way. For example, you might focus on a person who helped you; or on how you learned to text or tweet; or on a special book from your childhood; or on a person, place, or activity that led you to read or write a particular genre. Include images, videos, music, and other audio effects that are related to the event whether directly or metaphorically, as well as enough text to help readers understand the narrative.

27–51

58 Textual Analyses

rhetorical situations | genres | processes | strategies | research MLA / APA | media / design | readings

TORIE BOSCH

First, Eat All the Lawyers

Torie Bosch is editor of Future Tense, *a section of the online magazine* Slate *that is produced in collaboration with Arizona State University and the New American Foundation and that covers emerging technologies and their implications for society, public policy, and the future. Bosch's writing about politics, technology, and entertainment have been published in* AOL News, *the* Detroit News, Seventeen, *and other venues as well as in* Slate. *The following piece appeared in* Slate *in October 2011.*

THE SECOND SEASON of *The Walking Dead* premiered last week to ratings high enough to raise William Seabrook — the journalist who imported zombies to the United States with the 1929 novel *The Magic Island* — from the dead. More than 7 million tuned in to watch a show that is, honestly, not terribly compelling television. Bad-ass zombies aside, the plot is slow, the characters flat. And yet I and many others continue to clamor for zombies like zombies hunt for brains. Sensing our hunger, the studios and publishers keep the zombie pop culture coming: Colson Whitehead's "literary zombie novel" *Zone One* has just hit bookshelves, a movie version of Max Brooks' 2006 book *World War Z* will star Brad Pitt, and who could forget the tour de force that is *Pride and Prejudice and Zombies?*

What's new about the current zombie craze is its white-collar shine. No longer are zombies the beloved genre of the lonely, virgin teenage male, the macabre flipside of girls' obsession with unicorns. The undead have gone from lowbrow guilty pleasure to the favored monster of the erudite. (Sorry, Grendel.) At the risk of reading too deeply into a guilty pleasure, I can't help but believe that this current Era of the Dead draws its power from our economic malaise. If you work in the many white-collar fields that have suffered in this recession, zombies are the perfect representation of the fiscal horror show. The zombie apocalypse is a white-collar nightmare: a world with no need for the skills we have

developed. Lawyers, journalists, investment bankers — they are liabili-
ties, not leaders, in the zombie-infested world. (The exception to this
rule, of course, is doctors.)

In *The Walking Dead*, the strongest survivors come from blue-collar
backgrounds — cops, hunters, mechanics. Perhaps the weakest of the
band is Andrea, a former civil rights attorney who can't be trusted with
a gun and who is overly indulgent in grieving her sister, a college student,
who wasn't alert enough while peeing in the woods and got bit for her
neglectfulness. In the zombie apocalypse, your J.D. is worthless — which
is actually not so different from the real world of recent years. As we
watch humans battle zombies, we see a social order upended.

In *World War Z*, Max Brooks captured this fear in a scene from the
post-zombie reconstruction:

> You're a high-powered corporate attorney. You've spent most of
> your life reviewing contracts, brokering deals, talking on the phone.
> That's what you're good at, that's what made you rich and what

allowed you to hire a plumber to fix your toilet, which allowed you to keep talking on the phone. The more work you do, the more money you make, the more peons you hire to free you up to make more money. That's the way the world works. But one day it doesn't. No one needs a contract reviewed or a deal brokered. What it does need is toilets fixed. And suddenly that peon is your teacher, maybe even your boss. For some, this was scarier than the living dead.

We all worry about becoming obsolete; recently, my *Slate* colleague Farhad Manjoo sketched a frightening scenario in which robots take over industries like the law, medicine, even scientific discovery. The zombie apocalypse is the opposite scenario, in which our white-collar skills become worthless not through technical advance but through total system collapse. For blue-collar workers, the zombie stories are tales of comeuppance, of triumph: skills in auto maintenance, farming, plumbing, and electrical work — not to mention marksmanship — land blue-collar folks at the top of the new social order. This is not a bad thing, but it's nevertheless deeply disorienting to anyone who thought a college degree would mean never having to fix a generator.

These highbrow zombie stories are not just about watching the 5 newly humbled struggle to make sense of the topsy-turvy world. The suburbanite/urbanite viewer who can't hunt, can't slaughter animals, can't grow her own food, is meant to shudder at her ill-preparedness while watching. It's the existential fear of the economy writ large: I sometimes wonder what I would do if I lost everything. Move in with my mother? Crash on a generous friend's couch? Somehow put my supercharged typing skills to use? The zombie apocalypse scenario takes these fears and explodes them.

While watching *The Walking Dead*, I am reminded that I would be nothing but a drag in a survivalist scenario. There will be a greater supply than demand for storytellers. I've never gone fishing. I can't even make a fire without a lighter. I can't lie to myself and think that I would survive the initial chaos of a zombie invasion (or any other apocalyptic event). Realistically, I'd be one of the brain-devouring hordes, not a scrappy, fighting human. Indulging in these zombie films gives an outlet to more realistic fears of personal economic collapse. Colson Whitehead captures this feeling in *Zone One*. He writes:

> The dead had graduated with admirable GPAs, configured monthly contributions to worthy causes, judiciously apportioned their 401(k)s across diverse sectors according to the wisdom of their dead licensed financial advisers, and superimposed the borders of good school districts on mental maps of their neighborhoods, which were often included on the long list when magazines ranked cities with the Best Quality of Life. In short, they had been honed and trained so thoroughly by that extinguished world that they were doomed in this new one.

Obviously, these sentiments apply to other apocalypse tales — pandemics, nuclear holocaust (a la the late, sometimes-great TV show *Jericho*). But zombies make for true white-collar horror because most world-shattering disasters are short-term events. After a nuclear strike, the dead are dead, and the living can focus on rebuilding while avoiding fallout. Zombies, however, never stop, so danger persists past the initial cataclysm. Take Justin Cronin's *The Passage*, whose vampires are much more akin to traditional zombies than vampires. Cronin's evil vampires keep the humans down for generations; *World War Z* and *Zone One* are more optimistic about humans' ability to vanquish the undead, but any lengthy period of zombie chaos also means that should the humans retake the land, the infrastructure will have been roundly destroyed. White-collar workers will not be able to recline in their dusty Aeron chairs and return those calls they were about to make when the intern lumbered in, craving brains.

Should the economy recover, I suspect that we will abandon zombies as entertainment. The zombie boom will be a reminder of the frightening uncertainties of this decade. After all, we white-collar workers enjoy the illusion that our skills are meaningful. Once we no longer have to exorcise our fears of a society in which contract negotiation and SEO-optimization are nonsense, how will we terrify ourselves about the future? Perhaps we'll see a robot-apocalypse entertainment bubble.

rhetorical situations   genres   processes   strategies   research MLA / APA   media / design   readings

Engaging with the Text

1. Who is the intended **AUDIENCE** for Torie Bosch's essay? Point to one paragraph that makes the answer clear.

   5–8

2. What is the **THESIS** of Bosch's analysis? How does she **SUPPORT** her thesis? Do you agree with it? Why or why not?

   313–15

   70

3. Bosch's **TITLE** is a takeoff on a line from Shakespeare's play *Henry VI, Part 2*, in which a butcher who is discussing the need for a social revolution says, "The first thing we do, let's kill all the lawyers." How does the title relate to the main point of Bosch's essay? How effective is it, and how much of the effectiveness depends on the audience being familiar with the Shakespearean quotation?

   312–13

4. Bosch cites two long quotations, one by Max Brooks from *World War Z* and the other by Colson Whitehead from *Zone One*. What do these **QUOTATIONS** contribute to her analysis? What claims are they meant to support?

   463–67

5. *For Writing.* Select a successful television show, and using evidence from at least three episodes, **ANALYZE** what makes it a success. Select a particular aspect of the show to focus your analysis on and to organize your essay. For example, you might identify the underlying message of the show. Where else in the media does this message appears? Compare the show to other shows, websites, or books that deliver the same type of message and analyze how it succeeds.

   52–86

LAUREL THATCHER ULRICH

Well-Behaved Women Seldom Make History

Laurel Thatcher Urlich is professor of history at Harvard University, where she was appointed the 300th Anniversary University Professor. She is author and editor of a half-dozen books, including Good Wives: Image and Reality in the Lives of Women in Northern New England, 1650–1759 *(1982),* The Age of Homespun: Objects and Stories in the Creation of an American Myth *(2001), and* Well-Behaved Women Seldom Make History *(2007) from which the following essay was taken. Ulrich introduced the phrase "well-behaved women seldom make history" in a 1976 journal article titled "Vertuous Women Found: New England Ministerial Literature, 1668–1735," about how women were characterized in Puritan funeral sermons. Much to Ulrich's surprise, the phrase generated an explosion of cultural interest and now appears on greeting cards, T-shirts, bumper stickers, mugs, and plaques, among other places.*

SOME TIME AGO a former student e-mailed me from California: "You'll be delighted to know that you are quoted frequently on bumpers in Berkeley." Through a strange stroke of fate I've gotten used to seeing my name on bumpers. And on T-shirts, tote bags, coffee mugs, magnets, buttons, greeting cards, and websites.

I owe this curious fame to a single line from a scholarly article I published in 1976. In the opening paragraph, I wrote: "Well-behaved women seldom make history." That sentence, slightly altered, escaped into popular culture in 1995, when journalist Kay Mills used it as an epigraph for her informal history of American women, *From Pocahontas to Power Suits.* Perhaps by accident, she changed the word *seldom* to *rarely.* Little matter. According to my dictionary, *seldom* and *rarely* mean the same thing: "Well-behaved women *infrequently,* or on *few occasions,* make history." This may be one of those occasions. My original article

rhetorical situations   genres   processes   strategies   research MLA / APA   media / design   readings

was a study of the well-behaved women celebrated in Puritan funeral sermons.

In 1996, a young woman named Jill Portugal found the "rarely" version of the quote in her roommate's copy of *The New Beacon Book of Quotations by Women*. She wrote me from Oregon asking permission to print it on T-shirts. I was amused by her request and told her to go ahead; all I asked was that she send me a T-shirt. The success of her enterprise surprised both of us. A plain white shirt with the words "Well-behaved women rarely make history" printed in black roman type became a best-selling item. Portugal calls her company "one angry girl designs." Committed to "taking over the world, one shirt at a time," she fights sexual harassment, rape, pornography, and what she calls "fascist beauty standards."

Her success inspired imitators, only a few of whom bothered to ask permission. My runaway sentence now keeps company with anarchists, hedonists, would-be witches, political activists of many descriptions, and quite a few well-behaved women. It has been featured in *CosmoGirl*, the *Christian Science Monitor*, and *Creative Keepsake Scrapbooking Magazine*. According to news reports, it was a favorite of the pioneering computer scientist Anita Borg. The Sweet Potato Queens of Jackson, Mississippi, have adopted it as an "official maxim," selling their own pink-and-green T-shirt alongside another that reads "Never Wear Panties to a Party."

My accidental fame has given me a new perspective on American 5 popular culture. While some women contemplate the demise of feminism, others seem to have only just discovered it. A clerk in the Amtrak ticket office in D.C.'s Union Station told a fellow historian that all the women in her office wore the button. "I couldn't resist telling her that I was acquainted with you, and she just lit right up, and made me promise to tell you that the women at the Amtrak office thank you for all your 'words of wisdom.'"

. . .

The "well-behaved women" quote works because it plays into long-standing stereotypes about the invisibility and the innate decorum of the female sex. Many people think women are less visible in history than men because their bodies impel them to nurture. Their job is to bind the wounds, stir the soup, and bear the children of those whose mission it is to fight wars, rule nations, and define the cosmos. Not all those who make this argument consider women unimportant — on the contrary, they often revere the contributions of women as wives, mothers, and caregivers — or at least they say so. But they also assume that domestic roles haven't changed much over the centuries, and that women who perform them have no history. A New Hampshire pastor captured this notion when he wrote in his commonplace book in 1650, "Woman's the center & lines are men." If women occupy the fixed center of life, and if history is seen as a linear progression of public events, a changing panorama of wars and kingdoms, then only those who through outrageous behavior, divine intervention, or sheer genius step into the stream of public consequence have a history.

The problem with this argument is not only that it limits women. It also limits history. Good historians are concerned not only with famous people and public events but with broad transformations in human behavior, things like falling death rates or transatlantic migration. Here seemingly small actions by large numbers of people can bring about profound change. But this approach runs up against another imperative of history — its reliance on written sources. Until recent times most women (and a great many men) were illiterate. As a consequence their activities were recorded, if at all, in other people's writing. People who caused trouble might show up in court records, newspapers, or their masters' diaries. Those who quietly went about their lives were either forgotten, seen at a distance, or idealized into anonymity. Even today, publicity favors those who make — or break — laws.

But the difficulty is bigger than that. History is an account of the past based on surviving sources, but it is also a way of making sense out of the present. In the heat and confusion of events, people on all sides of an issue mine old stories for inspiration, enlightenment, or confirmation. Their efforts add to the layers of understanding attached to the original events, shaping what later generations know and care about. Scholars sometimes call these popular reconstructions of the past "memory" to distinguish them from formal history. But serious history is also forged in the tumult of change. History is not just what happened in the past. It is what later generations choose to remember.

. . .

Historians don't own history. But we do have a lot of experience sifting through competing evidence. Historical research is a bit like detective work. We re-create past events from fragments of information, trying hard to distinguish credible accounts from wishful thinking. One of our jobs is to explore the things that get left out when a person becomes an icon. Recent scholarship on the Sweet Potato Queens' heroine, Mae West, is a good example. There is no question about West's reputation for misbehavior. She said it herself: "When I'm bad, I'm better." Beginning her stage career at the age of six, she moved from playing the saintly Little Eva in *Uncle Tom's Cabin* to shimmying her way to fame. In uptight Boston, theater owners cut off the lights "with West's first ripple." But in New York she was the darling of urban sophisticates who wanted to explore the seamy side of life without leaving their theater seats. When she moved to Hollywood in the 1930s, censors tried to clean

Mae West, photographed in the 1930s.

up her scripts, but she knew how to fill even the blandest lines with sexual innuendo. *Variety* complained that "Mae couldn't sing a lullaby without making it sexy."

That is how Mae West made history. But what sort of history did   10 she make? Some recent studies focus on her debts to the male homosexuals whose outrageous impersonations defined *camp* in the 1920s. Others claim that her largest debt was to African American entertainers. West's shimmy, for example, ultimately derived from West African traditions adapted in rural dance halls, or "jooks." Her ballad "Honey let yo' drawers hang down low" (which may have inspired the Sweet Potato Queens' "Never Wear Panties to a Party") was a favorite in southern jooks. In the early twentieth century, West, the sexually active, streetwise girl from Brooklyn, gave middle-class audiences a glimpse of worlds that both fascinated and repelled. Like the legendary Godiva,* she allowed people to imagine the unimaginable. Because she was also a savvy businesswoman, she was able to live off other people's fantasies.

A first-year student at a California university told me that to make history, people need to do the unexpected. She offered the example of civil rights activist Rosa Parks, "who would not leave her seat." I like her emphasis on the unexpected. It not only captures the sense of history as the study of how things change, it offers a somewhat more complex way of understanding the contribution of a woman like Parks.

Was Parks a well-behaved woman? The Montgomery, Alabama, bus company did not think so. As the student from California recognized, Parks made history precisely because she dared to challenge both social norms and the law. Her refusal to obey the statute that required her to give up her seat to a white passenger sparked the 361-day-long boycott that thrust Martin Luther King into the public eye and led to a historic Supreme Court decision outlawing segregation on public transportation.

---

*Godiva: Lady Godiva, an eleventh-century Anglo-Saxon noblewoman who reportedly rode naked through the streets of Coventry to protest taxes imposed by her husband. [Editor's note]

rhetorical situations   genres   processes   strategies   research MLA / APA   media / design   readings

Yet Parks became an icon for the civil rights movement not only for her courage but because the media identified her as a hard-working seamstress who simply got tired of moving to the back of the bus. Few people outside Montgomery knew her as the politically conscious secretary of the local NAACP, nor understood how many years she and her husband had been working for social justice before that fateful day on the bus. In 1954 and 1955, Parks had attended workshops on desegregation sponsored by the radical Highlander Folk School in Tennessee, a public education project that Mississippi's Senator James Eastland excoriated as a "front for a conspiracy to overthrow this country."

Nor has popular history recorded the names of other Montgomery women — teenagers — whose arrests that year for refusing to give up their seats failed to ignite a movement. Years later, E. D. Nixon, president of the Montgomery NAACP, explained why he hadn't chosen any of these other women to make a historic stand against segregation. "OK, the case of Louise Smith. I found her daddy in front of his shack, barefoot, drunk. Always drunk. Couldn't use her. In that year's second case, the girl, very brilliant but she'd had an illegitimate baby. Couldn't use her. The last case before Rosa was the daughter of a preacher who headed a reform school for years. My interview of her convinced me that she wouldn't stand up to pressure. She were even afraid of me. When Rosa Parks was arrested, I thought, 'This is it!' 'Cause she's morally clean, she's reliable, nobody had nothing on her, she had the courage of her convictions." Parks's publicly acknowledged good behavior helped to justify her rebellion and win support for her cause. As one friend recalled, she "was too sweet to even say 'damn' in anger."

After Parks's death in the fall of 2005, the airways were filled with tributes celebrating the life of the "humble seamstress," the "simple woman" who sparked a revolution because her feet were tired. Reviewing these eulogies, syndicated columnist Ellen Goodman asked, "Is it possible we prefer our heroes to be humble? Or is it just our heroines?" She wondered if it wasn't time Americans got over the notion that women are "accidental heroines," unassuming creatures thrust into the public eye by circumstances beyond their control. Goodman noted that Parks and her compatriots spent years preparing for just such an opportunity.

Rosa Parks' mug shot, taken shortly after her arrest on December 1, 1955, for refusing to obey a bus driver's order to give up her seat to a white passenger.

She concluded: "Rosa Parks was 'unassuming'—except that she rejected all the assumptions about her place in the world. Rosa Parks was a 'simple woman'—except for a mind made up and fed up. She was 'quiet'—except, of course, for one thing. Her willingness to say 'no' changed the world."

The California student said that in contrast to Parks a "well-behaved   15 woman" is "a quiet, subservient, polite, indoors, cooking, cleaning type of girl who would never risk shame by voicing her own opinion." There is a delicious irony in this part of her definition. Notice that it associates a particular kind of work — cooking and cleaning — with subservience and passivity. Yet the boycott that made Parks famous was sustained by hundreds of African American domestic servants — cooks and maids — who walked to work rather than ride segregated buses. They too did the unexpected.*

Serious history talks back to slogans. But in the contest for public attention, slogans usually win. Consider my simple sentence. It sat quietly for years in the folds of a scholarly journal. Now it honks its ambiguous wisdom from coffee mugs and tailgates.

. . .

In my scholarly work, my form of misbehavior has been to care about things that other people find predictable or boring. My second book is a case in point. At a distance, the life of Martha Moore Ballard was the stuff from which funeral sermons were made. She was a "good wife" in every sense of the word, indistinguishable from all the self-sacrificing and pious women celebrated in Puritan eulogies. In conventional terms,

---

*Awele Makeba's powerful one-woman show, "Rage Is Not a 1-Day Thing," dramatizes the lives of sixteen little-known participants, male and female, black and white. For details see her website, http://www.awele.com/programs.htm. For a list of resources prepared for the fiftieth anniversary of the boycott in 2005, see http://www.teachingforchange.org/busboycott/busboycott.htm. Additional documents can be found in Stewart Burns, ed., *Daybreak of Freedom: The Montgomery Bus Boycott* (Chapel Hill and London: University of North Carolina Press, 1997). Herbert Kohl, *She Would Not Be Moved: How We Tell the Story of Rosa Parks and the Montgomery Bus Boycott* (New York and London: The New Press, 2005), urges teachers to move from the theme "Rosa Was Tired" to the more historically accurate concept "Rosa Was Ready."

she did not make history. She cherished social order, respected authority, and abhorred violence. As a midwife and healer, she relied on home-grown medicines little different from those found in English herbals a century before her birth. Her religious sentiments were conventional; her reading was limited to the Bible, edifying pamphlets, and newspapers. Although she lived through the American Revolution, she had little interest in politics. She was a caregiver and a sustainer rather than a mover and shaker.

Ballard made history by performing a methodical and seemingly ordinary act — writing a few words in her diary every day. Through the diary we know her as a pious herbalist whose curiosity about the human body led her to observe and record autopsies as well as nurse the sick, whose integrity allowed her to testify in a sensational rape trial against a local judge who was her husband's employer, and whose sense of duty took her out of bed at night not only to deliver babies but to care for the bodies of a wife and children murdered by their own husband and father. The power of the diary is not only in its sensational stories, however, but in its patient, daily recording of seemingly inconsequential events, struggles with fatigue and discouragement, conflicts with her son, and little things — like the smell of a room where a dead body lay. In Ballard's case, the drama really was in the humdrum. The steadiness of the diary provided the frame for everything else that happened.

. . .

Although I have received mail addressed to Martha Ballard and have been identified on at least one college campus as a midwife, I am only a little bit like my eighteenth-century subject. Like her, I was raised to be an industrious housewife and a self-sacrificing and charitable neighbor, but sometime in my thirties I discovered that writing about women's work was a lot more fun than doing it. I remember thinking one winter day how ironic it was that I was wrapped in a bathrobe with the heat of a wood stove rising toward my loft as I wrote about a courageous woman who braved snowstorms and crossed a frozen river on a cake of ice to care for mothers in labor. I felt selfish, pampered, and decadent. But I did not stop what I was doing. I did not know why I needed

rhetorical situations   genres   processes   strategies   research MLA / APA   media / design   readings

to write Martha's story, and I could not imagine that anybody else would ever want to follow me through my meandering glosses on her diary. I was astonished at the reception of the book. Even more important than the prizes was the discovery of how important this long-dead midwife's story was to nurses, midwives, and anonymous caregivers dealing with quite different circumstances today. These readers helped me to see that history is more than an engaging enterprise. It is a primary way of creating meaning. The meaning I found in Martha Ballard's life had something to do with my own life experience, but perhaps a lot more to do with the collective experiences of a generation of Americans coping with dramatic changes in their own lives.

When I wrote that "well-behaved women seldom make history," I   20
was making a commitment to help recover the lives of otherwise obscure women. I had no idea that thirty years later, my own words would come back to me transformed. While I like some of the uses of the slogan more than others, I wouldn't call it back even if I could. I applaud the fact that so many people—students, teachers, quilters, nurses, newspaper columnists, old ladies in nursing homes, and mayors of western towns—think they have the right to make history.

Some history-making is intentional; much of it is accidental. People make history when they scale a mountain, ignite a bomb, or refuse to move to the back of the bus. But they also make history by keeping diaries, writing letters, or embroidering initials on linen sheets. History is a conversation and sometimes a shouting match between present and past, though often the voices we most want to hear are barely audible. People make history by passing on gossip, saving old records, and by naming rivers, mountains, and children. Some people leave only their bones, though bones too make history when someone notices.

Historian Gerda Lerner has written: "All human beings are practicing historians. . . . We live our lives; we tell our stories. It is as natural as breathing." But if no one cares about these stories, they do not survive. People do not only make history by living their lives, but by creating records and by turning other people's lives into books or slogans.

Engaging with the Text

299–310 1. How does Laurel Thatcher Urlich **BEGIN** her essay? How does the opening relate to how the essay **ENDS**? How effective is her beginning in drawing the reader to her analysis of the slogan "Well-behaved women seldom make history"?

2. Urlich discusses the ambiguity of her slogan, noting that some read it as referring to the lack of women in histories or the lack of histories about women, whereas others read it as meaning that only by "misbehaving" do women make history. How does she relate this ambiguity to the broader issue of how history in general is written? Identify two examples she provides to illustrate the complexities of writing history.

3–4
313–15 3. What is the **PURPOSE** of Urlich's textual analysis of her slogan? How does the purpose relate to her **THESIS**?

70 4. What kind of **SUPPORT** does Urlich offer as evidence of the points she makes? Select three pieces of evidence in the essay and discuss how effective each is in supporting the point it is intended to support.

5. *For Writing.* Do a web search for "well-behaved women seldom [or rarely] make history" to identify three objects on which the slogan
52–86 appears, and write an essay **ANALYZING** how its meaning might be understood by those who purchase them. Describe the objects and those — whether businesses, organizations, or individuals — who are promoting them. What meaning do you think the promoters assume potential buyers will perceive? How closely does that meaning relate to the point Urlich originally made with this phrase? What does your analysis reveal about the role of slogans and history?

■ ▲ ○ ◆ ● □ 📖
rhetorical
situations
genres
processes
strategies
research
MLA / APA
media /
design
readings

DIANA GEORGE

Changing the Face of Poverty
Nonprofits and the Problem of Representation

Diana George is a professor of English at Virgina Polytechnic Institute and State University. She has written widely on culture, writing, and visual representation. She is the editor of Kitchen Cooks, Plate Twirlers, and Troubadours *(1999), a collection of essays by writing program administrators, and a coauthor of* Reading Culture *(with John Trimbur, 2006) and* Picturing Texts *(with Lester Faigley, Anna Palchik, and Cynthia Selfe, 2004). The following analysis comes from* Popular Literacy: Studies in Cultural Practices and Poetics *(2001). The endnotes are presented according to* The Chicago Manual of Style, *as they appeared in the original publication.*

> Constructively changing the ways the poor are represented in every aspect of life is one progressive intervention that can challenge everyone to look at the face of poverty and not turn away.
> — BELL HOOKS, OUTLAW CULTURE

As I WRITE THIS, Thanksgiving is near. I am about to go out and fill a box with nonperishables for the annual St. Vincent de Paul food drive. Christmas lights already outline some porches. Each day my mailbox is stuffed with catalogs and bills and with appeals from the Native American Scholarship Fund, the Salvation Army, WOJB — Voice of the Anishinabe, the Navaho Health Foundation, the Barbara Kettle Gundlach Shelter Home for Abused Women, Little Brothers Friends of the Elderly, Habitat for Humanity, and more. One *New Yorker* ad for Children, Inc. reads, "You don't have to leave your own country to find third-world poverty." Underneath the ad copy, from a black-and-white photo, a young girl in torn and ill-fitting clothes looks directly at the viewer. The copy continues, "In Appalachia, sad faces of children, like Mandy's, will haunt

> **ENCLOSED:** No Address Labels to Use Up.
> No Calendars to Look At.
> No Petitions to Sign.
>
> And No Pictures of Starving Children.

Text from the outer envelope of a 1998 Oxfam appeal.

you. There are so many children like her — children who are deprived of the basic necessities right here in America."*

The Oxfam promise that I quote above — to use no pictures of starving children — is surely an attempt to avoid the emotional overload of such images as the one Children, Inc. offers. Still, those pictures — those representations of poverty — have typically been one way nonprofits have kept the poor before us. In a culture saturated by the image, how else do we convince Americans that — despite the prosperity they see all around them — there is real need out there? The solution for most nonprofits has been to show the despair. To do that they must represent poverty as something that can be seen and easily recognized: fallen down shacks and trashed out public housing, broken windows, dilapidated porches, barefoot kids with stringy hair, emaciated old women and men staring out at the camera with empty eyes. In such images, poverty is dirt and rags and helplessness. In mail, in magazines, and in newspapers, ads echoing these appeals must vie for our time, attention, and dollars with Eddie Bauer, Nordstrom's, The Gap, and others like them whose polished and attractive images fill our days.

In the pages that follow . . . I examine a particular representation of poverty — publicity videos produced by Habitat for Humanity — in order to suggest that reliance on stereotypes of poverty can, in fact, work against the aims of the organization producing them. . . .

—————————

*The copy here has been revised, with the author's permission, to reflect the more recent Children, Inc., ad. [Editor's note]

You don't have to leave your own country to find third-world poverty.

In Appalachia, sad faces of children, like Mandy's, will haunt you. There are so many children like her— children who are deprived of the basic necessities right here in America.

You can sponsor a boy or girl in need through Children, Inc. Just $24 a month will help provide clothing, shoes, school supplies and food as well as a feeling that someone cares. We'll send you the picture and story of the child you will be helping. Please write, call or visit our website to enroll. Your help will mean so much.

Write to: **Children, Inc., 4205 Dover Road, Dept.RB5M6, Richmond, VA 23221-3267 USA**

❏ I wish to sponsor a ❏ boy, ❏ girl, in ❏ USA, ❏ Africa, ❏ Latin America, ❏ Middle East, ❏ Asia, ❏ Greatest need.

❏ I will give $24 a month ($288 a year). Enclosed is my gift for a full year ❏, the first month ❏.

❏ I can't sponsor, but I will help $ _____ .

www.children-inc.org
1-800-538-5381

Children
INCORPORATED
Share in their future

Name _____

Address _____ City _____ State _____ Zip Code _____

❏ Check or Money Order ❏ American Express ❏ Visa ❏ MasterCard

Card No. _____ Expiration Date _____

U.S. gifts are fully tax deductible. Annual financial statements are available on request.

An ad for Children, Inc.

Habitat for Humanity: A Case in Point

I have chosen Habitat for Humanity publicity videos for my focus because Habitat is a popular and far-reaching nonprofit with affiliates not only in the United States but throughout the world. Its goal is not a modest one: Habitat for Humanity aims to eliminate poverty housing from the globe. More than that, Habitat puts housing into the hands of the people who will be housed — into the hands of the homeowners and their neighbors. This is not another program aimed at keeping people in what has become known as the poverty or welfare cycle.

To be very clear, then, I am not criticizing the work of Habitat for Humanity. It is an organization that has done an amazing job of addressing what is, as cofounder Millard Fuller tells us again and again, a worldwide problem. What I would draw attention to, however, is how that problem of inadequate housing and its solution are represented, especially in publicity material produced and distributed by the organization, and how those representations can feed into the troubles that Habitat continues to have as it attempts to change the ways Americans think of helping others. What's more, the kinds of visual arguments Habitat and other nonprofits use to advocate for action or change have become increasingly common tools for getting the message to the public, and yet, I would argue, these messages too often fail to overturn cultural commonplaces that represent poverty as an individual problem that can be addressed on an individual basis. Habitat's catch phrase — A Hand Up, Not a Hand-Out — appeals to a nation that believes anyone can achieve economic security with just the right attitude and set of circumstances.

Habitat's basic program has a kind of elegance. Applicants who are chosen as homeowners put in sweat equity hours to build their home and to help build the homes of others chosen by Habitat. The organization then sells the home to the applicant at cost (that cost held down through Habitat's ability to provide volunteer labor and donated materials) and charges a small monthly mortgage that includes no interest. Unlike public assistance, which is raised or lowered depending on the recipient's circumstances, most Habitat affiliates do not raise mortgage

payments when homeowners get better jobs or find themselves in better financial shape. And once the house is paid for, it belongs to the homeowner.

Obviously, in order to run a program like this one, Habitat must produce publicity appeals aimed at convincing potential donors to give time, money, and material. Print ads, public service television and radio spots, commercial appeals linked to products like Maxwell House coffee, and publicity videos meant to be played for churches, volunteer organizations, and even in-flight video appeals on certain airlines are common media for Habitat.

Habitat publicity videos are typically configured as problem-solution arguments. The problem is that too many people have inadequate shelter. The solution is community involvement in a program like Habitat for Humanity. The most common setup for these productions is an opening sequence of images — a visual montage — in which we see black-and-white shots of rural shacks, of men and women clearly in despair, and of thin children in ragged clothing. The voice-over narrative of one such montage tells us the story:

> Poverty condemns millions of people throughout the world to live in deplorable and inhuman conditions. These people are trapped in a cycle of poverty, living in places offering little protection from the rain, wind, and cold. Terrible sanitary conditions make each day a battle with disease and death. And, for this, they often pay over half their income in rent because, for the poor, there are no other choices. Daily, these families are denied a most basic human need: a decent place to live. The reasons for this worldwide tragedy are many. They vary from city to city, country to country, but the result is painfully the same whether the families are in New York or New Delhi.[1]

It is a compelling dilemma.

Organizations like Habitat for Humanity, in order to convey the seriousness of this struggle and, of course, to raise funds and volunteer support for their efforts in addressing it, must produce all sorts of publicity. And in that publicity they must tell us quickly what the problem is and

what we can do to help. To do that, Habitat gives us a visual representation of poverty, a representation that mirrors the most common
understandings of poverty in America.

Now, there is nothing inherently wrong with that representation 10
unless, of course, what you want to do (as Habitat does) is convince the
American people to believe in the radical idea that those who have must
care for the needs of others, not just by writing a check, but by enabling
an entirely different lifestyle. For Americans, it is truly radical to think
that our poorer neighbors might actually be allowed to buy a home at
no interest and with the donated time and materials of others. It is a
radical notion that such a program means that these neighbors then
own that house and aren't obliged to do more than keep up with payments in order to continue owning it. And it is a radical idea that Habitat does this work not only in our neighborhoods (not isolated in
low-income housing developments) but throughout the world. Habitat
International truly believes that we are all responsible for partnering
with our neighbors throughout the world so that everyone might eventually have, at least, a simple decent place to live. Like the philosophy
behind many nonprofits, Habitat's is not a mainstream notion.

Still, that representation of poverty — clinging as it does to commonplaces drawn from FSA photographs in this century, from Jacob
Riis's nineteenth-century photos of urban poverty, and from documentaries of Third World hunger — has serious limitations, which must be
obvious to those who remember the moment that the Bush administration* confidently announced that, after looking everywhere, they had
discovered no real hunger in the United States. And that myth that
poverty cannot/does not actually exist in the heart of capitalism has
once again been reinforced in the 1998 Heritage Foundation report in
which Robert Rector echoed the perennial argument that there is little
true poverty in this country ("Myth").[2] Heritage Foundation's finding

---

*Bush administration: the administration of George H. W. Bush (1989–93). FSA: the
Farm Security Administration, which hired such prominent photographers as Walker
Evans and Dorothea Lange to document rural poverty in the 1930s. Jacob Riis (1849–1914):
Danish American social reformer. [Editor's note]

rhetorical situations genres processes strategies research MLA / APA media / design readings

comes despite figures from the National Coalition for the Homeless ("Myths and Facts About Homelessness"), which tell us that in 1997 nearly one in five homeless people in twenty-nine cities across the United States was employed in a full- or part-time job.[3]

In her call for a changed representation of poverty in America, bell hooks argues that in this culture poverty "is seen as synonymous with depravity, lack and worthlessness." She continues, "I talked with young black women receiving state aid, who have not worked in years, about the issue of representation. They all agree that they do not want to be identified as poor. In their apartments they have the material possessions that indicate success (a VCR, a color television), even if it means that they do without necessities and plunge into debt to buy these items."[4] Hers is hardly a noble image of poverty, but it is a true one and one that complicates the job of an organization like Habitat that must identify "worthy" applicants. This phenomenon of poverty in the center of wealth, in a country with its national mythology of hearty individuals facing the hardness of the Depression with dignity and pride, is certainly a part of what Manning Marable challenges when he asks readers not to judge poverty in the United States by the standards of other countries. Writing of poverty among black Americans, Marable reminds us that "the process of impoverishment is profoundly national and regional."[5] It does little good to compare the impoverished of this country with Third World poverty or, for that matter, with Depression Era poverty.

The solution in these Habitat videos is just as visible and compelling a representation as is the problem. The solution, it seems, is a modern-day barn raising. In clip after clip, Habitat volunteers are shown lined up to raise walls, to hammer nails, to cut boards, to offer each other the "hand up not a hand out," as these publicity messages tell us again and again. Like the barn-raising scene from Peter Weir's *Witness*, framed walls come together against blue skies. People who would normally live in very different worlds come together to help a neighbor. It is all finished in record time: a week, even a day. Volunteers can come together quickly. Do something. Get out just as quickly.

The real trouble with Habitat's representation, then, is twofold: it tells us that the signs of poverty are visible and easily recognized. And it suggests that one of the most serious results of poverty (inadequate shelter) can be addressed quickly with volunteer efforts to bring individuals up and out of the poverty cycle.

Of course, if Habitat works, what could be wrong with the representation? It is an organization so popular that it receives support from diametrically opposed camps. Newt Gingrich and Jesse Jackson have both pounded nails and raised funds for Habitat. This is what Millard Fuller calls the "theology of the hammer." People might not agree on political parties and they might not agree on how to worship or even what to worship, Fuller says, but they can all agree on a hammer. All can come together to build houses. Or, can they? 15

As successful as Habitat has been, it is an organization that continues to struggle with such issues as who to choose for housing, how to support potential homeowners, and how to convince affiliates in the United States to tithe a portion of their funds to the real effort of Habitat: eliminating poverty housing throughout the world, not just in the United States. And, even in the United States, affiliates often have trouble identifying "deserving" applicants or convincing local residents to allow Habitat homes to be built in their neighborhoods. There are certainly many cultural and political reasons for these problems, but I would suggest that the way poverty continues to be represented in this country and on tapes like those videos limits our understanding of what poverty is and how we might address it.

That limitation holds true for those caught in poverty as well as those wanting to help. What if, as a potential Habitat applicant, you don't recognize yourself or you refuse to recognize yourself in those representations? As Stanley Aronowitz points out in *The Politics of Identity*, that can happen very easily as class identities, in particular, have become much more difficult to pin down since World War II, especially with an expansion of consumer credit that allowed class and social status to be linked to consumption rather than to professions or even wages. In his discussion of how electronic media construct the *social imaginary*, Aronowitz talks of the working class with few media representations available to them as having fallen into a kind of "cultural homelessness."[6] How much more true is that of the impoverished in

this country who may be neither homeless nor ragged, but are certainly struggling every day to feed their families, pay rent, and find jobs that pay more than what it costs for daycare?

I have been particularly interested in this last question because of a difficulty I mentioned earlier, that of identifying appropriate applicants for Habitat homes or even getting some of the most needy families of a given affiliate to apply for Habitat homes. When I showed the video *Building New Lives* to Kim Puuri, a Copper Country Habitat for Humanity homeowner and now member of the affiliate's Homeowner Selection Committee, and asked her to respond, she was very clear in what she saw as the problem:

> When I see those pictures I usually think of Africa or a third-world country and NOT the U.S. It's not that they can't be found here, it's just that you don't publicly see people that bad off other than street people. If they could gear the publicity more to the geographical areas, it may make more of an impact or get a better response from people. It would mean making several videos. It may not be so much of a stereotype, but an association between Habitat and the people they help. People viewing the videos and pictures see the conditions of the people and feel that their own condition may not be that bad and feel they probably wouldn't qualify.[7]

What this Habitat homeowner has noticed is very close to what Stuart Hall describes. That is, the problem with this image, this representation, is not that it is not real enough. The problem has nothing to do with whether or not these are images of poverty as it exists in the world. There is no doubt that this level of poverty does exist in this country and elsewhere despite the Heritage Foundation's attempts to demonstrate otherwise. The problem is that this representation of poverty is a narrow one and functions to narrow the ways we might respond to the poor who do not fit this representation.

The representation I have been discussing is one that insists on constructing poverty as an individual problem that can be dealt with by volunteers on an individual basis. That is the sort of representation common in this country, the sort of representation Paul Wellstone objects to in a recent call to action when he says "We can offer no single description of American poverty." What it takes to break through such a representation is first, as Hall suggests, to understand it as a representation, to understand it as a way of imparting meaning. And the only way to contest that representation, to allow for other meanings, other descriptions, is to know more about the many dimensions of poverty in America. "More than 35 million Americans — one out of every seven of our fellow citizens — are officially poor. More than one in five American children are poor. And the poor are getting poorer," Wellstone writes.[8] But we can be certain that much of that poverty is not the sort pictured in those black-and-white images. And if it doesn't *look* like poverty, then how do we address it? How do we identify those "deserving" our help?

Indeed, as Herbert Gans has suggested, the labels we have chosen to place on the poor in this country often reveal more than anything "an ideology of undeservingness," by which we have often elided poverty and immorality or laziness or criminality. "By making scapegoats of the poor for fundamental problems they have not caused nor can change," Gans argues, "Americans can also postpone politically difficult and divisive solutions to the country's economic ills and the need to prepare the economy and polity for the challenges of the twenty-first century."[9] These are tough issues to confront and certainly to argue in a twenty-minute video presentation aimed at raising funds and volunteer support, especially when every piece of publicity must make a complex argument visible. 20

Notes

1. *Building New Lives* (Americus, Ga.: Habitat for Humanity International). This and other Habitat videos are directed primarily at potential volunteers for the organization or might be used to inform local residents about the work of Habitat.

2. Robert Rector, "The Myth of Widespread American Poverty," *The Heritage Foundation Backgrounder* (18 Sept. 1998), no. 1221. This publication is available on-line at <http://www.heritage.org/library/backgrounder/bg1221es.html>.

rhetorical situations   genres   processes   strategies   research MLA / APA   media / design   readings

3. Cited in Barbara Ehrenreich, "Nickel and Dimed: On (Not) Getting By in America," *Harper's* (January 1999), 44. See also Christina Coburn Herman's *Poverty Amid Plenty: The Unfinished Business of Welfare Reform*, NETWORK, A National Social Justice Lobby (Washington, D.C., 1999), from NETWORK's national Welfare Reform Watch Project, which reports that most studies of welfare use telephone surveys even though a substantial percentage of those needing aid do not have phone service (41 percent in the NETWORK survey had no operative phone) and, therefore, are not represented in most welfare reform reports. This report is available on-line at <http://www.network-lobby.org>.

4. bell hooks, "Seeing and Making Culture: Representing the Poor," *Outlaw Culture: Resisting Representations* (New York: 1994), 169.

5. Manning Marable, *How Capitalism Underdeveloped Black America* (Boston: South End Press, 1983), 54.

6. Stanley Aronowitz, *The Politics of Identity: Class, Culture, Social Movements* (New York: Routledge, 1992), 201.

7. Kim Puuri, personal correspondence with author.

8. Paul Wellstone, "If Poverty Is the Question," *Nation* (14 April 1997), 15.

9. Herbert J. Gans, *The War Against the Poor* (New York: Basic Books, 1995), 6–7.

Engaging with the Text

1. How, according to Diana George, is poverty represented by nonprofit agencies such as Habitat for Humanity? What problems does George identify as a result of such representation?

2. George opens her analysis with a bell hooks quote, followed by descriptions of how frequently she encounters charities near Thanksgiving. How do the quote by bell hooks and George's anecdote appeal to different **AUDIENCES?**

   5–8

3. The Children, Inc. ad that George refers to is reprinted here on p. 669. What does George mean by the "emotional overload" of this image? Why do you think the Oxfam envelope promises not to include images like this?

3–4 ■

4. What **PURPOSE** does George's textual analysis serve? Where is that purpose made explicit? What other purposes might her essay serve?

52–86 ▲

5. *For Writing.* Identify a print, TV, or web ad aimed at influencing your opinion on a political or social issue. **ANALYZE** the visuals (drawings, pictures, photographs) and the accompanying words in the ad to describe how the issue is represented. How effectively does the ad meet its goals? Can you identify any problems with how the issue is represented that might undermine those goals?

■ rhetorical situations
▲ genres
○ processes
◆ strategies
● research MLA / APA
□ media / design
▥ readings

BRIAN STELTER

"We Are the 99 Percent" Joins the Cultural and Political Lexicon

Brian Stelter is a journalist at the New York Times, *where he reports on television and the web. He has been writing for the* Times *since 2007 and is prominently featured in the documentary film* Page One: Inside the "New York Times," *which was released in 2011. The textual analysis below appeared in the* Times *in November 2011. The* Vanity Fair *article mentioned midway through this reading can be found on p. 746.*

WHATEVER THE LONG-TERM EFFECTS of the Occupy movement, protesters have succeeded in implanting "We are the 99 percent," referring to the vast majority of Americans (and its implied opposite, "You are the 1 percent," referring to the tiny proportion of Americans with a vastly disproportionate share of wealth), into the cultural and political lexicon.

First chanted and blogged about in mid-September in New York, the slogan become a national shorthand for the income disparity. Easily grasped in its simplicity and Twitter-friendly in its brevity, the slogan has practically dared listeners to pick a side.

"We are getting nothing," read the Tumblr blog *We Are the 99 Percent*, which helped popularize the percentages, "while the other 1 percent is getting everything."

Within weeks of the first encampment in Zuccotti Park in New York, politicians seized on the phrase. Democrats in Congress began to invoke the "99 percent" to press for passage of President Obama's jobs act — but also to pursue action on mine safety, Internet access rules and voter identification laws, among others. Republicans pushed back, accusing protesters and their supporters of class warfare; Newt Gingrich this week called the "concept of the 99 and the 1" both divisive and "un-American."

Perhaps most important for the movement, there was a sevenfold 5 increase in Google searches for the term "99 percent" from September

A protester in Los Angeles, where the police cleared a park near City Hall.

to October and a spike in news articles about income inequality throughout the fall, heaping attention on the issues raised by activists.

"The '99 percent,' and the '1 percent,' too, are part of our vocabulary now," said Judith Stein, a professor of history at the City University of New York.

Soon there were income calculators ("What Percent Are You?" asked *The Wall Street Journal*), music playlists (an album of Woody Guthrie covers, promoted as a "soundtrack for the 99 percent") and cheap lawn signs. And, inevitably, there were ads: a storefront near Union Square peddles "Gifts for the 99 percent." A trailer for a Showtime television series about management consultants, *House of Lies,* describes the lead characters as "the 1 percent sticking it to the 1 percent." A Craigslist ad for a three-bedroom apartment in Brooklyn has the come-on "Live Like the 1 Percent!" (in this case, in Boerum Hill).

rhetorical situations   genres   processes   strategies   research MLA / APA   media / design   readings

These days, the language of the Occupy movement is being reappropriated in new ways seemingly every day. CBS ran a radio spot that invited viewers to "occupy your couch." On Thanksgiving, people joked online about occupying the dinner table. Now, on Facebook, holiday revelers are inviting friends to "1 percent parties."

Slogans have emerged from American protest movements, successful and otherwise, throughout history. The American Revolution furnished the world with "Give me liberty or give me death" and the still-popular "No taxation without representation." The equal rights movement in the 1960s used the phrase "59 cents" to point out the income disparities between women and men. The civil rights movement embraced the song "We Shall Overcome" as a slogan. During the Vietnam War, protesters called on politicians to "Bring 'em Home" and "Stop the Draft." More recently, supporters of Mr. Obama shouted, "Yes, We Can."

The idea behind the 99 percent catchphrase has its roots in a 10 decade's worth of reporting about the income gap between the richest Americans and the rest, and more directly in May in a *Vanity Fair* column by the liberal economist Joseph E. Stiglitz titled "Of the 1%, by the 1%, for the 1%." The slogan that resulted in September identified both a target, the "1 percent," and a theoretical constituency, everyone else.

Rhetorically, "it was really clever," said David S. Meyer, a University of California, Irvine, professor who studies social movements. "Deciding whom to blame is a key task of all politics," he wrote in his blog about the phrase.

"It's something that kind of puts your opponents on the defensive," he said in an interview.

In some cases, even politicians who have been put on the defensive by the movement have resorted to the same rhetoric. When Philadelphia's mayor, Michael A. Nutter, announced last week that the protesters there had to make way for a construction project, he emphasized that the project would be "built by the 99 percent, for the 99 percent."

Xeni Jardin, the editor of the influential blog *Boing Boing*, which has featured the protests every day since they began, praised the slogan for capturing "a mounting sense of unfairness in America" and distilling it "into something very brief."

She also called it "fundamentally unfair," because within the so- 15
called 99 percent who have slept at occupations across the country, there
are many well-to-do college students but just as many, if not more,
homeless people. "There are many shades of gray," she said.

But attempts to mock or subvert the slogan seem not to have stuck;
as Ms. Jardin put it, "How do you make fun of numbers?" A Tumblr blog
that was set up to compete with *We Are the 99 Percent*, called *We Are the
53%* (referring to the estimated percentage of Americans who pay federal income taxes), has not been updated for two weeks.

Professor Stein at CUNY believes that the 99 percent rallying cry
will have limited effect in the future. "I don't think a good slogan is
enough to revivify a movement or our politics," she said.

But Professor Meyer said the catchphrase was useful in that it gave
continuity and coherence to a movement that is losing some of its camps
in major cities across the country. "'Occupy' takes its name from the
occupation," he said. "If Occupy continues without occupations, what
provides continuity with those people in Zuccotti Park? The slogan."

The slogan was chanted again early on Wednesday morning in Los
Angeles and Philadelphia as police there cleared out the Occupy camp
sites in each city. As they lost physical ground for their local movements, protesters told each other online, "You can't evict an idea."

Engaging with the Text

312–13
1. What role does the **TITLE** play in this essay? How appropriate is it, and
    how does it prepare readers for the analysis that follows? This title
    was the headline for the article in the print version of the *Times*: in
    the online version, the headline was "Camps Are Cleared, but '99 Per-
    cent' Still Occupies the Lexicon." Which do you think is more effective,
    and why?

52–86
69
2. An effective **TEXTUAL ANALYSIS** pays close attention to the **CONTEXT** of
    the text that is being analyzed. What contextual information does
    Brian Stelter provide about the slogan the "99 percent"? How effec-
    tive is this in helping you understand his analysis?

rhetorical situations   genres   processes   strategies   research MLA / APA   media / design   readings

3. What other political slogans does Stelter mention? How does the phrase the "99 percent" COMPARE AND CONTRAST with those other slogans? Discuss whether this recent one will have the same kind of staying power. Is it, as Judith Stein says in this essay, "part of our vocabulary now"?

348–55

4. What EVIDENCE does Stelter offer for the current cultural and political power of the slogans the "99 percent" and the "1 percent"? In what places are these phrases appearing? How effective do you think the slogan the "99 percent" is currently? How effective is the "1 percent"?

327–35

5. *For Writing.* Select a political slogan that has had staying power in the U.S. cultural and political lexicon, such as "Give me liberty, or give me death," "No taxation without representation," "We shall overcome," or some other slogan not mentioned by Stelter. Conduct a web search to identify both the circumstances that led to the development of the slogan and the most recent instances when it was invoked. Then write a TEXTUAL ANALYSIS that considers the following questions: What was the slogan originally responding to? Who first said or wrote it? How long has it been in the American cultural and political lexicon? When and where in the last few years has it been used?

52–86

ROY PETER CLARK

"A More Perfect Union": Why It Worked

Roy Peter Clark is the author of more than a dozen books on journalism and writing, including The Glamour of Grammar: A Guide to the Magic and Mystery of Practical English *(2010), and* Help! For Writers: 210 Solutions to the Problems Every Writer Faces *(2011). He has taught writing to people of all ages, from elementary-school children to college journalism students to professional journalists and even Pulitzer Prize–winning authors. He is the vice-president of the Poynter Institute for Media Studies, where he maintains a blog on writing. A frequent guest on television speaking about ethics in journalism and writing, Clark is also a founder of the National Writers' Workshop. The following textual analysis of a speech about race delivered by Barack Obama during his 2008 presidential campaign appeared in April 18, 2008, on Poynter.org. To access the online version of the analysis, including a link to a video of the speech, go to* wwnorton.com /write/fieldguidelinks.

MORE THAN A CENTURY AGO, scholar and journalist W.E.B. DuBois wrote a single paragraph about how race is experienced in America. I have learned more from those 112 words than from most book-length studies of the subject:

> After the Egyptian and Indian, the Greek and Roman, the Teuton and Mongolian, the Negro is a sort of seventh son, born with a veil, and gifted with second-sight in this American world, a world which yields him no true self-consciousness, but only lets him see himself through the revelation of the other world. It is a peculiar sensation, this double-consciousness, this sense of always looking at one's self through the eyes of others, of measuring one's soul by the tape of a world that looks on in amused contempt and pity. One ever feels his two-ness, — an American, a Negro; two souls,

rhetorical situations genres processes strategies research MLA / APA media / design readings

two thoughts, two unreconciled strivings; two warring ideals in one dark body, whose dogged strength alone keeps it from being torn asunder."

Much has been said about the power and brilliance of <u>Barack Obama's March 18 speech</u> on race, even by some of his detractors. The focus has been on the orator's willingness to say things in public about race that are rarely spoken at all, even in private, and his expressed desire to move the country to a new and better place. There has also been attention to the immediate purpose of the speech, which was to reassure white voters that they had nothing to fear from the congregant of a fiery African-American pastor, the Rev. Jeremiah Wright.

Barack Obama delivering "A More Perfect Union."

Amid all the commentary, I have yet to see an X-ray reading of the text that would make visible the rhetorical strategies that the orator and authors used so effectively. When received in the ear, these effects breeze through us like a harmonious song. When inspected with the eye, these moves become more apparent, like reading a piece of sheet music for a difficult song and finally recognizing the chord changes.

Such analysis, while interesting in itself, might be little more than a scholarly curiosity if we were not so concerned with the language issues of political discourse. The popular opinion is that our current president, though plain spoken, is clumsy with language. Fair or not, this perception has produced a hope that our next president will be a more powerful communicator, a Kennedy or Reagan, perhaps, who can use language less as a way to signal ideology and more as a means to bring the disparate parts of the nation together. Journalists need to pay closer attention to political language than ever before.

Like most memorable pieces of oratory, Obama's speech sounds better than it reads. We have no way of knowing if that was true of Lincoln's Gettysburg Address, but it is certainly true of Dr. King's "I Have a Dream" speech. If you doubt this assertion, test it out. Read the speech and then experience it in its original setting recited by his soulful voice.

The effectiveness of Obama's speech rests upon four related rhetorical strategies:

1. The power of allusion and its patriotic associations.
2. The oratorical resonance of parallel constructions.
3. The "two-ness" of the texture, to use DuBois' useful term.
4. His ability to include himself as a character in a narrative about race.

Allusion

Part of what made Dr. King's speech resonate, not just for black people, but for some whites, was its framing of racial equality in familiar patriotic terms: "This will be the day when all of God's children will be able to sing with new meaning, 'My country 'tis of thee, sweet land of liberty of thee I sing. Land where my fathers died, land of the pilgrim's

5

pride, from every mountainside, let freedom ring.' " What follows, of course, is King's great litany of iconic topography that carries listeners across the American landscape: "Let freedom ring from the snowcapped Rockies of Colorado! . . ."

In this tradition, Obama begins with "We the people, in order to form a more perfect union," a quote from the Constitution that becomes a recurring refrain linking the parts of the speech. What comes next is "Two hundred and twenty one years ago," an opening that places him in the tradition of Lincoln at Gettysburg and Dr. King at the Lincoln Memorial: "Five score years ago."

On the first page, Obama mentions the words *democracy, Declaration of Independence, Philadelphia convention, 1787, the colonies, the founders, the Constitution, liberty, justice, citizenship under the law, parchment, equal, free, prosperous,* and *the presidency.* It is not as well known as it should be that many black leaders, including Dr. King, use two different modes of discourse when addressing white vs. black audiences, an ignorance that has led to some of the hysteria over some of Rev. Wright's comments.

Obama's patriotic lexicon is meant to comfort white ears and soothe white fears. What keeps the speech from falling into a pandering sea of slogans is language that reveals, not the ideals, but the failures of the American experiment: "It was stained by this nation's original sin of slavery, a question that divided the colonies and brought the convention to a stalemate until the founders chose to allow the slave trade to continue for at least twenty more years, and to leave any final resolution to future generations." And "what would be needed were Americans in successive generations who were willing to do their part . . . to narrow that gap between the promise of our ideals and the reality of their time."

Lest a dark vision of America disillusion potential voters, Obama returns to familiar evocations of national history, ideals, and language:

- "Out of many, we are truly one"
- "survived a Depression"
- "a man who served his country"
- "on a path of a more perfect union"

- "a full measure of justice"
- "the immigrant trying to feed his family"
- "where our union grows stronger"
- "a band of patriots signed that document."

Parallelism

At the risk of calling to mind the worst memories of grammar class, I   10
invoke the wisdom that parallel constructions help authors and orators
make meaning memorable. To remember how parallelism works, think
of equal terms to express equal ideas. So Dr. King dreamed that one day
his four children "will not be judged by the color of their skin but by the
content of their character." (By *the content of their character* is parallel to
by the color of their skin.)

Back to Obama: "This was one of the tasks we set forth at the beginning of this campaign — to continue the long march of those who came
before us, a march for a more just, more equal, more free, more caring
and more prosperous America." If you are counting, that's five parallel
phrases among 43 words.

And there are many more:

". . . we may not have come from the same place, but we all want
to move in the same direction."

"So when they are told to bus their children to a school across town;
when they hear that an African America is getting an advantage in
landing a good job or a spot in a good college because of an injustice that they themselves never committed; when they're told that
their fears about crime in urban neighborhoods are somehow prej-
udiced, resentment builds over time."

". . . embracing the burdens of our past without becoming victims
of our past."

Two-ness

I could argue that Obama's speech is a meditation upon DuBois' theory
of a dual experience of race in America. There is no mention of DuBois

or two-ness, but it is all there in the texture. In fact, once you begin the search, it is remarkable how many examples of two-ness shine through:

- "through protests and struggles"
- "on the streets and in the courts"
- "through civil war and civil disobedience"
- "I am the son of a black man from Kenya and a white woman from Kansas."
- "white and black"
- "black and brown"
- "best schools . . . poorest nations"
- "too black or not black enough"
- "the doctor and the welfare mom"
- "the model student and the former gang-banger . . ."
- "raucous laughter and sometimes bawdy humor"
- "political correctness or reverse racism"
- "your dreams do not have to come at the expense of my dreams"

Such language manages to create both tension and balance and, without being excessively messianic, permits Obama to present himself as the bridge builder, the reconciler of America's racial divide.

Autobiography

There is an obnoxious tendency among political candidates to frame their life story as a struggle against poverty or hard circumstances. As satirist Stephen Colbert once noted of presidential candidates, it is not enough to be an average millionaire. To appeal to populist instincts it becomes de rigueur to be descended from "goat turd farmers" in France.

Without dwelling on it, Obama reminds us that his father was black   15
and his mother white, that he came from Kenya, but she came from Kansas: "I am married to a black American who carries within her the blood of slave and slave owners — an inheritance we pass on to our two precious daughters. I have brothers, sisters, nieces, nephews, uncles,

and cousins, of every race and every hue, scattered across three continents, and for as long as I live, I will never forget that in no other country on Earth is my story even possible."

The word *story* is revealing one, for it is always the candidate's job (as both responsibility and ploy) to describe himself or herself as a character in a story of his or her own making. In speeches, as in homilies, stories almost always carry the weight of parable, with moral lessons to be drawn.

Most memorable, of course, is the story at the end of the speech — which is why it appears at the end. It is the story of Ashley Baia, a young, white, Obama volunteer from South Carolina, whose family was so poor she convinced her mother that her favorite meal was a mustard and relish sandwich.

"Anyway, Ashley finishes her story and then goes around the room and asks everyone else why they're supporting the campaign. They all have different stories and reasons. Many bring up a specific issue. And finally they come to this elderly black man who's been sitting there quietly the entire time. . . . He simply says to everyone in the room, 'I am here because of Ashley.'"

During most of the 20th century, demagogues, especially in the South, gained political traction by pitting working class whites and blacks against each other. How fitting, then, that Obama's story points in the opposite direction through an old black man who feels a young white woman's pain.

Engaging with the Text

74 ▲
327–35 ◆

1. What four patterns does Roy Peter Clark identify to show **HOW THE TEXT WORKS**? What **EVIDENCE** does he offer to demonstrate these patterns? How do these patterns affect the message in the textual analysis?

12–15 ■

2. What is Clark's **STANCE** toward the speech? Identify one or more sentences that reveal the stance.

rhetorical situations ▲ genres ○ processes ◆ strategies ● research MLA / APA □ media / design ▮ readings

3. After reading Clark's analysis, click on the hyperlink to the transcript of the speech; then click on the recording of the speech in the "Multimedia" box on the left and read the transcript as you listen to the speech. How does seeing and hearing Obama's delivery of the speech help you understand Clark's analysis of it?

4. Why does Clark insert two links to Martin Luther King's "I Have a Dream" speech? How does King's speech relate to Obama's? What were both trying to achieve?

5. *For Writing.* Search for a speech on the web (such as one by a politician, an activist, or a music or film star). **IDENTIFY PATTERNS** in the speech to show how the text works and write an **ANALYSIS** of the speech that offers evidence from it to support the patterns you identify. Craft a thesis that states what effect these patterns have on the speech. Insert links to the speech, to pictures of the speaker, and to other relevant topics dealt within the speech.

408–11

52–86

59 Reports

rhetorical
situations

genres

processes

strategies

research
MLA / APA

media /
design

readings

ELEANOR J. BADER

Homeless on Campus

Eleanor J. Bader is a freelance writer and an instructor in the English Department at Kingsborough Community College in Brooklyn, New York. She is also the coauthor of Targets of Hatred: Anti-Abortion Terrorism *(2001). The following report appeared in the* Progressive, *a liberal political magazine. As you read, notice how Bader effectively incorporates specific examples to support the information she reports.*

AESHA IS A TWENTY-YEAR-OLD at Kingsborough Community College in Brooklyn, New York. Until the fall of 2003, she lived with five people — her one-year-old son, her son's father, her sister, her mother, and her mother's boyfriend — in a three-bedroom South Bronx apartment. Things at home were fine until her child's father became physically abusive. Shortly thereafter, Aesha realized that she and her son had to leave the unit.

After spending thirty days in a temporary shelter, they landed at the city's emergency assistance unit (EAU). "It was horrible," Aesha says. "We slept on benches, and it was very crowded. I was so scared I sat on my bag and held onto the stroller day and night, from Friday to Monday." Aesha and her son spent several nights in the EAU before being sent to a hotel. Sadly, this proved to be a temporary respite. After a few days, they were returned to the EAU, where they remained until they were finally moved to a family shelter in Queens.

Although Aesha believes that she will be able to stay in this facility until she completes her associate's degree, the ordeal of being homeless has taken a toll on her and her studies. "I spend almost eight hours a day on the trains," she says. "I have to leave the shelter at 5:00 a.m. for the Bronx where my girlfriend watches my son for me. I get to her house around 7:00. Then I have to travel to school in Brooklyn — the last stop on the train followed by a bus ride — another two hours away."

Reluctantly, Aesha felt that she had no choice but to confide in teachers and explain her periodic absences. "They've all said that as long as I keep up with the work I'll be OK," she says. But that is not easy for Aesha or other homeless students.

Adriana Broadway lived in ten places, with ten different families, during high school. A native of Sparks, Nevada, Broadway told the LeTendre Education Fund for Homeless Children, a scholarship program administered by the National Association for the Education of Homeless Children and Youth, that she left home when she was thirteen. "For five years, I stayed here and there with friends," she wrote on her funding application. "I'd stay with whoever would take me in and allow me to live under their roof." 5

Johnny Montgomery also became homeless in his early teens. He told LeTendre staffers that his mother threw him out because he did not get along with her boyfriend. "She chose him over me," he wrote. "Hard days and nights have shaped me." Much of that time was spent on the streets.

Asad Dahir has also spent time on the streets. "I've been homeless more than one time and in more than one country," Dahir wrote on his scholarship application. Originally from Somalia, he and his family fled their homeland due to civil war and ended up in a refugee camp in neighboring Kenya. After more than a year in the camp, he and his thirteen-year-old brother were resettled, first in Atlanta and later in Ohio. There, high housing costs once again rendered the pair homeless.

Broadway, Montgomery, and Dahir are three of the forty-four homeless students from across the country who have been awarded LeTendre grants since 1999. Thanks, in part, to these funds, all three have been attending college and doing well.

But few homeless students are so lucky. "Each year at our national conference, homeless students come forward to share their stories," says Jenn Hecker, the organizing director of the National Student Campaign Against Hunger and Homelessness. "What often comes through is shame. Most feel as though they should be able to cover their costs." Such students usually try to blend in and are reluctant to disclose either their poverty or homelessness to others on campus, she says. Hecker blames rising housing costs for the problem and cites a 2003 survey that

rhetorical situations   genres   processes   strategies   research MLA / APA   media / design   readings

found the median wage needed to pay for a two-bedroom apartment in the United States to be $15.21, nearly three times the federal minimum.

Even when doubled up, students in the most expensive states — Massachusetts, California, New Jersey, New York, and Maryland — are scrambling. "In any given semester, there are four or five families where the head of household is in college," says Beth Kelly, a family service counselor at the Clinton Family Inn, a New York City transitional housing program run by Homes for the Homeless.

Advocates for the homeless report countless examples of students sleeping in their cars and sneaking into a school gym to shower and change clothes. They speak of students who couch surf or camp in the woods — bicycling or walking to classes — during temperate weather. Yet, for all the anecdotes, details about homeless college students are hazy.

"I wish statistics existed on the number of homeless college students," says Barbara Duffield, executive director of the National Association for the Education of Homeless Children and Youth. "Once state and federal responsibility to homeless kids stops — at the end of high school — it's as if they cease to exist. They fall off the map."

Worse, they are neither counted nor attended to.

"Nobody has ever thought about this population or collected data on them because nobody thinks they are a priority to study," says Martha Burt, principal research associate at the Urban Institute.

Critics say colleges are not doing enough to meet — or even recognize — the needs of this group.

"The school should do more," says Aesha. "They have a child care center on my campus, but they only accept children two and up. It would have helped if I could've brought my son to day care at school." She also believes that the college should maintain emergency housing for homeless students.

"As an urban community college, our students are commuters," responds Uda Bradford, interim dean of student affairs at Kingsborough Community College. "Therefore, our student support services are developed within that framework."

"As far as I know, no college has ever asked for help in reaching homeless students," says Mary Jean LeTendre, a retired Department of Education administrator and creator of the LeTendre Education Fund. "Individual colleges have come forward to help specific people, but there is nothing systematic like there is for students in elementary and high school."

"There is a very low awareness level amongst colleges," Duffield adds. "People have this 'you can pull yourself up by your bootstraps' myth about college. There is a real gap between the myth and the reality for those who are trying to overcome poverty by getting an education."

Part of the problem is that the demographics of college attendance have changed. "Most educational institutions were set up to serve fewer, less diverse, more privileged students," says Andrea Leskes, a vice president with the Association of American Colleges and Universities. "As a result, we are not successfully educating all the students who come to college today. This means that nontraditional students — the older, returning ones as well as those from low income or other disenfranchised communities — often receive inadequate support services." 20

"It's not that colleges are not concerned, but attention today is not on serving the poor," says Susan O'Malley, chair of the faculty senate at the City University of New York. "It's not in fashion. During the 1960s, people from all over the country were going to Washington and making a lot of noise. The War on Poverty was influenced by this noise. Now the poor are less visible."

Mary Gesing, a counselor at Kirkwood Community College in Cedar Rapids, Iowa, agrees. "Nothing formal exists for this population, and the number of homeless students on campus is not tracked," she says. Because of this statistical gap, programs are not devised to accommodate homeless students or address their needs.

Despite these programmatic shortfalls, Gesing encounters two to three homeless students — often single parents — each semester. Some became homeless when they left an abuser. Others lost their housing because they could no longer pay for it due to a lost job, the termination of unemployment benefits, illness, the cessation of child support, or drug or alcohol abuse.

Kirkwood's approach is a "patchwork system," Gesing explains, and homeless students often drop out or fail classes because no one knows of their plight. "When people don't know who to come to for help they just fade away," she says.

"Without housing, access to a workspace, or access to a shower, students' lives suffer, their grades suffer, and they are more likely to drop classes, if not withdraw entirely from school. I've seen it happen," says Amit Rai, an English professor at a large, public university in Florida. "If seen from the perspective of students, administrators would place affordable housing and full access to health care at the top of what a university should provide." 25

Yet for all this, individual teachers — as well as administrators and counselors — can sometimes make an enormous difference.

B.R., a faculty member who asked that neither her name nor school be disclosed, has allowed several homeless students to sleep in her office during the past decade. "Although there is no institutional interest or involvement in keeping these students enrolled, a few faculty members really care about the whole student and don't shy away from helping," she says.

One of the students she sheltered lived in the space for three months, whenever she couldn't stay with friends. Like Aesha, this student was fleeing a partner who beat her. Another student had been kicked out of the dorm because her stepfather never paid the bill. She applied for financial assistance to cover the cost, but processing took months. "This student stayed in my office for an entire semester," B.R. says.

A sympathetic cleaning woman knew what was going on and turned a blind eye to the arrangement. "Both students showered in the dorms and kept their toothbrushes and cosmetics in one of the two department bathrooms which I gave them keys to," B.R. adds. "The administration never knew a thing. Both of the students finished school and went on to become social workers. They knew that school would be their saving grace, that knowledge was the only thing that couldn't be snatched."

Engaging with the Text

3–4 ■

1. What do you think is the **PURPOSE** of this report? How does this purpose affect the way the report is written? Point to examples from the text in your response.

2. This piece basically reports on the general topic of homeless college students. What is the author's specific point? How do you know? How else could she have made her point explicit?

306–10 ◆

3. Eleanor J. Bader **ENDS** her essay with a powerful quote from one of her informants, a teacher she calls B.R.: "[The students] knew that school would be their saving grace, that knowledge was the only thing that couldn't be snatched." What does B.R. mean by this observation? In what ways can an education help such students, and in what ways might it be misleading to think that an education alone will solve all of the problems these students face?

387–95 ◆

4. Consider the amount of **NARRATIVES** in this report. Why do you think Bader includes so many? What other kinds of support does she include, if any? What additional kinds of support might she have used to help accomplish her purpose?

5. *For Writing.* You may not be aware of services that are readily available on your campus. Find out what services are available at your school, and do some research on one of those services to learn who uses it and whether they're satisfied with it or think it could be improved. Write a **REPORT** on your findings. As an alternative, you may want to deliver your report as a website.

87–118 ▲

LINDA BABCOCK AND SARA LASCHEVER

Women Don't Ask

Linda Babcock is the James M. Walton Professor of Economics at Carnegie Mellon University where she founded and directs the Program for Research and Outreach on Gender Equity in Society. She has also been a visiting professor at the University of Chicago's Graduate School of Business, the Harvard Business School, and the California Institute of Technology. Sara Laschever is a writer and editor whose work has appeared in the New York Review of Books, *the* New York Times, *the* Village Voice, *the* Harvard Business Review, Vogue, Mademoiselle, *and the* Boston Phoenix, *among other publications. She has taught writing at Boston University. Babcock and Laschever's book,* Women Don't Ask: Negotiation and the Gender Divide *(2003), from which the following essay was taken, was called one of the seventy-five smartest books of all time by* Fortune *magazine. They are also coauthors of* Ask for It: How Women Can Use the Power of Negotiation to Get What They Really Want *(2008).*

A **FEW YEARS AGO,** when Linda was serving as the director of the Ph.D. program at her school, a delegation of women graduate students came to her office. Many of the male graduate students were teaching courses of their own, the women explained, while most of the female graduate students had been assigned to work as teaching assistants to regular faculty. Linda agreed that this didn't sound fair, and that afternoon she asked the associate dean who handled teaching assignments about the women's complaint. She received a simple answer: "I try to find teaching opportunities for any student who approaches me with a good idea for a course, the ability to teach, and a reasonable offer about what it will cost," he explained. "More men ask. The women just don't ask."

The women just don't ask. This incident and the associate dean's explanation suggested to Linda the existence of a more pervasive problem. Could it be that women don't get more of the things they want in life in part because they don't think to ask for them? Are there external pressures that discourage women from asking as much as men do — and even keep them from realizing that they can ask? Are women really less likely than men to ask for what they want?

To explore this question, Linda conducted a study that looked at the starting salaries of students graduating from Carnegie Mellon University with their master's degrees. When Linda looked exclusively at gender, the difference was fairly large: The starting salaries of the men were 7.6 percent or almost $4,000 higher on average than those of the women. Trying to explain this difference, Linda looked next at who had negotiated his or her salary (who had asked for more money) and who had simply accepted the initial offer he or she had received. It turned out that only 7 percent of the female students had negotiated but 57 percent (eight times as many) of the men had asked for more money. Linda was particularly surprised to find such a dramatic difference between men and women at Carnegie Mellon because graduating students are strongly advised by the school's Career Services department to negotiate their job offers. Nonetheless, hardly any of the women had done so. The most striking finding, however, was that the students who had negotiated (most of them men) were able to increase their starting salaries by 7.4 percent on average, or $4,053 — almost exactly the difference between men's and women's average starting pay. This suggests that the salary differences between the men and the women might have been eliminated if the women had negotiated their offers.

Spurred on by this finding, Linda and two colleagues, Deborah Small and Michele Gelfand, designed another study to look at the propensity of men and women to ask for more than they are offered. They recruited students at Carnegie Mellon for an experiment and told them that they would be paid between three and ten dollars for playing Boggle, a game by Milton Bradley. In Boggle, players shake a cube of tile letters until all the letters fall into a grid at the bottom of the cube. They must then identify words that can be formed from the letters vertically, horizontally, or diagonally. Each research subject was asked to play four rounds of the game, and then an experimenter handed him or her three dollars and said, "Here's three dollars. Is three dollars okay?" If a subject asked for more money, the experimenters would pay that participant ten dollars, but they would not give anyone more money if he or she just complained about the compensation (an indirect method of asking). The results were striking —

almost *nine times* as many male as female subjects asked for more money.*
Both male and female subjects rated how well they'd played the game
about equally, meaning that women didn't feel they should be paid less
or should accept less because they'd played poorly. There were also no
gender differences in how much men and women complained about the
compensation (there was plenty of complaining all around). The significant factor seemed to be that for men, unhappiness with what they were
offered was more likely to make them try to fix their unhappiness — by
asking for more.

In a much larger study, Linda, Michele Gelfand, Deborah Small, and ⁵
another colleague, Heidi Stayn, conducted a survey of several hundred
people with access to the Internet (subjects were paid ten dollars to log
on to a website and answer a series of questions).† The survey asked
respondents about the most recent negotiations they'd attempted or initiated (as opposed to negotiations they'd participated in that had been
prompted or initiated by others). For the men, the most recent negotiation they'd initiated themselves had occurred two weeks earlier on average, while for the women the most recent negotiation they'd initiated had
occurred a full month before. Averages for the second-most-recent negotiations attempted or initiated were about seven weeks earlier for men
and twenty-four weeks earlier for women.

These results suggest that men are asking for things they want and
initiating negotiations much more often than women — two to three times
as often.‡ Linda and her colleagues wanted to be sure that this discrepancy

---

*Only 2.5 percent of the female subjects but 23 percent of the male subjects asked
for more.

†The survey was hosted by Jonathan Baron's website at the University of
Pennsylvania.

‡Another interpretation is possible, however. Men may not really be doing more
negotiating than women; men and women may behave in the same ways but label or
describe their behavior differently. That is, what a man calls negotiation, a woman calls
something else. This interpretation seems less plausible because it suggests that men
and women define a common word in our language differently. But even if it is true, it
still has implications for behavior. If women aren't calling their interactions negotiations and men are, women may not be viewing those encounters as strategically and
instrumentally as men do and may therefore gain less from them in significant ways.

was not produced simply by memory lapses, however, so the survey also asked people about the *next* negotiation they planned to initiate. In keeping with the earlier findings, the negotiations planned by the women were much further in the future than those being planned by the men — one month ahead for the women but only one week ahead for the men. This means that men may be initiating *four* times as many negotiations as women. The sheer magnitude of this difference is dramatic, especially since respondents to the survey included people of all ages, from a wide range of professions, and with varied levels of education. It confirms that men really do take a more active approach than women to getting what they want by asking for it.

The more than 100 interviews we conducted . . . — with men and women from a range of professions (including full-time mothers) and from Britain and Europe as well as the United States — supported these findings.* When asked to identify the last negotiation in which they had participated, the majority of the women we talked to named an event several months in the past and described a recognized type of structured negotiation, such as buying a car. (The exceptions were women with small children, who uniformly said, "I negotiate with my kids all the time.") The majority of the men described an event that had occurred within the preceding week, and frequently identified more informal transactions, such as negotiating with a spouse over who would take the kids to soccer practice, with a boss to pay for a larger-size rental car because of a strained back, or with a colleague about which parts of a joint project each team member would undertake. Men were also more likely to mention more ambiguous situations — situations that could be construed as negotiations but might not be by many people. For the most part, the men we talked to saw negotiation as a bigger part of their lives and a more common event than the women did.

---

*Although we strove to make our sample as representative as possible of the full diversity of women in Western culture, we used the interviews only to illustrate the ideas in the book and did not try to ensure that our sample exactly matched current demographic patterns in the population. We also interviewed far more women than men.

rhetorical situations   genres   processes   strategies   research MLA / APA   media / design   readings

One particularly striking aspect of our findings was how they broke down by age. The changes brought about by the women's movement over the last 40 years had led us to expect greater differences between older men and women than between their younger counterparts. And indeed when we discussed the ideas . . . with younger women they often suggested that the problems we were studying were "boomer" problems, afflicting older women but not themselves. To our surprise, however, when we looked exclusively at respondents to the web survey who were in their twenties and early thirties, the gender differences in how often they initiated negotiations were similar to or slightly *larger* than the differences in older cohorts (with men attempting many more negotiations than women). In addition, both the starting salary study and the Boggle study used subjects who were in their twenties. This persuaded us that the tendency among women to accept what they're offered and not ask for more is far from just a "boomer" problem.

References

Babcock, L. 2002. Do graduate students negotiate their job offers? Carnegie Mellon University. Unpublished report.

Babcock, L., M. Gelfand, D. Small, and H. Stayn. 2002. Propensity to initiate negotiations: A new look at gender variation in negotiation behavior. Carnegie Mellon University. Unpublished manuscript.

Small, D., L. Babcock, and M. Gelfand. 2003. Why don't women ask? Carnegie Mellon University. Unpublished manuscript.

Engaging with the Text

110–11 ▲
312–15 ◆
327–35 ◆

1. Well-written reports require a tightly focused **TOPIC**. What are the topic and **THESIS** of "Women Don't Ask," and how do they relate to the **TITLE?**

2. What **EVIDENCE** is offered in this essay to support the thesis? How convincing do you find this evidence and the sources on which it depends?

3. What does the report say is the economic effect of not negotiating for a better starting salary? Why do you think there is a difference between women and men in whether and how they negotiate starting salaries? What gender differences account for how both negotiate more generally?

5–8 ■

4. Who is the intended **AUDIENCE** for this report? Who would most benefit from the information? Point to phrases in the report that make clear the audience.

87–118 ▲
327–35 ◆

5. *For Writing.* Replicate on a smaller scale the online survey or the interviews Babcock and Laschever conducted for this report. (You need not pay participants.) Analyze the responses you receive to determine whether there are differences in how the men and women participants negotiate. Write up your findings in a **REPORT;** be sure to support these findings with **EVIDENCE** (data, quotations, narratives). Cite Babcock and Laschever's report as an impetus for your study.

■ rhetorical situations
▲ genres
○ processes
◆ strategies
● research MLA / APA
□ media / design
▌ readings

JONATHAN KOZOL

Fremont High School

An educator, activist, and writer, Jonathan Kozol is known for his work as an advocate for social justice and public education. Currently on the editorial board of Greater Good Magazine, *Kozol is the author of over a dozen books, including* Fire in the Ashes: Twenty-five Years among the Poorest Children in America *(2012) and* The Shame of the Nation: The Restoration of Apartheid Schooling in America *(2005), from which the following selection is taken. In this piece, Kozol reports on one of the many schools he studied to write this book.*

FREMONT **H**IGH **S**CHOOL **IN** **L**OS **A**NGELES enrolls almost 5,000 students on a three-track schedule, with about 3,300 in attendance at a given time. The campus "sprawls across a city block, between San Pedro Street and Avalon Boulevard in South Central Los Angeles," the *Los Angeles Times* observes. A "neighborhood fortress, its perimeter protected by an eight-foot steel fence topped by spikes," the windows of the school are "shielded from gunfire by thick screens." According to teachers at the school, the average ninth grade student reads at fourth or fifth grade level. Nearly a third read at third grade level or below. About two thirds of the ninth grade students drop out prior to twelfth grade.

There were 27 homerooms for the first-year students, nine homerooms for seniors at the time I visited in spring of 2003. Thirty-five to 40 classrooms, nearly a third of all the classrooms in the school, were located in portables. Some classes also took place in converted storage closets — "windowless and nasty," said one of the counselors — or in converted shop rooms without blackboards. Class size was high, according to a teacher who had been here for six years and who invited me into her tenth grade social studies class. Nearly 220 classes had enrollments ranging between 33 and over 40 students. The class I visited had 40 students, almost all of whom were present on the day that I was there.

Unlike the staggered luncheon sessions I observed at Walton High, lunch was served in a single sitting to the students in this school. "It's

The school's slogan at the front entrance projects a positive outlook.

physically impossible to feed 3,300 kids at once," the teacher said. "The line for kids to get their food is very long and the entire period lasts only 30 minutes. It takes them 15 minutes just to walk there from their classes and get through the line. They get 10 minutes probably to eat their meals. A lot of them don't try. You've been a teacher, so you can imagine what it does to students when they have no food to eat for an entire day. The schoolday here at Fremont is eight hours long."

For teachers, too, the schedule sounded punishing. "I have six classes every day, including my homeroom," she said. "I've had *more* than 40 students in a class some years. My average class this year is 36. I see more than 200 students every day. Classes start at seven-thirty. I don't usually leave until four or four-thirty. . . . "

High school students, when I meet them first, are often more reluc-   5
tant than the younger children are to open up their feelings and express their personal concerns; but hesitation on the part of students did not prove to be a problem in this class at Fremont High. The students knew

The perimeter is protected by an eight-foot steel fence topped by spikes.

I was a writer (they were told this by their teacher) and they took no time in getting down to matters that were on their minds.

"Can we talk about the bathrooms?" asked a student named Mireya.

In almost any classroom there are certain students who, by force of the directness or unusual sophistication of their way of speaking, tend to capture your attention from the start. Mireya later spoke insightfully of academic problems, at the school, but her observations on the physical and personal embarrassments she and her schoolmates had to undergo cut to the heart of questions of essential dignity or the denial of such dignity that kids in squalid schools like this one have to deal with.

Fremont High School, as court papers document, has "15 fewer bathrooms than the law requires." Of the limited number of bathrooms that are working in the school, "only one or two . . . are open and unlocked for girls to use." Long lines of girls are "waiting to use the bathrooms," which are generally "unclean" and "lack basic supplies," including toilet paper. Some of the classrooms "do not have air-conditioning," so that students "become red-faced and unable to concentrate" during "the extreme heat of summer." The rats observed by children in their elementary schools proliferate at Fremont High as well. "Rats in eleven . . . classrooms," maintenance records of the school report. "Rat droppings" are recorded "in the bins and drawers" of the high school's kitchen. "Hamburger buns" are being "eaten off [the] bread-delivery rack," school records note.

No matter how many times I read these tawdry details in court filings and depositions, I'm always surprised again to learn how often these unsanitary physical conditions are permitted to continue in a public school even after media accounts describe them vividly. But hearing of these conditions in Mireya's words was even more unsettling, in part because this student was so fragile-seeming and because the need even to speak of these indignities in front of me and all the other students seemed like an additional indignity.

"The problem is this," she carefully explained. "You're not allowed   10 to use the bathroom during lunch, which is a 30-minute period. The only time that you're allowed to use it is between your classes." But "this is a huge building," she went on. "It has long corridors. If you have one class at one end of the building and your next class happens to be way down at the other end, you don't have time to use the bathroom and still get to class before it starts. So you go to your class and then you ask permission from your teacher to go to the bathroom and the teacher tells you, 'No. You had your chance between the periods. . . . '

"I feel embarrassed when I have to stand there and explain it to a teacher."

"This is the question," said a wiry-looking boy named Edward, leaning forward in his chair close to the door, a little to the right of where I stood. "Students are not animals, but even animals need to relieve themselves sometimes. We're in this building for eight hours. What do they think we're supposed to do?"

"It humiliates you," said Mireya, who went on to make the interesting statement that "the school provides solutions that don't actually work," and this idea was taken up by other students in describing course requirements within the school. A tall black student, for example, told me that she hoped to be a social worker or a doctor but was programmed

rhetorical situations   genres   processes   strategies   research MLA / APA   media / design   readings

into "Sewing Class" this year. She also had to take another course, called "Life Skills," which she told me was a very basic course — "a retarded class," to use her words — that "teaches things like the six continents," which she said she'd learned in elementary school.

When I asked her why she had to take these courses, she replied that she'd been told they were required, which reminded me of the response the sewing teacher I had met at Roosevelt Junior High School gave to the same question. As at Roosevelt, it turned out that this was not exactly so. What was required was that high school students take two courses in an area of study that was called "the Technical Arts," according to the teacher. At schools that served the middle class or upper middle class, this requirement was likely to be met by courses that had academic substance and, perhaps, some relevance to college preparation. At Beverly Hills High School, for example, the technical arts requirement could be fulfilled by taking subjects such as residential architecture, the designing of commercial structures, broadcast journalism, advanced computer graphics, a sophisticated course in furniture design, carving and sculpture, or an honors course in engineering research and design. At Fremont High, in contrast, this requirement was far more likely to be met by courses that were basically vocational.

Mireya, for example, who had plans to go to college, told me that she had to take a sewing class last year and now was told she'd been assigned to take a class in hair-dressing as well. When I asked the teacher why Mireya could not skip these subjects and enroll in classes that would help her to pursue her college aspirations, she replied, "It isn't a question of what students want. It's what the school may have available. If all the other elective classes that a student wants to take are full, she has to take one of these classes if she wants to graduate."

A very small girl named Obie who had big blue-tinted glasses tilted up across her hair interrupted then to tell me with a kind of wild gusto that she took hair-dressing *twice*! When I expressed surprise that this was possible, she said there were two levels of hair-dressing offered here at Fremont High. "One is in hair-styling," she said. "The other is in braiding."

Mireya stared hard at this student for a moment and then suddenly began to cry. "I don't *want* to take hair-dressing. I did not need sewing either. I knew how to sew. My mother is a seamstress in a factory. I'm trying to go to college. I don't need to sew to go to college. My mother sews. I hoped for something else."

"What would you rather take?" I asked.

"I wanted to take an AP class," she answered.

Mireya's sudden tears elicited a strong reaction from one of the boys 20 who had been silent up to now. A thin and dark-eyed student, named Fortino, with long hair down to his shoulders who was sitting on the left side of the classroom, he turned directly to Mireya.

"Listen to me," he said. "The owners of the sewing factories need laborers. Correct?"

"I guess they do," Mireya said.

"It's not going to be their own kids. Right?"

"Why not?" another student said.

"So they can grow beyond themselves," Mireya answered quietly. 25 "But we remain the same."

"You're ghetto," said Fortino, "so we send you to the factory." He sat low in his desk chair, leaning on one elbow, his voice and dark eyes loaded with a cynical intelligence. "You're ghetto — so you sew!"

"There are higher positions than these," said a student named Samantha.

"You're ghetto," said Fortino unrelentingly to her. "So sew!"

Mireya was still crying.

Several students spoke then of a problem about frequent substitute 30 teachers, which was documented also in court papers. One strategy for staffing classes in these three- and four-track schools when substitutes could not be found was to assign a teacher who was not "on track" — that is, a teacher who was on vacation — to come back to school and fill in for the missing teacher. "Just yesterday I was subbing [for] a substitute who was subbing for a teacher who never shows up," a teacher told the ACLU lawyers. "That's one scenario. . . ."

Obie told me that she stopped coming to class during the previous semester because, out of her six teachers, three were substitutes. "Come on now! Like — hello? We live in a rich country? Like the richest country in the world? Hello?"

The teacher later told me that three substitutes in one semester, if the student's words were accurate, would be unusual. But "on average,

rhetorical situations | genres | processes | strategies | research MLA / APA | media / design | readings

every student has a substitute teacher in at least one class. Out of 180 teacher-slots, typically 25 or so cannot be filled and have to be assigned to substitutes."

Hair-dressing and sewing, it turned out, were not the only classes students at the school were taking that appeared to have no relevance to academic education. A number of the students, for example, said that they were taking what were known as "service classes" in which they would sit in on an academic class but didn't read the texts or do the lessons or participate in class activities but passed out books and did small errands for the teachers. They were given half-credits for these courses. Students received credits, too, for jobs they took outside of school, in fast-food restaurants for instance, I was told. How, I wondered, was a credit earned or grade determined for a job like this outside of school? "Best behavior and great customer service," said a student who was working in a restaurant, as she explained the logic of it all to ACLU lawyers in her deposition.

The teacher gave some other examples of the ways in which the students were shortchanged in academic terms. The year-round calendar, she said, gave these students 20 fewer schooldays than the students who attended school on normal calendars receive. In compensation, they attended classes for an extra hour, up until three-thirty, and students in the higher grades who had failed a course and had to take a make-up class remained here even later, until six, or sometimes up to nine.

"They come out of it just totally glassed-over," said the teacher, and, 35 as one result, most teachers could not realistically give extra homework to make up for fewer days of school attendance and, in fact, because the kids have been in school so long each day, she said, "are likely to give less."

Students who needed to use the library to do a research paper for a class ran into problems here as well, because, as a result of the tight scheduling of classes, they were given no free time to use the library except at lunch, or for 30 minutes after school, unless a teacher chose to bring a class into the library to do a research project during a class period. But this was frequently impossible because the library was often closed when it was being used for other purposes such as administration of examinations, typically for "make-up tests," as I was told. "It's been closed now for a week because they're using it for testing," said Samantha.

"They were using it for testing last week also," said Fortino, who reported that he had a research paper due for which he had to locate 20 sources but had made no progress on it yet because he could not get into the library.

"You have to remember," said the teacher, "that the school's in session all year long, so if repairs need to be made in wiring or something like that in the library, they have to do it while the kids are here. So at those times the library is closed. Then, if there's testing taking place in there, the library is closed. And if an AP teacher needs a place to do an AP prep, the library is closed. And sometimes when the teachers need a place to meet, the library is closed." In all, according to the school librarian, the library is closed more than a quarter of the year.

During a meeting with a group of teachers later in the afternoon, it was explained to me in greater detail how the overcrowding of the building limited course offerings for students. "Even when students *ask* to take a course that interests them and teachers want to teach it," said one member of the faculty — she gave the example of a class in women's studies she said she would like to teach — "the physical shortages of space repeatedly prevent this." Putting students into service classes, on the other hand, did not require extra space. So, instead of the enrichment students might have gained from taking an elective course that had some academic substance, they were obliged to sit through classes in which they were not enrolled and from which they said that they learned virtually nothing.

Mireya had asked her teacher for permission to stay in the room with us during my meeting with the other teachers and remained right to the end. At five p.m., as I was about to leave the school, she stood beside the doorway of the classroom as the teacher, who was giving me a ride, assembled all the work she would be taking home. 40

"Why is it," she asked, "that students who do not need what we need get so much more? And we who need it so much more get so much less?"

rhetorical situations

genres

processes

strategies

research MLA / APA

media / design

readings

I told her I'd been asking the same question now for nearly 40 years and still had no good answer. She answered, maturely, that she did not think there was an answer.

Engaging with the Text

1. The **TITLE** of the book in which this essay appears is *The Shame of the Nation: The Restoration of Apartheid Schooling in America*. How does this piece illuminate and support the book title? Based on your reading of this report, what is the "shame of the nation" and how is "apartheid schooling" taking place in the United States even though schools were legally desegregated over thirty years ago?

312–13

2. What is the **PURPOSE** of Jonathan Kozol's report? What do you think Kozol hopes will happen because of his report? Given this purpose, who is the most important audience for this piece?

3–4

3. How does Kozol demonstrate that his information is **ACCURATE** and **WELL RESEARCHED**? What kinds of **EVIDENCE** does he use to support his points? To what degree do you find his information accurate?

71–72
327–35

4. Reread the final three paragraphs of Kozol's report. How effective is this **ENDING?** Do you think Kozol believes there is no answer to Mireya's question? Why or why not?

306–10

5. *For Writing.* Research a public high school near where you live — the school you attended or one near your college. Get permission from the school principal to **INTERVIEW** several teachers and students about their experiences with the curriculum, recreation facilities, lunch room, school library, and class sizes. Locate any recent newspaper accounts or school reports to supplement and verify the information you obtain from your interviews. Write a **REPORT** that **COMPARES** what you find out about the high school you researched with what Kozol reports about Fremont High. In what ways are the problems similar and in what ways are they different?

448–49

87–118
348–55

ALINA TUGEND

Multitasking Can Make You Lose . . . Um . . . Focus

Alina Tugend is a columnist for the New York Times *and the author of* Better by Mistake: The Unexpected Benefits of Being Wrong *(2011). Her work has also appeared in the* Los Angeles Times, *the* Atlantic, Family Circle, *and the* American Journalism Review, *as well as in anthologies and online magazines. This report on multitasking was published in the* New York Times *in 2008.*

As YOU ARE READING THIS ARTICLE, are you listening to music or the radio? Yelling at your children? If you are looking at it online, are you e-mailing or instant-messaging at the same time? Checking stocks?

Since the 1990s, we've accepted multitasking without question. Virtually all of us spend part of most of our day either rapidly switching from one task to another or juggling two or more things at the same time.

While multitasking may seem to be saving time, psychologists, neuroscientists and others are finding that it can put us under a great deal of stress and actually make us less efficient.

Although doing many things at the same time — reading an article while listening to music, switching to check e-mail messages and talking on the phone — can be a way of making tasks more fun and energizing, "you have to keep in mind that you sacrifice focus when you do this," said Edward M. Hallowell, a psychiatrist and author of *CrazyBusy: Overstretched, Overbooked, and About to Snap!* (Ballantine, 2006). "Multitasking is shifting focus from one task to another in rapid succession. It gives the illusion that we're simultaneously tasking, but we're really not. It's like playing tennis with three balls."

Of course, it depends what you're doing. For some people, listening to music while working actually makes them more creative because they are using different cognitive functions. 5

But despite what many of us think, you cannot simultaneously e-mail and talk on the phone. I think we're all familiar with what

Dr. Hallowell calls "e-mail voice," when someone you're talking to on the phone suddenly sounds, well, disengaged.

"You cannot divide your attention like that," he said. "It's a big illusion. You can shift back and forth."

We all know that computers and their spawn, the smartphone and cellphone, have created a very different world from several decades ago, when a desk worker had a typewriter, a phone and an occasional colleague who dropped into the office.

Think even of the days before the cordless phone. Those old enough can remember when talking on the telephone, which was stationary, meant sitting down, putting your feet up and chatting — not doing laundry, cooking dinner, sweeping the floor and answering the door.

That is so far in the past. As we are required, or feel required, to do 10 more and more things in a shorter period of time, researchers are trying to figure out how the brain changes attention from one subject to another.

A pedestrian walking and texting.

Earl Miller, the Picower professor of neuroscience at the Massachusetts Institute of Technology, explained it this way: human brains have a very large prefrontal cortex, which is the part of the brain that contains the "executive control" process. This helps us switch and prioritize tasks.

In humans, he said, the prefrontal cortex is about one-third of the entire cortex, while in dogs and cats, it is 4 or 5 percent and in monkeys about 15 percent.

"With the growth of the prefrontal cortex, animals become more and more flexible in their behavior," Professor Miller said.

We can do a couple of things at the same time if they are routine, but once they demand more cognitive process, the brain has "a severe bottleneck," he said.

Professor Miller conducted studies where electrodes were attached   15
to the head to monitor participants performing different tasks.

He found that "when there's a bunch of visual stimulants out there in front of you, only one or two things tend to activate your neurons, indicating that we're really only focusing on one or two items at a time."

David E. Meyer, a professor of psychology at the University of Michigan, and his colleagues looked at young adults as they performed tasks that involved solving math problems or classifying geometric objects.

Their 2001 study, published in *The Journal of Experimental Psychology*, found that for all types of tasks, the participants lost time when they had to move back and forth from one undertaking to another, and that it took significantly longer to switch between the more complicated tasks.

Although the time it takes for our brains to switch tasks may be only a few seconds or less, it adds up. If we're talking about doing two jobs that can require real concentration, like text-messaging and driving, it can be fatal.

The RAC Foundation, a British nonprofit organization that focuses   20
on driving issues, asked 17 drivers, age 17 to 24, to use a driving simulator to see how texting affects driving.

The reaction time was around 35 percent slower when writing a text message — slower than driving drunk or stoned.

All right, there are definitely times we should not try to multitask. But, we may think, it's nice to say that we should focus on one thing at a time, but the real world doesn't work that way. We are constantly interrupted.

A 2005 study, "No Task Left Behind? Examining the Nature of Fragmented Work," found that people were interrupted and moved from one project to another about every 11 minutes. And each time, it took about 25 minutes to circle back to that same project.

Interestingly, a study published last April, "The Cost of Interrupted Work: More Speed and Stress," found that "people actually worked faster in conditions where they were interrupted, but they produced less," said Gloria Mark, a professor of informatics at the University of California at Irvine and a co-author of both studies. And she also found that people were as likely to self-interrupt as to be interrupted by someone else.

"As observers, we'll watch, and then after every 12 minutes or so, for   25 no apparent reasons, someone working on a document will turn and call someone or e-mail," she said. As I read that, I realized how often I was switching between writing this article and checking my e-mail.

Professor Mark said further research needed to be done to know why people work in these patterns, but our increasingly shorter attention spans probably have something to do with it.

Her study found that after only 20 minutes of interrupted performance, people reported significantly higher stress, frustration, workload, effort and pressure.

"I also argue that it's bad for innovation," she said. "Ten and a half minutes on one project is not enough time to think in-depth about anything."

Dr. Hallowell has termed this effort to multitask "attention deficit trait." Unlike attention deficit disorder, which he has studied for years and has a neurological basis, attention deficit trait "springs entirely from the environment," he wrote in a 2005 *Harvard Business Review* article, "Overloaded Circuits: Why Smart People Underperform."

"As our minds fill with noise — feckless synaptic events signifying   30 nothing — the brain gradually loses its capacity to attend fully and gradually to anything," he wrote. Desperately trying to keep up with a multitude of jobs, we "feel a constant low level of panic and guilt."

But Dr. Hallowell says that despite our belief that we cannot control how much we're overloaded, we can.

"We need to recreate boundaries," he said. That means training yourself not to look at your BlackBerry every 20 seconds, or turning off your cellphone. It means trying to change your work culture so such devices are banned at meetings. Sleeping less to do more is a bad strategy, he says. We are efficient only when we sleep enough, eat right and exercise.

So the next time the phone rings and a good friend is on the line, try this trick: Sit on the couch. Focus on the conversation. Don't jump up, no matter how much you feel the need to clean the kitchen. It seems weird, but stick with it. You, too, can learn the art of single-tasking.

Engaging with the Text

318–22
1. According to Alina Tugend's research, what are the **EFFECTS** of multitasking? Tugend doesn't say much about the causes of this practice. Why do you think she doesn't treat causes? What do you think are the causes for multitasking?

108–9
2. How well does Tugend maintain a **TIGHT FOCUS** on her topic in this report? Given the claim she makes in her title, why might a tightly focused topic be important for helping readers understand the issue?

356–66
3. Tugend **DEFINES** several terms in her report. Locate one or more of the key terms she defines and discuss what these definitions contribute to this report.

12–15
4. What is Tugend's **STANCE** toward the practice of multitasking? Point out specific phrases that reveal her attitude. How appropriate is her stance, given her subject matter?

5. *For Writing.* Undertake your own study of multitasking. Spend time observing students, faculty, and staff in common spaces on your campus — the library, the student union, the dorms, and so on — to see how much multitasking occurs, if any. Speak with peers to find out their habits regarding multitasking. Write a **REPORT** on what you observe and what folks say about how beneficial or how detrimental multitasking can be.

87–118

rhetorical situations   genres   processes   strategies   research MLA / APA   media / design   readings

LAURA SULLIVAN

Escape from Alcatraz: A 47-Year Manhunt

Laura Sullivan is an award-winning NPR News investigative correspondent who has submitted reports that focus on social, legal, and political issues, especially those that affect disadvantaged people in the United States. The following report, posted to the NPR website in 2009, includes an audio clip and a slide show in addition to written text. To access the audio and slides, go to wwnorton.com/write/fieldguidelinks.

IT WAS CALLED **THE ROCK** — the country's only escape-proof prison. The federal penitentiary at Alcatraz was a cell house built on an island surrounded by the frigid waters of the San Francisco Bay.

In 1934, Alcatraz became the first high-security federal penitentiary in the United States. Built on the site of a military fortress, the prison was known for its extremely tight security and notorious prisoners, including Al Capone.

John Anglin, Frank Morris, and Clarence Anglin all had histories of robbing banks and escaping prison, both of which earned them a ticket to the Rock.

Only the worst of the worst were sent there, lifers like Frank Morris and John and Clarence Anglin. But from the moment the three men arrived, it was clear they did not intend to stay.

On June 12, 1962, they vanished, launching the largest manhunt of its time, one that has continued to this day.

Active Pursuit

The U.S. Marshals Service is still actively pursuing the case on the chance that the three men pulled off one of the most daring prison escapes in U.S. history.

"Leads still come in. I just got one a couple weeks ago," U.S. Marshal Michael Dyke said recently in his office in Oakland, California, as he pored over a stack of old file folders from the case.

"Here's one that says they were in a small town in Alabama living on the farm," Dyke says, flipping though pages. "Here's one saying they came to her house when she was a little girl, and she says her father told her as a child that Clarence Anglin used to come to her house regularly."

Dyke has been in charge of the 1962 Alcatraz escape for seven years now. It has always captured the public's — and Hollywood's —

5

rhetorical situations

genres

processes

strategies

research MLA / APA

media / design

readings

imagination: three bank robbers, a notorious prison, an ingenious plan. Back then, it filled the airwaves for months as newsreel footage showed the Coast Guard and police scouring the bay.

Even now, Dyke says it's hard not to root just a little for the bad guys, to wonder if maybe the three men found a way to freedom.

But it doesn't matter, Dyke says. He has a job to do.

"There's an active warrant and the Marshals Service doesn't give up 10 looking for people," he said. "In this case, this would be like saying, 'Well, yeah, they probably are dead. We're going to quit looking.' Well, there's no proof they're dead, so we're not going to quit looking."

Proof of death. It's the one thing that has flummoxed local police, the Coast Guard, the Bureau of Prisons, the FBI and the Marshals about this case for almost 50 years. Statistically, the majority of bodies that drown in the bay float to the top after a few days. In this case, not even one of the bodies surfaced. They all simply vanished.

Escaping Alcatraz

It all started when Morris and the Anglins devised an intricate plan more than six months earlier. They stole prison-issue raincoats to craft a boat and life vests. They molded soap and paper into life-sized heads with hair, lips and eyebrows, real-enough looking to place on their pillows and fool guards into thinking they were sleeping. They stole tools and kitchen spoons to chip away a hole in the back of their cells big enough to crawl through.

As U.S Park Ranger John Cantwell makes his way down the large corridor of the main cell house on Alcatraz, he stops in front of Morris' and the Anglins' cells.

"You can see the holes," he says, pointing to the back of the men's cells. "That's a fairly large hole to climb through. Those are the original holes that these convicts constructed."

Inside one of the cells, Cantwell picks up a cardboard vent cover 15 the men made to cover the holes. It still looks real.

"You hang a couple of coats, maybe a towel in front of it and it camouflages that portal into the utility corridor," he says.

The inmates found instructions for building life vests and a raft with an airtight seal in Popular Mechanics *magazine. One of the rafts was left behind.*

The utility corridor is a small passage right behind the cells. Cantwell squeezes in through a side door.

"If you look up you can see the plumbing they actually used as a ladder," he says.

At the top of the plumbing is a landing. Morris and the Anglins convinced officers to allow them to clean and paint this landing during the day, hidden behind a cloth. What they were really doing, however, was gluing their raincoat raft together using a technique they learned from *Popular Mechanics* magazine.

Cantwell points to the ceiling, which Morris and the Anglins were 20 supposed to paint.

"You can see the actual paint [line] where they stopped," he says. "So they did start their maintenance job, they did paint half the ceiling."

Soon the raft and life vests were ready. And on the night of June 11, 1962, the men climbed up the plumbing to the landing and pushed themselves through an air vent in the ceiling to the roof above.

Cantwell makes his way up an old rickety staircase and finds the air vent on the roof.

"All they had to do is just kick it off," giving the vent a tap with his foot. "They're on the roof now and they run across the rooftop trying not to make too much noise."

Cantwell runs to the edge of the roof and stops at a water pipe.   25

"They slid down the pipe, hopped over that fence, then went down that staircase, past the morgue," he says. "They ran past those water tanks, then down that hillside to the east side of the island. Where the smokestack is is basically where they entered the water."

"Totally Normal Night"

Bill Long was the lieutenant in charge of the cell block on the midnight to morning shift that night. He never heard a peep.

"Totally normal night for me," says Long, 85, who now lives in rural Pennsylvania. "I worked all night up through this."

His shift that night was quiet. But he remembers a few odd things that happened on the shift before his. A lieutenant reported a loud bang he described as a hubcap rolling on the floor — or was it an air vent being popped onto a roof? And another officer reported hearing what he thought were footsteps above him.

But it came to nothing, until Long ordered the morning count.   30

"The men went around the gallery to count and when they did the man on B1 didn't come back," Long said.

Long went to find him.

"He was hotfootin' it down toward me and he says, 'Bill, Bill, I got a guy who won't get up for count!'" Long remembers. "Well I said, 'Sarge, I'll get him up.' So I went down to the cell, get down on my knee, put my head against the bar. I reached my left hand through the bars and hit the pillow and hollered, 'Get up for count!'"

Then he says he almost had a heart attack.

"Bam, the head flopped off on the floor," Long said. "Oh, I thought   35 right then that there was a head that fell off on the floor. They said I jumped back four feet from the bars. I mean, the most unexpected thing you could almost imagine."

Long ran to the phone and sounded the alarm.

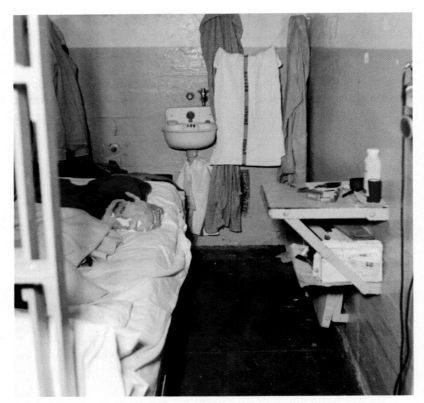

Former Alcatraz guard Lt. Bill Long discovered the prisoners' ruse the next morning, when he touched one of the papier-mache heads and it rolled off the bed. Long ran to the phone and sounded the alarm.

Fifteen-year-old Jolene Babyak, daughter of the acting warden, was lying in bed in the officer's quarters.

"The siren woke me up," she says. "They called my father and he opened the safe."

The safe held plans for action in case of an escape attempt.

"So he put that whole thing into motion," Babyak remembers. "They 40 called Washington, D.C. They alerted the newspapers. They used to say it was the biggest manhunt since the Lindbergh baby kidnapping."

rhetorical situations

genres

processes

strategies

research MLA / APA

media / design

readings

Boats scoured the bay and far out into the ocean. Officers searched every corner of the island. Local police for hundreds of miles looked for any sign of the men.

But Frank Morris, John Anglin and Clarence Anglin were never seen again.

Engaging with the Text

1. Laura Sullivan includes QUOTATIONS from several people in both her radio broadcast version and the online version of the report. What function do these quotations serve? What do they contribute to her report?

   463–67

2. What do the slide show, the time line, and the audio of the radio report add to the online version of the report? What, if any, other visual or audio elements might you recommend including in the online version of this report after having read the text and listened to the radio show?

3. What information do the captions on the pictures provide? How complete and how effective are the captions?

4. Take a look at the three wanted posters. What do you speculate happened to the three inmates — Frank Morris and Clarence and John Anglin? Do you think any of them will ever be caught? Why or why not?

5. *For Writing.* Locate an unusual room on your campus (such as one in the student union, the library, or your dorm) or in your neighborhood, and find out about its history. Ask a librarian at your school or public library to help you find out answers to questions like these: When was the room built? Why was it built? How has it been used? How is it used today? Try to locate past photographs of the room, and take some current ones. Interview people who have memories of the room; if it isn't on campus, find an older person or two who know about its history. Record the interview(s) as audio or video. Then write a REPORT on the room that includes written text, a slide show of pictures from the past to the present, and the audio or video recording(s) you made. At the end of your report, speculate on the future use of the room.

   87–118

60 Arguments

rhetorical situations ▪ genres ▲ processes ○ strategies ◆ research MLA / APA ● media / design ☐ readings ▯

ALEX WEISS

Should Gamers Be Prosecuted for Virtual Stealing?

Alex Weiss, a student at Arizona State University, wrote this essay as a blog posting for his "Work and Play in Contemporary Fiction/Digital Narrative" class. The online magazine Slate *published it in a section titled* Future Tense, *a partnership among* Slate, *Arizona State, and the New America Foundation. The purpose of this partnership, as noted by* Future Tense, *is "to explore emerging technologies and their transformative effects on society and public policy."*

THE MASSIVELY MULTIPLAYER ONLINE VIDEO GAME *RuneScape* was the site of a "virtual theft."

Last week, the Dutch Supreme Court made a curious ruling: It convicted a teenage gamer of stealing something that doesn't exist. The defendant stole two virtual items while playing *RuneScape*, a free massively multiplayer online [MMO] video game. According to the Associated Press, the defendant's attorney argued that the stolen amulet and shield "were neither tangible nor material and, unlike for example electricity, had no economic value." The court, however, disagreed, ruling that the time the 13-year-old victim spent in the game trying to earn the objects gave them value.

As a reformed online-gaming thief, this ruling makes no sense to me. It places too much value on the time people spend playing video games. Video games are not work or investments for which people should be compensated; they are escapism.

During my disappointing teenage years, I played an MMO set in space-capitalist hell titled *EVE Online*. *EVE* is the rat race imploded upon itself, a game that brings out the worst of its subscribers' humanity. In *EVE*, players can spend months working toward a goal, anything from starting a small in-game business to the production of a massive ship that requires billions of *EVE*'s in-game currency and months of man-hours.

The massively multiplayer online video game RuneScape *was the site of a "virtual theft."*

These projects may seem foolish to those outside of the gaming world, but they represent a great deal to their creators. And these hopes and dreams can be destroyed rapidly by another player who just wants to be a jerk. That's the whole point, actually.

EVE is one of the few MMOs that encourage players to use real 5 money to purchase in-game currency, called "isk," which in turn is used to build highly desirable objects in the virtual world. It is also the only game that actively allows thievery in the context of the game world. In fact, player satisfaction in *EVE* is based on taking chances and risking everything you've spent time building up. For instance, as *Kotaku* details, in 2010 pirates destroyed a ship that another player had filled with six years' worth of in-game subscription renewals. At the time, the six years' worth of play was valued at more than $1,000 in real money through *EVE*'s rather complicated financial system.

A few years ago, I could have been one of those pirates. In *EVE*, I enjoyed messing with people, making fake investments, engaging in corporation thievery, and even having an extended e-relationship with someone who thought I was a girl. I'd join corporations, running rainmaker scams by convincing the leadership that an antagonistic group was out to destroy everything we had built. Sometimes I even hired decoys to disrupt our supply lines just enough so that the monetary loss got their attention. After receiving the "bribe" money, they'd go away while I reaped the rewards of a now-trustworthy member of the target organization. After I had taken all I needed to take, I either blocked them or kept their enraged messages for posterity.

RuneScape, the game [the] Dutch minor was playing, is a bit different from both *EVE,* whose point is to engage in Bernie Madoff–esque shenanigans, and the more well-known *World of Warcraft*. *WoW* has a very strict policy against scamming, thievery, and even harsh language; violators can be banned, and victims' lost goods are refunded. The developers of *RuneScape,* however, didn't explicitly state that the thief couldn't do what he did, nor did they refund the victim his item. So here, we have a real-world court attempting to punish someone for behavior permitted within the realm. The real and virtual laws conflict, and it seems unfair to penalize the teenager for this. Reportedly, the player also beat up his victim, for which he should, of course, be punished. But attempting to bring real-world law into virtual realms — and putting monetary value on time spent immersed in a virtual world — seems dangerous.

Engaging with the Text

313–15

1. What is the **THESIS** of Alex Weiss's argument? How does he support the thesis? Do you agree with him? Why or why not?

2. At the end of his essay, Weiss writes that "attempting to bring real-world law into virtual realms — and putting monetary value on time spent immersed in a virtual world — seems dangerous." Given the ruling in the case at the Dutch Supreme Court, what policies and issues regarding behavior in online games need to be legally ironed out in the next few years? Who should be involved in the debates over how online games are policed?

12–15

3. What is Weiss's **STANCE** in this argument? How does he reveal his stance?

312–13

4. How does the **TITLE** function in this argument? How would you respond to the question posed in the title?

5. *For Writing.* In an essay, explore one of the issues that emerging technologies (such as social media, gaming, texting, and Skyping) are giving rise to. Explain the issue and take a stand on it, **ARGUING** for how it should be addressed and who should be included in the debate. Be sure to provide **CONVINCING EVIDENCE** (for which you need to do some research), to adopt **A TRUSTWORTHY TONE**, and to **CONSIDER OTHER POSSIBLE POSITIONS** on the issue.

323–41
136–37

rhetorical situations

genres

processes

strategies

research MLA / APA

media / design

readings

NICHOLAS CARR

Is Google Making Us Stupid?

Nicholas Carr has written widely on technology, business, and culture. His books include The Big Switch: Rewiring the World, From Edison to Google *(2008) and* The Shallows: What the Internet Is Doing to Our Brains *(2010). In addition to his blog* Rough Type, *in which he makes observations about the latest technologies and related issues, he regularly contributes to several periodicals. The following piece has been widely debated since its appearance as a cover article of the* Atlantic *in 2008. As you read, notice how Carr mixes in genres such as report and reflection to support his argument about the effects of the Internet on literacy, cognition, and culture.*

"**D**AVE, STOP. STOP, WILL YOU?** Stop, Dave. Will you stop, Dave?" So the supercomputer HAL pleads with the implacable astronaut Dave Bowman in a famous and weirdly poignant scene toward the end of Stanley Kubrick's *2001: A Space Odyssey.* Bowman, having nearly been sent to a deep-space death by the malfunctioning machine, is calmly, coldly disconnecting the memory circuits that control its artificial "brain." "Dave, my mind is going," HAL says, forlornly. "I can feel it. I can feel it."

I can feel it, too. Over the past few years I've had an uncomfortable sense that someone, or something, has been tinkering with my brain, remapping the neural circuitry, reprogramming the memory. My mind isn't going — so far as I can tell — but it's changing. I'm not thinking the way I used to think. I can feel it most strongly when I'm reading. Immersing myself in a book or a lengthy article used to be easy. My mind would get caught up in the narrative or the turns of the argument, and I'd spend hours strolling through long stretches of prose. That's rarely the case anymore. Now my concentration often starts to drift after two or three pages. I get fidgety, lose the thread, begin looking for something else to do. I feel as if I'm always dragging my wayward brain back to the text. The deep reading that used to come naturally has become a struggle.

Dave (Keir Dullea) removes HAL's "brain" in 2001: A Space Odyssey.

I think I know what's going on. For more than a decade now, I've been spending a lot of time online, searching and surfing and sometimes adding to the great databases of the Internet. The Web has been a godsend to me as a writer. Research that once required days in the stacks or periodical rooms of libraries can now be done in minutes. A few Google searches, some quick clicks on hyperlinks, and I've got the telltale fact or pithy quote I was after. Even when I'm not working, I'm as likely as not to be foraging in the Web's info-thickets reading and writing e-mails, scanning headlines and blog posts, watching videos and listening to podcasts, or just tripping from link to link to link. (Unlike footnotes, to which they're sometimes likened, hyperlinks don't merely point to related works; they propel you toward them.)

For me, as for others, the Net is becoming a universal medium, the conduit for most of the information that flows through my eyes and ears and into my mind. The advantages of having immediate access to such an incredibly rich store of information are many, and they've been

widely described and duly applauded. "The perfect recall of silicon memory," *Wired*'s Clive Thompson has written, "can be an enormous boon to thinking." But that boon comes at price. As the media theorist Marshall McLuhan pointed out in the 1960s, media are not just passive channels of information. They supply the stuff of thought, but they also shape the process of thought. And what the Net seems to be doing is chipping away my capacity for concentration and contemplation. My mind now expects to take in information the way the Net distributes it: in a swiftly moving stream of particles. Once I was a scuba diver in the sea of words. Now I zip along the surface like a guy on a Jet Ski.

I'm not the only one. When I mention my troubles with reading to friends and acquaintances — literary types, most of them — many say they're having similar experiences. The more they use the Web, the more they have to fight to stay focused on long pieces of writing. Some of the bloggers I follow have also begun mentioning the phenomenon. Scott Karp, who writes a blog about online media, recently confessed that he has stopped reading books altogether. "I was a lit major in college, and used to be [a] voracious book reader," he wrote. "What happened?" He speculates on the answer: "What if I do all my reading on the web not so much because the way I read has changed, i.e. I'm just seeking convenience, but because the way I THINK has changed?" 5

Bruce Friedman, who blogs regularly about the use of computers in medicine, also has described how the Internet has altered his mental habits. "I now have almost totally lost the ability to read and absorb a longish article on the web or in print," he wrote earlier this year. A pathologist who has long been on the faculty of the University of Michigan Medical School, Friedman elaborated on his comment in a telephone conversation with me. His thinking, he said, has taken on a "staccato" quality, reflecting the way he quickly scans short passages of text from many sources online. "I can't read *War and Peace* anymore," he admitted. "I've lost the ability to do that. Even a blog post of more than three or four paragraphs is too much to absorb. I skim it."

Anecdotes alone don't prove much. And we still await the long-term neurological and psychological experiments that will provide a definitive picture of how Internet use affects cognition. But a recently published study of online research habits, conducted by scholars from University College London, suggests that we may well be in the midst of a sea change in the way we read and think. As part of the five-year research program, the scholars examined computer logs documenting the behavior of visitors to two popular research sites, one operated by the British Library and one by a U.K. educational consortium, that provide access to journal articles, e-books, and other sources of written information. They found that people using the sites exhibited "a form of skimming activity," hopping from one source to another and rarely returning to any source they'd already visited. They typically read no more than one or two pages of an article or book before they would "bounce" out to another site. Sometimes they'd save a long article, but there's no evidence that they ever went back and actually read it. The authors of the study report:

> It is clear that users are not reading online in the traditional sense; indeed there are signs that new forms of "reading" are emerging as users "power browse" horizontally through titles, contents pages and abstracts going for quick wins. It almost seems that they go online to avoid reading in the traditional sense.

Thanks to the ubiquity of text on the Internet, not to mention the popularity of text-messages on cell phones, we may well be reading more today than we did in the 1970s or 1980s, when television was our medium of choice. But it's a different kind of reading, and behind it lies a different kind of thinking — perhaps even a new sense of the self. "We are not only *what* we read," says Maryanne Wolf, a developmental psychologist at Tufts University and the author of *Proust and the Squid: The Story and Science of the Reading Brain.* "We are *how* we read." Wolf worries that the style of reading promoted by the Net, a style that puts "efficiency" and "immediacy" above all else, may be weakening our capacity for the kind of deep reading that emerged when an earlier technology, the printing press, made long and complex works of prose commonplace. When we read online, she says, we tend to become "mere decoders of information." Our ability to interpret text, to make the rich

mental connections that form when we read deeply and without distraction, remains largely disengaged.

Reading, explains Wolf, is not an instinctive skill for human beings. It's not etched into our genes the way speech is. We have to teach our minds how to translate the symbolic characters we see into the language we understand. And the media or other technologies we use in learning and practicing the craft of reading play an important part in shaping the neural circuits inside our brains. Experiments demonstrate that readers of ideograms, such as the Chinese, develop a mental circuitry for reading that is very different from the circuitry found in those of us whose written language employs an alphabet. The variations extend across many regions of the brain, including those that govern such essential cognitive functions as memory and the interpretation of visual and auditory stimuli. We can expect as well that the circuits woven by our use of the Net will be different from those woven by our reading of books and other printed works.

Sometime in 1882, Friedrich Nietzsche* bought a typewriter — a Malling-Hansen Writing Ball, to be precise. His vision was failing, and keeping his eyes focused on a page had become exhausting and painful, often bringing on crushing headaches. He had been forced to curtail his writing, and he feared that he would soon have to given it up. The typewriter rescued him, at least for a time. Once he had mastered touch-typing, he was able to write with his eyes closed, using only the tips of his fingers. Words could once again flow from his mind to the page. 10

But the machine had a subtler effect on his work. One of Nietzsche's friends, a composer, noticed a change in the style of his writing. His already terse prose had become even tighter, more telegraphic. "Perhaps you will through this instrument even take to a new idiom," the friend wrote in a letter, noting that, in his own work, his "'thoughts' in music and language often depend on the quality of pen and paper."

Friedrich Nietzsche (1844–1900): nineteenth-century German philosopher whose work has been influential in several disciplines, including philosophy, literary studies, rhetoric, and linguistics. [Editor's note]

Friedrich Nietzsche and his Malling-Hansen Writing Ball.

"You are right," Nietzsche replied, "our writing equipment takes part in the forming of our thoughts." Under the sway of the machine, writes the German media scholar Friedrich A. Kittler, Nietzsche's prose "changed from arguments to aphorisms, from thoughts to puns, from rhetoric to telegram style."

The human brain is almost infinitely malleable. People used to think that our mental meshwork, the dense connections formed among the 100 billion or so neurons inside our skulls, was largely fixed by the time we reached adulthood. But brain researchers have discovered that that's not the case. James Olds, a professor of neuroscience who directs the Krasnow Institute for Advanced Study at George Mason University, says that even the adult mind "is very plastic." Nerve cells routinely break old connections and form new ones. "The brain," according to Olds, "has the ability to reprogram itself on the fly, altering the way it functions."

As we use what the sociologist Daniel Bell has called our "intellec-tual technologies" — the tools that extend our mental rather than our physical capacities — we inevitably begin to take on the qualities of those technologies. The mechanical clock, which came into common use in the 14th century, provides a compelling example. In *Technics and Civilization,* the historian and cultural critic Lewis Mumford described how the clock "disassociated time from human events and helped cre-ate the belief in an independent world of mathematically measurable sequences." The "abstract framework of divided time" became "the point of reference for both action and thought."

The clock's methodical ticking helped bring into being the scientific 15 mind and the scientific man. But it also took something away. As the late MIT computer scientist Joseph Weizenbaum observed in his 1976 book, *Computer Power and Human Reason: From Judgment to Calculation,* the conception of the world that emerged from the widespread use of time-keeping instruments "remains an impoverished version of the older one, for it rests on a rejection of those direct experiences that formed the basis for, and indeed constituted, the old reality." In deciding when to eat, to work, to sleep, to rise, we stopped listening to our senses and started obeying the clock.

The process of adapting to new intellectual technologies is reflected in the changing metaphors we use to explain ourselves to ourselves. When the mechanical clock arrived, people began thinking of their brains as operating "like clockwise." Today, in the age of soft-ware, we have come to think of them as operating "like computers." But the changes, neuroscience tells us, go much deeper than metaphor. Thanks to our brain's plasticity, the adaptation occurs also at a bio-logical level.

The Internet promises to have particularly far-reaching effects on cognition. In a paper published in 1936, the British mathematician Alan Turing proved that a digital computer, which at a time existed only as a theoretical machine, could be programmed to perform the function of any other information-processing device. And that's what we're seeing today. The Internet, an immeasurably powerful computing system, is subsuming most of our other intellectual technologies. It's becoming our

map and our clock, our printing press and our typewriter, our calculator and our telephone, and our radio and TV.

When the Net absorbs a medium, that medium is re-created in the Net's image. It injects the medium's content with hyperlinks, blinking ads, and other digital gewgaws, and it surrounds the content with the content of all the other media it has absorbed. A new e-mail message, for instance, may announce its arrival as we're glancing over the latest headlines at a newspaper's site. The result is to scatter our attention and diffuse our concentration.

The Net's influence doesn't end at the edges of a computer screen, either. As people's minds become attuned to the crazy quilt of Internet media, traditional media have to adapt to the audience's new expectations. Television programs add text crawls and pop-up ads, and magazines and newspapers shorten their articles, introduce capsule summaries, and crowd their pages with easy-to-browse info-snippets. When, in March of this year, the *New York Times* decided to devote the second and third pages of every edition to article abstracts, its design director, Tom Bodkin, explained that the "shortcuts" would give harried readers a quick "taste" of the day's news, sparing them the "less efficient" method of actually turning the pages and reading the articles. Old media have little choice but to play by the new-media rules.

Never has a communications system played so many roles in our lives — or exerted such broad influence over our thoughts — as the Internet does today. Yet, for all that's been written about the Net, there's been little consideration of how, exactly, it's reprogramming us. The Net's intellectual ethic remains obscure. 20

About the same time that Nietzsche started using his typewriter, an earnest young man named Frederick Winslow Taylor carried a stopwatch into the Midvale Steel plant in Philadelphia and began a historic series of experiments aimed at improving the efficiency of the plant's machinists. With the approval of Midvale's owners, he recruited a group of factory hands, set them to work on various metalworking machines, and recorded and timed their every movement as well as the operations of the machines. By breaking down every job into a sequence of small,

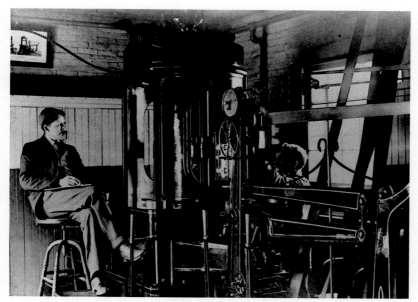

A testing engineer (possibly Taylor) observes a Midvale Steel worker c. 1885.

discrete steps and then testing different ways of performing each one, Taylor created a set of precise instructions — an "algorithm," we might say today — for how each worker should work. Midvale's employees grumbled about the strict new regime, claiming that it turned them into little more than automatons, but the factory's productivity soared.

More than a hundred years after the invention of the steam engine, the Industrial Revolution had at last found its philosophy and its philosopher. Taylor's tight industrial choreography — his "system," as he liked to call it — was embraced by manufacturers throughout the country and, in time, around the world. Seeking maximum speed, maximum efficiency, and maximum output, factory owners used time-and-motion studies to organize their work and configure the jobs of their workers. The goal, as Taylor defined it in his celebrated 1911 treatise, *The Principles of Scientific Management*, was to identify and adopt, for every job, the "one best method" of work and thereby to effect "the gradual substitution of science for rule of thumb throughout the mechanic arts." Once his system was applied to all acts of manual labor, Taylor assured his followers, it would bring about a restructuring not only of industry but of society, creating a utopia of perfect efficiency. "In the past the man has been first," he declared; "in the future the system must be first."

Taylor's system is still very much with us; it remains the ethic of industrial manufacturing. And now, thanks to the growing power that computer engineers and software coders wield over our intellectual lives, Taylor's ethic is beginning to govern the realm of the mind as well. The Internet is a machine designed for the efficient and automated collection, transmission, and manipulation of information, and its legions of programmers are intent on finding the "one best method" — the perfect algorithm — to carry out every mental movement of what we've come to describe as "knowledge work."

Google's headquarters, in Mountain View, California — the Googleplex — is the Internet's high church, and the religion practiced inside its walls is Taylorism. Google, says its chief executive, Eric Schmidt, is "a company that's founded around the science of measurement," and it is striving to "systematize everything" it does. Drawing on the terabytes of behavioral data it collects through its search engine and other sites, it carries out thousands of experiments a day, according to the *Harvard Business Review*, and it uses the results to refine the algorithms that increasingly control how people find information and extract meaning from it. What Taylor did for the work of the hand, Google is doing for the work of the mind.

The company has declared that its mission is "to organize the world's information and make it universally accessible and useful." It seeks to develop "the perfect search engine," which it defines as something that "understands exactly what you mean and gives you back exactly what you want." In Google's view, information is a kind of commodity, a utilitarian resource that can be mined and processed with industrial efficiency. The more pieces of information we can "access"   25

The Googleplex.

and the faster we can extract their gist, the more productive we become as thinkers.

Where does it end? Sergey Brin and Larry Page, the gifted young men who founded Google while pursuing doctoral degrees in computer science at Stanford, speak frequently of their desire to turn their search engine into an artificial intelligence, a HAL-like machine that might be connected directly to our brains. "The ultimate search engine is something as smart as people — or smarter," Page said in a speech a few years back. "For us, working on search is a way to work on artificial intelligence." In a 2004 interview with *Newsweek,* Brin said, "Certainly if you had all the world's information directly attached to your brain, or an artificial brain that was smarter than your brain, you'd be better off." Last year, Page told a convention of scientists that Google is "really trying to build artificial intelligence and to do it on a large scale."

Such an ambition is a natural one, even an admirable one, for a pair of math whizzes with vast quantities of cash at their disposal and a small army of computer scientists in their employ. A fundamentally scientific enterprise, Google is motivated by a desire to use technology, in Eric Schmidt's words, "to solve problems that have never been solved before," and artificial intelligence is the hardest problem out there. Why wouldn't Brin and Page want to be the ones to crack it?

Still, their easy assumption that we'd all "be better off" if our brains were supplemented, or even replaced, by an artificial intelligence is unsettling. It suggests a belief that intelligence is the output of a mechanical process, a series of discrete steps that can be isolated, measured, and optimized. In Google's world, the world we enter when we go online, there's little place for the fuzziness of contemplation. Ambiguity is not an opening for insight but a bug to be fixed. The human brain is just an outdated computer that needs a faster processor and a bigger hard drive.

The idea that our minds should operate as high-speed data-processing machines is not only built into the workings of the Internet, it is the network's reigning business model as well. The faster we surf across the Web — the more links we click and pages we view — the more opportunities Google and other companies gain to collect information about us and to feed us advertisements. Most of the proprietors of the commercial Internet have a financial stake in collecting the crumbs of data we leave behind as we flit from link to link — the more crumbs, the better. The last thing these companies want is to encourage leisurely reading or slow, concentrated thought. It's in their economic interest to drive us to distraction.

Maybe I'm just a worrywart. Just as there's a tendency to glorify technological progress, there's a countertendency to expect the worst of every new tool or machine. In Plato's *Phaedrus*, Socrates bemoaned the development of writing. He feared that, as people came to rely on the written word as a substitute for the knowledge they used to carry inside their heads, they would, in the words of one of the dialogue's characters, "cease to exercise their memory and become forgetful." And because they would be able to "receive a quantity of information without proper instruction," they would "be thought very knowledgeable when they are for the most part quite ignorant." They would be "filled with the conceit of wisdom instead of real wisdom." Socrates wasn't wrong — the new technology did often have the effects he feared — but he was shortsighted. He couldn't foresee the many ways that writing and reading would serve to spread information, spur fresh ideas, and expand human knowledge (if not wisdom).

The arrival of Gutenberg's printing press,* in the 15th century, set off another round of teeth gnashing. The Italian humanist Hieronimo Squarciafico worried that the easy availability of books would lead to intellectual laziness, making men "less studious" and weakening their minds. Others argued that cheaply printed books and broadsheets would undermine religious authority, demean the work of scholars and scribes, and spread sedition and debauchery. As New York University professor Clay Shirky notes, "Most of the arguments made against the printing press were correct, even prescient." But, again, the doomsayers were unable to imagine the myriad blessings that the printed word would deliver.

So, yes, you should be skeptical of my skepticism. Perhaps those who dismiss critics of the Internet as Luddites or nostalgists will be proved correct, and from our hyperactive, data-stoked minds will spring a golden age of intellectual discovery and universal wisdom. Then again, the Net isn't the alphabet, and although it may replace the printing press, it produces something altogether different. The kind of deep reading that a sequence of printed pages promotes is valuable not just for the knowledge we acquire from the author's words but for the intellectual vibrations those words set off within our own minds. In the quiet spaces opened up by the sustained, undistracted reading of a book, or by any other act of contemplation, for that matter, we make our own associations, draw our own inferences and analogies, foster our own ideas. Deep reading, as Maryanne Wolf argues, is indistinguishable from deep thinking.

If we lose those quiet spaces, or fill them up with "content," we will sacrifice something important not only in our selves but in our culture. In a recent essay, the playwright Richard Foreman eloquently described what's at stake:

> I come from a tradition of Western culture, in which the ideal (my ideal) was the complex, dense and "cathedral-like" structure of the

---

Johannes Gutenberg (1398–1468): a German goldsmith and printer credited with the invention of the printing press and the first mechanically printed Bible. [Editor's note]

highly educated and articulate personality — a man or woman who carried inside themselves a personally constructed and unique version of the entire heritage of the West. [But now] I see within us all (myself included) the replacement of complex inner density with a new kind of self — evolving under the pressure of information overload and the technology of the "instantly available."

As we are drained of our "inner repertory of dense cultural inheritance," Foreman concluded, we risk turning into "'pancake people' — spread wide and thin as we connect with that vast network of information accessed by the mere touch of a button."

I'm haunted by that scene in 2001. What makes it so poignant, and so weird, is the computer's emotional response to the disassembly of its mind: its despair as one circuit after another goes dark, its childlike pleading with the astronaut — "I can feel it. I can feel it. I'm afraid" — and its final reversion to what can only be called a state of innocence. HAL's outpouring of feeling contrasts with the emotionlessness that characterizes the human figures in the film, who go about their business with an almost robotic efficiency. Their thoughts and actions feel scripted, as if they're following the steps of an algorithm. In the world of 2001, people have become so machinelike that the most human character turns out to be a machine. That's the essence of Kubrick's dark prophecy: as we come to rely on computers to mediate our understanding of the world, it is our own intelligence that flattens into artificial intelligence.

Engaging with the Text

1. Sergey Brin has noted, "Some say Google is God. Others say Google is Satan. But if they think Google is too powerful, remember that with search engines, unlike other companies, all it takes is a single click to go to another search engine." How does Nicholas Carr's essay support or challenge this assertion? Why do you think this topic elicits such strong responses?

2. According to Carr, what has been the effect of the Internet on the way we read, think, and live? What EVIDENCE does he offer to support his claims? How does his discussion of the changes wrought by other technologies help him make his argument?

327–35

3. Where in his argument does Carr INCORPORATE OTHER VIEWPOINTS? Is this an effective strategy for his piece? Why or why not?

336–37

4. Why does Carr BEGIN and END by referring to HAL from the film *2001: A Space Odyssey*? How do the quotes he chooses from the film help him appeal to his AUDIENCE?

299–311

5–8

5. *For Writing.* What is your view of how technology is affecting the way we think, read, write, and live? Write an ARGUMENT in which you support or challenge Carr's conclusion that "as we come to rely on computers to mediate our understanding of the world, it is our own intelligence that flattens into artificial intelligence." Consider mixing in some REFLECTION on your own use of computers to help make your argument.

119–49
214–21

JOSEPH E. STIGLITZ

Of the 1%, by the 1%, for the 1%

Joseph E. Stiglitz is an American economist who won the 2001 Nobel Prize in economics and has authored over a dozen books, most recently Freefall: America, Free Markets, and the Sinking of the World *(2010). A professor at Columbia University, he is the former senior vice president and chief economist of the World Bank and served as chairman of the Council of Economic Advisers during the Clinton administration. Stiglitz is best known for his criticism of economists he has labeled "free-market fundamentalists" and of international economic institutions such as the World Bank. In 2011,* Time *named him one of the hundred most influential people in the world. "Of the 1%, by the 1%, for the 1%" appeared in* Vanity Fair *in 2011. For additional information about the 1%, see Brain Stelter's essay on p. 679.*

I T'S NO USE PRETENDING that what has obviously happened has not in fact happened. The upper 1 percent of Americans are now taking in nearly a quarter of the nation's income every year. In terms of wealth rather than income, the top 1 percent control 40 percent. Their lot in life has improved considerably. Twenty-five years ago, the corresponding figures were 12 percent and 33 percent. One response might be to celebrate the ingenuity and drive that brought good fortune to these people, and to contend that a rising tide lifts all boats. That response would be misguided. While the top 1 percent have seen their incomes rise 18 percent over the past decade, those in the middle have actually seen their incomes fall. For men with only high-school degrees, the decline has been precipitous — 12 percent in the last quarter-century alone. All the growth in recent decades — and more — has gone to those at the top. In terms of income equality, America lags behind any country in the old, ossified Europe that President George W. Bush used to deride. Among our closest counterparts are Russia with its oligarchs and Iran. While many of the old centers of inequality in Latin America, such as Brazil, have been striving in recent years, rather successfully, to improve the plight of the poor and reduce gaps in income, America has allowed inequality to grow.

rhetorical situations   genres   processes   strategies   research MLA / APA   media / design   readings

Economists long ago tried to justify the vast inequalities that seemed so troubling in the mid-19th century — inequalities that are but a pale shadow of what we are seeing in America today. The justification they came up with was called "marginal-productivity theory." In a nutshell, this theory associated higher incomes with higher productivity and a greater contribution to society. It is a theory that has always been cherished by the rich. Evidence for its validity, however, remains thin. The corporate executives who helped bring on the recession of the past three years — whose contribution to our society, and to their own companies, has been massively negative — went on to receive large bonuses. In some cases, companies were so embarrassed about calling such rewards "performance bonuses" that they felt compelled to change the name to "retention bonuses" (even if the only thing being retained was bad performance). Those who have contributed great positive innovations to our society, from the pioneers of genetic understanding to the pioneers of the Information Age, have received a pittance compared with those responsible for the financial innovations that brought our global economy to the brink of ruin.

Some people look at income inequality and shrug their shoulders. So what if this person gains and that person loses? What matters, they argue, is not how the pie is divided but the size of the pie. That argument is fundamentally wrong. An economy in which *most* citizens are doing worse year after year — an economy like America's — is not likely to do well over the long haul. There are several reasons for this.

First, growing inequality is the flip side of something else: shrinking opportunity. Whenever we diminish equality of opportunity, it means that we are not using some of our most valuable assets — our people — in the most productive way possible. Second, many of the distortions that lead to inequality — such as those associated with monopoly power and preferential tax treatment for special interests — undermine the efficiency of the economy. This new inequality goes on to create new distortions, undermining efficiency even further. To give just one example, far too many of our most talented young people, seeing the astronomical rewards, have gone into finance rather than into fields that would lead to a more productive and healthy economy.

Third, and perhaps most important, a modern economy requires 5 "collective action" — it needs government to invest in infrastructure, education, and technology. The United States and the world have benefited greatly from government-sponsored research that led to the Internet, to advances in public health, and so on. But America has long suffered from an under-investment in infrastructure (look at the condition of our highways and bridges, our railroads and airports), in basic research, and in education at all levels. Further cutbacks in these areas lie ahead. None of this should come as a surprise — it is simply what happens when a society's wealth distribution becomes lopsided. The more divided a society becomes in terms of wealth, the more reluctant the wealthy become to spend money on common needs. The rich don't need to rely on government for parks or education or medical care or personal security — they can buy all these things for themselves. In the process, they become more distant from ordinary people, losing whatever empathy they may once have had. They also worry about strong government — one that could use its powers to adjust the balance, take some of their wealth, and invest it for the common good. The top 1 percent may complain about the kind of government we have in America, but in truth they like it just fine: too gridlocked to re-distribute, too divided to do anything but lower taxes.

Economists are not sure how to fully explain the growing inequality in America. The ordinary dynamics of supply and demand have certainly played a role: laborsaving technologies have reduced the demand for many "good" middle-class, blue-collar jobs. Globalization has created a worldwide marketplace, pitting expensive unskilled workers in America against cheap unskilled workers overseas. Social changes have also played a role — for instance, the decline of unions, which once represented a third of American workers and now represent about 12 percent.

But one big part of the reason we have so much inequality is that the top 1 percent want it that way. The most obvious example involves tax policy. Lowering tax rates on capital gains, which is how the rich receive a large portion of their income, has given the wealthiest Americans

rhetorical situations

genres

processes

strategies

research MLA / APA

media / design

readings

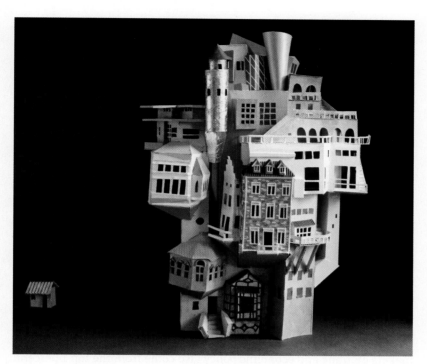

The top 1 percent may have the best houses, educations, and lifestyles, says the author, but "their fate is bound up with how the other 99 percent live."

close to a free ride. Monopolies and near monopolies have always been a source of economic power — from John D. Rockefeller at the beginning of the last century to Bill Gates at the end. Lax enforcement of antitrust laws, especially during Republican administrations, has been a godsend to the top 1 percent. Much of today's inequality is due to manipulation of the financial system, enabled by changes in the rules that have been bought and paid for by the financial industry itself — one of its best investments ever. The government lent money to financial institutions at close to 0 percent interest and provided generous bailouts on favorable terms when all else failed. Regulators turned a blind eye to a lack of transparency and to conflicts of interest.

When you look at the sheer volume of wealth controlled by the top 1 percent in this country, it's tempting to see our growing inequality as a quintessentially American achievement — we started way behind the pack, but now we're doing inequality on a world-class level. And it looks as if we'll be building on this achievement for years to come, because what made it possible is self-reinforcing. Wealth begets power, which begets more wealth. During the savings-and-loan scandal of the 1980s — a scandal whose dimensions, by today's standards, seem almost quaint — the banker Charles Keating was asked by a congressional committee whether the $1.5 million he had spread among a few key elected officials could actually buy influence. "I certainly hope so," he replied. The Supreme Court, in its recent *Citizens United* case, has enshrined the right of corporations to buy government, by removing limitations on campaign spending. The personal and the political are today in perfect alignment. Virtually all U.S. senators, and most of the representatives in the House, are members of the top 1 percent when they arrive, are kept in office by money from the top 1 percent, and know that if they serve the top 1 percent well they will be rewarded by the top 1 percent when they leave office. By and large, the key executive-branch policy-makers on trade and economic policy also come from the top 1 percent. When pharmaceutical companies receive a trillion-dollar gift—through legislation prohibiting the government, the largest buyer of drugs, from bargaining over price—it should not come as cause for wonder. It should not make jaws drop that a tax bill cannot emerge from Congress unless big tax cuts are put in place for the wealthy. Given the power of the top 1 percent, this is the way you would *expect* the system to work.

America's inequality distorts our society in every conceivable way.   10 There is, for one thing, a well-documented lifestyle effect — people outside the top 1 percent increasingly live beyond their means. Trickle-down economics may be a chimera, but trickle-down behaviorism is very real. Inequality massively distorts our foreign policy. The top 1 percent rarely serve in the military — the reality is that the "all-volunteer" army does not pay enough to attract their sons and daughters, and

patriotism goes only so far. Plus, the wealthiest class feels no pinch from higher taxes when the nation goes to war: borrowed money will pay for all that. Foreign policy, by definition, is about the balancing of national interests and national resources. With the top 1 percent in charge, and paying no price, the notion of balance and restraint goes out the window. There is no limit to the adventures we can undertake; corporations and contractors stand only to gain. The rules of economic globalization are likewise designed to benefit the rich: they encourage competition among countries for *business,* which drives down taxes on corporations, weakens health and environmental protections, and undermines what used to be viewed as the "core" labor rights, which include the right to collective bargaining. Imagine what the world might look like if the rules were designed instead to encourage competition among countries for *workers.* Governments would compete in providing economic security, low taxes on ordinary wage earners, good education, and a clean environment — things workers care about. But the top 1 percent don't need to care.

Or, more accurately, they think they don't. Of all the costs imposed on our society by the top 1 percent, perhaps the greatest is this: the erosion of our sense of identity, in which fair play, equality of opportunity, and a sense of community are so important. America has long prided itself on being a fair society, where everyone has an equal chance of getting ahead, but the statistics suggest otherwise: the chances of a poor citizen, or even a middle-class citizen, making it to the top in America are smaller than in many countries of Europe. The cards are stacked against them. It is this sense of an unjust system without opportunity that has given rise to the conflagrations in the Middle East: rising food prices and growing and persistent youth unemployment simply served as kindling. With youth unemployment in America at around 20 percent (and in some locations, and among some socio-demographic groups, at twice that); with one out of six Americans desiring a full-time job not able to get one; with one out of seven Americans on food stamps (and about the same number suffering from "food insecurity") — given all this, there is ample evidence that something has blocked the vaunted "trickling down" from the top 1 percent to everyone else. All of this is having the predictable effect of creating alienation — voter turnout among those in their 20s in the last election stood at 21 percent, comparable to the unemployment rate.

In recent weeks we have watched people taking to the streets by the millions to protest political, economic, and social conditions in the oppressive societies they inhabit. Governments have been toppled in Egypt and Tunisia. Protests have erupted in Libya, Yemen, and Bahrain. The ruling families elsewhere in the region look on nervously from their air-conditioned penthouses — will they be next? They are right to worry. These are societies where a minuscule fraction of the population — less than 1 percent — controls the lion's share of the wealth; where wealth is a main determinant of power; where entrenched corruption of one sort or another is a way of life; and where the wealthiest often stand actively in the way of policies that would improve life for people in general.

As we gaze out at the popular fervor in the streets, one question to ask ourselves is this: When will it come to America? In important ways, our own country has become like one of these distant, troubled places.

Alexis de Tocqueville once described what he saw as a chief part of the peculiar genius of American society — something he called "self-interest properly understood." The last two words were the key. Everyone possesses self-interest in a narrow sense: I want what's good for me right now! Self-interest "properly understood" is different. It means appreciating that paying attention to everyone else's self-interest — in other words, the common welfare — is in fact a precondition for one's own ultimate well-being. Tocqueville was not suggesting that there was anything noble or idealistic about this outlook — in fact, he was suggesting the opposite. It was a mark of American pragmatism. Those canny Americans understood a basic fact: looking out for the other guy isn't just good for the soul — it's good for business.

The top 1 percent have the best houses, the best educations, the best doctors, and the best lifestyles, but there is one thing that money doesn't seem to have bought: an understanding that their fate is bound

up with how the other 99 percent live. Throughout history, this is something that the top 1 percent eventually do learn. Too late.

Engaging with the Text

1. What **REASONS** does Joseph E. Stiglitz offer to support the claim in his argument that "what matters . . . is not how the [economic] pie is divided but the size of the pie" is fundamentally wrong? How do the statistics in this argument function as convincing **EVIDENCE.** Identify two statistics Stiglitz cites and discuss the role they play in making his argument convincing.

   326–27

   327–35

2. Stiglitz points to an economic theory called marginal productivity. What is the theory and how is it relevant to his argument?

3. At the end of his argument, Stiglitz writes that though the top 1 percent have "the best houses, the best educations, the best doctors, and the best lifestyles," they don't understand that "their fate is bound up with how the other 99 percent live" — and that "throughout history, this is something that the top 1 percent eventually do learn. Too late." What is the main point Stiglitz is making here? How does this point relate to the **BEGINNING** of his argument?

   299–306

4. What **STANCE** does this argument take? Identify two passages in the argument that make clear the writer's stance. How trustworthy do you find the tone?

   12–15

5. *For Writing.* At the beginning and ending of his argument, Stiglitz points out that the inequality in America is something "even the wealthy will come to regret." Research a time in history when a privileged group learned the lesson too late and lost their power. Write an essay that **NARRATES** and **DESCRIBES** what happened and how it relates to the current economic situation in the United States.

   387–95

   367–75

GRANT PENROD

Anti-Intellectualism: Why We Hate the Smart Kids

The following essay won second place in the Arizona State University Printer's Devil Contest, an annual competition open to all students enrolled in writing classes at Arizona State. Grant Penrod wrote the essay for a first-year composition course.

THE FOOTBALL TEAM FROM MOUNTAIN VIEW HIGH SCHOOL won the Arizona state championship last year. Again. Unbeknownst to the vast majority of the school's student body, so did the Science Bowl Team, the Speech and Debate Team, and the Academic Decathlon team. The football players enjoyed the attentions of an enthralled school, complete with banners, assemblies, and even video announcements in their honor, a virtual barrage of praise and downright deification. As for the three champion academic teams, they received a combined total of around ten minutes of recognition, tacked onto the beginning of a sports assembly. Nearly all of the graduating seniors will remember the name and escapades of their star quarterback; nearly none of them will ever even realize that their class produced Arizona's first national champion in Lincoln-Douglas Debate. After all, why should they? He and his teammates were "just the nerds."

This instance finds plentiful company in the experiences of everyday life; intellectuals constantly see their efforts trivialized in the rush to lavish compliments elsewhere. However, such occurrences present only a faint silhouette of true anti-intellectualism; trivialization seems insignificant when compared with the outright disdain for the educated harbored by much of society. That academia's proponents provoke the wrath of the populace is certain. As an illustration, a commentator under the screen name ArCaNe posted the following quote on *Talking-Cock.com*, an online discussion board: "Man how I hate nerds . . . if I ever had a tommygun with me . . . I would most probably blow each one of their . . . heads off." Were this statement alone in its extremism, it could

rhetorical situations

genres

processes

strategies

research MLA / APA

media / design

readings

be written off a joke. Unfortunately, it represents just one statement along countless similar sites and postings, a veritable cornucopia of evidence attesting to society's distaste for intellectuals. The question, then, is not whether anti-intellectualism exists, but rather why it exists. Several factors seem to contribute to the trend, including social stereotypes, public examples, and monetary obsession. Any or all of these factors can contribute to anti-intellectualism, and the result is a crushing disregard for the lives and achievements of fellow human beings.

Perhaps the most obvious cause of anti-intellectualist tendencies, harmful social stereotypes begin to emerge as early as in high school. The idea of the "geek" or "nerd" of the class is a familiar one to most students, and it is not a pleasant one. One online venter, Dan6erous, describes the image well: "A+ this and . . . got a 1600 on my SAT and got all AP class[es] next year woohoo. That's all these people care about don't they have lives damn nerds." In this respect, the trend to dislike intellectuals stems at least in part from an inescapable perception that concern for grades and test scores excludes the coexistence of normal social activities. Sadly, this becomes somewhat of a self-fulfilling prophecy; "nerds" are excluded from social activity because of their label, and that label in turn intensifies through the resulting lack of social contact. The cycle seems unbreakable. Of course, not all "nerds" are socially excluded; most high school students could readily name a few intelligent people with at least a degree of popularity. The point, though, is that the *image* of intellectualism is disliked as anti-social, and the harms of even a fallacious perception to this effect spread to all of the intelligentsia.

This argument, however, merely accounts for the perpetuation of anti-intellectual feelings. Those feelings must also *originate* somewhere, possibly in the examples set by public figures. Certainly the image presented by modern celebrities suggests that intellectualism has no ties to success and social legitimacy. As an illustration, a Web site hosted by *Angelfire.com* features a compilation of the names of famous high school dropouts ("Noted Dropouts"). With such well-known cultural icons as Christina Aguilera, Kid Rock, L. L. Cool J., and Sammy Sosa qualifying for such a list, any drive toward intelligence or education becomes laughable in the eyes of media-inundated young people ("Noted Dropouts"). Thus, intellectualism loses the respect that its rigor would otherwise tend to earn it. Uneducated success extends far beyond just singers and sports stars, too; even the current President of the United States* presents the image of the success of nonintellectualism. His reputation as a "C" student is widely touted, and his public speeches hardly exonerate his intellectual image. The fact that such a vital public figure can get away with saying things like "It's clearly a budget. It's got a lot of numbers in it," and "There needs to be a wholesale effort against racial profiling, which is illiterate children" reflects rather poorly on the regard in which most Americans hold intelligence (Lewis).

Sadly, the aforementioned examples of uneducated success are even 5 further entrenched by the prodigious wealth of the celebrities involved. For example, Sammy Sosa earned an intimidating eighteen million dollars during the year 2002 ("Celebrity 100"). Indeed, as a writer for *The Carillon* put it, "In more than a few cases athletes' incomes surpass the gross national product of some third-world countries" (Brejak). In the eyes of an ever-watchful public, just the existence of such amazingly affluent yet strikingly uneducated individuals would seem to call into question the necessity and even legitimacy of intellectualism. Certainly, most of the people effected by these media images are teenagers, but these budding young anti-intellectuals carry the sentiments of education-bashing on into their adult lives as well. As an illustration, Robert T. Kiyosaki (no longer a teenager) claims in his book *If You Want to Be Rich and Happy, Don't Go to School?* that education is now merely an archaic institution that continues to cling to obsolete practices (Rev. of *If You Want to Be Rich*). The tendency to forgo enlightenment for "success" even leaks into the college community now: a recent article by Ethan Bronner states that "in the survey . . . 74.9 percent of freshmen chose being well off as an essential goal while only 40.8 percent" selected "developing a philosophy" as a similar goal. Indeed, Americans seem enamored with wealth at the expense of intellectualism. Unfortunately for them, this supposed negative correlation between brains and buying power doesn't even exist:

---

*President: George W. Bush was president at the time of this essay. [Editor's note]

"People holding doctorate degrees earned more than twice the salary of high school graduates" in the year 2000 ("Census").

Regardless of the causes of anti-intellectualism, the effects are clear and devastating; society looks down on those individuals who help it to progress, ostracizing its best and brightest. Some may blame television or general societal degradation for the fall of the educated, but at heart the most disturbing issue involved is the destruction of promising personalities; ignoring intellectuals both in school and later on in life crushes its victims, as illustrated in the following lines:

> My loud and bitter screams aren't being heard
> No one is there to hear them or to care
> They do not come cuz I'm a nerd
> Dealing with this pain is a lot to bear. (Casey F.)

For the sake of the smart kids, we all need to "lay off" a little.

Works Cited

ArCaNe. "Re: A Gifted Student." *TalkingCock.com*. TalkingCock.com, 2 Sept. 2001. Web. 21 Apr. 2009.

Brejak, Matt. "Money, Contracts and Switzerland." *Carillon*. U. of Regina, 28 Oct. 1999. Web. 24 Apr. 2009.

Bronner, Ethan. "College Freshmen Aiming for High Marks in Income." *New York Times*. New York Times, 12 Jan. 1998. Web. 28 Apr. 2009.

"The Celebrity 100—Jocks." *Forbes.com*. Forbes.com Inc., 20 Jun. 2002. Web. 1. Oct. 2003.

"Census 2000: Education." *BDASUN*. Bermuda Sun, 18 Dec. 2002. Web. 21 Apr. 2009.

Dan6erous. Online posting. *Chilax.com*. Chilax.com, 31 Aug. 2003. Web. 1 Oct. 2003.

F., Casey. "My loud and bitter screams aren't being heard." *TeenMag.com*. Hearst Communications, Inc., 9 Apr. 2002. Web. 1 Oct. 2003.

Lewis, Jone Johnson, comp. "Bushisms Quotes." *WisdomQuotes.com*. N.p., 2009. Web. 28 Apr. 2009.

"Noted High School and Elementary School Dropouts." *Celebrity Research Lists*. Angelfire.com, 14 Apr. 2009. Web. 28 Apr. 2009.

Rev. of *If You Want to Be Rich and Happy, Don't Go to School?* by Robert T. Kiyosaki. *EducationReformBooks.net.* World Prosperity, Ltd., n.d. Web. 28 Apr. 2009.

Engaging with the Text

1. Grant Penrod claims that the effects of anti-intellectualism are "clear and devastating," arguing that society "ostracizes its best and brightest." What **REASONS** and **EVIDENCE** does he provide to support his claim? Do you find his argument persuasive? Why or why not?

326–35 ◆

2. What does Penrod's **TITLE** tell us about his intended **AUDIENCE?** What values do you think he assumes they hold? How does he **APPEAL** to these readers? Do you think he is successful?

312–13 ◆
5–8 ■
137 ▲

3. Penrod suggests that intellectuals are disliked in part because of the "perception that concern for grades and test scores excludes the coexistence of normal social activities" — and that this becomes a "self-fulfilling prophecy; 'nerds' are excluded from social activity because of their label, and that label in turn intensifies through the resulting lack of social contact." Do you agree? Why or why not?

4. To support his claim that anti-intellectualism is fueled in part by the media, Penrod names celebrities from sports, music, and politics who became successful without the benefit of an education. Do you agree with Penrod that the success of these celebrities is partly responsible for anti-intellectualism? Why or why not? What **EVIDENCE** could be offered to **REFUTE** this argument?

327–35 ◆
337

5. *For Writing.* Penrod identifies "nerds" as one stereotypical high school group. "Jocks" are another familiar stereotype. How were students **CLASSIFIED** into stereotyped groups at your high school? Were the classifications fair? Who did the classifying? What were the consequences for members of the group and for other students? Write an essay about one of these groups that **ARGUES A POSITION** on what factors motivated the stereotyping. You'll need to support your argument with reasons and evidence, such as facts, statistics, and anecdotes.

342–47 ◆
119–49 ▲

DAVID SIROTA

Kenneth Cole Gets Schooled

David Sirota, a political journalist who has also worked on political campaigns, writes a nationally syndicated column and is author of three books, Hostile Takeover *(2007),* The Uprising *(2008), and* Back to Our Future *(2011). His journalistic writing has also appeared in such publications as the* New York Times, *the* Nation, Wired, Slate, Salon, *and* In These Times, *where he serves as a senior editor. He hosts an award-winning show on a Denver radio station and often appears on television as a guest on news and opinion shows as well as Comedy Central's Colbert Report. The following argument appeared in* Salon *on April 30, 2012. To access the online version, including hyperlinks, go to* wwnorton.com/write/fieldguidelinks.

IT WAS ALWAYS BOUND TO GO THERE, but few likely expected it would be so blatant. I'm talking about the ongoing campaign against organized labor; for decades deeply rooted in American political culture, the crusade has been periodically amplified in popular culture as well, from 1954's *On the Waterfront* all the way to the *Sopranos'* depiction of mob-controlled unions (and sometimes pop culture and political culture have even fused). So it was only a matter of time before vilifying rank-and-file union members would be commodified into a consumer brand by a company looking for an edge in the high-end retail market.

That's where Kenneth Cole now comes in. The clothing designer has just launched a new crusade to tie his expensive clothing and shoes line to the elite's movement du jour: the fight to demonize public school-teachers and their unions. In a billboard and Web-based campaign, Cole's foundation portrays the national debate over education as one that supposedly pits "Teachers' Rights vs. Students' Rights."

"Should underperforming teachers be protected?" asks the foundation's website.

When asked about the campaign, one of Cole's spokeswomen insisted the company isn't trying to insult teachers or unions, saying,

"It's something in the news and being debated, and we wanted to provide a forum where people could discuss it as well." But with the company using the same loaded language as the conservative political activists trying to undermine public education and teachers' unions, the corporate P.R.-speak is, to say the least, unconvincing.

No, Cole's campaign is thinly veiled ideological propaganda, and it comes with myriad problems, not the least of which is the simple fact that almost nobody believes "underperforming teachers" should be protected. That includes the nation's biggest teachers' unions, which have been outspoken in backing "accountability" reforms for teacher tenure. So right off the bat, Cole is constructing a straw man, one that has served over the years to pretend that public employee unions in general and teachers' unions specifically are about nothing more than making sure bad employees get to keep their jobs.

Of course, there is a legitimate debate among state lawmakers and school boards about how to determine what an "underperforming teacher" is. Should a teacher be considered subpar if her students perform poorly on standardized tests? Should any teacher-to-teacher peer

review be included in performance evaluations? And should any factors other than tests and grades — say, student poverty levels — be considered when using student achievement to judge a particular teacher?

As evidenced by the language of his new campaign, Cole, like the anti-union activists in the larger corporate-sponsored education "reform" movement, doesn't want those questions asked, much less answered, for pondering them raises the very queries about power and wealth that Cole's fellow 1 percenters don't want to discuss.

For instance, actually taking an honest look at America's education system brings up queries about why other less economically stratified nations have unionized teachers and far better academic results than here in America. It also forces us to ask why it just so happens that wealthy unionized districts in America do so well — but poorer districts have such problems. All of that consequently compels us to consider issues like poverty and funding disparities between rich and poor districts — issues that inherently threaten the status quo, and thus the interests of the super-wealthy. And so under the veneer of the term "reform" and with the backing of seemingly altruistic philanthropy via foundations like Cole's, the super-wealthy work to avoid substance and instead define the education policy discourse on reductionist slogans like "underperforming teachers."

Perhaps the biggest problem with Cole's campaign, though, is how it forwards the "us-versus-them" notion that teachers' rights to due process in the workplace are automatically at odds with their students' interests. This so fundamentally misunderstands how education works that it perfectly underscores why a clothing corporation doesn't have much credibility on education issues.

Think about it: We need our best teachers to work in the public 10 schools that educate the most at-risk populations. Why? Because with decades of social science research proving that achievement is driven mostly by out-of-classroom factors (poverty, family dysfunction, etc.), those are the schools that need the most skilled pedagogues to overcome comparatively difficult odds for success. But why would a good teacher opt to work in such a school without basic protections — protections designed to make sure the at-risk population's achievement-suppressing disadvantages aren't used as a rationale to fire her? She probably wouldn't.

In this way, "Teachers' Rights vs. Students' Rights" is the mirror opposite of how things actually work. Without extending teachers' rights to, say, be evaluated fairly or to challenge a termination, it would be difficult — if not impossible — for public schools to recruit the best teachers to the specific at-risk schools that need them the most.

Most likely, these inconvenient truths are of little concern to someone like Kenneth Cole. According to Gotham Schools, he sends his kids to private school, making him part of the larger trend of elites who are trying to foist radical policies onto public schools, knowing their own kin won't be hurt by those policies.

But, you ask, wouldn't a clothing mogul with no kids in public school be averse to a divisive crusade against teachers, if only to circumvent a controversy? Even if he is a political activist, wouldn't he refrain from such a campaign for fear of losing customers?

These are fair questions, and they highlight how Cole's campaign may say something hugely important — and troubling — about the long-term future of education politics in America.

Recall that Cole is in a zeitgeist industry that is all about lashing branded chic to the popular fad of the moment. That means his move probably reflects what he believes to be an ascendant cause célèbre — one that he thinks he isn't joining *in spite of* his company, but *in support of* its profit-making objectives. Put another way, he probably believes he will *gain* customers if he ties his company to anti-teacher, anti-union themes. 15

Sure, that gamble could be wrong — and I hope it is. I hope America sees just how wrongheaded and ideologically extreme the crusade against public schools, teachers and unions is.

But as a successful mogul, Cole's clearly got skill as a cultural seer; and if someone like him sees mass profit potential in not-so-subtly bashing teachers and unions, it's a scary sign that such unhinged anti-teacher sentiment could be going more mainstream than ever.

Update: After a mass outcry from teachers, Kenneth Cole announced on Twitter Monday that it is removing the billboard. In its statement, the

company said "We misrepresented the issue — one too complex for a billboard — and are taking it down." It has also taken down the campaign on the accompanying website.

Engaging with the Text

1. What is David Sirota's **THESIS**? How does he **SUPPORT** this thesis?   313–15 143

2. Click on the hyperlinks in the online text. What function do these links serve? What do they add to the text? How important are they to Sirota's argument?

3. What does Sirota's **TITLE** mean? How is it relevant to his argument? How does it relate to the picture at the beginning of the text?   312–13

4. In his **ENDING,** Sirota says that "if someone like him [Kenneth Cole] sees mass profit potential in not-so-subtly bashing teachers and unions, it's a scary sign that such unhinged anti-teacher sentiment could be going more mainstream than ever." What does he mean by this claim? According to the essay, what is the message of the Kenneth Cole ad campaign? Who, in Sirota's view, benefits by the "bashing" of teachers and unions? Who suffers? Do you agree or disagree with Sirota's argument? — and why?   306–10

5. *For Writing.* Respond to Sirota's essay, either defending his argument or refuting it. To support your claims, include (either in the text or as links) visuals such as photos, graphs, or video. Decide on a specific **AUDIENCE** to target — teachers, politicians, conservatives, liberals, students, parents, or some other group — and make sure your argument will both appeal to and be understood by that audience.   5–8

61 Evaluations

rhetorical
situations

genres

processes

strategies

research
MLA / APA

media /
design

readings

JODY ROSEN

Born This Way
Lady Gaga's New Album Is a Pop Rapture

American author and journalist Jody Rosen is the music critic for the online magazine Slate *and a frequent contributor to other publications such as the* New York Times, *the* Nation, *and* Rolling Stone. *He is also author of the book* White Christmas: The Story of an American Song (2002) *and editor of* Jewface (2006), *a controversial collection of early twentieth-century songs with Jewish characters. The following evaluation appeared in* Slate *in 2011. It was among the first reviews published of Lady Gaga's album* Born This Way.

THE RAPTURE DID NOT ARRIVE AS SCHEDULED this weekend, but Lady Gaga's new album showed up, bringing with it enough sound and fury to please the most exacting eschatologist. *Born This Way* is windswept, end-times pop music: pummeling beats, huge choruses, screeching hair-metal guitar solos, crescendos straight out of a Broadway curtain closer. There has been a notable plus-sizing of pop in recent years, with everyone from indie rockers to southern rappers embracing music on a vast and symphonic scale. But Gaga has decided to outdo them all, to put out a record that is bigger, more emphatic, more ferociously campy than anyone's. It's one thing to title a ballad "The Edge of Glory" — to belt out lyrics about "hanging on a moment of truth" and "dancing in the flames" over the gustiest possible power chords. It's another, in the middle of that maelstrom, to unleash a saxophone solo of the sort that hasn't been heard since 1987. This is the place where pop schlock becomes, if you will, rapturous — where a song slips the surly bonds of earth, gusting heavenward to touch the cloudbank where Jesus, or Meatloaf, gazes down from a golden throne.

Of course, you'd expect nothing less from Lady Gaga. The most impressive thing about *Born This Way* is simply that it is *acceptably* audacious: It manages to reach the bar that Gaga sets higher each time she releases a video or appears on a red carpet wearing New York sirloin.

She's pulled off her act by sweating the details. Beneath its roar, *Born This Way* is a model of fine, small-bore songcraft. The music is intricately arranged, with every synthesizer strain, beat, and computer-generated vocal fillip slotted precisely in place. Gaga and her collaborators (including the Mexican producer Fernando Garibay, DJ White Shadow, and longtime comrade RedOne) focus on dynamics, building slow-boiling introductions that erupt into booming refrains. Those huge choruses are Gaga's specialty, but her tunes would hold up if played on an acoustic guitar.

Not that you'd want to hear them that way. Big is the point: big sound, big sentimentality, big silliness. In nearly every song, Gaga flirts with absurdity, charging right up to the line where catharsis turns into comedy. A song like the album-opener "Marry the Night" feels almost like a science experiment. Can we reanimate the corpses of Pat Benatar and Bonnie Tyler? How many windy pop-rock clichés can be pumped into a modern club anthem before it bursts? On the album cover, Gaga appears with circa 1985-style big hair, and in "Hair," she sings a ridiculous liberation anthem about teased tresses. ("This is my prayer / That I'll die living just as free as my hair!") Then there's "Americano," about a lesbian wedding in East L.A. It's a cabaret-style ballad, awash in Latin kitsch: swooping "gypsy" strings, flamenco guitars, castanets.

In these songs, Lady Gaga draws on a tradition of camp that extends from drag queen cabaret to Broadway and disco. Gay men are Gaga's core constituency and, not coincidentally, her cause; for Gaga, activism and careerism are one in the same. Exhibit A on *Born This Way* is the title track, which hitches a melody from Madonna to some inspirational sloganeering: "Whether life's disabilities / Left you outcast, bullied, or teased / Rejoice and love yourself today / 'Cause baby you were born this way / No matter gay, straight, or bi / Lesbian, transgendered life."

These lyrics do not roll trippingly off the tongue. Gaga can be hard to take when she tries to be high-minded. And when she tries to be high-concept. "I've made it my goal to revolutionize pop music," she's said, but the self-consciousness with which she undertakes that mission sometimes has a distancing effect. "Judas," her current single, screeches to a halt for a rap that sounds like an excerpt from a bad cultural studies seminar: "In the most Biblical sense / I am beyond repentance / Fame   5

rhetorical situations   genres   processes   strategies   research MLA / APA   media / design   readings

Lady Gaga performing "Born This Way."

hooker, prostitute wench, vomits her mind/ But in the cultural sense / I just speak in future tense." Even for those of us who love thinking about pop music "in the cultural sense" — who make a living pondering pop stars' mind-vomit — a song like this is a bummer. Beyoncé makes music that is just as fascinatingly multivalent as Gaga's, and she does it without interrupting her songs to provide Cliffs Notes.

But Gaga's real concern isn't politics or conceptual art — or even hair. It is, for lack of a better term, rock 'n' roll. Remember, she wasn't born this way. Before she was Lady Gaga, pop revolutionary, disco queen, and Muppet dress fancier, she was Stefani Germanotta, a young singer-songwriter with a good voice, reasonable piano skills, and a desire to be the next Tori Amos or Fiona Apple. Or was it the next Def Leppard? One of the new album's standout songs is "You and I," a straightforward pop-rock power ballad, produced by "Mutt" Lange, the studio legend behind albums like Leppard's *Hysteria*.

Gaga is a rocker at heart. She has little feel for, or interest in, black music; there's almost no hip-hop on her records. Her songs are powered by blunt foursquare house beats — a European sound that, thanks to Gaga, has become the default pulse of American pop.

Yet on the new album, this Europhile stakes claim to her Americanness. Forget Madonna: Gaga's new muse is Bruce Springsteen. She swathes song after song in Springsteen's open-road romanticism. (That's Clarence Clemons playing sax on "The Edge of Glory" and "Hair.") Sonically, *Born This Way* is a club record; spiritually, it's *Born to Run*, with Springsteen's Marys and Wendys recast in the lead roles. In "Highway Unicorn (Road 2 Love)," Gaga sings: "She's just an American riding a dream. . . . She's a free soul, burning roads / With a flag in her bra." Gaga's thudding music has something in common with Springsteen's, too — it's a disco-fied update of the Boss' walloping "dinosaur beat." It's an overwhelming sound. In the album's best moments, it simply drowns out all the white noise that surrounds Lady Gaga: You stop thinking about Gaga's newest dress or Tweet or *succès de scandale* — you stop puzzling over Gaga in the cultural sense — and surrender to the music's crude power. You just dance.

rhetorical situations

genres

processes

strategies

research MLA / APA

media / design

readings

Engaging with the Text

1. Who is the intended **AUDIENCE** for Jody Rosen's review of *Born This Way*? Where in the essay are there clues about the intended audience?

5–8

2. If you've listened to the album, do you agree with Rosen's assessment in the beginning of the review that *Born This Way* is "a record that is bigger, more emphatic, and more ferociously campy than anyone's"? If you haven't heard it, does Rosen provide enough **EVIDENCE** to back up his assertion?

327–35

3. With whom does Rosen **COMPARE AND CONTRAST** Lady Gaga? How are these comparisons useful to his assessment of the album?

348–55

4. What is Rosen's **STANCE** in this essay? How does he establish that his discussion is **KNOWLEDGEABLE**?

12–15
169

5. *For Writing.* Visit the part of *Billboard's* website that identifies recently released albums and select one to review. In your **EVALUATION,** consider how this album ranks against other new releases and why. Write for an audience who is already interested in either the artist(s) or the genre of music on the album.

164–72

MICHIKO KAKUTANI

The End of Life as She Knew It

Michiko Kakutani is a book critic at the New York Times. *In 1998, she was awarded the Pulitzer Prize for Criticism. The following review of Joan Didion's memoir,* The Year of Magical Thinking *(2005), was originally published in the* Times. *For a selection from Didion's book,* *see p. 932.*

IN JOAN DIDION'S WORK, there has always been a fascination with what she once called "the unspeakable peril of the everyday" — the coyotes by the interstate, the snakes in the playpen, the fires and Santa Ana winds of California. In the past, that peril often seemed metaphorical, a product of a theatrical imagination and a sensibility attuned to the emotional and existential fault lines running beneath society's glossy veneer: it was personal but it was also abstract.

There is nothing remotely abstract about what has happened to Ms. Didion in the last two years.

On Christmas Day 2003, her daughter Quintana, who had come down with flulike symptoms, went to the emergency room at Beth Israel North Hospital in New York City. Suffering from pneumonia and septic shock, she was suddenly in the hospital's intensive-care unit, hooked up to a respirator and being given a potent intravenous drug cocktail.

Five days later, Ms. Didion's husband of 40 years, John Gregory Dunne, sat down to dinner in their Manhattan apartment, then abruptly slumped over and fell to the floor. He was pronounced dead — of a massive heart attack — later that evening.

"The Broken Man," what Quintana as a young girl used to call "fear   5 and death and the unknown," had come for her father, even as it had come to wait for her in the I.C.U.

"Life changes fast," Ms. Didion would write a day or two later. "Life changes in the instant. You sit down to dinner and life as you know it ends."

rhetorical situations　genres　processes　strategies　research MLA / APA　media / design　readings

Like those who lost loved ones in the terrorist attacks of 9/11, like those who have lost friends and family members to car accidents, airplane crashes, and other random acts of history, Ms. Didion instantly saw ordinary life morph into a nightmare. She saw a shared existence with shared rituals and shared routines shatter into a million irretrievable pieces.

In her devastating new book, *The Year of Magical Thinking,* Ms. Didion writes about the year she spent trying to come to terms with what happened that terrible December, a year she says that "cut loose any fixed idea I had ever had about death, about illness, about probability and luck, about good fortune and bad, about marriage and children and memory, about grief, about the ways in which people do and do not deal with the fact that life ends, about the shallowness of sanity, about life itself."

Throughout their careers, Ms. Didion and Mr. Dunne wrote about themselves, about their marriage, their nervous breakdowns, the screenplays they worked on together, and the glittering worlds they inhabited in New York and Los Angeles. Writing for both of them was a way to find out what they thought; the construction of a narrative was a means of imposing a pattern on the chaos of life.

And so, almost a year after the twin calamities of December 2003, 10 Ms. Didion began writing this volume. It is an utterly shattering book that gives the reader an indelible portrait of loss and grief and sorrow, all chronicled in minute detail with the author's unwavering reportorial eye. It is also a book that provides a haunting portrait of a four-decade-long marriage, an extraordinarily close relationship between two writers, who both worked at home and who kept each other company almost 24 hours a day, editing each other's work, completing and counterpointing each other's thoughts.

"I could not count the times during the average day when something would come up that I needed to tell him," Ms. Didion writes. "This impulse did not end with his death. What ended was the possibility of response."

Like so many of her fictional heroines, Ms. Didion says she always prized control as a means of lending life at least the illusion of order, and in an effort to cope with what happened to her husband and daughter, she turned to the Internet and to books. "Read, learn, work it up, go to the literature," she writes. "Information is control." She queried doctors, researched the subjects of grief and death, read everything from Emily Post on funeral etiquette to Philippe Ariès's *Western Attitudes toward Death.*

When Quintana suffered a relapse in March 2004 — she collapsed at the Los Angeles airport and underwent emergency neurosurgery at the U.C.L.A. Medical Center for a massive hematoma in her brain — Ms. Didion began researching the doctors' findings. She skimmed the appendices to a book called *Clinical Neuroanatomy* and studied *Intensive Care: A Doctor's Journal* in an effort to learn what questions to ask Quintana's doctors.

During those weeks at U.C.L.A., Ms. Didion says she realized that many of her friends in New York and California "shared a habit of mind usually credited to the very successful": "They believed absolutely in their own management skills. They believed absolutely in the power of the telephone numbers they had at their fingertips, the right doctor, the major donor, the person who could facilitate a favor at State or Justice." For many years, she shared those beliefs, and yet at the same time she says she always understood that "some events in life would remain beyond my ability to control or manage them" and that "some events would just happen. This was one of those events."

Nor could she control her own thoughts. Try as she might to sup-   15
press them, memories of her life with Mr. Dunne — of trips they had taken with Quintana to Hawaii, of homes where they had lived in Los Angeles and Manhattan, of walks and meals shared — continually bobbed to the surface of her mind, creating a memory "vortex" that pulled her back in time only to remind her of all that she had lost. She began trying to avoid places she might associate with her husband or daughter.

The magical thinking of denial became Ms. Didion's companion. She found herself "thinking as small children think, as if my thoughts or wishes had the power to reverse the narrative, change the outcome." She authorized an autopsy of her husband, reasoning that an autopsy could show what had gone wrong, and if it were something simple — a change in medication, say, or the resetting of a pacemaker — "they might still be able to fix it."

She similarly refused to give away his shoes, reasoning that it would be impossible for him to "come back" without anything to wear on his feet. When she heard that Julia Child had died, she thought: "this was finally working out: John and Julia Child could have dinner together."

In an effort to get her mind around what happened, Ms. Didion ran the events of December 30 through her mind again and again, just as she ran several decades of family life through her mind, looking for a way to de-link the chain of causation. What if they hadn't moved to New York so many years ago? What if Quintana had gone to a different hospital? What if they still lived in Brentwood Park in their two-story Colonial house with the center-hall plan?

Even when Quintana seems to be making a recovery, Ms. Didion finds it difficult to work: she has a panic attack in Boston, trying to cover the Democratic convention, and puts off finishing an article, thinking that without John, she has no one to read it. She feels "fragile, unstable," worried that when her sandal catches on the sidewalk, she will fall and there will be no one to take her to the emergency room. She takes to wearing sneakers about town and begins leaving a light on in the apartment throughout the night.

In this book, the elliptical constructions and sometimes mannered 20 prose of the author's recent fiction give way to stunning candor and piercing details that distinguished her groundbreaking early books of essays, *Slouching Towards Bethlehem* and *The White Album*. At once exquisitely controlled and heartbreakingly sad, *The Year of Magical Thinking* tells us in completely unvarnished terms what it is to love someone and lose him, what it is to have a child fall sick and be unable to help her.

It is a book that tells us how people try to make sense of the senseless and how they somehow go on.

The tragic coda to Ms. Didion's story is not recounted in these pages: the death — from an abdominal infection — of Quintana in August, a year and eight months after she first fell ill and a year and eight months after the death of her father.

Engaging with the Text

299–306

1. Michiko Kakutani waits until the eighth paragraph of her book review to mention the title of the book she's reviewing, Joan Didion's *The Year of Magical Thinking*. How does she **BEGIN** her text, and how does this beginning appeal to readers? What would be the effect had she opened by referring to the book?

463–67

2. Kakutani peppers her review with **QUOTATIONS** from Didion's memoir. What function do these quotations serve? What role, in general, do quotations play in evaluations?

3. Kakutani does not explicitly state her opinion of Didion's book, but how do we know what she thinks? Identify passages that reveal her evaluation.

3–4

4. One **PURPOSE** of a book review is to help potential readers decide whether or not a book is worth reading. Does this review achieve that purpose? Why or why not? What other purpose might it serve? What other goals might Kakutani have had in writing it?

164–72
168–69

5. *For Writing.* Write a review **EVALUATING** a book you've read — a novel, a how-to book, a textbook, whatever. Be sure to develop **CRITERIA** to determine the book's strengths and weaknesses and to cite specific examples from the book to support your evaluation.

rhetorical situations   genres   processes   strategies   research MLA / APA   media / design   readings

DANA STEVENS

The Help
A Feel-Good Movie That Feels Kind of Icky

Dana Stevens is a movie critic for the online magazine Slate *and cohost of the* Slate Culture Gabfest *podcast. Her work has also appeared in the* New York Times, *the* Washington Post Book World, *the* Atlantic, *and a blog titled* High Sign, *which Stevens wrote under the pseudonym Liz Penn. She has also appeared several times on the television talk show* Charlie Rose. *The following review appeared in* Slate *in August 2011.*

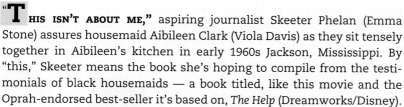

"**T**HIS ISN'T ABOUT ME,**"** aspiring journalist Skeeter Phelan (Emma Stone) assures housemaid Aibileen Clark (Viola Davis) as they sit tensely together in Aibileen's kitchen in early 1960s Jackson, Mississippi. By "this," Skeeter means the book she's hoping to compile from the testimonials of black housemaids — a book titled, like this movie and the Oprah-endorsed best-seller it's based on, *The Help* (Dreamworks/Disney).

Skeeter — a brainy, ambitious white woman freshly graduated from Ole Miss — eventually convinces the skeptical Aibileen of her good faith, and together they produce an oral history scandalous enough to turn Jackson's Junior League on its ear. But it's never clear whether we, the audience, should believe Skeeter's disclaimer or not, since the movie sort of *is* about her. *The Help,* written and directed by Tate Taylor from the novel by Kathryn Stockett, belongs to the *Driving Miss Daisy* tradition of feel-good fables about black-white relations in America, movies in which institutional racism takes a backseat to the personal enlightenment of one white character.

It's hard to actively hate *The Help,* a movie so solicitous of the audience's favor that it can't help but win it some of the time. Viola Davis and Octavia Spencer are tremendous as the stolid Aibileen and her hot-tempered best friend and fellow housekeeper, Minny; these two women are funny, smart, and righteous, and every moment we spend in their company is a delight. Some of the smaller performances are quite fine, too, especially Jessica Chastain as a ditzy new arrival in town. There are several solid laughs, and at least two instances when I had to scramble for a tissue. But after awhile all this emotional dexterity starts to resemble emotional manipulation. *The Help* is a high-functioning tearjerker, but the catharsis it offers feels glib and insufficient, a Barbie Band-Aid on the still-raw wound of race relations in America.

Skeeter's idea for the book begins to take shape when Minny's employer, the bitchy queen bee Hilly Holbrook (Bryce Dallas Howard) starts a campaign to pass a bill requiring separate "colored" bathrooms for houses with domestic help. When Minny defiantly uses her boss's bathroom, Hilly summarily fires her, and Minny, after taking sly revenge, goes to work for Celia Foote (Chastain), a nouveau-riche newlywed whom Hilly has chosen as her sworn enemy.

While the white women of Jackson spar over social status, bridge 5 clubs, and charity fundraisers, the town's black maids, who are bused

Viola Davis and Octavia Spencer in The Help.

in each morning from the poorer side of town, struggle to make a living and send their children to school. A few characters, like Skeeter's ailing mother (Allison Janney), are given a trajectory from racial obliviousness to semi-enlightenment, but for the most part, whites in this movie are either pure-of-heart crusaders or sneering bigots.

Similarly, some of the black characters (most notably Skeeter's aged former nanny Constantine, played by a frail-looking Cicely Tyson) border on saintly stereotypes from a sentimental abolitionist-era novel. This moral Manichaeism makes for satisfying melodrama — in fact, one of the two scenes that made me cry involved the angelic Constantine. But it also lets the viewer off the hook by making racism seem like a quaint artifact of the days when there were openly racist Hillys bullying self-evidently blameless Constantines.

If *The Help* contained more moments in which Skeeter's good will wasn't enough — in which, despite her best intentions, she blundered by unintentionally patronizing one of her interview subjects and had to confront her own received ideas about race — contemporary viewers might recognize a moment we've actually lived through, rather than being encouraged to congratulate ourselves on how far we've come.

Then again, if glossily inspiring movies about African-American lives didn't get made, would a different, more challenging kind get made in their place? Part of me wants to say that it's fine for *The Help*, book and movie, to exist as a pop-cultural phenomenon. The story simplifies and reduces the civil rights movement, yes, but at least it's *about* it. That's not nothing given the insulated bubble in which most movies marketed at women take place (the blithely apolitical *Eat Pray Love* comes to mind). *The Help* raises the eternal question faced by minority groups who have to fight for space onscreen (that is to say, anyone but white men): Do we count ourselves glad to make any inroads we can, or do we demand rich, nuanced, subtle representations right from the start? I get the feeling that *The Help*'s reception will be sharply divided by that question — a division which may in itself be this movie's most valuable contribution.

Engaging with the Text

169 ▲

1. In what ways does Dana Stevens make her review of *The Help* a **BALANCED ASSESSMENT** of the film? What is her major criticism of it? If you haven't seen it, does her review make you want to? Why or why not? If you've seen it, how convincing do you find the review? Why?

312–13 ◆

2. How does Stevens's **TITLE** prepare you for her review? Is it an accurate representation of the way she evaluates the film?

313–15 ◆
327–35

3. What is the **THESIS** of this review? What **EVIDENCE** does Stevens offer to support her thesis?

4. Stevens ends her review by stating: "I get the feeling that *The Help*'s reception will be sharply divided by that question — a division which may in itself be this movie's most valuable contribution." What question is she referring to? What are some of the ways you think it will be debated? In what way would this debate be a "valuable contribution"?

164–72 ▲

5. *For Writing.* Select a movie that you have mixed feelings about. It might be one that is currently in theaters or one that is on DVD or the web. Write an **EVALUATION** of the movie that shows why you have both a positive and a negative assessment of it. Write a title for your review that signals the mixed evaluation.

CONSUMER REPORTS

Fast Food: Four Big Names Lose
36,733 Readers Rate the Food, Value, Staff, and Speed at 53 Chains

The following report appeared in the August 2011 issue of Consumer Reports, *a magazine dedicated to testing products and services and reporting the results of such tests to consumers so they can make informed choices. In this case,* Consumer Reports *relied on the ratings in a survey of 36,733 readers. As you read, notice the criteria the writer uses to evaluate the subject — fast food restaurants.*

NEXT TIME YOU HAVE A CRAVING FOR FAST FOOD, think twice about slowing down for Burger King, KFC, McDonald's, or Taco Bell.

In our first major survey of quick-service restaurants (industry-speak for fast-food chains), subscribers who made a total of more than 98,000 visits to 53 chains said those four biggies were worse than many others. The main reason: the uninspiring food, though they also had so-so service. Readers said those chains, which boast of supersized value, don't even offer much bang for the buck. Other major chains with relatively low scores: sandwich shops Arby's and Quiznos and pizza joints Domino's and Pizza Hut.

By contrast, our survey revealed good deals and even better meals at dozens of less-ubiquitous fast-food restaurants. Readers gave 21 of them especially high marks for food; 11 stood out for value. In-N-Out Burger (264 restaurants in Arizona, California, Nevada, Texas, and Utah), Chipotle Mexican Grill (1,100 nationwide), Chick-fil-A (1,536 nationwide), and Papa Murphy's Take 'N' Bake Pizza (1,250 in 37 states and Canada) ranked at the top of their type, and offered speedy and solicitous service that the industry giants couldn't match. (Most restaurant counts are approximate.)

Our survey's other key findings:

Diners want better food. Many restaurants scored higher for service—specifically, speed and politeness—than for food. At chains with the highest scores for food, 42 to 54 percent of patrons called the fare excellent, but at Burger King, KFC, McDonald's, and Taco Bell, no more than 11 percent of patrons did. In fact, 15 to 19 percent of respondents who ate at one of those chains thought the food was fair, poor, or very poor. At Sbarro, an international Italian chain trying to emerge from bankruptcy, 27 percent of patrons judged the food fair, poor, or very poor.

Cheap food may not be a bargain. Fifty-four percent of those surveyed cited low prices as a reason for picking a particular fast-food restaurant, and savvy shoppers can often score discounts by downloading coupons and other perks from a chain's website and social-media pages. But despite the low prices, just 19 percent of all respondents said they got excellent value for their money. In-N-Out Burger, Papa Murphy's, and CiCi's Pizza offered the best value; Sbarro, Round Table Pizza, and KFC, the worst.

5

rhetorical situations   genres   processes   strategies   research MLA / APA   media / design   readings

Who makes the best fries?

By Wendy's own reckoning, its spuds were sort of duds. Ken Calwell, the chain's chief marketing officer before being named Papa Murphy's Pizza president, conceded that Wendy's never enjoyed McDonald's reputation for tasty french fries. So Wendy's went back to the kitchen and came out with a revamped fry, made from russet potatoes, with the skin on for added flavor and texture, cooked in trans-fat-free oil, and dusted with sea salt.

Wendy's says its new fries are so good that they beat McDonald's by a wide margin in a recent independent consumer taste test. To see for ourselves, we had two sensory experts taste fries from those two chains and from Burger King, Five Guys, Fuddruckers, and KFC in the New York tristate area.

Bottom line. Wendy's has the right to brag, and we scored its fries Very Good. Our experts gave Wendy's a slight edge over McDonald's because its fries were "a bit more potato-y." The others were close too, except Burger King; its fries tasted fatty, had less-intense potato flavor, and rated only Good.

Wendy's: Distinct potato flavor enhanced by browned and earthy taste of skins. Crispy outside, moist inside. Quality somewhat inconsistent.

Five Guys: Big baked-potato flavor complemented by oil and salt. Crispness and doneness were variable.

McDonald's: Moderate potato and browned flavors with crispy texture.

KFC: Flavorful seasoned wedges with extra-crispy coating and peppery kick. Very soft interior.

Fuddruckers: Spicy wedges with garlic, black pepper, salt, and paprika, sometimes distributed unevenly. Interiors slightly dry and mealy; edges lightly crisped. Some earthy skin flavor and bitterness.

Burger King: Relatively low in flavor; coating detracts from quality. Fatty taste has about the same intensity as potato flavor.

Diners want a better experience. Whether they ordered cafeteria-style, at a counter, or at a drive-thru, or had food delivered, readers were much less pleased overall with fast-food restaurants than with casual full-service eateries like Cracker Barrel, Outback Steakhouse, and Red Lobster. Sixty percent of respondents said they were completely or very satisfied with their fast-food dining experiences vs. 68 percent of casual-restaurant patrons.

Sometimes fast food isn't. The slowest places to get fast food were KFC, Popeyes, and Pizza Hut.

Consumers talk thin but eat fat. Despite their reputation for blowing a diet to smithereens, fast-food restaurants offer plenty of healthful options. Hardee's (1,900 in 30 states and nine countries) and Carl's Jr. (1,100 worldwide) recently started selling charbroiled turkey burgers; Subway (34,679 in 98 countries), egg-white omelets; and Little Caesars (thousands from coast to coast), pizza crust and sauce with no animal products.

Trouble is, there aren't many takers. "Indulgence wins over health- 10 fulness every time," says Darren Tristano, executive vice president of Technomic, a food-service research and consulting firm in Chicago. When asked if they had eaten a healthful meal during their most recent visit to a fast-food restaurant, only 13 percent of those surveyed said yes. At pizza chains, just 4 percent said they'd ordered something healthful.

Subway, with a "Fresh Fit" menu and spokesman Jared Fogle (an everyday guy who lost 245 pounds partly by living on the chain's low-fat subs), had the most diet-conscious eaters: Almost half of respondents who ate there said they chose a nutritious meal. But not all sandwiches are created equal, even at Subway, where the footlong Italian B.M.T. sub packs 900 calories and 40 grams of fat.

Winners and Losers

Are some of the biggest and best-known chains low-rated because of the Walmart syndrome, in which the public enjoys taking potshots at

Sinking sub!

Subway is known for its healthful menu offerings, notably low-fat subs like the Turkey Breast & Black Forest Ham sandwich pictured below. But not every choice at Subway is a smart one. The footlong Italian B.M.T., with cheese, ham, pepperoni, salami, and veggies, is packed with more than a day's worth of sodium and more than half of a day's recommended fat allotment.

SIX-INCH Turkey Breast & Black Forest Ham
on nine-grain wheat bread: 280 calories, 4 grams of fat, and 820 milligrams of sodium

FOOTLONG Italian B.M.T.
on nine-grain wheat bread: 900 calories, 40 grams of fat, and 3,000 milligrams of sodium

the 800-pound gorilla? Not according to Tristano. "The large chains are consistent and they're everywhere, but they do get lower scores for their overall experience," he says. "It's not high quality that's driving traffic, it's good value, drive-thru, and convenience."

Fortunately, if you like fast food of any type, there are plenty of good choices.

For burger fans, the best restaurants include In-N-Out Burger, rated highest of all 53 chains, Burgerville (39 in Oregon and Washington), Five Guys Burgers and Fries (750 nationwide and in Canada), Culver's (428 mainly in the Midwest), and Back Yard Burgers (120 mostly in the South and East).

FAST-FOOD FACT

A better burger? Thirty-six percent of Burgerville diners in our survey said they ordered a healthful meal. No other burger joint came close. Though its burgers are about as nutritious as the rest, the chain may benefit from a "halo" effect from what it calls its "fresh, local, sustainable" food and reliance on "pastured, vegetarian-fed, and antibiotic-free" beef.

For Mexican food, Chipotle, Rubio's 15 Fresh (180 in the West), Qdoba (500 nationally), and Baja Fresh (255 in 24 states and Dubai) earned high marks for food and service.

One chicken chain topped the rest: Chick-fil-A. (It has come under criticism, but not for its food: A franchisee ruffled feathers earlier this year by donating food for events by a group reportedly opposing gay marriage, prompting company president and chief operating officer Dan Cathy to respond in a video. "Providing food to these events," he said in part, "is not an endorsement.")

Crave a top-notch wedge, hero, hoagie, or sub served quickly with a smile on the side? Try Jason's Deli (200 in 28 states), Firehouse Subs (426 in 24 states), Jersey Mike's Sub (500 nationwide), Potbelly Sandwich Shop (200 in 11 states and Washington, D.C.), Jimmy John's Gourmet Sandwiches (1,000 nationwide), or Schlotzsky's (327 nationwide).

The single standout for pizza: Papa Murphy's Take 'N' Bake Pizza, which has an unconventional concept: Patrons order a pizza to bake at home.

The Big Picture

On average, our survey respondents bought lunch or dinner at a fast-food chain four times a month; 13 percent did so 10 or more times. Although three-quarters said the sagging economy didn't affect how often they ate fast food, 22 percent said they eat out at fast-food restaurants less often than they used to because of financial concerns.

Still, fast-food restaurants have weathered the recession better than 20 white-tablecloth and casual restaurants, many of which were forced to offer discounts such as smaller portions at lower prices. "The restaurant

rhetorical situations   genres   processes   strategies   research MLA / APA   media / design   readings

How good are the chains' main dishes?

We asked 25,079 subscribers who recently bought the pizza chains' pizza, chicken chains' grilled or roasted chicken, sandwich chains' subs, and Mexican chains' tacos and burritos this question: On a scale of 1 to 10, from least delicious to most delicious you've ever eaten, how would you rate the taste?

The tables reveal that some house specialties came close to our readers' standards for excellence, but CiCi's Pizza, Del Taco, Little Caesars, Sbarro, and Taco Bell earned significantly lower scores than most chains for the foods that best define them. Domino's, which with fanfare changed its core recipe in December 2009, seeking a better pie, came in fifth place, behind Papa Murphy's and other pizza joints. KFC chicken was rated less tasty than chicken from most rival chains.

Among burger chains (which we covered in October), burgers at In-N-Out Burger and Five Guys Burgers and Fries were standouts. Burger King and Wendy's fared better than McDonald's, whose burgers ranked lowest of all.

Mexican food	Taste
Chipotle Mexican Grill	7.7
Rubio's Fresh Mexican Grill	7.5
Qdoba Mexican Grill	7.4
Moe's Southwest Grill	7.3
Baja Fresh Mexican Grill	7.2
Taco John's	6.6
Del Taco	6.1
Taco Bell	6.0

Chicken	Taste
Chick-fil-A	7.6
Boston Market	7.4
Popeyes Louisiana Kitchen	7.4
El Pollo Loco	7.4
Zaxby's	7.2
Bojangles' Famous Chicken 'n Biscuits	7.1
Church's Chicken	7.0
KFC	6.6

Sandwiches and subs	Taste
Firehouse Subs	8.0
Jason's Deli	7.8
Jersey Mike's Subs	7.7
Schlotzsky's	7.7
Jimmy John's Gourmet Sandwiches	7.6
Potbelly Sandwich Shop	7.4
Togo's	7.4
McAlister's Deli	7.2
Quiznos	7.1
Subway	6.8
Arby's	6.8

Pizza	Taste
Papa Murphy's Take `N´ Bake Pizza	7.8
Round Table Pizza	7.3
Papa John's	6.9
Pizza Hut	6.6
Domino's Pizza	6.1
CiCi's Pizza	5.8
Little Caesars	5.7
Sbarro	5.7

industry is immediately affected by how flush consumers feel, so the recession had a huge impact," says Robin Lee Allen, executive editor of *Nation's Restaurant News,* a trade publication. But things are picking up. After three dismal years, the National Restaurant Association, a trade group, forecasts that restaurant sales will grow by an estimated 3.6 percent this year, to $604 billion. Twenty-seven percent of that total is expected to be spent at fast-food restaurants. Their food is relatively inexpensive to begin with, and they've attracted new customers determined to keep eating out but on a tighter budget.

Many chains keep customers coming back with limited-time promotions like Whataburger's Chop House Cheddar Burger and super-cheap options such as Domino's pizza-and-chicken-wing package, $5.99 each. The tactic of mixing low-price choices (think Dollar Menu), patented specialties (McDonald's Big Mac), and some pricier items (Burger King's A1 Steakhouse XT burger) is called barbell or tiered pricing. Its goal is to lure customers with a few heavily advertised loss leaders, then tempt them to buy more profitable items.

FAST-FOOD FACT

Pizza snobs? In the Boston-to-New York corridor and in Chicago, you're likely to find a mom-and-pop pizza shop on almost every corner. Readers who live in these areas gave pizza chains much lower scores than those who live in the rest of the U.S.

That's effective, but experts wonder whether rising commodity and fuel costs will lead to price hikes that cause a double whammy: fewer cars at the drive-thru and fewer customers buying profitable fare.

To enhance the customer experience (and the perception of value), many chains are upgrading their facilities. McDonald's, for instance, is replacing its classic yellow-and-red interiors with muted yellows, greens, and oranges and exchanging its fiberglass chairs for wood and faux-leather ones. In addition, most franchises will add a second drive-thru window; some will also add a TV or two.

Besides remodeling, some chains are allowing customers to place orders online for pickup; expanding their selection of snacks and breakfast items; adding grilled

rhetorical situations · genres · processes · strategies · research MLA / APA · media / design · readings

items; reducing fat and sodium; and catering to customers with diabetes or gluten intolerance.

How to Avoid Temptation

Some states and towns have passed or are considering regulations requiring restaurants to display nutrition information at the point of sale, so it's in your face when you order. Does that keep diners from overindulging? A handful of small studies show mixed results.

Researchers at Yale University reported in a 2009 study that they observed 303 adults in New Haven, Connecticut, and found that a group that saw calorie counts before ordering consumed 14 percent fewer calories than a group that didn't. A study by New York University researchers who analyzed the ordering habits of consumers in low-income areas suggested that those who were exposed to calorie counts before ordering didn't make healthier choices.

Another recent study by researchers at Duke–National University of Singapore Graduate Medical School focused on one fast-food chain in King County, Washington, where local legislation requires calorie counts. It found that the labeling had no effect on consumer behavior in the year after the law's implementation.

A provision in the Patient Protection and Affordable Care Act of 2010 requires consistent calorie labeling of menus at food establishments with 20 or more locations. But that part of the legislation is progressing slowly. In April the Food and Drug Administration issued guidelines on implementing the rule, and it's awaiting comments. Allen of *Nation's Restaurant News* says the final rule is expected to be published by year's end and to go into effect six months later.

Even before the rule takes effect, there are plenty of ways for you to ensure that healthfulness wins over indulgence:

Visit websites. Many fast-food chains post figures for fat, calories, and sodium.

Have it your way. Many chains will hold the mayo or cheese, go easy on sauces, substitute skim milk for whole, or serve dressings on the side. Being able to customize was a key reason many respondents visited sandwich shops.

Ratings: Fast-food chains

in order of reader score

BETTER < < < < > > > > WORSE

Restaurant	Reader score (0–100)	Food	Value	Staff	Speed
BURGERS					
In-N-Out Burger	88				
Burgerville	83				
Five Guys Burgers and Fries	83				
Culver's	82				
Back Yard Burgers	82				
Whataburger	80				
Fuddruckers	80				
White Castle	78				
Checkers	77				
Hardee's	76				
Sonic	76				
Krystal	75				
Carl's Jr.	75				
Wendy's	75				
Jack in the Box	74				
A&W Restaurants	74				
Burger King	71				
McDonald's	71				
MEXICAN					
Chipotle Mexican Grill	82				
Rubio's Fresh Mexican Grill	80				
Qdoba Mexican Grill	79				
Baja Fresh Mexican Grill	78				
Moe's Southwest Grill	77				
Taco John's	73				
Taco Bell	72				
Del Taco	71				

Restaurant	Reader score (0–100)	Food	Value	Staff	Speed
CHICKEN					
Chick-fil-A	83				
El Pollo Loco	76				
Boston Market	76				
Zaxby's	76				
Bojangles' Famous Chicken 'n Biscuits	76				
Popeyes Louisiana Kitchen	73				
Church's Chicken	72				
KFC	67				
SANDWICHES AND SUBS					
Jason's Deli	83				
Firehouse Subs	83				
Jersey Mike's Subs	82				
Potbelly Sandwich Shop	81				
Jimmy John's Gourmet Sandwich Shop	81				
Schlotzsky's	80				
Togo's	78				
Subway	77				
McAlister's Deli	77				
Arby's	73				
Quiznos	73				
PIZZA					
Papa Murphy's Take 'N' Bake Pizza	86				
Round Table Pizza	75				
Little Caesars	74				
Papa John's	74				
CiCi's Pizza	73				
Pizza Hut	70				
Domino's Pizza	68				
Sbarro	63				

Guide to the Ratings

Ratings are based on a survey of 36,733 *Consumer Reports* subscribers who told us about 98,253 dining experiences at 53 hamburger, pizza, chicken, sandwich, and Mexican fast-food chains from April 2009 to June 2010. Respondents are not necessarily representative of the national population. Reader score is a measure of overall satisfaction. A score of 100 would mean all respondents were completely satisfied with their experience; 80 means they were very well satisfied on average; 60, fairly well satisfied. Differences of 5 points are meaningful. Other results reflect how well each chain did compared with the rest in food quality, perceived **value**, politeness of **staff**, and **speed** of service.

rhetorical situations | genres | processes | strategies | research MLA / APA | media / design | readings

Beware of certain words. When you see "battered," "creamy," "crispy," "crusted," "sautéed," or "stuffed," read "fattening." Look for roasted, broiled, baked, grilled, charbroiled, steamed, poached, or blackened food.

Summon your willpower. Don't supersize unless you plan to feed the entire family. Opt for a single patty instead of a double- or triple-decker, the standard soft drink rather than the Bunyonesque option, and a turkey or veggie burger instead of beef. More chains carry unsweetened tea, flavored water, and coffee as alternatives to sodas. Try a side salad with low-fat dressing, and for dessert, try sliced apples with a fat-free caramel sauce instead of a vanilla shake. At Sonic, the apples and sauce are 110 calories, vs. 480 calories for the shake.

Engaging with the Text

1. What **CLEARLY DEFINED CRITERIA** did *Consumer Reports* use to evaluate quick-service restaurants? Are these appropriate for the assessing these restaurants?   ▲ 168–69

2. Examine the **CHARTS** on p. 785 and at the end of the evaluation on p. 788. How helpful are the charts in summarizing the evaluations in the text? Do the data they present match your experience at any of the quick-service restaurants listed? Why or why not?   593–95

3. The article ends with the section "How to Avoid Temptation." Why do you think *Consumer Reports* included this section? What are the suggestions for avoiding temptation? Can you think of any others that would be useful?

4. How does *Consumer Reports* use **HEADINGS** to help readers throughout the essay? How do the headings function?   588–89

5. *For Writing.* Create your own survey to **EVALUATE** student hangout spots. Have students in your class, your dorm, or your program fill out the survey, rating various spots for different criteria such as food, music, atmosphere, and décor. Tabulate the results and decide which are the most popular spots and which are less favored and why. Write an essay that presents the survey results for students on your campus to help them identify good places to go.   ▲ 164–72

ROBERTA SMITH

An Online Art Collection Grows Out of Infancy

Roberta Smith shares with Holland Cotter the position of chief art critic at the New York Times, where she is the first woman to hold that title. She lectures on contemporary art and has written widely on that field; at the Times, she writes about decorative arts, popular and outsider art, visual arts, architecture, and design. She was awarded the Frank Jewett Mather Award for Art Criticism in 2003 by the College Art Association, and was named one of the 100 most powerful critics in contemporary art in 2010 by ArtReview Guide. The following evaluation of the Google Art Project *appeared in the* Times *on April 11, 2012. To access the online version, which includes several illustrations as well as hyperlinks to the project and the sites of various museums, go to* wwnorton.com/write/fieldguidelinks.

I **DON'T KNOW HOW MANY** wonders of the world there are by now, but it is possible that the Google Art Project will someday join the list.

The greatly expanded second iteration of this online compilation of self-selected art museums and artworks was unveiled last week. It makes available images of more than 32,000 works in 31 mediums and materials, from the collections of 151 museums and arts organizations worldwide, forming a broad, deep river of shared information, something like a lavishly illustrated art book fused with high-end open storage.

But world-wonder status will not happen tomorrow. The project has plenty of limitations and some bugs to work out. Numerous important museums have remained aloof, for one thing, including the Louvre, the Prado, the Centre Pompidou, Stedelijk in Amsterdam, Topkapi Palace in Istanbul and every Swiss museum of note.

Others, having joined, participate grudgingly, whether protective of their own Web sites or unwilling to deal with copyright permissions that apply to art not yet in the public domain; this includes vast

The expanded second iteration of the Google Art Project.

quantities of 20th-century Modernist material, which remains in very short supply here.

To cite one glaring gap: Although there are now more than 6,500 names on the list of artists (cumbersomely alphabetized by first name, with no option to reconfigure by last name), the site still does not include a single work by Picasso. There is also apparently nothing by Georges Braque, Marcel Duchamp, Kazimir Malevich or Max Beckmann and only a single painting by Matisse, thanks to the Toledo Museum of Art. Post-war American and European art fares no better; none of the main Abstract Expressionists are represented. No Beuys, Fontana or Manzoni. Nothing notable by Johns, Rauschenberg or Warhol (although the Art Institute of Chicago has managed to put up a very nice 1961 painting by Twombly).

But that will undoubtedly change. One of the glories of the Google Art Project is that it is a collective, additive work in progress that allows any museum or art-related organization to join and upload as many — or as few — high-resolution images of artworks as it chooses. At some point some museum somewhere is going to tackle the Picasso rights problem.

In the meantime the grand potential of the project and of its collaborative structure is fully evident in the new version. In all, it ranges through several millenniums of art history and also across actual space in ways that boggle the mind, and it ushers in a new era of interconnected access both to world art and among the institutions that preserve it. It is light-years beyond the first version, which had its debut early last year and featured 17 participating museums from Europe and the United States and a selection of just over 1,000 works in a single medium — painting — that represented but a few centuries of Western art.

At the time the air was thick with wait-and-see caution. Now museums large and small from around the globe have jumped aboard, joining early adopters like the Metropolitan Museum of Art, the Museum of Modern Art, the Gemäldegalerie in Berlin and the National Gallery, London.

Some newcomers are similar in stature and location, including the Kunsthistoriches in Vienna, the Art Institute of Chicago, the National

The Fortune Teller (1630–39), a work by Georges de La Tour that was uploaded by the Metropolitan Museum of Art.

rhetorical situations   genres   processes   strategies   research MLA / APA   media / design   readings

Gallery of Scotland, the Philadelphia Museum of Art, the National Gallery of Art in Washington, the Musée d'Orsay in Paris and the Museum of Fine Arts, Boston.

Others are much further afield in terms of geography or mission. There are major museums from Mexico City, Australia, Japan, India, Taiwan, Austria, and Israel, as well as the new Museum of Islamic Art in Qatar. There are several artist museums, including those dedicated to Edvard Munch (Oslo), Frida Kahlo (Mexico City), Norman Rockwell (Stockbridge, Mass.) and Fernando Botero (Bogotá, Colombia). And there are definite moments of weirdness. The Ayala Museum in Makati, the Philippines, has uploaded 15 images of painted dioramas depicting scenes from Philippine history. The 20-year-old Olympics Museum in Lausanne, Switzerland — the single Swiss participant — is displaying lots of fairly awful statues of athletes.

There seems to be a general consensus that 50 to 250 images of artworks per museum is the appropriate number, but there are some wonderful, slightly insane exceptions. The top contributor is the Yale

Edvard Munch's Separation *(1896), which the Munch Museum in Oslo has placed in the Google Art Project.*

Center for British Art, which has uploaded images of 5,414 paintings, sculptures, prints and drawings by 580 artists — about 10 to 12 percent of its entire collection and everything in the public domain that appears on its own Web site — including scores of works by John Constable and J. M. W. Turner. The J. Paul Getty Museum has come close to the number of works it usually has on view at its two sites in Los Angeles, with 3,325 images of works by 713 artists — including a large and dazzling portion of its photography collection and, for some reason, battalions of small terra cotta oil lamps dating from the first to the fourth centuries.

(Curatorial quirks like these may make you pine for the ability to view works in a museum's collection organized by artist or medium, but that's still not an option. The option to organize by nationality or culture would also be nice.)

The first time around, the dazzlement of the Google Art Project lay especially in its fantastically magnified mega-pixel images of 17 paintings — one from each museum — and gallery views that enabled visitors to take virtual tours. You either zoomed in on magnified surfaces of paintings and brush strokes or zoomed through galleries.

These options still exist (although not all the partners have them yet), but now it is the sheer plethora of images of art objects that dominates, along with the seamless movement among them. You get to the art much faster than on most museum Web sites, and the images start sliding past like butter. You can choose to unspool them in single, double or triple bands, while proceeding collection by collection or filtering according to medium or artist. (Call up, for example, the 42 works by Manet.)

As the cursor glides over an image, its title, date, artist and collection appear beside it. Click and you get a larger image of this work, which you can explore with magnification. Click again, on "details," and you get written information about the piece, which will vary tremendously according to institution (though there is a pervasive avoidance of dimensions). Also a link to the museum itself, which can sometimes lead you to delve beneath the lateral stream of images. 15

rhetorical situations　genres　processes　strategies　research MLA / APA　media / design　readings

At one point in my initial explorations I filtered the artworks according to the medium "silk," and 158 images — including Chinese ink paintings, French tapestries and a ball gown from the House of Worth — popped up. I investigated an embroidered wall hanging from 17th-century China and within three clicks was watching a 14-minute video of curators at the Wilanow Palace Museum in Warsaw discussing (with subtitles) their collection of Asian art and an obsession with the East that began with a Polish king, Jan III Sobieski (1629-96).

Overall the greater number and diversity of participants makes the collective nature of the endeavor much clearer and more exciting. The Google Art Project is a forum for institutional self expression and contrasting artistic values and views of history in which the institutions themselves step out of the picture, at least initially. They make their presences felt not from their own little plots of digital real estate with customized, brand-oriented Web designs but within a single and rather plain format, through bodies of artworks that contrast and can be mingled with other bodies of artworks. It is similar to what happens in the human mind.

That these bodies of work tell us as much about the museums' attitudes toward the Google Art Project, as they do about the history of art, is to be expected. Clearly, some of these institutions are not yet committed to the idea of sharing what they have with the world through this new platform; and of course the fact that it's part of the Google empire would give any thinking curator pause. Still, the Google Art Project looks like a big wave of the future. Resistance may be futile, and even now ambivalent participation seems unbecoming.

For example the Museum of Modern Art's contribution — which jumps from 22 Post-Impressionist works, including van Gogh's *Starry Night,* to 86 works dating from the early 1980s forward — seems almost shabby in its omissions. And the Tate Modern in London has uploaded no artworks at all: it offers a barren, museum-view tour of the empty Turbine Hall that virtually sniffs: If you want to see our stuff, visit our site. You want to say: No thanks, I'm busy. I'm swimming in art here, with no end in sight.

Engaging with the Text

169 ▲

1. How does Roberta Smith achieve a **BALANCED AND FAIR ASSESSMENT** of the *Google Art Project*? Identify four sentences that offer evidence of her balanced evaluation.

2. Click on the hypertext links in the evaluation. Where do they take you, and why do you think Smith linked to those specific sites? What do they have in common? How do they differ? How does Smith use the strategy of **COMPARISON** with regard to the links?

348–55 ◆

3. Click on the link for the *Google Art Project* and spend some time browsing that site. What is your favorite museum catalogued on the site? Identify at least one piece of art on the site that you find interesting. Click on the artwork and then on the Details link for it; jot down the information that is provided.

5–8 ■

4. Who is the intended **AUDIENCE** for this evaluation? Where in the text is the nature of the intended audience most evident?

164–72 ▲
169

5. *For Writing.* Locate a website that you find particularly good or particularly bad and write an **EVALUATION** of it. Be sure to provide a **BALANCED AND FAIR ASSESSMENT,** for no site is all good or all bad. Include a screen shot of the site's homepage, a link to the site and guidance for navigating it, and links to other sites that offer good comparison and contrast to support your evaluation.

Memoirs 62

DAVID SEDARIS

Us and Them

Humorist David Sedaris is the author of several collections of personal essays, and stories, including Me Talk Pretty One Day *(2000),* When You Are Engulfed in Flames *(2008), and* Squirrel Seeks Chipmunk: A Modest Bestiary *(2010). He is a frequent commentator on National Public Radio and a playwright whose works include* SantaLand Diaries & Seasons Greetings: 2 Plays *(1998), as well as works coauthored with his sister, Amy Sedaris. The following essay comes from Sedaris's book-length memoir* Dress Your Family in Corduroy and Denim.

WHEN MY FAMILY FIRST MOVED to North Carolina, we lived in a rented house three blocks from the school where I would begin the third grade. My mother made friends with one of the neighbors, but one seemed enough for her. Within a year we would move again and, as she explained, there wasn't much point in getting too close to people we would have to say good-bye to. Our next house was less than a mile away, and the short journey would hardly merit tears or even good-byes, for that matter. It was more of a "see you later" situation, but still I adopted my mother's attitude, as it allowed me to pretend that not making friends was a conscious choice. I could if I wanted to. It just wasn't the right time.

Back in New York State, we had lived in the country, with no sidewalks or streetlights; you could leave the house and still be alone. But here, when you looked out the window, you saw other houses, and people inside those houses. I hoped that in walking around after dark I might witness a murder, but for the most part our neighbors just sat in their living rooms, watching TV. The only place that seemed truly different was owned by a man named Mr. Tomkey, who did not believe in television. This was told to us by our mother's friend, who dropped by one afternoon with a basketful of okra. The woman did not editorialize — rather, she just presented her information, leaving her listener to make of it what she might. Had my mother said, "That's the craziest thing I've ever heard in my life," I assume that the friend would have agreed, and had she said, "Three cheers for Mr. Tomkey," the friend likely would have agreed as well. It was a kind of test, as was the okra.

To say that you did not believe in television was different from saying that you did not care for it. Belief implied that television had a master plan and that you were against it. It also suggested that you thought too much. When my mother reported that Mr. Tomkey did not believe in television, my father said, "Well, good for him. I don't know that I believe in it, either."

"That's exactly how I feel," my mother said, and then my parents watched the news, and whatever came on after the news.

Word spread that Mr. Tomkey did not own a television, and you began 5 hearing that while this was all very well and good, it was unfair of him to inflict his beliefs upon others, specifically his innocent wife and children. It was speculated that just as the blind man develops a keener sense of hearing, the family must somehow compensate for their loss. "Maybe they read," my mother's friend said. "Maybe they listen to the radio, but you can bet your boots they're doing *something*."

I wanted to know what this something was, and so I began peering through the Tomkeys' windows. During the day I'd stand across the street from their house, acting as though I were waiting for someone, and at night, when the view was better and I had less chance of being discovered, I would creep into their yard and hide in the bushes beside their fence.

Because they had no TV, the Tomkeys were forced to talk during dinner. They had no idea how puny their lives were, and so they were not ashamed that a camera would have found them uninteresting. They did not know what attractive was or what dinner was supposed to look like or even what time people were supposed to eat. Sometimes they wouldn't sit down until eight o'clock, long after everyone else had finished doing the dishes. During the meal, Mr. Tomkey would occasionally pound the table and point at his children with a fork, but the moment he finished, everyone would start laughing. I got the idea that he was imitating someone else, and wondered if he spied on us while we were eating.

When fall arrived and school began, I saw the Tomkey children marching up the hill with paper sacks in their hands. The son was one grade lower than me, and the daughter was one grade higher. We never spoke, but I'd pass them in the halls from time to time and attempt to view the world through their eyes. What must it be like to be so ignorant and alone? Could a normal person even imagine it? Staring at an Elmer Fudd lunch box, I tried to divorce myself from everything I already knew: Elmer's inability to pronounce the letter *r*, his constant pursuit of an intelligent and considerably more famous rabbit. I tried to think of him as just a drawing, but it was impossible to separate him from his celebrity.

One day in class a boy named William began to write the wrong answer on the blackboard, and our teacher flailed her arms, saying, "Warning, Will. Danger, danger." Her voice was synthetic and void of emotion, and we laughed, knowing that she was imitating the robot in a weekly show about a family who lived in outer space. The Tomkeys, though, would have thought she was having a heart attack. It occurred to me that they needed a guide, someone who could accompany them through the course of an average day and point out all the things they were unable to understand. I could have done it on weekends, but friendship would have taken away their mystery and interfered with the good feeling I got from pitying them. So I kept my distance.

In early October the Tomkeys bought a boat, and everyone seemed greatly relieved, especially my mother's friend, who noted that the motor was definitely secondhand. It was reported that Mr. Tomkey's father-in-law owned a house on the lake and had invited the family to use it whenever they liked. This explained why they were gone all weekend, but it did not make their absences any easier to bear. I felt as if my favorite show had been canceled. 10

Halloween fell on a Saturday that year, and by the time my mother took us to the store, all the good costumes were gone. My sisters dressed as witches and I went as a hobo. I'd looked forward to going in disguise to the Tomkey's door, but they were off at the lake, and their house was dark. Before leaving, they had left a coffee can full of gumdrops on the

front porch, alongside a sign reading DON'T BE GREEDY. In terms of Halloween candy, individual gumdrops were just about as low as you could get. This was evidenced by the large number of them floating in an adjacent dog bowl. It was disgusting to think that this was what a gumdrop might look like in your stomach, and it was insulting to be told not to take too much of something you didn't really want in the first place. "Who do these Tomkeys think they are?" my sister Lisa said.

The night after Halloween, we were sitting around watching TV when the doorbell rang. Visitors were infrequent at our house, so while my father stayed behind, my mother, sisters, and I ran downstairs in a group, opening the door to discover the entire Tomkey family on our front stoop. The parents looked as they always had, but the son and daughter were dressed in costumes — she as a ballerina and he as some kind of a rodent with terry-cloth ears and a tail made from what looked to be an extension cord. It seemed they had spent the previous evening isolated at the lake and had missed the opportunity to observe Halloween. "So, well, I guess we're trick-or-treating *now,* if that's okay," Mr. Tomkey said.

I attributed their behavior to the fact that they didn't have a TV, but television didn't teach you everything. Asking for candy on Halloween was called trick-or-treating, but asking for candy on November first was called begging, and it made people uncomfortable. This was one of the things you were supposed to learn simply by being alive, and it angered me that the Tomkeys did not understand it.

"Why of course it's not too late," my mother said. "Kids, why don't you . . . run and get . . . the candy."

"But the candy is gone," my sister Gretchen said. "You gave it away last night."   15

"Not *that* candy," my mother said. "The other candy. Why don't you run and go get it?"

"You mean *our* candy?" Lisa said. "The candy that we *earned?*"

This was exactly what our mother was talking about, but she didn't want to say this in front of the Tomkeys. In order to spare their feelings, she wanted them to believe that we always kept a bucket of candy lying around the house, just waiting for someone to knock on the door and ask for it. "Go on, now," she said. "Hurry up."

My room was situated right off the foyer, and if the Tomkeys had looked in that direction, they could have seen my bed and the brown paper bag marked MY CANDY. KEEP OUT. I didn't want them to know how much I had, and so I went into my room and shut the door behind me. Then I closed the curtains and emptied my bag onto the bed, searching for whatever was the crummiest. All my life chocolate has made me ill. I don't know if I'm allergic or what, but even the smallest amount leaves me with a blinding headache. Eventually, I learned to stay away from it, but as a child I refused to be left out. The brownies were eaten, and when the pounding began I would blame the grape juice or my mother's cigarette smoke or the tightness of my glasses — anything but the chocolate. My candy bars were poison but they were brand-name, and so I put them in pile no. 1, which definitely would not go to the Tomkeys.

Out in the hallway I could hear my mother straining for something to talk about. "A boat!" she said. "That sounds marvelous. Can you just drive it right into the water?"   20

"Actually, we have a trailer," Mr. Tomkey said. "So what we do is back it into the lake."

"Oh, a trailer. What kind is it?"

"Well, it's a *boat* trailer," Mr. Tomkey said.

"Right, but is it wooden, or you know . . . I guess what I'm asking is what *style* trailer do you have?"

Behind my mother's words were two messages. The first and most obvious was "Yes, I am talking about boat trailers, but also I am dying."   25
The second, meant only for my sisters and me, was "If you do not immediately step forward with that candy, you will never again experience freedom, happiness, or the possibility of my warm embrace."

I knew that it was just a matter of time before she came into my room and started collecting the candy herself, grabbing indiscriminately, with no regard to my rating system. Had I been thinking straight, I would have hidden the most valuable items in my dresser drawer, but instead, panicked by the thought of her hand on my doorknob, I tore off the wrappers and began cramming the candy bars into my mouth, desperately, like someone in a contest. Most were miniature, which made them easier to accommodate, but still there was only so much room, and it

rhetorical situations

genres

processes

strategies

research
MLA / APA

media / design

readings

was hard to chew and fit more in at the same time. The headache began immediately, and I chalked it up to tension.

My mother told the Tomkeys she needed to check on something, and then she opened the door and stuck her head inside my room. "What the *hell* are you doing?" she whispered, but my mouth was too full to answer. "I'll just be a moment," she called, and as she closed the door behind her and moved toward my bed, I began breaking the wax lips and candy necklaces pulled from pile no. 2. These were the second-best things I had received, and while it hurt to destroy them, it would have hurt even more to give them away. I had just started to mutilate a miniature box of Red Hots when my mother pried them from my hands, accidentally finishing the job for me. BB-size pellets clattered onto the floor, and as I followed them with my eyes, she snatched up a roll of Necco wafers.

"Not those," I pleaded, but rather than words, my mouth expelled chocolate, chewed chocolate, which fell onto the sleeve of her sweater. "Not those. Not those."

She shook her arm, and the mound of chocolate dropped like a horrible turd upon my bedspread. "You should look at yourself," she said. "I mean, *really* look at yourself."

Along with the Necco wafers she took several Tootsie pops and half a dozen caramels wrapped in cellophane. I heard her apologize to the Tomkeys for her absence, and then I heard my candy hitting the bottom of their bags. 30

"What do you say?" Mrs. Tomkey asked.

And the children answered, "Thank you."

While I was in trouble for not bringing my candy sooner, my sisters were in more trouble for not bringing theirs at all. We spent the early part of the evening in our rooms, then one by one we eased our way back upstairs, and joined our parents in front of the TV. I was the last to arrive, and took a seat on the floor beside the sofa. The show was a Western, and even if my head had not been throbbing, I doubt I would have had the wherewithal to follow it. A posse of outlaws crested a rocky hilltop, squinting at a flurry of dust advancing from the horizon, and I thought again of the Tomkeys and of how alone and out of place they had looked in their dopey costumes. "What was up with that kid's tail?" I asked.

"Shhhh," my family said.

For months I had protected and watched over these people, but now, with one stupid act, they had turned my pity into something hard and ugly. The shift wasn't gradual, but immediate, and it provoked an uncomfortable feeling of loss. We hadn't been friends, the Tomkeys and I, but still I had given them the gift of my curiosity. Wondering about the Tomkey family had made me feel generous, but now I would have to shift gears and find pleasure in hating them. The only alternative was to do as my mother had instructed and take a good look at myself. This was an old trick, designed to turn one's hatred inward, and while I was determined not to fall for it, it was hard to shake the mental picture snapped by her suggestion: here is a boy sitting on a bed, his mouth smeared with chocolate. He's a human being, but also he's a pig, surrounded by trash and gorging himself so that others may be denied. Were this the only image in the world, you'd be forced to give it your full attention, but fortunately there were others. This stagecoach, for instance, coming round the bend with a cargo of gold. This shiny new Mustang convertible. This teenage girl, her hair a beautiful mane, sipping Pepsi through a straw, one picture after another, on and on until the news, and whatever came on after the news.

Engaging with the Text

312–13 ◆   1. David Sedaris **TITLES** his essay "Us and Them." Whom does this title refer to? With whom are we meant to sympathize — "us" or "them"? How do you know?

187 ▲   2. Successful memoirs tell a **GOOD STORY**. Do you think "Us and Them" meets that requirement? Why or why not? Refer to the text in your response.

rhetorical situations   genres   processes   strategies   research MLA / APA   media / design   readings

3. Sedaris describes two handwritten signs from Halloween night. The first is attached to a "coffee can full of gumdrops" telling trick or treaters "DON'T BE GREEDY." The second graces young Sedaris's bag of candy: "MY CANDY. KEEP OUT." What significance do these two signs have in the story? What do they tell us about Sedaris?

4. How would you characterize Sedaris's **STANCE?** What specific passages indicate his attitude about the events he recalls?

12–15

5. *For Writing.* Recall a time when a person or event taught you something about yourself, something that perhaps you could not fully understand until now. Write a **MEMOIR** that describes the person or narrates the event. Include **VIVID DETAIL** and be sure to make clear what **SIGNIFICANCE** the person or event had in your life.

183–90
187–88

JUDITH ORTIZ COFER

The Myth of the Latin Woman

Judith Ortiz Cofer is the Regents' and Franklin Professor of English and Creative Writing at the University of Georgia. She is a prolific writer, known as a poet, a short-story writer, a novelist, an essayist, and an autobiographer. Her works, some intended for a young-adult audience, include the novels The Meaning of Consuelo *(2003) and* If I Could Fly *(2011), the books of poems* Terms of Survival *(1987) and* Reaching for the Mainland *(1995), and the bilingual picture book* ¡A Bailar! Let's Dance! *(2011), to name just a few of her many book-length publications. The following essay comes from her memoir* The Latin Deli: Prose and Poetry *(1993).*

ON A BUS TRIP TO LONDON FROM OXFORD UNIVERSITY where I was earning some graduate credits one summer, a young man, obviously fresh from a pub, spotted me and as if struck by inspiration went down on his knees in the aisle. With both hands over his heart he broke into an Irish tenor's rendition of "María" from *West Side Story*. My politely amused fellow passengers gave his lovely voice the round of gentle applause it deserved. Though I was not quite as amused, I managed my version of an English smile: no show of teeth, no extreme contortions of the facial muscles — I was at this time of my life practicing reserve and cool. Oh, that British control, how I coveted it. But María had followed me to London, reminding me of a prime fact of my life: you can leave the Island, master the English language, and travel as far as you can, but if you are a Latina, especially one like me who so obviously belongs to Rita Moreno's gene pool, the Island travels with you.

This is sometimes a very good thing — it may win you that extra minute of someone's attention. But with some people, the same things can make you an island — not so much a tropical paradise as an Alcatraz, a place nobody wants to visit. As a Puerto Rican girl growing up in the United States and wanting like most children to "belong," I resented the stereotype that my Hispanic appearance called forth from many people I met.

rhetorical situations

genres

processes

strategies

research MLA / APA

media / design

readings

Our family lived in a large urban center in New Jersey during the sixties, where life was designed as a microcosm of my parents' casas on the island. We spoke in Spanish, we ate Puerto Rican food bought at the bodega, and we practiced strict Catholicism complete with Saturday confession and Sunday mass at a church where our parents were accommodated into a one-hour Spanish mass slot, performed by a Chinese priest trained as a missionary for Latin America.

As a girl I was kept under strict surveillance, since virtue and modesty were, by cultural equation, the same as family honor. As a teenager I was instructed on how to behave as a proper señorita. But it was a conflicting message girls got, since the Puerto Rican mothers also encouraged their daughters to look and act like women and to dress in clothes our Anglo friends and their mothers found too "mature" for our age. It was, and is, cultural, yet I often felt humiliated when I appeared at an American friend's party wearing a dress more suitable to a semi-formal than to a playroom birthday celebration. At Puerto Rican festivities, neither the music nor the colors we wore could be too loud. I still experience a vague sense of letdown when I'm invited to a "party" and it turns out to be a marathon conversation in hushed tones rather than a fiesta with salsa, laughter, and dancing — the kind of celebration I remember from my childhood.

I remember Career Day in our high school, when teachers told us 5 to come dressed as if for a job interview. It quickly became obvious that to the barrio girls, "dressing up" sometimes meant wearing ornate jewelry and clothing that would be more appropriate (by mainstream standards) for the company Christmas party than as daily office attire. That morning I had agonized in front of my closet, trying to figure out what a "career girl" would wear because, essentially, except for Marlo Thomas on TV, I had no models on which to base my decision. I knew how to dress for school: at the Catholic school I attended we all wore uniforms; I knew how to dress for Sunday mass, and I knew what dresses to wear for parties at my relatives' homes. Though I do not recall the precise details of my Career Day outfit, it must have been a composite of the above choices. But I remember a comment my friend (an Italian-American) made in later years that coalesced my impressions of that day. She said that at the business school she was attending the Puerto Rican girls always stood out for wearing "everything at once." She meant, of course, too much jewelry, too many accessories. On that day at school, we were simply made the negative models by the nuns who were themselves not credible fashion experts to any of us. But it was painfully obvious to me that to the others, in their tailored skirts and silk blouses, we must have seemed "hopeless" and "vulgar." Though I now know that most adolescents feel out of step much of the time, I also know that for the Puerto Rican girls of my generation that sense was intensified. The way our teachers and classmates looked at us that day in school was just a taste of the culture clash that awaited us in the real world, where prospective employers and men on the street would often misinterpret our tight skirts and jingling bracelets as a come-on.

Mixed cultural signals have perpetuated certain stereotypes—for example, that of the Hispanic woman as the "Hot Tamale" or sexual firebrand. It is a one-dimensional view that the media have found easy to promote. In their special vocabulary, advertisers have designated "sizzling" and "smoldering" as the adjectives of choice for describing not only the foods but also the women of Latin America. From conversations in my house I recall hearing about the harassment that Puerto Rican women endured in factories where the "boss men" talked to them as if sexual innuendo was all they understood and, worse, often gave them the choice of submitting to advances or being fired.

It is custom, however, not chromosomes, that leads us to choose scarlet over pale pink. As young girls, we were influenced in our decisions about clothes and colors by the women — older sisters and mothers who had grown up on a tropical island where the natural environment was a riot of primary colors, where showing your skin was one way to keep cool as well as to look sexy. Most important of all, on the island, women perhaps felt freer to dress and move more provocatively, since, in most cases, they were protected by the traditions, mores, and laws of a Spanish/Catholic system of morality and machismo whose main rule was: *You may look at my sister, but if you touch her I will kill you.* The extended family and church structure could provide a young woman with a circle of safety in her small pueblo on the island; if a man "wronged" a girl, everyone would close in to save her family honor.

This is what I have gleaned from my discussions as an adult with older Puerto Rican women. They have told me about dressing in their best party clothes on Saturday nights and going to the town's plaza to promenade with their girlfriends in front of the boys they liked. The males were thus given an opportunity to admire the women and to express their admiration in the form of *piropos*: erotically charged street poems they composed on the spot. I have been subjected to a few piropos while visiting the Island, and they can be outrageous, although custom dictates that they must never cross into obscenity. This ritual, as I understand it, also entails a show of studied indifference on the woman's part; if she is "decent," she must not acknowledge the man's impassioned words. So I do understand how things can be lost in translation. When a Puerto Rican girl dressed in her idea of what is attractive meets a man from the mainstream culture who has been trained to react to certain types of clothing as a sexual signal, a clash is likely to take place. The line I first heard based on this aspect of the myth happened when the boy who took me to my first formal dance leaned over to plant a sloppy overeager kiss painfully on my mouth, and when I didn't respond with sufficient passion said in a resentful tone: "I thought you Latin girls were supposed to mature early" — my first instance of being thought of as a fruit or vegetable — I was supposed to *ripen*, not just grow into Womanhood like other girls.

It is surprising to some of my professional friends that some people, including those who should know better, still put others "in their place." Though rarer, these incidents are still commonplace in my life. It happened to me most recently during a stay at a very classy metropolitan hotel favored by young professional couples for their weddings. Late one evening after the theater, as I walked toward my room with my new colleague (a woman with whom I was coordinating an arts program), a middle-aged man in a tuxedo, a young girl in satin and lace on his arm, stepped directly into our path. With his champagne glass extended toward me, he exclaimed, "Evita!"

Our way blocked, my companion and I listened as the man half- 10 recited, half-bellowed "Don't Cry for Me, Argentina." When he finished, the young girl said: "How about a round of applause for my daddy?" We complied, hoping this would bring the silly spectacle to a close. I was becoming aware that our little group was attracting the attention of the other guests. "Daddy" must have perceived this too, and he once more barred the way as we tried to walk past him. He began to shout-sing a ditty to the tune of "La Bamba" — except the lyrics were about a girl named María whose exploits all rhymed with her name and gonorrhea. The girl kept saying "Oh, Daddy" and looking at me with pleading eyes. She wanted me to laugh along with the others. My companion and I stood silently waiting for the man to end his offensive song. When he finished, I looked not at him but at his daughter. I advised her calmly never to ask her father what he had done in the army. Then I walked between them and to my room. My friend complimented me on my cool handling of the situation. I confessed to her that I really had wanted to push the jerk into the swimming pool. I knew that this same man — probably a corporate executive, well educated, even worldly by most standards — would not have been likely to regale a white woman with a dirty song in public. He would perhaps have checked his impulse by assuming that she could be somebody's wife or mother, or at least *some-body* who might take offense. But to him, I was just an Evita or a María: merely a character in his cartoon-populated universe.

Because of my education and my proficiency with the English language, I have acquired many mechanisms for dealing with the anger I experience. This was not true for my parents, nor is it true for the many Latin women working at menial jobs who must put up with stereotypes about our ethnic group such as: "They make good domestics." This is another facet of the myth of the Latin woman in the United States. Its origin is simple to deduce. Work as domestics, waitressing, and factory jobs are all that's available to women with little English and few skills. The myth of the Hispanic menial has been sustained by the same media phenomenon that made "Mammy" from *Gone with the Wind* America's idea of the black woman for generations; María, the housemaid or counter girl, is now indelibly etched into the national psyche. The big and the little screens have presented us with the picture of the funny Hispanic maid, mispronouncing words and cooking up a spicy storm in a shiny California kitchen.

This media-engendered image of the Latina in the United States has been documented by feminist Hispanic scholars, who claim that such portrayals are partially responsible for the denial of opportunities for upward mobility among Latinas in the professions. I have a Chicana friend working on a Ph.D. in philosophy at a major university. She says her doctor still shakes his head in puzzled amazement at all the "big words" she uses. Since I do not wear my diplomas around my neck for all to see, I too have on occasion been sent to that "kitchen," where some think I obviously belong.

One such incident that has stayed with me, though I recognize it as a minor offense, happened on the day of my first public poetry reading. It took place in Miami in a boat-restaurant where we were having lunch before the event. I was nervous and excited as I walked in with my notebook in my hand. An older woman motioned me to her table. Thinking (foolish me) that she wanted me to autograph a copy of my brand new slender volume of verse, I went over. She ordered a cup of coffee from me, assuming that I was the waitress. Easy enough to mistake my poems for menus, I suppose. I know that it wasn't an intentional act of cruelty, yet of all the good things that happened that day, I remember that scene most clearly, because it reminded me of what I had to overcome before anyone would take me seriously. In retrospect I understand that my anger gave my reading fire, that I have almost always taken doubts in my abilities as a challenge — and that the result is, most times, a feeling of satisfaction at having won a convert when I see the cold, appraising eyes warm to my words, the body language change, the smile that indicates that I have opened some avenue for communication. That day I read to that woman and her lowered eyes told me that she was embarrassed at her little faux pas, and when I willed her to look up at me, it was my victory, and she graciously allowed me to punish her with my full attention. We shook hands at the end of the reading, and I never saw her again. She has probably forgotten the whole thing but maybe not.

Yet I am one of the lucky ones. My parents made it possible for me to acquire a stronger footing in the mainstream culture by giving me the chance at an education. And books and art have saved me from the harsher forms of ethnic and racial prejudice that many of my Hispanic *compañeras* have had to endure. I travel a lot around the United States, reading from my books of poetry and my novel, and the reception I most often receive is one of positive interest by people who want to know more about my culture. There are, however, thousands of Latinas without the privilege of an education or the entree into society that I have. For them life is a struggle against the misconceptions perpetuated by the myth of the Latina as whore, domestic, or criminal. We cannot change this by legislating the way people look at us. The transformation, as I see it, has to occur at a much more individual level. My personal goal in my public life is to try to replace the old pervasive stereotypes and myths about Latinas with a much more interesting set of realities. Every time I give a reading, I hope the stories I tell, the dreams and fears I examine in my work, can achieve some universal truth which will get my audience past the particulars of my skin color, my accent, or my clothes.

I once wrote a poem in which I called us Latinas "God's brown   15
daughters." This poem is really a prayer of sorts, offered upward, but also, through the human-to-human channel of art, outward. It is a prayer for communication, and for respect. In it, Latin women pray "in Spanish to an Anglo God / with a Jewish heritage," and they are "fervently hoping / that if not omnipotent / at least He be bilingual."

Engaging with the Text

187
313–15

1. A strong memoir includes **VIVID DETAILS** to bring the past back to life. How do the details Judith Ortiz Cofer includes support her **THESIS?** Identify two of these details and explain how they help her make her case that Latinas are poorly understood and grossly stereotyped.

306–10

2. How does Cofer **END** her essay? What is the significance of the ending?

3–4

3. What is the **PURPOSE** of this memoir? What do you think Cofer hopes it to achieve? Where in the essay does she make that hope explicit?

rhetorical situations   genres   processes   strategies   research MLA / APA   media / design   readings

4. Cofer explains that the way Puerto Rican women dress in Puerto Rico is "read" very differently by other people than when they dress in the same way elsewhere in the United States. What is the difference between the two responses? What does she say to explain why in one place the young women are respected and revered and in the other are disrespected and treated rudely? What role do you think dress should play in how people read other people?

5. *For Writing.* Think about the way you dress. What image are you trying to create through your clothing and accessories? How do others *read* your image? Do they read it in ways you mean it to be read or in other ways that go against your intentions? Write a **MEMOIR,** one that reflects on both the past and the present, that addresses these questions.

▲ 183–90

ILIANA ROMAN

First Job

Iliana Roman is the mother of three children and owner of a hair salon. Her road to that end was long and winding. At seventeen, she became pregnant and dropped out of high school. She held several jobs — at a sporting goods store, an electronics store, and a car dealership — while studying to attain her GED, taking business classes at a community college, and enrolling in cosmetology school. Today she is a successful salon owner with several employees. Roman says her father served as her inspiration to work hard at something she loved. When he helped her buy her salon, she promised him that she "would do this right." She explained, "When I was younger and left school, that was very irresponsible of me. But I wised up; I don't want to mess up in life again." This essay first appeared in the edited collection Help Wanted: Tales from the First Job Front *(2000).*

MY PARENTS HAVE PROPERTY IN PUERTO RICO, but I was raised here in the States. They took me back and forth so I know both languages. When she was younger, my mom worked, but once she had children she became a homemaker. My dad's worked for the Park District for years; he's a head attendant for the parks now. He also works on cars — that's his hobby. He loves work, he *has* to work, he's not a person to sit at home and let life waste.

In high school, I got pregnant. I wish I'd have finished school before having kids. I was seventeen when I had my first boy, nineteen the second, and twenty-one my daughter. I lived with my boyfriend — we weren't legally married, but we were like married. I had everything you could want: a house, everything brand-new. I wanted to go back to school, but my boyfriend stopped working so I had to work and take care of the kids.

I was about to get married, but when I saw that my boyfriend was changing, I broke the engagement. He started drinking. I didn't want

the children to see that. My father raised me with good values, so I said to my boyfriend, "You gotta go your way, I gotta go my way." My dad said, "Come back home." Thank God for him! It was the best thing I ever did, because it helped me accomplish everything I wanted to accomplish.

I was twenty-five when I left my boyfriend. I finally got my GED and went to community college to study business. My children motivate me. You can always do better in life, and I'm always one to do better, better, better.

I started working at Sportmart when I was eighteen, and I worked 5 there for eight years. I started as a regular cashier and was promoted to an assistant, and then from there I took off. They gave me decent raises, too. I worked with the computers, I did payroll, and I took care of customer complaints. When I left, I was a cash-control manager. I did finances, daily cash, balanced their books. I'm good at numbers.

They hesitated with me because I was so young. But I always wanted to learn more and more and more. I talked them into teaching me things; I proved myself. I showed them I was serious, convinced them to give me more responsibility. I was motivated, and my work performance was excellent. I've always been dedicated to my work, whatever it is. I've always loved coming in early. I've always been cool and calm, and known what to say and what not to say.

It was a good company to work for because I learned a skill, and they encouraged me. Payroll, computers — I did not know anything about either of those. I didn't know how to balance books. I learned all of that on the job. I think if you set your mind to learn something you'll learn it; there's no stopping you. Basically, I knew how to treat people, I knew how to relate to people. That's something I was taught at home, how to consider people. That was what I had when I started.

I loved that job so much — I loved the people I worked with, I loved the company. I quit because I wanted to go back to school, and I also had to take care of my kids. The manager was a total jerk about it; he was like an obstacle. I wanted to work fewer hours, but I could have still done the job. All I was asking was to leave work early. He didn't want that; he was mad about that. I think he liked me but I didn't like him in the same way, so he was punishing me. As much as I loved working there, I wanted the education *more*. I didn't want to stay there forever; there's more in the world than just one place.

But it was a big decision to leave that job. I cried. But we all have to do what we have to do in life. I got another job at an electronics store, at Circuit City, doing basically the same thing as at the sporting goods store. They knew my skills and they wanted me to work, work, work. I was working full-time, long hours, and I started slacking off in school. I had to drop out. It was like the end of the world, like I was incomplete.

After that, I worked at a car dealership to get the experience. It was   10 like a little challenge for me. I didn't see women selling cars and I thought a woman *could* do it — and sure enough, I did it! They had fantastic sales managers at the dealership and they taught me. It was interesting. Consumers aren't educated; they have no knowledge of the car industry. People are indecisive about what they want. They have an idea, but you have to convince them of what is right for them. OK, they want a Caravan and they don't know which one to get, the Chevy or the Dodge. You have to sell *yourself* a little bit, in order for them to believe you. And you have to know the differences between cars, between competitors.

It worked out. But when they saw I was getting good at it, they wanted more hours from me. And at the time I'd started cosmetology school. I quit in order to finish my cosmetology certificate — you have to put in hundreds of hours. I got my license last March. Since I was twelve years old, I've loved that beauty, glamor-girl stuff, and I wanted to learn about it. We learned on mannequins and then on clients.

When we do chemicals, like for coloring hair, I'm very careful about what I'm doing because it's a big responsibility. We learned a lot of science. We deal with strong chemicals, so we had to study anatomy — you can actually damage someone's scalp if you don't follow instructions. We had to learn about the functioning of the body, circulation, and the muscles in the face.

I grew up watching my aunts — they're cosmetologists. One of them started in cosmetology school, but she never finished. I said, "If I'm going to do that, I'm going to *finish*." So that's something I was proud of,

because I *did* it, thanks to my father and mother, of course, because they helped so much. Sometimes we don't appreciate the kind of support we have and that's wrong. If I'd listened to them about school in the first place, I could have done this years ago. I could have done who *knows* what!

When I finished cosmetology school, I didn't want to work for anybody. I felt in my heart that I was ready to have my own business. I was always one to have my hair and nails nice, so that part's easy. And I also have this knowledge from the sporting goods store about managing money. My dad was there for me; he helped me. He told me, "If you take it seriously and finish cosmetology school, I will buy you your own salon."

There was a hair salon a few blocks from where we lived, and the 15 owner was ill and needed to sell the business. I was born and raised in this neighborhood, and I know the area's getting better. I thought it would be a good place to be, a good investment. We bought it and remodeled — my father did a lot of the work. The remodeling wasn't very expensive at all because my family helped. They broke down walls and they painted. So *much* was given to me. It was an old-fashioned salon. We went from Pepto-Bismol pink to a more art-deco look. It was slow, but I got things how I wanted.

The clients from before were older. Some still come, but not as many. I don't know if they feel they've been pushed out, but to me they are always welcome — I don't neglect anybody. But I have a bigger clientele now; I made it more profitable. People saw the salon looking more modern, so now there are younger people, more my age. I see people with money coming to the neighborhood. You'd think they would change the environment, be all mean, but I don't notice anything like that — they're easy to get along with. I have lawyers, doctors, police officers, business people, professional people.

When I was ready to hire a staff, I got in touch with friends from the cosmetology school. I've learned that sometimes friends and business don't mix. I hired two friends, and they took advantage of me — they thought they could get away with things. They would smoke and not clean up after themselves. They tried to make their *own* schedule;

they'd be on the phone all the time. To them it was like I was not a boss; I was their friend. Like this is easy money; it is *not* easy money, it's a responsibility.

They would come in an hour or two late and I'd say, "You can't do that. This is a job. In order to have this place run, you have to be on time." I had several appointments for one girl and she called me ten minutes from her starting time and said, "I'm going to be late." I said, "What do you mean? I have clients waiting for you and I'm supposed to be doing other things. How can you do this to me?!" There are times I've run the whole place by myself because people didn't show up. So those two don't work for me anymore.

The one quit because I was so upset with her. I said, "Fine. I'm still your friend. But remember, I have to run a business." Maybe she took it the wrong way, but I feel I'm still being a friend. It's just that I have to do my job and run this business right. The place doesn't run itself — I run the place.

The other one, she was just terrible. She'd gone to the cosmetology school, but her skills weren't good. I look at it this way: being young, being pretty, being skillful is good in this business. I looked back and thought, "Was it just because she was beautiful that I thought she'd be good?" You have to *be* good, not just *look* good. If someone's not real pretty but knows how to look her best and has skills, I will hire her in a heartbeat. I learned from experience.   20

It's not easy running your own business. I have to budget myself. I think when you first start out, you should be careful and not spend too much money, just work with what you have. If I have extra money, I buy more shampoos and extra chemicals. I'm not one to think let's buy more until the bills are paid, until the rent is paid. It's something we all have to do: make sure the bills are paid.

I've taken all my other work experiences and brought them to this shop. I already knew how to do books and how to present myself and how to treat people. In the sporting goods store, I dealt with people's emotions, their complaints. This is different, but in a way it's the same. I love dealing with clients and customers. Of course, people always have their problems, and sometimes they don't even know why they're arguing

or mad, but you do not go at their level. You compromise — you let them speak their mind.

People's appearance means a lot to them, and also, they're coming to me to relax. A stylist and a psychologist are a little alike. People come to you about their problems too, so you're doing two things at once. Some clients treat you like family. I take care of the client just as well as if I were taking care of myself. That's how I feel. With customers and clients, you're trying to satisfy them in what they want. To me it's easy, 'cause I'm a good listener. Sometimes they just want to let you know how they feel and how stressed out they are. You've got to really observe the person; don't have assumptions about what they might want. I like to study people, watch and understand their reactions.

Like Saturday, one of my clients, she just moved to Chicago from Idaho. She needed her hair fixed because she had a bad haircut. She told my stylist she wanted a certain look, but with the haircut she had, it was impossible. My stylist was confused about how to satisfy her. There was a way to create the *illusion* of what she wanted, but the client didn't understand that. I had to jump in and make her feel comfortable. My stylist is Colombian, so I don't know if the client felt she wasn't skillful because of her accent or what. But I stepped in and calmed the client down. It worked out. When I started explaining what we could do, she felt at ease and let her hair be cut so she could get what she wanted. *And* she ended up getting a manicure and a pedicure.

I have my hair salon, but I want to do something more. I want my salon to run itself so I can study real estate. I want to earn more money. And being a real estate agent, you can work at home, arrange your own time. I know I'm a good salesperson, so if I set my mind to it I think I can do it. People always want to buy homes, but they just don't know which one.

You have to have a positive attitude. Always think you can do it; determine what you want out of life. I've never been afraid to ask questions because I've always wanted to *know* — I've always wanted to learn. Education is the best. Even when you're old and gray, keep learning. Learning does *good* for you. That's something no one can take away from you — no one.

These little girls from the neighborhood come up to me, they think I'm a teenager and they're amazed that I'm a mom. I tell them not to drop out of school. I say, "Yeah, I started young. But if I could do it again, I'd have finished school before becoming a mom." They say, "You went back to school?!" I say, "Yes, and I'm thinking about going back again." They look up to me — I try to set a good example.

I *have* to work. No way could I be a housewife and not work, ever. Women do not have to be at home and just the husband works. If I get married, the man has to accept that I am a businesswoman. But I'm not thinking about marriage. My priorities are my business and my children.

I want my children to see what I saw in my father: work, work, work. I want to be my kids' idol, to take those values from home, like I took them from my dad. I don't want my sons to be deadbeats or to be in gangs — that's a waste in society. So I show them a different way. One of my boys wants to become a veterinarian, the other wants to join the FBI — he wants to do good for society. My daughter wants to become a police officer. My family, we're a minority and we've proved many people wrong — we don't fit their stereotype.

When I first opened I knew this was a serious job, something that   30
I had to devote myself to 100 percent, 110 percent. It's going on five months since I opened, and we're doing real well. I'm still scared, of course, but I don't think you should worry as long as you've done your very best. It takes a lot of energy, but hey . . . my family gives me the energy! I made a promise to my dad that I would do this right. When I was younger and left school, that was very irresponsible of me. But I wised up. I don't want to mess up in life again. He did so much for me. I do not want to let him down.

Engaging with the Text

1. What is the **SIGNIFICANCE** of this memoir to Iliana Roman? How does she make the significance clear? Select a phrase or section from the memoir that shows the significance.
187–88

2. When Roman was selling cars, she learned that "you have to sell *yourself* a little bit, in order for them to believe you. And you have to know the differences between cars, between competitors." How is this lesson relevant to a writer's **STANCE** in an essay? What is Roman's stance in this memoir?
12–15

3. How is this memoir **ORGANIZED?** How effective is the organization?
190

4. How does Roman **BEGIN** her memoir? How is the beginning related to the **ENDING?** How are these effective ways to open and close the memoir?
299–311

5. *For Writing.* Write a **MEMOIR** about a time you made the wrong decision or took the wrong action. Explain the consequences and how they affected your life following the event. What is the effect today? Be sure that you offer a good story about the event and clearly explain the significance of it. Remember that **VIVID DETAILS** give life to a memoir.
183–90
187

ABIGAIL ZUGER

En Route

Abigail Zuger is associate professor of clinical medicine at Columbia University College of Physicians and Surgeons in New York City and senior attending physician at St. Luke's–Roosevelt Hospital Center there, where she is an internist and a specialist in infectious diseases, particularly HIV. Author of the book Strong Shadows: Scenes from an Inner City AIDS Clinic *(1995), she is also a frequent contributing writer to the* New York Times *and other national publications. The following memoir appeared in the anthology* Becoming a Doctor, *edited by Lee Gutkind and published in 2010.*

IT IS A BALMY JULY NIGHT IN NEW YORK CITY, 1981. *The fluorescent lights in the hallway of ward 16E of Bellevue Hospital never dim, but after dinner things slowly settle down. Visitors leave at eight. The nurses change shift at eleven. By midnight, everything is quiet. An intern balancing blood tubes, needles, and syringes on a clipboard heads into a darkened room. The night nurse wheels the medication cart down to the far end of the ward and begins to give out the night meds.*

In a four-bed room way at the far end of the hall, a young woman named Nilda is standing next to her bed looking out the window.

She knows the view well: river, tugboats, and bridge to the left, sunrise over Brooklyn to the right, moonrise over Queens straight ahead. She has been in this room for three weeks now. Two months ago she spent two weeks over on 16W and got to see the sun set beside the Empire State Building. A month before that, it was 16E again, but only for a few days. She had to leave early that time, to go pay her rent.

Her problem never changes. It is fever, always fever. No one can figure out why. She knows the routine now as well as the interns do, and she knows pretty much all the interns now, too. She meets them in rotation night after night, when her fever spikes high and they come in to draw her blood. But the tests for all the various problems heroin addicts can get — endocarditis, hepatitis, cellulitis, pneumonia, blood clots — just keep coming back negative. So, after a few weeks in the hospital she gathers her things together, feeling a little stronger from the regular meals and the bed rest and the forced detox, and goes back home. Back to her apartment, that dump. Back to heroin. Back to fevers, sweats, feeling weak. Then back to Bellevue. This has become her routine. It's not so bad. Sometimes she helps the nurses feed the other patients in her room — three old, old ladies, one Spanish, one black, one Chinese, all asleep, all snoring.

Nilda is waiting for the intern. She was 103.8 at the last temperature check. 5 They always draw blood for culture when she is this hot. That's how they check for endocarditis, an infection in the heart from shooting drugs. By now she must have had blood cultures a hundred times, and they are always negative. They all know she doesn't have endocarditis. But still they draw more blood, the nice ones probing for the few good veins she has left in her hands and arms, the impatient ones just going for the big veins in her groin or her neck. Jerks. But she always lets them. She has no choice. She knows she is sick. She is getting scared. She used to be a big woman, even with the drugs. Now she is a stick. Her old man moved out last month. The city took the kids long ago. She might as well be here as anywhere.

The overhead light in the room snaps on. The old ladies keep snoring.

"Hi," says the intern. Both of them blink in the sudden light. "It's only me."

And indeed, it was only me, three weeks into my internship, midway through a long, sleepless night on call. I was up all night, every third night, those days, zooming around the corridors of Bellevue fueled exclusively by nerves and fear. You couldn't even get a cup of coffee in that place from the time the cafeteria closed at 7 p.m. till 3 a.m., when a truck that peddled snacks pulled into the back parking lot. I had drawn blood from poor Nilda so many times by then that I could navigate her skinny hands and wrists without even looking. Among us all, we had drawn at least forty sets of blood cultures, all negative, and yet my resident made us draw more. We all knew that he had pretty much no idea what to do with Nilda, but he had to do something, of course, and so we kept drawing her blood.

This was now more than twenty-five years ago. In theory, I had been a doctor for about seven weeks. In actuality, I still had quite some time to go. In actuality, I'm still working on it. Sitting at my clinic desk in the mornings, looking at my list of patients for the day, I catch myself thinking, "Good lord, these people need a doctor." Instead, what they have is me, an amphibious creature still in the process of evolving. Sometimes what I am at the moment is exactly what a patient needs. Sometimes the need and the reality are so wildly disparate that catastrophe results. And sometimes, as years pass, we grow into each other, water against stone, a long, slow process.

I don't know that I am particularly backward in my evolutionary progress. I suspect I am right in the middle of the pack. There are some practitioners — you may well have met one or two yourself — who never make it at all. Forget the diploma on the wall: medical school comes and goes far too quickly to have much of an impact. Almost everyone is aware of this fact but medical students, who take themselves and their perceived mission (to memorize every piece of information they will ever have to know) very seriously. In my day we loaded ourselves up with notebooks and index cards; now they use portable computers. Either way, students hoard facts and treatment guidelines like squirrels hoard nuts, hiding them in accessible places against the coming of that long, dark winter between graduation and retirement, during which they assume they will never be able to be uncertain or to ask anyone a question ever again.

Little do they know, poor things, that medical facts have a shelf life just like nuts. Most of them will spoil before they are ever used. New ones will show up unannounced. A study some years ago methodically evaluated the lifespan of a body of medical knowledge and found a half-life of forty-five years. In other words, half of what you learn in medical school is obsolete by the time you are in your sixties (and presumably think you know what you are doing). Nobody is going to tell you which half.

My particular circumstances are even more extreme: I spend my workdays taking care of patients with a disease that did not exist when I was in school. Nothing like AIDS had ever been dreamed of. I graduated

10

and landed in an entirely new world, full of naked, unprocessed facts without journals or textbooks to organize them for us. Nilda baffled us, and so did the dozens and then hundreds of patients who came after her, clogging the system with their dire illnesses and our inability to figure them out. Patients came to the hospital and stayed for weeks and months; if we sent them home, they came right back. The disease had no name back then, let alone any algorithms for thinking its problems through. It stripped doctors of everything that medical school tried to teach them: their facts and their confidence simultaneously. It changed everything.

Sometimes I amuse myself thinking back to two of the attending doctors I met during medical school, who epitomized fairly standard operating modes. Call them Dr. Data and Dr. Confidence. Neither would last a moment in my world.

Dr. Data was a fact man: he had maintained the mind-set of a medical student from graduation onward. He was evidence-based all the way: he practiced as the very latest studies and nomograms told him to. He aimed to provide the best care to all comers, by which he generally meant the same care, validated in large clinical trials, based on scientific evidence.

Dr. Data was a cardiologist. Lean, trim, a runner, he refused to take   15
care of anyone who smoked. He was quite proud of himself for this unusual detail of his practice; he had thought of it all by himself. Sitting in his pleasant consultation room, he would break the news to would-be patients with a certain straight-faced glee. I could have sworn he sent the occasional wink toward the student observing from a corner.

"First things first," he would tell the patient after the initial history and physical exam. "If you smoke, you are just wasting my time. We are just wasting each other's time. Go home, quit smoking, make an appointment to come back. I can't do anything for you if you undo it all with cigarettes. Good to see you." He would stand, shake hands, open the door, and the patient would head out to the great beyond without a peep. I don't know how many of them came back. Should Dr. Data still be in practice, under Medicare's current plans to pay physicians for getting good results and penalize them for getting bad ones he would be in clover.

Were he to be sitting in my chair on a Monday morning, banishing patients from his presence for their array of addictions, bad habits, and human frailties, he would be out of work by Tuesday noon.

Dr. Confidence operated at the opposite end of the spectrum. He made his progress through the hospital abdomen first, bow tie second, starched white coat buttoned from top to bottom, sleeves secured with cufflinks around pudgy wrists. He seemed to know no actual medicine at all. On rounds with Dr. Confidence the usual patterns were reversed: we students were the ones who taught him a thing or two, quoting the newest studies as he nodded appreciatively and made notes on file cards. Not that he ever used the information: his patients kept getting antique tests, old drugs given in weird ways the other attendings had abandoned long ago. Dr. Confidence was a standing joke. We pitied his patients.

Imagine my surprise when an idle conversation at a high school reunion unearthed the incredible fact that one of my friends — sharp, sophisticated, nobody's fool — was one of them. That she had actually sought him out, on the strong recommendation of her aunt, whose life Dr. Confidence had saved. The aunt had been deathly ill with a disease called (here my friend, an English major and science hater, stuttered a little but pressed on) systemic lupus erythematosus. Dr. Confidence had saved her life by treating her with a powerful new drug, prednisone. The whole family saw him now. He was great. They worshipped him.

I just stared at her. Prednisone for lupus. A fourth-grader with a copy of the *Merck* manual would know to give someone prednisone for lupus. That was the drug you gave, and it wasn't new, not by a long shot, not by decades. But Dr. Confidence in all his starched self-assured godlike presence had managed to transform a completely straightforward clinical transaction into an act of personal triumph. 20

I enjoy the image of Dr. Confidence sitting at my desk, white-coated, bow-tied, trying to preserve the illusion of divine omniscience and control with a patient who was diagnosed with AIDS twenty years ago, who was told then that he had eighteen months to live, and who has in the interim made his own survival his life's career. Our patients have no time or tolerance for medical bloviation. They are simply not in the

mood. They have watched the sands shift so wildly, they have defied so many dire, confident predictions, that the only certain way to gain their confidence is to share their uncertainties.

But if neither Dr. Data nor Dr. Confidence would survive in my world, then who does? If a doctor is not to be a scientist or a shaman, what then?

I am certainly not the first to ask this question. One widely quoted answer was voiced by Dr. Francis W. Peabody, an eminent Boston physician who told a class of Harvard students in 1925 that "the secret of the care of the patient is in caring for the patient." Nicely put, but still, what exactly does that mean? Who is the doctor to be, in this caring role? A parent, a friend, a policeman? A guardian angel, an alter ego, a parole officer? There are no prototypes that fit completely, and no rules for creating new ones. There is only trial and error.

My biggest success to date, I think, has been with Audrey, long a supremely difficult patient. She is a small, flamboyant woman, with a gigantic wardrobe of wigs, scarves, dresses, boots, and snakeskin pants. She dresses according to mood, some days as prim and demure as any youngish senior citizen (her records say she is sixty-three, she admits to sixty-seven, but sometimes forgets and gives dates that calculate out to sixty-nine). Other days she is a teenager, and others a movie star. In fact, Audrey started out life as a man, but no one has to know that piece of information. She refuses to discuss it.

Whoever she is on any particular day, Audrey stays in control; that goes for her own behavior, and for everyone else's, too. She takes her AIDS medications precisely, and her infection has been under optimal control for years. She watches her weight. She has a slew of therapists, whom she sees on an as-needed basis. Her cocaine use is episodic — pretty much alternating with her stints in therapy. She does not like to be confined by arbitrary, man-made barriers such as, say, appointment times, and pretty much shows up in my office whenever she feels the need.

There was a time when I would see her name on my list and groan at the prospect of another mentally bruising session with Audrey and her achy knee, her recurrent headaches, her weight loss, her weight gain, her troubled relationships, her difficulty urinating — and no, no examination of her private parts is ever permitted. Audrey was impossible. She knew exactly what she needed, be it antibiotics or nutritional supplements, or migraine medication, or the latest prescription diet drug, or an X-ray of her perfectly normal knee, and battered me till I finally said yes, just to cut my losses and get on to the next patient.

One month a few years ago it all got out of hand. Audrey was in the clinic every day, sometimes twice a day, for every passing twinge. She was anxious, she finally confided. She had a big show coming up. She was in a cabaret class and the final exam was to be a public performance.

It was our clinic nurse who had the great idea. And so, one evening a few weeks later the nurse, the clinic manager, and I forked over a cover charge, ordered our two-drink minimum in a little dark cellar nightclub, and watched Audrey slink up on stage in a sequined gown and croon "Smoke Gets in Your Eyes." She was truly wonderful. She was triumphant. She brought down the house, and we gave her a standing ovation.

From that night on, Audrey has been a changed person with us. She has stopped banging on doors and waits patiently to be seen. She makes and keeps appointments. She tells me she is blessed to have me in her life. She has actually said the following words: "Anything you say, Doctor." Suddenly she is happy to behave like a patient and let me behave like a doctor, all because I once treated her like a person, not a patient. Is that, perhaps, the secret of caring for the patient?

Or is it even simpler than that? Way back in that long-ago July of my internship year, Nilda and I spent an awful lot of time together, for the simple reason that my blood-drawing skills were not, at that point, all they might have been. I knew Nilda's hands and wrists up and down, but I still had terrible trouble getting her blood. Those were the days when I actually dreamed about drawing her blood, I dreaded it so much: I dreaded the pain I inflicted, and the bruises I produced, and the occasional humiliating outcome of having to confess the next morning that I had simply been unable to get it. I never went for the big veins in the

rhetorical situations   genres   processes   strategies   research MLA / APA   media / design   readings

groin or neck like some of the others did because I was far too scared. Instead, I wrapped hot towels around Nilda's poor thin hands and hoped the veins would appear.

One early morning, waiting in Nilda's room for her towel-encased hands to yield a usable vein, I noticed that her covered dinner tray was still lying on the bedside table, untouched. "I hate fish," she said, shrugging. As it happens, I hate fish too. I looked at my watch. It was 3 a.m., just the hour for the life-saving snack truck to be pulling up to the hospital's back door. I was beyond starving. I never ate meals, back then. There was never time.

I ran down to the truck and bought two giant doughnuts and two cups of coffee. We ate and drank side by side, sitting on the edge of Nilda's bed.

That Christmas I got a card from Nilda, addressed to me at the hospital. Shortly thereafter came a phone call from the emergency room of some hospital in Brooklyn, where she had shown up, suddenly blind in one eye. She had told them I was her doctor. After that I never heard from or about her again.

Not infrequently, these days, when I hear my colleagues spinning fulsome phrases about the doctor-patient relationship, or when I think about all the forces that can help a poor frightened intern crawl a few yards out of the primal muck of confusion onto a firmer shore, I wonder if anyone else realizes that sometimes it can all boil down to a doughnut.

Engaging with the Text

1. How does Abigail Zuger **BEGIN** her essay? How effective is this beginning? How else might she have begun her essay?

   ◆ 299–306

2. Zuger **COMPARES AND CONTRASTS** two attending doctors she met while she was in training to become a doctor herself. How does she describe the two doctors? Why does she say "Neither would last a moment in my world"? What does she mean by this statement?

   ◆ 348–55

187–88 ▲

3. What is the **SIGNIFICANCE** of Zuger's memoir of this time in her life? What is the insight we should take away from her essay?

5–8 ■

4. Who is the intended **AUDIENCE** for this memoir? Who would be best suited to hear Zuger's message?

5. *For Writing.* At the heart of this essay is the message that everyone deserves to be treated humanely and with respect. Recall a time when you took part in an event that helped you to realize (even if it is only now that you realize) that all people deserve to be treated this way. Write an essay that narrates the event; describe what happened in detail so your audience gets the message that everyone deserves to be treated humanely.

■ rhetorical situations
▲ genres
○ processes
◆ strategies
● research MLA / APA
□ media / design
▜ readings

SULEIKA JAOUAD

Finding My Cancer Style

Suleika Jaouad, a writer who in her twenties developed a bone-marrow disorder that turned into acute myeloid leukemia (AML), has chronicled her battle with cancer in a New York Times blog, Life, Interrupted, *where this memoir was posted. Jaouad offers advice to those coping with life-threatening diseases in two other online forums as well: on Twitter and on her personal blog,* Secrets of Cancerhood. *Her writing has also appeared on the Huffington Post. To access the online version of this reading, which incorporates a slide show and links to all of* Life, Interrupted, *including videos and Facebook chats, go to* wwnorton.com/ write/fieldguidelinks.

ONE YEAR AGO, ALMOST TO THE DAY, I asked my hairdresser to cut off 16 inches of my hair. It was a pre-emptive strike. A few days later I would be admitted to the oncology unit at Mount Sinai Hospital in Manhattan to undergo chemotherapy to treat leukemia. Everyone knows that chemo takes your hair. I wanted to take control of what I could before the poison did its damage. But I left the hair salon in tears, my braids in a plastic bag.

When I was given a cancer diagnosis at the age of 22, sitting in a doctor's office less than a mile from my childhood home, I remember watching my dad burying his face in his hands. My mom rubbed my back with her open palm. The room fell silent for 30 seconds, or maybe it was three minutes. Then I managed to blurt out two questions: Was I going to make it through this? My doctor told me that my leukemia was "high risk." I would need to begin treatment immediately. The second thing I asked was whether I was going to lose my hair.

As I tried to prepare for my first round of chemo, I scoured the Internet, read the pamphlets my doctor had given me and paged through the cancer books that friends and relatives had dropped off at the house. I was still catching up on the basic details of my disease, its treatment and its prognosis. I had no idea how to prepare for the havoc it would wreak on my appearance — the part of the cancer experience that the world can see.

As the Gatorade-red poison made its way into my veins, my body began to morph within the first week. Many of my physical transformations — new surgical scars, drastic weight loss, chronic mouth sores and (maybe worst of all) infertility — were invisible to the world, the silent imprint of disease. With all of these things going on, I was surprised to find myself preoccupied by one of the more temporary side effects of chemo: the impending loss of my hair.

On balance with battling my disease, worrying about hair loss   5
seemed petty. It's only hair, I kept telling myself. It would grow back. But I couldn't shake the idea that soon, everywhere I went, baldness would be my dominant (or at least most noticeable) physical trait. When you're bald, cancer leads. Everything else follows. While much of what a cancer patient experiences is deeply personal, losing your hair is an undeniably public affair.

For the first few weeks after I lost my hair last year, I avoided going out in public. The mirror can be an onerous thing to a cancer patient, and I no longer recognized myself. Maybe I could wait it out behind the shuttered windows of my bedroom, I thought. I wanted to avoid the stares from strangers — even if most of them were just out of curiosity. I never expected cancer to make me so self-conscious.

Chemotherapy is a swift, sure stylist. Seeking inspiration and solidarity, I tried reading popular books about cancer that I found in the self-help section of the local bookstore. Many of the books sought to recast cancer as an empowering experience, even something that could be "sexy" or "cool." But I couldn't connect with that kind of upbeat gospel. Maybe it was too soon. I felt unsexy. I felt uncool.

Without my hair, my curvy hips or my full eyebrows, I felt less feminine than ever. Sometimes I thought I looked more like the local store mannequin — bald, pale and razor thin — than the real women who shopped there. I hid beneath hats and headscarves, which I'd built a collection of since getting out of the hospital. But even hats felt like "cancer clothes."

Cancer may not be a choice, but style is. I was drawn to the idea of recreating myself — a cancer makeover. Once my hair was a few inches long again, I dyed it purple and wore it as a mohawk.

rhetorical situations · genres · processes · strategies · research MLA / APA · media / design · readings

I also couldn't wear any of my old pants or dresses — they were too   10
big now — so I had to replace a lot my clothes. I started wearing a brown
leather jacket that a friend had lent me. I wore long earrings that would
have been obscured by the long hair I'd always had. One day I saw a pair
of boots with spikes on the heels in a store window, and I bought them on
the spot. Some people told me my new look was "tough" or "edgy." I didn't
feel always very tough, but I liked experimenting with a tough uniform.

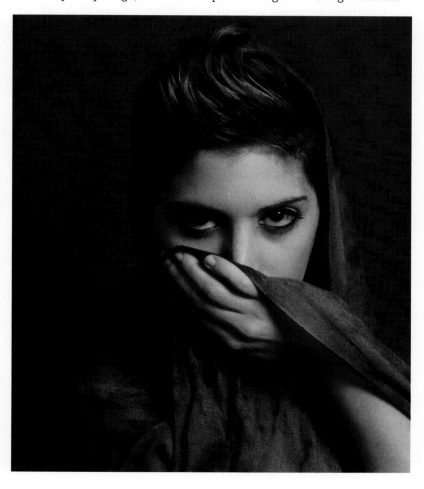

As my hair began to grow back, I was still drawing the stares of strangers in public. But this time people weren't staring from a distance. They were coming right up to me. But none of them mentioned cancer — people were interested in where I got my hair cut or what hair styling product I was using.

I'm just figuring it out as I go. A month before my transplant this spring, I went to the barber for a buzz cut and left with "hair tattoos." In a cavernous basement barbershop in downtown New York City that has a sign listing the dozens of languages spoken there, a stylist named Miguel buzzed my mohawk and grooved a spiral design in the one-inch layer that remained.

rhetorical situations

genres

processes

strategies

research MLA / APA

media / design

readings

Today, I'm bald again. It's been 57 days since my bone marrow transplant. I'm back to wearing a summer hat or a shawl on my head. I'm still a long way from the girl with long, wavy brown hair. Sometimes I dream of having my old hair back. But it'll be a long time before that happens. For now, I've got a new hair tattoo in mind. This time, I think I'll design it myself.

Engaging with the Text

1. Look carefully at the slide show that accompanies this essay. How fully do the pictures convey the meaning of this memoir? What (if anything) do they express that the text doesn't — or vice versa? Develop a title or label for each picture that makes clear its relationship with the text.

2. What is the **PURPOSE** of this memoir? How can you tell? Where in the essay does the purpose become very clear? 3–4

3. Of all the devastating results of her chemotherapy, which one haunted Suleika Jaouad most deeply? Why do you think that is?

4. A memoir relies on vivid details to bring the story and its significance to light. Pick out three details from this piece that you think are particularly effective. Why and how are these three so effective?

5. *For Writing.* Think of a time when either you or a friend or a family member dealt with a difficult period in life, such as physical illness or injury, deep disappointment, or marital stress. Write a **MEMOIR** that describes in **VIVID DETAIL** that period of your life as you either coped or helped someone else cope with the stressful times. Include photos, whether depicting the people involved or metaphorically illustrating particular points, and a piece of music that captures the mood of the memoir. 187 / 183–90

63 Profiles

rhetorical
situations

genres

processes

strategies

research
MLA / APA

media /
design

readings

NATASHA SINGER

On Campus, It's One Big Commercial

Natasha Singer is a reporter for the Sunday Business section of the New York Times, *covering business and marketing trends and privacy issues connected to the collection and sale of consumer data. She has also worked as a reporter in its daily Business section, covering the pharmaceutical industry and medical ethics, and developed the Skin Deep column for the Style section. She has also served as a correspondent for* Outside *magazine, a health and beauty editor at* W *magazine, and an editor-at-large of the Russian edition of* Vogue. *The following essay appeared in the September 10, 2011, issue of the* New York Times.

IT'S MOVE-IN DAY here at the University of North Carolina, and Leila Ismail, stuffed animals in tow, is feeling some freshman angst.

A few friendly upperclassmen spring into action.

But wait: there is something odd, or at least oddly corporate, about this welcome wagon. These U.N.C. students are all wearing identical T-shirts from American Eagle Outfitters.

Turns out three of them are working for that youth clothing chain on this late August morning, as what are known in the trade as "brand ambassadors" or "campus evangelists" — and they have recruited several dozen friends as a volunteer move-in crew. Even before Ms. Ismail can find her dorm or meet her roommate, they cheerily unload her family's car. Then they lug her belongings to her dorm. Along the way, they dole out American Eagle coupons, American Eagle water canisters and American Eagle pens.

Ms. Ismail, 18, of Charlotte, welcomes the help. "I'll probably always remember it," she says. 5

American Eagle Outfitters certainly hopes so, as do a growing number of companies that are hiring college students to represent brands on campuses across the nation.

At the University of North Carolina, Kimmy Summers, wearing cap, is a "brand ambassador" for American Eagle Outfitters. She helped freshmen on move-in day.

This fall, an estimated 10,000 American college students will be working on hundreds of campuses — for cash, swag, job experience or all three — marketing everything from Red Bull to Hewlett-Packard PCs. For the companies hiring them, the motivation is clear: college students spent about $36 billion on things like clothing, computers and cellphones during the 2010-11 school year alone, according to projections from Re:Fuel, a media and promotions firm specializing in the youth market. And who knows the students at, say, U.N.C., better than the students at U.N.C.?

Corporations have been pitching college students for decades on products from cars to credit cards. But what is happening on campuses today is without rival, in terms of commercializing everyday college life.

Companies from Microsoft on down are increasingly seeking out the big men and women on campus to influence their peers. The students most in demand are those who are popular — ones involved in athletics, music, fraternities or sororities. Thousands of Facebook friends help, too. What companies want are students with inside knowledge of school traditions and campus hotspots. In short, they want students with the cred to make brands seem cool, in ways that a TV or magazine ad never could.

"We are the people who understand what kinds of things the students will be open to," says Alex Stegall, a Carolina junior who recruited about 20 members of her sorority for the American Eagle promotion. "It's marketing for the students, by the students."

It's a good deal for the student marketers, who can earn several hundred to several thousand dollars a semester in salary, perks, products and services, depending on the company. But the trend poses challenges for university officials, especially at a time when many schools are themselves embracing corporate sponsorships to help stage events for students.

Just how far one big company — Target — has permeated this university was evident at freshmen welcome week in late August, at what students and administrators alike characterized as a touchstone party for the class of 2015.

As part of the official university program, Target sponsored a welcome dinner on a Friday. Then, on Saturday, for the first real social event for freshmen, it hired buses to ferry students to a Target superstore in Durham for late-night shopping, says Winston B. Crisp, the university's vice chancellor for student affairs.

From the school's point of view, Mr. Crisp says, the excursion is both social and practical. It's a convenient way for freshmen to pick up last-minute items. Equally important, he says, is that shopping at midnight keeps freshmen away from alcohol-fueled parties on their first weekend. University administrators supervise the event, he says, and control the marketing messages.

But Mr. Crisp says he was unaware of the American Eagle effort on his campus. He worried aloud that students and parents might mistake such promotions as having the university's imprimatur.

"They are not supposed to be using the opportunity to help people move in as a way of forwarding commercial ventures," he said, standing near the cash registers at Target that evening, as upperclassmen handed out free VitaminWater, Combos and packages of macaroni and cheese. He added: "So it's a bit of a dilemma."

In an e-mail message on Friday, Jani Strand, a spokeswoman for American Eagle, wrote: "We all were under the impression that U.N.C. officials had been contacted and were aware of the event. We apologize for any confusion." She said the company views its on-campus activities as beneficial for students as well as the brand.

Many college students are the heads of a household of one. But if a company can hook them early, it often has customers for life. And the choices students make — about shampoo, clothing, computers, smartphones and so on — can become the lifetime habits of future families or business executives, says Lisa Baker, director of education marketing at Hewlett-Packard, which has long promoted its laptops to universities.

What's more, she says, college students tend to maintain deep connections to their parents, siblings and high school friends, so their likes and dislikes can influence purchases back home.

"We think of them as a bridge," Ms. Baker says of undergraduates. "They will have influence back in the home and influence going forward." 20

Traditional marketing techniques — like national advertising campaigns on MTV or in *Rolling Stone* — don't resonate with college students the way they used to, says Matt Britton, chief executive of Mr. Youth, a marketing agency in Manhattan. Nowadays, companies need student ambassadors to create marketing events, like mural painting or video contests, that are relevant to their particular schools, he says. Students who participate tend to promulgate brand messages.

"They are engaging in real activities to move the needle on major brands," he says.

His company has developed Internet and on-campus campaigns for dozens of brands, including Nike, Microsoft, H.P. and Ford. It charges corporate clients $10,000 to $48,000 a campus per semester for

rhetorical situations   genres   processes   strategies   research MLA / APA   media / design   readings

brand-ambassador programs, he says. (American Eagle works with a different firm, Youth Marketing Connection, on its ambassador activities.)

This fall, Mr. Youth plans to hire more than 5,000 college students among the 150,000 who submitted profiles to its student recruitment network. The company uses behavioral profiling to match the personalities of brands and students.

Consider Alyssa Nation, 21, a junior at the University of Central 25 Florida in Orlando and a brand ambassador for H.P. laptops with Intel processors. Even when she is not officially on duty, she puts on her H.P. logo shirt, takes her company-issue laptop and positions herself at a campus Wi-Fi hotspot.

"I love technology, and I love interacting with people, so it's perfect," says Ms. Nation, a communications major.

Among her duties: setting up a laptop display table in the student union. First, she says, she tells freshmen who ask for advice that she is paid to promote H.P. products. Then she makes recommendations, depending on the student.

"I can tell they believe me," she says. "There's a completely different trust level when it's peer-to-peer marketing."

She also posts to H.P.'s Facebook site for students and uses her own Facebook account, with more than 1,300 friends, and her Twitter account to promote H.P. student discounts and contests.

"I am constantly marketing on Facebook and Twitter," she says, "to 30 the point where my friends threaten to block me because I am constantly posting about H.P."

Last semester, Ms. Nation painted the H.P. logo and Web site address on her car, using washable markers. She posted photos of the car on Facebook and recruited 15 friends to paint their cars, too.

The University of Central Florida is only one of several dozen colleges where H.P. has ambassadors.

"It would be difficult for a brand to be able to tap into all those unique activities at all of those schools," says Ms. Baker of H.P.

Just before 10 on a Saturday night in August, hundreds of U.N.C. freshmen line up outside the campus bookstore, waiting for a fleet of buses to take them to Target. At the front of the line is Dasia Robinson, a senior and, for the day, a Target brand ambassador. She has a soft spot for Target, she says. On her first weekend at U.N.C., she met four students during a similar Target event. They became her best friends.

"Target incorporated their brand into the fact that we are college students," she says. "I really do appreciate that."   35

She revs up the new Carolina Tar Heels. "Tar!" she yells.

"Heels!" the crowd yells back.

The Target student reps stand out: they are wearing red T-shirts that say "COLLEGE," punctuated by Target's bull's-eye logo.

"This is our first big college experience," says Viraj Patel, 18, standing in line next to freshman friends from high school.

University of North Carolina students shop at a Target party as part of the university's welcoming week in Chapel Hill, N.C. U.N.C.'s mascot, Rameses the Ram, and Bullseye, the Target mascot, danced with students at the store to music played by a D.J.

rhetorical situations genres processes strategies research MLA / APA media / design readings

When the first bus arrives, the students rush forward as if it were 40 Black Friday. Twenty minutes later, the first bus arrives at the Super-Target. Mr. Crisp, the U.N.C. vice chancellor, greets the students and alerts those following on Twitter.

"First bus load at Target!!! Let the fun begin!!" Mr. Crisp posts @vice-crispy. A little later, he posts: "Target is rocking!!! Come on out!"

By midnight, the store is crowded with freshmen pushing shopping carts full of lamps, pillows, cases of soda and free junk food. "Mac and cheese, everyone!" an upperclassmen yells, tossing packages at passing students. One student wins a refrigerator and a year's supply of Coca-Cola.

This year, 66 universities and colleges are taking part in private shopping events at Target as part of welcome weeks for freshmen. At U.N.C., where the company has been sponsoring the event since 2007, the night is already a tradition. Upperclassmen drop by to party with the freshmen.

A D.J. spins tunes between clothing racks. Students dance the wobble. Target's mascot, Bullseye the Dog, joins in with Carolina's Rameses the Ram.

Over the course of the evening, about 2,200 Carolina students make 45 their way through the aisles. Mr. Crisp describes the party as the school's "signature event" for the start of the school year. "It's late night. It's fun," he says, adding: "It's an opportunity for us to gather them together on a Saturday night in a healthy, safe environment."

Students at Chapel Hill — there are nearly 19,000 undergraduates this semester — do things the Carolina Way. Many often wear the school color, sky blue. Few ever wear Prussian blue, the color of Duke, Carolina's archrival. They stand up throughout sports events and root — loudly — for the Tar Heels. They like to pitch in.

Companies that hire students co-opt such local knowledge. It's easy for the three American Eagle student marketers here to enlist friends via Facebook and campus listservs for the move-in event. In return, the company outfits the volunteers with free T-shirts in navy blue, the corporate color of American Eagle, that read "A.E. Move-In Crew."

"We are a welcoming community. We're not going to let you move in and struggle," says David Artin, 20, a senior and fraternity member who volunteered. "We are going to help you move in the Carolina way."

For American Eagle, the strategy has the potential to increase sales not only among the freshmen but also among the volunteers. After all, people are most likely to act on suggestions from people they know and trust, says J. Andrew Petersen, an assistant professor of marketing at U.N.C.'s Kenan-Flagler Business School. In this case, the upperclassmen are already friends with the company's student representatives, he says, and now they feel their own personal link to the brand.

"The 50 people who volunteered think American Eagle is being very 50 nice," Professor Petersen says.

Participating in the move-in event seems to have made an impression on Kiley Pontrelli, 20, who volunteered along with friends from her sorority.

"When you know that the company is not just there to get your money, they're actually willing to, like, help you as an individual in whatever way possible, it makes you respect them a lot more," Ms. Pontrelli says. "I'm definitely going to give American Eagle, like, a second thought when I go by next time."

Not everyone is comfortable with all this student-to-student marketing.

Across campus, on a plaza somewhere between the free Pepsi truck and the free Ben & Jerry's ice cream wagon, Rachel Holtzman and a few other students are painting a sign promoting their own group: the Center for Social Justice.

"Although you want to support your friends, you may not always 55 be interested in supporting the company," says Ms. Holtzman, 19, a sophomore majoring in health policy and management. "It's hard when the two things have an unclear line."

On-campus marketing is intended to reach students where they eat, sleep, study and sweat.

Red Bull, which has student brand managers at 300 universities and colleges, sponsors everything from chariot races to music lectures.

rhetorical situations · genres · processes · strategies · research MLA / APA · media / design · readings

The Carolina students Amanda Day, left, and Rachel Holtzman painted a sign for the Center for Social Justice at the school. They expressed some concerns about commercial marketing campaigns on the campus.

Student representatives for Microsoft Windows give interactive product demonstrations each week to peers on more than 300 campuses.

American Eagle plans to stage freshmen move-in events at 50 campuses and works with university recreation centers to outfit intramural sports teams and fitness instructors. It also holds an annual academic competition for marketing students and flies the finalists to its Pittsburgh headquarters to present their cases to top executives. The company has even introduced a vintage-looking U.N.C. T-shirt that comes in, natch, Carolina blue.

It's a multipronged effort intended to make students feel they are personally involved in the brand, says Cathy McCarthy, American Eagle's senior director of campus marketing. The events, she says, are intended to amplify campus culture, not alter it. She flew in to observe the move-in event at U.N.C.

For its efforts, American Eagle gains insight from students about how to market to them, she says. Brand ambassadors, she says, acquire skills that can lead to a job at the company. [60]

"There's a two-way dialogue with our core customer," Ms. McCarthy says. "There's opportunity for recruitment as well."

Mr. Britton of Mr. Youth says the real change on campus is that companies are marketing through students, not to them. "The only difference now is that, as opposed to it being executed by, you know, field service reps who weren't their age, who didn't really speak their language," he says, "it's being executed by their peers."

Some universities welcome such programs, and the career experience they may provide, but others prohibit such activities, he says.

The lines aren't always clear. U.N.C. officials, for example, say they don't currently have a clear handle on how many students work as brand ambassadors — but it could be several hundred or more. "I don't think we have a good grip on it," Mr. Crisp says. "We are going to need to get a good grip on it."

He is blunt about the fact that student-to-student marketing has only recently come to the school's attention. Asked how U.N.C. is handling it, he acknowledges, "Honestly, not very well." [65]

The challenge, he says, is to balance potential student employment opportunities against practices that could manipulate undergraduates or dilute the U.N.C. experience.

"Corporations have become very savvy about hiring students to be their representatives on campus, and a lot of the stuff that they're doing we have no knowledge of — and so they are not things we are sponsoring or supporting," Mr. Crisp says. "How we police that and how we deal with our students, who after all are our students, is probably something we need to spend some more time thinking about."

Back at Target, Nitin Goel, a wiry, gum-chewing 18-year-old in low-slung jeans, is loaded down with free mac and cheese. He's carrying a friend's new beanbag chair.

Earlier that night, waiting for the Target bus by the campus bookstore, Mr. Goel had pledged allegiance to Wal-Mart, where he had shopped all his life. Now he doesn't seem quite so sure.

rhetorical situations   genres   processes   strategies   research MLA / APA   media / design   readings

"This was definitely the highlight of my orientation," he says.   70
It's a great day to be a Tar Heel.

Engaging with the Text

1. What is the **PURPOSE** of this profile? How successful is it in achieving its purpose?   ■ 3–4

2. A good **PROFILE** is a **FIRSTHAND ACCOUNT** of the person, place, or event at the center of it. How do you know this is a firsthand account? Point to at least three places in the essay that offer evidence that the writer participated in the event she is describing.   ▲ 191–204 / 199

3. How does Natasha Singer **BEGIN** her profile? How effective is this beginning? How else might she have opened this piece?   ◆ 299–306

4. What are your views about on-campus marketing? Have you had experience with it, either as a brand spokesperson or as a potential customer? Should it be regulated or banned? Why or why not? Do you have items of clothing with name brands on them? After reading this essay, do you feel any differently about these pieces? Why or why not?

5. *For Writing.* Identify an event that takes place on your campus weekly, monthly, or every semester. Participate in or attend the event, interview other participants or attendees, and write a **PROFILE** of it. Consider the main impression you want to convey about the event — remember that you need to find an **INTERESTING ANGLE** —and use **ENGAGING DETAILS** and **DIALOGUE** to convey that impression.   ▲ 191–204 / 198–99   ◆ 376–81

NATHANIEL RICH

Marlen Esparza: Going the Distance

Nathaniel Rich is author of the novels The Mayor's Tongue *(2008) and* Odds Against Tomorrow *(2013), as well as the nonfiction book* San Francisco Noir: The City in Film Noir from 1940 to the Present *(2005). Rich has written reviews, essays, and criticism for the* Paris Review, *the* New York Review of Books, *the* New York Times, Harper's Magazine, Slate, *and* Vogue, *in which the following profile appeared in July 2012.*

R UDY SILVA, THE HEAD COACH OF HOUSTON'S ELITE BOXING GYM, was preparing a group of fighters for an upcoming tournament when he noticed, the way a bull might notice a fly buzzing around its snout, a child standing beside him.

"Can I train with you?"

When Silva looked over — and down — he saw a thin, bony girl with long legs, hair past her shoulders, and a bright smile. She was eleven years old but seemed younger; she came up to his waist.

Silva figured she was just looking to kill time. His gym was in Pasadena, Texas, a working-class Hispanic city on Houston's southeastern margin, and children often showed up when they had no place else to go. Silva advised the girl to see his assistant, who was teaching a group of children how to throw a punch. He told her that he didn't waste his time with beginners.

"Besides," he added, "I don't train females."   5

The girl was back the next day. Silva again refused to train her, but as he worked with his fighters he kept getting distracted by what she was doing at the other end of the gym. Most beginners tire easily, but this little girl was inexhaustible, bouncing and whaling away at the punching bag with a deranged intensity. She had no technique, of course, but she did have *something*. At the end of practice, Silva pulled her over.

"Hey, kid," he said. "What's your name?"

"Marlen."

"And you're serious about this?"

"Yes," she said. "I really want to box."   10

He asked about school. The girl explained that she had been sent to a disciplinary program because she'd talked back to her teacher too many times.

"I'll train you," said Silva, "but only under two conditions. First, you have to behave and return to your old school."

"OK," she said, nodding, wide-eyed.

"Second," he said, "I'm not going to train you like a girl. I'm going to train you like a man."

Twelve years later, women's boxing has grown from a curiosity into an   15 Olympic sport, with Marlen Esparza its most astonishing and graceful star. Esparza is now 69–2 in her career, which gives her a 97 percent winning percentage. By comparison, Cassius Clay had an amateur record of 99–8 (93 percent); Floyd Mayweather, Jr., was 84–6 (93 percent); and Mike Tyson was 48–6 (89 percent). Esparza has been ranked number one in her weight class since she was sixteen.

I met Esparza in March, during the 2012 U.S. Women's National Championships. She had won the past six nationals; with a seventh championship she would have set a new amateur record. But for the first time in her career, Esparza had not entered the tournament. That was because the previous week she had won the only competition that mattered to her anymore: the U.S. Olympic trials. Women's boxing is making its debut at the London Games this summer, and Esparza will represent the U.S. in the flyweight division.

So at home in Pasadena that week, Esparza found herself in an unprecedented situation. For the first time in twelve years, Silva was asking her to relax. Her preparation for the Olympic trials had been her most rigorous yet, and her body needed rest — at least a couple of weeks' worth. But Esparza did not know how to rest. Every afternoon at 5:00 p.m., she was back at the gym, lacing up her gloves, shadowboxing, and punching bags with the speed and cutthroat intensity of a saw-scaled viper. Had she even had a chance to enjoy her victory?

"I thought that when I won the Olympic trials I was going to be the happiest person in the whole world," she says. "And I was happy. But

As women's boxing makes its long-awaited debut at the Olympics, all eyes are on Marlen Esparza, America's best hope for the gold.

it wasn't like I thought it was going to be. I had already imagined it in my head so many times. It was real before it happened."

Esparza's father, David, had not been as confident. "I've never been more stressed out," he says of the trials. "My head was about to explode." It is difficult for him to talk about her Olympic achievement without betraying his emotions. "This," he says, "was what we've been waiting for all our lives."

David may have been waiting most of his life for one of his chil- 20 dren to become a boxing legend, but he never suspected it would be his younger daughter. A boxing fanatic since his childhood in Juárez — he idolized the Mexican legend Salvador Sánchez — David taught his two sons how to box around the time that they learned to read. He invited his friends to bring their sons over to fight his sons in his living room. The fathers would watch from the couch, shouting out instructions.

The other women in the house — Marlen's older sister, Dalila, and her mother, Carmen, whose family is also from Juárez — had no interest in boxing, but Marlen was always desperate to compete against her brothers. When her younger brother was nine, David asked Marlen to take him to boxing lessons. She refused unless she could train, too. David, whose work as an industrial welder on oil rigs prevented him from taking his son to the gym himself, reluctantly granted his approval. Two weeks later Marlen was training with Silva, and her brother had quit.

Silva, an officer in the Houston Police Department who spends his days patrolling Jefferson Davis, a public high school in a different working-class Hispanic neighborhood, didn't go easy on the little girl. He assigned her to a group with twelve- and thirteen-year-old boys and pushed them through exaggeratedly strenuous routines — running sprints, jumping rope, and punching bags — with five seconds of rest between sets. By the end of the second day, several of the boys burst into tears and, rather than embarrass themselves further in front of the younger girl, gave up boxing altogether. "They were getting tired, and she was constantly going and going, back and forth with the sprints," says Silva today, laughing. "I thought, This thing done backfired on me!" Six months later, after Esparza was readmitted to her regular school, her mother came to the gym to thank Silva personally. "She's totally changed," she said. "We haven't been getting any calls from teachers. What do you do when she talks to back to you?"

"We don't do that here," Silva said.

To this day Carmen remains somewhat baffled by her daughter's passion for boxing. Her father, however, came around early. "She changed my mind at her very first fight," he says. "Me being a boxing expert, I couldn't believe it. For a girl, she was excellent. Marlen attacked that other little girl like a pit bull, like a grasshopper. She was going pow-pow-pow-pow-pow-pow-pow!" David jabs the air with each pow. "Her determination and stamina surprised me. I was jumping up and down. That other girl was just trying to survive! She was being brutalized. Pow-pow-pow-pow-pow-pow-pow!"

When Esparza's parents divorced two years later, it was decided that Marlen live with her father, so that he could more closely supervise her training. For Marlen's *quinceañera*, David gave her a gold necklace. The medallion is a boxing glove inscribed with her initials. But she refused it.

"It's a guy's necklace!" she says to me, rolling her eyes. "It's huge."

"It's solid gold," David protests.

"You know what my sister got? A car and a trip to Cancún!"

I notice that David is wearing the necklace.

Strangers do not take Esparza for a boxer. A track-and-field athlete, perhaps, or a runner, but at five feet three and 112 pounds she is neither brawny nor particularly fierce-looking. The same cannot be said of her U.S. teammates in the lightweight (132-pound) and middleweight (165-pound) divisions. In photographs of the three Olympic hopefuls after the trials, Esparza looks like the kid sister, tagging along, even though she is the most accomplished of the fighters and six years older than the middleweight, a fearsome seventeen-year-old from Flint, Michigan, named Claressa Shields. Esparza's ponytail, tight V-neck sweater, strawberry nail polish, and giddy energy give her an adolescent, even girlish quality. This makes a certain amount of sense because around the time she began high school, her life outside boxing stopped.

She dated one boy, "but it wasn't ever serious, because my boxing was serious." Rudy allowed her to attend her senior prom, but her curfew was 10:00 p.m.; he sat at her kitchen table, waiting up for her. He let her participate in extracurricular activities, but only ones that would make her a better boxer. When she was fourteen, Silva told her to join her high school's cross-country team in order to increase her stamina. She took her team to district championships and might have gone even further had Silva not pulled her from a number of meets in order to compete in conflicting boxing tournaments. "Her coach loved Marlen," says Silva. "But she hated me." Then Silva ordered Esparza to join the swimming team. Finally, after she won her first nationals, he made her join the debate team.

"I knew then that she was going to blow the doors open for women's boxing," says Silva. "I thought, She's going to be in front of the camera a lot."

After graduating in 2007 from Pasadena High School, where she was class president and earned a 4.6 GPA, she was accepted to Rice University and the University of Texas. At seventeen Esparza was already a two-time national champion, and she announced to Silva that she had nothing else to prove. More importantly, she wanted to be the first person in her family to graduate from college. But Silva asked her to reconsider. "Just keep winning," he told her, "and people will have to notice. Good things will come."

But in 2008 this didn't seem likely. Of the 28 Olympic sports at the Beijing Games, boxing was the only one closed to female athletes. The International Olympic Committee had cited concerns over safety. Some boxing coaches were more outspoken: "Women should be showing off their beautiful faces," said a prominent Cuban coach, "not getting punched in the face."

Besides, Esparza had not fared well in international competitions. 35 Whereas women's boxing in America is dominated by fighters trained like their male counterparts, in a straight-ahead style based on power and precision, women's boxers abroad rely more heavily on quickness and guile. Punches come at strange angles; Esparza refers to the style as "noodle arms" and likens it to fighting an octopus. When she began competing in world championships, she found herself losing matches decisively without absorbing a single hard blow. (Her international record is not nearly as gaudy as her U.S. record, which is kept separately; she is currently ranked ninth in the world.) Over the last three years Esparza has trained herself in the international style, which for a boxer is like learning a foreign language.

Her persistence was rewarded in 2009, when the International Olympic Committee announced that women's boxing would debut at the London Games. Though in the United States the sport remains relatively obscure, its popularity has surged internationally — particularly in Britain, where the number of registered female fighters has increased more than tenfold over the last seven years. After the announcement,

Nike signed Esparza to a sponsorship deal; Coca-Cola and CoverGirl have followed. She decided to quit her job — she had been working with her mother, a dental assistant — and focus on training for the only title left for her to win.

"It's superembarrassing," she says, "but one reason that I would like, maybe, to be somewhat famous is that I want to wear a Vera Wang dress when I get married. Sleek, old-fashioned, romantic, with some sort of lace." But she can't talk about this with a straight face — soon she's laughing again, her high, carbonated laugh. "I've thought about it a hundred times. I even buy bridal magazines sometimes. I want David Tutera to do my wedding. I'm obsessed with getting married, but I don't even have a boyfriend." She shakes her head. "Rudy's going to be like, What the heck — you said that out loud?"

I asked her if it's been worth it — the long hours, the seclusion, the intense, single-minded focus.

"It's miserable, actually. It's torture. I get mad. I don't date. I haven't gone out in a long time. It's just depressing. Thank God I don't have Facebook, because if I did, I'd be jealous of everybody. I don't want to know what I'm missing."

Even by Olympic standards, Esparza's training regimen is extraordinarily rigorous. In the weeks before a competition she eats only organic food. She weighs herself three times a day, though it is hardly necessary — her knowledge of her body is so precise that at all times she can guess her exact weight, to the half-pound. She never drinks alcohol. Each morning she either swims or lifts weights under the supervision of trainers. In the evening she spends two and a half hours in the boxing gym with Silva. She also runs three to four miles every day. She kept to this regimen every single day of the week, for six years, until a couple of months ago, when a prominent sports nutritionist explained to Silva that the human body needs time to rest and recuperate during intensive training. Silva was incredulous, but after cautious experimentation, he noticed that Esparza was stronger and had more energy when allowed one day off per week.

"That's all we knew," says Silva, with a shrug. "We just thought the harder you train, the better you'll perform."

40

rhetorical situations | genres | processes | strategies | research MLA / APA | media / design | readings

"Rudy lives a life of telling people what to do," says Esparza. "All day he's the master. He goes to work and tells everyone what to do, then he comes to the gym and tells everyone what to do." But she's not complaining. "It's perfect the way it is. I just agree with whatever Rudy says. It makes everybody's life easier." She laughs. "I don't have to think. My only job is to show up and win."

Esparza plans on quitting after the Olympics, though that might be difficult if she is offered a lucrative professional contract. But this seems unlikely. While male fighters can earn millions for a title bout, female professionals rarely make more than $10,000 for a title and often must fight abroad. There is hope in women's boxing that the Olympics will draw attention, and advertising dollars, to the sport, but Esparza believes that broad acceptance of women fighters will take much longer. "We finally have some momentum," she says, "but I don't think women will be considered the main event, or get paid for boxing, in my generation. Maybe in my lifetime. We're about 10 percent there."

If no major offers materialize after the Games, Esparza will attend college and then medical school, where she intends to pursue an unlikely field. After a dozen years of delivering pain, physical and psychological, to other fighters, she hopes to be an anesthesiologist.

Esparza now practices at a gym built last year by the Fellowship of the Nations church, where she is a congregant. Tacked on the walls are posters of Esparza and black-and-white stills of Salvador Sánchez, Muhammad Ali, Rocky Marciano. There is also a photograph of Maurice "Termite" Watkins, a legend in the Houston boxing world, who in 1974 was the first sixteen-year-old to make the U.S.A. Olympic boxing team, and as a professional fought for the world title. An active church member, Watkins oversees the gym and mentors Esparza. He believes she will win the gold. 45

"I've never seen anyone work harder than Marlen," Watkins says. "I was an amateur with some of the best amateurs in history, and I was a pro with some of the best pros in history — Leonard, Ali, Frazier, Foreman. I put her in that caliber of fighter. She is already going to go down in history as one of the great amateurs. And in the last six months I've seen her reach another level. She and Rudy are bringing it all together now. She's unreal."

Boxer Manny Pacquiao has taken an interest in her career, as has Houston's mayor, Annise Parker. "Marlen Esparza is an inspiration and a role model," she wrote in an e-mail. "Houston is proud to have Marlen among its best homegrown athletes, and she will have the entire city's support as she continues her journey."

"It's not just about me anymore," acknowledges Esparza at the gym, between rounds of shadowboxing. Then a buzzer rings and she starts punching again. Watching Esparza in her gloves and purple tank top and sparkling scarlet Nike boxing boots, her ponytail bouncing as she weaves and ducks and pistons her fists in the air, I find myself feeling sorry for her imaginary opponent. Esparza has talked about accessing her anger in the ring, but the expression on her face is not rage, at least not entirely. There is something mournful, too. It is as if her invisible opponent has wronged her, and she is determined to exact revenge.

Then it's over. She takes off the gloves and tape, and is again her giggling, playful self. I ask her what goes through her head when she is boxing.

"It's a feeling of being free," she says. "The headgear is like a mask. 50 When you put it on, you feel like you can do anything. You're not even you anymore." She points to the ring. "When I'm in there," she says, "I can do whatever I want."

Engaging with the Text

1. How does Nathaniel Rich use **QUOTATIONS** in his profile of Marlan Esparza? Whom does he quote? Why do you think he chose those people to quote? What do the quotations contribute to this profile?   *463–67*

2. The subject of a profile must be interesting either because it is unusual or because it is something ordinary that is written about in an intriguing way. In what ways is Marlen Esparza an **INTERESTING SUBJECT?** What makes her as a person and her story unusual?   *198*

3. What is Rich's **STANCE** toward his subject, Esparza? Identify one passage (or more) that indicates this stance.   *12–15*

rhetorical situations   genres   processes   strategies   research MLA / APA   media / design   readings

4. With whom does Rich compare Marlen Esparza? Identify two passages where Rich compares Esparza to someone else. How effective are these comparisons? How do they help a reader understand the subject of this profile?

5. *For Writing.* Identify a leader on your campus—someone in sports, in student government or publications, in fraternity or sorority life, in extracurricular activities such as theater or debate or skateboarding, and so on. **INTERVIEW** the leader and those who surround her or him. Write a **PROFILE** of this person, and include relevant quotations from your interviews to help readers gain a clear picture of the subject.

378–80
191–204

ROB BAKER

Jimmy Santiago Baca: Poetry as Lifesaver

Rob Baker is a freelance creative writer who was teaching English and creative writing at Barrington High School in Illinois when he wrote the following profile. It appeared in a 2008 issue of the Council Chronicle, *a monthly magazine published by the National Council of Teachers of English (NCTE). As you read, notice how Baker focuses his profile on the significance of poetry for Baca, using details from Baca's life to support his point.*

CHICANO POET JIMMY SANTIAGO BACA was born with rattlesnake poison in his blood. In January, 1952, just before his mother gave birth, she was bitten by a rattler. The healer who tended to her wound and then brought Baca into the world said that because of the venom Baca would be able to see in the dark and that he would change many times throughout his life, just as a snake sloughs its skin. And change many times he did.

As related in his award-winning autobiography, *A Place to Stand*, Baca's parents abandoned him when he was seven; he lived briefly with his grandparents and then in a series of detention centers from which he constantly ran away. He attended junior high, but dropped out after less than a year because he could not keep up academically nor mesh with the "normal" kids who had families. As a teenager, he lived a haphazard existence on the streets of Albuquerque, fighting, drinking, and doing drugs. He worked piecemeal jobs — loading food on planes, operating a vending machine route, a handyman business. Then, during stints in California and Arizona, he became a very successful drug dealer.

That he would morph into a renowned poet is perhaps the least likely change anyone would have predicted for Baca who, as a young adult, could barely read or write, who "hated books, hated reading," who had "never owned a book and had no desire to own one." And this change probably wouldn't have happened if Baca hadn't been sentenced, at age 21, to five to ten years in prison.

rhetorical situations genres processes strategies research MLA / APA media / design readings

Jimmy Santiago Baca.

To read of Baca's prison years is to marvel at the human capacity for survival and renewal. In a place more reminiscent of Dante's *Inferno* than of an institution for rehabilitation, where blood was shed more often than light, and where the inmates' chronic lassitude, fear, and anger led to depression, murder, rape, and paranoia, Baca — remarkably — endured, and exited not only sane and alive, but as a poet.

Chance encounters catalyzed Baca's transformation. A couple years into his incarceration, Baca received a letter from a man as part of a church program to write to prisoners without families. As a result of their continued correspondence, Baca painstakingly taught himself to read and write, activities that helped bring purpose into his monotonous days. The man then put Baca in touch with a poet friend. Poetry changed Baca's life forever.

"I believe something in my brain or something in my nervous system was impacted by poetry, by the way the lines and the words were arranged," said Baca. "I was such an emotional animal and I had never read any poetry. When I read it, it just tolled so many bells in my head, it was like, 'Wow! I can actually communicate like this. There are actually people who talk like this and write like this.' I was just absorbed into it, into the vortex of this ecstasy."

Baca published poems while still in prison. His first collection, *Immigrants in Our Own Land* (Louisiana State University Press, 1979), came out just after his release.

Baca's writing explores his fractured family and personal life, his prison experiences, and his ethnicity. In addition to his autobiography, he has penned ten poetry collections, a book of short stories, and a screenplay, the 1993 film *Blood In, Blood Out*.

"Language gave me a way to keep the chaos of prison at bay and prevented it from devouring me," he wrote in his prologue to *A Place to Stand*. "It was a resource that allowed me to confront and understand my past . . . and it opened a way toward the future that was based not on fear or bitterness or apathy but on compassionate involvement."

In another life change, Baca ultimately morphed into a teacher. He began by working with gang members who regularly congregated near his home, though his initial contact with them seemed more likely to result in violence than poetry. One night, when the youths hanging out

rhetorical situations genres processes strategies research MLA / APA media / design readings

on his street were particularly raucous, Baca went outside in his pajamas, baseball bat in hand. He told them that they had awakened his baby and that they had to leave.

"They said, 'We ain't got no other place to go,'" Baca recounted. "So I said, 'All right, meet me at St. Anne's church tomorrow and I'll ask the priest if we can use the barracks there.' And you know what? They all met me there and I had my first workshop ever, and I realized with a sort of vague ignorance that I was really gifted at working with kids."

Baca now does many workshops a year and receives frequent visits from public school educators who come to observe his techniques. He says he's "very much into Latin American poets," but he also uses more frequently taught poets such as William Carlos Williams, Denise Levertov, Lawrence Ferlinghetti, and Walt Whitman.*

> Language gave me a way to keep the chaos of prison at bay and prevented it from devouring me. It was a resource that allowed me to confront and understand my past.

Baca encourages students to tell the stories no one else has: the stories of their own lives. He also encourages students to use poetry to discuss issues they might not normally talk about. "Most of the time there are subtle protocols you have to abide by. You're sitting at a table with friends, there are certain things you don't talk about. With these kids, ninety percent of their lived experience is stuff you don't talk about."

Baca believes poetry is able to reach the people he works with — people often considered by society to be "the worst of the worst" — because "there's nothing that is required for you to speak poetically from your heart."

To Baca, his mission as a teacher — and the role of poetry in general — is nothing less than to save lives. 15

"My job is simply to keep the light inside [my students] burning. That's it. My job is to make sure they do not fall into despair. And I guess

---

*William Carlos Williams (1883–1963), Denise Levertov (1923–97), Lawrence Ferlinghetti (b. 1919), and Walt Whitman (1819–92): American poets who composed in free verse. With the exception of Whitman, all wrote during the twentieth century. [Editor's note]

that's the answer to why I work with unwed mothers, I go to prisons, I work with homeless and gang kids, because their light's starting to go off, to dim, and I have to come in there and fire it up, and I do that with poetry, and I do that with commitment, and I do that with compassion."

Engaging with the Text

1. Rob Baker begins his profile of the poet Jimmy Santiago Baca with an ANECDOTE. How does this anecdote foreshadow the changes Baca experiences during his life? What role does language play in those changes?

   305

2. What ENGAGING DETAILS does Baker provide in his profile to create an impression of Baca as someone who sees "his mission as a teacher — and the role of poetry in general — [as] nothing less than to save lives"?

   199

3. This piece was published in a magazine for English teachers. How does Baker shape his profile of Baca to appeal to that AUDIENCE? How might his profile be different if he had written it for an audience of high school students? prison inmates?

   5–8 ■

4. How much BACKGROUND on Baca does Baker provide in this profile? Why is this background important? How does it help the reader better understand who Baca is today?

   198

5. *For Writing.* Identify someone with an interesting career, job, or hobby that has played a significant role in his or her life. Interview that person and write a PROFILE that demonstrates how that hobby or job has changed him or her. Use DIALOGUE and engaging details to help reveal your subject's character.

   191–204
   376–81 ◆

ALEX WILLIAMS

Drawn to a Larger Scale

Alex Williams is a staff reporter for the Styles section of the New York Times, *where he writes about technology, style, and education. The following profile appeared in the* Times *in April 14, 2010.*

H OW DID A 32-YEAR-OLD COLLEGE DROPOUT from the bayou of Louisiana, with no formal training in art — well, to be frank, no training at all — end up with a one-man show in a New York gallery and a client list that includes Robert Downey Jr. and Orlando Bloom?

For Scott Campbell, it all started at a tattoo studio in the Lower Haight district of San Francisco. "I'm just the dirty kid who snuck in the back door," said Mr. Campbell, who said that he got the bulk of his art education tattooing teenage gang members in San Francisco in the 1990s.

Indeed, as he sat in the Smile, a restaurant on Bond Street, with his friend Dan Colen, a fellow artist, and with his lank dirty-blond hair brushing the top of his collar and his ink-stained forearms peeking out of his shirt, Mr. Campbell looked like a kid in Salvation Army vintage who sells Minor Threat albums at Bleecker Bob's — never mind that his button-down shirt was Loden Dager, that his jeans were from Earnest Sewn and that his lunky diver's watch was a Rolex (a family piece handed down to him by an uncle in the Navy Seals, Mr. Campbell explained).

And that tattoo career? It took off in 2005, four years after he moved to New York and opened his studio, Saved Tattoo, in the then-emerging neighborhood of Williamsburg, Brooklyn.

One day an impatient Australian came in and commissioned a small 5 bird in flight on his left forearm. The next day, Mr. Campbell said, *Entertainment Tonight* came with cameras, grilling him on what kind of tattoo he had just given Heath Ledger. The two became friends — "the sweetest guy, so open," he said of Mr. Ledger. "The third time I hung out with him, I had keys to his house."

It became a pattern, as Mr. Campbell became something of a celebrity tattoo artist, charging as much as $300 an hour ($1,000 minimum) to ink customers like Courtney Love and Josh Hartnett. After Mr. Campbell tattooed three of Sting's adult children, he said, the singer and his wife, Trudie Styler, put him up at their house in London when he was there for a gallery show in October (he said he paid Sting back by giving him a tattoo, a meditation labyrinth on his back). And he said he recently went gallery hopping with Marc Jacobs, who sports a tattoo of his two bull terriers on his shoulder, courtesy of Mr. Campbell. The nature of his craft, he said, helps to explain these friendships. "Tattooing is a very intimate exchange," he said.

"You have your hands on someone, you're communicating with them, and they're very yielding," he continued. "There's no cool-guy factor, no barriers."

It's easy to see why Mr. Campbell might have been welcomed into the inner circle of celebrity. He's charming in a not-too-forced way, can fluidly swing the conversation from Greek art to the Dead Kennedys to motorcycles, and he has an appealing back story.

He grew up in rural Louisiana in a fishing village called Hermitage. "I hated it when I was a kid," said Mr. Campbell, whose father owned a small oil-services company. As a teenager, he would order William S. Burroughs novels from New York and dream about the world beyond. "I felt like everything I was passionate about was something that was mail-order from somewhere else."

His rebelliousness inspired him to get his first tattoo — a skull on his leg — at 15, to his mother's horror. "When I was a kid, she sat me on her lap and said: 'Scotty, you could murder, and I'd still be proud to call you my son. But if you get a tattoo, I'll shoot you myself,' " he recalled.

Early on, Mr. Campbell toyed with the idea of a middle-class life. At the University of Texas he studied biochemistry and planned a career as a medical illustrator. Eventually, his restlessness took over. "I have the attention span of a gerbil," he said. He dropped out, spent a few years in San Francisco, where he worked in that tattoo parlor, before

rhetorical situations   genres   processes   strategies   research MLA / APA   media / design   readings

Scott Campbell, a tattoo artist, will have a gallery show of his fine-art work. His life has been a continuous line of adventure, starting when he was a teenager in the Louisiana bayou.

bumming around Asia and Europe, where he tattooed for cash, and then landing in Williamsburg in 2001.

Inspired by the street sensibilities of artists (and tattoo clients) like Mr. Colen and Dash Snow, he dabbled in mixed-media art — United States currency (above) that he etches with a laser, for example — around 2004. The painter Michael Bevilacqua, a friend, encouraged him to exhibit his work in group shows, Mr. Campbell said. The work started to sell.

Last April, Mr. Campbell's solo show at OHWOW, a gallery in Miami, sold out, said Al Moran, its director. It was evidence that Mr. Campbell had the stature needed to carry a solo show on April 29 at the gallery's new space in Manhattan, on Crosby Street — its first since moving to the city. "All sorts of people were coming" to the Miami show, Mr. Moran said. "Tattoo kids were coming in, and museums were coming in."

Mr. Campbell said he is nervous to show in New York. But added, philosophically, "If the art world shuns me, I can still do tattoos."

Engaging with the Text

312–13
1. What is the meaning of Alex Williams's **TITLE** "Drawn to a Larger Scale"? How does it relate to his profile of Scott Campbell?

12–14
2. What **STANCE** does Williams take toward the subject of his profile? Where in the essay do you see evidence of this stance?

199
3. What are some of the **ENGAGING DETAILS** Williams offers in his profile? How do they contribute to bringing his subject to life?

4. Having read this profile, how do you account for Campbell's success in the world of tattoos? What sets him apart from the many other tattoo artists around the country?

378–80
5. *For Writing.* **INTERVIEW** a professional artist in your community, whether at your school or outside, to find out why he or she chose to pursue an artistic career and the particular medium or media in which he or she works. Write a **PROFILE** of the person that includes background information from the interview.

191–204

rhetorical situations   genres   processes   strategies   research MLA / APA   media / design   readings

BILL PENNINGTON

Defying the Odds: Victor Cruz

Bill Pennington is a sportswriter for the New York Times. *A former beat writer covering the New York Giants, he has become best known for writing on golf; in 2008, he began the* Times' *weekly golf column,* On Par. *A six-time winner of the Associated Press Sports Editors national writing award, Pennington also won a Deadline Club award from the Society of Professional Journalists for his examination of the real monetary value of the NCAA athletic scholarship. The following profile appeared in the* New York Times *on February 4, 2012. To access the online version, including hyperlinks, go to* wwnorton.com/write/fieldguidelinks.

PAMELA MARSH-WILLIAMS, the associate dean for undergraduate advising at the University of Massachusetts, had never met Victor Cruz. But she had seen his academic record.

"And it was not good," Marsh-Williams said.

Cruz, a second-year wide receiver on the football team, needed a C average to remain at the university. He was not close to that — in any recent semester. Cruz, then 20, was dismissed from the institution and his football scholarship was revoked.

It was the second time in two years that UMass had kicked him out.

In desperation, Cruz scheduled a meeting with Marsh-Williams. His 5 mother, Blanca Cruz, who had raised him in a single-parent home, made the drive to central Massachusetts from the family home in Paterson, N.J.

"Victor's mother was distraught and overwhelmed emotionally because she said there was nothing waiting for Victor back home," Marsh-Williams said Friday, looking back on the 2007 conversation in her office. "UMass was supposed to be his gateway out of a tough neighborhood, and she feared for what would happen if he went back. She worried he would never get out.

"I understood, but I explained that we had standards and he could not stay. If I had been betting right then, I would have bet that I would never see him again."

Three years later, Marsh-Williams had her living room television tuned to a preseason football game, although she was not really watching it. She heard a familiar name, looked up at the replay of a spectacular touchdown catch, but nothing unusual registered. After another touchdown reception, she heard the announcers mention UMass. She looked closer at the television screen.

"And I recognized Victor," Marsh-Williams said of Cruz, who had three touchdown catches in the game for the Giants. "I was blown away — just completely stunned. Who would have thought that? I couldn't believe it was the same person."

The improbable ascent of Victor Cruz has been a popular story line   10
approaching this year's <u>Super Bowl</u> — a narrative that parallels the late-season resurrection of the Giants. And much of the focus has been on Cruz's misjudged athletic credentials, casting him as the ultimate disregarded football underdog.

But long before he was an undrafted free agent in search of an N.F.L. team, Cruz was on his way to being just another talented player who flunks out of college unprepared and untrained to do much of anything.

"I was going to be another inner-city kid working at Wendy's or some mall," Cruz said Thursday, preparing for Sunday's Super Bowl against the New England Patriots. "In fact, that is what I was. I came home and worked in a clothing store at the Garden State Plaza. I could have been there the rest of my life."

What happened over the next year, however, altered Cruz's life story in a most implausible way. Cruz is now the darling of the Super Bowl: Madonna mimicked his salsa end zone dance at a news conference, and his No. 80 uniform is the best-selling football jersey in the country. A little more than four years ago, Cruz, by his own estimation, was a "one-in-a-million shot to accomplish anything at all."

He said: "I had two strikes against me and I needed a home run just to get back to college. The last open windows were closing. Things like the N.F.L. and the Super Bowl were not in my thoughts. I mean, come on, man, don't be talking crazy."

rhetorical situations   genres   processes   strategies   research MLA / APA   media / design   readings

Trouble on the Street

It was not the first bump in the road Cruz had endured. The son of Blanca Cruz and Michael Walker, a Paterson firefighter, Cruz lived in the city's downtrodden Fourth Ward.

"It was a very tough place to grow up," said Benjie Wimberly, Cruz's high school football coach at Paterson Catholic High School and now a New Jersey legislator. "Drugs, gangs — there was trouble around many street corners if you wanted it. But his mom is a very strong woman, and his father was involved in his life, too."

Cruz's parents never married, but Walker made sure to teach his son to play football even though his mother preferred less violent sports like baseball and basketball. Victor ended up participating in them all, and took karate, too.

"Part of the plan for Vic," Wimberly said, "was to keep him busy; don't let him be idle, and he will be productive."

Cruz was a star receiver and kick returner at Paterson Catholic, albeit one who was only 5 feet 9 inches and 165 pounds. Football Championship Subdivision colleges were interested, but Cruz did not score high enough on his College Boards to qualify for an N.C.A.A. scholarship when he graduated in 2004.

Don Brown, the coach at UMass, called Bridgton Academy in Maine, a one-year postgraduate school that welcomes many athletes in need of physical maturation and academic improvement, to see if they would admit Cruz.

"And pretty soon I went off to Maine, where there was nothing but snow and one traffic light in the town," Cruz said. "I asked about a laundromat and they told me it was 30 minutes away."

But as he was in high school, Cruz was the leading receiver at Bridgton, too.

"He did all the things you see him doing now," said Rick Marcella, his coach at Bridgton. "He made one of the best catches I've seen in 30 years of coaching — twisting and turning like a cat, then snatching it out of the air with one hand."

Victor Cruz in 2004 at Bridgton Academy, a school in Maine. Cruz grew up in the Fourth Ward of Paterson, New Jersey.

Cruz, like all students, was sent to a two-hour study hall nightly. He retook the College Boards in December, exceeded the required N.C.A.A. threshold and was a redshirt freshman at UMass in the fall of 2005.

But he was not necessarily studying.

"We hope that once the students leave the structure here, they will take the study habits they learned and use them in college," Marcella said. "But it doesn't always happen that way. There are many distractions for a 19-year-old in college, some of them female."

Cruz said this week, "I wasn't doing any bad things; I just wasn't acting like a college student who understood that college is about learning and getting a degree."

For the 2006 season, Cruz was academically ineligible with a 1.7 grade point average and was sent back to Paterson to regroup.

25

■ rhetorical situations
▲ genres
○ processes
◆ strategies
● research MLA / APA
□ media / design
▮▮ readings

"He was never a bad kid, never in trouble," said Brown, who is now the defensive coordinator at Connecticut. "Even back then, he had that great smile that lit up a room. He just didn't make going to class or doing his homework a priority."

By the time Cruz landed in the office of Marsh-Williams, he was 30 multiple credits short of athletic eligibility — more than could be made up in one semester.

"I told him he could return to UMass, but first he would have to go home to New Jersey and find a new accredited institution where he could take several core courses that would be transferrable," Marsh-Williams said. "He would have to pay for it and he would have to figure out all the details himself. And he would have to get good grades.

"I remember that Victor did not say much. He quietly took notes."

A Humiliating Return

Back in Paterson, at first, Cruz stayed at home, almost unwilling to go outside.

"It was too embarrassing," he said last week. "If I went out, then people would see me and they'd ask, 'What are you doing here?' The neighborhood thought I was off doing great things at UMass, and I'd have to tell them the truth. That was humbling."

Cruz saw his future, and it was working at a mall in Paramus, N.J., 35 for little pay. That future had no football in it, either, except what he watched on television.

"I did some soul-searching and I decided I could change, and if I did, my future would change with it," Cruz said.

He enrolled at Passaic County Community College, eventually earning a solid B to B-plus average.

But one day, his older brother, Milek, called crying into the telephone. His father, who had recently been injured in an automobile accident, had died. Police investigating the death believed it to be a suicide. Cruz was devastated.

"That was a very hard thing on a young man trying to remake his life," Wimberly said. "Mike was a great guy who was always there for

Vic. He would get so excited for Vic, sometimes I thought he would jump on the field."

Cruz said last week that during youth football games in Paterson, his father did just that — run onto the field to hug him after a nice catch or run. 40

This year, his first playing in the N.F.L. regular season, Cruz has a ritual to start each game. He runs to the far end zone opposite the players' entrance tunnel and drops to a knee.

"I say a prayer and I talk to my father," he said. "I have a conversation with him for a moment because I feel he's there and I want him to know that."

Walker's death in 2007 served to redouble Cruz's focus on his studies.

"I had to be the man of the family," he said. "It was up to me not to waste the opportunities I had been given. I had to study and work. There was still light at the end of the tunnel for me, and while it might have been dim, I had to run to it with everything in me."

With several acceptable grades in multiple <u>community college</u> classes, Cruz was reinstated as a UMass student in late 2007. 45

"When he came back, he understood what mattered and he understood how to take care of it," Brown said. "There was never any turning back. And he still had that smile and infectious energy that uplifted everyone."

By the 2008 season, Cruz's junior year of eligibility, he led the team with more than 1,000 receiving yards. As a senior, now 6 feet and 200 pounds, he performed even better.

"The coaches in our conference were very glad to see Victor leave," Brown said, laughing. "They had seen enough."

N.F.L. scouts, however, had not seen enough size or speed — or competition against elite talent — to call his name on draft day. Cruz later went to an open workout day for undrafted free agents at the Meadowlands. It was the league's version of a local casting call for <u>*American Idol*</u>.

The Giants invited Cruz to training camp, but they also investigated his background and learned all about the dismissal from UMass. 50

"I viewed him with a lot of caution because of that," Kevin Gilbride, the Giants' offensive coordinator, said Thursday. "He had a lot of the

After being kicked out of Massachusetts for academic reasons, Cruz returned for his junior year and led the team in receiving.

tools we look for in a slot receiver — enough size, shifty — but we did wonder: will he have the capacity or the willingness to learn everything we need our slot receivers to learn?"

Gilbride said Cruz struggled at first. But the coaches saw a determination that impressed them. For example, when Cruz was on injured reserve and missed the 2010 regular season, he attended the wide receivers film prep meetings anyway.

"I'm not surprised now when I'm told that he toughed it out in other life situations," Gilbride said. "We were very hard on him and put him through some demanding coaching. Victor would just smile and do it better the next time."

In the wake of the 2011 regular season, the best by a first-year wide receiver in Giants history (82 receptions and 1,536 yards), Cruz signed with the marketing giant IMG. He became a father recently when his longtime girlfriend, Elaina Watley, gave birth to their daughter. An autobiography may be coming. His Q rating is high enough that he turned down "Dancing With the Stars" without pause.

Not bad for a wide receiver who was still seeking his first N.F.L. regular-season catch only five months ago. 55

"I can't say I saw this coming," Marsh-Williams of UMass said. "He certainly refocused against the odds when he had to. He succeeded because of it. Victor proved us wrong, I'm happy to say."

Engaging with the Text

3–4
1. What is the **PURPOSE** of Bill Pennington's profile of Victor Cruz? What is the message it offers about the role of effort in life?

299–311
2. How does the **BEGINNING** prepare the reader for Pennington's profile? How does the beginning relate to the **ENDING?** How effective do you find the beginning and ending?

313–15
3. Shortly after this profile was published, the New York Giants won the 2012 Super Bowl. How is this fact relevant to this profile? What does it contribute to the **THESIS** of the profile?

4. Click on the hypertext links in the text and in the "Multimedia" sidebar. How do the links in the text function? Listen to the six interviews at the sidebar links. What do they contribute to the profile? What does the 2004 picture of Cruz at Bridgton Academy add?

191–204
5. *For Writing.* Write a **PROFILE** of an interesting teacher or student at your school. Secure the person's permission, and then research his or her background and arrange a brief interview in which the person discusses a topic around which you can organize your profile. Record the interview using either video or just audio, and take some photos of the person as well. Then decide on a design for the profile. Will you keep the pictures and links to the interview in sidebars, or incorporate them or some of them into the text? Be sure to include any necessary 198–99 **BACKGROUND INFORMATION** and **ENGAGING DETAILS.**

rhetorical situations   genres   processes   strategies   research MLA / APA   media / design   readings

Proposals **64**

MICHAEL CHABON

Kids' Stuff

Michael Chabon has published a dozen books, about half of them novels, beginning with The Mysteries of Pittsburgh *(1988) and most recently,* The Yiddish Policemen's Union *(2007) and the serialized novel* Gentlemen of the Road *(2007). In 2001, he was awarded a Pulitzer Prize for Fiction for his novel* The Amazing Adventures of Kavalier & Clay, *which explores the lives of two Jewish comic book artists in the 1940s. In addition to his novels, Chabon has written short-story and essay collections, newspaper serials, screenplays, children's and young-adult books, and comics. "Kids' Stuff" originated as a keynote speech at the 2004 Eisner Awards, known as the "Oscar awards of the comics industry."*

FOR AT LEAST THE FIRST FORTY YEARS OF THEIR EXISTENCE, from the Paleozoic pre-Superman era of *Famous Funnies* (1933) and *More Fun Comics* (1936), comic books were widely viewed, even by those who adored them, as juvenile: the ultimate greasy kids' stuff.* Comics were the literary equivalent of bubblegum cards, to be poked into the spokes of a young mind, where they would produce a satisfying — but entirely bogus — rumble of pleasure. But almost from the first, fitfully in the early days, intermittently through the fifties, and then starting in the mid-sixties with increasing vigor and determination, a battle has been waged by writers, artists, editors, and publishers to elevate the medium, to expand the scope of its subject matter and the range of its artistic styles, to sharpen and increase the sophistication of its language and visual grammar, to probe and explode the limits of the sequential panel, to give free rein to irony, tragedy, autobiography, and other grown-up-type modes of expression.

Also from the first, a key element — at times the central element — of this battle has been the effort to alter not just the medium itself but

---

*Greasy kids' stuff: a phrase used in 1960s advertisements for Vitalis, a men's haircare product, to disparage competing brands. [Editor's note]

rhetorical situations   genres   processes   strategies   research MLA / APA   media / design   readings

the public perception of the medium. From the late, great Will Eisner's lonely insistence, in an interview with the *Baltimore Sun* back in 1940 (1940!), on the artistic credibility of comics, to the nuanced and scholarly work of recent comics theorists, both practitioners and critics have been arguing passionately on behalf of comics' potential to please — in all the aesthetic richness of that term — the most sophisticated of readers.

The most sophisticated, that is, of *adult* readers. For the adult reader of comic books has always been the holy grail, the promised land, the imagined lover who will greet the long-suffering comic-book maker, at the end of the journey, with open arms, with acceptance, with approval.

A quest is often, among other things, an extended bout of inspired madness. Over the years this quest to break the chains of childish readership has resulted, like most bouts of inspired madness, in both folly and stunning innovation. Into the latter category we can put the work of Bernard Krigstein or Frank Miller, say, with their attempts to approximate, through radical attack on the conventions of panel layouts, the fragmentation of human consciousness by urban life; or the tight, tidy, miniaturized madness of Chris Ware. Into the former category — the folly — we might put all the things that got Dr. Frederic Wertham so upset about EC Comics in the early fifties, the syringe-pierced eyeballs and baseball diamonds made from human organs; or the short-lived outfitting of certain Marvel titles in 1965 with a label that boasted "A Marvel Pop Art Production"; or the hypertrophied, tooth-gnashing, blood-letting quote unquote heroes of the era that followed Miller's *The Dark Knight Returns*. An excess of the desire to appear grown up is one of the defining characteristics of adolescence. But these follies were the inevitable missteps and overreaching in the course of a campaign that was, in the end, successful.

Because the battle has now, in fact, been won. Not only are comics   5 appealing to a wider and older audience than ever before, but the idea of comics as a valid art form on a par at least with, say, film or rock and roll is widely if not quite universally accepted. Comics and graphic novels are regularly reviewed and debated in *Entertainment Weekly*, the *New York Times Book Review*, even in the august pages of the *New York Review of Books*. Ben Katchor won a MacArthur Fellowship, and Art Spiegelman a Pulitzer Prize.

A *modern* Batman cover.

A Batman cover from the heyday of the child-focused audience.

But the strange counterphenomenon to this indisputable rise in the reputation, the ambition, the sophistication, and the literary and artistic merit of many of our best comics over the past couple of decades is that over roughly the same period comics readership has declined. Some adults are reading better comics than ever before; but fewer people overall are reading any — far fewer, certainly, than in the great sales heyday of the medium, the early fifties, when by some estimates* as many as 650 million comic books were sold annually (compared to somewhere in the neighborhood of 80 million today). The top ten best-selling comic books in 1996, primarily issues making up two limited series, Marvel's *Civil Wars* and DC's *Infinite Crisis*, were all superhero books, and, like the majority of superhero books in the post–*Dark Knight*, post-*Watchmen* era, all of them dealt rather grimly, and in the somewhat hand-wringing fashion that has become obligatory, with the undoubtedly grown-up issues of violence, freedom, terrorism, vigilantism, political repression, mass hysteria, and the ambivalent nature of heroism. Among the top ten best-selling titles in 1960 (with an aggregate circulation, for all comics, of 400 million) one finds not only the expected *Superman* and *Batman* (decidedly sans ambivalence) but *Mickey Mouse, Looney Tunes,* and the classic sagas of *Uncle Scrooge*. And nearly the whole of the list for that year, from top to bottom, through *Casper the Friendly Ghost* (#14) and *Little Archie* (#25) to *Felix the Cat* (#47), is made up of kids' stuff, more or less greasy.

To recap — Days when comics were aimed at kids: huge sales. Days when comics are aimed at adults: not so huge sales, and declining.

The situation is more complicated than that, of course. Since 1960 there have been fundamental changes in a lot of things, among them the way comics are produced, licensed, marketed, and distributed. But maybe it is not too surprising that for a while now, fundamental changes and all, some people have been wondering: what if there were comic books for children?

---

*See, for example, www.comichron.com.

Leaving aside questions of creator's rights, paper costs, retail consolidation, the explosive growth of the collector market, and direct-market sales, a lot of comic-book people will tell you that there is simply too much competition for the kid dollar these days and that, thrown into the arena with video games, special-effects-laden films, the Internet, iPods, etc., comics will inevitably lose out. I find this argument unconvincing, not to mention a cop-out. It is, furthermore, an example of our weird naïveté, in this generation, about how sophisticated we and our children have become vis-à-vis our parents and grandparents, of the misguided sense of retrospective superiority we tend to display toward them and their vanished world. As if in 1960 there was not a *ton* of cool stuff besides comic books on which a kid could spend his or her considerably less constricted time and considerably more limited funds. In the early days of comics, in fact, unlike now, a moderately adventuresome child could find all kinds of things to do that were not only fun (partly because they took place with no adult supervision or mediation), but absolutely free. The price of fun doesn't get any more competitive than that.

I also refuse to accept as explanation for anything the often- 10 tendered argument that contemporary children are more sophisticated, that the kind of comics that pleased a seven-year-old in 1960 would leave an ultracool kid of today snickering with disdain. Even if we accept this argument with respect to "old-fashioned" comics, it would seem to be invalidated by the increasing sophistication of comic books over the past decades. But I reject its very premise. The supposed sophistication — a better term would be *knowingness* — of modern children is largely, I believe, a matter of style, a pose which they have adapted from and modeled on the rampant pose of knowingness, of being wised up, that characterizes the contemporary American style, and has done at least since the late fifties–early sixties heyday of *Mad* magazine (a publication largely enjoyed, from the beginning, by children). Even in their irony and cynicism there is something appealingly insincere, maladroit, and, well, *childish* about children. What is more, I have found that even my own children, as knowing as they often like to present themselves, still take profound pleasure in the old comics that I have given them to read. My older son has still not quite recovered from the heartbreak he felt, when he was seven, reading an old "archive edition" of *Legion of Superheroes,* at the tragic death of Ferro Lad.

Children did not abandon comics; comics, in their drive to attain respect and artistic accomplishment, abandoned children. And for a long time the lovers and partisans of comics were afraid, after so many years of struggle and hard work and incremental gains, to pick up that old jar of greasy kid stuff again, and risk undoing all the labor of so many geniuses and revolutionaries and ordinary, garden-variety artists. Comics have always been an arriviste art form, and all upstarts are to some degree ashamed of their beginnings. But shame, anxiety, the desire to preserve hard-won gains — such considerations no longer serve to explain the disappearance of children's comics. The truth is that comic-book creators have simply lost the habit of telling stories to children. And how sad is that?

When commentators on comics address this question, in the hope of encouraging publishers, writers, and artists to produce new comic books with children in mind, they usually try formulating some version of the following simple equation: create more child readers now, and you will find yourselves with more adult readers later on. Hook them early, in other words. But maybe the equation isn't so simple after all. Maybe what we need, given the sophistication of children (if we want to concede that point) and the competition for their attention and their disposable income (which has always been a factor), is not simply *more* comics for kids, but more *great* comics for kids.

Easy, I suppose, for me to say. So although I am certain that there are many professional creators of comics — people with a good ear and a sharp eye for and a natural understanding of children and their enthusiasms — who would be able to do a far better job of it, having thrown down the finned, skintight gauntlet, I now feel obliged to offer, at the least, a few tentative principles and one concrete suggestion on

rhetorical situations   genres   processes   strategies   research MLA / APA   media / design   readings

how more great comics for kids might be teased into the marketplace, even by amateurs like me. I have drawn these principles, in part, from my memories of the comics I loved when I was young, but I think they hold true as well for the best and most successful works of children's literature.

1) Let's not tell stories that we think "kids of today" might like. That is a route to inevitable failure and possible loss of sanity. *We should tell stories that we would have liked as kids.* Twist endings, the unexpected usefulness of unlikely knowledge, nobility and bravery where it's least expected, and the sudden emergence of a thread of goodness in a wicked nature, those were the kind of stories told by the writers and artists of the comic books that I liked.

2) Let's tell stories that, over time, build up an intricate, involved, involving mythology that is also accessible and comprehensible at any point of entry. The *intricacy*, the accretion of lore over time, should be both inventive and familiar, founded in old mythologies and fears but fully reinterpreted, reimagined. It will demand, it will ache, to be mastered by a child's mythology-mastering imagination. The *accessibility* will come from our making a commitment to tell a full, complete story, or a complete piece of a story, in every issue. This kind of layering of intricate lore and narrative completeness was a hallmark of the great "Superman-family" books (*Adventure, Jimmy Olsen, Superboy*) under the editorship of Mort Weisinger. 15

3) Let's cultivate an unflagging readiness as storytellers to retell the same stories *with endless embellishment*. Anybody who thinks that kids get bored by hearing the same story over and over again has never spent time telling stories to kids. The key, as in baroque music, is repetition with *variation*. Again the Mort Weisinger–edited *Superman* books, written by unflagging story-tellers like Edmond Hamilton and Otto Binder, were exemplary in this regard. The proliferation of theme and variation there verges, at times, on sheer, splendid madness.

4) Let's blow their little minds. A mind is not blown, in spite of whatever Hollywood seems to teach, merely by action sequences, things exploding, thrilling planetscapes, wild bursts of speed. Those are all good

things; but a mind is blown when something that you always feared but knew to be impossible turns out to be true; when the world turns out to be far vaster, far more marvelous or malevolent than you ever dreamed; when you get proof that everything is connected to everything else, that everything you know is wrong, that you are both the center of the universe and a tiny speck sailing off its nethermost edge.

So much for my principles: here is my concrete suggestion. If it seems a little obvious, or has already been tried and failed, then I apologize. But I cannot help noticing that in the world of children's *literature*, an overwhelming preponderance of stories are stories *about* children. The same is true of films for children: the central characters are nearly always a child, or a pair or group of children. Comic books, however, even those theoretically aimed at children, are almost always about adults or teenagers. Doesn't that strike you as odd? I suggest that a publisher should try putting out a truly thrilling, honestly observed and remembered, richly imagined, involved and yet narratively straightforward comic book for children, *about children*.

My oldest son is ten now, and he likes comic books. In 1943, if you were a ten-year-old, you probably knew a dozen other kids your age who were into Captain Marvel and the Submariner and the Blue Beetle. When I was ten, in 1973, I knew three or four. But in his class, in his world, my son is all but unique; he's the only one he knows who reads them, studies them, seeks to master and be worthy of all the rapture and strangeness they still contain. Now, comic books are so important to me — I have thought, talked, and written about them so much — that if my son did not in fact like them, I think he would be obliged to loathe them. I have pretty much *forced* comics on my children. But those of us who grew up loving comic books can't afford to take this handcrafted, one-kid at-a-time approach anymore. We have to sweep them up and carry them off on the flying carpets of story and pictures on which we ourselves, in entire generations, were borne aloft, on carpets woven by Curt Swan and Edmond Hamilton, Jack Kirby and Stan Lee, Chris Claremont and John Byrne. Those artists did it for us; we who make comics today have a solemn debt to pass it on, to weave bright carpets of our own. It's our duty, it's our opportunity, and I really do believe it will be our pleasure.

rhetorical situations   genres   processes   strategies   research MLA / APA   media / design   readings

Engaging with the Text

1. Good proposals present a **WELL-DEFINED PROBLEM** so readers understand the need for action to implement a solution. What problem does Michael Chabon define and present? How persuasively does he make the case for the existence and seriousness of the problem?

   ▲ 208

2. Chabon does not accept the argument made by comic-book people that the reason comic books today are being published more for adults than for children is because "there is simply too much competition for the kid dollar these days and that, thrown into the arena with video games, special-effects-laden films, the Internet, iPods, etc., comics will inevitably lose out." Why does he find this position unconvincing? What is your opinion on why the sales of comic books are declining and why so few are for children?

3. What are the four principles Chabon offers for creating great comics for kids? What **REASONS** does he offer for these principles?

   ◆ 326–27

4. What is the **PURPOSE** for Chabon's proposal? Who is its intended **AUDIENCE?**

   ■ 3–4
5–8

5. *For Writing.* Research some children's pastimes — such as card games, board games, or jigsaw puzzles — to identify one that has declined in popularity over the last fifty years. How would you propose bringing it back? What would it take to get kids interested in this pastime today? Write a **PROPOSAL** that outlines your ideas for reinvigorating the pastime.

   ▲ 205–13

DENNIS BARON

Don't Make English Official — Ban It Instead

Dennis Baron is a professor of English and linguistics at the University of Illinois at Urbana-Champaign. His essays on the history of English usage, language legislation, and technology and literacy have been widely published in newspapers and magazines. His books include The English-Only Question: An Official Language for Americans? *(1992) and* A Better Pencil: Reading, Writers, and the Digital Revolution *(2009). He also serves as a consultant to policy makers, lawyers, and journalists on questions concerning language. The following proposal originally appeared in the* Washington Post.

CONGRESS IS CONSIDERING, and may soon pass, legislation making English the official language of the United States. Supporters of the measure say that English forms the glue that keeps America together. They deplore the dollars wasted translating English into other languages. And they fear a horde of illegal aliens adamantly refusing to acquire the most powerful language on earth.

On the other hand, opponents of official English remind us that without legislation we have managed to get over ninety-seven percent of the residents of this country to speak the national language. No country with an official language law even comes close. Opponents also point out that today's non-English-speaking immigrants are picking up English faster than earlier generations of immigrants did, so instead of official English, they favor "English Plus," encouraging everyone to speak both English and another language.

I would like to offer a modest proposal to resolve the language impasse in Congress. Don't make English official, ban it instead.

That may sound too radical, but proposals to ban English first surfaced in the heady days after the American Revolution. Anti-British sentiment was so strong in the new United States that a few superpatriots wanted to get rid of English altogether. They suggested replacing English with Hebrew, thought by many in the eighteenth century to be

rhetorical situations

genres

processes

strategies

research MLA / APA

media / design

readings

the world's first language, the one spoken in the garden of Eden. French was also considered, because it was thought at the time, and especially by the French, to be the language of pure reason. And of course there was Greek, the language of Athens, the world's first democracy. It's not clear how serious any of these proposals were, though Roger Sherman* of Connecticut supposedly remarked that it would be better to keep English for ourselves and make the British speak Greek.

Proposals to ban English first surfaced shortly after the American Revolution.

Even if the British are now our allies, there may be some benefit to banning English today. A common language can often be the cause of strife and misunderstanding. Look at Ireland and Northern Ireland, the two Koreas, or the Union and the Confederacy. Banning English would prevent that kind of divisiveness in America today.

Also, if we banned English, we wouldn't have to worry about whose English to make official: the English of England or America? of Chicago or New York? of Ross Perot or William F. Buckley?†

We might as well ban English, too, because no one seems to read it much lately, few can spell it, and fewer still can parse it. Even English teachers have come to rely on computer spell checkers.

Another reason to ban English: it's hardly even English anymore. English started its decline in 1066, with the unfortunate incident at Hastings.‡ Since then it has become a polyglot conglomeration of French, Latin, Italian, Scandinavian, Arabic, Sanskrit, Celtic, Yiddish and Chinese, with an occasional smiley face thrown in.

More important, we should ban English because it has become a world language. Remember what happened to all the other world languages: Latin, Greek, Indo-European? One day they're on everybody's

---

Roger Sherman (1721–93): American revolutionary leader and signer of the Declaration of Independence and the U.S. Constitution. [Editor's note]

†*William F. Buckley Jr.* (1925–2008): conservative political commentator. *Ross Perot*: American industrialist and independent presidential candidate. [Editor's note]

‡*Hastings*: port on south coast of England, site of Saxon army's defeat by the invading Norman forces led by William of Normandy (c. 1028–87). [Editor's note]

tongue; the next day they're dead. Banning English now would save us that inevitable disappointment.

Although we shouldn't ban English without designating a replacement for it, there is no obvious candidate. The French blew their chance when they sold Louisiana. It doesn't look like the Russians are going to

> We might as well ban English . . . no one seems to read it much lately.

take over this country anytime soon — they're having enough trouble taking over Russia. German, the largest minority language in the U.S. until recently, lost much of its prestige after two world wars. Chinese is too hard to write, especially if you're not Chinese. There's always Esperanto, a language made up a hundred years ago that is supposed to bring about world unity. We're still waiting for that. And if you took Spanish in high school you can see that it's not easy to get large numbers of people to speak another language fluently.

In the end, though, it doesn't matter what replacement language we pick, just so long as we ban English instead of making it official. Prohibiting English will do for the language what Prohibition did for liquor. Those who already use it will continue to do so, and those who don't will want to try out what has been forbidden. This negative psychology works with children. It works with speed limits. It even worked in the Garden of Eden.

Engaging with the Text

299–306 ◆

1. Dennis Baron **BEGINS** his essay by presenting two views on whether or not English should be the official language of the United States. What is the central problem that both sides are trying to address? Is this an effective beginning? Why or why not? How else might he have begun?

2. Baron signals that his proposal is meant to be read as satire when he writes "I would like to offer a modest proposal to resolve the language impasse in Congress. Don't make English official, ban it instead." Here

rhetorical situations   genres   processes   strategies   research MLA / APA   media / design   readings

Baron alludes to Jonathan Swift's "A Modest Proposal," an essay that is a tour de force of satire. If we aren't meant to take his proposal at face value — and we aren't — what is the **PURPOSE** of Baron's proposal? What, in other words, is the real argument he is making?

3–4

3. Baron offers six **REASONS** for accepting his "solution." What are those reasons? What is the central point that holds these different reasons together?

326–27

4. If Baron's purpose is not actually to propose banning English in America, why do you think he chose to use the proposal genre to put forth his argument? What other **GENRES** might he have used?

9–11

5. *For Writing.* Identify a current hotly debated issue in the country, your state, your town, or your school. **PROPOSE** an outlandish solution for the problem and provide a plausible, if ironic, argument for your solution. Be sure to anticipate — and respond to — possible objections to your proposed solution.

205–13

MEGAN HOPKINS

Training the Next Teachers for America
A Proposal for Reconceptualizing Teach For America

Megan Hopkins was a doctoral student in the Graduate School of Education and Information Studies at the University of California, Los Angeles at the time she wrote this proposal. It appeared in a 2008 issue of Phi Delta Kappan, *a journal that addresses education policy and practice. As you read, notice how Hopkins uses evidence from several studies to support her proposal for improving the Teach For America program. Hopkins documents her sources according to* The Chicago Manual of Style, *as required for articles published in* Phi Delta Kappan.

SOON AFTER I BEGAN my first year as a Teach For America (TFA) corps member, I realized how underprepared I felt teaching first grade. Not only was I unsure how to manage and organize my classroom, but I also lacked the necessary content and pedagogical knowledge to teach my students effectively. Perhaps most important, I did not have deep understandings of or appreciation for the experiences of my students or their community. The five-week training institute I attended during the prior summer had not been enough to develop my educational "toolkit" or to prepare me to provide my students with the type of education that might begin to equalize their chances in the system.

Although I grew as an educator over time and am still committed to working in education, it was an uphill battle. And, like most other TFA corps members, I left teaching within the first three years. Since my involvement with Teach For America, the organization has made considerable efforts to refine its preparation model, yet the program continues to draw criticism for teacher underpreparation and low retention rates.

In light of my experience and this continuing criticism, I wish to recommend alterations in the preparation of corps members that would: (1) extend the TFA commitment to three years; (2) convert the first year of teaching to a residency training year, offering classroom training with expert veteran teachers while corps members also complete coursework

toward certification; and (3) offer incentives for corps members to teach longer than three years. I recommend these changes with the goal of improving the effectiveness of corps members and motivating TFA teachers to remain in their assignments for longer than two or three years. These changes could help TFA fulfill its mission of creating leaders who will make lasting changes in the field of education, while also enhancing program quality during the time these potential leaders serve in our nation's most underresourced schools.

These recommendations could be supported, in part, by the Teaching Residency Act, introduced by Sen. Barack Obama (D-Ill.), and the Preparing Excellent Teachers Act, introduced in the House by Rep. Rahm Emanuel (D-Ill.). Both bills, introduced last summer, would enable prospective teachers to work under the wing of expert mentor teachers for an academic year while they complete their coursework for certification. The bills aim to expand the reach of highly successful models for urban teacher residencies — programs that provide substantial preparation for carefully selected novice teachers who commit to teaching for a minimum of three to four years in the districts that sponsor them. The passage of this legislation would create an opportunity for Teach For America to embrace promising new strategies for teacher preparation and induction.

Why Change TFA?

Recent research on corps members' effectiveness suggests the need for a change in TFA's approach. The TFA model assumes that extensive formal teacher training is not essential for its recruits — most of them graduates of top colleges with strong leadership abilities and a desire to improve educational opportunities for the nation's children.

Yet the reality is that Teach For America teachers are initially less successful in supporting student learning than are traditionally prepared teachers who are fully certified when they enter the profession.[1] One study found that TFA recruits had more positive effects on students' math achievement as corps members finished their certification and training; however, they continued to have negative effects on elementary students' reading achievement throughout all the years of the study.[2]

A small study comparing the performance of the students of 41 beginning and experienced TFA teachers with that of the students of other teachers in their schools reported that the TFA-taught students performed as well as the others in reading and better than the others in math. But the teachers of the comparison group were even less likely to be trained or certified than the TFA teachers.[3] The slight increases in mathematics achievement that the more experienced TFA teachers contributed were not substantial.

While the research is limited to comparing student performance on standardized tests, and it is arguable whether these tests accurately measure student achievement, these studies show that TFA corps members are not, in fact, as successful as the organization assumes they will be. Particularly when they begin teaching, TFA teachers are less successful than their peers who receive more formal training.

In addition to criticism involving the preparation of its teachers, Teach For America is often criticized for its high turnover rates, as studies have found that 80 percent or more of corps members have left their teaching positions by the end of the third year, just when they are beginning to be more successful. This figure compares to about 30 percent to 40 percent of traditionally certified teachers in the same districts who leave by the end of the third year.[4] Districts — and their schools and students — bear the cost of this high level of attrition, and not surprisingly, some district officials have expressed concerns about this turnover rate. For example, Chicago administrators have indicated their desire for TFA corps members to stay longer, noting the longer tenures of other recruits and emphasizing their own responsibility to be "conscientious consumers" when making hiring decisions.[5] These observations suggest that TFA should consider incentives for corps members who are willing to remain longer in the classroom.

What Approaches Might Improve the Model?

In comparative international studies of teacher preparation, the U.S. has been shown to undervalue preservice training. In particular, it is much less likely in the U.S. than in other developed nations that prospective

teachers will learn to teach under the wing of a master teacher while they are learning about curriculum, instruction, learning, and child development. Most European countries include a full year of closely supervised clinical practice in a school associated with the university as part of universal preservice preparation. Other countries, such as Japan, require extensive on-the-job training for teachers in their initial "apprenticeship," with coaching and 60 days per year of seminars and classroom visits providing guidance and support that prepare novice teachers to lead their own classrooms.[6] Master teachers supervise beginning teachers by observing, suggesting areas for improvement, and discussing effective instructional strategies.

Similarly, in an attempt to strengthen teacher preparation in the U.S. and to alter experienced teachers' roles in teacher training, some schools and universities across the country are collaborating to create professional development schools. These schools are designed to support the learning of new and experienced teachers and to restructure schools of education.[7] In partnership with universities, veteran teachers serve as mentors for new teachers and work with university faculty members to develop the preparation curriculum and make decisions about instructional practices. Not only do such schools promote collaboration and provide hands-on training for new teachers, but they also redefine the roles of experienced teachers by giving them an opportunity to take on leadership positions. Studies show that teachers trained in professional development schools feel better prepared, more often apply theory to practice, are more confident and enthusiastic about teaching, and are more highly rated than teachers prepared in other ways.[8]

More recently, shortages of high-quality teachers have led large urban school districts to initiate their own versions of the professional development school approach. For example, the Boston Public Schools and the Boston Plan for Excellence collaborated to create the Boston Teacher Residency; Chicago implemented the Academy for Urban School Leadership through a nonprofit agency chartered by the city schools; and Denver started the Boettcher Teachers Program in two of its schools, with the help of the Boettcher Foundation, the Public Education and Business Coalition, and the University of Denver.[9] Together, these programs form the Coalition of Urban Teacher Residencies. Each program builds on a medical residency approach to train new teachers, very much like the professional development school model. The programs recruit recent college graduates and midlife career changers to complete a year-long paid residency with an expert mentor teacher while they also take coursework toward certification and a master's degree in education. When they have completed a year-end portfolio evaluation and the required coursework, program graduates begin teaching independently within their residency districts the following year. They continue to receive mentoring while they begin to teach. Finally, program participants must commit to teach in the district for at least three or four years. This model of preparation brings committed, well-prepared individuals into high-need urban schools with the hope of keeping them there.

A Teach for America Residency

In view of TFA teachers' limited preparation and considering the promise of these innovative approaches, I recommend that Teach For America develop a residency training model with the following features:

1. *Extend the program's current two-year commitment to three years.* Corps members will serve as residents during their first year. Then they will go on to teach on their own for at least two subsequent years.

2. *Require all first-year corps members to complete a residency year in an experienced teacher's classroom within their placement district and at (or near) their placement grade level.* During this year, corps members will co-teach with a mentor teacher who is deemed highly effective at raising student achievement. The mentor teacher, in collaboration with a TFA program director or university instructor, will scaffold the corps member's training, so that the corps member first observes the mentor teacher and discusses instructional strategies and eventually leads the classroom while the mentor assesses and provides feedback on the corps member's performance. During this year of residency, not only will corps members acquire collaborative skills and instructional

rhetorical situations   genres   processes   strategies   research MLA / APA   media / design   readings

expertise, but they will also gain an understanding of the community context in which they will teach, and they will complete coursework for certification.

3. *Cluster TFA "residents" at high-performing urban schools.* Each of the programs in the Coalition of Urban Teacher Residencies concentrates its participants at a small number of schools that have a large number of expert teachers and adept administrators. Like prospective teachers who train in professional development schools, residents under this model would collaborate within a school community that provides a positive culture and support.

4. *Offer courses through a university partner for first-year corps members to obtain certification and a master's degree.* During the residency year, corps members will also take courses through a local partner university so that they may complete their teacher certification requirements and have the opportunity to obtain a master's degree. While TFA currently partners with local universities in most of its placement sites, stronger relationships between TFA and these partners — and between coursework and clinical experiences — must be developed if residents are to integrate theory and practice and apply what they are learning.

5. *Provide incentives to teach longer than three years.* A range of incentives could be offered, including opportunities to take on leadership roles, as well as stipends and forgivable loans for accepting additional responsibilities. Teachers who serve for longer than three years could also serve as liaisons among members of the partnership and provide support and professional development to novice teachers. After gaining substantial teaching experience, these longer-term corps members could serve as mentors in one of the residency training schools and partner with university colleagues in offering support and coursework.

Challenges to Implementation

Since these strategies would require an overhaul of Teach For America's approach to teacher preparation, there are many issues to address before proceeding.

Funding. School districts currently provide full salaries to TFA corps   15
members. A different funding structure would need to be developed to
support first-year corps members during their residency year, as many
districts could not afford to support two teachers for a single classroom.
Additional funds would also be needed to compensate mentor teachers
and longer-term TFA teachers who took on leadership roles, although
these roles already exist in a number of districts. Some possibilities
follow:

- As the Chicago teacher residency does, TFA and the districts could
  adopt a graduated pay scale that would pay first-year corps members
  less than the normal first-year teacher salary, while longer-term corps
  members would receive a stipend in addition to their regular salary
  for fulfilling a mentor or leadership role. In addition, teachers who
  decided to remain at their placement sites for longer than their com-
  mitments could be granted forgivable student loans, with a specific
  percentage of the balance forgiven for each additional year teaching
  at the site. Federal funds are available to help underwrite such programs to keep teachers in high-need schools.

- Model first-year funding on the Boston Teacher Residency (BTR)
  model. This program offers a small stipend ($10,000) to first-year res-
  idents. In addition, residents must pay tuition of $10,000 for their uni-
  versity coursework, but BTR offers them a no-interest loan to cover
  this cost, which is reduced and ultimately eliminated if residents
  remain as teachers in the district for three years. Teach For America
  could use a similar approach.

- If Teach For America alters its approach to include a year of residency,
  it may be able to reduce its summer institute training or even replace
  it with training administered within the cities or school districts where
  corps members are placed, thereby greatly reducing the costs. Corps
  members may be better served by completing an intensive training
  in their placement district under the guidance of an expert mentor
  teacher from that district so that they can acquire knowledge about
  the specific context in which they will teach.

- Instead of devoting funding to recruitment and to expanding the corps at the current rapid rate, Teach For America could use this funding to implement the preparation model proposed. While this may hinder TFA from meeting its expansion goals, the model would produce a number of high-quality teachers who would be likely to remain for more than two or three years at their placement sites. This would reduce the demand for new teachers and provide greater benefit to districts, schools, and students.

Capacity. If Teach For America desires to initiate these changes, it will need to consider its capacity to do so. One issue will be recruiting enough mentor teachers to match the number of first-year corps members. TFA currently recruits veteran teachers for its summer institute, and these people are certainly candidates for mentoring positions during the school year. Furthermore, because TFA has been placing teachers in some cities for over 10 years, there are some sites that have a reasonable number of alumni still in teaching, and they would be an excellent pool of mentors and could also provide connections to other experienced teachers.

In addition, the organization would need to form partnerships with local universities and with local school districts. Thus far, Teach For America has been successful at securing such partnerships within each placement city, but none has thus far been as involved as this new strategy would require. New models of coursework may need to be developed, and instructors may need to be hired. The Boston Teacher Residency has a curriculum coordinator who works to develop the coursework and to seek university faculty members to help design and to teach each of the required courses. The Chicago Residency works with National-Louis University and the University of Illinois at Chicago to design and offer coursework that is linked to the clinical experience.

Existing structures. Teach For America would have to make some decisions about the existing structures of the organization. For example, it would have to consider making changes to or eliminating the summer institute to supply funding for a new system. It would also have to consider the current support systems within each placement city. For example, the roles and responsibilities of program directors would change within this model, as they not only would work with corps members but also would collaborate with mentor teachers, school principals, and university faculty members.

Possible objections. If the Teach For America commitment is extended to three years, some applicants may be reluctant to apply, thus limiting the pool of highly qualified candidates. However, better training and support should encourage other recruits, and the incentives offered in the third year and beyond should overcome some resistance. Surveying and conducting focus groups with current corps members regarding the use of a residency model would help TFA determine which kinds of recruits would be interested in participating in a longer-term alternative track. Furthermore, some school districts will prefer the model, as it provides better-prepared entrants who have a better chance of staying in teaching longer. This improvement may encourage districts to contribute funds, just as a growing number are creating residency and intern programs of their own.

Next steps. Before implementing a programwide change, Teach For America would be wise to pilot the new strategy in one placement site and assess its effectiveness. Such a site should be chosen after assessing such resources as the availability of mentor teachers, the number of effective schools to serve as residency sites, and the potential for district and university support. New strategies should be implemented for no less than three years before evaluating results, as this would provide enough time for at least one cohort of corps members to complete their service under the new model.

Conclusion

While these proposals would require substantial redesign of the TFA model, the results are likely to be worth the investment. Teach For America has the potential to effect large-scale change in the field of

rhetorical situations   genres   processes   strategies   research MLA / APA   media / design   readings

education. It recruits highly qualified, motivated corps members who appreciate the importance of equal educational opportunities, and many go on to devote their lives to this mission. However, these bright individuals are not as effective in the classroom as they could be, and their students do not perform as well as students in classrooms where teachers have more formal training. Corps members who are given a full year to learn effective instructional practices and to fully prepare to work within the context of their placement site will be better prepared to enter their classrooms as skilled teachers. If TFA can prepare its recruits to be more successful in their classrooms from the beginning of their service, it may be able to achieve its vision more effectively, so that, as the TFA mission states, "One day, all children in this nation will have the opportunity to attain an excellent education."

Notes

1. Ildiko Laczko-Kerr and David C. Berliner, "The Effectiveness of 'Teach For America' and Other Under-Certified Teachers on Student Academic Achievement: A Case of Harmful Public Policy," *Education Policy Analysis Archives,* 6 September 2002, http://epaa.asu.edu/epaa/v10n37; Linda Darling-Hammond et al., "Does Teacher Preparation Matter? Evidence About Teacher Certification, Teach For America, and Teacher Effectiveness," www.schoolredesign.net/binaries/teachercert.pdf, 2005; and Thomas J. Kane, Jonah E. Rockoff, and Douglas O. Staiger, "What Does Certification Tell Us About Teacher Effectiveness? Evidence from New York City," Working Paper 12155, National Bureau of Economic Research, Cambridge, Mass., April 2006.

2. Donald Boyd et al., "How Changes in Entry Requirements Alter the Teacher Workforce and Affect Student Achievement," *Education Finance and Policy,* vol. 1, 2006, pp. 176–216.

3. Paul Decker, Daniel Mayer, and Steven Glazerman, *The Effects of Teach For America on Students: Findings from a National Evaluation* (Princeton, N.J.: Mathematica Policy Research, MPR Reference No: M-8792750, 2004).

4. Boyd et al., op. cit.; Darling-Hammond, op. cit.; and Kane, Rockoff, and Staiger, op. cit.

5. Bess Keller, "Chicago Wants TFA to Commit Longer," *Education Week,* 22 September 2004, p. 14.

6. Harold W. Stevenson and James W. Stigler, *The Learning Gap* (New York: Simon & Schuster, 1992).

7. Linda Darling-Hammond, Marcella L. Bullmaster, and Velma L. Cobb, "Rethinking Teacher Leadership Through Professional Development Schools," *Elementary School Journal,* vol. 96, 1995, pp. 87–106.

8. Renee L. Clift and Patricia Brady, "Research on Methods Courses and Field Experiences," in Marilyn Cochran-Smith and Kenneth M. Zeichner, eds., *Studying Teacher Education: The Report of the AERA Panel on Research and Teacher Education* (Mahwah, N.J.: Erlbaum, 2005), pp. 309–424; Gloria A. Neubert and James B. Binko, "Professional Development Schools: The Proof Is in the Performance," *Educational Leadership,* February 1998, pp. 44–46; and Suzanne Yerian and Pamela L. Grossman, "Preservice Teachers' Perceptions of Their Middle-Level Teacher Education Experience: A Comparison of a Traditional and a PDS Model," *Teacher Education Quarterly,* Fall 1997, pp. 85–101.

9. Information about the Boston Teacher Residency is available at www.bpe.org/btr; information about the Academy for Urban School Leadership, at www.ausl-chicago.org; and information about the Boettcher Teachers Program, at www.boettcherteachers.org.

Engaging with the Text

1. Megan Hopkins identifies specific problems with the Teach For America program and proposes three changes to help solve those problems. What specific changes does she suggest? How does she build a convincing **ARGUMENT** to persuade readers to accept the solutions she proposes?

208

306–10

2. Hopkins **ENDS** her proposal with a powerful quotation from the Teach For America mission statement: "One day all children in this nation will have the opportunity to attain an excellent education." How effective is this ending? In what ways would Hopkins's proposed solutions contribute to this goal?

rhetorical situations   genres   processes   strategies   research MLA / APA   media / design   readings

3. Who is the intended **AUDIENCE** for this proposal? How does the content of the proposal as well as its place of publication lead you to identify this particular audience?

5–8

4. How does Hopkins **ANTICIPATE QUESTIONS** about and potential objections to her proposal? Point to two specific passages in which she anticipates questions and objections. Can you think of any additional questions about or potential objections to her proposal that she has not addressed?

208

5. *For Writing.* Writing from the perspective of a teacher, Hopkins proposes ways to reconceptualize the Teach For America program to help it better realize its "potential to effect large-scale change in the field of education." Consider your own experience as a student. What aspect of your education — class sizes, teaching methods, required courses, peer mentoring, and so on — might be improved? Write a **PROPOSAL** that identifies one or more problems with your education as you have experienced it and argues for your recommended solutions.

205–13

PETER SINGER

The Singer Solution to World Poverty

Australian philosopher Peter Singer is the Ira W. DeCamp professor of bioethics at Princeton University and a professor in the Center for Applied Philosophy and Public Ethics at the University of Melbourne in Australia. The author of numerous books, among them Animal Liberation *(revised edition 2001),* One World: Ethics and Globalization *(2002), and* The Life You Can Save: Acting Now to End World Poverty *(2009), he is considered one of the founders of the modern animal rights movement. The following proposal was first published in 1999 in the* New York Times Magazine.

IN THE BRAZILIAN FILM CENTRAL STATION, Dora is a retired schoolteacher who makes ends meet by sitting at the station writing letters for illiterate people. Suddenly she has an opportunity to pocket $1,000. All she has to do is persuade a homeless nine-year-old boy to follow her to an address she has been given. (She is told he will be adopted by wealthy foreigners.) She delivers the boy, gets the money, spends some of it on a television set, and settles down to enjoy her new acquisition. Her neighbor spoils the fun, however, by telling her that the boy was too old to be adopted — he will be killed and his organs sold for transplantation. Perhaps Dora knew this all along, but after her neighbor's plain speaking, she spends a troubled night. In the morning Dora resolves to take the boy back.

Suppose Dora had told her neighbor that it is a tough world, other people have nice new TVs too, and if selling the kid is the only way she can get one, well, he was only a street kid. She would then have become, in the eyes of the audience, a monster. She redeems herself only by being prepared to bear considerable risks to save the boy.

At the end of the movie, in cinemas in the affluent nations of the world, people who would have been quick to condemn Dora if she had not rescued the boy go home to places far more comfortable than her apartment. In fact, the average family in the United States spends almost

one-third of its income on things that are no more necessary to them than Dora's new TV was to her. Going out to nice restaurants, buying new clothes because the old ones are no longer stylish, vacationing at beach resorts — so much of our income is spent on things not essential to the preservation of our lives and health. Donated to one of a number of charitable agencies, that money could mean the difference between life and death for children in need.

All of which raises a question: in the end, what is the ethical distinction between a Brazilian who sells a homeless child to organ peddlers and an American who already has a TV and upgrades to a better one — knowing that the money could be donated to an organization that would use it to save the lives of kids in need?

Of course, there are several differences between the two situations   5
that could support different moral judgments about them. For one thing, to be able to consign a child to death when he is standing right in front of you takes a chilling kind of heartlessness; it is much easier to ignore an appeal for money to help children you will never meet. Yet for a utilitarian philosopher like myself — that is, one who judges whether acts are right or wrong by their consequences — if the upshot of the American's failure to donate the money is that one more kid dies on the streets of a Brazilian city, then it is, in some sense, just as bad as selling the kid to the organ peddlers. But one doesn't need to embrace my utilitarian ethic to see that, at the very least, there is a troubling incongruity in being so quick to condemn Dora for taking the child to the organ peddlers while, at the same time, not regarding the American consumer's behavior as raising a serious moral issue.

In his 1996 book *Living High and Letting Die,* the New York University philosopher Peter Unger presented an ingenious series of imaginary examples designed to probe our intuitions about whether it is wrong to live well without giving substantial amounts of money to help people who are hungry, malnourished, or dying from easily treatable illnesses like diarrhea. Here's my paraphrase of one of these examples:

Bob is close to retirement. He has invested most of his savings in a very rare and valuable old car, a Bugatti, which he has not been able to insure. The Bugatti is his pride and joy. In addition to the pleasure he gets from driving and caring for his car, Bob knows that its rising market value means that he will always be able to sell it and live comfortably after retirement. One day when Bob is out for a drive, he parks the Bugatti near the end of a railway siding and goes for a walk up the track. As he does so, he sees that a runaway train, with no one aboard, is running down the railway track. Looking farther down the track, he sees the small figure of a child very likely to be killed by the runaway train. He can't stop the train and the child is too far away to warn of the danger, but he can throw a switch that will divert the train down the siding where his Bugatti is parked. Then nobody will be killed — but the train will destroy his Bugatti. Thinking of his joy in owning the car and the financial security it represents, Bob decides not to throw the switch. The child is killed. For many years to come, Bob enjoys owning his Bugatti and the financial security it represents.

Bob's conduct, most of us will immediately respond, was gravely wrong. Unger agrees. But then he reminds us that we, too, have opportunities to save the lives of children. We can give to organizations like Unicef or Oxfam America. How much would we have to give one of these organizations to have a high probability of saving the life of a child threatened by easily preventable diseases? (I do not believe that children are more worth saving than adults, but since no one can argue that children have brought their poverty on themselves, focusing on them simplifies the issues.) Unger called up some experts and used the information they provided to offer some plausible estimates that include the cost of raising money, administrative expenses, and the cost of delivering aid where it is most needed. By his calculation, $200 in donations would help a sickly two-year-old transform into a healthy six-year-old — offering safe passage through childhood's most dangerous years. To show how practical philosophical argument can be, Unger even tells his readers that they can easily donate funds by using their credit card and calling one of these toll-free numbers: (800) 367-5437 for Unicef; (800) 693-2687 for Oxfam America.

> You shouldn't take that cruise, redecorate the house, or get that pricey new suit. After all, a $1000 suit could save five children's lives.

Now you, too, have the information you need to save a child's life. How should you judge yourself if you don't do it? Think again about Bob and his Bugatti. Unlike Dora, Bob did not have to look into the eyes of the child he was sacrificing for his own material comfort. The child was a complete stranger to him and too far away to relate to in an intimate, personal way. Unlike Dora, too, he did not mislead the child or initiate the chain of events imperiling him. In all these respects, Bob's situation resembles that of people able but unwilling to donate to overseas aid and differs from Dora's situation.

If you still think that it was very wrong of Bob not to throw the   10 switch that would have diverted the train and saved the child's life, then it is hard to see how you could deny that it is also very wrong not to send money to one of the organizations listed above. Unless, that is, there is some morally important difference between the two situations that I have overlooked.

Is it the practical uncertainties about whether aid will really reach the people who need it? Nobody who knows the world of overseas aid can doubt that such uncertainties exist. But Unger's figure of $200 to save a child's life was reached after he had made conservative assumptions about the proportion of the money donated that will actually reach its target.

One genuine difference between Bob and those who can afford to donate to overseas aid organizations but don't is that only Bob can save the child on the tracks, whereas there are hundreds of millions of people who can give $200 to overseas aid organizations. The problem is that most of them aren't doing it. Does this mean that it is all right for you not to do it?

Suppose that there were more owners of priceless vintage cars — Carol, Dave, Emma, Fred and so on, down to Ziggy — all in exactly the same situation as Bob, with their own siding and their own switch, all sacrificing the child in order to preserve their own cherished car. Would that make it all right for Bob to do the same? To answer this question affirmatively is to endorse follow-the-crowd ethics — the kind of ethics that led many Germans to look away when the Nazi atrocities were being committed. We do not excuse them because others were behaving no better.

We seem to lack a sound basis for drawing a clear moral line between Bob's situation and that of any reader of this article with $200 to spare who does not donate it to an overseas aid agency. These readers seem to be acting at least as badly as Bob was acting when he chose to let the runaway train hurtle toward the unsuspecting child. In the light of this conclusion, I trust that many readers will reach for the phone and donate that $200. Perhaps you should do it before reading further.

Now that you have distinguished yourself morally from people who   15
put their vintage cars ahead of a child's life, how about treating yourself and your partner to dinner at your favorite restaurant? But wait. The money you will spend at the restaurant could also help save the lives of children overseas! True, you weren't planning to blow $200 tonight, but if you were to give up dining out just for one month, you would easily save that amount. And what is one month's dining out, compared to a child's life? There's the rub. Since there are a lot of desperately needy children in the world, there will always be another child whose life you could save for another $200. Are you therefore obliged to keep giving until you have nothing left? At what point can you stop?

Hypothetical examples can easily become farcical. Consider Bob. How far past losing the Bugatti should he go? Imagine that Bob had got his foot stuck in the track of the siding, and if he diverted the train, then before it rammed the car it would also amputate his big toe. Should he still throw the switch? What if it would amputate his foot? His entire leg?

As absurd as the Bugatti scenario gets when pushed to extremes, the point it raises is a serious one: only when the sacrifices become very significant indeed would most people be prepared to say that Bob does nothing wrong when he decides not to throw the switch. Of course, most people could be wrong; we can't decide moral issues by taking opinion polls. But consider for yourself the level of sacrifice that you would demand of Bob, and then think about how much money you would have to give away in order to make a sacrifice that is roughly equal to that. It's almost certainly much, much more than $200. For most middle-class Americans, it could easily be more like $200,000.

Isn't it counterproductive to ask people to do so much? Don't we run the risk that many will shrug their shoulders and say that morality, so conceived, is fine for saints but not for them? I accept that we are unlikely to see, in the near or even medium-term future, a world in which it is normal for wealthy Americans to give the bulk of their wealth to strangers. When it comes to praising or blaming people for what they do, we tend to use a standard that is relative to some conception of normal behavior. Comfortably off Americans who give, say, 10 percent of their income to overseas aid organizations are so far ahead of most of their equally comfortable fellow citizens that I wouldn't go out of my way to chastise them for not doing more. Nevertheless, they should be doing much more, and they are in no position to criticize Bob for failing to make the much greater sacrifice of his Bugatti.

At this point various objections may crop up. Someone may say: "If every citizen living in the affluent nations contributed his or her share I wouldn't have to make such a drastic sacrifice, because long before such levels were reached, the resources would have been there to save the lives of all those children dying from lack of food or medical care. So why should I give more than my fair share?" Another, related objection is that the government ought to increase its overseas aid allocations, since that would spread the burden more equitably across all taxpayers.

Yet the question of how much we ought to give is a matter to be 20 decided in the real world — and that, sadly, is a world in which we know that most people do not, and in the immediate future will not, give substantial amounts to overseas aid agencies. We know, too, that at least in the next year, the United States government is not going to meet even the very modest United Nations–recommended target of 0.7 percent of gross national product; at a moment it lags far below that, at 0.09 percent, not even half of Japan's 0.22 percent or a tenth of Denmark's 0.97 percent. Thus, we know that the money we can give beyond that theoretical "fair share" is still going to save lives that would otherwise be lost. While the idea that no one need do more than his or her fair share is a powerful one, should it prevail if we know that others are not doing their fair share and that children will die preventable deaths unless we do more than our fair share? That would be taking fairness too far.

Thus, this ground for limiting how much we ought to give also fails. In the world as it is now, I can see no escape from the conclusion that each one of us with wealth surplus to his or her essential needs should be giving most of it to help people suffering from poverty so dire as to be life-threatening. That's right: I'm saying that you shouldn't buy that new car, take that cruise, redecorate the house, or get that pricey new suit. After all, a $1,000 suit could save five children's lives.

So how does my philosophy break down in dollars and cents? An American household with an income of $50,000 spends around $30,000 annually on necessities, according to the Conference Board, a nonprofit economic research organization. Therefore, for a household bringing in $50,000 a year, donations to help the world's poor should be as close as possible to $20,000. The $30,000 required for necessities holds for higher incomes as well. So a household making $100,000 could cut a yearly check for $70,000. Again, the formula is simple: Whatever money you're spending on luxuries, not necessities, should be given away.

Now, evolutionary psychologists tell us that human nature just isn't sufficiently altruistic to make it plausible that many people will sacrifice so much for strangers. On the facts of human nature, they might be right, but they would be wrong to draw a moral conclusion from those facts. If it is the case that we ought to do things that, predictably, most of us won't do, then let's face that fact head-on. Then, if we value the life of a child more than going to fancy restaurants, the next time we dine out we will know that we could have done something better with our money. If that makes living a morally decent life extremely arduous, well, then that is the way things are. If we don't do it, then we should at least know that we are failing to live a morally decent life — not because it is good to wallow in guilt but because knowing where we should be going is the first step toward heading in that direction.

When Bob first grasped the dilemma that faced him as he stood by that railway switch, he must have thought how extraordinarily unlucky he was to be placed in a situation in which he must choose between the

life of an innocent child and the sacrifice of most of his savings. But he was not unlucky at all. We are all in that situation.

Engaging with the Text

1. What is the **PURPOSE** of Peter Singer's proposal? What is he actually proposing? What action does he want us to take? Point to passages where his purpose is made explicit.

    3–4

2. Singer begins his essay with reference to the Brazilian film *Central Station* and follows it with a hypothetical **SCENARIO.** What role do the film and the scenario play in his proposal? What do they contribute to the persuasiveness of his argument? Do you find them effective? Why or why not?

    331–32

3. Singer argues that "whatever money you're spending on luxuries, not necessities, should be given away." To what degree do you agree with this claim? How much faith in this claim does Singer himself appear to have?

4. What **QUESTIONS** does Singer anticipate? How does he address potential naysayers?

    208

5. *For Writing.* Think of a large societal problem (for example, poverty, pollution, or unemployment) and how the actions of individuals might help alleviate it (volunteering at a food bank, recycling soda cans, restructuring a company to create more positions). Describe the problem and write a **PROPOSAL** for how you and other individuals can help to solve it.

    205–13

JOHN BOHANNON

Dance vs. PowerPoint: A Modest Proposal

John Bohannon is a science journalist who writes for Discover, Science, and Wired magazines. For his reporting on collaborative research in Gaza, he won the 2006 Reuters environmental journalism award. In 2008, under the pseudonym "Gonzo Scientist," he created an annual "Dance Your Ph.D." contest, in which doctoral students in science and social science must explain their dissertations through interpretive dance.

During the summer of 2011, Walter de Brouwer, curator of TEDˣ Brussels, admired the "Dance Your Ph.D." contest and invited Bohannon to give a talk about it at TEDx Brussels. Bohannon responded that instead of showing dance videos during his lecture, he "wanted to use live dancers on stage in lieu of PowerPoint." He worked with the Black Label Movement dance troupe, choreographer Carl Flink, and the composer Greg Brosofske to put together a performance that argues for the superiority of dance over PowerPoint by imitating Jonathan Swift's satire "A Modest Proposal." Bohannon's goal, he said, was "preventing the artists of the United States of America from being a burden to their parents or country and . . . making them beneficial to the public." The performance of "Dance vs. PowerPoint: A Modest Proposal" took place on November 11, 2011.

On the following pages you'll see snapshots of the performance from beginning to end. See if you could imagine how this could have been said in a PowerPoint. To see the online version, go to <u>wwnorton.com/write/fieldguidelinks</u>.

Engaging with the Text

1. How does John Bohannon **BEGIN** his "modest proposal"? How effective is this beginning given Bohannon's **PURPOSE** in this piece?

299–306

3–4

313–15

2. Bohannon doesn't state the **THESIS** of his proposal explicitly until 5:58 minutes into the video. Why do you think he didn't announce it at the very beginning? Why might he have thought he needed to focus on his argument for the **SOLUTION** up front?

208

208

3. The **PROBLEM** that Bohannon's proposal tries to solve is that "bad *PowerPoint* presentations are a serious threat to the global economy." What do you see as the pros and cons of *PowerPoint* vs. live streaming performance or video? Do you think Bohannan makes a **CONVINCING ARGUMENT** for his proposed solution? Why or why not? How would his proposal be different and how effective would it be if he had used written text only? What does video do for his proposal?

208

4. What is Bohannon's **STANCE** in this proposal? Point to at least one phrase he says that reveals this stance.

12–15

5. *For Writing.* Whether or not you've already read Swift's "Modest Proposal," *Google* it and read it. Then think of a present-day problem that could be solved with an unexpected approach and write a satirical **PROPOSAL** for the solution. Include visuals — photos, drawings, video, or some combination — to illustrate your proposal, and consider using audio as well. Make clear that you are writing a satire by the exaggerated way you phrase the problem, such as Bohannon does when he states that "bad *PowerPoint* presentations are a serious threat to the global economy."

205–13

65 Reflections

rhetorical situations   genres   processes   strategies   research MLA / APA   media / design   readings

DAVE BARRY

Guys vs. Men

Dave Barry is a well-known humorist who is the author of thirty books and countless columns. Two of his books — Dave Barry Turns 40 *(1990) and* Dave Barry's Greatest Hits *(1988) — served as the basis for the TV sitcom* Dave's World, *which ran for four seasons from 1993 to 1997. In 1988, Barry was awarded a Pulitzer Prize for Commentary. Formerly a syndicated columnist, he has had writing published in over 500 newspapers in the United States and abroad. The following reflection is from his book* Dave Barry's Complete Guide to Guys.

MEN ITSELF IS A SERIOUS WORD, not to mention *manhood* and *manly*. Such words make being male sound like a very important activity, as opposed to what it primarily consists of, namely, possessing a set of minor and frequently unreliable organs.

But men tend to attach great significance to Manhood. This results in certain characteristically masculine, by which I mean stupid, behavioral patterns that can produce unfortunate results such as violent crime, war, spitting, and ice hockey. These things have given males a bad name.* And the "Men's Movement," which is supposed to bring out the more positive aspects of Manliness, seems to be densely populated with loons and goobers.

So I'm saying that there's another way to look at males: not as aggressive macho dominators; not as sensitive, liberated, hugging drummers; but as *guys*.

And what, exactly, do I mean by "guys"? I don't know. I haven't thought that much about it. One of the major characteristics of guyhood is that we guys don't spend a lot of time pondering our deep innermost feelings. There is a serious question in my mind about whether guys

---

*Specifically, "asshole."

actually *have* deep innermost feelings, unless you count, for example, loyalty to the Detroit Tigers, or fear of bridal showers.

But although I can't define exactly what it means to be a guy, I can   5
describe certain guy characteristics, such as:

Guys Like Neat Stuff

By "neat," I mean "mechanical and unnecessarily complex." I'll give you an example. Right now I'm typing these words on an *extremely* powerful computer. It's the latest in a line of maybe ten computers I've owned, each one more powerful than the last. My computer is chock-full of RAM and ROM and bytes and megahertzes and various other items that enable a computer to kick data-processing butt. It is probably capable of supervising the entire U.S. air-defense apparatus while simultaneously processing the tax return of every resident of Ohio. I use it mainly to write a newspaper column. This is an activity wherein I sit and stare at the screen for maybe ten minutes, then, using only my forefingers, slowly type something like:

Henry Kissinger looks like a big wart.

I stare at this for another ten minutes, have an inspiration, then amplify the original thought as follows:

Henry Kissinger looks like a big fat wart.

Then I stare at that for another ten minutes, pondering whether I   10
should try to work in the concept of "hairy."

This is absurdly simple work for my computer. It sits there, humming impatiently, bored to death, passing the time between keystrokes via brain-teaser activities such as developing a Unified Field Theory of the universe and translating the complete works of Shakespeare into rap.*

In other words, this computer is absurdly overqualified to work for me, and yet soon, I guarantee, I will buy an *even more powerful* one. I won't be able to stop myself. I'm a guy.

------

*To be or not? I got to *know*.
Might kill myself by the end of the *show*.

Probably the ultimate example of the fundamental guy drive to have neat stuff is the Space Shuttle. Granted, the guys in charge of this program *claim* it has a Higher Scientific Purpose, namely to see how humans function in space. But of course we have known for years how humans function in space: They float around and say things like; "Looks real good, Houston!"

No, the real reason for the existence of the Space Shuttle is that it is one humongous and spectacularly gizmo-intensive item of hardware. Guys can tinker with it practically forever, and occasionally even get it to work, and use it to place *other* complex mechanical items into orbit, where they almost immediately break, which provides a great excuse to send the Space Shuttle up *again*. It's Guy Heaven.

Other results of the guy need to have stuff are Star Wars, the recreational boating industry, monorails, nuclear weapons, and wristwatches that indicate the phase of the moon. I am not saying that women haven't been involved in the development or use of this stuff. I'm saying that, without guys, this stuff probably would not exist; just as, without women, virtually every piece of furniture in the world would still be in its original position. Guys do not have a basic need to rearrange furniture. Whereas a woman who could cheerfully use the same computer for fifty-three years will rearrange her furniture on almost a weekly basis, sometimes in the dead of night. She'll be sound asleep in bed, and suddenly, at 2 A.M., she'll be awakened by the urgent thought: *The blue-green sofa needs to go perpendicular to the wall instead of parallel, and it needs to go there RIGHT NOW.* So she'll get up and move it, which of course necessitates moving other furniture, and soon she has rearranged her entire living room, shifting great big heavy pieces that ordinarily would require several burly men to lift, because there are few forces in Nature more powerful than a woman who needs to rearrange furniture. Every so often a guy will wake up to discover that, because of his wife's overnight efforts, he now lives in an entirely different house.

(I realize that I'm making gender-based generalizations here, but my feeling is that if God did not want us to make gender-based generalizations, She would not have given us genders.)

15

Guys Like a Really Pointless Challenge

Not long ago I was sitting in my office at the *Miami Herald*'s Sunday magazine, *Tropic,* reading my fan mail,* when I heard several of my guy coworkers in the hallway talking about how fast they could run the forty-yard dash. These are guys in their thirties and forties who work in journalism, where the most demanding physical requirement is the ability to digest vending-machine food. In other words, these guys have absolutely no need to run the forty-yard dash.

But one of them, Mike Wilson, was writing a story about a star high-school football player who could run it in 4.38 seconds. Now if Mike had written a story about, say, a star high-school poet, none of my guy coworkers would have suddenly decided to find out how well they could write sonnets. But when Mike turned in his story, they became *deeply* concerned about how fast they could run the forty-yard dash. They were so concerned that the magazine editor, Tom Shroder, decided that they should get a stopwatch and go out to a nearby park and find out. Which they did, a bunch of guys taking off their shoes and running around barefoot in a public park on company time.

This is what I heard them talking about, out in the hall. I heard Tom, who was thirty-eight years old, saying that his time in the forty had been 5.75 seconds. And I thought to myself: This is ridiculous. These are middle-aged guys, supposedly adults, and they're out there *bragging* about their performance in this stupid juvenile footrace. Finally I couldn't stand it anymore.

"Hey!" I shouted. "*I* could beat 5.75 seconds."   20

So we went out to the park and measured off forty yards, and the guys told me that I had three chances to make my best time. On the first try my time was 5.78 seconds, just three-hundredths of a second slower than Tom's, even though, at forty-five, I was seven years older than he. So I just *knew* I'd beat him on the second attempt if I ran really, really hard, which I did for a solid ten yards, at which point my left hamstring muscle, which had not yet shifted into Spring Mode from Mail-Reading Mode, went, and I quote, "pop."

---

*Typical fan letter: "Who cuts your hair? Beavers?"

I had to be helped off the field. I was in considerable pain, and I was obviously not going to be able to walk right for weeks. The other guys were very sympathetic, especially Tom, who took the time to call me at home, where I was sitting with an ice pack on my leg and twenty-three Advil in my bloodstream, so he could express his concern.

"Just remember," he said, "*you didn't beat my time.*"

There are countless other examples of guys rising to meet pointless challenges. Virtually all sports fall into this category, as well as a large part of U.S. foreign policy. ("I'll bet you can't capture Manuel Noriega!"* "Oh YEAH??")

Guys Do Not Have a Rigid and Well-Defined Moral Code

This is not the same as saying that guys are bad. Guys *are* capable of 25 doing bad things, but this generally happens when they try to be Men and start becoming manly and aggressive and stupid. When they're being just plain guys, they aren't so much actively *evil* as they are *lost*. Because guys have never really grasped the Basic Human Moral Code, which I believe was invented by women millions of years ago when all the guys were out engaging in some other activity, such as seeing who could burp the loudest. When they came back, there were certain rules that they were expected to follow unless they wanted to get into Big Trouble, and they have been trying to follow these rules ever since, with extremely irregular results. Because guys have never *internalized* these rules. Guys are similar to my small auxiliary backup dog, Zippy, a guy dog[†] who has been told numerous times that he is *not* supposed to (1) get into the kitchen garbage or (2) poop on the floor. He knows that these are the rules, but he has never really understood *why*, and sometimes he gets to thinking: Sure, I am *ordinarily* not supposed to get into the garbage, but obviously this rule is not meant to apply when there are certain extenuating[‡] circumstances, such as (1) somebody just threw

---

Manuel Noriega: former military dictator in Panama; he was removed from power by the United States in 1989. [Editor's note]

[†]I also have a female dog, Earnest, who *never* breaks the rules.

[‡]I am taking some liberties here with Zippy's vocabulary. More likely, in his mind, he uses the term *mitigating.*

away some perfectly good seven-week-old Kung Pao Chicken, and (2) I am home alone.

And so when the humans come home, the kitchen floor has been transformed into GarbageFest USA, and Zippy, who usually comes rushing up, is off in a corner disguised in a wig and sunglasses, hoping to get into the Federal Bad Dog Relocation Program before the humans discover the scene of the crime.

When I yell at him, he frequently becomes so upset that he poops on the floor.

Morally, most guys are just like Zippy, only taller and usually less hairy. Guys are *aware* of the rules of moral behavior, but they have trouble keeping these rules in the forefronts of their minds at certain times, especially the present. This is especially true in the area of faithfulness to one's mate. I realize, of course, that there are countless examples of guys being faithful to their mates until they die, usually as a result of being eaten by their mates immediately following copulation. Guys outside of the spider community, however, do not have a terrific record of faithfulness.

I'm not saying guys are scum. I'm saying that many guys who consider themselves to be committed to their marriages will stray if they are confronted with overwhelming temptation, defined as "virtually any temptation."

Okay, so maybe I *am* saying guys are scum. But they're not *mean-spirited* scum. And few of them — even when they are out of town on business trips, far from their wives, and have a clear-cut opportunity — will poop on the floor.

Engaging with the Text

1. Dave Barry claims that he isn't able to say what he means by the term "guys" because "one of the major characteristics of guyhood is that we guys don't spend a lot of time pondering our deep innermost feelings," and yet in this piece — indeed even this sentence — he identifies specific characteristics of "guys" that suggest he has indeed

rhetorical situations · genres · processes · strategies · research MLA / APA · media / design · readings

pondered this state of maleness thoroughly. How do you account for this contradiction?

2. Despite his assertion that he can't define the term, Barry essentially provides an **EXTENDED DEFINITION** of the term "guy," detailing several characteristics. What are the characteristics of guys, according to Barry? Do you agree with these characteristics and his description of each? What other characteristics would you add, if any? 358–64

3. Barry includes several **EXAMPLES** of the behavior he identifies as characteristic of guys. Identity several passages that include such examples and discuss what these contribute to his reflection. 363

4. What is Barry's **STANCE** toward his topic of guys? Point to specific passages that reveal that stance. Is this stance appropriate for Barry's **PURPOSE?** Why or why not? 12–15

   3–4

5. *For Writing.* Identify a specific group of people, animals, things, or places, and reflect on what distinguishing characteristics are shared by its members. Write a **REFLECTION** on the group that identifies those major characteristics. Study Barry's reflection to see what techniques he uses to elicit a smile or chuckle. Try your hand at one or more of these. 214–21

GEETA KOTHARI

If You Are What You Eat, Then What Am I?

Geeta Kothari's stories and essays have been published in numerous newspapers, journals and anthologies. She teaches writing at the University of Pittsburgh and is the editor of Did My Mama Like to Dance? and Other Stories about Mothers and Daughters (1994). *The following reflection first appeared in 1999 in the* Kenyon Review, *a literary journal published at Kenyon College. As you read, notice how Kothari incorporates vivid anecdotes to illustrate the competing cultural experiences that complicate her sense of identity.*

> To belong is to understand the tacit codes of the people you live with.
> —MICHAEL IGNATIEFF, *BLOOD AND BELONGING*

THE FIRST TIME MY MOTHER and I open a can of tuna, I am nine years old. We stand in the doorway of the kitchen, in semidarkness, the can tilted toward daylight. I want to eat what the kids at school eat: bologna, hot dogs, salami — foods my parents find repugnant because they contain pork and meat byproducts, crushed bone and hair glued together by chemicals and fat. Although she has never been able to tolerate the smell of fish, my mother buys the tuna, hoping to satisfy my longing for American food.

Indians, of course, do not eat such things.

The tuna smells fishy, which surprises me because I can't remember anyone's tuna sandwich actually smelling like fish. And the tuna in those sandwiches doesn't look like this, pink and shiny, like an internal organ. In fact, this looks similar to the bad foods my mother doesn't want me to eat. She is silent, holding her face away from the can while peering into it like a half-blind bird.

"What's wrong with it?" I ask.

She has no idea. My mother does not know that the tuna everyone   5
else's mothers made for them was tuna *salad*.

rhetorical situations   genres   processes   strategies   research MLA / APA   media / design   readings

"Do you think it's botulism?"

I have never seen botulism, but I have read about it, just as I have read about but never eaten steak and kidney pie.

There is so much my parents don't know. They are not like other parents, and they disappoint me and my sister. They are supposed to help us negotiate the world outside, teach us the signs, the clues to proper behavior: what to eat and how to eat it.

We have expectations, and my parents fail to meet them, especially my mother, who works full-time. I don't understand what it means, to have a mother who works outside and inside the home; I notice only the ways in which she disappoints me. She doesn't show up for school plays. She doesn't make chocolate-frosted cupcakes for my class. At night, if I want her attention, I have to sit in the kitchen and talk to her while she cooks the evening meal, attentive to every third or fourth word I say.

We throw the tuna away. This time my mother is disappointed. I   10 go to school with tuna eaters. I see their sandwiches, yet cannot explain the discrepancy between them and the stinking, oily fish in my mother's hand. We do not understand so many things, my mother and I.

When we visit our relatives in India, food prepared outside the house is carefully monitored. In the hot, sticky monsoon months in New Delhi and Bombay, we cannot eat ice cream, salad, cold food, or any fruit that can't be peeled. Definitely no meat. People die from amoebic dysentery, unexplained fevers, strange boils on their bodies. We drink boiled water only, no ice. No sweets except for jalebi, thin fried twists of dough in dripping hot sugar syrup. If we're caught outside with nothing to drink, Fanta, Limca, Thums Up (after Coca-Cola is thrown out by Mrs. Gandhi) will do. Hot tea sweetened with sugar, served with thick creamy buffalo milk, is preferable. It should be boiled, to kill the germs on the cup.

My mother talks about "back home" as a safe place, a silk cocoon frozen in time where we are sheltered by family and friends. Back home, my sister and I do not argue about food with my parents. Home is where they know all the rules. We trust them to guide us safely through the maze of city streets for which they have no map, and we trust them to feed and take care of us, the way parents should.

Finally, though, one of us will get sick, hungry for the food we see our cousins and friends eating, too thirsty to ask for a straw, too polite to insist on properly boiled water.

At my uncle's diner in New Delhi, someone hands me a plate of aloo tikki, fried potato patties filled with mashed channa dal and served with a sweet and a sour chutney. The channa, mixed with hot chilies and spices, burns my tongue and throat. I reach for my Fanta, discard the paper straw, and gulp the sweet orange soda down, huge drafts that sting rather than soothe.

When I throw up later that day (or is it the next morning, when a   15
stomachache wakes me from deep sleep?), I cry over the frustration of being singled out, not from the pain my mother assumes I'm feeling as she holds my hair back from my face. The taste of orange lingers in my mouth, and I remember my lips touching the cold glass of the Fanta bottle.

At that moment, more than anything, I want to be like my cousins.

In New York, at the first Indian restaurant in our neighborhood, my father orders with confidence, and my sister and I play with the silverware until the steaming plates of lamb biryani arrive.

What is Indian food? my friends ask, their noses crinkling up.

Later, this restaurant is run out of business by the new Indo-Pak-Bangladeshi combinations up and down the street, which serve similar food. They use plastic cutlery and Styrofoam cups. They do not distinguish between North and South Indian cooking, or between Indian, Pakistani, and Bangladeshi cooking, and their customers do not care. The food is fast, cheap, and tasty. Dosa, a rice flour crepe stuffed with masala potato, appears on the same trays as chicken makhani.

Now my friends want to know, Do you eat curry at home?   20

One time my mother makes lamb vindaloo for guests. Like dosa, this is a South Indian dish, one that my Punjabi mother has to learn from a cookbook. For us, she cooks everyday food — yellow dal, rice, chapati, bhaji. Lentils, rice, bread, and vegetables. She has never referred to anything on our table as "curry" or "curried," but I know she has made chicken curry for guests. Vindaloo, she explains, is a curry too. I under-

stand then that curry is a dish created for guests, outsiders, a food for people who eat in restaurants.

I look around my boyfriend's freezer one day and find meat: pork chops, ground beef, chicken pieces, Italian sausage. Ham in the refrigerator, next to the homemade bolognese sauce. Tupperware filled with chili made from ground beef and pork.

    He smells different from me. Foreign. Strange.

    I marry him anyway.

    He has inherited blue eyes that turn gray in bad weather, light brown 25 hair, a sharp pointy nose, and excellent teeth. He learns to make chili with ground turkey and tofu, tomato sauce with red wine and portobello mushrooms, roast chicken with rosemary and slivers of garlic under the skin.

    He eats steak when we are in separate cities, roast beef at his mother's house, hamburgers at work. Sometimes I smell them on his skin. I hope he doesn't notice me turning my face, a cheek instead of my lips, my nose wrinkled at the unfamiliar, musky smell.

I have inherited brown eyes, black hair, a long nose with a crooked bridge, and soft teeth with thin enamel. I am in my twenties, moving to a city far from my parents, before it occurs to me that jeera, the spice my sister avoids, must have an English name. I have to learn that haldi = turmeric, methi = fenugreek. What to make with fenugreek, I do not know. My grandmother used to make methi roti for our breakfast, cornbread with fresh fenugreek leaves served with a lump of homemade butter. No one makes it now that she's gone, though once in a while my mother will get a craving for it and produce a facsimile ("The cornmeal here is wrong") that only highlights what she's really missing: the smells and tastes of her mother's house.

    I will never make my grandmother's methi roti or even my mother's unsatisfactory imitation of it. I attempt chapati; it takes six hours, three phone calls home, and leaves me with an aching back. I have to write translations down: jeera = cumin. My memory is unreliable. But I have always known garam = hot.

If I really want to make myself sick, I worry that my husband will one day leave me for a meat-eater, for someone familiar who doesn't sniff him suspiciously for signs of alimentary infidelity.

Indians eat lentils. I understand this as absolute, a decree from an unidentifiable authority that watches and judges me.

So what does it mean that I cannot replicate my mother's dal? She and my father show me repeatedly, in their kitchen, in my kitchen. They coach me over the phone, buy me the best cookbooks, and finally write down their secrets. Things I'm supposed to know but don't. Recipes that should be, by now, engraved on my heart.

Living far from the comfort of people who require no explanation for what I do and who I am, I crave the foods we have shared. My mother convinces me that moong is the easiest dal to prepare, and yet it fails me every time: bland, watery, a sickly greenish yellow mush. These imperfect limitations remind me only of what I'm missing.

But I have never been fond of moong dal. At my mother's table it is the last thing I reach for. Now I worry that this antipathy toward dal signals something deeper, that somehow I am not my parents' daughter, not Indian, and because I cannot bear the touch and smell of raw meat, though I can eat it cooked (charred, dry, and overdone), I am not American either.

I worry about a lifetime purgatory in Indian restaurants where I will complain that all the food looks and tastes the same because they've used the same masala.

Engaging with the Text

367–75
218

1. Geeta Kothari uses food as a way to explore the larger issue of cultural identity. How does she **DESCRIBE** Indian and American food? What **SPECIFIC DETAILS** does she include to help her readers understand the pulls of both American and Indian culture?

312–13

2. A good **TITLE** indicates what the piece is about and makes readers want to read it. How well does this title do those things? How does Kothari answer the question her title asks?

rhetorical situations · genres · processes · strategies · research MLA / APA · media / design · readings

3. How does Kothari **BEGIN**? Is this an effective beginning? Why or why not? How does it signal to readers what Kothari will address in the rest of the piece?

299–306

4. For Kothari, cultural identity shapes, and is shaped by, the foods one eats and the ways one eats them. Her reflection reveals a struggle over two cultures — Indian and American — and she worries that she cannot locate herself fully in either. At the end of her text, she notes: "I worry that this antipathy toward dal signals something deeper, that somehow I am not my parents' daughter, not Indian, and because I cannot bear the touch and smell of raw meat . . . I am not American either." What does it mean to live on the border between two cultures in the ways Kothari describes?

5. *For Writing.* Think about the kinds of foods you grew up with and the ways they were similar or dissimilar to those of your peers. Write an essay **REFLECTING** on the role food has played in your own sense of your cultural heritage and identity.

214–21

ALEX HORTON

The Ides of March

Alex Horton is a staff writer at the U.S. Department of Veteran Affairs (VA), where he writes for VAntage Point, *a blog that helps veterans communicate with the VA. He is best known, however, for his personal blog,* Army of Dude, *which he began while serving in the army in Iraq; it focused on veterans' issues and U.S. foreign policy and was nominated twice for a military blog award. Horton's writing has also appeared in the* New York Times *blog* At War, *the* St. Petersburg Times, *and* Time *magazine's* Battleland. *He has been the subject of profiles by CNN, BBC, NPR's* All Things Considered, *the* Washington Post, *and other media outlets. The following reflection was posted on* Army of Dude *on March 20, 2011. Horton explains that when his platoon learned in early 2007 that they would be moving to a more dangerous area of Iraq sometime in mid-March — information that they couldn't share with their families for security reasons — he sent his parents an email with a link to an article about the area, accompanied simply by the message "Beware the Ides of March."*

SINCE MOST OF **BATTLE COMPANY, SECOND PLATOON**, disbanded we've moved on. Careers have been launched, schools attended and families started. We're not the kids that filled out Army uniforms so long ago. As close as we were then, both geographic distance and the rigors of post-military life have left us isolated. There was a time that you could reach in any direction and grab the shoulder of a brother. These days, the best we can muster is a phone call or an email, with makeshift reunions of a few men happening quick and infrequently.

> *We went camping and I let him borrow a tent not knowing it had a hole in it. He walked out of the tent the next morning soaked from the knees down.*
> — Dozer

March is for moving forward. But for second platoon, the month is swallowed by memories of a particular man in a particular place on a particular day: March 14, 2007. Brian Chevalier, a lean and baby-faced Georgia boy, was the driver for first squad. He faced the enemy before the rest of his squad every time they mounted up. I never heard him complain about a thankless job like ferrying infantryman into battle.

> *Thompson and me were on CQ and fucking Chevy came by covered in mud and looking like he just got tag teamed by a bunch of forest animals. He celebrated his 21st birthday at the casino, tried to walk to post and passed out in a ditch.* — Dodo

There was no whimper, no cries for mother or last words when 5 Chevy died. The explosion that blew him out of the Stryker made him, for a brief moment, a creature of flight. He didn't suffer. The next few hours were spent fighting out of a kill zone expertly crafted by gunmen lying in wait. In our unit's history, The Ides of March became a bloody smear on the calendar.

On the first anniversary of Chevy's death, many of the guys around Ft. Lewis were able to get together, along with a CBS reporter to cover the story. We sang and drank and traded memories about Chevy. Three years later, it's not so easy. Many of us relied on Facebook to tell the same old stories or share new ones.

> *I remember that fool planning his redneck wedding. Also remember him telling Hernandez that he wouldn't be his battle buddy to the chow hall in Mosul. After a while he would hide out in his room just to avoid him.* — Dodo

I've never worked or went to school on March 14. Last year I spent the day with Dodo and another friend in New York, but last week I found myself alone. I decided to spend the day where another group of young men struggled and died: Antietam. The park system contains two monuments to the 20th Infantry NY Regulars, which were the predecessors of our unit, 5th Battalion 20th Infantry Regiment. The engagement is remembered with a striped battle streamer on the regimental colors. Us, though, we remember Chevy with late night phone calls and laughter through tears.

20th Infantry monument at Antietam National Battlefield.

We have moved on since then, but March carries a weight that loads us down. Spring is just around the corner, but not for our best.

> *In that kid I saw the best in all of you. No matter how bad it got, he and you all persevered. He would remind me that you all were kids and to lighten up. Leave fucking with the Army of Dude for another day. It was an honor to serve with each and everyone of you. As long as we don't forget him, he will live longer than all of us.* — Richard Kellar, Chevy's squad leader

10

■ rhetorical situations
▲ genres
○ processes
◆ strategies
● research MLA / APA
□ media / design
▶ readings

Engaging with the Text

1. What does Alex Horton's **TITLE** refer to? (Do some research if necessary to find out.) How well does it fit his reflection? How effective is it? Why?

312–13

2. Horton's reflection includes **QUOTATIONS** from other soldiers who knew Brian Chevalier, the soldier who died in battle. What do these quotations contribute to the reflection and the narrative it focuses on?

463–67

3. Antietam National Park marks the place where the Battle of Antietam took place during the Civil War on September 17, 1862. According to the park's website, it was "the bloodiest one-day battle in American history." Why do you think Horton decided to go to Antietam National Park? What was he looking for? What is the larger **PURPOSE** of his reflection?

3–4

4. Horton concludes that "We have moved on since then, but March carries a weight that loads us down. Spring is just around the corner, but not for our best." What does he mean by this **ENDING**? How effective is it? This conclusion is followed by one last quotation from Chevalier's squad leader, Richard Kellar. Why is this an appropriate place for this final quotation?

306–10

5. *For Writing.* What day or time of the year or event in history (either recent or not) brings one of your own past experiences to mind? Write a **REFLECTION** on that experience and relate it to the day or time of the year or to the historical event. Include quotations from people who were with you during the experience that help reveal its significance and the reaction to it that you are working through in your reflection.

214–22

JOAN DIDION

Grief

Joan Didion has written several novels and many journalistic works but is perhaps best known for her collections of essays, including Slouching Toward Bethlehem *(1968),* The White Album *(1979), and* Political Fictions *(2001). The following reflection comes from Didion's National Book Award–winning memoir,* The Year of Magical Thinking *(2005), which chronicles her experiences following the death of her husband. (For a review of this book, see p. 770.) As you read, pay attention to how Didion structures her text, moving the reader through time from her early childhood to her adulthood and interweaving her reflections about how to make sense of life after the loss of a loved one.*

GRIEF TURNS OUT TO BE A PLACE none of us know until we reach it. We anticipate (we know) that someone close to us could die, but we do not look beyond the few days or weeks that immediately follow such an imagined death. We misconstrue the nature of even those few days or weeks. We might expect if the death is sudden to feel shock. We do not expect this shock to be obliterative, dislocating to both body and mind. We might expect that we will be prostrate, inconsolable, crazy with loss. We do not expect to be literally crazy, cool customers who believe that their husband is about to return and need his shoes. In the version of grief we imagine, the model will be "healing." A certain forward move-ment will prevail. The worst days will be the earliest days. We imagine that the moment to most severely test us will be the funeral, after which this hypothetical healing will take place. When we anticipate the funeral we wonder about failing to "get through it," rise to the occasion, exhibit the "strength" that invariably gets mentioned as the correct response to death. We anticipate needing to steel ourselves for the moment: will I be able to greet people, will I be able to leave the scene, will I be able even to get dressed that day? We have no way of knowing that this will not be the issue. We have no way of knowing that the funeral itself will be anodyne, a kind of narcotic regression in which we are wrapped in

rhetorical situations | genres | processes | strategies | research MLA / APA | media / design | readings

the care of others and the gravity and meaning of the occasion. Nor can we know ahead of the fact (and here lies the heart of the difference between grief as we imagine it and grief as it is) the unending absence that follows, the void, the very opposite of meaning, the relentless succession of moments during which we will confront the experience of meaninglessness itself.

As a child I thought a great deal about meaninglessness, which seemed at the time that most prominent negative feature on the horizon. After a few years of failing to find meaning in the more commonly recommended venues I learned that I could find it in geology, so I did. This in turn enabled me to find meaning in the Episcopal litany, most acutely in the words *as it was in the beginning, is now and ever shall be, world without end,* which I interpreted as a literal description of the constant changing of the earth, the unending erosion of the shores and mountains, the inexorable shifting of the geological structures that could throw up mountains and islands and could just as reliably take them away. I found earthquakes, even when I was in them, deeply satisfying, abruptly revealed evidence of the scheme in action. That the scheme could destroy the works of man might be a personal regret but remained, in the larger picture I had come to recognize, a matter of abiding indifference. No eye was on the sparrow. No one was watching me. *As it was in the beginning, is now and ever shall be, world without end.* On the day it was announced that the atomic bomb had been dropped on Hiroshima those were the words that came immediately to my ten-year-old mind. When I heard a few years later about mushroom clouds over the Nevada test site those were again the words that came to mind. I began waking before dawn, imagining that the fireballs from the Nevada test shots would light up the sky in Sacramento.

Later, after I married and had a child, I learned to find equal meaning in the repeated rituals of domestic life. Setting the table. Lighting the candles. Building the fire. Cooking. All those soufflés, all that crème caramel, all those daubes and albóndigas and gumbos. Clean sheets, stacks of clean towels, hurricane lamps for storms, enough water and food to see us through whatever geological event came our way. *These*

Quintana Dunne, John Gregory Dunne, and Joan Didion in 1981.

*fragments I have shored against my ruins,** were the words that came to mind then. These fragments mattered to me. I believed in them. That I could find meaning in the intensely personal nature of my life as a wife and mother did not seem inconsistent with finding meaning in the vast indifference of geology and the test shots; the two systems existed for me on parallel tracks that occasionally converged, notably during earthquakes. In my unexamined mind there was always a point, John's and my death, at which the tracks would converge for a final time. On the Internet I recently found aerial photographs of the house on the Palos Verdes Peninsula in which we had lived when we were first married, the house to which we had brought Quintana home from St. John's Hospital in Santa Monica and put her in her bassinet by the wisteria in the box garden. The photographs, part of the California Coastal Records Project, the point of which was to document the entire California coast-

---

These fragments I have shored against my ruins: a line from T. S. Eliot's poem *The Waste Land* (1922). [Editor's note]

rhetorical situations   genres   processes   strategies   research MLA / APA   media / design   readings

line, were hard to read conclusively, but the house as it had been when we lived in it appeared to be gone. The tower where the gate had been seemed intact but the rest of the structure looked unfamiliar. There seemed to be a swimming pool where the wisteria and box garden had been. The area itself was identified as "Portuguese Bend landslide." You could see the slumping of the hill where the slide had occurred. You could also see, at the base of the cliff on the point, the cave into which we used to swim when the tide was at exactly the right flow.

The swell of clear water.

That was one way my two systems could have converged.

We could have been swimming into the cave with the swell of clear water and the entire point could have slumped, slipped into the sea around us. The entire point slipping into the sea around us was the kind of conclusion I anticipated. I did not anticipate cardiac arrest at the dinner table.

Engaging with the Text

1. Joan Didion reflects on what she thought grief would be and how different it turned out to be when her husband died. What role does this contrast — between what she thought would happen and what she actually experienced — play in the way she STRUCTURES her thoughts?

   ▲ 218

2. How would you characterize Didion's STANCE? Does it seem appropriate for her topic? Why or why not? What does her tone convey about her stance toward her subject?

   ◼ 12–15

3. How does Didion DESCRIBE her "rituals of domestic life"? What specific details does she supply? What DOMINANT IMPRESSION of her domestic life is created by these details? Why is that impression important to Didion?

   ◆ 367–75
   373–74

4. What is the PURPOSE of Didion's reflection? Where is that purpose made most explicit?

   ◼ 3–4

5. *For Writing.* Grief is a powerful and sometimes surprising emotion. Think about a time when you experienced a strong emotion — such as grief, anger, or elation. Consider how this emotion affected you, and write an essay that REFLECTS on this emotion and your experience of it.

   ▲ 214–21

ARMANDO MONTAÑO

The Unexpected Lessons of Mexican Food

Armando Montaño (1989–2012) wrote the following essay during his senior year at Grinnell College, where he graduated in 2012 with a major in Spanish and a concentration in Latin American studies and served as news editor for the school newspaper. He had a passion for journalism, and he loved talking about writing. "It's wonderful," he said about his editors' comments on a story he wrote as an intern for the Associated Press. "They keep giving me feedback, and they said today, 'This is a helluva story, but here's how to make it EVEN better.'" In high school, he was a guest columnist for the Denver Post; *in college, he interned for the* New York Times, *the* Seattle Times, *and the* Chronicle of Higher Education. *He was working for the Associated Press in Mexico City when he died there in June 2012. This essay, in which he reflects on his mixed ethnic heritage, was first published in* Salon *in March 2012. To access the original online version, including comments, go to* wwnorton.com/write/fieldguidelinks.

I FIRST DISCOVERED COOKING AT AGE 5, when the earthy smell of boiling pinto beans lured me into the kitchen. It was my dad. He dripped them into an oily skillet and smashed them into a lumpy paste. I started pulling on his apron straps, begging to know the name of the concoction.

"Your grandmother always made this," he said, stirring the bubbling brown stew and pinching in cumin. "I'll teach you how to make it. Here, try it." He raised the dripping spoon to my mouth. The mild tingle of cumin and the soft squish of beans lingered on my palate, like a spicy fingerprint.

For as long as I can remember, I've felt the push and pull of growing up biracial in America. In the Mexican side of my family I was known as the white one. Even though I spoke Spanish, it was the formal kind learned from classrooms and reading, rather than the one you pick up by bartering with local shop owners over the price of firm avocados, or arguing with parents over a ridiculous curfew. On the other side, my cousins called me a "Wexican," a white Mexican despite my similarly toned skin.

Cooking, however, taught me to channel my frustrations by creating foods through the addition of sour cream, cilantro, cayenne pepper and tender meat. I could make a food that doesn't have to be Mexican or American.

Since I was 6, my cultural anthropologist father took me on his research projects along the border in South Texas. He wanted to show me the tiny corner in his hometown that birthed the iconic Latino food: the nacho.

We ended our 14-hour drive from Colorado as the sun began to set behind the sandy wasteland known as West Texas. We pulled into the Best Western for refuge, the only hotel for almost a hundred miles. The Anglo man gawked at my dark-skinned father and his freckled child, and answered our unasked question: "We're out of rooms." He shuffled his papers to avoid eye contact. As my father dragged me closer to the counter, he strengthened his grip on my tiny hand and asked why the parking lot was empty if they were out of rooms.

"Conference," the man said, glaring at my father and me without blinking.

We spent the night on a ratty mattress supported by cinder blocks at another motel a few miles away. When dawn came, we started our trip again as if nothing happened.

"I hate white people," I muttered as we approached the sign welcoming us to my dad's hometown, Eagle Pass. He jerked the car off the road and pounded the brake. He sighed, wiped the sweat from his forehead and glasses, and demanded that I never utter those words again. "How would your mother feel if she heard you say that?" he said.

We arrived at our destination, Eagle Pass, Texas. We weaved through the bustling streets of downtown, lined with banks, money exchanges and a line outside of the local meat market and bakery that snaked past a convenience store where people bought icy Cokes while they waited. From here, we saw the concrete bridge connecting Mexico and the United States over the Rio Grande River. During the '60s, my dad crafted lures on both sides when he fished for catfish, carp, turtles and alligator. Now, the heat sensors and armed guards stop him from crossing as freely. We parked in front of an old hotel and began to wander around town.

Inside the Mancha Meat Market and Bakery, a sharp, sweet smell of caramelized sugar filled the room, emerging from the side ovens cooking sweet bread glazed in a strawberry coat. On Saturdays, however, the stench of bloody, uncooked cow head lurks toward the empanadas and sweet bread.

Barbacoa, slow-cooked beef, had served as the Mancha family's specialty for 70 years. Every week they divide up several beef heads, place its remains in thigh-high containers, lower it into a hot pit, lined with mesquite coals, behind the bakery, and wake up at 6 a.m. the next morning to find the juicy aroma of tender meat, inviting you for a breakfast treat. On Sunday they used to sell well over a hundred pounds of meat for $3 a pound. Hordes of Mexican and Anglo mothers wait patiently to get their bounty for dinner that evening. There were only two weekends when Eagle Pass was left without barbacoa: once when elder Mancha died in the early '90s from heart disease, and the other when his wife joined him several years later.

Being one of the first Hispanics to get a Ph.D. in his program at the University of Pennsylvania weighed down my father whenever he returned to Texas. He liked to keep his accomplishments tucked away from most people. When he stopped by his friends' bakeries, banks and law offices in Eagle Pass they always greeted him with endearing shouts and playful insults. But underneath the handful of dinner invites and barbecues, he felt a gradual separation with his past.

Sometimes, I think my dad tries to repair his link back to Texas through his students, especially the minority ones. He directed the ethnic studies and chaired the anthropology departments, and in his spare time takes on a mentor role for the first generation and students of color. At lunch he sketches their life plans on ketchup-stained napkins and tells them not to take any crap from losers. Most of those students go to grad school or work as a professional in a high-powered "something." Not once during these meetings did I ever hear him tell students how to go back to their old lives, Santa Fe, Detroit or Los Angeles, after college. Likely, he was trying to figure it out for himself.

We trekked along the international bridge against a stationary line of   15
cars waiting to enter the United States. Our two-hour wait in customs

seemed like nothing compared to their four-hour wait in the unforgiving Texas heat. The sound of nearby dogs barking and angry shouting in Spanish caused me to jump, but before I could turn around, my dad tugged at my shirt, a signal for me to keep going.

The dim glow from the Moderno's antique lamps and wooden tables made it feel like a speakeasy, rather than a restaurant. During the 1950s it served Mexican as the hangout for Mexican and Texas politicians, including President Lyndon Johnson and Maverick County Judge Roberto Bibb, conniving the different ways the Mexican vote would be delivered. As in those days, people still spent their dollars on beer, milanesa and, according to folk legend, the famous nachos, invented in this restaurant.

The waiter brought our mountain of freshly hot tortilla chips, each with some refried pinto beans, topped with a small slice of cheddar cheese and crowned with a deep green slice of jalapeno. We scarfed down the nachos like a horde of hungry javelinas. For the next 10 minutes we communicated in grunts and moans, only aware of the

explosion of flavor in our mouths and the flow of dense cheese bubbling in our stomach.

The nacho, according to my father's stories, represents the fusion between the Spanish colonizers' new-world dairy and the Aztecs' corn and chile. Throughout the centuries, the recipe morphed, first with the independence of Texas and California from Mexico, and then the immigration boom in the 20th century. By the 1980s, even though Cortez and Montezuma had withered into the pages of history, their spirits live on in the hot plates of these fried delicacies.

In my junior year of college, I decided go on my own adventure south of the border. But this time, I flew past Piedras Negras and landed in Buenos Aires, where the Mexican restaurants left my mouth bitter and my wallet dry. The Argentine diet consists of rich cheese, juicy steak and fluffy bread, carried over by the millions of Western European immigrants at the beginning of the 20th century. The country's distance and lack of immigrants from Mexico left Argentines confused over the simplest of Mexican dishes. The huevos rancheros scraped against my mouth, and the weak margarita left me thirsty. I missed spicy food so much that my biweekly trip to the Bolivian vendor for jalapeños resembled a drug deal more than a produce purchase. Something needed to change.

So I started cooking. I spent the day before my feast assembling the 20 ingredients from all over town. The Bolivian woman from down the street sold me the jalapeños, a 10-minute subway ride took me to the dietary shop where I bought dried black beans, and a long bus ride brought me to the only Mexican restaurant that hustled individual tortillas for a dollar apiece.

I made Guillermo cook the black beans, while I diced the tomatoes into fine cubes. Even though he claimed vegetarianism, he rarely ate beans and pulverized them in the skillet with childlike curiosity and enthusiasm. He never knew Mexican food beyond the posh restaurants in the gentrified neighborhood of the city, and saw this as an authentic way to learn about Mexican culture from a real live Mexican.

rhetorical situations   genres   processes   strategies   research MLA / APA   media / design   readings

"I'm technically American, Guillermo," I told him as I started slicing the avocados. "My dad is first generation and my mom is white. I'm considered Hispanic."

"Well, you're the only Mexican I know," he said. "If you speak Spanish, cook Mexican food, and have Montaño as a last name, I don't see how you could be anything else."

The waterfall of beaten eggs I poured into the sizzling skillet engulfed the fried tortilla cubes, until the batter thickened.

"It's a Mexican peasant dish," I said sprinkling in the peppers. 25 "When the ingredients in your house were just about to go bad, you threw them all in a pan and ate it."

Guillermo and his friends took hearty spoonfuls from the skillet, and before I could stab a piece of egg for myself, they wanted more. I slathered the beans Guillermo flattened into a rough paste over a fried tortilla chip, topped it off with a thick piece of cheddar and a single jalapeño slice, and offered it to Guillermo. He ate it all in one greedy bite. After a few seconds of hurried chewing, he stopped, opened his mouth and screamed.

"IT'S TOO HOT! IT FEELS LIKE HELL ON MY TONGUE!" he said right before he gulped down two glasses of strong margaritas. Several hours later, and a bottle of tequila later, he passed out on his bed finally knowing what "real" Mexican food tasted like.

For the next couple of months in Argentina, I cooked regularly for my Argentine friends and told stories about cooking with my dad. The entire time, they noticed how my syntax and vocabulary differed from theirs. Even though I spoke Spanish as a second language, they always referred to me as their "Mexican friend."

My dad and I eat at Chipotle when we don't feel like cooking or want to get out of the house. I order a veggie burrito stuffed with grilled peppers, wet black beans, sticky white rice and cheese. My dad usually orders the same, but tortilla-less, because of his doctor-mandated hypoglycemic diet. Even though he likes to call Chipotle "the Mexican PF Chang," he likes the taste and has befriended everyone who works there.

We know the Mexican women behind the counter and we always tell stories about Piedras Negras, while they lament Mexico City and brag about their children winning college scholarships.

Engaging with the Text

1. How did cooking help Armando Montaño cope with the "push and pull" of growing up biracial in America? Identify one of the challenges he faced and how cooking helped with it.

2. What is the **PURPOSE** of this reflection? Where in the text does that purpose become evident?

   3–4 ◼

3. When it was originally published in *Salon*, this reflection generated a number of comments. Read through the comments. What topics do they cover? On what topics is there disagreement? What appears to be the central argument of these comments?

4. A good reflection needs **SPECIFIC DETAILS.** Identify three specific details in this essay and explain what they contribute to the power of Montano's reflection.

   218 ▲

5. *For Writing.* Do you identify with a certain ethnicity, race, religion, region, or something else? What activities make you feel that identity most strongly? Music? Dance? Food? Places? Language? Sounds? Write an essay about that activity and how it **REFLECTS** your sense of identity.

   214–21 ▲

Texts That Mix Genres **66**

DAVID RAMSEY

I Will Forever Remain Faithful
How Lil Wayne Helped Me Survive My First Year Teaching in New Orleans

David Ramsey was a social studies and writing teacher in the Recovery School District in New Orleans when he wrote this essay, which first appeared in 2008 in the Oxford American: The Southern Magazine for Good Writing. *He is currently a third-grade teacher at Victory Youth Training Academy in the city's Ninth Ward. His writings on both food and music have been published in magazines such as* Slate *and* Men's Journal *and anthologies such as* Best Music Writing *(2009),* Best American Food Writing *(2011) and* Cornbread Nation 5 *(2010). Ramsey also writes fiction, and in 2010 one of his short stories won an award for fiction given by the University of New Orleans.*

1.

Complex magazine: What do you listen to these days?

Lil Wayne: Me! All day, all me.

2. Like a white person, with blue veins

In my first few weeks teaching in New Orleans' Recovery School District, these were the questions I heard the most from my students:

1. "I gotta use it." (This one might sound like a statement, but it's a request — May I use the bathroom?)

2. "You got an ol' lady?" (the penultimate vowel stretched, lasciviously, as far as it'll go).

3. "Where you from?"

4. "You listen to that Weezy?"

I knew that third question was coming. Like many RSD teachers, I was new, and white, and from out of town. It was the fourth question, however, that seemed to interest my students the most. Dwayne Carter, aka

Lil Wayne, aka Weezy F. Baby, was in the midst of becoming the year's biggest rapper, and among the black teenagers that made up my student population, fandom had reached a near-Beatlemania pitch. More than ninety percent of my students cited Lil Wayne on the "Favorite Music" question on the survey I gave them; about half of them repeated the answer on "Favorite Things to Do."

For some of my students, the questions *Where are you from?* and *Do you listen to Lil Wayne?* were close to interchangeable. Their shared currency — as much as neighborhoods or food or slang or trauma — was the stoned musings of Weezy F. Baby.

The answer was, sometimes, yes, I did listen to Lil Wayne. Despite 5 his ubiquitous success, my students were shocked.

"Do you have the mix tapes?" asked Michael, a sixteen-year-old ninth grader. "It's all about the mix tapes."

The following day, he had a stack of CDs for me. Version this, volume that, or no label at all.

And that's just about all I listened to for the rest of the year.

3. My picture should be in the dictionary next to the definition of definition

Lil Wayne slurs, hollers, sings, sighs, bellows, whines, croons, wheezes, coughs, stutters, shouts. He reminds me, in different moments, of two dozen other rappers. In a genre that often demands keeping it real via being repetitive, Lil Wayne is a chameleon, rapping in different octaves, paces, and inflections. Sometimes he sounds like a bluesman, sometimes he sounds like a Muppet baby.

Lil Wayne does his share of gangsta posturing, but half the time 10 he starts chuckling before he gets through a line. He's a ham. He is heavy on pretense, and thank God. Like Dylan, theatricality trumps authenticity.

And yet — even as he tries on a new style for every other song, it is always unmistakably him. I think of Elvis's famous boast, "I don't sound like nobody." I imagine Wayne would flip it: "Don't *nobody* sound like me."

Lil Wayne

4.

Every few weeks, Michael or another student — for this piece, the names of my students have been changed — would have a new burned CD that was supposedly *Tha Carter III*, Lil Wayne's long-anticipated sixth studio album. "This one's official," they would say. I learned to be skeptical even as I enjoyed the new tracks. Nothing "official" would come

around until school was out for summer, but Lil Wayne created hundreds of new songs in 2007 and the first half of 2008. *Vibe* magazine took the time to rank his best seventy-seven songs of 2007, and that was not a comprehensive list. These songs would end up on the Internet, which downloaders could snag for free. He also appeared for guest verses on dozens of other rappers' tracks. He thusly managed to rate as the "Hottest MC in the Game" (according to MTV) and the "Best MC" (according to *Rolling Stone*), despite offering nothing new at the record store.

While Wayne claimed to do every song "at the same ability or hype," the quality varied widely. He wrote nothing down (he was simply too stoned, he explained), rapping off the top of his head every time the spirit moved him, which was pretty much all the time. The results were sometimes tremendous and sometimes awkward, but that was half the fun. His oeuvre ended up being a sort of unedited reality show of his wily subconscious.

5. Ain't 'bout to pick today to start running

During the first few days of school, Darius, one of my homeroom students, kept getting in trouble for leaving classes without permission. At the end of the second day, he pulled me aside to tell me why he kept having to use the bathroom: he had been shot in the leg three times and had a colostomy bag.

When I visited him in the hospital a few weeks later — he was there 15 for follow-up surgery — he told me about the dealers who shot him. Darius's speaking voice is a dead ringer for Lil Wayne's old-man rasp. "I told them, Do what you need to do, you heard me? I ain't scared, you heard me?"

Then he leaned over and pointed, laughing, to Sponge Bob on the television.

6.

Lil Wayne, rumor has it, briefly went to the pre-Katrina version of our school. Same name and location, but back then it was a neighborhood high school. The building was wrecked in the storm. Our school, a charter school, is housed in modulars (my students hate this euphemism — they're trailers) in the lot in back. Sometimes I went and peeked in the windows of the old building, and it looked to me like no one had cleaned or gutted it since the storm. It was like a museum set piece. There was still a poster up announcing an open house, coming September 2005.

7.

I taught fifth-grade social studies, eighth-grade writing, ninth-grade social studies. Sometimes I felt inspired, sometimes deflated.

One time, a black student vehemently defended his one Arab classmate during a discussion about the Jena 6: "If you call him a terrorist, that's like what a cop thinks about us." Another day, when I was introducing new material about Africa, a student interrupted me — "I heard them niggas have AIDS!"

8. Pain, since I've lost you — I'm lost too

Our students are afraid of rain. A heavy morning shower can cut attendance in half. I once had a student write an essay about her experience in the Superdome. She wrote, without explanation, that she lost her memory when she lost her grandmother in the storm. I was supposed to correct the grammar, so that she would be prepared for state testing in the spring.

20

9. Keep your mouth closed and let your eyes listen

Lil Wayne is five-foot-six and wiry, sleepy-eyed, covered in tattoos, including teardrops under his eyes. His two camera poses are a cool tilt of the head and a sneer. He means to look sinister, I think, but there is something actually huggable about him. He looks like he could be one of my students — and some of my students like to think they look like him.

The other day, I saw Cornel West on television say that Lil Wayne's physical body bears witness to tragedy. I don't even know what that

means, but I do think that Wayne's artistic persona is a testament to *damage*.

10.

One of my favorite Lil Wayne hooks is the chorus on a Playaz Circle song called "Duffle Bag Boy." In the past year, he started singing more, and this was his best turn. He sounds a little like the neighborhood drunk at first as he warbles his way up and down the tune, but his singing voice has an organically exultant quality that seems to carry him to emotional delirium. After a while, he's belting out instructions to a drug courier with the breathy urgency of a Baptist hymn. By the end of the song, the standard-order macho boast, "I ain't never ran from a nigga and I damn sure ain't 'bout to pick today to start running," has been turned by Lil Wayne into a plea, a soul lament.

11.

On New Orleans radio, it seems like nearly every song features Lil Wayne. My kids sang his songs in class, in the hallways, before school, after school. I had a student who would rap a Lil Wayne line if he didn't know the answer to a question.

   An eighth grader wrote his Persuasive Essay on the topic "Lil Wayne   25
is the best rapper alive." Main ideas for three body paragraphs: *Wayne has the most tracks and most hits, best metaphors and similes, competition is fake.*

12. My flow is art, unique — my flow can part a sea

Once I witnessed a group of students huddled around a speaker listening to Lil Wayne. They had heard these songs before, but were nonetheless gushing and guffawing over nearly every line. One of them, bored and quiet in my classroom, was enthusiastically, if vaguely, parsing each lyric for his classmates: "You hear that? *Cleaner than a virgin in detergent.* Think on that."

Pulling out the go-to insult of high schoolers everywhere, a girl nearby questioned their sexuality. "Y'all be into Lil Wayne so much you sound like girls," she said.

They just kept listening. Then one of the boys was simply overtaken by a lyrical turn. He stood up, threw up his hands, and began hollering. "I don't care!" he shouted. "No homo, no homo, but that boy is cute!"

13.

Lil Wayne on making it: "When you're really rich, then asparagus is yummy."

Lil Wayne on safe sex: "Better wear a latex, cause you don't want that late text, that 'I think I'm late' text." 30

Lil Wayne on possibly less safe sex: "How come there is two women, but ain't no two Waynes?"

14.

Okay, but it's not any one line, it's that *voice*. Just the way he says "car in park" in his cameo on Mario's "Crying Out for Me" remix; it's a soft growl from another planet. It sounds like a threat and a comfort and a come-on all at once.

15. I am just a Martian, ain't nobody else on this planet

Right before you become a teacher, you are told by all manner of folks that it will be (1) the hardest thing you've ever done, and (2) the best thing you've ever done. That seems like a recipe for recruiting wannabe martyrs. In any case, high stakes can blind you to the best moments. One day, I was stressing over what I imagined was my one-man quest to keep Darius in school and out of jail, and missed that a heated dispute between two fifth graders was escalating. Finally, I asked them what was wrong.

"Mr. Ramsey," one of the boys pleaded, "will you *please* tell him that if you go into space for a year and come back to Earth that all your family will be dead because time moves slower in space?"

rhetorical situations   genres   processes   strategies   research MLA / APA   media / design   readings

**16. And to the kids: drugs kill. I'm acknowledging that.
But when I'm on the drugs, I don't have a problem with that.**

On one of his best songs, the super-catchy "I Feel Like Dying," Lil Wayne 35
barely exists. He always sounds high, but on this song he sounds as
though he has already passed out.

A lot of the alarmism about pop music sending the wrong message
to impressionable youth seems mostly overwrought to me, but I'll cop
to feeling taken aback at ten-year-olds singing, "Only once the drugs are
done, do I feel like dying, I feel like dying."

First time I heard a fifth grader singing this in falsetto, I said: "*What
did you say?*"

He said: "Mr. Ramsey, you know you be listening to that song. Why
you tripping?"

My students always ask me why I'm tripping at precisely the
moments when the answer seems incredibly obvious to me.

17.

After Michael cussed out our vice principal, I did a home visit. Michael 40
was one of the biggest drug dealers in his neighborhood, and also one
of my best students.

His mother was roused from bed. She looked half-gone, dazed. Then
she started crying, and hugged me, pulled my head into her body. "No
one's ever cared like this," she said. "Bless you. Thank you."

Michael smiled shyly. "I just want to get in my right grade," he told me.

"We'll find a way to make that happen," I told him.

A few weeks later, I gave him a copy of a *New Yorker* piece on Lil Wayne.

"Actually, that was good," he said, later. "You teach me to write like 45
that?"

18. Born in New Orleans, raised in New Orleans . . . .

You live here as a newcomer and locals are fond of saying "this is New
Orleans" or "welcome to New Orleans" by way of explanation. They use
it to explain absurdity, inefficiency, arbitrary disaster, and transcendent

fun. Enormous holes in the middle of major streets, say, or a drunken man dressed as an insect in line behind you at the convenience store.

Our challenge in the schools is to try to reform a broken system (the "recovery" in Recovery School District doesn't refer to the storm — the district was created before Katrina, when the state took over the city's failing schools) amidst a beautiful culture that is sometimes committed to cutting folks a little slack.

I have heard the following things speciously defended or excused by New Orleans culture: truancy, low test scores, drug and alcohol addiction, extended families showing up within the hour to settle minor school-boy scuffles, inept bureaucracy, lazy teachers, students showing up hungover the day after Mother's Day . . . .

19.

Once, a girl's older sister looked askance at one of my best students after school, and about five minutes later there was a full-on brawl in the parking lot. I lost my grip on the student I was holding back and she jumped on top of another student's mother and started pounding.

On the pavement in front of me was a weave and a little bit of blood. 50 One of my ninth graders was watching the chaos gleefully while I tried to figure out how to make myself useful. He was as happy as I've ever seen him. He shrugged beatifically. "This is *New Orleans!*" he shouted, to me, to himself, to anyone who might be listening.

20.

Sometimes my students tell me they are sick of talking about the storm. Sometimes it's all they want to talk about. Might be the same student. Some students have told me it ruined their lives, some students have told me it saved their lives. Again, sometimes the same student will say both.

21.

From an interview in early 2006:

AllHipHop.com: On the album, did you ever contemplate doing a whole track dedicated to the Hurricane Katrina tragedy?

Lil Wayne: No, because I'm from New Orleans, brother. Our main focus is to move ahead and move on. You guys are not from New Orleans and keep throwing it in our face, like, 'Well, how do you feel about Hurricane Katrina?' I f—king feel f—ked up. I have no f—king city or home to go to. My mother has no home, her people have no home, and their people have no home. Every f—king body has no home. So do I want to dedicate something to Hurricane Katrina? Yeah, tell that b—h to suck my d—k. That is my dedication.

22. I am the beast! Feed me rappers or feed me beats.

Lil Wayne mentions Katrina in his songs from time to time. He has a track that rails against Bush for his response to the storm. But, to his credit, he doesn't wallow in his city's famous tragedy.

The world needs to be told, and reminded, of what happened here. But New Orleans is bigger and more spirited than the storm. So its favorite son can be forgiven for refusing to let it define him. For my students, Lil Wayne is good times and good memories, and enduring hometown pride. All they ask of him is to keep making rhymes, as triumphant and strange as the city itself.

23. Ever since I was little, I lived life numb

Michael stopped coming to school. His mother told me, "He's a man ₅₅ now. There's nothing more I can do."

Darius got kicked out for physically attacking a teacher.

I have lots of happy stories, so I don't mean to dwell on these two, but I guess that's just what teachers do in the summer months, replay the ones that got away.

24.

I read over this, and I got it all wrong. I fetishize disaster. I live in the best city in the world and all I can write about is hurricanes and dropouts.

25.

One time, after they finished a big test I gave them last period, my students started happily singing Lil Wayne's "La La La" on their way outside.

"Come on, Ramsey, sing along, you know it."   60

And so I did. "Born in New Orleans, raised in New Orleans, I will forever remain faithful New Orleans . . . ."

That I *wasn't* from New Orleans didn't much matter, so long as I was game to clap and dance and sing. It was a clear and sunny day, Lil Wayne was the greatest rapper alive, and school was out. It was time to have fun.

Engaging with the Text

1. How does David Ramsey **ORGANIZE** his text? Why do you think he chose to organize it in this way? What role do the **HEADINGS** throughout the essay play in the organization? What is the source of those headings?

   238
   588–89

2. Ramsey notes that New Orleans natives often say to newcomers, "this is New Orleans." What does that phrase mean? How is it used in the essay?

3. This essay both narrates a first year teaching and reviews Lil Wayne's music. What is the **PURPOSE** of the essay? What are we meant to take away from it? How are Ramsey's students and Lil Wayne's lyrics related?

   3–4

4. Throughout his essay, Ramsey inserts **DIALOGUE.** How does the dialogue function in this essay? Whom does he quote, and how is their role central to the essay?

   376–81

5. *For Writing.* Select a favorite artist, and think about how that artist's work relates. Write an essay **ANALYZING** or **REFLECTING** on his or her work. Include images of the work. If you write about a musician and are writing online, add audio.

   52–86
   214–21

rhetorical situations   genres   processes   strategies   research MLA / APA   media / design   readings

ALISON BECHDEL

Fun Home

Alison Bechdel became a cartoonist and writer after growing up in Lock Haven, Pennsylvania, where both her parents were high school English teachers; her father also ran a family-owned funeral home that his children called the "fun home." This selection is from Fun Home: A Family Tragicomic *(2006), a best-selling graphic memoir that was chosen by* Time *magazine as number-one of its "10 Best Books" of 2006. In it, Bechdel chronicles her childhood and her coming to recognize both her own homosexuality and her father's, which she learned of only after his death. Before publishing* Fun Home, *she had become known for her cartoon strip* Dykes to Watch Out For, *which followed the lives of a group of lesbian characters over twenty-five years; the strips were published in gay and lesbian newspapers and eventually on the web, as well as in twelve book-length collections. In 2012, Bechdel published another graphic memoir,* Are You My Mother?, *which focuses on her relationship with her mother. Bechdel's work has also appeared in* Ms., Slate, *the* Village Voice, *the* Advocate, Out, *and many comic books and anthologies.*

IF THIS WAS A PREMONITORY DREAM, I CAN ONLY SAY THAT ITS CONDOLENCE-CARD ASSOCIATION OF DEATH WITH A SETTING SUN IS MAUDLIN IN THE EXTREME.

YET MY FATHER DID POSSESS A CERTAIN RADIANCE--

--PERHAPS DUE TO HIS HABIT OF EXCESSIVE, EVEN IDOLATROUS, SUNBATHING--

OFF TO CHURCH

--AND SO HIS DEATH HAD AN INEVITABLY DIMMING, CREPUSCULAR EFFECT. MY COUSIN EVEN POSTPONED HIS ANNUAL FIREWORKS DISPLAY THE NIGHT BEFORE THE FUNERAL.

WHY?

WELL, UH...OUT OF RESPECT FOR YOUR DAD.

I HAD BEEN HOPING FOR A MORE BLUNT RESPONSE, LIKE, "BECAUSE YOUR FATHER JUST DIED, YOU IDIOT."

MY NUMBNESS, ALONG WITH ALL THE MEALY-MOUTHED MOURNING, WAS MAKING ME IRRITABLE. WHAT WOULD HAPPEN IF WE SPOKE THE TRUTH?

THE LORD MOVES IN MYSTERIOUS WAYS.

THERE'S NO MYSTERY! HE **KILLED HIMSELF** BECAUSE HE WAS A MANIC-DEPRESSIVE, CLOSETED **FAG** AND HE COULDN'T FACE LIVING IN THIS SMALL-MINDED SMALL TOWN ONE MORE **SECOND**.

I DIDN'T FIND OUT.

THE LORD MOVES IN MYSTERIOUS WAYS.

YES. HE DOES.

I'D KILL MYSELF TOO IF I HAD TO LIVE HERE.

WHEN I THINK ABOUT HOW MY FATHER'S STORY MIGHT HAVE TURNED OUT DIFFERENTLY, A GEOGRAPHICAL RELOCATION IS USUALLY INVOLVED.

BEECH CREEK — Bruce Bechdel, 44, of Maple Avenue, Beech Creek, well-known funeral director and high school teacher, died of multiple injuries suffered when he was struck by a tractor-trailer along Route 150, about two miles north of Beech Creek at 11:10 a.m. Wednesday.

He was pronounced dead on arrival at Lock Haven Hospital while standing on the berm, police said.

Bechdel was born in Beech Creek on April 8, 1936 and was the son of Dorothy Bechdel Bechdel, who survives and lives in Beech Creek, and the late Claude H. Bechdel.

He operated the Bruce A. Bechdel Funeral Home in Beech Creek and was also an English teacher at Bald Eagle-Nittany

Institute of Mortuary Science.

He served in the U.S. Army in Germany.

Bechdel was president of the Clinton County Historical Society and was instrumental in the restoration of the Heisey Museum after the 1972 flood and in 1978 he and his wife, the former Helen Fontana, received the annual Clinton County Historical Society preservation for the work at their Victorian house in Beech

IF ONLY HE'D BEEN ABLE TO ESCAPE THE GRAVITATIONAL TUG OF BEECH CREEK, I TELL MYSELF, HIS PARTICULAR SUN MIGHT NOT HAVE SET IN SO PRECIPITATE A MANNER.

s a member of the n Society of America, d of directors of the k Playhouse, National Council of Teachers of English, Phi Kappa Psi fraternity and was a deacon at the Blanchard

gardening and stepped onto the roadway. He was struck by the right front portion of the truck

degree from The Pennsylvania State University. He was also a graduate of the Pittsburgh

PERHAPS THE PECULIAR TOPOGRAPHY REALLY DID EXERT SOME KIND OF PULL.

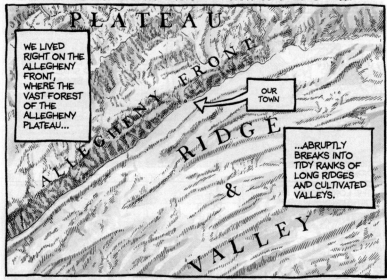

PLATEAU

WE LIVED RIGHT ON THE ALLEGHENY FRONT, WHERE THE VAST FOREST OF THE ALLEGHENY PLATEAU...

ALLEGHENY FRONT

OUR TOWN

...ABRUPTLY BREAKS INTO TIDY RANKS OF LONG RIDGES AND CULTIVATED VALLEYS.

RIDGE & VALLEY

THE APPALACHIAN RIDGES--MANY LONGER THAN HADRIAN'S WALL--HISTORICALLY DISCOURAGED CULTURAL EXCHANGE. MY GRANDMOTHER, FOR EXAMPLE, WAS A BECHDEL EVEN BEFORE SHE MARRIED MY GRANDFATHER. AND IN OUR TOWN OF 800 SOULS, THERE WERE 26 BECHDEL FAMILIES LISTED IN THE PHONE BOOK.

THIS DESPITE THE FACT THAT PEOPLE COULD EASILY DRIVE AROUND THE MOUNTAINS BY THE TIME MY FATHER WAS A CHILD.

DAD

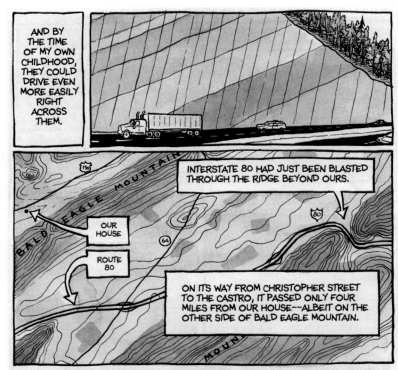

OUR SUN ROSE OVER BALD EAGLE MOUNTAIN'S HAZY BLUE FLANK.

(WE SAW LOTS OF SUNRISES IN 1974, THANKS TO THE ENERGY CRISIS AND THE YEAR-ROUND DAYLIGHT SAVINGS TIME IT ENTAILED.)

AND IT SET BEHIND THE STRIP MINE-POCKED PLATEAU...

...TYPICALLY WITH SOME DEGREE OF PYROTECHNIC SPLENDOR, DUE TO PARTICULATES FROM THE PRE-CLEAN AIR ACT PAPER MILL TEN MILES AWAY.

WITH SIMILAR PERVERSITY, THE SPARKLING CREEK THAT COURSED DOWN FROM THE PLATEAU AND THROUGH OUR TOWN WAS CRYSTAL CLEAR PRECISELY BECAUSE IT WAS POLLUTED.

MINE RUNOFF HAD LEFT THE WATER TOO ACIDIC TO SUPPORT LIFE OF ANY KIND.

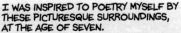

IN THE FOREGROUND STANDS A MAN, MY SAD PROXY, GAZING ON THE UNTIMELY ECLIPSE OF HIS CREATIVE LIGHT.

WE HAD A HUGE, OVERSIZE COLORING BOOK OF E.H. SHEPARD'S ILLUSTRATIONS FOR *THE WIND IN THE WILLOWS*.

SPRING
spring is very nice youknow
not a bit of ice or snow!
LiLACS tu lips and daffodils
peak their heads inthewindowsill.

I NEVER WROTE ANOTHER POEM. AND SOON, I ABANDONED COLOR TOO.

DAD HAD READ ME BITS OF THE STORY FROM THE REAL BOOK. IN ONE SCENE, THE CHARMING SOCIOPATH MR. TOAD PURCHASES A GYPSY CARAVAN.

I WAS FILLING THIS IN ONE DAY WITH MY FAVORITE COLOR, MIDNIGHT BLUE.

WHAT ARE YOU DOING? THAT'S THE *CANARY-COLORED* CARAVAN!

SEVERAL YEARS AFTER DAD DIED, MOM WAS USING OUR OLD TAPE RECORDER TO REHEARSE FOR A PLAY. SHE READ FROM THE SCRIPT, LEAVING PAUSES WHERE IT WAS HER CHARACTER'S TURN TO SPEAK.

WHEN SHE CHECKED TO MAKE SURE THE MACHINE WAS RECORDING PROPERLY...

...SHE REALIZED THAT SHE WAS TAPING OVER MY FATHER'S VOICE.

BUT IT WAS *ALL* THAT SUSTAINED THEM, AND WAS THUS ALL-CONSUMING.

FROM THEIR EXAMPLE, I LEARNED QUICKLY TO FEED MYSELF.

IT WAS A VICIOUS CIRCLE, THOUGH. THE MORE GRATIFICATION WE FOUND IN OUR OWN GENIUSES, THE MORE ISOLATED WE GREW.

OUR HOME WAS LIKE AN ARTISTS' COLONY. WE ATE TOGETHER, BUT OTHERWISE WERE ABSORBED IN OUR SEPARATE PURSUITS.

AND IN THIS ISOLATION, OUR CREATIVITY TOOK ON AN ASPECT OF COMPULSION.

Engaging with the Text

312–13

1. The **TITLE** of Alison Bechdel's graphic autobiography, *Fun Home,* refers both to the funeral home in which she spent a lot of time while growing up and to the fun house in an amusement park. Describe the characteristics that distinguish a fun house from other kinds of buildings.
367–70 In what ways do the **DETAILS** in this excerpt suggest the idea of an amusement park fun house? Why do you think Bechdel selected this
3–4 analogy? What does it suggest about the **PURPOSE** of her memoir?

2. What role do the graphic images play in helping Bechdel tell her story? What details do they provide that the words do not, and vice versa?

312–17

3. What strategies does Bechdel use in the text and graphics to **GUIDE READERS** through her narrative and help them relate to her struggle to understand her identity? How effective are these strategies in helping readers follow her story?

4. One of the key features of a text that mixes genres is that it needs a
238 **CLEAR FOCUS.** In what ways does Bechdel's piece accomplish this feature? In your response, consider both the images and the words.

387–95

5. *For Writing.* Create your own graphic **NARRATIVE** essay that details an early experience of some kind that you had, whether at home, at school, or elsewhere. Think about what insights you want to provide your readers in your account, and focus your piece to convey them. Pay attention to the graphic as well as verbal details you include. You need not draw graphics yourself; if you prefer, you can use images you find elsewhere and integrate them with your own words.

ANU PARTANEN

Finland's School Success
What Americans Keep Ignoring

Anu Partanen is a Finnish writer who splits her time between Finland and the United States and writes for both Finnish- and English-language magazines and newspapers, including the Atlantic, *the* New York Times, *and* Fortune *magazine. She has also worked on the Finnish television show* Pressiklubi (The Press Club), *where she debated news trends and current affairs, and taught magazine writing at a Finnish university. The following essay appeared in the* Atlantic *in December 2011.*

EVERYONE AGREES the United States needs to improve its education system dramatically, but how? One of the hottest trends in education reform lately is looking at the stunning success of the West's reigning education superpower, Finland. Trouble is, when it comes to the lessons that Finnish schools have to offer, most of the discussion seems to be missing the point.

The small Nordic country of Finland used to be known — if it was known for anything at all — as the home of Nokia, the mobile phone giant. But lately Finland has been attracting attention on global surveys of quality of life — *Newsweek* ranked it number one last year — and Finland's national education system has been receiving particular praise, because in recent years Finnish students have been turning in some of the highest test scores in the world.

Finland's schools owe their newfound fame primarily to one study: the PISA survey, conducted every three years by the Organization for Economic Co-operation and Development (OECD). The survey compares 15-year-olds in different countries in reading, math, and science. Finland has ranked at or near the top in all three competencies on every survey since 2000, neck and neck with superachievers such as South Korea and Singapore. In the most recent survey in 2009 Finland slipped slightly, with students in Shanghai, China, taking the best scores, but

Finnish schools assign less homework and engage children in more creative play.

the Finns are still near the very top. Throughout the same period, the PISA performance of the United States has been middling, at best.

Compared with the stereotype of the East Asian model — long hours of exhaustive cramming and rote memorization — Finland's success is especially intriguing because Finnish schools assign less homework and engage children in more creative play. All this has led to a continuous stream of foreign delegations making the pilgrimage to Finland to visit schools and talk with the nation's education experts, and constant coverage in the worldwide media marveling at the Finnish miracle.

So there was considerable interest in a recent visit to the U.S. by   5 one of the leading Finnish authorities on education reform, Pasi Sahlberg, director of the Finnish Ministry of Education's Center for International Mobility and author of the new book *Finnish Lessons: What Can the World Learn from Educational Change in Finland?* Earlier this month, Sahlberg stopped by the Dwight School in New York City to speak with

educators and students, and his visit received national media attention and generated much discussion.

And yet it wasn't clear that Sahlberg's message was actually getting through. As Sahlberg put it to me later, there are certain things nobody in America really wants to talk about.

During the afternoon that Sahlberg spent at the Dwight School, a photographer from the *New York Times* jockeyed for position with Dan Rather's TV crew as Sahlberg participated in a roundtable chat with students. The subsequent article in the *Times* about the event would focus on Finland as an "intriguing school-reform model."

Yet one of the most significant things Sahlberg said passed practically unnoticed. "Oh," he mentioned at one point, "and there are no private schools in Finland."

This notion may seem difficult for an American to digest, but it's true. Only a small number of independent schools exist in Finland, and even they are all publicly financed. None is allowed to charge tuition fees. There are no private universities, either. This means that practically every person in Finland attends public school, whether for pre-K or a Ph.D.

The irony of Sahlberg's making this comment during a talk at the 10 Dwight School seemed obvious. Like many of America's best schools, Dwight is a private institution that costs high-school students upward of $35,000 a year to attend — not to mention that Dwight, in particular, is run for profit, an increasing trend in the U.S. Yet no one in the room commented on Sahlberg's statement. I found this surprising. Sahlberg himself did not.

Sahlberg knows what Americans like to talk about when it comes to education, because he's become their go-to guy in Finland. The son of two teachers, he grew up in a Finnish school. He taught mathematics and physics in a junior high school in Helsinki, worked his way through a variety of positions in the Finnish Ministry of Education, and spent years as an education expert at the OECD, the World Bank, and other international organizations.

Now, in addition to his other duties, Sahlberg hosts about a hundred visits a year by foreign educators, including many Americans, who want to know the secret of Finland's success. Sahlberg's new book is partly an attempt to help answer the questions he always gets asked.

From his point of view, Americans are consistently obsessed with certain questions: How can you keep track of students' performance if you don't test them constantly? How can you improve teaching if you have no accountability for bad teachers or merit pay for good teachers? How do you foster competition and engage the private sector? How do you provide school choice?

The answers Finland provides seem to run counter to just about everything America's school reformers are trying to do.

For starters, Finland has no standardized tests. The only exception 15 is what's called the National Matriculation Exam, which everyone takes at the end of a voluntary upper-secondary school, roughly the equivalent of American high school.

Instead, the public school system's teachers are trained to assess children in classrooms using independent tests they create themselves. All children receive a report card at the end of each semester, but these reports are based on individualized grading by each teacher. Periodically, the Ministry of Education tracks national progress by testing a few sample groups across a range of different schools.

As for accountability of teachers and administrators, Sahlberg shrugs. "There's no word for accountability in Finnish," he later told an audience at the Teachers College of Columbia University. "Accountability is something that is left when responsibility has been subtracted."

For Sahlberg what matters is that in Finland all teachers and administrators are given prestige, decent pay, and a lot of responsibility. A master's degree is required to enter the profession, and teacher training programs are among the most selective professional schools in the country. If a teacher is bad, it is the principal's responsibility to notice and deal with it.

And while Americans love to talk about competition, Sahlberg points out that nothing makes Finns more uncomfortable. In his book Sahlberg quotes a line from Finnish writer named Samuli Paronen: "Real winners do not compete." It's hard to think of a more un-American idea, but when it comes to education, Finland's success shows that the

Finnish attitude might have merits. There are no lists of best schools or teachers in Finland. The main driver of education policy is not competition between teachers and between schools, but cooperation.

Finally, in Finland, school choice is noticeably not a priority, nor is engaging the private sector at all. Which brings us back to the silence after Sahlberg's comment at the Dwight School that schools like Dwight don't exist in Finland.

"Here in America," Sahlberg said at the Teachers College, "parents can choose to take their kids to private schools. It's the same idea of a marketplace that applies to, say, shops. Schools are a shop and parents can buy what ever they want. In Finland parents can also choose. But the options are all the same."

Herein lay the real shocker. As Sahlberg continued, his core message emerged, whether or not anyone in his American audience heard it.

Decades ago, when the Finnish school system was badly in need of reform, the goal of the program that Finland instituted, resulting in so much success today, was never excellence. It was equity.

Since the 1980s, the main driver of Finnish education policy has been the idea that every child should have exactly the same opportunity to learn, regardless of family background, income, or geographic location. Education has been seen first and foremost not as a way to produce star performers, but as an instrument to even out social inequality.

In the Finnish view, as Sahlberg describes it, this means that schools should be healthy, safe environments for children. This starts with the basics. Finland offers all pupils free school meals, easy access to health care, psychological counseling, and individualized student guidance.

In fact, since academic excellence wasn't a particular priority on the Finnish to-do list, when Finland's students scored so high on the first PISA survey in 2001, many Finns thought the results must be a mistake. But subsequent PISA tests confirmed that Finland — unlike, say, very similar countries such as Norway — was producing academic excellence through its particular policy focus on equity.

That this point is almost always ignored or brushed aside in the U.S. seems especially poignant at the moment, after the financial crisis and Occupy Wall Street movement have brought the problems of inequality in America into such sharp focus. The chasm between those who can afford $35,000 in tuition per child per year — or even just the price of a house in a good public school district — and the other "99 percent" is painfully plain to see.

Pasi Sahlberg goes out of his way to emphasize that his book *Finnish Lessons* is not meant as a how-to guide for fixing the education systems of other countries. All countries are different, and as many Americans point out, Finland is a small nation with a much more homogeneous population than the United States.

Yet Sahlberg doesn't think that questions of size or homogeneity should give Americans reason to dismiss the Finnish example. Finland *is* a relatively homogeneous country — as of 2010, just 4.6 percent of Finnish residents had been born in another country, compared with 12.7 percent in the United States. But the number of foreign-born residents in Finland doubled during the decade leading up to 2010, and the country didn't lose its edge in education. Immigrants tended to concentrate in certain areas, causing some schools to become much more mixed than others, yet there has not been much change in the remarkable lack of variation between Finnish schools in the PISA surveys across the same period.

Samuel Abrams, a visiting scholar at Columbia University's Teachers   30
College, has addressed the effects of size and homogeneity on a nation's education performance by comparing Finland with another Nordic country: Norway. Like Finland, Norway is small and not especially diverse overall, but unlike Finland it has taken an approach to education that is more American than Finnish. The result? Mediocre performance in the PISA survey. Educational policy, Abrams suggests, is probably more important to the success of a country's school system than the nation's size or ethnic makeup.

Indeed, Finland's population of 5.4 million can be compared to many an American state — after all, most American education is managed at the state level. According to the Migration Policy Institute, a research organization in Washington, there were 18 states in the U.S. in 2010 with

an identical or significantly smaller percentage of foreign-born residents than Finland.

What's more, despite their many differences, Finland and the U.S. have an educational goal in common. When Finnish policymakers decided to reform the country's education system in the 1970s, they did so because they realized that to be competitive, Finland couldn't rely on manufacturing or its scant natural resources and instead had to invest in a knowledge-based economy.

With America's manufacturing industries now in decline, the goal of educational policy in the U.S. — as articulated by most everyone from President Obama on down — is to preserve American competitiveness by doing the same thing. Finland's experience suggests that to win at that game, a country has to prepare not just some of its population well, but all of its population well, for the new economy. To possess some of the best schools in the world might still not be good enough if there are children being left behind.

Is that an impossible goal? Sahlberg says that while his book isn't meant to be a how-to manual, it is meant to be a "pamphlet of hope."

"When President Kennedy was making his appeal for advancing 35 American science and technology by putting a man on the moon by the end of the 1960's, many said it couldn't be done," Sahlberg said during his visit to New York. "But he had a dream. Just like Martin Luther King a few years later had a dream. Those dreams came true. Finland's dream was that we want to have a good public education for every child regardless of where they go to school or what kind of families they come from, and many even in Finland said it couldn't be done."

Clearly, many were wrong. It is possible to create equality. And perhaps even more important — as a challenge to the American way of thinking about education reform — Finland's experience shows that it is possible to achieve excellence by focusing not on competition, but on cooperation, and not on choice, but on equity.

The problem facing education in America isn't the ethnic diversity of the population but the economic inequality of society, and this is precisely the problem that Finnish education reform addressed. More equity at home might just be what America needs to be more competitive abroad.

Engaging with the Text

1. According to this essay, what are some of the major differences between how schools are run in the United States and how they are run in Finland? Identify at least three differences, pointing to the sentences that reveal them.

312–13
2. What is the answer to the implied question in the **TITLE** of this essay? What do Americans keep ignoring about Finland's school success? Why do you think Americans have not yet adopted the Finnish system of education? How would a similar system fare in the United States?

306–10
3. How does Anu Partanen **END** her essay? Do you agree with her conclusion? Why or why not?

327–35
432–52
4. What kind of **EVIDENCE** does Partanen provide to support her argument? How does she use **SOURCES**? How convincing is the evidence and the sources of it?

119–49
164–72
214–21
5. *For Writing.* Write an essay responding to Partanen's argument. Do you believe the Finnish system would improve education in the United States, or not? For another perspective, you might read Jonathan Kozol's essay "Fremont High School" on p. 705. In your essay, you might mix several genres — to **ARGUE** your own position, **EVALUATE** schools you've attended, **REFLECT** on your own education, and soon.

SOJOURNER TRUTH

Ain't I a Woman?

Sojourner Truth, born into slavery in 1797 and given the name Isabella Baumfree, was sold several times before she obtained her freedom when New York State abolished slavery on July 4, 1827. After a profound religious experience, she became an inspired preacher and in 1843 changed her name to Sojourner Truth. She dictated her memoirs, The Narrative of Sojourner Truth: A Northern Slave, *to Oliver Gilbert, and they were published by the prominent abolitionist William Lloyd Garrison in 1850. She became a traveling speaker, giving talks throughout the country on abolition, women's rights, and her life as a slave. In 1854, she delivered the following oration at the Ohio Woman's Rights Convention in Akron. It became her most famous speech.*

WELL, CHILDREN, where there is so much racket there must be something out of kilter. I think that 'twixt the negroes of the South and the women at the North, all talking about rights, the white men will be in a fix pretty soon. But what's all this here talking about?

That man over there says that women need to be helped into carriages, and lifted over ditches, and to have the best place everywhere. Nobody ever helps me into carriages, or over mud-puddles, or gives me any best place! And ain't I a woman? Look at me! Look at my arm! I have ploughed and planted, and gathered into barns, and no man could head me! And ain't I a woman? I could work as much and eat as much as a man — when I could get it — and bear the lash as well! And ain't I a woman? I have borne thirteen children, and seen most all sold off to slavery, and when I cried out with my mother's grief, none but Jesus heard me! And ain't I a woman?

Then they talk about this thing in the head; what's this they call it? [member of audience whispers, "intellect"] That's it, honey. What's that got to do with women's rights or negroes' rights? If my cup won't hold but a pint, and yours holds a quart, wouldn't you be mean not to let me have my little half measure full?

Then that little man in black there, he says women can't have as much rights as men, 'cause Christ wasn't a woman! Where did your Christ come from? Where did your Christ come from? From God and a woman! Man had nothing to do with Him.

If the first woman God ever made was strong enough to turn the world upside down all alone, these women together ought to be able to turn it back, and get it right side up again! And now they is asking to do it, the men better let them. 5

Obliged to you for hearing me, and now old Sojourner ain't got nothing more to say.

Engaging with the Text

299–311

1. How does Sojourner Truth **BEGIN** her speech? How effective is her beginning? How does it relate to her **ENDING?**

2. Throughout the speech, Truth repeats the phrase "Ain't I a woman?" What purpose does this phrase serve in the speech? What is she comparing herself to when she ends a sentence, "And ain't I a woman?" What else might she have said and then used this phrase?

313–15
13

3. What is Truth's **THESIS?** Why do you think she chose to speak about this issue? What do you think she was hoping would happen soon? How would you describe her **TONE?** And how does that tone relate to her thesis?

5–8
12–15

4. Who is Truth's **AUDIENCE** for this speech? Where in the text are there clues to her targeted audience? How effective is her **STANCE** for this audience?

5. *For Writing.* Consider a position that you feel you have been denied unfairly — cheerleader, lead in a play, student president, store manager, lead guitarist, whatever. Write a three-to-five-minute speech in which you show how you are just as qualified for that position as someone else who holds it. Come up with a phrase that captures your argument as Truth does with "Ain't I a woman?" and use it as a refrain throughout your speech.

rhetorical situations · genres · processes · strategies · research MLA / APA · media / design · readings

MICHAEL KIMMELMAN

A Ballpark Louder Than Its Fans

Michael Kimmelman has written columns and criticism on music, art, European politics and culture, and architecture. He began the Abroad column for the New York Times *in 2007 and reported from Berlin until 2011, when he was named the newspaper's architecture critic. Previously he had served as a music critic and then the chief art critic for the* Times. *He is also the author of several books, including* The Accidental Masterpiece *(2005),* Oscar Niemeyer *(2009), and* Portraits: Talking with Artists at the Met, the Modern, the Louvre, and Elsewhere *(1998). In addition, Kimmelman is a pianist who regularly performs in concerts in New York and Europe. He has hosted several television shows and appears in the documentary film* My Kid Could Paint That *(2007). The following essay was published in the* Times *on April 27, 2012. To access the online version, which includes a slide show as well as hyperlinks, go to* wwnorton .com/write/fieldguidelinks.

A**FTER 20 YEARS OF RETRO-STYLE BALLPARKS** since the opening of Oriole Park at Camden Yards in Baltimore, nearly all decked out with brick facades and calculated quirks that came to seem as predictable and interchangeable as the old doughnut-shaped arenas, Major League Baseball has its first unapologetic 21st-century stadium.

Lumbering and dizzyingly white in the Florida sun, the new Marlins Park is an elliptical concrete, steel and glass boulder looming above the low-rise houses and empty lots of the Little Havana neighborhood. With retail on the outside and a public plaza in front, it's designed partly to gin up some street life. Economic development is supposed to follow — that was the rationale for the public financing that covered most of the $634 million project ($515 million for the park itself) and contributed to the recall of Miami-Dade County's mayor. Cities are always building new stadiums with the justification that they'll catalyze the local economy. They rarely do.

Fans outside the stadium. Miami-Dade County paid nearly $350 million for the bulk of construction, with the Marlins kicking in $161.2 million.

At the same time, the ballpark is unlikely to satisfy aficionados of the latest trends in architecture, but it is nonetheless a modern building, with genuine panache, as opposed to another pastiche. Give the team's owner, Jeffrey Loria, credit. An art dealer, he cares more than most about aesthetics and took a gamble — part old-school civic improvement plan, part marketing strategy — that Miamians will recognize themselves in the stylishness of the place.

He has festooned concourses and stairwells with art, photographs and sculpture. Most fans will no doubt focus more on the grass field, air-conditioning and retractable roof, which slides over the entry plaza onto slender, palm-shaped pillars, illuminated by pulsing lights. Because of the oppressive heat and rain, the roof isn't likely to be opened for more than a dozen or so games a year, but even when it is closed, there are sweeping views of the city skyline through 60-foot-tall windows.

The challenge now will be filling the park's seats. With a capacity of 37,442, this is one of the smallest arenas in the big leagues, but Miamians

5

have notoriously stayed away from Marlins games in droves. Mr. Loria and the city are banking, as so many other owners and cities have, that a new stadium can change a team's and a neighborhood's fortunes.

Can it? The Miami Marlins, until this year the Florida Marlins, have labored since their inaugural season in 1993 in a 75,000-seat suburban football arena, where the Dolphins play, which can be as much as an hour's drive from downtown, with lousy sightlines, crippling summer-time humidity and no roof. The *Miami Herald's* Marlins beat reporter, Clark Spencer, told me on a recent night that he used to pass the time with colleagues in the press booth counting attendance.

"Once we counted 80-something people," he said, "and that included some confused foreign tourists."

Mr. Loria, who took over in 2002, argued that it was pointless to spend money on top players without a domed stadium. Detractors said he was blackmailing the city into paying for a new park, meanwhile pocketing revenue-sharing millions from other teams that were meant to go toward a beefier payroll.

But then in 2007, Miami officials consented to a new stadium on the site of the former Orange Bowl, a couple of miles from downtown. The city provided the land and $13 million. Miami-Dade County paid nearly $350 million for the bulk of construction, with the Marlins kicking in $161.2 million. The pliant architecture firm Populous, formerly HOK Sport, which designed Yankee Stadium and nearly every retro ball-park during the last two decades, was hired to do the architecture.

Orel Hershiser, the pitcher turned ESPN analyst, got in first dibs as 10 critic on opening night when, apropos the swooping *Star Trek* curves on the outside, he said that the stadium looked "like a cruise ship had a baby with a spaceship."

Almost endearingly, when we met, Mr. Loria countered with a few wishful comparisons to the Getty Center in Los Angeles and Frank Lloyd Wright's Guggenheim Museum. He said the inspiration for the stadium's electric color scheme, with its fluorescent-green outfield wall, was the palette of the Spanish painter Joan Miró. Public art and native plantings are meant to lend his building's exterior what might be called an aspirational gravitas.

Inside Mr. Loria has also installed giant reproductions of paintings by blue-chip modernists like Roy Lichtenstein on or near the main concourse, called the Promenade, amid a souk of food stalls hawking $12 mahi-mahi tacos and $14 Cuban sandwiches. Nobody seemed to take much notice of the art the other night, fans clustering instead four-deep before a bobble-head-doll display. But Mr. Loria professed not to care. The goal is a mix of visual distractions.

These include two narrow saltwater aquariums behind home plate, giving off a bright blue glow. The intended spirit is light-hearted. For the same reason that Florida's hockey team never installed a panther cage in its rink, it's now clear why no one had put an aquarium in a backstop before. Animal rights activists were traumatized after the team tested the glass with a pitching machine.

The game aside, the main attraction is clearly the kinetic sculpture by the Pop maestro of kitsch, Red Grooms, in left-center field: marlins spin, flamingos flap and water splashes whenever a Marlin hits a homer. Miamians have been competing to come up with a name for it (the Marlinator and the Marlinstrosity are two, so far). This over-the-top gizmo is to the Mets' homely home-run apple what the video game *Call of Duty* is to a jack-in-the-box. Considering how few homers have been hit so far, the fences might need to be brought in before too long to make sure it is exercised.

Mr. Hershiser was close to the mark about the architecture. Stadiums these days emulate cruise ships. They've got their first-class cabins and exclusive restaurants and nightclubs. (The one at Marlins Park even has a swimming pool.)   15

The game is no longer necessarily the point for many people who buy a ticket. Baseball used to be a sport of reverie, with the murmur of the crowd, the chatter of announcers on transistor radios and the crack of bats. Now parks are entertainment palaces, telling us when to cheer and selling us overpriced food and merchandise. The longest line I saw on the Promenade was to get into the team's souvenir store.

Retro stadiums catered to nostalgia for an era before steroids and artificial turf, but even the past gets old. Fans may someday come to long for the doughnut stadiums. I almost miss Shea. Whether the trop-

The kinetic sculpture by Red Grooms.

The pool within the nightclub at Marlins Park.

ical colors and aquariums at Marlins Park will appeal to local Latino fans, on whom Miami is relying to fill most of the seats, or play to outsiders' clichés of the city, time will tell.

Sightlines are good. Those at the top and behind the outfield fences feel close to the action, and field-level seats benefit from the narrow foul territory. With the roof closed, Marlins Park is chilled to a dry 75 degrees, a family-friendly environment in which to pass a hot summer day or night. Angled walls and cantilevered ramps on the building's outside create a few elegant geometries, and multicolored tiles provide decorative pizzazz. It's more than what you find in the grim concrete corridors of Yankee Stadium.

Yes, baseball isn't what it used to be — the modern game panders to the corporations and rich patrons who buy luxury boxes and seats behind home plate. But stadiums are about as close as many cities come today to creating large-scale public spaces. They attract untold numbers of fans who might never have gone to a game back when baseball was played before cigar-chomping men in jackets and fedoras.

"A lot of us weren't expecting something this nice," said Adam   20
Brownstein, a 38-year-old native Miamian, who spoke for what seemed
like every resident I met.

Ten clubs have opened new homes since 2001. The Phillies thrive
in Citizens Bank Park, where they keep winning. Pittsburgh flounders in
PNC Park — which may be the most beautiful of all the parks to be built
in recent years — because the Pirates are perennial losers.

Now that Mr. Loria has gotten his new stadium, he is doling out big
money for marquee players, talking about World Series games played with
the roof open, under the stars. Through seven home games, according to
ESPN, the Marlins have sold an average of more than 29,000 tickets.

If the Marlins are bottom dwellers in late September, that home-
run sculpture may come to seem forlorn, the new team uniforms clown-
ish and the cost of the stadium a renewed scandal.

But that's then. For now, Miami has reason to cheer.

Engaging with the Text

1. The primary **GENRE** in this text is evaluation of a new arena. What
    other genres are used? Point out two examples of other genres.

    25

2. Michael Kimmelman uses an effective **COMPARISON** when he writes
    about Marlins Park's home-run display: "This over-the-top gizmo is
    to the Mets' homely home-run apple what the video game *Call of Duty*
    is to a jack-in-the-box." What does he mean by this comparison? What
    does it say about Miami's new ballpark?

    348–55

3. This essay was published in the *New York Times*, a newspaper with a
    national and international **AUDIENCE.** What more specific audience
    does it intend to address within that broad group? How can you tell?

    5–8

4. Click on the hyperlinks in the text and look at the slide show in the
    online version of the article. Because of space limitations, only a few
    of these photos could be included in the print version. The links and
    additional photos give readers a better visual conception and more
    background knowledge of Marlins Park, but they have to spend more

time to get these benefits. Besides these considerations of space and time, what other trade-offs are involved in the choice between print and electronic media, either in journalism or elsewhere?

5. *For Writing.* Visit a nearby sports facility. Study the facility closely — inside and out, if it's enclosed — and watch how people interact in it. (For example, what parts get the most use or attention? Where are the longest lines?) How would you **DESCRIBE** the facility? What distinguishes it from other facilities of the same kind? What is your **EVALUATION** of it? How well does it serve the teams, sports, or players it was intended for? Write an essay like Kimmelman's that addresses these questions and any other aspects of the facility that interest you (such as the reasons it was built in the style and location it was or the costs of its construction and maintenance). Include photos of the facility in your essay, and if you're writing online, try to include some hyperlinks to sources for additional information.

367–75 ◆

164–72 ▲

rhetorical situations   genres   processes   strategies   research MLA / APA   media / design   readings

Acknowledgments

IMAGE ACKNOWLEDGMENTS

27 Courtesy of Emily Vallowe; 37, 39 Courtesy of Sofia Gomez; 52 Courtesy of Hannah Berry; 54 Courtesy of The Clarks Companies; 56 Courtesy of Sorel; 57 Courtesy of Emily Nussbaum; 58 Aby Baker/Getty Images; 62 © The New York Times/Redux; 64 Seth Wenig/AP; 79 Jeff Darcy/The Plain Dealer; 82 The Granger Collection, New York/The Granger Collection; 87 Courtesy of Michaela Cullington; 95 © Colin McPherson/Corbis; 100 © 2010 Larry D. Moore/Wikimedia Commons; 101 (left) Charles Bennett/AP; 101 (right) Mark Duncan/AP; 105 Courtesy of The Atlantic; 106 The Advertising Archives; 124 Courtesy of Heather Douglas; 125 Photo Researchers/Getty Images; 127 Wikimedia Commons; 129 Bettmann/Corbis; 131 Courtesy of Andrew Leonard; 132–34 YouTube; 157 Courtesy of Jessica Ann Olson; 164 ConsumerReports.org; 165 Courtesy of Ali Heinekamp; 166 The Kobal Collection; 183 John Amis/AP; 191 Courtesy of Christian Danielsen; 193 John Burgess © The Press Democrat, Santa Rosa, CA; 202 Courtesy of Dan Meyer; 205 Courtesy of Michael Granof; 209 Heather Ainsworth/The New York Times/Redux; 214 Wikimedia Commons; 235 Steye Raviez/Hollandse Hoogte/Redux; 303 Jim Mone/AP; 333 © Reagan Louie; 334 RecycleManiacs.org; 345 Courtesy of Michiganapples.com; 352 (top) From Stiglitz, Joseph, *Economics*. New York: Norton; 352 (middle and bottom) © GOOGLE; 361 © Swim Ink 2, LLC/CORBIS; 372–73 The Advertising Archives; 385 Courtesy of The Other Side of Fifty — othersideoffifty.com; 426 www.wordle.net/create; 435 (top) The Journal of Social History; 435 (bottom) The Smithsonian Magazine; 437, 441–42 The University of Wyoming Library; 496 From *At Day's Close: Night in Times Past* by A. Roger Ekirch. Copyright © 2005 by A. Roger Ekirch. Used by permission of W. W. Norton & Company. This selection may not be reproduced, stored in a retrieval system, or transmitted in any form or by any means without the prior written permission of the publisher; 504 Jerry Weinberger, "Pious Princes and Red-Hot Lovers: The Politics of Shakespeare's *Romeo and Juliet*," *The Journal of Politics* 65 (2003), p. 350. Copyright © 2003, Southern Political Science Association. Reprinted with the permission of Cambridge University Press; 505 (left) Jim Krueger; 505 (right) D1ILL/Corbis; 509 Courtesy of Forum on Religion and Ecology, Yale University and J. Baird Callicott; 512 Reprinted with permission of EBSCO Publishing, 2008; 525 Bettmann/CORBIS; 543 From *Endless Forms Most Beautiful: The New Science of Evo Devo and the Making of the Animal Kingdom* by Sean B. Carroll. Copyright © 2005 by Sean B. Carroll. Used by permission of W. W. Norton & Company. This selection may not be reproduced, stored in a retrieval system, or transmitted in any form or by any means without the prior written permission of the publisher; 549 Lisa

TEXT ACKNOWLEDGMENTS

for America," *Phi Delta Kappan*, June 2008, pp. 721–725. Reprinted by permission of the author.

Alex Horton: "The Ides of March," *Army of Dude*, March 30, 2011. Reprinted by permission of Alex Horton.

Stephanie Huff: "Metaphors and the Counterfeit Nature of Our Society." Reprinted by permission of the author.

Suleika Jaouad:" Life, Interrupted: Finding My Cancer Style," NYTimes.com, June 7, 2012. © 2007, The New York Times. All rights reserved. Used by permission and protected by the Copyright Laws of the United States. The printing, copying, redistribution, or retransmission of the Material without express written permission is prohibited.

Michiko Kakutani: "The End of Life as She Knew It" from *The New York Times*, 10/4/2005. © 2005 The New York Times. All rights reserved. Used by permission and protected by the Copyright Laws of the United States. The printing, copying, redistribution, or retransmission of the Material without express written permission is prohibited.

Michael Kimmelman: "A Ballpark That May Be Louder than the Fans" *The New York Times*, April 27, 2012. © 2007 The New York Times. All rights reserved. Used by permission and protected by the Copyright Laws of the United States. The printing, copying, redistribution, or retransmission of the Material without express written permission is prohibited.

Geeta Kothari: "If You Are What You Eat, Then What Am I?" Reprinted by permission of the author.

Jonathan Kozol: From *The Shame of the Nation* by Jonathan Kozol, copyright © 2005 by Jonathan Kozol. Used by permission of Crown Publishers, a division of Random House, Inc.

Andrew Leonard: "Black Friday: Consumerism Minus Civilization" Salon.com, November 25, 2011. Reprinted with permission.

Lawrence Lessig: "Some Like It Hot" — *Wired Magazine* article, from *Free Culture* by Lawrence Lessig, copyright © 2004 by Lawrence Lessig. Used by permission of The Penguin Press, a division of Penguin Group (USA) Inc.

Joanna MacKay: "Organ Sales Will Save Lives." Reprinted by permission of the author.

Malcolm X: From *The Autobiography of Malcolm X* by Malcolm X and Alex Haley, Copyright © 1964 by Alex Haley and Malcolm X. Copyright © 1965 by Alex Haley and Betty Shabazz. Used by permission of Random House, Inc.

William Moller: "Those Who Live in Glass Houses" from *Yankees Dollar* blog, May 5, 2009. Reprinted by permission of the author.

Armando Montaño: "The Unexpected Lessons of Mexican Food" from Salon.com, March 17, 2012. Reprinted with permission.

Shannon Nichols: "'Proficiency.'" Reprinted by permission of the author.

Emily Nussbaum: "In Defense of Liz Lemon" *The New Yorker*, February 23, 2012. Copyright © 2012 Condé Nast. All rights reserved. Originally published in *The New Yorker*. Reprinted by permission.

Matthew O'Brien: "The Strange (and Formerly Sexist) Policy of Engagement Rings" The Atlantic Online, April 2012. Copyright © 2012 The Atlantic Media Co., as published in The Atlantic Online. Distributed by Tribune Media Services.

Jessica Ann Olson: "Annotated Bibliography on Global Warming." Reprinted by permission of the author.

Anu Partanen: "What Americans Keep Ignoring about Finland's School Success" Originally published in *The Atlantic Monthly*, Dec. 29, 2011. Reprinted by permission of the author.

Bill Pennington: "Catching On after a Last Chance" *The New York Times*, February 4, 2012. © 2012, The New York Times. All rights reserved. Used by permission and protected by the Copyright Laws of the

Glossary / Index

A

abstract, 150–54, 244 A writing GENRE that summarizes a book, an article, or a paper, usually in 100–200 words. Authors in some academic fields must provide, at the top of a report submitted for publication, an abstract of its content. The abstract may then appear in a journal of abstracts, such as *Psychological Abstracts*. An *informative abstract* summarizes a complete report; a briefer *descriptive abstract* provides only a brief overview; a *proposal abstract* (also called a TOPIC PROPOSAL) requests permission to conduct research, write on a topic, or present a report at a scholarly conference. Key Features: SUMMARY of basic information • objective description • brevity

   descriptive, 151, 154
   design and, 588
   example, 565
   generating ideas and text for, 153
   headings and, 588
   informative, 150–51, 154
   key features of, 152
   lab reports and, 179
   objective description in, 152

Note: This glossary/index defines key terms and concepts and directs you to pages in the book where you can find specific information on these and other topics. Please note the words set in SMALL CAPITAL LETTERS are themselves defined in the glossary/index. *Page numbers in italics indicate visuals.*

   organizing, 154
   proposal, 151–52, 154
   reports and, 150
   rhetorical situation and, 152–53
   summarizing and, 153
   thesis statement and, 153
   writing, 152–54

academic searches, the web and, 447

academic writing, 19–24 Writing done in an academic or scholarly context, such as for course assignments. Key Features: evidence that you've carefully considered the subject • clear, appropriately qualified THESIS • response to what others have said • good reasons supported by evidence • acknowledgment of multiple perspectives • carefully documented sources • confident, authoritative STANCE • indication of why your topic matters • careful attention to correctness

   consideration of the subject, 19
   correctness and, 23
   documentation and, 21
   multiple perspectives, 21
   reasons and evidence, 20–21
   response to others, 20
   rhetorical situation and, 23–24
   stance and, 21–22, 24
   thesis, 19–20
   thinking about, 23–24
   topic, 22

acknowledgment
   collaborating and, 477

antecedent, 284   The noun or pronoun to which a pronoun refers. In <u>Maya</u> lost <u>her</u> wallet, Maya is the antecedent of *her*.

APA style, 22, 480–83, 533–74   A system of DOCU-MENTATION used in the social sciences. APA stands for the American Psychological Association. *See also detailed directory at back of book*

appendix, 180   A section at the end of a written work for supplementary material that would be distracting in the main part of the text.

application letters, 229–34   Letters written to apply for a job or other position. Key Features: succinct indication of qualifications • reasonable and pleasing tone • conventional, businesslike form

arguing, 323–41   A STRATEGY that can be used in any kind of writing to support a claim with REASONS and EVIDENCE.

arguing a position, 119–49, 244, 247, 726–63   A writing GENRE that uses REASONS and EVIDENCE to support a CLAIM or POSITION and, sometimes, to persuade an AUDIENCE to accept that position. Key Features: clear and arguable position • necessary background • good reasons • convincing support for each reason • appeal to readers' values • trustworthy TONE • careful consideration of other positions

audience, 5–8   Those to whom a text is directed — the people who read, listen to, or view the text. Audience is a key part of every text's RHETORICAL SITUATION. *See also specific genres and strategies*

authorities, 328–29   People or texts that are cited as support for a writer's ARGUMENT. A structural engineer may be quoted as an authority on bridge construction, for example. *Authority* also refers to a quality conveyed by a writer who is knowledgeable about his or her subject.

B

bandwagon appeal, 339   A logical FALLACY that argues for thinking or acting a certain way just because others do.

begging the question, 339   A logical FALLACY that argues in a circle, assuming as a given what the writer is trying to prove.

block quotation, 465, 522, 562   In a written work, a long QUOTATION that is set off, or indented, from the main text and presented without quotation marks. In MLA style: set off text more than four typed lines, indented ten spaces (or one inch) from the left margin; in APA style, set off quotes of forty or more words, indented five spaces (or one-inch half) from the left margin.

brainstorming   A PROCESS for GENERATING IDEAS AND TEXT by writing down everything that comes to mind about a topic, then looking for patterns or connections among the ideas.

design, 15–18, 271, 565–620 The way a text is arranged and presented visually. Elements of design include font, color, illustration, layout, and white space. One component of a RHETORICAL SITUATION, design plays an important part in how well a text reaches its AUDIENCE and achieves its PURPOSE.

multimedia, 579   Using more than one medium of delivery, such as print, speech, or electronic. Often used interchangeably with MULTIMODAL.

multimodal, 579   Using more than one mode of expression, such as words, images, sound, links, and so on. Often used interchangeably with MULTIMEDIA.

N

narration, 272, 387–95   A STRATEGY for presenting information as a story, for telling "what happened." It is a pattern most often associated with fiction, but it shows up in all kinds of writing. When used in an essay, a REPORT, or another academic GENRE, narration is used to support a point — not merely tell an interesting story for its own sake. It must also present events in some kind of sequence and include only pertinent detail. Narration can serve as the ORGANIZING principle for a whole text.

organizing   Arranging parts of a text so that the text as a whole has COHERENCE. The text may use one STRATEGY throughout or may combine several strategies to create a suitable organization.

outlining, 259, 263–64 A PROCESS for GENERATING IDEAS AND TEXT or for organizing or examining a text. An *informal outline* simply lists ideas and then numbers them in the order that they will appear; a *working outline* distinguishes supporting from main ideas by indenting the former; a *formal outline* is arranged as a series of headings and indented subheadings, each on a separate line, with letters and numerals indicating relative levels of importance.

P

parallelism, 284 A writing technique that puts similar items into the same grammatical structure. For example, every item on a to-do list might begin with a command: *clean, wash, buy*; or a discussion of favorite hobbies might name each as a gerund: *running, playing basketball, writing poetry.*

paraphrasing, 21, 462–74 Rewording someone else's text using about the same number of words but not the phrasing or sentence structure of the original. Paraphrasing is generally called for when a writer wants to include the details of a passage but does not need to quote it word for word. Like a QUOTATION or SUMMARY, a paraphrase requires DOCUMENTATION.

response, 275–76   A PROCESS of writing in which a reader gives the writer his or her thoughts about the writer's title, beginning, THESIS, support and DOCUMENTATION, ORGANIZING, STANCE, treatment of AUDIENCE, achievement of PURPOSE, handling of the GENRE, ending, and other matters.

restrictive element. *See* essential element

résumé, 222–29   A GENRE that summarizes someone's academic and employment history, generally written to submit to potential employers. DESIGN and word choice depend on whether a résumé is submitted as a print document or in an electronic or scannable form. Key Features: organization that suits goals and experience • succinctness • design that highlights key information (for print) or that uses only one font (for scannable).

revision, 276–79 The PROCESS of making substantive changes, including additions and cuts, to a draft so that it contains all the necessary content and presents it in an appropriate organization. During revision, writers generally move from whole-text issues to details with the goals of sharpening their focus and strengthening their position. *See also specific genres and strategies*

rewriting, 279–81 A PROCESS of composing a new draft from another perspective — with a different POINT OF VIEW, AUDIENCE, STANCE, GENRE, or MEDIUM, for example.

rhetorical situation, 1–24 The context in which writing or other communication takes place, including PURPOSE, AUDIENCE, GENRE, STANCE, and MEDIA/DESIGN. *See also specific genres and strategies*

S

secondary source, 432–33 An ANALYSIS or INTERPRETATION of a PRIMARY SOURCE. In writing about the Revolutionary War, a researcher would likely consider the Declaration of Independence a primary source and a textbook's description of how the document was written a secondary source.

stance, 12–15, 22, 271   A writer's or speaker's attitude toward his or her subject — for example, reasonable, neutral, angry, curious. Stance is conveyed through TONE.

strategy, 272, 297–418 A pattern for ORGANIZING text to ANALYZE CAUSE AND EFFECT, ARGUE, CLASSIFY AND DIVIDE, COMPARE AND CONTRAST, DEFINE, DESCRIBE, EXPLAIN A PROCESS, NARRATE.

style In writing, the arrangement of sentences, CLAUSES, PHRASES, words, and punctuation to achieve a desired effect; also, the rules of capitalization, punctuation, and so on recommended for DOCUMENTATION of a source.

tone, 13–14   The way a writer's or speaker's STANCE toward the readers and subject is reflected in the text.

topic, 423–24   The specific subject written about in a text. A topic should be narrow enough to cover, not too broad or general, and needs to be developed appropriately for its AUDIENCE and PURPOSE.

topic proposal, 211–13   A statement of intent to examine a topic; also called a proposal ABSTRACT. Some instructors require a topic proposal in order to assess the feasibility of the writing project that a student has in mind. Key Features: concise discussion of the subject • clear statement of the intended focus • rationale for choosing the subject • mention of resources

Submitting Papers for Publication by W. W. Norton & Company

We are interested in receiving writing from college students to consider including in our textbooks as examples of student writing. Please send this form with the work that you would like us to consider to Marilyn Moller, Student Writing, W. W. Norton & Company, 500 Fifth Avenue, New York NY 10110.

Text Submission Form

Student's name _____

School _____

Address _____

Department _____

Course _____

Writing assignment the text responds to _____

_____

_____

_____

_____

Instructor's name _____

(continued next page)

Please write a few sentences about what your primary purposes were for writing this text. Also, if you wish, tell us what you think you learned about writing from the experience writing it.

_____

_____

_____

_____

_____

_____

_____

Contact Information

Please provide the information below so that we can contact you if your work is selected for publication.

Name _____

Permanent address _____

Email _____

Phone _____

A Directory to MLA Style

A Directory to APA Style

APA IN-TEXT DOCUMENTATION

APA REFERENCE LIST

A Menu of Readings